Humanistic Foundation of Criminal Law

Xingliang Chen

Humanistic Foundation of Criminal Law

中国人民大学出版社
CHINA RENMIN UNIVERSITY PRESS

Springer

Xingliang Chen
School of Law
Peking University
Beijing, China

The translation of this book is sponsored by *B&R book program.*

ISBN 978-981-19-9763-1   ISBN 978-981-19-9764-8 (eBook)
https://doi.org/10.1007/978-981-19-9764-8

Jointly published with China Renmin University Press.
The print edition is not for sale in China (Mainland). Customers from China (Mainland) please order the print book from: China Renmin University Press.

This Springer imprint is published by the registered company Springer Nature Singapore Pte Ltd.
The registered company address is: 152 Beach Road, #21-01/04 Gateway East, Singapore 189721, Singapore

Preface

When a scholar begins to sum up academic career, his or her academic creativity is withering. The collection named Science of Criminal Law written by Chen Xingliang is a summary of my research career in the science of criminal law, which is clear proof of my withering academic creativity.

The study of the science of criminal law is my lifelong career. I began to learn criminal law in 1978 when I was enrolled in the Law Department of Peking University in February as a student in Grade 1977. The year 1978 is known as the first year of China's reform and opening-up. The third Plenary Session of the 11th Central Committee of the Communist Party of China held in December 1978 determined the policy of reform and opening-up. The restoration and reconstruction of China's legal system were marked by the passing of seven laws, including Criminal Law, on July 1, 1979. From 1949 to 1979, there was no criminal law or civil law in China, not to mention administrative law. Criminal Law promulgated in 1979 is the first criminal law for socialist China. The law began to be drafted in 1950, with a total of 33 drafts, and was hastily promulgated in 1979. Criminal law was drafted during the political honeymoon period between China and the Soviet Union. Although our country broke with the Soviet Union in politics, the criminal law still retained the obvious traces of Soviet Russia. Meanwhile, Chinese criminal jurists who grew up in the 1950s mainly received academic training in criminal jurisprudence in Soviet Russia. They returned to teach at colleges and universities after 20 years of waste, reviving the academic tradition of criminal jurisprudence in Soviet Russia. We were their first formal students. Criminal Law, which was adopted on July 1, 1979, took effect on January 1, 1980. According to the course arrangement, our grade began to learn criminal law in September 1979. That is to say, we started studying criminal law before it came into force. The course continued until July 1980. In one year, we finished the general and specific provisions of criminal law. As for criminal law, we only had a rough grasp of the articles of law. We didn't know the legal principles of criminal law, let alone knew the reason behind these principles. As for the judicial practice, since Criminal Law had just been implemented, many charges didn't have real cases, which made us poorly understand. When I was in college, the academic world in China was in shambles, just emerging from the "Cultural Revolution". The most devastating legal discipline was almost in ruins. We went through this process. It is hard to imagine now that we spent the entire four years at college without a formal textbook for every subject. We finished our studies without a textbook. Therefore, we read a lot of books unrelated to law. Out of my interest, I read a large number of philosophical works available in the library at that time, mainly from the seventeenth century in the West, including British, French and German philosophical works. I was fascinated by the German classical philosophy represented by Kant and Hegel. It was easier for me to understand German classical philosophy, one of the sources of Marxism, because I had a certain basic knowledge of Marxist philosophy. This reading experience, to a certain extent, not only fostered my philosophical temperament but also had a significant impact on my subsequent criminal law research. My research on criminal law philosophy in the late 1980s and early 1990s was a derivative of this reading experience. The title of my undergraduate thesis completed at the end of 1981 was *On the Nature of Crime*, which was an ontological topic. This topic also showed my academic preference at that time. However, this paper was very unsuccessful. It just repeated Marxist political discourse on the class nature of crime and lacked the required academic nature. Therefore, the thesis score was good rather than excellent. My undergraduate criminal law test score was only good. I was not interested in criminal law at that time. Later, an accidental reason made me embark on the academic career of criminal law.

When I graduated from Peking University in February 1982, Chinese society was in great need of talented people. Most of my classmates were assigned to the Supreme People's Court, the Supreme People's Procuratorate and Central Authority. Some students went back to work at the high courts and procuratorates in the provinces. Some students engaged in academic research at colleges and universities as teachers. Those who were younger went on studying at the university, pursuing their master's degrees. I was admitted to the Law Department of Renmin University of China. It was renamed law school in 1988. I began to study criminal law under the instruction of Prof. Gao Mingxuan and Prof. Wang Zuofu, two famous criminal jurists in China.

In February 1982, I came to Renmin University of China from Peking University. Renmin University of China became the second university where I received legal education. It was there that I received the most classical academic training in the science of criminal law with obvious traces of Soviet Russia. The thesis for my master's degree was supervised by Prof. Wang Zuofu. The title was *On Justifiable Defense in China's Criminal Law*. This was a paper close to judicial practice, which was also my first paper writing. The paper was 40,000 words at the time of the thesis defense. Later, it was extended to more than 200,000 words. In 1987, it was published by China Renmin University Press under the title of *On Justifiable Defense*, which became my first book. By the time I got my doctor's degree of law in March 1988, I had skillfully mastered the science of criminal law of Soviet Russia which had been localized in China, which became the academic basis of my research on the science of criminal law.

In December 1984, when I got my master's degree, I stayed for teaching in the Law Department of Renmin University of China, so I pursued my doctor's degree as a full-time teacher. Of course, there were not many class hours at that time, which did not affect the doctoral study. My doctoral thesis was approved in March 1988. The thesis supervised by Prof. Gao Mingxuan was entitled *Theory of Joint Crime* with a total number of 280,000 words. It was the first time I had finished a long paper. Although the doctoral thesis took the provisions of China's criminal law on joint crime as the basic clue, it drew on the works written and translated during the Republic of China. For example, most of them were Japanese works from the 1930s and 1940s. I tried to graft these academic views into the theory of joint crime in China's criminal law. Among them, the theoretical model centered on the dual distinction between principal offender and accomplice was used to shape the theoretical image of joint crime in China's criminal law. Later, my doctoral thesis was extended to more than 500,000 words and was published by China Social Sciences Press in 1992. The above two books revised on the basis of my master's thesis and doctoral thesis were the outcome of my early study of criminal law based on the science of criminal law of Soviet Russia, which laid my academic foundation.

I had been teaching at Law School of Renmin University of China from 1984 to 1998, engaged in academic research on criminal law. At Law School of Renmin University of China, I was promoted from teaching assistant to professor. I was appointed teaching assistant in December 1984, lecturer in December 1987, associate professor in September 1989, professor in June 1993 and doctoral supervisor in 1994. I returned to teach at Law School of Peking University, my Alma Mater, in January 1998. As a teacher at a university, my main job is certainly to teach students. However, for faculty at a research university, academic research is also where their mission and reputation rest. Therefore, I have devoted considerable energy to the academic research of criminal law. I have witnessed the evolution of the criminal rule of law in China, and also participated in the development of criminal law research in China. As far as I am concerned, I have made efforts and contributions to both improving the academic level of criminal law research in China and expanding the theoretical domain of criminal law research in China. My research fields are mainly in the following five aspects.

Philosophy of Criminal Law

Philosophy of Criminal Law, which was published by China University of Political Science and Law Press in 1992, could be called the longest book on criminal law at that time. It was also the book that made me famous. I was 35 years old at that time, 10 years after I graduated from Peking University with an LLB. *Philosophy of Criminal Law* was a summary of my study and research of criminal law in the past 10 years. It completed my theoretical improvement and reflection on Chinese criminal jurisprudence from the source of Soviet Russian criminal jurisprudence. Moreover, it determined the academic direction of my further research. It was the first book in the whole law circle in China to study departmental laws with the philosophical method, so it attracted people's attention. On the basis of *Philosophy of Criminal Law*, I published *Human Nature Foundation of Criminal Law* by China Founder Publishing House in 1996 and *Value Structure of Criminal Law* by China Renmin University Press in 1998. The above three books constituted my philosophy of criminal law research trilogy and became a unique aspect of my criminal law academic research.

My research on the philosophy of criminal law was carried out in a quite unique academic environment. It was also an academic ability for me to try to overcome difficulties and seek a future for the extremely poor criminal jurisprudence in China. As mentioned earlier, when I entered the criminal law academia in the mid-1980s, China's criminal law theory was still a "copy" of the criminal jurisprudence of Soviet Russia though some explanations were made in combination with China's newly promulgated Criminal Law. However, generally speaking, the criminal law theory in China at that time was rather superficial, which could not quench my thirst for knowledge. By the time I got my doctorate in 1988, I had already mastered the existing criminal law. At that time, China's academic community was not yet open to the outside world, and it was in an isolated academic environment. Based on my dissatisfaction with the current situation of criminal law theory which was confined to low-level interpretation of laws, I thought that the way out of criminal law theory lay in upgrading from criminal law hermeneutics to the philosophy of criminal law. Therefore, in the name of the philosophy of criminal law, I systematized the existing criminal law knowledge, and tried to explore the way out of China's criminal jurisprudence. In the trilogy of the philosophy of criminal law, *Philosophy of Criminal Law* was based on the systematic description of the knowledge of criminal law in Soviet Russia with the relationship between crime and punishment as the center to construct a theoretical system of science of criminal law. The book could be regarded as a philosophic transformation of criminal law knowledge in Soviet Russia. If *Philosophy of Criminal Law* was mainly about the knowledge of criminal law, *Human Nature Foundation of Criminal Law* and *Value Structure of Criminal Law* would be metaphysical studies of criminal law. The latter two books could actually be classified as works of jurisprudence rather than criminal jurisprudence. It was an effort to seek a breakthrough in the science of criminal law by absorbing knowledge from philosophy and other disciplines under gloomy academic circumstances. The study of the philosophy of criminal law lasted from 1990 to 1996, which was the golden period of my life from 33 to 38 years of age. Although the study of the philosophy of criminal law had brought me a high reputation, it was only my academic training period for the real study of criminal jurisprudence. It was the study of the philosophy of criminal law that enabled me to grasp the essence and philosophy of criminal law and overlook criminal law research from academic perspectives.

Dogmatics of Criminal Law

China completed a large-scale revision of Criminal Law in 1997. From then on, I turned my academic attention to the provisions of Criminal Law. At the age of 40, I published a book titled *Notes on Criminal Law* by People's Public Security University of China Press in March 1997. It was a criminal law book full of notes based on the provisions, which was my return from the philosophy of criminal law to criminal law hermeneutics. "Shuyi" in the original Chinese title of this book was a specific term. It not only contained the meaning of explanation but also had the meaning of dredging. In the Tang Dynasty, there was a famous book called *Code of the Tang Dynasty*, which had been handed down through the ages, and it was regarded as the most important book on the science of law in ancient China. The Chinese title of *Notes on Criminal Law* had obviously imitated the Chinese title of *Code of the Tang Dynasty* as both of the two Chinese titles contained "Shuyi". It also showed that I tried to draw useful knowledge from the science of law in ancient China, which was a special discipline. The science of the law was different from modern jurisprudence. Jurisprudence was transplanted from abroad in the late Qing Dynasty, mainly from Japan which absorbed German criminal law knowledge. Because my book was all notes on the provisions of Criminal Law article by article, its content quickly became outdated over time. It became the only book of mine that was not revised or republished. This time, it was not included in the collection of my books on the science of criminal law.

I published *Ontological Criminal Jurisprudence* by the Commercial Press in 2001. It was another book focusing on criminal law itself after *Notes on Criminal Law*. However, *Ontological Criminal Jurisprudence* was completely different from *Notes on Criminal Law*. The latter was a book which annotated the provisions of Criminal Law article by article, while there were no provisions of Criminal Law in the former book which took legal principles of Criminal Law as the object. *Ontological Criminal Jurisprudence* was the follow-up book of *Notes on Criminal Law*. I tried to complete the process of refining and sublimation from provision explanations to expositions of legal principles. The word "Ontological" in the title of *Ontological Criminal Jurisprudence* came from Kant's philosophy and had the meaning of thing-in-itself. I regarded the provision as the representation of things and the legal principle as the thing-it-self hidden in the provision. Therefore, *Ontological Criminal Jurisprudence* was a pure description of the legal principles of criminal law. It should be pointed out that China's criminal jurisprudence was still in a state of isolation for academic research during the 1980s. It was since the early 1990s that China has been open to the outside world and academic exchanges with foreign countries have been carried out. In particular, the publication of translated works on criminal jurisprudence from Britain, the USA, Germany and Japan in China has opened an academic window for Chinese criminal law scholars. These foreign academic exchanges were carried out with Japan at first and with Germany later, and provided, to a considerable extent, academic resources for the study of criminal jurisprudence in China. The academic community of criminal law began to reflect on China's traditional criminal jurisprudence, which broke a path of transformation for contemporary criminal law knowledge in China.

I published *Normative Criminal Jurisprudence* by China University of Political Science and Law Press in 2003. It was my first textbook on criminal law, or a book on the system of criminal law. The book took provisions of China's Criminal Law as the central clue, and completely developed the knowledge of the general theory of criminal law and the specific discussion of criminal law so as to meet the needs of classroom teaching. The book is now in its third edition and has been extended on a large scale. *Normative Criminal Jurisprudence* had a relatively simple explanation of the legal principles of the general provisions of criminal law, and its focus was the analysis of the specific provisions of criminal law. China's Criminal Law is a unified criminal code. All the charges are stipulated in one criminal code. There are nearly 500 charges in the criminal code, and no other law can create a charge. *Normative Criminal Jurisprudence* analyzed the constitutive elements of these charges one by one. The book analyzed the key charges in great detail, which was referential for grasping the legal characteristics of these crimes. In addition to the provisions of Criminal Law, China also has a judicial interpretation system. The Supreme People's Court and the Supreme People's Procuratorate can interpret the application of law in trials and prosecutions. The judicial interpretation has legal effect and can be invoked in written judgments. Since the implementation of Criminal Law, the Supreme People's Court and the Supreme People's Procuratorate has made a large number of judicial interpretations, which in fact become statute-like norms. The norms in *Normative Criminal Jurisprudence* included not only the provisions of criminal law but also judicial interpretations. Therefore, the book tried its best to integrate judicial interpretation into the description of legal principles. The book was constantly revised as judicial interpretations were issued.

I published a book titled *Dogmatics of Criminal Jurisprudence* by China Renmin University Press in 2010. This was a book that systematically recounted the knowledge of criminal law in Germany and Japan by taking the three-class system of crime theory as the central clue and comparing the four-element system of crime theory. The book talked about the dogmatics of criminal jurisprudence. The book took Dogma as its core idea and the three-class system of crime theory as its logical framework. The book systematically recounted the basic principles of dogmas of criminal law in considerable depth and breadth. It fully demonstrated the academic charm of criminal jurisprudence which took dogmatics as the content. The book made a comparative study of the three-class system of crime theory and the four-element crime constitution theory. It was a localized knowledge transformation of the three-class system of crime theory. It cleared the ground for the introduction of a three-class system of crime theory. The book was my academic effort to promote the transformation of contemporary criminal law knowledge in China by replacing criminal law knowledge based on criminal jurisprudence of Soviet Russia with German and Japanese criminal law knowledge.

Rule of Criminal Law

I returned to teach at Law School of Peking University, my Alma Mater, in January 1998, which was another turning point in my life. Meanwhile, I worked as a part-time deputy procurator-general of Beijing Haidian District People's Procuratorate from 1997 to 1999. This temporary post enabled me to further understand the judicial practice and especially made me develop a personal understanding of the actual operation of China's criminal procedure, which was of great help to my later research on the rule of criminal law. To a certain extent, my academic horizon went beyond criminal jurisprudence, and I established the concept of criminal integration, that is, the whole criminal jurisprudence, which broadened my theoretical horizon. My book *On Rule of Criminal Law*, which was published by China Renmin University Press in 2007, was a result of my efforts in this field. It was a book facing the reality of rule of law. The book was structured with the actual operation of criminal justice, and the central clue of criminal justice system reform ran throughout the whole book. The book discussed the general principles of the rule of criminal law. Based on the concept of the rule of criminal law, I conducted legal research on police power, prosecutorial power, the right to defense and judicial power to seek the rational basis, describe the operation mechanism and discuss the scientific setting of these powers (rights). Meanwhile, I also studied reeducation-through-labor and community correction. In particular, reeducation-through-labor is a unique system in China with a certain nature of security measures. However, since the power to decide security measure is monopolized by public security organs, security measure is being abused day by day with increasing intensity. In this part of the book, I clearly put forward the reform idea of disintegrating reeducation-through-labor and making it judicial.

The rule of criminal law is a practical issue that I have been paying close attention to for the past 20 years or more. It is also based on the theoretical thinking of criminal law in China's current social situations. It is an academic contribution to promoting rule of law in this field. Although there is a huge gap between reality and the ideal, which inevitably makes us disappointed, academic efforts are still worthwhile. At present, China is at a critical moment of building a country under the rule of law, which needs both courage and the thought of reform.

Theory of Knowledge on Criminal Law

I published the article titled *The Theory of Social Harmfulness: A Reflective Review* in the first issue of the *Chinese Journal of Law* in 2000. It was the beginning of my reflection on China's criminal jurisprudence influenced by Soviet Russia. Social harmfulness was a core concept in criminal jurisprudence of Soviet Russia and was considered an essential feature of crime. It was on the basis of social harmfulness that the theoretical system of criminal jurisprudence of Soviet Russia was constructed.

China's criminal jurisprudence also inherited the theory of social harmfulness, and on the basis of it, China inherited the four-element crime constitution system, which formed the basic theoretical framework of China's criminal jurisprudence. The criticism of the theory of social harmfulness became my entry point to the academic exposure and criticism of criminal jurisprudence in Soviet Russia. In 2006, in the fifth issue of *Political Science and Law Forum*, I published the article titled *Removal of Soviet Russian Influence on Law Knowledge*, explicitly proposing removing criminal law knowledge from Soviet Russia. From the perspective of the sociology of knowledge, the article criticized the criminal jurisprudence of Soviet Russia and discussed the trend of criminal law knowledge in China. The conclusion was reflected in my article titled *The Process of Dogmatics of Criminal Law Knowledge* published in the sixth issue of *Chinese Journal of Law* in 2011. My view was to absorb German and Japanese criminal law knowledge and to construct the knowledge system of dogmatics of criminal law in China. In this process, it was urgent to complete the transformation from the four-element crime constitution theory from Soviet Russia to the three-class system of crime theory from Germany and Japan. Of course, the transformation of criminal law knowledge in China has not been completed, and the four-element crime constitution system is still the general theory, but the three-class system of crime theory has begun to be popular among law schools and judicial circles. Based on the above considerations, I published two books, namely *Knowledge Transformation of Criminal Law (Academic History)* and *Knowledge Transformation of Criminal Law (Methodology)*, in 2012 by China Renmin University Press, which put an end to my 10-year research on criminal law knowledge in China. The study of the theory of knowledge on criminal law made me withdraw from the specific norms and legal principles of criminal law and examined the methodology and academic history of criminal jurisprudence. It was a meta-scientific problem of criminal jurisprudence, and it was also the final destination of my research on criminal jurisprudence.

Case Criminal Jurisprudence

There is another unique field in my criminal law research, which is case criminal jurisprudence. The traditional research of criminal jurisprudence in China is based on the articles of Criminal Law, which is related to the existence of the judicial interpretation system but the nonexistence of the case system in China. However, the importance of precedents to the application of law is self-evident. Therefore, thorough criminal jurisprudence research will inevitably extend the theory to the case. A few years ago, although there was no case system in China, judicial materials such as the Bulletin of the Supreme People's Court and selected cases published by the Criminal Division of the Supreme People's Court provided possibilities for the study of criminal cases. In law school, I had been offering the course of criminal law case study for Master's degree candidates majoring in criminal law, which was popular among the students as a supplement to the study of the generality of criminal law and specific discussion of criminal law. Under such circumstances, I used the relevant cases published by the Criminal Division of the Supreme People's Court as materials to conduct research on case criminal jurisprudence. I published Case Criminal Jurisprudence (two volumes) by China Renmin University Press in 2009. The book started with the cases, and launched the legal theory description, and case analysis and legal theory research were integrated into the book, which became a new aspect of criminal jurisprudence research.

China officially established the case system in 2010. It is a case system with Chinese characteristics, which is called the case guidance system. This case system is completely different from that of Germany and Japan. It operates in the way that the Supreme People's Court issues guiding cases from time to time. The guiding cases issued by the Supreme People's Court have the effect of reference in the trials of lower courts. The reference here neither has full binding force nor is completely free of it, but it has weak binding force. Although these guiding cases cannot be cited in the written judgments, conflicts between the judgment and the guiding case may be used as grounds for appeal. Although the case guidance system still has a strong administrative nature, which is presented in the way of issuance rather than the rule and order formed spontaneously in the process of trial, it is, after all, a new way to provide rules, which is of great significance to judicial practice in China. The key function of the case system is to form operable judicial rules through specific cases, so it is an important task to extract the judicial rules. As a chief expert, I have undertaken the task of compiling *China Case Guidance System*, a major national social science project, since 2010. At the beginning of 2013, I published a book called *"General Compilation of Criminal Guiding Cases Judgment Gist of People's Courts" (two volumes)* by Peking University Press. On the basis of selecting the existing criminal guiding cases, the book extracted the gist of judgments which is instructive to the criminal trial, and expounded the gist of judgments in jurisprudence so as to provide a reference for judicial authorities.

Criminal jurisprudence belongs to departmental jurisprudence, which is closely related to civil rights. Therefore, a scholar who specialized in criminal law is not only an addict to articles of law but also a social thinker. He should not only have the ideal of a national rule of law but also have a vision of civil society. He should not only have love for the victim but also have compassion for the accused.

As I know, the doctrine of a legally prescribed punishment for a specified crime is a core proposition of criminal jurisprudence. It is the starting point and the destination of criminal law. In my theoretical research of criminal law, this doctrine is extremely important. The 1979 Criminal Law of China did not stipulate the principle of a legally prescribed punishment for a specified crime. The system of analogy was, on the contrary, stipulated in the 1979 Criminal Law. The Criminal Law was revised in 1997, abolishing the system of analogy and stipulating the principle of a legally prescribed punishment for a specified crime. Therefore, China's Criminal Law embarked on the road of legally prescribed punishment for a specified crime. Before and after China's Criminal Law stipulated the principle of a legally prescribed punishment for a specified crime, I wrote in-depth papers on the doctrine of a legally prescribed punishment for a specified crime. The papers were compiled into a book called

Doctrine of a Legally Prescribed Punishment for a Specified Crime, which was published by China Legal Publishing House in 2010. On the back cover of the book, I wrote the colophon, expressing my understanding of the doctrine. It said, "Doctrine of a legally prescribed punishment for a specified crime: the return of justice and the arrival of legal theory." The doctrine should be a way of thinking in criminal law and run through the whole criminal law system. Although China's Criminal Law has stipulated the principle of a legally prescribed punishment for a specified crime, it is only the beginning, and it will go through a difficult process of judicialization of legally prescribed punishment for a specified crime. For quite a long period of time, the scholars of criminal law in China still have to strive to realize the principle.

Integrated criminal jurisprudence is also worth advocating. Liszt put forward the proposition of integrated criminal jurisprudence, which still had guiding significance for the research of criminal jurisprudence in China today. My predecessor, Prof. Chu Huaizhi, a professor from Law School, Peking University, put forward the idea of criminal integration, which pursued the rational internal structure of criminal law (horizontal coordination) and the restriction before and after the operation of criminal law (vertical coordination). As a methodology, criminal integration emphasizes the deep integration of various criminal law relations. It should be noted that both integrated criminal jurisprudence and criminal integration look at criminal law from the perspective of system theory, opposing the isolated study of criminal law and advocating the analysis of criminal law in the whole legal system and social relations. I quite agree with this methodology of criminal law research. Since the research field of criminal law itself is relatively narrow, we must broaden the research field of criminal law and deepen its research level. We should take dogmatics as the center for criminal law research. If the dogmatics of criminal law is to study criminal law within criminal law, we also need to study the philosophy of criminal law above the criminal law, the sociology of criminal law outside the criminal law, the case criminal jurisprudence under the criminal law, and so on. Apart from the theoretical study of criminal law, scholars of criminal law should also pay attention to social reality and national rule of law. Only in this way can we not only make criminal jurisprudence a kind of dogmatics of law but also make it have a practical effect.

Criminal law is national, and its effect has national boundaries. However, criminal law knowledge and criminal law theory are universal and can cross national boundaries. Therefore, I always think that China's criminal jurisprudence should be integrated into, rather than separate from, the knowledge system of the world's criminal jurisprudence. In this case, China should learn advanced criminal law theory from Germany, Japan, Britain, the United States and other developed countries ruled by law. Relatively speaking, due to historical reasons, China draws lessons from the legal system of the continental law system, including legal technology and thinking methods. Therefore, it is more convenient for us to absorb the knowledge of German and Japanese criminal law. From the perspective of the evolution path of China's criminal jurisprudence since the 1980s, criminal jurisprudence also developed in the academic opening to the outside world. At first, China introduced the knowledge of criminal law from Japan, and later from Germany. At first, China introduced the general knowledge of criminal law, and then gradually introduced a specific discussion of criminal law. China has experienced a development process from the translation and publication of books on the criminal law system (textbooks) to the translation and publication of monographs on criminal jurisprudence. The criminal law knowledge from Germany and Japan has played an important role in promoting the development of China's criminal jurisprudence. Chinese scholars apply imported criminal law knowledge to solve the problems in China's criminal legislation and criminal justice, and the practical function of that knowledge is also very obvious. We can say that China's criminal jurisprudence is integrating into the system of German and Japanese criminal law knowledge.

The collection named "Science of Criminal Law Written by Chen Xingliang" will be published on the basis of revision and arrangement of my published books. My earlier books were published by various publishing houses. First of all, I would like to express my sincere thanks to the editors of various publishing houses for their hard work in the process of publishing my books. More than 20 books of mine have been included in "A Series of Books Written by Chinese Contemporary Jurists" published by China Renmin University Press in 2006. At present, as a summary of my academic career, my personal monographs have been revised and published under the name "Science of Criminal Law Written by Chen Xingliang". I would like to express my appreciation to the editors of China Renmin University Press for their dedication, carefulness and professionalism in publishing my books. I have been taking research as a goal and treating writing as my career for the past 30 years. Although the work is exhausting physically and mentally, I pursue my career persistently and wholeheartedly. This is, of course, the duty of a scholar. However, the more I put into my research, the more I owe my family. Therefore, I would like to express my gratitude to my wife, Mrs. Jiang Ying, for her understanding and assistance all along.

It has been 30 years since I published my first book titled *On Justifiable Defense* by China Renmin University Press in 1987. The 30 years are the golden years of my academic research. During this period, I have published dozens of monographs, edited dozens of books and two continued publications, namely *The Review of Criminal Law (40 volumes)* and *The Interpretation of Criminal Law (9 volumes)*, and published hundreds of papers. "Science of Criminal Law Written by Chen Xingliang" includes my books published in the past 30 years in 18 volumes, more than 10 million words in total, which are in the following 14 categories:

1. *Philosophy of Criminal Law*
2. *Human Nature Foundation of Criminal Law*
3. *Value Structure of Criminal Law*
4. *Knowledge Transformation of Criminal Law (Methodology)*
5. *Knowledge Transformation of Criminal Law (Academic History)*
6. *On Rule of Criminal Law*
7. *On Justifiable Defense*
8. *On Joint Crime*
9. *General Theory of the Application of Criminal Law (Vol. 1)*

10. *General Theory of the Application of Criminal Law (Vol. 2)*
11. *Normative Criminal Jurisprudence (Vol. 1)*
12. *Normative Criminal Jurisprudence (Vol. 2)*
13. *Case Criminal Jurisprudence (Vol. 1)*
14. *Case Criminal Jurisprudence (Vol. 2)*
15. *Noumena Criminal Jurisprudence*
16. *Dogmatics of Criminal Jurisprudence*
17. *Oral Instruction of Criminal Jurisprudence (Vol. 1)*
18. *Oral Instruction of Criminal Jurisprudence (Vol. 2)*

Academic research is a process of gradual accumulation, and everyone is just a node in the knowledge chain formed by a discipline. As a scholar who has been on the academic stage of criminal law in China since the 1980s, I am so fortunate that my academic life can continue to the 2020s, along with the restoration and reconstruction of the rule of criminal law and the revival of criminal law discipline as well as the integration and transformation of criminal law knowledge. In the academic history of criminal law, the works collected in "Science of Criminal Law Written by Chen Xingliang" are just "passers-by". The current academic significance of these works is gradually disappearing, while their significance in academic history is gradually increasing. One day, they will be curio pieces in the academic museum of criminal law. This is the fate of history.

In the process of editing the collection of "Science of Criminal Law Written by Chen Xingliang", there is always an exclamation that the books and I are both old. I know that the book here is not in the general sense, but refers to the writing of calligraphy. However, in the corresponding sense with "I", any kind of understanding of the "book" here is not important, and the consciousness and understanding of "both old" is real and profound. For a writer, what could be more exciting than a book written by him growing old with him?

Finally, I would like to thank China Renmin University Press for its great kindness to me. As I mentioned earlier, my first book titled *On Justifiable Defense* was published by China Renmin University Press in 1987. Since 2006, "Chen Xingliang's Criminal Law Research Series" has been included in "A Series of Books of Contemporary Chinese Jurists" by China Renmin University Press, which published the collection of "Science of Criminal Law Written by Chen Xingliang" for me this time. I would also like to thank Mr. Liu Weidong, president of Beijing Guanheng Criminal Defense Institute, for his generous donation and financial support for the publication of the collection. As a lawyer with an LLM under my guidance, Liu Weidong practiced the rule of law in his career and became an elite. As his teacher, I am very honored.

The preface ends.

Haidian, Beijing, China
September 2017

Xingliang Chen

Contents

Chapter 1
Introduction

Hume, a famous British philosopher, points out that it is evident, that all the sciences have a relation, greater or less, to human nature; and that however wide any of them may seem to run from it, they still return by one passage or another.[1] The content of criminal law is to regulate human behaviors. The existence and application of any kind of criminal law norm are essentially reasonable only when it is based on the scientific hypothesis[2] of human nature. Therefore, the original thinking of criminal law is bound to extend the theoretical tentacles to the human nature issue with ultimate significance.

1 The Analytical Framework for Human Nature

Human nature, also known as human original nature, is the basic character of human beings. In theory, human nature is a charming and controversial issue. Moreover, the understanding of human nature is quite different between Chinese and western cultural views. For a Chinese, the mere mention of human nature naturally brings to his mind the debate between good nature and evil nature. Therefore, Chinese philosophy mainly defines human nature from the perspective of ethics. However, in western philosophy, although the good and evil of nature is a question related to human nature, the study of human nature mainly focuses on the debate between reason and experience. Whether a man is rational or experiential has become an eternal theme of western theory of human nature. It not only affects the world outlook and methodology, but is the basis of all sciences. The human nature discussed in this book is mainly understood in the debate between reason and experience of human nature. This is a prerequisite definition.

---

[1] Hume [1], p. 6.

[2] "Hypothesis" means "given". As for the reason why it is called the hypothesis of human nature, please refer to Perdue et al. [2].

X. Chen, *Humanistic Foundation of Criminal Law*,
https://doi.org/10.1007/978-981-19-9764-8_1

1.1 Rational Man

The rational man is the rational assumption of human nature. It is the human nature view in Rationalism philosophy. This rational human nature view originated in ancient Greek philosophy and reached its peak in modern Hegel's philosophy.

The discussion of human nature in ancient Greece began with Socrates, the renowned ancient Greek philosopher. Pre-Socratic philosophers show more concern for the noumenon of the universe. Ever since Socrates famously proposes "know thyself", philosophers have turned to the study of man himself. This is the famous transition from cosmic noumenon to human noumenon in western philosophy history. Human nature is brought into the research perspective of the philosophers under this historical background. Socrates' contribution to the understanding of human nature lies in the proposition that virtue is knowledge. Socrates emphasizes that knowledge comes from reason, and to know things is to use reason to determine the concepts of things. Only by determining concepts can we realize the essential understanding of things and achieve true knowledge. This shows that Socrates defines human nature by knowledge. Following Socrates, Plato also makes an in-depth discussion of human nature, and puts forward Plato's Tripartite Theory of human nature. According to Plato, a person is made up of body and soul. Plato divided the soul into three parts, namely lust, spirit and reason. The soul is a combination of these three parts or factors. Each of these factors plays a role in an individual's life and behavior. However, there is a certain hierarchical relationship among the three: reason is the highest, spirit is the second, and lust is the lowest. In the understanding of human nature, it is undoubtedly great progress from Socrates' knowledge monism to Plato's tripartite theory of reason, spirit and appetite, because Plato realizes the complexity of human nature. In particular, Plato's emphasis on reason has a certain significance. Aristotle, following Plato, further emphasizes the importance of reason. Aristotle, on the basis of life experience, believes that in order to figure out the nature of eudaimonia, we must study human nature, that is, to indicate the functions peculiar to man. Aristotle points out, "The function of man is definitely not only life, because even plants have life. What we're trying to find out is a uniquely human function. Therefore, the growing life cannot be regarded as the special function of a man. Secondly, the so-called life of sensation is not a special function of a man, because even horses, oxen and all animals have it. The special function of a man is to lead a rational life based on rational principles."[3] In this sense, a man is a rational animal. Of course, Aristotle does not deny that there is an element of unreason in human nature. Aristotle believes that there are three elements in the human soul, namely feeling, reason and desire, or the soul has an irrational part and a rational part. In the irrational part, it is the characters of living things. However, the soul has another nature, which is the reason. People who can or cannot control themselves have rational parts in their souls. In addition to reason, there seems to be in the soul a different nature, which resists and rebels against reason, just as the same happens to the soul as to the paralyzed parts of the body. In the same way, the immoderate man, under impulse, will be contrary

[3] Zhou [3], p. 208.

to reason. However, in the body, we see the opposite movement, but we cannot see it in the soul. In the soul, however, in addition to reason, there is something that is contrary to reason and rebels against it. In Aristotle's view, the vegetative desire to grow is an irrational part. It is associated with greed and general desires, and has nothing in common with reason, but it accepts and submits to reason. For those who are temperate or brave, their souls are rational. Therefore, Aristotle thinks that reason and unreason both have duality. The duality of reason shows that reason overcomes unreason and becomes the reason. The duality of unreason is reflected in the turning of unreason into reason under the guidance of reason.[4] Aristotle's genius lies in dialectically discussing the rational nature of man, revealing that man's nature is the unity of opposites between reason and unreason. Aristotle also divides reason into active reason and passive reason. Active reason refers to the pure rational activity, while passive reason refers to cognition derived from feeling. It should be noted that the passive reason Aristotle here refers to is, in fact, human experience. Thus, Aristotle does not make a complete distinction between reason and experience. Of course, he puts the active reason of man paramount. In this sense, Aristotle is still a rationalistic philosopher. In ancient Greek philosophy after Aristotle, the Stoic School further elaborates on the rational nature of man. The Stoic School inherits from Aristotle the proposition that man is a rational animal, but naturalizes this reason and believes that rational life is a life in accordance with nature. The Stoic School believes that the universe is an orderly whole and that man is a part of it. Therefore, man should live in accordance with the order of nature. When a man becomes a rational animal, he regards a rational instinct as his true self. Therefore, man's pursuit and realization of his own nature are good, because man is a natural part of the whole universe, and his own nature is the natural nature of the whole universe. Thus, according to the Stoic School, living in accordance with nature is the supreme good. What is the universal law? In Stoic philosophy, it is the reason that permeates all things, that is, the God who governs and prescribes all things. The Stoic School equates reason with nature and deifies it, showing the tendency of mystifying reason.

Through the historical changes of Roman times, human reason turned to religion and formed the so-called religious reason. Thomas Aquinas, the chief exponent of medieval empirical philosophy, affirms that, man, like all other animals, seeks to develop his capabilities to the fullest and to perfect his nature. But some animals have consistent purposes, and some don't. Desires for life, health, safety, joy, power, fame, love, and knowledge are not evil, but they cannot be regarded as the supreme good. What, then, is the supreme good? Aquinas cites Aristotle to argue that the supreme good is the activities of reason. Only when reason is perfect can all actions be perfect. Its value lies in the perfection of the inner soul and self-improvement. Because the object of rational contemplation is vast and sacred, the soul can achieve omniscience and wisdom, and reach the state of perfection and beauty. Then, what objects would satisfy it? Aquinas believes that it is not the enjoyment of wealth, fame, power and carnal desires, but the love and pursuit of God. It is the contemplation of God that leads to a godlike state and true happiness. Thus, Aquinas regards

[4] See [4], pp. 22–24.

reason as a tool to get close to God, which shows the characteristics of religious reason. Religious reason breeds mysticism and eventually leads to the birth of modern humanistic reason. The spiritual awakening of modern reason is marked by Italian humanism and Luther's Protestant Reformation, thus forming the Renaissance movement. Humanism condemns the obscurantism of religious theology with the pursuit of the liberation of human nature and faith in improving human nature with knowledge of reason. At the same time, humanism boldly and passionately pursues the happiness and joy of human beings' real life, affirming the value and significance of life, eulogizing the natural nature of life, and fiercely attacking the religious reason with asceticism as its content in the Middle Ages. Therefore, humanism cannot be both rational and anti-rational, and it can only be said that religious reason is replaced by humanistic reason, which promotes the growth of the modern capitalist spirit. Luther's Protestant Reformation initiates the enlightenment of human rational thought, because the ideological basis of the religious reform is the affirmation of human self-consciousness and the conviction of human rational free value. The full affirmation of the inner subject's independence and freedom makes each individual's self-consciousness obtain unprecedented spiritual liberation and freedom. Luther believes that the magisterium system and all the laws that constrain and enforce people from it are external and heteronomous; only faith in the heart can produce conscious good deeds. This is the spiritual self-discipline of man, that is, human rational self-consciousness derived from faith.

From the seventeenth and eighteenth centuries, with the rise of the Enlightenment, Europe entered the age of Reason. The Enlightenment then was called on by reason to sweep away all ignorance, and to reflect rationally on the social system and all its ideologies at that time. Engels points out, "The great men, who in France prepared men's minds for the coming revolution, were themselves extreme revolutionists. They recognized no external authority of any kind whatever. Religion, natural science, society, political institutions—everything was subjected to the most unsparing criticism; everything must justify its existence before the judgment-seat of reason or give up existence."[5] Under the guidance of this rational world view, rational man became the assumption of human nature in the seventeenth and eighteenth centuries. The founder of modern rationalism is Descartes, a famous French philosopher. Descartes bases his philosophy on clear ideas and thinks that reason is the gift of man, and man is different from beasts because of his rational endowment. Therefore, only from a rational concept of human beings, from a clear concept, can man obtain correct knowledge. Descartes thinks that the rational concept or the rational cognitive ability of human beings is innate and everyone has it. That capacity for right judgment and for distinguishing true and false, which is, in fact, what we call conscience or reason, is naturally possessed by all men equally. Since man is distinguished from beasts by the capacity of reason or thought, the essential principle for establishing man is the principle of thought. Thinking is human nature. Starting from the premise that the essence of man is thinking reason, Descartes establishes the principle of universal doubt and the supreme principle of philosophical subjectivity of "I

[5] See [5], p. 719.

think therefore I am". Descartes believes that since man has thinking reason, there is nothing that cannot make thinking reason doubt. From the universe and nature to the human world, from the concept of nature to ethics, everything is in doubt of thinking. Through doubting, thinking establishes what is positive and negates what is negative; through doubting, thinking confirms its authority and supremacy. Although all things may be doubted by thinking, the thinking which is doubted by thinking cannot be doubted. Because only the existence of the thinking person, that is, the existence of the thinking subject, can the doubt of thinking proceed. Therefore, "I think therefore I am" is a universal proposition established by thinking and thinking entities. Human subjectivity and existence have been promoted to an unprecedented supreme position. The emphasis on and admiration for the reason make Descartes conclude that only the rational demonstration can be forever obeyed. Reason, according to Descartes, is human judgment and the ability to distinguish between true and false. Everyone is born with reason. It is human nature and the essence of self. Descartes regards reason as the conscience possessed by everyone who has this gift, so everyone has the ability to correctly judge and distinguish true and false. Descartes is a dogmatist and rationalist, believing in the ability of human reason to grasp true and universal knowledge. By virtue of the self-evident concepts and principles inherent in the soul, Descartes undertakes to establish an all-embracing theory which, like the propositions of geometry, must be obeyed by reason. Spinoza, who has the same confidence, thinks that the purpose of philosophy is also the acquisition of complete knowledge of things, which can only be achieved by clear and definite thinking. If we start from the self-evident principle and prove it at every step, we can establish a system of truth like mathematics.[6] In Spinoza's view, man is a part of nature, just a special style that embodies the essence of the entity in a certain way. As a special style of entity, the thought and extension of man are body and soul. The essence of man is a unity of body and soul. Nature's nature is man's nature. According to Spinoza's analysis, the soul can imagine and associate freely through the external object image provided by the body, and further form the connection of ideas, that is, memory. Therefore, he draws an important conclusion that reason is the same for all men. Spinoza investigates the relationship between human emotion and reason, and believes that emotion is not inherent in human nature, but is stimulated by external objects after the contact between the body and external objects. Emotions are feelings that make physical activities increase or decrease, smooth or baffling. According to Spinoza, emotions can bring disasters to people, and therefore they must be controlled by reason. Thus, Spinoza puts forward the theory of the unity of knowledge and virtue that the development stage of morality and emotion is compatible with the development stage of knowledge. In the lower stage, according to his view, man's emotions are passive, and the soul's knowledge of matters is partial, fragmentary, and unclear, and is only impressionistic emotional knowledge. Adapted to this knowledge, emotions can only take the form of passive, blind and narrow enthusiasm. At this stage, people are often driven and enslaved by lust, and weak in controlling emotions. In order to be freed from slavery, man must transcend the lower stage and reach the higher

[6] See [6], pp. 55–56.

stage of reason. At the stage of reason, the soul has a correct concept, which is from one-sided, fragmentary and unclear knowledge to complete, systematic and clear knowledge. The cognition of nature and necessity is attained, and true knowledge is acquired. In connection with the correct concept of the soul and true knowledge, the emotion develops into an active will. A will is an effort to maintain one's existence under the guidance of reason. It is only at this stage that a soul or reason can become the master of lust and show the initiative of a will. Spinoza emphasizes the consistency and identity of rational knowledge capacity and rational action capacity, which embodies the characteristics of rationalist ethics.

The French materialist philosophers in the eighteenth century inherited the tradition of rationalism, but they also had a strong color of utilitarianism. Hervetius applies materialist sensualism to the study of human nature, and establishes the theory of utilitarian ethics on this basis. Hervetius regards man as a part of nature, a machine powered by senses. Everything that the human body does comes down to physical sensation. Human desire, emotion, will, thought and behavior are determined by the physical sensation of the body. The tendency towards pleasure and the avoidance of pain, therefore, is human nature. It is an immutable law. According to Hervetius, people come into the world only with the capacity for feelings, that is, carnal and physical sensations. The capacity for reason develops from this capacity of feelings. Under the influence of external objects, people feel happiness or pain through feelings, and yield hope and disappointment, anxiety and fear through memory and imagination. According to repeated experience and lessons, people pursue what is pleasant and avoid what is painful. Therefore, the pursuit of happiness and avoidance of suffering has become the only motivation and reason for people's behaviors. Hervetius emphasizes that the physical sensation of human beings, human selfishness, pleasure pursuit and pain avoidance, and the pursuit of self-interest are the motive power of human behaviors. However, he also believes that individuals and a society are inseparable, and individuals must form a society to meet their own needs. How do we combine private interests with public interests? Hervetius thinks that one must resort to reason on this issue. Reason will tell people that as members of society, they must estimate the consequences of their behaviors, and sometimes if they do not give up their present happiness, they will have painful consequences later. Thus, although Hervetius emphasizes human sensation, which has empirical factors, in the end, he restricts people's sensation from a rational point of view in order to comply with the needs of social interests. Therefore, reason is still the highest principle in Hervetius' understanding of human nature. Holbach, another French materialist philosopher, believes that moral science, just like natural science, should start from objective facts and their relations, and be based on certain and natural principles. It is necessary to study the causes of human behaviors scientifically in accordance with realistic human relations and human nature. According to Holbach, the reliable foundation of morality is human nature. Man is made up of substances, and he is a rational physical body that can think. Man has a reason as well as sensibility. Since man has senses and reason, it is human nature to act upon them. Whatever makes their bodies feel happy, they pursue; whatever makes their bodies feel painful, they run away. Therefore, it is human nature to seek pleasure and avoid suffering. The function of human reason is to give the man a purpose and to be able to propose the appropriate means of action to achieve his purpose. A rational man is one who is able to choose the most reliable means to achieve his proposed purpose by experience. According to Holbach, morality is necessary for human beings, and it is based on human reason. Moral obligations are inevitable and certain, and they are as long as human life. In his opinion, virtue is the moral attribute of obligatory behaviors. Such moral attributes can be formed in individuals, which is the result of reason overcoming desires and deliberating cognition, and the result of civilization defeating nature. Thus, Holbach also emphasizes the importance of reason to morality. This utilitarianism is, to be precise, a kind of rational utilitarianism. This is also evident in the writings of Bentham, a British philosopher. Bentham's utilitarian thought originates from French materialist ethics, especially Hervetius, who has a profound influence on him. In *An Introduction to the Principles of Morality and Legislation*, Bentham takes the pursuit of pleasure and avoidance of suffering as the basis for demonstrating the principle of utilitarianism. Bentham believes that it is a natural instinct of all people to seek pleasure and avoid suffering. Nature has placed mankind under the governance of two sovereign masters, pain and pleasure. It is for them alone to point out what we ought to do, as well as to determine what we shall do. On the one hand the standard of right and wrong, on the other the chain of causes and effects, is fastened to their throne. That is to say, Bentham regards to pleasure and pain as standards of how people should behave, and he attributes the standard of moral judgment to human feelings of pain and pleasure. If the balance of one action which brings more pleasure than pain is more than the balance of the other activities which brings more pleasure than pain, the former action is better than the latter one. Of all possible actions, the one which contains the greatest surplus of pleasure over pain is the greatest good. Pleasure and pain not only provide the standards of values needed to examine jurisprudence, but also point out the causes of human behaviors and reveal the cause-and-effect chain of human behaviors. Not only can legislators skillfully make use of it to formulate laws governing human behaviors, but also ethicists can establish moral principles by virtue of it. Bentham points out that the utilitarian principle recognizes that man is ruled by pleasure and pain, and bases its system on a such rule. The purpose of the system is to build a welfare system under the guise of reason and law. Thus, the core and purpose of Bentham's whole system is utilitarianism. The pursuit of utility is not only the duty of reason, but also the important task of law enforcement. The legislator's duty is simply to reconcile private interests with public welfare. Therefore, Bentham proposes the slogan of the greatest happiness for the greatest number of people, and this utilitarian calculation and prediction completely depends on the rational ability of man. When evaluating the sensationalist ethics of Holbach and others, Soviet ethicists point out that the trinity of "natural morality-reason-law" is a common topic constantly repeated by Voltaire, Diderot, Holbach, Helvetius, Rousseau and others, despite their differences in philosophy and politics. The inclusion of reason in ethical theory is a return to the Cartesian tradition. The theoretical weakness of sensationalist ethics lies in that it secretly changes the standard of moral evaluation. It talks about both experience and reason, both receptivity as the basis of morality and the rationality of the will, and both private interests and social interests.[7]

Human rational spirit developed to the peak of rationalism in German classical philosophy in the eighteenth century. In Kant's view, man is a rational being, and only reason can determine man and his moral value. Ethics in the past was heteronomous, that is, drawing moral principles from causes other than human nature. They either seek the moral bases from the world of external experience or derive moral principles from the will of God; they either find moral bases in social laws and authorities or make the morality depend on the natural requirements of people, emphasizing the joy of behaviors, happiness and interests. According to Kant, none of these heteronomous ethics has really found a basis for moral values. Therefore, they neither find the universal necessary law of actions, nor reveal the law of freedom. In order to find the universal necessary law of actions and the bases of moral values, we must start from the rational essence of man and recognize the value of rational being as a purpose. According to Kant, man is certainly an animal with sensual desires, but the difference between man and an animal is not sensual desires, but reason. The will of man is free because it is rational in nature. The reason why man is moral is that reason can give himself and mankind a code of conduct, so that people do not obey the emotional desires and drives and do not fall into the herd. Kant regards man as a rational animal or a rational being. The reason why the will of man is free is that it is rational. In Kant's system, a will is the practical capacity of reason, the practical reason. Therefore, the will is the starting point of Kantian ethics. The will as the starting point is a universal good will. This good will comes from man's reason itself. In Kant's view, the law of practical reason and the law of morality cannot be based on perceptual experience, but must be based on the good will of reason. The moral law of universal necessity is derived from the good will of reason, which is the categorical imperative. According to Kant, there is only one categorical imperative as the law of morality, the fundamental law of practical reason: "Act only on that maxim through which you can at the same time will that it should become a universal law." Kant emphasizes the good will and the categorical imperative, so that the moral basis and the standard of values move from the outside of the subject to the inside of the subject, from the emotional aspect to the rational aspect, and the moral heteronomy is changed into the moral self-discipline. Kant's argument of the law of freedom is to demonstrate the universal necessity of the will self-discipline based on the categorical imperative of reason. Hegel, a famous German philosopher, on the basis of the rationalism tradition created by Kant, combines the great achievements of German rationalism, pushes human reason to the extreme, elevates the human rational spirit to the spirit of the universe noumenon, and establishes an amazing philosophical system of objective idealism. Hegel believes that reason is the soul of the world, and reason lives in the world. Reason constitutes the intrinsic, inherent, and profound nature of the world. In other words, the reason is the general character of the world. As reason is the master and entity of the universe, the reason is the infinite content of all things and the essence and truth of all things. The whole

[7] See [7], p. 413.

universe, including human history and spirits, operates and develops in a rational order. Therefore, Hegel believes that reason comes before natural objects, and the visible nature, spiritual world and historical process are all governed by rational decisions. Thus, Hegel puts forward the concept of the absolute idea. In Hegel's view, his philosophy, as the highest cognition of absolute existence, can start from the concrete idea with the direct regulation of concept, so as to grasp the absolute existence which is identical with spirit and nature or thought and being in the higher form of human reason, namely the absolute idea.

The rational assumption of human nature is the basic point of rationalist philosophy. Modern rationalism philosophy was initiated by Descartes, and developed to the peak of absolute rationalism by Hegel after Kant's critique of pure reason, and human rational self-knowledge entered a stage of conscious maturity.[8] Rationalist philosophy does not deny the irrational factors in human nature, but tries to eliminate the opposition between reason and unreason with rational principles, so that human nature is built on the basis of rational principles.

1.2 Empirical Man

Empirical man is the empirical hypothesis of human nature and the view of human nature in empiricism philosophy. Although the empirical view of human nature is not as great as the rational view of human nature in western culture, it also has an impact on western civilization that cannot be underestimated. Especially since the nineteenth century, with the decline of rationalism, empiricism has been manifested in various forms and has become the mainstream of modern western philosophy.

In ancient Greek philosophy, along with the rise of rationalism, empiricism began to emerge and manifested itself in the form of unreason. For example, in the theory of Aristotle, a famous ancient Greek philosopher, there is an idea that reason and unreason are the same. Aristotle holds that the soul has two parts, namely reason and unreason, and human's inner nature has the contradiction between reason and unreason. Aristotle's ethical values make man distinguish himself from animals with his unique reason, and make a man become a rational man. However, he objectively sees the biological and natural nature of man's transition from animals. Epicurus is the representative of empiricism in ancient Greek philosophy. Epicurus advocates the epistemological theory of sensation. He believes that things exist outside, independent of human consciousness. The senses are the only reliable source and standard of cognition. Epicurus thinks that nothing can refute perception. The same perception cannot refute the same perception because they have the same criteria; different perceptions do not refute different perceptions, because they do not judge the same thing. In his view, reason is the way to know things, but reason itself depends on feelings. Reason is a derivative, and without feeling it cannot provide reliable knowledge. Nor can the concept refute perception, on which the concept depends. To deny

[8] See [8], p. 84.

sensation is to deny the standard of truth, and at the same time to lose the possibility of all behaviors and reliability of belief. The error of cognition, according to Epicurus, lies neither in the senses nor in the perception, but in the judgment, for without the judgment of the senses and perception, there would be nothing to judge the wrong judgment which you condemn. Nor do we misjudge what we perceive when we are sane. In the same way, doubts and opinions in thought cannot become truth because they have not been judged and demonstrated by experience. Epicurus emphasizes that all opinions must be empirically demonstrated before they can be judged. Obviously, Epicurus emphasizes the role of feelings in cognition, which has tinged with empiricism.

In the Middle Ages, religious theology used reason to establish its theoretical system and formed religious reason. However, at the same time, the fideism peculiar to religion inevitably led to the negation of human reason, thus moving towards empiricism characterized by sensationalism. With the return of modern rationalism, empiricism also became popular, and especially a strong ideological trend of empiricism philosophy formed in Britain. In modern British philosophy, Bacon is the representative of empiricist philosophers. Bacon values experience but despise reason. He says, "The understanding must not therefore be supplied with wings, but rather hung with weights, to keep it from leaping and flying." Bacon believes that human cognition is the reflection of objective things. Knowledge comes from the imitation of nature, and the truth of existence is consistent with the truth of knowledge. For Bacon, knowledge is the cognition of the laws of nature. What really exists in nature is nothing but the pure individual actions of individual bodies according to certain laws; but in philosophy, it is this law, and the study, discovery, and interpretation of this law, form the basis of knowledge and activity. Bacon emphasizes the effect of sensory experiences and practical activities on cognition, and believes that knowledge comes from sensory experiences, and that human beings should investigate and transform knowledge on the basis of practice to establish a scientific system. Bacon emphasizes experience, but he does not completely exclude reason. While emphasizing that experience is the source and foundation of knowledge, he advocates that perceptual cognition should be elevated to rational cognition. Bacon believes that the sensory experiences should not be allowed to drift, but they must be given rational guidance in accordance with certain laws, in order to obtain real knowledge. Why is Bacon an empiricist since he also talks about reason? In this regard, the US philosopher Thilly points out that we can put Bacon into the empiricism school, although his empiricism is incomplete and inconsistent. He believes that all knowledge, except the apocalypse, arises from the sensation, and that only individual things exist. Spirits or reason can process the materials provided by the senses; knowledge is rational and empirical; reason itself does not yield truth. At the same time, he talks of the capacities of the mind as if they were innate. A soul is a material. However, there is also a soul of reason, of which we know nothing, and it belongs to religion. Theology was excluded from physics and became part of the unprofitable branch of metaphysics.[9] Starting from empiricism, Bacon establishes the inductive method and challenges the

[9] See [6], p. 26.

deductive method of rationalism. The inductive method, which is based on empirical facts and eliminates the fallacies brought by rationalism, is regarded by Bacon as the sole scientific method of understanding.

After Bacon, the British philosopher Hume is also a famous empiricist. Hume doubts and belittles reason, and emphasizes and exaggerates the roles of emotion and intuition. Hume denies the existence of any material or spiritual entity outside of human sensation. He believes that cognition cannot go beyond the scope of subjective sensation. All that exists in the world are sensation and perception, except for which nothing is known. In *An Enquiry Concerning Human Understanding*, Hume says, "I shall venture to affirm, as a general proposition, which admits of no exception, that the knowledge of this relation is not, in any instance, attained by reasonings a priori; but arises entirely from experience, when we find that any particular objects are constantly conjoined with each other. Let an object be presented to a man of ever so strong natural reason and abilities; if that object is entirely new to him, he will not be able, by the most accurate examination of its sensible qualities, to discover any of its causes or effects. Adam, though his rational faculties are supposed, at the very first, entirely perfect, could not have inferred from the fluidity and transparency of water that it would suffocate him, or from the light and warmth of the fire that it would consume him. No object ever discovers, by the qualities which appear to the senses, either the causes which produced it, or the effects which will arise from it; nor can our reason, unassisted by experience, ever draw any inference concerning real existence and matter of fact."[10] Since no belief can be obtained by inference or reason, and we do obtain innumerable beliefs anyway, the traditional rationalist idea of man as an independent and rational actor should be discarded, according to Hume.

The rise of positivism of Comte, a famous French philosopher, is a further challenge to rationalism. Comte puts forward the proposition that "observation is superior to the imagination", which inhibits human reason and has an obvious tendency toward empiricism. As the US philosopher Thilly points out, Comte is on the side of empirical thinkers. He belongs to the class of philosophers chiefly represented by Hume and Diderot.[11] Comte believes that all science must develop on the basis of observed facts. Observation and experiment are the fundamental means for people to explore all things and phenomena. Perceptual experience obtained by observation is the source of cognition. Therefore, Comte places great emphasis on the role of the senses. Comte believes that if one loses an important sense, or if one gains a new sense, he can at least perceive a group of facts. Therefore, Comte places sensation in an unusually important position: the study of phenomena is carried out only through sensation. In the case of loss of sensation, or in the case of simple qualitative changes of sensation, it is conceivable what kind of results will be produced in the research. Starting from such sensationalism, Comte suppresses the role of rational thinking and imagination, and advocates that people's cognition can only be phenomenological and cannot make any detailed evaluation beyond this limit. To attempt to explain the

[10] See [9], p. 28.

[11] See [6], p. 276.

inner nature of existence, the origin and end of all things, the nature of all phenomena, and the forms of discovery, is not only utopian and useless, but it even endangers all the foundations of true science. The result of this repression of rational cognition is that Comte regards perceptual sensory experiences as the only factor and measure that determines the development of cognition and he concludes that only experience provides us with the only measure of our power. Here, Comte's positive philosophy shows the obvious empiricist tendency recognized by people. The reason why Comte emphasizes that all knowledge must be subordinate to observation is that people's cognition is restricted to the field of a single fact and phenomenon given directly by observation, so that cognition is led by sensation and experience.[12]

In the twentieth century, with the disillusionment of the French Enlightenment, the development of rationalism encountered a profound crisis, which provided an opportunity for the origin of modern irrationalism philosophy. Modern irrationalism tries its best to highlight the individuality and unrepeatability of man as the subject. It puts the non-rational elements in human psychological factors, such as will, emotion, intuition and instinct, in the first place, and emphasizes the decisive role of non-rational psychological factors in human cognition and behaviors.[13]

1.3 The Unity of Rational Man and Empirical Man

"The history of philosophy is, to a large extent, the history of the clashes of human temperaments," the US pragmatist philosopher James says astonishingly. The rationalist and the empiricist are regarded by James as two philosophical equivalents of temperament. James points out empiricist' means your lover of facts in all their crude variety, 'rationalist' means your devotee to abstract and eternal principles. No one can live an hour without both facts and principles, so it is a difference rather of emphasis, yet it breeds antipathies of the most pungent character between those who lay the emphasis differently; and we shall find it extraordinarily convenient to express a certain contrast in men's ways of taking their universe, by talking of the 'empiricist' and of the 'rationalist' temper. These terms make the contrast simple and massive. These two nouns make the contrast simple but powerful. The use of these two nouns to describe people often makes their contrast simpler but more powerful than the people they indicate. Human nature may have various kinds of interweaving and combinations, so, if I, by making the two nouns add some features of the secondary regulation respectively, explain more fully what my mind refers to when I mention empiricists and rationalists, please take my behavior as an arbitrary measure to some extent. Historically we find the terms 'intellectualism' and 'sensationalism' used as synonyms of 'rationalism' and 'empiricism'. Well, nature seems to combine most frequently with intellectualism an idealistic and optimistic tendency. Empiricists on the other hand are not uncommonly materialistic, and their optimism is apt to be

[12] See [10], p. 49.

[13] See [11], p. 45.

decidedly conditional and tremulous. Rationalism is always monistic. It starts from wholes and universals, and makes much of the unity of things. Empiricism starts from the parts, and makes the whole a collection-is not averse therefore to calling itself pluralistic. Rationalism usually considers itself more religious than empiricism, but there is much to say about this claim, so I merely mention it. It is a true claim when the individual rationalist is what is called a man of feeling, and when the individual empiricist prides himself on being hard-headed. In that case, the rationalist will usually also be in favor of what is called free-will, and the empiricist will be a fatalist—I use the terms most popularly current. The rationalist finally will be of dogmatic temper in his affirmations, while the empiricist may be more skeptical and open to discussion. James divided the qualities of rationalism and empiricism into two categories, 'tender-minded' and 'tough-minded', as follows[14]:

The tender-minded	The tough-minded
Rationalistic	Empiricist
(going by "principles")	(going by "facts")
Intellectualistic	Sensationalistic
Idealistic	Materialistic
Optimistic	Pessimistic
Religious	Irreligious
Free-willist	Fatalistic
Monistic	Pluralistic
Dogmatical	Skeptical

The contrast between rationalism and empiricism that James sets out here is correct in a sense, but certainly not absolutely correct. In fact, the two pairs of categories of reason and experience and rationalism and empiricism are difficult to distinguish. Thilly, a US philosopher, once pointed out that modern philosophy is classified as rationalism or empiricism on the basis that it takes reason or experience as the source or criteria of knowledge. To avoid misunderstanding, the following points must be emphasized: (1) Rationalism can be referred to as an attitude that affirms that the standard of knowledge is reason rather than revelation or authority. In this sense, all modern systems of philosophy are rationalistic; according to this characteristic, we classify them as modern philosophy. (2) Rationalism can be referred to as the view that true knowledge consists of universal and necessary judgments, and that the purpose of thought is to formulate a system of truth in which propositions are logically related to one another. This is a mathematical concept of knowledge that almost all new thinkers regard as ideal. Whether or not they believe that this ideal is realizable, they only recognize that knowledge that fits a mathematical model is true knowledge. (3) There is also the question of the origin of knowledge, to which modern philosophy has different answers: (a) True knowledge cannot come from sensory perception or experience, but it must have its foundation in thought or reason. If truth is the

[14] See [12], pp. 8–9.

natural possession of reason or truth is inherent in reason, it is the natural, innate, or transcendental truth. Well-established truth springs from thought itself. This is also called rationalism, although some people prefer to call it intuitionism or transcendentalism. (b) There is no innate truth, and all knowledge springs from sensory perception or experience. Consequently, the so-called apodeictic propositions are not at all apodeictic or absolutely certain, but they can only give people probabilistic knowledge. This view is called empiricism or sensationalism. Thilly thinks that the empiricists may accept rationalism in the first and second senses; they may consider only such knowledge genuine as gives us absolute certainty, and, at the same time, deny the possibility of attaining real knowledge except perhaps in mathematics. If by empiricism we mean that our world of experience is the object of philosophy, that philosophy has to interpret it, then all modern philosophy is empirical. If we mean by it that we cannot know without experience, that pure thought, or thought absolutely independent of sense perception, is impossible, then, again, modern philosophy is largely empirical. Keeping all this in mind, we may characterize philosophers as rationalists (apriorists) or empiricists (sensationalists), according to the answers they give to the question of the origin of knowledge. Closely connected with the question of the origin is the question of the certainty or validity of knowledge. Both schools of early modern times agree that sense knowledge is not absolutely certain; rationalists declare that only rational or a priori truths, clearly and distinctly perceived truths, are certain; empiricists generally deny that there are such a priori truths, and hold that clearly and distinctly perceived truths are not necessarily certain.[15] This shows that only in the origin of knowledge can rationalism and empiricism be truly distinguished.

Modern rationalism develops the view of reason from two aspects, essentialism and epistemology. It involves not only the understanding of human nature, but also the methodology of world cognition. It should be mentioned that the hypothesis of rational man contains a certain degree of truth, which reveals the difference between human beings and animals to a certain extent, and thus explains human nature. This rational view of human nature has had a profound influence on the humanities and has penetrated all fields of knowledge. In politics, it is political rationalism, which refers to the rational observation and contemplation of human society and its political system, as well as self-conscious political and historical activities. As the US philosopher Thilly put it, “Modern spirit is the spirit of resisting the medieval society and its system and thought, and also the self-extension of human reason in the field of thought and action.”[16] Political Man *(Homo Politicus)*, envisaged by political rationalism, is a rational man who participates in democracy mainly through the election. In the election, any voter is a rational voter, whose voting behavior is rational voting behavior. Rational voting behavior refers to voters’ choice to maximize their perceived (or expectant) benefits. In other words, any action the actor decides to take must maximize the benefits he or she perceives, or else the actor will make other

[15] See [6], pp. 14–15.

[16] See [6], p. 148.

choices, so any voter must be rational.[17] Political rationalism produces a positive view of politics, and people who hold this view tend to be optimistic. They have reasons to be optimistic about the realization of the supreme good through political activities because human reason can be the ultimate recourse of human beings. In their view, man's unique gift lies in his reason. Reason is the glory and pride of mankind. The proposition that man is a rational animal states that reason and lust are antithetical. The former symbolizes good, and the latter symbolizes evil. However, people can consciously use reason to guide their actions and suppress the "evil" lust in their hearts. Socrates and Plato both stress that reason is the highest part of the human soul. The goal of human struggles and the meaning of progress is to achieve the perfection of reason in man and in society.[18] In economy, modern rationalism is the laissez-faire of the classical economic school. Economic man (*homo economicus*), as conceived of by the classical economic school, is also a rational man. For example, Adam Smith, a famous British economist, believes that human beings are rational. The pursuit of personal economic interests is the basis of all human activities. It is also human instinct. This egoistic instinct of economic man forms an irresistible natural economic force, which cannot be restricted. Therefore, Adam Smith advocates laissez-faire in economy, opposing state intervention and advocating adjusting the social economy by the market mechanism, which is like an invisible hand.[19] All the theories above are based on reason. However, human reason is not innate. It comes from social life, and it is subject to the limits of social life. In other words, man's rational capacities are extremely limited. To exaggerate the function of reason without limits is bound to lead to absurdity. A more scientific view of reason should not be the absolute and infinite reason, but relative and finite reason. Simon, a famous US scholar, once described finite reason very incisively. He believes that reason is to choose satisfactory alternative behavior with a value system that evaluates the consequences of behavior. Reason can be divided into objective reason and subjective reason. Objective reason means that a certain value can really be maximized in a given situation. Subjective reason refers to the maximization of a decision's value relative to the decision maker's subjective knowledge. In Simon's opinion, actual behavior determines objective reason, at least in the following three aspects: (1) In accordance with the requirements of reason, the behavioral agent should have complete knowledge and foresight about the consequence of each choice. In fact, understanding the consequences is always fragmentary. (2) Since consequences are in the future, imagination must make up for the lack of experience when we assign value to such consequences. Yet the expectation of value cannot be complete. (3) In accordance with the requirements of reason, one can think of only a few possible action plans. Simon goes on to discuss the limits of reason: (1) The incompleteness of knowledge. Reason means being fully aware of the exact consequence of each choice. In fact, a man's knowledge of the conditions of his actions can be no more than fragmentary; he knows very little of the laws which enable him to infer future

[17] See [13], p. 117.

[18] See [14].

[19] See [15], p. 18.

consequences from his knowledge of present conditions. (2) Foresight of difficulty. The ability to track the shifting value elements of its imagined consequences and the ability to give consistent tradeoffs to the post-experience that these elements lead to. (3) Range of possible actions.[20]

I should say that finite reason is correct. It takes into account the complexity and variability of the human environment and makes a relatively objective evaluation of human rational ability. In fact, man has not only reason, but also irrational elements, such as passion and impulse, which reflect animal instincts. The British philosopher Russell once pointed out that all human activities take place from two sources: impulse and desire. Impulse is the instinctual part of human nature. Instinct is the need for survival and development shared by all human beings and lower animals. In addition to impulse, a man's actions are governed by desires. Desire is conscious. It is connected with human reason, manifested as the pursuit of a certain purpose. From impulse and desire, Russell makes a conclusion that human nature lies between the individual and society. Therefore, sociality and individuality are two basic elements of human nature, which is the human nature foundation of ethics, according to Russell.[21]

Modern empiricism denies the apriority of human cognition, especially emphasizing the individuality of human beings and the difference between individual cognition, which contains certain cognition of truth. The opposition between empiricism and rationalism is also reflected in various fields of knowledge. In politics, it is political empiricism. Sartori, a US scholar, once compared the difference between empirical democracy and rationalist democracy, believing that both take people's sovereignty as the starting point. However, the characteristic of Anglo-US democratic theory—the model of empirical democracy—is that it is a theory of ways and means of discussing democratic politics. On the contrary, in Article 1 of *The Constitution of the Weimar Republic*, which of course is the model of constitutional rationalism, we can read "die Staatsgewalt geht vom volke aus" (The power of the State comes from people). This premise provides the basis for a carefully structured deductive argument. That is because people in British are concrete people. The French word for people and its synonym is an abstract entity, a whole arising out of abstract speculation consistent with the rational Gestalt.[22] Political empiricism produces a negative view of politics, believing in the supremacy of evil and haunted by dark consciousness. The negative political view holds that since human nature is unreliable, power in human hands will inevitably be used for evil. Therefore, in order to avoid the corruption of power resulting in totalitarian autocracy, it is necessary to take precautions from the system.[23] The British scholar Wallas "discovered" the irrational factor in politics, believing that most people's political behavior, which is based on instincts and emotions, is irrational. It turns out that since a man's capacity for conscious reasoning is imperfect, the fear and impulse

---

[20] See [16], pp. 79–81.

[21] See [17], p. 30.

[22] Giovanni [13], p. 57.

[23] See [14].

of the moment may be more reliable than the process of reasoning, but even the decision to comply with the impulse becomes a behavioral problem because he has a choice, Wallas points out. Burke believes that man's capacity for political reasoning is extremely limited. All his life he exhorts the British to conform to convention, that is, to conform on principle to habitual political impulses.[24] In economics, the assumption of a rational economic man in classical economics is also seriously challenged. For example, the British economist Hodgson points out that the concept of reason is very special indeed, and it is in the most important position at least in the orthodox theories. However, economists use the word "reason" more arrogantly than other social scientists. They often assert that any statement of irrational behavior is derogatory to human prestige or absurd. However, a brief glance at the other social sciences, particularly sociology and anthropology, reveals the complexities and unanswered questions about the word "reason". It would be much better if economists dabble in such literature, crossing more frequently the artificial boundaries that often exist between the social sciences.[25] The hypothesis of empirical man, discarding abstract human nature, laying human nature on the basis of social reality, and revealing the individuality of human nature, has a certain scientific nature. However, the hypothesis of empirical man exaggerates the role of feelings too much. It does not recognize the rational factors in human nature, and denies common human nature or commonality in human nature, which also has defects.

To sum up, I think the rational man and empirical man are not diametrically opposed. There are both rational factors and empirical factors in human nature. Human nature has both commonality and particularity, and the two have dialectical unity. Only by adhering to the principle of duality between reason and experience of human nature can we scientifically reveal human nature and lay a reasonable human nature foundation for criminal law.

2 Analysis Approaches to Human Nature

The analysis of human nature involves methodologies. The analysis approaches to human nature are mainly related to the understanding of human beings. That is, whether human beings are individual people or social people. Therefore, there is a difference between individualism and holism in methodology.

2.1 Individualism

The individualistic methodology in the analysis of human nature is to elucidate human nature from the perspective of the individual. Individualism holds that society

[24] See [18], p. 121.
[25] See [19], p. 88.

is composed of countless individuals, and there is no society without individuals. Therefore, the analysis of society must start from individuals, and there is no way to explain society otherwise.

The methodology of individualism originates from the atomism of Democritus, an ancient Greek philosopher. Democritus believes that everything in the world is made of atoms, and that atoms are always in motion. Atoms can be big or small. Everything is made up of atoms in different combinations and collisions of size, number, order, shape and position. Man is also made of atoms. The human soul is made up of atoms of the most delicate, tactful, and sensitive kind. When body atoms and soul atoms join, human life is born. And there is one soul atom for every two body atoms. Every day we breathe, we absorb soul atoms from the air. When the soul atom is separated from the body atom, the vessel of soul atom in the body is broken, and human life ends. In Democritus' opinion, a man is a union of body atoms and soul atoms. Human nature arises from the union of body atoms and soul atoms. The manifestation of the material and moving atoms in society is man's activity and the development of an independent personality. Democritus thus famously proposes that man is a small world.[26] In the late 18th and early nineteenth centuries, in the writings of utilitarianists and liberalists, individualistic methodologies began to permeate the social sciences. The earliest elaboration of the methodology of individualism can be found in the writings of the eighteenth and nineteenth centuries freethinkers such as Jeremy Bentham. John Stuart Mill writes, "The laws of the phenomena of society are, and can be, nothing but the laws of the actions and passions of human beings united together in the social state." This is the personal law of human nature. Mill goes on to say, "Men are not, when brought together, converted into another kind of substance, with different properties." The term individualistic methodology was coined by Schumpeter in 1908. However, it is Mises who makes the word more widely known. He points out that the principles of the methodology of individualism include the recognition that "all actions are human actions; when the behavior of individual members is excluded, there will be no existence and reality of social groups."[27] The methodology of individualism has exerted great influence in the fields of political science, law, economics, psychology and other social sciences.

The methodology of individualism starts from individuals and emphasizes that all explanations of social phenomena must be analyzed and elucidated from the perspective of individuals. The individualism methodology's causality view, which attributes everything to individuals, has a deeper meaning: the explanation of social phenomena, even a circuitous path, must be from the part (individual) to the whole (society), not the other way round. The core idea of the methodology of individualism is "the principle of individual purposefulness," which holds that individual purposefulness is the sufficient cause of all social behavior.

[26] See [20], p. 107.

[27] Hodgson [19], p. 64.

2.2 Holism

The holistic methodology of human nature analysis refers to the interpretation of human nature from the social sense and the full attention to the influence of social factors on human nature. Holism holds that although the society is composed of individuals, the individuals here are not disorderly and scattered, and the society is not simply the sum of countless individuals. Society has its own development law, which inevitably determines the behavior of individuals. Therefore, human nature can only be explained by society as a whole.

The methodology of holism comes from the ancient Greek philosopher Aristotle's idea that man is a social animal. Aristotle believes that human beings, as social animals, cannot live alone and exist individually, and only in society can human beings survive and develop. As a methodology of social science, holism developed in modern times. Especially Dürkheim, a famous French sociologist, made great contributions to it. In the book *The Rules of Sociological Method*, Dürkheim systematically expounds on the methodology of holism. Dürkheim first distinguishes social phenomena from individual phenomena, believing that social phenomena have a special character. They are ways of acting, thinking and feeling that exist outside of the body, and at the same time exert a coercive force on each individual. The word "social" has a definite meaning only when it is applied to a synthetic phenomenon, a phenomenon detached from the individual phenomenon already formed. Individual phenomena are different from social phenomena. Social phenomena cannot be explained by individual consciousness, but only by the nature of society itself. Social phenomena are far beyond the individual in both time and space. It has a kind of authority to force individuals, forcing individual behavior and thinking mode, so that individuals feel its pressure, by the society as a whole on each individual, which is the special mark of social phenomenon. According to this principle, society is not a simple sum of individuals. Society is formed by the combination of individuals, but the system formed by this combination shows a special situation and has its own unique nature. There can be no collective consciousness without individual consciousness, which is a necessary condition but not a sufficient one. This individual consciousness must be combined into certain forms. Social life is the product of this combination, and only this combination can explain social life. Therefore, Dürkheim puts forward the famous assertion that "social phenomena are explained by society."[28] It can be said that Dürkheim's sociology is based on the methodology of holism.

The methodology of holism starts with people in society and emphasizes that human nature should be explained by the whole society. This method breaks through the narrow thought scope of individualism limited to the individual understanding of human nature, and puts human nature in the broad vision of society, which is undoubtedly great progress in explaining human nature.

---

[28] See [21], pp. 5, 81 and 82.

2.3 *The Unity of Individualism and Holism*

The opposition of individualism and holism in methodology leads to different interpretations of various social phenomena, thus forming the opposition of various schools of thought. Xie Yong, a Chinese scholar, has sharply revealed the opposition between the two methodological thoughts always existing in the western criminology theory, which is the opposition between individualism and holism. As methodologies, the opposition between the two focuses on their different logical priorities for theoretical interpretation. Holism holds that social phenomena can only be explained by social phenomena, so the causes of criminal phenomena should be determined mainly on the macroscopic level of causality, rather than relying on the explanation of the criminal's individual psychology. Individualism believes that the causes of social phenomena can only be truly and ultimately answered in individual behavior and psychology. Leaving this basis and attempting to find causal relationships between social phenomena can only be regarded as running after the less important things, forgetting the important or seeking roses in December. Xie Yong points out that one of the main reasons why neither individualistic criminology nor holistic criminology can establish a reliable and effective theory on the causes of crimes is that they do not fully understand the methodological significance contained in the following fact. That is, individual criminal behavior and social crimes as a whole belong to different things. Therefore, the laws governing them should not be the same. In our theoretical analysis, we cannot leave this hierarchy isolation of things alone and blindly pursue a "unified and comprehensive" theoretical explanation. Both holism and individualism fail in their tendency to apply, openly or covertly, concepts, judgments or modes of analysis acquired at one level to another. However, the interaction mode of individualism is more mysterious. It simply moves its foothold to a certain position between the above two levels, trying to build a bridge between the two levels. However, a series of problems in the current theoretical construction of criminology have shown that these methods are not helpful, but lead the practical research astray. Therefore, Xie Yong proposes that criminology should find a new theoretical strategy for development. The key link is that it recognizes and emphasizes the relative isolation between the phenomenon of social crimes at the macro level and the behavior of individual crimes at the micro level. It advocates the establishment and development of theories on two levels and resolutely resists the temptation of "cross-level explanation."[29] Although what is said here is a theoretical problem of criminology, it is of great significance to the general methodology of human nature analysis. I believe that the theoretical structure of a discipline is determined by the nature of a discipline. Criminology, economics and other disciplines can be divided into macro and micro levels by the theoretical structure, thus forming macro criminology and micro criminology, macroeconomics and microeconomics. Any cross-level interpretation is not desirable here. Undoubtedly, macro theories focus on the holistic approach, while micro theories focus on the individualistic approach. However, when any discipline

[29] See [22], p. 3.

explains a social phenomenon, it still has a general explanation. For example, criminology. Although it can explain the phenomenon of a crime from both macro and micro aspects, as the basis of these two explanations, there must be a general explanation of the phenomenon of a crime, which is the task of theoretical criminology. In the course of this general explanation, a crime can neither be treated as a social phenomenon detached from the individual perpetrator, nor be treated as a purely individual phenomenon detached from society. In this sense, a crime is a crime. Isn't there a comprehensive methodology involved in giving this general explanation?

Solomon Asch points out that the subjects of our study are not simple individuals, but social individuals who have a place in the social order…In order to understand the individual, we must study it in the context of its group; and to understand this group, we must examine the individuals, because it is the interrelated behavior of these individuals that constitutes a social group.[30] Therefore, this is sociological interaction theory. In my opinion, man has the duality of the individual and the society, and dialectical analysis should pay full attention to this duality of man. Therefore, the individual and the society are not opposite, but interactive; our free characters and abilities are formed in the social and economic environment. The basic element of society is not the abstract individual, but the social individual. He forms society and is organized by society. In Patrick Berman's words, we should avoid "fruitless polarization between individuals and society." It is wrong to stress the primacy of individuals or society.[31] From this point of view, I believe that as a methodology, individualism and holism should be organically unified. For the interpretation of human nature, neither the individual nor the society can all be come down to. Human nature can only be explained by the unity of individuals and society, which is a comprehensive explanation.

It should be pointed out that individualism and holism are different from methodology and axiology. Individualistic methodology cannot be equated with ethical individualism, and holistic methodology cannot be equated with ethical collectivism. The British economist Hodgson, for example, talks about it when he talks about the methodology of individualism. A further difficulty in discussing the subject, he points out, is that the term "individualistic methodology" has an ideological connotation. In fact, it has become commonplace for advocates and opponents alike to confuse the "individualistic methodology" with the "individualism" in political changes. However, the link between political individualism and methodological individualism is only supported by things assumed by proponents or critics or by lax arguments, and this link has never been rigorously demonstrated.[32] As a matter of fact, there is a phenomenon that ethical individualism often adopts the holistic approach, while ethical holism often adopts the individualistic approach.

[30] Hodgson [19], p. 83.

[31] Hodgson [19], pp. 61–62.

[32] Hodgson [19], pp. 61–62.

References

1. [UK] Hume, *A Treatise of Human Nature*, vol. 1 (The Commercial Press, Beijing, 1980)
2. [US] Perdue et al., *Sociological Theory: Explanation, Paradigm, and Ideology* (Hebei People's Publishing House, Shijiazhuang, 1992)
3. F. Zhou (ed.), *Selected Works of Western Ethics* (The Commercial Press, Beijing, 1964)
4. [Ancient Greece] Aristotle, *The Nicomachean Ethics* (China Social Sciences Press, Beijing, 1990)
5. *Karl Marx Frederick Engels Selected Works*, vol. 3, 2nd edn. (People's Publishing House, Beijing, 1995)
6. [US] Thilly, *A History of Philosophy*, vol. 2 (The Commercial Press, Beijing, 1979)
7. [Soviet Union] A. Guseynov et al., *Brief History of Ethics* (Renmin University of China Press, Beijing, 1992)
8. Y. Feng, *The Sorrow and Joy of Reason: The Critique of Reason and Non-reason* (People's Publishing House, Beijing, 1993)
9. [UK] Hume, *An Enquiry Concerning Human Understanding* (The Commercial Press, Beijing, 1957)
10. L. Ou, *Comte and His Positivism* (Shanghai Academy of Social Science Press, Shanghai, 1987)
11. G. Su, *Rationality and Its Limitation: Introduction to Weber's Thoughts* (Shanghai People's Press, Shanghai, 1988)
12. [US] J. William, *Pragmatism: A New Name for Some Old Ways of Thinking* (The Commercial Press, Beijing, 1979)
13. [US] S. Giovanni, *The Theory of Democracy Revisited* (People's Oriental Publishing & Media, Beijing, 1993)
14. J. Liu, *Good and Evil: Two Political Views and National Capabilities*, no. 5 (Reading, 1994)
15. P. Hu (Chief Editor), *Chinese Market Economy Complete Book* (Huaxia Publishing House, Beijing, 1993)
16. [US] Simon, *Administrative Behavior* (Beijing College of Economics Press, Beijing, 1988)
17. [UK] Russell, *Human Society in Ethics and Politics* (China Social Sciences Press, Beijing, 1992)
18. [UK] W. Graham, *Human Nature in Politics* (Zhejiang People's Publishing House, Hangzhou, 1988)
19. [UK] Hodgson, *Manifesto of Modern Institutional Economics* (Peking University Press, Beijing, 1993)
20. Compiled by the Teaching and Research Section of the Section of Foreign Philosophy of the Department of Philosophy of Peking University, *Ancient Greek and Roman Philosophy* (Joint Publishing, Beijing, 1957)
21. [France] Dürkheim, *The Rules of Sociological Method* (Huaxia Publishing House, Beijing, 1988)
22. Y. Xie, *Introduction to Study of Criminology* (Hunan Publishing House, Changsha, 1992)

Chapter 2
Human Nature Foundation Held by the Classical School of Criminology

Ōtsuka Hitoshi, a Japanese criminal jurist, points out that the opposition between the classical school of criminology and the positivist school of criminology stems from their different understanding of the human nature of a criminal who is the subject of the crime. A crime is committed by a man on whom punishment is judged. Therefore, as the object of criminal law, human nature must often be considered. It can be said that the understanding of human nature determines the nature of criminal jurisprudence.[1] It should be said that this judgment incisively reveals the root cause of the divergence between the classical school of criminology and the positivist school of criminology. However, the differences between the two schools on human nature are not only limited to the understanding of criminals' human nature, but also involve the understanding of legislators' and judicial persons' human nature, which is precisely based on the different understanding of general human nature. Only by starting from human nature can we clarify the theoretical context and opposition points of the two schools.

1 Assumption About Human Nature

The assumption about the human nature of the classical school of criminology is a rational man. Rational man is the assumption that any human being has the rational capacity for freedom of will. Starting from this, the classical school of criminology constructed the first theoretical system of criminal jurisprudence in modern times.

---

[1] See [1], p. 2.

X. Chen, *Humanistic Foundation of Criminal Law*,
https://doi.org/10.1007/978-981-19-9764-8_2

1.1 Human Nature Analysis of Crimes

Starting from the rational assumption about human nature, the classical school of criminology holds that the criminal has freedom of will in nature and chooses to commit a crime based on this freedom of consciousness, so he should bear the criminal liability for the consequences of his behavior.

The representative figures of the classical school of criminology are Beccaria, Bentham, Feuerbach, Kant and Hegel. Although they differ in some views, they share the same rational assumption of the criminal's freedom of will, which is the humanistic foundation of the classical school of criminology.

Kant regards criminal law as a categorical imperative to human reason, and believes that a person's ability to act in accordance with his own expression constitutes his life. The ability of man to act according to his own expression itself contains man's rational choice, which constitutes will.[2] Kant's assumption of the rational man comes from the autonomy of will. The so-called autonomy of the will is every rational existing will as the will of common legislation. Kant points out that nature now concludes that man (with every rational being) is the purpose itself in the destination country. That is, no one (not even God) can use him only as a means; he himself is always a purpose. The nature of the person who incarnates ourselves must therefore be sacred to us. The reason for this conclusion is that man is the subject of a moral imperative, which is itself sacred…This moral imperative is based on his autonomy of will. This will, as a free will, at the same time corresponds, according to his universal law, to that thing which he was to obey.[3] In Kant's view, the reason why people are human beings lies in the fact that their reason enables their will to be free and their morality to be self-disciplined, which is the transcendence of man's perceptual existence. Therefore, according to Kant, the reason why a person should be punished is that he committed a crime under the control of freedom of will, which is the only legitimate basis for the punishment of the criminal. Hegel believes that man is a rational animal, and the criminal also has the freedom of will to commit a crime. Therefore, he concludes that punishment contains the criminal's own law, so to punish him is to honor him as a rational being.[4] It can be seen that Hegel's theory of criminal law is based on the rational assumption of human nature. In Hegel's view, there can be no crime without freedom of will. For example, Hegel points out that kids, idiots, madmen and so on have no or only limited capacity for responsibility in their own actions when examining the capacity for responsibility. The subjective determination of this capacity for responsibility also contains uncertainty, and the degree of uncertainty is related to the strength of self-will and thinking. However, this uncertainty can only be considered in terms of dementia, madness and childhood. For this determinate state alone annihilates the qualities of thought and freedom of will, and permits the actor to be considered as a man lacking the dignity

[2] See [2], p. 10.

[3] See [3], p. 134.

[4] See [4], p. 103.

of a thinking man and the dignity of a will.[5] Thus, Hegel regards freedom of will as the foundation of the capacity for responsibility. Without freedom of will, there is no capacity for responsibility, so we should not bear criminal responsibility for our behavior. Beccaria believes that people have the instinct to seek benefits and avoid harm. Criminal law cannot change this nature, but can only use this nature, making the best use of the circumstances to prevent the occurrence of crimes. Therefore, Beccaria points out that the force that drives us to seek happiness is like the force of gravity, which is only limited by the resistance it encounters. The result of this force is a mixture of all kinds of human behavior. If they conflict and violate each other, punishment called "political constraint" is in place to prevent the evil consequences. However, it does not eliminate the cause of conflict because it is man's indivisible sense.[6] Feuerbach also assumes that people have the nature of seeking benefits and avoiding harm, and choose and decide their own behavior according to the principle of utility, thus putting forward the theory of psychological compulsion. The theory of psychological compulsion is intended to intimidate citizens through the promulgation of criminal law. The reason why this threat can be effective is that criminals have rational judgment ability.

It should be pointed out that there is a difference between the libertarianism advocated by Kant and Hegel and that advocated by Beccaria and Feuerbach. The former may be called transcendental libertarianism and the latter perceptual libertarianism. Kant talks about freedom of will in the sense of autonomy of will. According to Kant, human beings, as rational beings, have freedom of will, and can legislate for themselves and enforce the law, so they should be responsible for their own actions. Kant believes that a rational will can be his own only if he acts under the control of the idea of freedom. Thus, in the sphere of practice, this idea must be ascribed to all rational beings. That is to say, morality is only meaningful if we recognize freedom of will.[7] Hegel also regards freedom of will as a transcendental proposition and rejects the practice of demonstrating freedom of will in an empirical sense. He points out that with regard to the freedom of the will, we may recollect the older method of cognition. It simply presupposed the representation of the will and attempted to set up a definition of the will by extracting it from this representation; then, in the manner of the older empirical psychology, the so-called proof of the will's freedom was derived from the various feelings and phenomena of ordinary consciousness, such as remorse, guilt, and the like, which could allegedly be explained only in terms of a free will. But it is more convenient simply to adhere to the notion that freedom is given as a fact of consciousness in which we must simply believe. The deduction is that the will is free and the nature of the will and freedom is possible only within the context of the whole. The basic features of this premise are that spirit is initially intelligence and that the determinations through which it proceeds in its development, from feeling to representational thinking to thought, are the way by which it produces itself as will which, as practical spirit in general, is the proximate

---

[5] See [5], p. 75.

[6] See [6], p. 68.

[7] See [7], p. 433.

truth of intelligence.[8] The sensible libertarianism advocated by Beccaria and Feuerbach demonstrates man's freedom of will through the method of experience as Hegel says. Beccaria and Feuerbach both start from the principle of the utility of people seeking benefits and avoiding harm, believing that people's behavior is guided by interests and external objective necessity controls people's freedom of will. Thus, the freedom of will here is not a transcendental self-discipline, but a heteronomy. However, heteronomy here does not mean the negation of people's freedom of will, but this freedom of will can be guided and controlled, so it is available in reality. Through the setting of interests, and the implementation of rewards and punishments, people's behavior can be standardized to achieve a certain utilitarian purpose. These two different theories of freedom of will come from a different understanding of what the reason means. Kant and Hegel think that reason and sensibility are opposite. The former does not depend on the latter at all, and it has a super-perceptual source and goal. In the opinion of Beccaria et al., the basis of rationality lies in sensibility and in the law of nature that exists objectively. What is natural is reasonable, and vice versa. The reason is to make people's nature get the fullest satisfaction; the reason is people's clear understanding of their own vital interests. Its function is to overcome people's blindness in the pursuit of material benefits, so that people can obtain the maximum benefits through more effective methods and shortcuts.[9]

In the theory of criminal law, there is a debate about whether Beccaria is a libertarian. For example, Wald, a US criminologist, believes that the development of modern criminology can be divided into three frames of reference. The first frame of reference is classical criminology, which advocates libertarianism and holds that criminal behavior is free choice. The second frame of reference is demonstration criminology, which advocates determinism and holds that crime is caused by forces beyond the control of the individual. The third frame of reference is the behavioral theory of criminal law, which advocates interactionism and focuses on the operational behavior of criminal law rather than criminal behavior. All criminological views can be incorporated into these three frames of reference. Wald classes Beccaria's criminological view as classical criminology, arguing that its basic explanation of crime is libertarianism.[10] Quinney and Wildeman, two US criminologists, also point out that the classical school of criminology represents the highest peak of humane rationalism in the eighteenth century. In the study of human behavior, this humane rationalist method is applied earlier than the scientific method. Guided by the assumption that man is rational and capable of controlling his destiny, classical writers focus on the connection between the people and the legal structure of the state. Their response to the legal practice of the time is to protest the inconsistency and injustice between the criminal law and its enforcement, and to envisage its reform so as to bring it into line with what they call the conception of human nature. The publication of Beccaria's *On Crimes and Punishments* created the classical school of criminology

[8] See [4], pp. 10–11.

[9] See [8], p. 45.

[10] See [9], pp. 10–11.

in that era.[11] And even Ferri, who belongs to the positivist school of criminology, also confirms that Beccaria is a libertarian. Ferri points out that if you look closely at Beccaria's ideas for the major reforms of medieval criminal justice, you will find that this great classical school reform took a very slow step, because its theoretical and practical foundations of criminal justice were still based on medieval and ancient notions of individual moral responsibility.[12] The concept of individual moral responsibility here refers to the theory of criminal responsibility based on freedom of will. However, Huang Feng, a Chinese scholar, believes that Beccaria is not a libertarian but a mechanical determinist. According to this view, freedom of will means that one's will can be independent of the laws of objective cause and effect, and one can determine one's actions according to a supernatural or transcendental idea of good and evil. However, we find no such argument in *On Crimes and Punishments*. Huang Feng believes that Beccaria does not simply avoid the discussion of the causes of crimes with libertarianism. On the contrary, he tries to explain the inevitable connection between various political, economic and social factors and conditions and crimes from the standpoint of mechanical materialism. Although *On Crimes and Punishments* does not have a chapter devoted to this subject, if the arguments scattered throughout the chapters are gathered together, one can find that the unified view of mechanical determinism runs through Beccaria's interpretation.[13]

Obviously, Huang Feng here uses the transcendental freedom of will to analyze Beccaria, and thus comes to the conclusion that Beccaria denies freedom of will. I disagree with this view. Indeed, Beccaria does not simply attribute the crimes to freedom of will, which is different from Kant and Hegel. In his evaluation of Hegel's libertarianism, Marx says that Hegel does not regard the criminal as a simple object, that is, the slave of justice, but raises the criminal to the status of a free and self-determined person, so it is desirable. However, at the same time, libertarianism is absurd to use the character of man's "free will", instead of the real motivation of a particular person's behavior and all the characteristics formed under the influence of various social conditions, so it is also unscientific.[14] Different from Kant and Hegel, Beccaria does not simply sum up the causes of crimes with freedom of will, but explains the causes of crimes from people's nature which seeks benefits and avoids harm. Beccaria, for example, points out that it is impossible to restrict human restlessness by the rules of well-behaved geometry; just as the constant and simple laws of nature cannot prevent the planets from interfering with each other in their motion, it is impossible for human laws to prevent entanglements and deviance under the infinite and diametrically opposed gravitational forces of pleasure and pain. This is just the imagination of a few people when they give orders. As Beccaria points out, what our situation will be like if everything that might lead us to commit a crime must be banned? Then people have to stop using their senses. If there is one incentive which makes people commit a real crime, there are a thousand incentives

[11] See [10], pp. 35–36.

[12] See [11], p. 10.

[13] See [8], pp. 41 and 47.

[14] See [5], p. 84.

which make people take those petty action that a bad law would call crimes.[15] In addition, Beccaria discusses the influence of people's desire, character, customs, climate, population and geographical conditions on crime. Huang Feng quotes a passage written by Marx and Engels on 18th-century French materialism to illustrate the depth of Beccaria's views. The passage goes, "We don't need to be very smart to find out that materialistic theories about human goodness and equality on intelligence, about experience, habits, omnipotence of education, about the external environment impact on people, about the significance of the industry, about the rationality of the pleasure and so on, have inevitable links with communism and socialism...Since man is not free in the materialistic sense, in other words, since man gets freedom not because he escapes the negative force of some things, but because he has the positive force to show his real personality, we shall not punish the criminal behavior of individuals, and shall destroy the roots of crime against society, and make everyone have the necessary social activity places to show his important vitality. Now that man's personality is shaped by his environment, we must make the environment conform with human nature."[16] Just as Marx and Engels put it, if people are not free, they should not be punished for their criminal acts. But Beccaria, whose theory of criminal law is precisely based on the theory of individual moral responsibility, did not draw this conclusion. In this sense, we cannot deny that Beccaria is a libertarian, but what Beccaria advocates are the perceptual libertarianism. Xie Yong, a Chinese scholar, points out that the key is to confuse two related but different issues when we discuss the difference in understanding between the affirmation and negation of Beccaria as a libertarian. One question is what causes people to commit crimes, and the other is what is the foundation of individual criminal responsibility, or the foundation of punishments. Beccaria, deeply influenced by Helvétius' materialistic sense theory, apparently enumerates many environmental stimuli that lead people to commit crimes in order to answer the question of the cause of crimes. However, he does not lead to the foundation of individual punishments. I believe that no one can do this, because mechanical environmental determinism and the theory of individual criminal responsibility are difficult to reconcile. In fact, for Beccaria, individual criminal responsibility is difficult to exist in theory in the form of unstated axioms. Beccaria himself may not have explicitly borrowed any form of libertarianism, but his main theories, especially the principle of symmetry between crimes and punishments, require free will as a logical premise.[17]

Frankly speaking, the above comments are very insightful. However, what I do not agree with is the view that mechanical environmental determinism and the theory of individual criminal responsibility are difficult to reconcile. In Beccaria's opinion, environmental determinism and the theory of individual criminal responsibility are in the same furnace. In terms of the cause of a crime, a crime is regarded by Beccaria as the inevitable result of people's seeking benefits and avoiding harm in a certain

[15] See [6], p. 104.

[16] Marx and Engel [12], pp. 166–167.

[17] See [13], p. 84.

environment. On the foundation of the penalty, freedom of will is an indispensable prerequisite. As Hans Toch, a US criminologist, points out, "Classical criminology is all firmly based on the will psychology. These criminologists all believe that every criminal act is the result of temptation and free will."[18] Beccaria's harmony between environmental determinism and the theory of individual criminal responsibility comes from a famous judgment made by Helvétius and Holbach, two 18th-century French materialists, which state that the environment determines man, and man determines the environment. For example, Helvétius emphasizes that the environment determines a person's morality. The reason why people are hypocritical, insidious and narrow in their moral characters is closely related to the social system in which people live. Social economic and political factors play an important role in the formation of people's moral characters. Then, how can we change the moral characters of people and the moral value of a society? According to the theoretical premise of Helvétius, it is logical to conclude that the social system must be changed. But how do you change the social system? He thinks that the solution is to change the legislation. And to change the legislation depends on the opinions of good legislators. Thus, Helvétius, like other French materialists, fell into an insoluble antinomy: the environment determines the opinion, and the opinion determines the environment; environment determines morality, and morality determines the environment. Holbach is the same. In his opinion, public opinion, politics, law, and especially education can determine people's thoughts and moral qualities. This is an important conclusion he draws from the premise of materialist epistemology. However, since he does not understand the dialectical relationship between the environment and education, politics and law, he falls into the idealism that opinions determine the environment.[19] In Beccaria's opinion, the reason why people commit crimes is the result of the instinct to seek benefits and avoid harm, but it is precisely this human nature that can be used to prevent crimes. Beccaria points out that it is better to prevent crimes than to punish them. This is the fundamental principle of good legislation, which is the art of conducting men to the maximum of happiness, and to the minimum of misery, if we may apply this mathematical expression to the good and evil of life.[20] To punish crimes is to prevent crimes by taking advantage of the human nature of seeking benefits and avoiding harm. Therefore, there is a self-evident logical premise: in the face of benefits and harm, people have the ability to choose freely upon wills. It is necessary to commit a crime under the temptation of "benefits", for it is free because it passes through the criminal's senses; under the deterrence of "harm"—penalty, people do not commit crimes, which is also the result of freedom of will. It should be said that necessity and freedom are relative, and it is on this point that Beccaria found the harmony between environmental determinism and the theory of individual criminal responsibility. However, reconciliation is not dialectical unity after all, just as the 18th-century French materialist philosophers

---

[18] Toch [14], p. 212.

[19] See [7], pp. 345 and 365.

[20] See [6], p. 104.

fell into the antinomy situation that the environment determines man, and man determines the environment, Beccaria also failed to scientifically reveal the dialectical relationship between behavioral determinism and libertarianism. In short, Beccaria is a libertarian in criminal law. Specifically speaking, criminals have freedom of will, which is an undeniable fact.

It is from the freedom of the criminal's will that classical school of criminology constructs the objectivism theory of crime constitution. Whether the transcendental freedom of will of Kant and Hegel or the perceptual freedom of will of Beccaria and Feuerbach is an abstract person in the court of reason. Everybody is equal before reason. Therefore, on the premise of freedom of will, the only basis for a crime is the objective harm of the act, and there is no need to consider the subjective and subject factors of the criminal. Beccaria asserts that crimes are only to be measured by the injury done to society.[21] To demonstrate this point, Beccaria rejects the following two points of view on the criteria for criminalization. One is the theory of intention, which holds that the criminal's intention is the true standard to measure the crime. The second is the theory of sin, which holds that the severity of sin is the true standard to measure a crime. According to Beccaria, the intention depends on the actual impression of objects on the senses, and on the previous disposition of the mind; both which will vary in different persons, and even in the same person at different times, according to the succession of ideas, passions, and circumstances. Upon that system, it would be necessary to form, not only a particular code for every individual, but a new penal law for every crime. Men, often with the best intention, do the greatest injury to society, and with the worst, do it the most essential services.[22] From the above argument, Beccaria seems to be an effect theorist who does not consider the motivation of human thought. Therefore, intention is not a sufficient criterion for identifying a crime. As for the theory of sin, Beccaria points out that the absurdity of it will be evident after a sober study of the relation between man and man, man and God. The degree of sin depends on the malignity of the heart, which is impenetrable to finite being. How then can the degree of sin serve as a standard to determine the degree of crimes? If that were admitted, men may punish when God pardons, and pardon when God condemns; and thus act in opposition to the Supreme Being.[23] Beccaria's objection to the theory of intention and the theory of sin is reasonable because these two views are very prone to judicial tyranny. However, these arguments also reflect Beccaria's objectivism theory of crime constitution.

Kant is a motive theorist in ethics, but a full effect theorist in law. Kant's effect theory in law is derived from his doctrine of retribution. However, a further study of the contradiction between Kant's ethical motive theory and legal effect theory reveals that it originates from his profound thought: "the subjectivity of morality and the objectivity of law".[24] In other words, Kant makes a strong distinction between

[21] Beccaria [6], p. 67.

[22] See [6], p. 67.

[23] See [6], p. 68.

[24] Kiichiro [15], p. 13.

morality and law. Kant divides the dynamic basis of social behavior into two categories. One is external and empirical. The other is internal and subjective. The former is legal, which is enforced by force. The latter, which comes from awareness of the inner obligation, from the inner nature of things, is moral. This distinction is evident in Kant's unpublished materials during his lifetime. Law is only about actions, while morality is only about beliefs. Legitimacy involves actions, even though all such actions are supposed to result from force. Ethics is concerned with the principle of what these actions should look like if they were not the result of any compulsion, but merely of moral beliefs. Kant believes that action for the sake of all mankind and his happiness (which is considered to be the highest happiness) is moral. Legal relations are directed against the ultimate will of the individual and their external, cold connection.[25] Obviously, Kant's idea of the distinction between morality and law is very important for understanding Kant's thought of criminal law. So Kant expounds the retributive punishment theory that the murderer must be put to death, and believes that this is based on the concept of judicial power based on the rational universal law. Justice will do so. Kant also criticizes Beccaria's views on the abolition of the death penalty. He points out that Beccaria, out of sympathy with human feelings, insists that all capital punishment is inherently wrong and unjust. Beccaria argues that the death penalty could not have been included in the earliest civic contracts. If so, every one of the people must agree that when he murders any one of his fellow citizens, he shall die. Beccaria, however, argues that such consent is impossible because no one would do this with their life. According to Kant, Beccaria's argument is all sophistry and a reversal of rights. No man suffers punishment because he is willing to suffer it, but because he has once determined to affirm an act worthy of punishment, for in fact what anyone is willing to experience will never be punishment, and no one can be willing to suffer punishment. The sentence "if I murder anyone, I will be punished" means nothing more than "I myself obey the law as well as all other citizens". If there is a criminal among men, the law he breaks certainly includes criminal law. A person who, as one of the co-legislators, makes criminal law is not necessarily the same person (as a subject) who is punished under that law. Because as a prisoner, he cannot be considered to have his vote in the legislature. The legislator is regarded as intellectually just and noble. If any man should make a penal law to punish himself as a criminal, it must be determined by the reason of legislation which is purely judicial. This reason makes him see himself as a possible sinner, so he sees himself as another human being. He and everyone else in the civil union are subject to the penal code. In other words, it is not for the people to judge individually, but for the public courts of justice (except criminals) to impose capital punishment. It cannot be argued that the social contract contains the consent of each person to allow himself to be punished and to do the same with himself and his life. If the right to punish must rest on the promise of the erring person, then he is supposed to be willing to be punished, and it is necessary to make him perceive that he himself should be punished. Thus, the prisoner becomes his own judge. The greatest fallacy of this sophistry lies in the belief that the prisoner's sentence must be decided by his own

[25] See [16], p. 458.

reason, that he is responsible for suffering the loss of his life. As a sentence, it must be based on his determination to end his own life. In this way, what we call the executor of the right is also the judge of the right. The two kinds of persons are combined into one person.[26] According to Kant's reasoning, Beccaria believes that the death penalty can only be based on a person's determination to end his own life, which in fact amounts to suicide. Beccaria proves the unrighteousness of the death penalty from the fact that a person has no right to commit suicide. In fact, the debate between Beccaria and Kant on the abolition of the death penalty is a debate between utilitarianism and doctrine of retribution. Beccaria thinks that the indiscriminate use of capital punishment never converts people from evil to good, so the death penalty is not a right of law. Beccaria does not hesitate to insist on the death penalty under the two circumstances that it was the fundamental and only means of preventing social unrest and preventing others from committing crimes.[27] Kant believes that the death penalty is the right of revenge,[28] but there is no fundamental difference between Kant and Beccaria on the point of conviction and punishment according to the harm caused by objective actions. Hegel completely unites Kant with Beccaria. Beccaria is quite right in demanding that a person be executed only with his consent. But the prisoner had already given such consent by his conduct. Not only the nature of the crime, but also the will of the criminal himself demands that the harm he has committed be set aside.[29] Hegel expresses his legal retribution in his peculiar philosophical language, that is, the idea of criminalization of objective actions externalized by human reason. He points out that the harm done to the prisoner is not only intrinsically just, because it is at the same time his will to be intrinsically present, his free existence, his law, and therefore it is just; Moreover, it is a law established in the prisoner himself, that is to say, a law established in his will to be achieved and in his actions. In fact, his action, as the action of a rational man, implies that it is something universal, and that by this action the criminal has laid down a law which he recognizes for himself in his action, and to which he should therefore be subordinate as to his own law.[30] In classical school of criminology, Feuerbach elaborates on the principle of a legally prescribed punishment for a specified crime and establishes the crime constitution theory of objectivism centered on behavior. He pointed out, "The constitution of a crime is, from the point of view of the law, the sum of the elements of each act or fact contained in the illegal act."[31] Although Feuerbach is quite sure that the subjective factors of the actor, intentional or negligent, are the conditions of criminal responsibility, they are not included in the elements of crimes. As Trainin, a famous Soviet criminal jurist, points out, "Classical criminal jurists believe that a crime is criminal responsibility—the quality of the behavior, not the subject. It is on this objective

[26] See [17], pp. 169–170.

[27] See [6], p. 44.

[28] See [2], p. 166.

[29] See [18], p. 104.

[30] See [18], p. 103.

[31] Trainin [19], p. 15.

basis that the classical representatives establish their theory of crime constitution."[32] Therefore, Trainin calls it objective structure of crime constitution. The humanistic foundation of the objective structure of crime constitution is the libertarianism based on the rational assumption of the criminal.

1.2 Human Nature Analysis of Penalty

The assumption of the criminal's reason made by the classical school of criminology has also become the humanistic foundation of its penalty. However, Beccaria and Feuerbach, from perceptual libertarianism, introduce the utilitarian penalty theory which takes general prevention as its content. Kant and Hegel, from transcendental libertarianism, introduce the penalty theory in the doctrine of retribution with regard to justice as its content. Although there are significant differences between utilitarianism and the doctrine of retribution in the choice of penalty value, they are common in the humanistic foundation of penalty. The difference only lies in the divergence of views within the classical school of criminology.

Starting from the rational hypothesis of the criminal, Beccaria endows the penalty with the utilitarian purpose of general prevention. This theory is also called the theory of deterrence, which is opposed to the theory of retribution. David, a US scholar, has different views on whether there is a factor of the theory of retribution in Beccaria's thought of criminal law. He believes that Beccaria is consistent with Hegel's theory of retribution in advocating the ladder of crime and punishment as they both believe that different penalties may be imposed on specific crimes because various crimes cause different harmful consequences to society under different social conditions.[33] David also points out that Beccaria always combines utilitarianism with doctrine of retribution, and that he generally places more emphasis on the former.[34] Huang Feng, a Chinese scholar, agrees with David's view that Beccaria faces contradiction in the reason for penalty. On the one hand, Beccaria believes that penalty is a deterrent tool in the hands of the state and exists to maintain the normal order of a society; on the other hand, he points out that just penalty is the embodiment of the right of freedom of every member of society and exists as the avenger of the social contract. Beccaria, out of a kind desire, tries to theoretically unite the two reasons of order and justice. He considers penalties "necessary" for the maintenance of order and "just" for the personal benefit of every member of society. And he uses the words "necessary" and "just" as interchangeable synonyms in his book. However, he cannot explain why some penalties that are "necessary" from the point of view of maintaining social order (such as the death penalty) have no sufficient justification for their existence from the point of view of defending individual rights. Therefore, Huang Feng believes that Beccaria takes the absolutist

---

32 Trainin [19], p. 15.

33 See [20].

34 See [21].

standard of justice as the limitation of defense, and takes bourgeois individualism as the basis of his penal utilitarianism.[35] Xie Yong, a Chinese scholar, also believes that, whether in terms of Beccaria's personal thoughts, or in terms of the guiding trend of the whole classical criminology, paricidas is the basis of its penalty theory.[36] I think there seem some reasons for that, but it is not true. According to Huang Feng, the necessary penalty refers to the penalty limit advocated by utilitarianism, while the just penalty refers to the penalty limit advocated by the doctrine of retribution. But in Beccaria's viewpoint, what is necessary and what is just are not entirely used in the above opinions. They are, as Huang Feng says, often interchangeable. The key point here is that the standard of justice in utilitarianism is quite different from that in the doctrine of retribution. The justice standard of utilitarianism is the greatest happiness of the greatest majority of people, while the justice standard of the doctrine of retribution is that everyone has fallen into his right place. Beccaria is a full utilitarian on penalty justice standard. For example, in regard to the origin of the power of penalty, Beccaria points out that it is this need (which refers to the ending of the war of the natural society, and building a civil society by social contracts—the quoter's note) that forces people to cede part of their freedom, and there is no doubt that everyone wishes to give as little freedom as possible to the public preservation, as long as it is enough for others to protect him. The crystallization of this least amount of freedom forms the power of punishment. Anything extra is monopolization of power, not justice, fiction not rights. Penalty is inherently unjust if it exceeds the need to protect the public interests of the community.[37] It is made clear that, in Beccaria's view, the standard of justice can only be required by the public interests. In addition to it, the standard of justice also has a standard of humanity. There is no doubt that Beccaria is a compassionate humanitarian. In *On Crimes and Punishments*, Beccaria inveighs against the cruelty of punishments, which are often carried out in the name of retribution—the atonement. Beccaria points out that the intent of punishments is not to torment a sensible being, nor to undo a crime already committed. Is it possible that torments, and useless cruelty, the instruments of furious fanaticism, or of impotency of tyrants, can be authorized by a political body? Which, so far from being influenced by passion, should be the cool moderator of the passions of individuals. Can the groans of a tortured wretch recall the time past, or reverse the crime he has committed?[38] This shows that Beccaria rejects rather than accepts the doctrine of retribution in the form of atonement, let alone takes it as the basis of the theory of punishment. Beccaria also discusses the relationship between cruel punishment and the utilitarian purpose of crime prevention. He believes that the severity of punishments, though not immediately contrary to the public good, or to the end for which they were intended, viz., to prevent crimes, be useless; then such severity would be contrary to those beneficent virtues, which are the consequence of enlightened reason, which instructs the sovereign to wish rather to govern men in a

---

[35] See [8], p. 89.

[36] See [13], p. 82.

[37] See [6], p. 9.

[38] See [6], p. 42.

state of freedom and happiness, than of slavery. It would also be contrary to justice, and the social compact.[39] Moreover, Beccaria thinks that there are yet two other consequences of cruel punishments, which counteract the purpose of their institution, which was, to prevent crimes. The first arises from the impossibility of establishing an exact proportion between the crime and punishment; for though ingenious cruelty hath greatly multiplied the variety of torments, yet the human frame can suffer only to a certain degree, beyond which it is impossible to proceed, be the enormity of the crime ever so great. The second consequence is impunity. Human nature is limited no less in evil than in good. Excessive barbarity can never be more than temporary; it is impossible that it should be supported by a permanent system of legislation; for if the laws are too cruel, they must be altered, or anarchy and impunity will succeed.[40] From a humanitarian point of view, Beccaria advocates the leniency of the penalty, and even proposes the abolition of the death penalty. Then, utilitarianism and humanity are both standards of justice. Should we obey utilitarianism or humanity when the two are in conflict? Huang Feng, a Chinese scholar, thinks that Beccaria does not solve this problem and that it is an uncoordinated contradiction existing in Beccaria's penalty philosophy.[41] In fact, Beccaria has solved this problem from the perspective of utilitarianism. In other words, humanity should be subordinate to utility. The limitation humanity puts on utility is only reflected in that the punishment should not exceed the necessary limit of crime prevention. Punishment must be no more severe than deterring people from committing crimes in order to make it just. Punishment is tyrannical and cruel when it is unnecessary. As Beccaria points out that punishment may produce the effect required, it is sufficient that the evil it occasions should exceed the good expected from the crime; including in the calculation the certainty of the punishment, and the privation of the expected advantage. All severity beyond this is superfluous, and therefore tyrannical.[42] Beccaria cleverly takes limited utility as a measure of the cruelty of punishment; the punishment that is not necessary to prevent crime is cruel and unjust. This is more clearly reflected in Beccaria's attitude towards capital punishment. As we all know, Beccaria was the first person in western history to put forward the abolition of the death penalty. He makes this argument mainly on humanitarian grounds, but this by no means means the rejection of utilitarian factors. He puts forward this problem in the name of utilitarianism and justice. Beccaria's formal formulation is whether capital punishment is really beneficial and just in a well-organized society. Obviously, whether the death penalty is necessary is a priority for Beccaria. The injustice of the death penalty is simply that it cannot be a right of the State. Because citizens were not willing to give others the power over their own life and death in the earliest days when they signed the social contracts. Beccaria's main reason for abolishing the death penalty is that it is unnecessary and replaceable. Beccaria believes that the death penalty has never changed people from bad to good and is therefore unnecessary. More importantly,

---

[39] See [6], p. 11.

[40] See [6], pp. 43–44.

[41] See [8], p. 89.

[42] See [6], p. 42.

Beccaria thinks that capital punishment can be replaced by lifelong penal servitude. This is because what has a greater impact on the human mind is not the intensity of punishment, but the continuity of punishment. The spectacle of execution, terrible as it is, is temporary. If the criminal is turned into a forced labor convict, and is made to pay for the society he has violated with his own toil, then the lesson of loss of freedom is long and painful. This is the most powerful deterrent to crimes. This effective restraint is a constant reminder that if I commit such a sin, I too will be in such long-suffering. Therefore, it is more powerful than the complicated and confusing idea of death. As a rational person, the criminal will not choose the road that causes him to lose his freedom completely and permanently after weighing, no matter how much benefit the crime can bring him. Beccaria argues, therefore, that the intensity of the lifelong penal servitude that replaces the death penalty is enough to change any determined mind.[43] However, once from the utilitarian point of view, the death penalty is necessary. Beccaria does not hesitate to choose utility, so Beccaria is not a complete abolitionist of the death penalty. Beccaria points out that the death of a citizen cannot be necessary but in one case. When, though deprived of his liberty, he has such power and connections as may endanger the security of the nation; when his existence may produce a dangerous revolution in the established form of government. But even in this case, it can only be necessary when a nation is on the verge of recovering or losing its liberty; or in times of absolute anarchy, when the disorders themselves hold the place of laws. But in a reign of tranquility; in a form of government approved by the united wishes of the nation; in a state fortified from enemies without, and supported by the strength within, and opinion, perhaps more efficacious; where all power is lodged in the hands of the true sovereign; where riches can purchase pleasures and not authority, there can be no necessity for taking away the life of a subject. This is the second reason why the death penalty is considered a just and necessary punishment.[44] Therefore, Beccaria is a complete utilitarian advocate of the theory of deterrence.

Feuerbach inherited Beccaria's theory of deterrence. Starting from the rational hypothesis of criminals, he puts forward such a slogan full of utilitarian implications as "intimidate by law", and takes the theory of psychological compulsion as theoretical support. Feuerbach believes that the root of all illegal acts lies in the sources of spiritual trends and motivations that lead to criminal acts, which drive people to break the law. Therefore, a state's first line of defense against crimes should be moral education. However, education is far from a panacea, and there will always be people who defy education and have spiritual trends to break the law. This determines that a state must also establish a second line of defense for the purpose of eliminating spiritual trends to break the law, namely recourse to psychological compulsion. Feuerbach believes that people's spiritual trends to break the law are not created out of anything, but are seduced and driven by the potential happiness in illegal behavior and the unpleasant feelings brought by the failure to obtain such happiness. Thus, Feuerbach tries to find the theoretical basis of the utilitarian principle of seeking

[43] See [6], pp. 46–47.

[44] See [6], pp. 45–46.

benefits and avoiding harm. Feuerbach points out that if illegal behavior is made to contain some kind of pain, people who have the spiritual trend to break the law have to make a careful balance between the pleasure and pain that illegal behavior may bring. When the pain contained in the illegal behavior is greater than the joy in it, the subject will, based on the instinct of abandoning the smaller and seeking the greater, avoid the pain which is greater than the pain of not breaking the law, and pursue the joy which is greater than the joy of breaking the law. The subject will repress the spiritual trend to break the law by himself so that it does not develop into a criminal act. That's what Feuerbach's theory of psychological compulsion is all about. Then, how can psychological compulsion be achieved? Feuerbach believes that punishment must be connected with the spiritual trend to break the law by means of a certain intermediary, which is the citizens' conviction that pain and crimes are inseparable and that certain illegal behavior will inevitably lead to certain penalties and sanctions. Without such conviction, citizens are unlikely to recognize the pain involved in an illegal act, much less to abandon the spiritual trend to break the law out of the motive of avoiding such pain. And the only way to establish the conviction that pain and crimes are inseparable is through the threat of law. In Feuerbach's view, the law clearly stipulates the penalties for various crimes, and at the same time declares that any crime must be punished. In this way, the person who attempts to commit a crime, no matter what kind of criminal trend he has, is facing the threat of punishment, and will not carry out any crime because of this threat, so as to achieve the purpose of preventing crimes for a state.

Starting from the criminal's rational hypothesis, Kant gets the theory of moral retribution. Kant points out, "Public justice can serve as its principle. In the balance of justice, the needle is not tilted to one side. In other words, the evil which any man does to an individual among the people may be seen as evil to himself. Therefore, we can also say, "If you slander another, you slander yourself; if you steal from another, you steal from yourself; if your strike another, you strike yourself; if you kill another, you kill yourself. That is the right to retaliate."[45] Kant even argues that this is the only principle that governs public courts. The principle can be used to determine explicitly just punishments in both quality and quantity. Kant then extends the principle of equal retribution, which is actually the rational manifestation of retaliation. Therefore, in Kant's view, the criterion of justice can only be the retribution of the same form. From the point of view of equal retribution, Kant points out that the murderer must be put to death. In this case, there are no legal replacements or substitutes that can satisfy the principle of justice by their increase or decrease. There is no such thing as life, no comparison between lives. No matter how painful, there is no alternative but to die. Therefore, there is no equality between murder and revenge for murder. We have to execute the criminal according to the law. Kant puts forward an example that even if a Civil Society resolved to dissolve itself with the consent of all its members—as might be supposed in the case of a People inhabiting an island resolving to separate and scatter themselves throughout the whole world—the last Murderer lying in the prison ought to be executed before the resolution was carried out. This ought to

[45] Kant [2], p. 165.

be done in order that every one may realize the desert of his deeds, and that blood guiltiness may not remain upon the people; for otherwise they might all be regarded as participators in the murder as a public violatioil of Justice.[46]

Hegel also advocates doctrine of retribution, which is based on the rational assumption of the criminal. For what is contained in the criminal's action is not only the conception of the crime, the self-being and self-making rational aspect of the crime, which the State should assert to be valid, regardless of the consent of the individual, but also the rationality of form, which is the desire of the individual. Hegel believes that punishment contains the prisoner's own law, so to punish him was to honor him as a rational being. If we do not seek the concept and measure of punishment from the prisoner's conduct, he will not gain this respect.[47] Because the penalty is derived from the criminal's reason, this kind of penalty has the meaning of retribution. Hegel points out that retribution is the internal connection and identity between two requirements with different phenomena and different external existences. When the retribution for crimes takes on, this retribution has the appearance of an alien rule which was not his. But punishment, as we have already seen, is after all only the manifestation of crimes; that is to say, it is necessarily the second half that takes the first half as its premise. Retribution, firstly, will encounter this reproach, and it appears to be something immoral or revenge, and therefore may be regarded as something personal. But it is not something personal but the concept that does retribution. In the Bible, God says, "Vengeance is mine." If we derive from the word retribution the notion of a special preference of the subjective will, it must be pointed out that retribution is simply the form the crime takes to turn against itself. Eumenides[48] fell asleep, but the crime woke them up. So criminal behavior is to eat one's own bitter fruit.[49] Hegel's doctrine of retribution is characterized by legal retribution, which is restrained retribution confined to legal forms. It is retribution of equal value and therefore different from Kant's retribution of equal amount. According to Hegel, it is easy to draw the absurd conclusion of penal retaliation from Kant's retribution of an equal amount. For example, an eye for an eye, a tooth for a tooth. We can also imagine that the actor is one-eyed or has lost all his teeth. The only exception, of course, is the death penalty for murder. Hegel points out that although retribution is not equal in species, it is different in the case of murder, and the death penalty must be imposed. The reason is that because life is the whole sphere of human determination, punishment cannot exist only in a value—life is priceless—but only in depriving the life of the murderer.[50] More importantly, Hegel emphasizes that the retributive significance of punishment lies in the affirmation of legal order. He points out that through a crime, something is altered, and the thing exists in this alteration; but this existence is the opposite of the thing itself, and is to that extent within itself null and void. The nullity is that right as right has been cancelled. For right, as an

[46] See [2], pp. 166–167.

[47] See [22], p. 103.

[48] The goddess of vengeance in Greek mythology, also called Nemesis.

[49] See [22], p. 106.

[50] See [22], pp. 106–107.

absolute, cannot be cancelled, so that the expression of crime is within itself null and void, and this nullity is the essence of the effect of crime. But whatever is null and void must manifest itself as such—that is, it must itself appear as vulnerable. The criminal act is not an initial positive occurrence followed by the punishment as its negation, but is itself negative, so that the punishment is merely the negation of the negation. Actual right is thus the cancellation of this infringement, and it is in this very circumstance that it demonstrates its validity and proves itself as a necessary and mediated existence.[51] It should be pointed out that although Hegel's legal doctrine of retribution gets rid of Kant's vulgar form of retribution of equal amount, Marx points out that this theory of punishment as the result of the individual will of the criminal is only the speculative expression of the ancient "retributive punishment"—eye for eye, tooth for tooth, blood for blood.[52]

The theory of deterrence of Beccaria and Feuerbach and the theory of retribution of Kant and Hegel seem to give people the impression of consistency in the appearance of the design of penalty rules.

In the case of the kinds of punishments, Beccaria, starting from the utilitarian purpose of crime prevention, thinks that punishments should accord with the nature of crimes as far as possible. This principle dramatically further reinforces the vital link between crimes and punishments. This similarity is particularly useful for comparing the motive of the crime with the retribution of the punishment. This similarity changes the mind and directs it to the opposite goal when the seductive lawbreaking idea strives to pursue one goal.[53] This view of the similarity between crimes and punishments is based on the popular associationistic psychology of the day. Associationistic psychology attributes all psychological phenomena to the association of ideas. Hume, for example, believes that these qualities produce a connection between ideas, and that when one idea appears, it naturally gives rise to another. It is evident that, in the course of our thought, in the constant alternation of our ideas, our imagination easily passes from one idea to another which is like it, and that this nature alone is sufficient to be the principle of connection and association of the imagination. This is Hume's Similarity Law.[54] According to this similarity law, Beccaria believes that if the evil result caused by the punishment is offset by the possible benefits of the crime, and if the benefits deprived by the punishment are exactly the interests pursued by the criminal, then it will make people feel that the crime is unprofitable. Doctrine of retribution is even more assiduous in demanding that punishment should be similar to the nature of the crime. Kant's retribution of an equal amount goes without saying. Hegel advocates that the cancellation of crime is retribution in so far as the latter, by its concept, is an infringement of an infringement, and in so far as crime, by its existence, has a determinate qualitative and quantitative magnitude, so that its negation, as existent, also has a determinate magnitude. But this identity of crime and retribution, which is based on the concept, is not an equality in the

[51] See [22], p. 100.

[52] See [23], p. 579.

[53] See [6], p. 57.

[54] See [24], p. 22.

specific character of the infringement, but in its character in itself—in terms of its value.[55] Hegel also focuses on the concept of equivalence, which, according to the general idea of retribution, should be to deal with a man as he deals with you. Only in this way can the general feeling of the nation and the individual towards crimes be satisfied, but such equivalence in the character is virtually impossible. Hegel believes that the inherent stipulation reflected by the concept of retribution is the inevitable connection between crimes and punishments, that is, punishments should be imposed upon crimes, which is the inherent equivalence. As for the qualitative and quantitative equivalence of crimes and punishments, it is only an external equivalence. The external character equivalence is only ever close to satisfaction.[56] "Close" here refers to the similarity of crimes and punishments in external characters rather than complete equivalence.

Not only in the kinds of punishments, but also in the relationship between crimes and punishments, the theory of deterrence and the theory of retribution in the classical school of criminology both advocate that there is a causal and necessary connection between them. In the theory of deterrence, Beccaria insists on the certainty and timeliness of penalty, so as to enhance the deterrence effect of the penalty. As for the certainty of penalty, Beccaria points out that the most powerful constraint on crimes is not the severity of penalty, but the certainty of penalty. The inevitability of this penalty makes it lenient without losing its effect. As Beccaria points out, the certainty of a small punishment will make a stronger impression, than the fear of one more severe, if attended with the hopes of escaping.[57] Regarding the timeliness of punishment, Beccaria points out that the more rapid and timely the punishment of a crime is, the more just and beneficial it is. The shorter the time between crimes and punishments, the more prominent and continuous the connection between the two concepts in people's minds, so that people naturally regard the crime as a cause and the punishment as an indispensable and inevitable result.[58] Feuerbach also emphasizes the establishment of citizens' conviction of the inevitability of punishments, and the relationship between crimes and punishments is clearly stipulated by law (legally prescribed punishment for a specified crime), which is to play a general minacious psychological compulsion role.[59] The theory of retribution in classical school of criminology also emphasizes the inevitability between crimes and punishments, that is, the inevitability of punishments, but this is not for the purpose of utility, but the requirement of justice. Kant holds that criminal law is the categorical imperative, and that all crimes must be punished and that he got the punishment he deserved are the inevitable requirements of justice. Kant points out that we should not follow the Pharisaic maxim "it is better that one man should die than that the whole people should perish", the criminal cannot be asked to crawl through the winding path of utilitarianism like a serpent to find something in his favor that would save him from

[55] See [22], p. 104.

[56] See [22], p. 105.

[57] See [6], p. 59.

[58] See [6], p. 56.

[59] See [25], p. 220.

just punishments, or even from deserved sanctions. If justice and righteousness perish, human life would no longer have any value in the world. Starting from absolutism, Kant believes that punishments cannot be replaced, because justice would cease to be justice, if it were bartered away for any consideration whatever.[60] Hegel also discusses the necessary causal relationship between crimes and punishments. It is a relationship of retributive justice. This relationship is naturally derived from the reason of the criminal, so it has justice. On this point, Hegel opposes the psychological basis of the deterrence theory held by Beccaria, Feuerbach and others. Beccaria et al. borrow Hume's law of causality and space–time proximity in associationistic psychology as the psychological basis of theory of deterrence. Hume points out that since the senses, in changing their objects, must undergo regular changes, receiving them according to the order in which they approach each other, imagination must also, by the force of long habit, acquire the same mode of thought, and pass through the different parts of space and time in the process of imagining its objects. As to the relation of causation, it may be said that there is no relation so strong in imagination as causality between the objects of ideas, which causes one idea to evoke another more rapidly.[61] Hegel believes that superficial views such as the theory of intimidation would set aside the objective examination of justice. Yet this is the very point of primacy and substance in the examination of crimes. This naturally leads to the following results. The moral view, that is, the subjective aspect of the crime, becomes essential, and the subjective aspect of the crime is mixed up with some vulgar psychological ideas, thinking that stimulation and emotional impulse are too strong in comparison with reason. In addition, it is mixed with some coercive and psychological factors that influence people's ideas (Freedom does not seem to have the same possibility to reduce people's ideas to something purely accidental). Hegel also directly criticizes Feuerbach's theory of psychological compulsion, pointing out that intimidation may at last inspire people to assert their freedom against intimidation, but intimidation, after all, throws justice aside. Psychological coercion can refer only to qualitative and quantitative differences within crime, not to the nature of crime itself, and any legal codes which may have originated in this doctrine consequently have no proper foundation.[62] It should be said that Hegel's critique of the theory of deterrence is justified, but the theory of retribution, which bases punishments on an empty concept of justice, is hardly well founded.

The most delicate display of the design of punishments made by the classical school of criminology is the crime and punishment ladder. The classical school of criminology advocates a balance between crime and punishment. Beccaria points out that the public is concerned not only that crimes do not occur, but that they cause as little harm to society as possible. Therefore, the greater the harm of crimes to the public interest, the stronger the force to urge people to commit crimes, the more powerful the means to stop people from committing crimes should be. This

[60] See [2], pp. 164–165.

[61] See [24], p. 23.

[62] See [22], p. 102.

requires that the punishment be proportional to the crime.[63] This balance of crime and punishment is mainly considered from the perspective of deterrence. Beccaria points out that if pleasure and pain are the two motives that govern the perceived, and if the invisible legislator arranges rewards and punishments in the motives that drive men to the best works, then, the improper distribution of rewards and punishments will lead to a more common but more neglected contradiction, that is, the object of punishments is the crime it causes itself. If two crimes against society in different degrees are punished equally, there will be no more powerful means to stop the larger crime that can bring greater benefits. Whoever sees that the death penalty applies to killing a pheasant, killing a person, or forging an important document, and no distinction will be made between these crimes, moral emotions will be destroyed. On this basis, Beccaria puts forward the idea of the crime and punishment ladder. He points out that since the necessity of uniting in society being granted, together with the conventions, which the opposite interests of individuals must necessarily require, a scale of crimes may be formed, of which the first degree should consist of those which immediately tend to the dissolution of society, and the last, of the smallest possible injustice done to a private member of that society. Between these extremes will be comprehended, all actions contrary to the public good, which are called criminal, and which descend by insensible degrees, decreasing from the highest to the lowest.[64] Once the scale of crimes and punishments has been established, they can be made to be symmetrical to each other: light punishments for misdemeanor crimes and heavy punishments for serious crimes. It not only provides people with a list to determine whether a certain act constitutes a crime, but also provides citizens with a crime price list, which acts as a deterrent. The idea of the ladder of crimes and punishments proposed by Beccaria shows a measurement relationship between crimes and punishments. Beccaria even argues that how much punishment resistance can be used to counteract the gravitational force of crimes is a problem that can be solved with geometrical precision. Beccaria also compares the legislator to a deft architect. It is his duty to correct the harmful orientations, and to bring into perfect harmony those orientations which form the strength of the building. As Huang Feng, a Chinese scholar, comments, Beccaria is not satisfied with the abstract theory of the nature, purpose and function of penalty as some criminal jurists in the past, but tries to find the rules for the accurate use of penalty and its best benefits. Beccaria's literacy in mathematics and physics lead him to explore these rules from the perspective of political arithmetic and penal mechanics. In Beccaria's thoughts, the punishment should not be arbitrarily estimated, anyone more or less will have a positive or negative impact on the result after the equal sign. The effect of punishment depends to a large extent on its application procedures and methods, just as a force will have different effects under different conditions. Punishments should not rely on some gruesome images to intimidate people's minds, but should rely on their own hierarchy, accuracy, timeliness and certainty, to influence people's calculation of pros and cons, so as to prevent them from committing crimes that are useless to others

[63] See [6], p. 65.

[64] See [6], pp. 65 and 66.

and themselves.[65] It should be said that Beccaria's thought on the scale of crimes and punishments has reached the highest level of its time, which is a qualitative leap in the concept of human criminal law and has so far been praised by people. Bentham is another scholar who proposes and designs rules for the proportionality of crimes and punishments from a utilitarian point of view. Bentham points out that Montesquieu recognizes the need for proportionality and Beccaria stresses its importance. However, they just make recommendations. They don't explain. They don't tell us what proportionality consists of.[66] Bentham lays out the main rules for determining proportionality. These rules are as follows. The first rule is that the pain of the penalty must outweigh the benefit of the crime. In order to prevent a crime, the power of inhibiting motives must be greater than that of seducing motives. The penalty for being a feared object must outweigh the crime of a temptation object. An insufficient punishment is worse than a severe punishment because an insufficient punishment is an evil that should be thrown away thoroughly, from which nothing good can be obtained. This is true for the public because such punishments seem to imply that they enjoy the crimes; this is also true for criminals because the punishments have not made them better. The second rule is that the less certain the punishment is, the more severe it should be. No one wants to commit a crime unless there is a hope of impunity. If a punishment arises precisely from the profit of the crime, and it is unavoidable, then no one commits a crime. In all crimes, there is a calculation of chance of success and failure. In order to balance the chance of being punished, the weight of punishments must be increased. The following proposition is correct. The more certain the penalty, the less severe it is required. This is a benefit from the clarity of the law as well as a good procedural method. For the same reason, the punishments should follow the crimes as closely as possible, since their psychological effect will diminish with time. Furthermore, the interval increases the uncertainty of punishment by providing new opportunities to escape sanctions. The third rule is that when two crimes are linked, the serious crime should be punished with a severe punishment, thus making it possible for the offender to stop the crime at the stronger stage. When a person has the ability and desire to commit two crimes, they can be linked. A robber may simply be content with robbery, or may begin with murder and end with robbery. The punishment for murder should be harsher than for robbery in order to deter him from committing a more severe crime. If there is a corresponding punishment for every evil committed, it means that this rule is perfectly practiced. The same punishment for different crimes often prompts a person to commit a more severe crime. The fourth rule is that the heavier the crime, the stronger the reason for applying severe punishments to reduce its occurrence. We must not forget that the bitterness of punishments is a sure price for uncertain benefits. The application of heavy sentences to petty crimes is precisely to prevent large expenditures for petty evils. The fifth rule is that the same sentence should not be applied to all criminals for the same crime, and certain circumstances that may affect feelings must be considered. Finally, Bentham points out that it should be seen

[65] See [8], p. 112.

[66] See [26], p. 68.

that the proportionality of crime and punishment should not be such a mathematical proportionality so as to avoid excessive detail, complexity and ambiguity of the law. Simplicity and clarity should be more important values. Sometimes complete proportionality may be sacrificed in order to give the penalty a more dramatic effect, and to better encourage hatred of the evils of the preparatory crimes.[67] It can be seen that Bentham put forward more systematic legal rules on the basis of inheriting Beccaria's balanced crime and punishment ladder design. Although Hegel does not calculate the exact amount of punishment, he also believes that there is a value equivalence between crimes and punishments. Hegel pointed out, "In the case of crime, whose basic determination is the infinite aspect of the deed, that aspect which is only externally specific disappears all the more readily, and equality remains merely the basic measure of the criminal's essential deserts, but not of the specific external shape which the retribution should take. It is only in terms of this specific shape that theft and robbery [on the one hand] and fines and imprisonment etc. [on the other] are completely unequal, whereas in terms of their value, i.e., their universal character as injuries, they are comparable. It is then, as already remarked, a matter for the understanding to seek an approximate equivalence in this common value. If we do not grasp either the connection, as it is in itself, between crime and its nullification, or the thought of value and the comparability of crime and punishment in terms of value, we may reach the point (see Klein's *Elements of Penal Law*, Sect. 9) of regarding a proper punishment as a purely arbitrary association of an evil with an illicit action."[68] In this passage, Hegel's language is very obscure, but his thoughts are quite profound. According to Hegel's point of view, punishments can only be equal in value, but not in character, because the manifestations of crimes are varied. This is Hegel's idea that the basic stipulation of crimes lies in the infinity of acts. Acts are unlimited and the law is limited, so the criminal law's provisions on criminal acts are always highly generalized. For example, homicide is an abstract reflection of various homicidal acts in a society. The external characteristics of various homicide cases disappear because they do not affect the characterization. Only the essential feature of the crime of illegally depriving others of life reflects the illegal value of the homicide, and thus determines the severity of the punishment it should receive. From the external point of view, there are as few as one or two hundred kinds of crimes and as many as four or five hundred kinds of crimes in a country. And punishment, generally can only be about ten kinds. It is impossible for punishments to be like retaliation in which the external characteristics of crimes and punishments are exactly the same. Thus, as Hegel points out, there is a marked disparity between the crimes and fines of theft and robbery and the penalties of imprisonment. Although the external characters are not the same, the internal value can be compared and thus may be close to the same, which is to achieve the equivalence of crimes and punishments. Hegel's thought of the equivalence of crimes and punishments does not come from the precise calculation, but from the requirement of justice. Justice requires to find the concept and measure of punishment from the criminal's behavior, which is retribution.

---

[67] See [26], pp. 68–70.

[68] Hegel [22], p. 106.

Undoubtedly, there is a difference in nature between the equilibrium of crimes and punishments proposed by Beccaria and the equivalence of crimes and punishments proposed by Hegel. The former takes the need for deterrence as the criterion for determining the relationship between crimes and punishments. The latter uses the satisfaction of retribution as an index to determine the relationship between crimes and punishments. However, some people do not see the profound difference between the two in theory, but confuse the two. For example, David, a US scholar, points out, "On this point, we can see that Beccaria and Hegel are in agreement. Both of them believe that different punishments may be imposed on various specific crimes because, under different social conditions, various crimes have different harmful consequences for society."[69] Obviously, this view is difficult to establish. In my opinion, Beccaria and Hegel have very different starting points. Hegel draws the conclusion that crimes and punishments are equivalent from the perspective of retribution. Beccaria, on the other hand, does not regard the symmetry of crime and punishment as the requirement of retribution, but as the requirement of using the law of human psychological activities to exert the intimidating effect of punishments. So, is Beccaria's utilitarianism thorough? Xie Yong, a Chinese scholar, believes that Beccaria is clearly aware that the existing punishment is unjust from the point of view of utilitarianism or the intention of criminal punishment doctrine. He is not, however, ready to give up these penalties, or even reduce them, insisting on the "symmetry of crime and punishment". If stealing a sack of wheat results in three-month hard labor, the offender, whether he is a hungry boy or she is a poor mother who wants to save her son or daughter, shall not lose one day of the three-month hard labor. Of course, Beccaria or other classical criminologists might hold that the three-month hard labor is too harsh to be necessary, and thus allow the legal "price" of the crime to drift downwards. Once the new price is clearly written into the penal code, it will treat everyone equally. Therefore, the unchanging principle here is "symmetry of crime and punishment", while the utilitarian view is only reflected in the technical link of "cost accounting" for specific criminal acts. Such utilitarianism is obviously incomplete, and it is rightly criticized by the positive school of criminology, which really represented the utilitarian concept of crime. "Classical criminology replaced the absolutist concept of justice with eclectic theory, holding that absolute justice has the right of punishment, but this right is modified by the interests of civilized life in real society. This is, in fact, the theory on which they reformed the penal code."[70] In my opinion, utilitarianism with general deterrence as the core runs through Beccaria's thought. Of course, as a humanitarian, humanitarian requirements in his thoughts are also very clear. These two seem to contradict, but in fact unite with utilitarianism. The design of Beccaria's crime and punishment ladder, although it contains the restriction of punishment based on humanitarian requirements, is ultimately out of the need for deterrence. As Huang Feng, a Chinese scholar, says, Beccaria's theory of symmetry pays more attention to the macroscopic hierarchy of the whole penalty system, and thinks that only through the hierarchy of the penalty ladder can we provide people

[69] David [27].

[70] Xie [13], p. 83.

with a practical utilitarian standard, so that they can give up the unprofitable criminal ideas after weighing the advantages and disadvantages, so as to achieve the purpose of punishments to maintain the normal social order.[71]

In the classical school of criminology, the most fundamental difference between the theory of deterrence and the theory of retribution is the purpose of punishments. The theory of deterrence takes crime prevention as the purpose of punishment. Beccaria points out that the purpose of punishments is neither to torture a perceiver nor to eliminate the crime that has been committed. On the basis of denying the doctrine of retribution, Beccaria puts forward the concept of double-sided prevention of the purpose of punishments. He points out that the purpose of punishments is only to prevent crimes from re-injuring citizens, and to discipline others not to recommit the same errors.[72] The so-called preventing criminals from re-infringing citizens here refers to the individual preventive purpose of punishments. And the so-called admonishing others not to recommit the same errors refers to the general preventive purpose of punishments. Following Beccaria, Bentham clearly points out that the purpose of punishments is to prevent crimes, saying "any punishment is harm, and all punishments are evil. According to the utilitarian principle, if punishments are deemed necessary, it is only to ensure the exclusion of the greater evil."[73] Bentham also divides the purpose of punishments into general prevention and individual prevention for the first time. According to Bentham's point of view, punishment is necessary only if it has a certain function of repelling evil and can exclude a greater evil. Therefore, Bentham believes that the penalty should not be applied in the following four cases. (1) Abusive; (2) Ineffective; (3) Excessive; (4) Too expensive. Abuse of punishments occurs in the following cases. There are no actual crimes, no first or second level of evil. The second-level evil here refers to the horror of the crime, while the first-level evil refers to the plot that determines the degree of horror; or the viciousness just outweighs the compensability created by the collateral goodness. Ineffective punishments refer to punishments that have no effect on the will and thus cannot prevent similar behavior. Bentham believes that the punishments applied to those who do not know the law, those who act unintentionally, and those who commit wrongdoing innocently due to misjudgment or force majeure are all ineffective. Although people such as children, the mentally handicapped and idiots can be influenced by rewards and threats to some extent, they lack sufficient awareness of the future prohibited by punishments. In their cases, the sentences are also ineffective. Excessive punishments mean that the application of punishments is excessive when the same effect can be obtained by more moderate means such as guidance, demonstration, request, probation and praise. Expensive punishments mean that if the evil of the punishment exceeds the evil of the crime, the legislator is to inflict greater pain rather than prevent it, and to eliminate the lesser evil at the cost of the greater one.[74] Bentham believes that in the above four cases, the punishments should

[71] See [8], p. 115.

[72] See [6], p. 42.

[73] See [28], pp. 493–494.

[74] See [26], pp. 66–67.

not be applied, mainly because it is difficult to obtain the effect of crime prevention. He believes that the way to achieve general prevention is by means of the deterrent effect of punishments. Bentham cites robbery as an example. He points out, "It can be said that a past crime of robbery may contain a weakening of the political decree designed to prevent such a crime. This political decree prevents robbery by declaring a stable sentence for anyone who commits robbery...If the punishment is finally implemented, the harmfulness of such crimes will finally stop."[75] As for the realization of the individual prevention purpose of punishments, it mainly depends on three factors. That is, by detaining criminals in certain places, they lose the physical ability to commit crimes; eliminate criminal desires by virtue of moral transformation; and fear of punishments by means of legal intimidation or terror. Again, take robbery as an example. Bentham puts it bluntly, "Wherever robbery happens with impunity, there is no shame in the robber."[76] The result can only lead to recidivism. Although Beccaria and Bentham are two-faced preventers, it does not mean that individual prevention is equal to general prevention. Both great masters show appreciation for general prevention. In particular, Bentham points out undisguisedly, "In any case, the main purpose of punishment is general prevention."[77] Beccaria and Bentham's special love for general prevention leads to the rise of general preventionism held by Feuerbach and Filangieri. Feuerbach is known for his theory of legislative deterrence. According to his theory of psychological compulsion, the reason why criminals commit crimes is mainly because of the temptation of happiness in illegal behavior and the oppression of potential pain when they cannot get happiness. Therefore, the price list of crimes and punishments must be clearly stipulated in the form of statute law. Based on the deterrent effect of criminal legislation, potential criminals have to psychologically weigh the pros and cons of crime according to the utilitarian principle of seeking advantages and avoiding disadvantages, and give up the joy of crime due to the suffering of the terrifying prison bars. They have to consciously suppress the mental trend of breaking the law, so that it does not turn into criminal behavior. Unique in the general preventer camp is Filangieri's theory of execution deterrence. According to Filangieri, the purpose of punishment is not to pursue the deterrent effect that punishment may produce when it is established in law on paper, but to make people frightened by the vivid scene of its execution. He puts it bluntly, "The public is prevented from committing crimes by the terror of the execution of the punishments which they witness."[78]

The theory of deterrence takes crime prevention, here mainly refers to general prevention as the purpose of punishments, which is obviously an inevitable conclusion derived from its utilitarianism. The theory of retribution has put forward a sharp criticism of this. Kant points out that juridical punishment can never be administered merely as a means for promoting another good either with regard to the criminal

[75] See [28], p. 493.

[76] See [28], p. 493.

[77] Bentham [29], p. 396.

[78] Filangieri [30].

himself or to civil society, but must in all cases be imposed only because the individual on whom it is inflicted has committed a crime. For one man ought never to be dealt with merely as a means subservient to the purpose of another, nor be mixed up with the subjects of real right. Against such treatment his inborn personality has a right to protect him, even although he may be condemned to lose his civil personality. He must first be found guilty and punishable, before there can be any thought of drawing from his punishment any benefit for himself or his fellow citizens.[79] This shows that Kant does not deny that moral retribution for crimes will bring warning effects, but in any case, crime prevention, whether general prevention or individual prevention, cannot be regarded as the purpose of punishments. Kant discusses this issue from the principle of justice, and believes that crime is the only premise of punishment. This is mainly out of a concern that utilitarianism might punish the innocent. In fact, the deterrence of the theory of deterrence is also limited to the principle that the punishment can only be applied to the offender and the degree of the punishment is proportional to the nature of the crime. Therefore, Kant's concern is unnecessary except for the extreme theory of deterrence. Of course, Kant's ethical thought that a person should not be used only as a means to achieve the purpose of others is worthy of attention. It is based on Kant's thought that people are purposes. In Kant's view, the purpose is not the subjective purpose that is usually called. If the purpose is subjective, it means that it is only established as the concrete object to be achieved by the action, and only as the condition for the possibility of the action. This subjective purpose must be special, accidental, and not universally necessary, and therefore only belongs to a means or a tool of a higher purpose. As a practical rule, it only expresses its value in the erotic relationship with the actor, so it has only relative value, not absolute value. On the contrary, if the purpose is purely rational, then it is a purpose suitable for all rational beings, an objective purpose with universal inevitability. This purpose, as a practical principle, casts aside all subjective, special and accidental purposes, that is, throws aside all substantive purposes, and retains only purely pro forma principles, thus constituting the universally inevitable and objective ground of the will. This kind of purpose with reason itself as the purpose has absolute value. It is a purpose in itself, not taking any other object as a purpose. It has value in itself, not because of other conditions. It is the value basis of all purposes as means or tools.[80] It is from the ethical proposition that man is the purpose that Kant denies punishing a man as a means to promote another kind of good, thus denying the purpose of punishment to prevent crimes. Hegel, like Kant, also rejects the deterrent view of the purpose of punishments. Hegel points out that the theory of punishments is one of the most failed topics in modern positive jurisprudence. Because in this theory reason is not enough, the nature of the problem depends on concepts. It certainly cannot be considered reasonable to regard the crime and its sublation (which is subsequently prescribed as a penalty) as merely a general scourge, so that another scourge should be adopted simply because it already exists. This shallow character of evil is assumed to be the primary thing in various theories

[79] See [2], p. 164.

[80] See [7], p. 431.

of punishments, such as the theory of prevention, the theory of warning, the theory of intimidation, the theory of correction, and what the punishment produces is likewise superficially defined as good. However, the problem is neither evil nor this or that good, but certainly lawlessness and justice. Hegel also sharply criticizes Feuerbach's theory of psychological compulsion. Hegel points out that Feuerbach's theory bases punishment on threat and maintains that, if anyone commits a crime in spite of the threat, the punishment must follow because the criminal knew about it in advance. But to what extent is the threat compatible with right? The threat presupposes that human beings are not free, and seeks to coerce them through the representation of an evil. But right and justice must have their seat in freedom and the will, and not in that lack of freedom at which the threat is directed. To justify punishment in this way is like raising one's stick at a dog; it means treating a human being like a dog instead of respecting his honor and freedom.[81] Therefore, Hegel denies that punishments have the purpose of preventing crime, and thinks that punishments can only be a kind of legal retribution.

The difference between the theory of deterrence and the theory of retribution in the purpose of punishments in the classical school of criminology is determined by their different understandings of the freedom of will. What Kant and Hegel advocated is transcendental libertarianism. According to this libertarianism, human beings, as rational beings, are completely beyond sensibility and experience. Human beings themselves are self-content purposes and cannot be used as tools. Therefore, the freedom of human wills is absolute. For example, Kant believes that when people do any action, as long as they are not insane, they do it under the control of their conscious wills. Here is the autonomy of the will, with the freedom of decisions and choices. You can do it or not, and you can do this or that. Although the reason for what to do in the end can be found in the law of causation, the decision and choice at that time are free, and it is possible to decide and choose to follow or not to follow the moral law. Therefore, a person is morally responsible for his actions.[82] It can be seen that, according to Kant and Hegel's transcendental libertarianism, the basis of punishments lies only in human reason itself, and the purpose of punishments is only to satisfy rational demands through retribution. Beccaria, Bentham and Feuerbach advocate perceptual libertarianism. According to this libertarianism, although people have the freedom to choose their own behavior, this freedom is not transcendental and super-perceptual, but is dominated by people's nature of seeking advantages and avoiding disadvantages. Therefore, legislators can use the principle of utilitarianism to regulate human behavior through the freedom of human wills. Therefore, it is possible to prevent crimes by punishing offenders. It should be pointed out that although the theory of deterrence and the theory of retribution have differences in the understanding of freedom of will, their theories of punishments are both based on the assumption of rational people with freedom of wills, which is the common humanistic foundation.

---

[81] See [22], pp. 101 and 102.

[82] See [31], p. 289.

1.3 Human Nature Analysis of Legislation

The classical school of criminology is a rational hypothesis not only for the criminal, but also for the legislator. The legislator, as a rational person, can make perfect provisions for all criminal acts in advance. Therefore, in general, those who support the classical school of criminology are enthusiastic advocates of the penal code, especially the doctrine of a legally prescribed punishment for a specified crime.

The doctrine of a legally prescribed punishment for a specified crime requires that crimes and punishments be explicitly stipulated in the form of words. This is actually to see the penal code as a kind of contract between citizens and the state. This idea comes from the social contract theory. Beccaria inherits Montesquieu's thought on the social contract theory, from which he expounds on the origin of law and the generation of punishment power. Beccaria points out that, laws are the conditions under which men, naturally independent, united themselves in society. Weary of living in a continual state of war, and of enjoying a liberty which became of little value, from the uncertainty of its duration, they sacrificed one part of it to enjoy the rest in peace and security. The sum of all these portions of the liberty of each individual constituted the sovereignty of a nation; and was deposited in the hands of the sovereign, as the lawful administrator. But it was not sufficient only to establish this deposit; it was also necessary to defend it from the usurpation of each individual, who will always endeavor to take away from the mass, not only his own portion, but to encroach on that of others.[83] This shows that, according to Beccaria, the right to punish is a right formed by citizens who transfer as little of their freedom as possible to the state through a social contract. This right is limited by law. Beccaria points out that the laws only can determine the punishment of crimes; and the authority of making penal laws can only reside with the legislator, who represents the whole society united by the social compact. No magistrate then, (as he is one of the society,) can, with justice, inflict on any other member of the same society, punishment that is not ordained by the laws. But as a punishment, increased beyond the degree fixed by the law, is the just punishment, with the addition of another; it follows, that no magistrate, even under a pretense of zeal, or the public good, should increase the punishment already determined by the laws.[84] Beccaria here expresses the view of using the law to limit the right of punishments, which reflects the protection of civil rights. The law is expressed in the form of clauses. A law is a text. Beccaria highly praises the certainty of writing, especially pointing out the importance of writing in social management. Beccaria points out that without written laws, no society will ever acquire a fixed form of government, in which the power is vested in the whole, and not in any part of the society; and in which the laws are not to be altered but by the will of the whole, nor corrupted by the force of private interest. Experience and reason shew us, that the probability of human traditions diminishes in proportion as they are distant from their sources. How then can laws resist the inevitable force of time, if there be not a lasting monument of

---

83 See [6], pp. 8–9.

84 See [6], p. 11.

the social compact?[85] Beccaria's admiration for the written things makes him firmly believe that only written laws can bring the behavior of citizens into the track of reason in a definite and infallible form, and thereby limit the arbitrariness of judges. Therefore, Beccaria puts forward a clear requirement for legislation, holding that the vagueness of the law is a drawback. Legislators should make necessary corrections to doubtful phrases, strive for accuracy, and prevent the deadly free interpretation that is the source of arbitrariness and favoritism. Beccaria is even more opposed to making laws in a language that the people do not understand. This puts people in a position of dependence on a few legal interpreters, and people cannot control their own freedom or handle their own destinies. This language turns dignified public codes and records almost into a private book. Beccaria believes that crimes will be less frequent, in proportion as the code of laws is more universally read, and understood; for there is no doubt, but that the eloquence of the passions is greatly assisted by the ignorance and uncertainty of punishments.[86] Therefore, Beccaria concludes with a general axiom. In order not to make the penalty an atrocity inflicted by a person or some people on other citizens, the penalty should by its very nature be public, prompt, necessary, and as light as possible under the given conditions, commensurate with the crimes, and stipulated by law.[87] Here the punishments should be prescribed by law, which means that the crimes and punishments should be legal. This is Beccaria's idea of legal crimes and punishments. It can be said that the doctrine of a legally prescribed punishment for a specified crime is the essence of Beccaria's legislative thought.

Bentham, directly inheriting Beccaria's ideas, carries utilitarianism more thoroughly into legislation. Bentham says that I remember very clearly that I get the first hint of this principle (calculation of pleasure and happiness) from Beccaria's little treatise on crimes and punishments. Beccaria says that man's happiness is joy and pain, and good legislation is the art that leads man to the greatest happiness and the least misery if we can use mathematical formulas to calculate the good and evil of life.[88] Bentham believes that legislative theory includes two aspects. One is the nature of the law, that is, the standard for measuring the quality of the law and the change in its value. The second is the form of the law, that is, the compilation of the code and its value. As for the nature of law, Bentham believes that the utilitarian principle of seeking benefits and avoiding harm should be introduced as the criterion that must be followed in legislation. How do measure and estimate whether the established law conforms to or violates this utilitarian principle? Bentham believes that the judgment should be made by a detailed calculation of pain and pleasure. Specifically, three aspects should be considered. (1) Looking at the assumed behavior of the draft bill, for anyone, whether suffering is more than pleasure or pleasure is more than suffering. If suffering is more than pleasure, then it is not good for people, which is a violation of the principle of avoiding suffering and seeking pleasure; if happiness

[85] See [6], p. 15.
[86] See [6], p. 15.
[87] See [6], p. 109.
[88] See [32], p. 349.

is better than suffering, then it is beneficial to people, and of course it conforms to the principle of avoiding suffering and seeking pleasure. (2) Seeing whether the presumed content of the draft bill covers all related parties in turn. This means that it must be measured against the overall interests of a society. (3) Looking at the proportion of the number of people who benefit from and suffer from the content stipulated in the draft bill. If there are more people who benefit than those who suffer, it is in line with the utilitarian principle. On the contrary, it violates the utilitarian principle, and such a draft bill should be discarded. Bentham believes that since the law is made by the state, and the purpose of the law is to seek "the greatest happiness of the greatest number of people", when making legislation, when deciding and assigning people's rights and obligations, the general happiness of the citizens must be taken as a benchmark. This utilitarian principle is carried out in criminal legislation, which is to prevent the occurrence of crimes to the maximum extent with as few penalties as possible. Different crimes are punished differently, and the punishment must be strengthened as the lure increases. Bentham thinks that, according to the requirements of legal definitions and legislative principles, a code must meet the following conditions. (1) It must be complete. That is to say, to present the whole law in a very adequate manner. This law need not be supplemented by explanatory notes or precedents. (2) It must be universal. That is to say, the norms in the code must be universally achievable. (3) It must be concise and precise, that is to say, to express the entire content of the law in short clauses. Legal terms and connotations should be unified and accurate, and should not be contradictory or ambiguous. (4) It must be well-structured and have a reasonable layout. If these conditions are not met, it cannot be called a code, let alone a good code.[89] Under the historical background of British case law culture, Bentham's loud voice and advocacy for codification are indeed commendable. Bentham examines British law with the utilitarian philosophy as the standard, and believes that the common law is the product of accidental historical events, not the result of rational designs. Its ancient concept, complex court organization and cumbersome litigation procedures not only fail to guarantee people's safety and promote the happiness of the majority, but are also a major obstacle to social reform. Therefore, Bentham strongly advocates the reform of British law. The main ways are to codify the code, fully implement the codification, and draft the constitution, the criminal code and the civil code. Although Bentham's reform proposal was resisted and unaccepted, it still had a profound impact on the reform of British law in the nineteenth century. In particular, the rules of formulating the criminal code proposed by Bentham have a very positive significance for fully embodying the doctrine of a legally prescribed punishment for a specified crime. Bentham points out that the choice of punishments is the result of considering many factors. They should have the sensibility of quantity, equality, proportionality, similarity with crimes, demonstration, economy, improvement, popularity, etc. A certain type of punishments must not have the above attributes at the same time. In order to find the structures that we need, we must combine them to make them different and organically combined. If a code based on these principles happens to be a project,

[89] See [32], pp. 351–352.

then it may be seen as unrealistic fantasy. A criminal code is being constructed according to these principles. This code follows these rules so carefully that it has no more striking features than its clarity, brevity and precision. None of the criminal legislation known to date has achieved half of the above-mentioned goals, and it is undoubtedly more complex, more vague and more difficult to understand.[90]

In the classical school of criminology, Feuerbach is the most powerful advocate of doctrine of a legally prescribed punishment for a specified crime and makes it a positive law principle. Feuerbach inherits the utilitarian thought of Beccaria and Bentham, and takes the doctrine of a legally prescribed punishment for a specified crime as the foundation of criminal law.[91] Feuerbach believes that human beings are animals that avoid unhappiness, pursue pleasure, and weigh interests. If the punishment is pre-specified as the consequence of the crime, and the punishment stipulated by the law is executed immediately when the crime is committed, then people will reasonably weigh the small unpleasantness caused by not committing the crime and the big unpleasantness caused by the punishment. In order to avoid big unhappiness and suppress small unhappiness without committing crime, it is necessary to predetermine the relationship between crimes and punishments in law.[92] Thus it can be seen that the doctrine of a legally prescribed punishment for a specified crime is the inevitable conclusion of Feuerbach's theory of psychological compulsion. Feuerbach's doctrine of a legally prescribed punishment for a specified crime actually contains the assumption of the human nature of the legislator. That is, the legislator is also a rational person. He can legalize crimes and punishments through legislation, and intimidate all criminals through punishments.

As mentioned above, the utilitarianism in the classical school of criminology derives the principle of doctrine of a legally prescribed punishment for a specified crime from the rational assumption of legislators, thus constructing its complete criminal legislation theory. The doctrine of retribution in the classical school of criminology assumes the same human nature to the legislators as utilitarianism, and the principle of a legally prescribed punishment for a specified crime should also be included in their thinking. Of course, since Kant and Hegel are mainly philosophers, their discussion of criminal law is not as systematic as that of Beccaria, Bentham and Feuerbach. Therefore, it is impossible to find direct discussion of doctrine of a legally prescribed punishment for a specified crime from their speeches. However, the ideological essence of doctrine of a legally prescribed punishment for a specified crime can still be found in the discourses of Kant and Hegel. Kant is a social contract theorist. He believes that human beings originally lived in a state of nature, and everyone enjoyed the innate freedom. But a man was bound to abuse his liberty in dealing with others. As a result, the state of nature almost became a state of war, with a lack of security. And because people have the need to be gregarious, and realize that entering a civilized society can develop their own talents, they set up a state. Therefore, Kant believes that the state is a union organized by many

[90] See [26], p. 83.
[91] See [33], p. 13.
[92] See [34].

people living according to the law. In the state, people live in an order prescribed by law. Only in a civilized society can human talents develop perfectly. As the only rational animal on the earth, the natural ability to exercise reason in man can be fully developed not in a single person but only in all human beings. It is because human beings are rational that they can leave the state of nature and establish an order prescribed by law. This kind of life in which the law regulates the relationship between people is a civilized society. Only in such a society can human reason be fully developed. Therefore, Kant believes that a crime is a violation of the law, and the punishment can only be limited within the scope of the law. Kant points out that every transgression of a law only can and must be explained as arising from a Maxim of the transgressor making such wrong-doing his rule of action; for were it not committed by him as a free being, it could not be imputed to him. But it is absolutely impossible to explain how any rational individual forms such a Maxim against the clear prohibition of the law giving reason; for it is only events which happen according to the mechanical laws of nature that are capable of explanation. Now a transgressor or criminal may commit his wrong-doing either according to the Maxim of a Rule supposed to be valid objectively and universally, or only as an exception from the Rule by dispensing with its obligation for the occasion. In the latter case, he only diverges from the Law, although intentionally. He may, at the same time, abhor his own transgression, and without formally renouncing his obedience to the Law only wish to avoid it. In the former case, however, he rejects the authority of the Law itself, the validity of which, however, he cannot repudiate before his own reason, even while he makes it his rule to act against it. His Maxim is therefore not merely defective as being negatively contrary to the Law, but it is even positively illegal, as being diametrically contrary and in hostile opposition to it.[93] Here, from the perspective of law, Kant expounds that the essence of a crime is the violation of the law, including the intentional violation and the negligent violation. Therefore, crimes can only be convicted in accordance with the law. Starting from the proposition of "objective reality of law", Hegel emphasizes that law as law must be expressed as positive law. Hegel opposes the natural law school's theory of dividing natural law and human law. He denies that there is an inherent natural law in the natural state of human beings, and believes that law is positive. The positive nature of the law here is that, firstly, in terms of form, any law in a certain country must be expressed in an effective form. Secondly, in terms of content, it contains some positive factors, which are the final provisions required by the actual judgment. Hegel points out that law is what is law in itself and is posited in its objective positing. That is to say, in order to make it available to consciousness, thought defines it explicitly and announces it as something legal and effective. Through this provision, the law becomes a general positive law.[94] From this, Hegel distinguishes customary law from law, opposes the replacement of law by customs, and advocates the promulgation of statute law. In response to the German school of historical law's emphasis on customs and against the formulation of a unified German code, Hegel points out that customary

[93] See [2], pp. 150–151.

[94] See [22], p. 218.

laws are different from laws only in that they are subjective and known incidentally, so they themselves are relatively uncertain, and the universality of thought is also relatively vague. Furthermore, knowing this or that aspect of the law, and knowing the law in general, is a skill owned by a few people by chance. Some argue that customary laws, because they are in the form of habits, should have the advantage of being a part of life. But it's a fantasy. Because the existing laws of a nation do not cease to be customs just because they are written and compiled. When the customary law has been compiled and assembled, as it must be in slightly civilized peoples, the compilation is a code. Precisely because it is merely a compilation, it is obviously deformed, obscure and mutilated. The main difference between it and a real code is that the real code grasps and expresses the universality of the various principles of law and their prescription from the thinking. As we all know, the domestic law of the United Kingdom is contained in statutes (enacted laws) and so-called unwritten laws. In fact, these unwritten laws are also written; to gain knowledge of unwritten laws, one can only and must read several quarto books full of unwritten laws. There is astonishing confusion, both in British judiciary and in its legislative cause, as described by experts. They refer in particular to the situation where, because unwritten laws are contained in the judgments of courts and judges, judges become regular legislators. Judges are bound by the authority of precedents, which express no other than unwritten laws. But it can also be said that they are not bound by them, because they have a set of unwritten laws, so they have the right to make judgments on past judgments and determine whether they conform to unwritten laws. To deny that a civilized nation and its law circle have the ability to codify codes is a great insult to this nation and its law circle. Because the problem here is not to build a new legal system whose content is brand new, but to know, that is, to understand and observe the prescribed universality of legal content, and then apply it to particular things.[95] Obviously, Hegel considers a code to be a form of positive law superior to customary law and unwritten law. Because the content of customary law is ambiguous and the form of unwritten law is confusing, only the written code can grasp the universality of various principles of law from the thinking. At the same time, Hegel also finds out the contradiction between the stability and adaptability of law. He pointed out that, on the one hand, simple and universal determinations are required for the public legal code, but on the other, the nature of the finite material in question leads to endless further determinations. The scope of the law ought on the one hand to be that of a complete and self-contained whole, but on the other hand, there is a constant need for new legal determinations. But since this antinomy is merely a product of the specialization of universal principles which themselves remain unchanged, the right to a complete legal code remains intact, as does the right [which requires] that these simple and universal principles should be capable of comprehension and formulation without reference to, and in distinction from, their specialization.[96] Therefore, Hegel believes that it can only be overcome by the distinction between legislation and judiciary. Legislation is the stipulation of the

[95] See [22], pp. 218–220.

[96] See [22], p. 225.

general principles of law, and judiciary applies these principles to special objects. Here, Hegel does not deny the relative incompleteness of a code. He points out that the demand for a complete code, that is, a code that appears to be absolutely complete without further stipulation—a requirement that is chiefly the fault of the Germans—and, on the grounds that the code cannot be revised so completely, argues that something so-called incomplete should be allowed to come into being, that is, something incomplete should not be allowed to become reality. Both of the above cases stem from a misunderstanding of the nature of finite objects like private law. In fact, the so-called integrity of private law is only a permanent approach to integrity. Hegel clearly points out that the universal law in the past has always been the Ten Commandments of Moses, and now it is absurd to not create a law like "you shall not kill" on the pretext that it is impossible to complete the code.[97] This shows that Hegel, like other scholars of the classical school of criminology, advocates formulating a written code, which is what human reason should and can do. This is also the inevitable conclusion drawn from the rational assumption of legislators.

1.4 Human Nature Analysis of Administration of Justice

The rational assumption of human nature in the classical school of criminology is also applicable to the judicial persons, here mainly refers to the judges. Beccaria believes that the judicial person is the just judge. He is a third party relative to the monarch and the accused. Beccaria points out that the sovereign, who represents the society itself, can only make general laws to bind the members; but it belongs not to him to judge whether any individual has violated the social compact, or incurred the punishment in consequence. For in this case there are two parties, one represented by the sovereign, who insists upon the violation of the contract, and the other is the person accused, who denies it. It is necessary then that there should be a third person to decide this contest; that is to say, a judge, or magistrate, from whose determination there should be no appeal; and this determination should consist of a simple affirmation, or negation of fact.[98] However, in order to prevent judicial arbitrariness, Beccaria also advocates strict restrictions on the power of the judicial person, and regarded the judge's trial of the case as a syllogistic logical reasoning. The major premise is the general law; the minor premise is whether the behavior conforms to the law; and the conclusion is freedom or punishment. At the same time, Beccaria also denies that judges have the power to interpret criminal law. Beccaria points out that there is nothing more dangerous than the common axiom: the spirit of the laws is to be considered. To adopt it is to give way to the torrent of opinions. This may seem a paradox to vulgar minds, which are more strongly affected by the smallest disorder before their eyes, than by the most pernicious, though remote,

[97] See [18], pp. 225–226.

[98] See [6], p. 11.

consequences produced by one false principle adopted by a nation.[99] Therefore, in Beccaria's design, the judicial person is only a tool to apply the law mechanically. According to Hegel, legislation is the general principle of law, while judiciary applies it to special objects. Therefore, the judicial person can only apply within the scope stipulated by law. Hegel points out that the pure positiveness of law mainly lies in the direct application of the universal not only to the particular, but also to the individual. For a person who has committed a certain crime, should the stick be 40 or 40 minus 1, should he be fined five yuan or four yuan, 2.3 cents, should he be sentenced to one year in prison or 364 days, or one years and one day, two days or three days? It is impossible to make reasonable stipulations on what is fair, nor can it be determined by applying the stipulations derived from the concept. However, one more or less cane, more or less fine of one yuan or one cent, more or less sentence of one week or one day in prison are unjust. Reason itself admits that contingency, contradiction and illusion each have their own, indeed, limited domains and rights, and does not attempt to make these contradictions even and just. There is only a question of practical application here, namely that provisions and rulings are to be made anyway, regardless of the method (as long as it is within the limits). Making such a decision is a form of self-assurance, which is abstract subjectivity. This subjectivity can be resolved entirely within the limits mentioned above, and fixed for the sake of certainty. Otherwise, insist that this is an integer as a reason for the decision, or a reason that the number 40 minus 1 might contain. The law generally does not affirm this final stipulation required by reality, and leaves it to the judge to decide. It only limits him between a maximum and a minimum. But this does not solve the problem, because the minimum and the maximum are each an integer, so it does not prevent the judge from making such a limited, purely affirmative stipulation; on the contrary, this is something that necessarily falls within the purview of the judge.[100] Hegel regards judiciary as something contingent or individual, in order to distinguish it from the affirmation of necessity or universality by legislation. Therefore, Hegel obviously does not view judiciary as completely mechanically as Beccaria, but still regards judiciary as the process of applying universally prescribed law to individual events, whose status and function are far less important than legislation. In a word, based on the idea of separation of legislation and judiciary, the classical school of criminology strictly limits the discretional activities of judges.

2 Cultural Background

The classical school of criminology's rational hypothesis about human nature and the theoretical system of criminal law constructed from it are the product of certain historical conditions. In order to deeply understand the criminal law thought of the

[99] See [6], pp. 12–13.

[100] See [22], pp. 222–223.

classical school of criminology, it is necessary to explore the cultural background of the classical school of criminology.

2.1 Metaphysical Methodology

The term metaphysics comes from the title of a book written by Aristotle, the ancient Greek philosopher, which is called *Metaphysics*. However, this title was not used by Aristotle; it was added by a descendant who edited the work. According to the legend, Andronicos, who edited Aristotle's writings, first compiled materials about natural things and their motion into a book called *Physics*. Later, he compiled materials on abstract problems such as the existence of general principles into this book. At that time there was no name for it, and it was later named *The Later Chapters of Physics*. It has the meaning of discussing the problem of non-empirical objects. This is the origin of the title of *Metaphysics*, which means "after physics". This book was introduced into China and was translated as *Metaphysics* according to its content. Because there is a saying in *The Book of Changes* in ancient China that "The metaphysical is called the Tao, and the physical is called the implement", based on this, Yan Fu translated the Chinese title of the book *The Later Chapters of Physics* into *Metaphysics*, which has been passed down to this day. In modern philosophy, the term metaphysics, as a basic concept of philosophy, has two different meanings. One is metaphysics in the ontological sense. The other is metaphysics in the sense of methodology. As a theory that pursues ontology, metaphysics refers to the kind of philosophical theory that studies supersensory and non-empirical objects. In this sense, metaphysics is opposed to positive knowledge of empirical objects. It belongs to the speculative theory with metaphysical nature and is the knowledge of sensible things. What metaphysics pursues is the essence of existence as being and the ultimate reality in all real objects. This theory of existence is usually regarded as a first principle in philosophy. In modern philosophy, although some philosophers oppose taking metaphysics as the basis of philosophical theories, from the perspective of its dominant tendency and basic nature, modern philosophy can be considered to be basically metaphysical theories, of which Cartesian philosophy and Hegelian philosophy are the most typical. A strong anti-metaphysics trend has arisen in contemporary philosophy, but metaphysics still occupies an important position in many philosophical schools. Of course, its content has changed a lot, and it has a major difference with the traditional metaphysical theories from ancient times to modern times. Another meaning of metaphysics, that is, the concept of metaphysics as a theory of methods, is determined by Hegel. In this sense, metaphysics represents a way of thinking that is different from the dialectical way of thinking. The basic characteristic of the metaphysical way of thinking is that it sees things as isolated, absolutely static, frozen. This approach is concentrated in a rigid view of concepts. The essence of its thought is to fundamentally deny the rationality and legitimacy of the viewpoint of contradiction (identity of opposites). Metaphysics as methodology and metaphysics as ontology are two concepts that are different from each other.

Because each of them has its own special provisions and confronts with different theories or viewpoints. But there is some kind of internal connection between them, so it is possible for Hegel to extend and transform it from the concept of ontology into the concept of methodology. This inner connection is that noumenon is the core concept of metaphysical theory. As the ultimate reality and ultimate essence, noumenon has always been regarded as an absolute existence with eternal nature. Once people grasp this kind of existence, the knowledge and theory will have the ultimate and absolute nature and become the eternal truth. Therefore, as long as the metaphysical viewpoint on ontology is extended to the concepts and theories that express it, the metaphysical thinking method will be formed. From the perspective of methodological metaphysics, it is an objective fact that people rarely deny that the phenomena experienced are in constant flow and change. The so-called isolated, static and unchanging views are mainly for the ontology that is hidden or contained in or behind the phenomenon, as well as the concepts or theories that express this eternal ontology. Here, according to the metaphysical point of view, we can only admit that existence is existence, and cannot be non-existence at the same time. Truth is truth, and cannot be false at the same time. This is the essence of metaphysical thinking method. Therefore, the solidified viewpoint and the abstract ontology theory are interlinked with each other, and even presuppose each other. Hegel derives the metaphysical concept of invariance from ontological metaphysics. In this definition, it can be said that it only further reveals the characteristics or nature of the thinking method of invariance of metaphysical ontology.[101] The metaphysics methodology that I am talking about here as the humanistic background of the classical school of criminology refers not only to the ontology of metaphysics, but also to the methodology. In a more important sense, it refers to the ontology.

Metaphysical thinking began in ancient Greece. The original metaphysical thinking was mainly about the fundamental problems of the world. The ancient Greek philosophers assume that beyond the empirical facts, there is the eternal foundation, which is the noumenon of the world. As Windelband, a German philosopher, points out, it refers to what is a thing or what is the nature of a thing. This question is already contained in the Miletus School's concept of the "primitive foundation" (*apcin*). This question assumes that the prevailing, primitive and naive way of thinking about the world has been shaken, although this assumption has not yet been clearly recognized in consciousness.[102] Therefore, the initial theoretical form of metaphysics is ontology, which is based on Aristotle's *Metaphysics*. Although ontology is a philosophical theory, in essence it expresses a unique way that people use human points of view to look at things. The question of ontology will be raised, which means that people are not satisfied with the phenomenal knowledge about things obtained from the senses. Only by taking visible real things as non-free beings, and assuming that there is another invisible thing behind them that dominates and determines them, can we ask the question of seeking or exploring ontology. Therefore, the question of

---

[101] See [35], p. 45.

[102] See [36], p. 83.

ontology shows that people have secretly divided the object into two kinds of existence. One is the existence of human senses, and the other is the real reality of things. The search for noumenon is to transcend the present existence of sensory things to discover the hidden but real existence. Therefore, ontology is the basic theoretical form of ancient philosophy. This theory has the following characteristics. (1) The exogenous philosophy that pursues the innate essence. Ancient philosophy usually divided the object into two kinds of existence in theory. One is the external, accidental and phenomenal existence, and the other is the internal, inevitable and authentic existence. The task of philosophy is to get rid of the disturbance of phenomena, to go deep behind the facts to grasp its true details, and to pursue the ultimate value of life in the world and life. The pursuit of external transcendence of essence and power is the highest goal of ancient philosophy. (2) The philosophy of absolute rationalism in pursuit of ultimate truth. In the ancient concept, cognitive reason is the first place in the spiritual activity, which is regarded as the overriding and decisive thing. Philosophy is a cognitive theory of reason, and culture is also a cognitive culture dominated by reason. The purpose of reason is to grasp the truth and to seek truth is the fundamental purpose of spiritual activities. The highest truth is the absolute grasp of that eternity, so philosophy becomes the highest authority of the whole spiritual activity. (3) A philosophical way of thinking that pursues absolute unity between polar opposites. According to the traditional concept, the highest absoluteness can only be the single essence, and it is because of this that it becomes the highest absoluteness, otherwise it is not an eternal thing. Therefore, the pursuit of absolute unity and dogmatic monism are the highest principles of ancient philosophy as well as their ultimate goal. Therefore, the purpose of splitting existence into two is to seek the absoluteness of unity, which is the concept of substance in ancient philosophy. The metaphysics of modern philosophy began with Descartes, a German philosopher. According to Descartes, the first part of true philosophy is metaphysics. Metaphysics includes principles of knowledge, such as the definition of important attributes of God, the immateriality of the soul, and all the simple and clear conceptions of human beings. Descartes believes that metaphysics should have a definite and self-evident starting point, which is "I think, therefore I am". Starting from the proposition "I think, therefore I am", Descartes simultaneously proposes matter and thought, two opposite entities. These two things are incompatible. They have their own independent natures. The existence in reality can only be either this or that, and it is absolutely impossible for a thing to have dual essence at the same time. From this, Descartes' dualism can be logically deduced. The central problem of ontological theory after Descartes is to overcome the opposition of this dual entity and establish a single entity based on the "black or white" thinking logic based on the principle of law of contradiction. From the perspective of ontology, the essence of this problem is the relationship between thinking and existence. To solve this problem, two ontological philosophies, that is, modern materialism and modern idealism, have been formed. After the interpretation of Spinoza and others, the ontology of materialism reached its peak in the eighteenth century by French philosophers. In the eighteenth century, French philosophers mainly relied on the achievements of mechanics of machinery, and by extending it to all fields, they not only used the laws of mechanics to explain physical phenomena, chemical phenomena, and life phenomena, but also used it to explain human spiritual phenomena. Thus, everything that exists comes down to a mechanical causal necessary connection. Any supernatural existence is denied. The whole world becomes just one entity, that is, the different manifestation of a physical entity. Kant, a famous German philosopher, made an important transition from ontology to epistemology. Kant, by means of reconciling contradictory dualism, promoted philosophy to change its emphasis on the original role of the object to the active role of the subject. Although Kant also admits the existence of ontology, he attributes it to the world of things-in-itself that no cognitive reason can grasp. According to Kant, the thing-in-itself is unknowable. All people can know is the phenomenal world. Phenomenon is only the appearance produced in the human mind by external objects acting on the senses, and it does not represent the state of the external world. In this way, Kant completely overthrows the previous ontology theories in scientific forms that used intellectual methods to describe the physical conditions, all of which boils down to fictional theories. Kant believes that the categories used in rational activities belong to the innate thinking function of human beings. It can only play the role of cognition when combined with perceptual experience. And all that perceptual experience can provide is intuitive materials about concrete things. Once reason tries to know the thing-in-itself, it transcends empirical intuitive realm and must be caught in the conflict between different propositions that can neither be verified nor repudiated. This is what Kant calls the dilemma of antinomy. Therefore, according to Kant, noumenon is just a thing-in-itself, which belongs to the thing which we do not know, but which exists. In this way, Kant turns ontology into a metaphysical theory about super-empirical existence. Kant overthrows the ontological theory that appears in the form of science but has dogmatic nature, not to deny the ontology, but to change the ontological theory with the mechanical causal point of view, and to re-establish an ontological theory with the free will causality point of view. Kant's ontology is also a metaphysical ontology, but it does not belong to the metaphysical theory of nature, but to the metaphysical theory of morality. After Kant, after Fichte and Schelling's philosophical exploration from different angles, Hegel finally established the last ontology system in the development of traditional philosophy. In this regard, Marx once points out that the metaphysics in the seventeenth century, defeated by the French Enlightenment, especially the French materialism in the eighteenth century, has a successful and substantial restoration in German philosophy, especially in the German speculative philosophy in the nineteenth century. After Hegel's genius in combining the metaphysics in the seventeenth century with all subsequent metaphysics and German idealism and establishing an all-embracing realm of metaphysics, the attack on speculative metaphysics and all metaphysics, as in the eighteenth century, was again combined with the attack on theology.[103] The biggest characteristic of Hegel's ontological theory is to subjectify noumenon and endow noumenon with a noumenon of dynamic development. The noumenon established by Hegel is the absolute idea. In order to complete the development system of the absolute idea, combined with the development history of human cognition, it

[103] See [37], p. 159.

has absorbed almost all the knowledge achievements created by human beings, thus building an all-embracing knowledge system covering various fields of knowledge. Thus, it can be seen that metaphysics, as an ontological theory as well as a way of thinking, once dominated for a long time before the nineteenth century, and had a significant impact on the academic research at that time.

The classical school of criminology is the school of criminal law that comes into being in this metaphysical ideological atmosphere. In particular, in this school, Kant and Hegel were famous philosophers at that time, and their criminal law thoughts were just reflections of their philosophical thoughts on criminal law. For example, Kant's theory of law, as its title indicates, is a metaphysical theory of law and an important part of the moral metaphysical theory. Kant points out that moral laws are valid laws only insofar as they can be rationally founded on transcendental principles and understood as necessary and metaphysical arguments. Any transcendental system of knowledge contains some pure concepts. Therefore, practical philosophy—which regards not character, but freedom of will as its object—must presuppose and need moral metaphysics.[104] As for Hegel, he calls his legal theory a philosophy of law. We can clearly see the close relationship between his legal thought and his philosophical thought. Hegel points out that the science of right is a part of philosophy. It has therefore to develop the Idea, which is the reason within an object, out of the concept; or what comes to the same thing, it must observe the proper immanent development of the thing itself.[105] Thus it can be seen that Kant and Hegel use a transcendental metaphysical speculative way to study criminal law. Beccaria's thought is more materialistic, which is different from Kant and Hegel, but there is something in common in metaphysics, because Beccaria also discusses criminal law questions with metaphysics. This is mainly manifested in Beccaria's persistent pursuit of justice and humanity.

The metaphysical method of the classical school of criminology on crimes is manifested in the human nature interpretation of crime noumenon. In the Middle Ages, theology ruled Europe, and people's thoughts all wore the shackles of theology. Therefore, in this era, the essence of crime was the result of conflict between individuals and a society caused by certain physiological and psychological desires of human beings in ancient Greece, and it transformed into the result of the influence of superhuman forces outside the real world. In a word, from a natural interpretation of the essence of a crime to a supernatural interpretation. The so-called supernatural interpretation of the essence of a crime here refers to taking a crime as a kind of behavior imposed on people by a supernatural external force, which is the result of a demonic action. On this point, two US criminologists, Richard Quinney and John Wildeman make the following account. When most of the writings of early social philosophers focus on the relationship between crimes and various factors in the spiritual world, they generally attribute crimes to the influence of forces outside the real world. Wald calls this interpretation of crimes "the study of demons". It can be found that this diabolical interpretation takes various forms. The primitive, yet

[104] See [2], pp. 15 and 17.

[105] See [22], p. 2.

unwritten, animism, thought that evil spirits caused crimes. In the Middle Ages, evil spirits were blamed for crimes and other aberrations. Tyzas devotes a great deal of attention to this cause. He mainly discusses the social causes of crimes and abnormal mental problems, attributing them to the results of evil spirits. The notions of "evil" and "lack of morality" were universally accepted and pervaded most writings from the 16th to the early nineteenth centuries. Criminals are considered to be people who in some way have an abnormal relationship with monsters outside the world.[106] From the eighteenth century, Enlightenment thinkers broke through the shackles of medieval religious theology and reconsidered the essence of crime. Enlightenment thinkers change the medieval view that crime is explained by supernatural power, and discuss the crime philosophically. Rousseau, for example points out that a man who does evil becomes a traitor to his motherland because of his crimes since he is attacking social rights. He breaks the laws of the motherland, so he is no longer a member of the state, and he even goes to war against the state. The preservation of the state is then incompatible with the preservation of himself, and one of the two must be destroyed. To punish a criminal with a death sentence is to treat him as an enemy rather than as a citizen. The prosecution and the judgment are proofs and declarations that he has broken the social contract, so that he is no longer a member of the state.[107] Obviously, Rousseau regards crime as breaking the social contract and thus violating the public will of a society. As Locke points out, when a criminal violates natural law, he shows that he lives according to rules other than reason and justice. And the rules of reason and justice are the measures of human behavior which God has set for the mutual security of mankind. Therefore, whoever neglects and undermines the restraint that protects mankind from damage and violence is dangerous to mankind. Since this is an aggression against all mankind, against the peace and security of all mankind stipulated by natural law, everyone, by virtue of his right to safeguard mankind in general, has the right to stop or, if necessary, destroy all the things that are bad for them, and everyone can give the one who breaks natural law misfortune that can cause him to repent, so that he and his example can make others dare not do the same again.[108] There is no doubt that Locke regards crime as an act against natural law and legitimate rational rules. Enlightenment thinkers explain human behavior not by supernatural forces, but by human factors. In their study of crime, they connect crime with law, thereby denying the supernatural interpretation of the essence of crime in the Middle Ages. The classical school of criminology is deeply influenced by enlightenment thought, and also adopts a humanistic natural interpretation in the interpretation of crime, especially it attributes the crime to the freedom of human will, which is completely a metaphysical interpretation.

The metaphysical method of the classical school of criminology on the issue of punishments is mainly manifested in the interpretation of the purpose of punishments. Kant and Hegel's theory of retribution interprets punishments with justice, and exerts the concepts of moral retribution and legal retribution. Divine doctrine

---

[106] See [10], p. 34.

[107] See [38], p. 47.

[108] See [39], pp. 7–8.

of retribution dominated in the Middle Ages. Divine doctrine of retribution takes God's will as the reason for retribution, and believes that crime is a violation of God's order or Heaven's will, and the state's punishments for criminals is to uphold God's will and make retribution. For example, St. Augustine, a famous Christian thinker in ancient Rome, points out that a crime is the mother of slavery and the first reason for human obedience. It appears not beyond the guidance of the highest God, but according to the guidance of the highest God. There is no injustice in the highest God. Only the highest God knows best how to impose proper punishments for crimes.[109] The divine doctrine of retribution interprets the noumenon of punishments in secular society with the insubstantial will of God, and its absurdity is self-evident. Kant denies the divine retribution and advocates moral retribution. The meaning of the punishment is to achieve moral justice. Hegel advocates legal retribution. He concludes the meaning of the punishment to achieve legal justice. Although the theories of retribution of Kant and Hegel are different in content, they are completely consistent in pursuing retributive justice of punishments. The theories of deterrence held by Beccaria, Bentham and Feuerbach interpret punishments with utility and puts forward the thought of general prevention. In the Middle Ages, punishments often appear in a cruel form, and their bloody scenes clearly have intimidation. However, Beccaria et al. set legal limits on punishment deterrence from the perspective of humanitarianism. They advocate a legally prescribed punishment for a specified crime and balance between crime and punishment, so as to realize the effective guarantee of civil freedom.

The ontological mode of thinking adopted by metaphysical methodology has left obvious traces in the theory of classical school of criminology. In particular, the metaphysical absolutist notions of the supremacy of thinking, the rational hypothesis of criminals and legislators in classical school of criminology, the utility calculation ability of the offender, the rational essence of the offenders' freedom of will, the creative power of the legislators' all-encompassing legal system, even theoretical critical thinking, logic capabilities on language expressions and so on. All of the above have the marks of metaphysical methodology.

2.2 *The Conception of Nature of Mechanism*

Introducing the research results of the natural sciences into the research field of the social sciences was a popular fashion in the European academic circles in the seventeenth and eighteenth centuries after the Enlightenment. People try to use the latest discoveries of natural sciences to explain various social phenomena, so that social sciences have been deeply branded by natural sciences. What may be applied to nature, which we now understand as the course of history, can also be applied to all the departments of social history, and to all the sciences which deal with human (and divine) matters. In a sense, we can say that any kind of new ideas is the result

[109] See [28], p. 93.

of interaction and infiltration between natural sciences and social sciences. In this case, the development of social sciences cannot help but be influenced by natural sciences.

The revolution of modern natural sciences began with Copernicus. Copernicus was an astronomer as well as a mathematician. The main question he pondered was what motion the planets should have in order to produce the simplest and most harmonious celestial geometry. As a result of thinking, Copernicus proposed the heliocentric theory. He moved the coordinate reference system of planetary motion from the Earth to the stars. This involved a revolution in physics and mathematics, and was enough to destroy Aristotle's physics and astronomy. Copernicus made people see the world with new visions. The earth descended from the center of the universe to a lower status, which was one of the planets. Such a change would not necessarily mean relegating human beings from the lofty status of the wisest of all creatures, but it would certainly cast doubt on the reliability of beliefs. Therefore, Copernicus' astronomy not only destroyed Ptolemy's theory, which was incorporated schoolmen into its own system, but also influenced people's thoughts and beliefs in more important aspects. Copernicus's theory caused a revolution in astronomy, and, in fact, it also caused a revolution in general scientific thought. After Copernicus, in astronomy, Kepler induced and proved three propositions or laws of planetary motion. These three laws later became the basis of Newton's astronomy. The following are the three general inductions that have survived in science under the name of Kepler's Law. (1) The orbit of the planet is an ellipse with the sun at one of its focal points. (2) The area swept in orbit by the connection between the center of the sun and the center of the planet is proportional to time. (3) The square of the time a planet takes in its orbit is directly proportional to the cube of its average distance from the sun. Galileo further developed the natural sciences, which at that time took astronomy as a breakthrough. Copernicus and Kepler proved that the motion of the Earth and other planets can be expressed mathematically. Galileo felt that the parts of the earth also moved mathematically in local motion. Hence, what he wanted to discover was not why the object falls, but how it falls, that is, according to what mathematical relationship it falls. This was a great discovery in the scientific method. When evaluating Galileo, British scholars point out that Galileo's philosophical thought is close to Kepler on the one hand, and Newton on the other hand. Like Kepler, he was looking for mathematical relationships between natural phenomena, but he was not looking for mystical causes, but to understand the eternal laws that govern changes in nature, regardless of whether natural reasons are understood by human beings or not. It can be seen that Galileo has been far away from the schoolmen's man-centered philosophy. In this philosophy, the whole nature is created for man. However, in Galileo's view, God endows nature with this strict mathematical inevitability, and then creates human understanding through nature, so that human understanding can explore a few secrets of nature after making great efforts.[110] Through the efforts of Copernicus, Keppler, Galileo and others, science entered the era of the first thorough comprehensiveness in history, which was the Newtonian era. Newton also started his

[110] See [40], p. 199.

thinking from astronomy. Galileo's research showed that there must be a reason for the planets and moons to orbit and not fly straight into space. Galileo regards this cause as a force, but it remains to be proven whether this force exists. According to Voltaire, Newton found a clue to the problem when he saw apples fall to the ground in his orchard. This phenomenon led him to guess why objects fell, and made him wonder how far the Earth's suction could reach. Since this attractive force is felt as much in the deepest mines as it is in the highest mountains, could it reach the moon and be the reason why objects do not fly in a straight line, but keep falling towards the Earth? In 1685, Newton overcame computational difficulties and proved that a ball of gravitational matter attracted objects outside it as if all the mass were concentrated in its center. With this valid proving, a simplified method of treating the sun, the planets, the Earth, and the moon as if they were all a single particle made sense, and thus raised the calculations from rough approximations to extremely precise proving. This achievement cleared the way for Newton's original research. Hence, he tried to relate the forces of the heavenly bodies to the forces of the Earth that attract objects to fall. The gravity of the Earth can be seen as having a center and being right at the center of the Earth to verify his hypothesis. The distance between the Earth and the moon is about 60 times the radius of the Earth, which has a radius of 4,000 miles. Thus, he calculated that the Moon leaves the straight path and falls towards the Earth at a speed of about 0.0044 feet per second. If the inverse-square law is correct, this force should be $(60)^2$ times, that is, 3,600 times, stronger on the Earth's surface than on the moon's surface, so the velocity of the falling object on the ground is $3{,}600 \times 0.0044$, or about 16 feet per second. This is consistent with the facts of contemporary observations, so the proving is fully established. Newton thus proved that an apple or a stone that usually falls to the ground, and the moon, which orbits solemnly in the sky, are governed by the same unknown cause. This cause is gravity, as Newton calls it. As Newton points out, gravity is only a name given to the causes of objects falling, planets in closed orbits around the sun, etc. Experimental philosophy cannot determine what the cause is because there are no proper observations to make. Experimental philosophers can only point out how gravity works, how much velocity increases in a given time when an object falls, etc., as Galileo does when he finds that the falling object is accelerating. Speculating about the cause of gravity X, and describing it as a mysterious force or a vortex in the universe, is worthless to experimental philosophy because all such explanations are of a hypothetical nature. Newton points out that it will be nonsense to tell us that everything has a mysterious particularity by which it works and produces obvious effects. But to deduce from phenomena two or three general principles of motion, and to tell us afterwards that the natures and functions of all corporeal things are based on these obvious principles, is a great advance in philosophy, otherwise the cause of these principles has not yet been discovered. Therefore, after consideration, I think it is better not to put forward the principles of the above-mentioned motion, because these principles cover a very wide range, and it is better to let others discover their causes.[111] It can be seen that, as a scientist, Newton pays attention to the knowledge provided by experiments,

[111] See [41], p. 188.

but he is not limited to experiments. He advocates using the known to explain the unknown and using deduction. Newton distinguishes between principles provided by experiments and principles provided by intuition. Newton believes that the starting point of physical–mathematical deduction should be the effect or law observed from the experiment, and the deduction should lead to the explanation or prediction of other observable effects. These scientific methods adopted by Newtonian mechanics gave people great encouragement at the time. General principles could be deduced from the observation of individual phenomena. At the same time, it also led people to establish the belief that the world was a huge machine built according to the laws of mathematics. The concrete manifestation of this belief in rationalistic philosophy is dualism. Rationalists hope that God can guarantee the consistency between what is in the mind and what is in reality, and guarantee the objective validity of innate knowledge. This belief persisted for 300 years. The mechanistic world view dominated throughout modern times. Modern philosophy was deeply influenced by the mechanistic conception of nature, not only because philosophy must draw knowledge nutrition from science, but more importantly, at that time, philosophy and science were not completely separated. At the same time, some philosophers were scientists themselves and made great contributions to the development of science. Among these philosophers, Descartes, a French philosopher, was foremost. Descartes was fascinated by the mathematical methods developed in the physical science. Descartes believes that not all ideas that can be treated mathematically are equally important, and that only ideas given intuitively can provide the most reliable starting point for deductive methods of mathematical properties. Motion, extension and God are such ideas. The idea of God is the main basis of the Cartesian system, because God creates extension and puts motion into the universe. Since motion is only given to the universe at one blow at the time of creation, the total amount of motion in the world must be a constant. Using this method of argumentation, Descartes comes to his principle of conservation of momentum. Descartes is convinced that all the remarkable features of nature can be deduced from unquestionable and definite principles and demonstrated in a mathematical manner. In the Cartesian system, all material things are machines governed by the same mechanical laws, and so it is with animals, plants, and inorganic matter, as it is with the human body. In this way he excludes the traditional notion that nature is always constituted according to a certain hierarchy. He rules out the idea that all things in the world form a huge chain, which starts from the perfect God at the edge of the universe, passes through the heavenly gods and angels of different ranks, and ends with various ranks of people, animals, plants and minerals. According to Descartes, the inorganic and organic worlds are homologous mechanical system composed of qualitatively identical objects. Each of these objects obeys quantitative mechanical laws that are analyzed and revealed by mathematical methods. The world is not as heterogeneous as the scholastic philosophers say it is, but is made up of a variety of different objects. Each of these objects, through pure classification of the qualitative system, finds a certain rank in this space system according to its different soul. In addition to the mechanical world, Descartes believes that there is also a spiritual world, in which man belongs only to the material reality in which he participates by means of his soul. After the advantages of Cartesian philosophy, the traditional view that everything in the universe is on a vertical ladder gradually disappeared and was replaced by another concept. That is, the universe is made up of two different parallel sides (one mechanical and the other spiritual), and only man has both sides at the same time. Since the time of Descartes, this dualism has been a fundamental view in European thought. Descartes believes that human reason has the ability to grasp certain and common knowledge. He is a dogmatist as well as a rationalist. Drawing on self-evident concepts and principles inherent in the mind, he engaged in building an all-embracing theory. This theory, like a proposition of geometry, must be obeyed by reason. Inheriting the thought of Descartes, Spinoza, a famous Dutch philosopher, believes that the purpose of philosophy is to obtain complete knowledge about things, which can only be achieved by clear and definite thinking. If we proceed from self-evident principles and prove every step of the way, we can construct systems of truth like mathematics. Descartes gives examples of the use of geometric methods in the appendix to his *Meditations*. Spinoza uses the same approach in his early writings on Cartesian philosophy and in his major work, *The Ethics*, which is from definitions and axioms to propositions. Such propositions are demonstrated by him in geometrical order, in which each proposition occupies its due place. A proposition is followed by an inference, that is, a necessary consequence of a proposition. There are also explanations, where the propositions are informally discussed and compared in more detail. Russell, a famous British philosopher, remarks that a modern scholar cannot conceive of any rigorous proving of what he purportedly seeks to establish, and must be impatient with the details in proving, which in fact are not worth mastering. It is enough to read the narratives of the propositions and then study the commentaries, which contain much of the essence of *The Ethics*. But if Spinoza uses the geometric method, that also shows a lack of knowledge. It is the essence and lifeblood of Spinoza's philosophical system to claim that everything is possible to prove, not only in metaphysics but also in ethics, so proving must be mentioned. We cannot accept his method because we cannot accept his metaphysics. We cannot believe that the interconnectedness of the parts of the universe is a logical connection, because we believe that scientific laws must be discovered by observation, not by reasoning alone. But in Spinoza's view, the geometric method is indispensable, and is closely related to the most fundamental part of his theory.[112] Indeed, as Russell says, the method of geometric proving is an integral part of Spinoza's theory. The mechanistic conception of nature had a great influence on French materialism in the eighteenth century. French materialism in the eighteenth century was a mechanical materialism. In explaining materialism, Dampier points out that the word materialism, according to its loose usage, is often understood as a synonym for atheism, or to express any philosophy that is incompatible with popular orthodoxy. But in our opinion, it has a stricter meaning. It is the belief that the hard, impenetrable, dead matter, or Newton's solid, impenetrable particle, or the complex fundamental particle of modern physics, is the only ultimate reality of the universe. Thought and consciousness are but by-products of matter.

[112] See [42], p. 96.

There is no reality under or beyond matter.[113] The French materialists in the eighteenth century regarded motion as the inherent property and way of existence of matter, demonstrated the motility of matter, and regarded moving matter as the only substance that existed independently outside consciousness and acted on our senses. However, they use the mechanical point of view to explain the properties and motion of matter, and even use the mechanical point of view to explain the thought and consciousness and even human beings. There are limitations to the mechanism. For example, La Mettrie's *Man is a Machine* describes man as a machine. He points out that man is such a complex machine that it is impossible to have a clear conception of it from the very beginning and give it a definition. Because of this, the research that the greatest philosophers have done congenitally, that is, with the help of spiritual wings, turns out to be all in vain. Only by nurture, that is to say, only by trying to dissect the mind through the organs of the human body, can we—I cannot discover human nature itself explicitly, but at least—approach the utmost probability on this subject.[114]

In the historical background of the mechanistic conception of nature in the seventeenth and eighteenth centuries, the criminal law theory held by Beccaria, the founder of the classical school of criminology, was deeply marked by the mechanism. Beccaria was very fond of mathematics and physics during his studies at Pavia University. He was deeply influenced by Newtonian mechanics, and with his profound natural science accomplishment, he won the title of Little Newton. In *On Crimes and Punishments*, Beccaria's famous book, traces of Newtonian mechanics can be found in both the understanding of the nature of things and the expression of ideas. From the understanding of the nature of things, Beccaria compares the force of personal well-being to universal gravitation. This force manifests itself in a complex series of human actions, and can only be suppressed by resistance in the opposite direction. Beccaria calls the punishment political resistance. Using the political resistance to punishments can prevent the harmful consequences that may arise from the conflict of these actions. However, at the same time, he believes that punishments can only suppress or counteract these gravitational forces, but cannot eliminate the causes that produce them, because these gravitational forces arise from people's inherent sensitivity. Beccaria also compares the legislator to an ingenious architect. He believes that it is the duty of the architect to remove the harmful effects of universal gravity and to apply it where it will make the buildings strong. According to Newton's law of universal gravitation, gravity is the nature of all matter in the universe. All objects, whether macroscopic or microscopic, animate or inanimate, abide by this law. The entire universe is a well-ordered causal series that strictly follows the laws of mechanics. In Beccaria's view, society is also a universe, which also obeys certain laws of mechanics. And the mission of social scientists is simply to discover such laws. Crime is the result of the sensitivity in human nature that strives for personal peace and happiness. And the penalty is the political resistance against this gravitational force—that's Beccaria's formula. The criminal law theory

[113] See [40], p. 281.

[114] See [43], p. 242.

of the classical school of criminology is based on this formula, which can be said to be a replica of Newton's law of mechanics in the field of criminal law. On this basis, Beccaria further puts forward the view that punishments and crimes are balanced or symmetrical (*Proporzione fra i delitti e le pene*). Here the word "Proporzione", which can be translated as equilibrium or symmetry, refers to the equal proportion or ratio between two objects. For example, Newton's third law of mechanics is that reaction and action are always equal and opposite; in other words, the interactions between two objects are always equal in magnitude and opposite in direction.[115] It can be seen that the proportional relationship between such objects is the basic concept of Newtonian mechanics in the study of momentum and external force, action and reaction. According to this proportional relationship, people can infer the change of the momentum of the object when the external force that the object bears is known; when we know the force of the object, the reaction force can be inferred. We apply this proportional relationship of forces between objects to crimes and punishments, making them interacting counterparts. The function of punishments is to prevent the occurrence of crime, so the intensity of punishments depends on the need for general prevention. In Beccaria's view, even this intensity of punishments can be precisely calculated geometrically. Regarding this point, as Huang Feng, a Chinese scholar, points out, Beccaria is not satisfied with the abstract theory of the nature, purpose and function of punishments like some criminal jurists in the past. He seeks to find the rules for precisely applying the punishment to its best effect. His literacy in mathematics and physics leads him to explore these rules from the perspective of political arithmetic and penal mechanics. In his thought, punishments should not be arbitrarily estimated, and anyone more or less will have a positive or negative impact on the result after the equal sign. The effect of the punishment depends to a large extent on its application procedures and methods, just as a force will have different effects under different conditions. Punishments should not rely on some creepy horror image to intimidate the mind. Punishments should rely on their own level, accuracy, timeliness and certainty to influence people's calculation of pros and cons, so as to prevent them from committing crimes that are not beneficial to others or themselves.[116] In addition, Beccaria also uses a lot of Newtonian mechanics language in the process of expressing his thought, making it vivid. For example, Beccaria points out that this is the fundamental principle of good legislation, which is the art of conducting men to the maximum of happiness, and to the minimum of misery, if we may apply this mathematical expression to the good and evil of life. But the means hitherto employed for that purpose, are generally inadequate, or contrary to the end proposed. It is impossible to reduce the tumultuous activity of mankind to absolute regularity; for, midst the various and opposite attractions of pleasure and pain, human laws are not sufficient entirely to prevent disorders in society. Such, however, is the chimera of weak men, when invested with authority. To prohibit a number of indifferent actions, is not to prevent the crimes which they may produce.[117] In the final summary of *On*

[115] See [40], p. 228.

[116] See [8], p. 112.

[117] See [6], p. 104.

Crime and Punishment, Beccaria summarizes the content of the book as a general axiom. The word axiom here is obviously a term in geometry. In the classical school of criminology, Bentham is also influenced by mechanism. Bentham is known as a utilitarian, who believes that people are governed by the principle of utility. He points out that nature places human beings under the rule of two kings, namely pain and pleasure. Only they can dictate what we should do and decide what we are going to do. The standard of right and wrong is one side, and the chain of cause and effect is one side, both of which are tied to their golden thrones. Everything we can do, say, and think is subject to them. All we can do to break free from submission to them can only illustrate and affirm this relationship of submission. A man may pretend to scold their empire, but, in reality, he can only continue to obey it. The principle of utility recognizes this relationship of obedience as the cornerstone of that system whose purpose is to establish happiness by rational and legal means.[118] According to Bentham's utilitarian principle, human beings are constrained by two factors, pain and pleasure. It is human nature to draw on advantages and avoid disadvantages. By manipulating pain and pleasure, legislators can effectively control people's behavior. From a mechanical point of view, both Beccaria and Bentham believe that human behavior is dominated by external perceptual forces, but neither of them denies the freedom of human will, which is clearly a characteristic of Cartesian dualism.

2.3 Individual-Based Values

Every school has its own unique values. As a school of criminal law, the classical school of criminology also has its specific criminal law value. This criminal law value is an individual-based concept with the protection of human rights as the core content.

The individual-based values of the classical school of criminology come from the cultural tradition of humanism that has arisen in continental Europe since the Renaissance. The Renaissance in Italy played a very important role in the development of modern European civilization. The themes of the Renaissance were the discovery of individuals and the discovery of reason. In the Middle Ages, both aspects of human consciousness—inner introspection and external observation alike—had been under a common veil, in sleeping or semi-awake states. This veil was woven of belief, fantasy and childish prejudice. Looking out through it, the world and history were covered with a strange color. Human beings were conscious of themselves only as members of a race, a nation, a party, a family, or a community—only through certain general categories. In Italy, this veil was the first to dissipate, and it became possible to objectively deal with and consider everything in the country and the world. At the same time, the subjective aspect also emphasized and expressed itself accordingly. Man became a spiritual individual, and thus knew himself. When this driving force for the highest personal development is combined with a character that is strong,

[118] See [28], p. 483.

colorful, and has mastered all the cultural elements of the time, then there is a unique Italian "versatile person"—"I' uomo universel" (all-rounder).[119] When Engels talked about the characters of the Renaissance, he once pointed out affectionately, "This is the greatest and progressive change that mankind has never experienced. This is a time when giants are needed and produced—giants in thinking ability, passion and character, in versatility and knowledge."[120] The discovery of the individual in the Renaissance led to the origin of the individual-based value concept, which was clearly reflected in natural law advocated by the Enlightenment thinkers in the seventeenth and eighteenth centuries.

As a legal theory in the Enlightenment period, the core content of natural law is two assumptions. One is the assumption about the state of nature, and the other is the assumption about the social contract. Hobbes describes the state of nature from the perspective that human nature is evil. He thinks that man is natural. Everyone tries to save his life. People pursue what is beneficial to life, avoid what is unfavorable to life, and engage in activities in accordance with the principle of seeking advantages and avoiding disadvantages. This makes self-preservation the basic driving force of all human activities. Human beings act according to the principle of self-preservation, which is a right granted by nature. This self-right is that each person uses his own strength to preserve his freedom according to his own wishes. In this case, the state of nature gives rise to a war of all against all (*bellum omuiurn contra omnes*). Hobbes points out that since the human condition is one in which everyone is at war against everyone, in this case, everyone is ruled by his own reason. Anything at his disposal can help him fight the enemy and save his life. Therefore, in this case, everyone has a right over everything, even over each other's bodies.[121] In order to bring peace to mankind and avoid a state of war, people transfer their rights to each other. This mutual transfer of rights is what people call a contract. Hobbes points out that whenever a man transfers his right, or renounces his right, it is always either because of the consideration that the other party has transferred him some right, or because he hopes to obtain some other advantage from it. Because this is a voluntary action, and anyone's voluntary action is for some kind of benefit to himself. Unlike Hobbes, Locke does not describe a state of nature as a state of war. Locke believes that a state of nature is a state of freedom and equality. The fundamental features of this state of nature are as follows. (1) This is a state of complete freedom. Within the natural law, people act as they see fit in dealing with property and personal matters. (2) This is a state of natural equality. People are of the same species and equal, and their powers and jurisdictions are mutual and equivalent. All are equal and have no affiliation. (3) This is also a state in which freedom cannot be abused. This is not a state of war, but a state of peace, fraternity and coexistence. Locke points out that a state of nature is dominated by natural law that everyone should abide by. And reason, that is, natural law, teaches all human beings who consciously obey reason. Since people are all equal and independent, no one can harm the life, health, liberty or property of

---

[119] See [44], pp. 125 and 131.

[120] See [45], pp. 261–262.

[121] See [46], p. 94.

others.[122] Since the state of nature is so beautiful, why are people willing to give up their realm of freedom and subject themselves to the domination and control of any other right? Locke believes that although people enjoy rights in the state of nature, this enjoyment is very unstable, and there is a constant threat of being violated by others. Since everyone is like him in the air of a king, everyone is equal to him, and most people do not strictly observe justice, his possession of property in this state is very insecure and very unreliable. That is to say, the state of nature cannot protect people's property, so they have to unite into a state. The state of nature is so for three reasons. (1) In the state of nature, there is a lack of a definite, prescribed, and well-known law as a standard for judging right and wrong and a common measure for judging all disputes between people. Because although there is natural law, some people have prejudice because of their interests, and some people are ignorant because of a lack of research on natural law, and these people do not think natural law is binding upon them. (2) In the state of nature, there is no known and impartial judge who has the power to judge all disputes in accordance with the established law. Because if everyone is the judge and executor of natural law, it is inevitable to favor oneself and act according to the psychology of revenge, resulting in unfair judgment. (3) In the state of nature, there is often a lack of power to support the correct judgment and make it duly execute. In such a case, as Locke says, the only way for anyone to give up his natural liberty and to be subject to the constraints of civil society is to agree with others to form a community together for their mutual comfortable, safe and peaceful life in order to enjoy their property in security and to have greater protection against encroachment by anyone outside the community. Thus, Locke argues that political societies all originate from voluntary unions and mutual agreements in which people freely choose their rulers and forms of government.[123] Thus it can be seen that although Hobbes and Locke have different understandings of the state of nature, they both expounded on the conclusion of a social contract to end the state of nature and establish a political society. This social contract theory reflects the guarantee of individual rights of citizens. As Peter Stein and John Shand, two British scholars, point out, the two social contracts that constitute the basis of a society proposed by Hobbes and Locke have different characteristics, but both social contracts start with the individual in a state of nature. One of the consequences of such an emphasis on the individual is the theory of individual non-transferable rights.[124]

The theory of natural law strengthens the individual-based values, the core of which is to protect the individual freedom and rights of citizens through the law, and to limit the power of the government. Locke clearly points out that the purpose of the law is not to abolish or restrict freedom, but to protect and expand it. This is because in all human states capable of being governed by law, where there is no law, there is no freedom. This is because freedom means freedom from constraint and violence by others, and there can be no such freedom where there is no law.[125] In order to protect

[122] See [39], p. 6.

[123] See [39], pp. 59 and 63.

[124] See [47], p. 145.

[125] See [48], p. 36.

civil liberties, Locke puts forward the theory of separation of powers. Locke believes that a state has three powers, namely, legislative power, executive power and foreign power. Legislative power is the power to make and promulgate laws. Executive power is the power to enforce the law. Foreign power is the power to declare war, make peace, conclude a treaty, etc. Each of these three powers should be executed by an organ. The key of the theory of separation of powers lies in restricting power with power and preventing its arrogation. Montesquieu further develops the theory of separation of powers, making it constitute a political philosophy of separation of the three powers. Montesquieu points out that from the nature of things, it is necessary to restrain power with power in order to prevent abuse of power.[126] Montesquieu divides state power into three types, namely, legislative power, executive power and judicial power. Compared with Locke's ideas, the characteristic of Montesquieu's ideas in the history of the theory of separation of powers lies not in his idea of separation of powers, but in his theory of checks and balances. It is about "mutual approval system" and "coordinated advance" of three kinds of state power.[127] Montesquieu points out that a citizen's political freedom is a state of peace of mind. This peace of mind arises from the perception that everyone thinks he is safe. To enjoy this liberty, there must be a government under whose rule one citizen does not fear another. Liberty ceases to exist when legislative and executive powers are concentrated in the same person or organ, because people will fear that this king or parliament will make tyrannical laws and enforce them tyrannically. If the judicial power is not separated from the legislative and executive powers, then there is no liberty. If the judicial power and the legislative power are combined, the life and liberty of citizens will be arbitrarily exercised, because the judge is the legislator. If the judicial power and the executive power are combined, the judge will have the power of the oppressor. If the same person, or the same body composed of important figures, nobles or commoners, exercises these three powers, namely, the power to make laws, the power to enforce public decisions, and the power to judge private crimes or disputes, all is over.[128] Thus it can be seen that the starting point of Montesquieu's theory of separation of the three powers is also to protect civil liberties.

Individual basis is also known as individualism. Hayek, a famous Austrian scholar, profoundly distinguishes two kinds of individualism. One is true individualism, the development of which began with John Locke. The other is false individualism, which is represented by the French Enlightenment scholar Rousseau and others. It is called false individualism because it always has a tendency to evolve into the enemy of individualism—socialism or collectivism. According to Hayek, the essential characteristics of true individualism are as follows. First, it is primarily a social theory aimed at understanding the forces that determine human social life; second, it is a set of political behavior norms derived from this social outlook. Hayek points out that the philosophical basis for these two individualistic distinctions lies in the assumption of human reason. True individualism holds that, in general, reason plays a fairly

[126] See [49], p. 154.

[127] See [50], p. 67.

[128] See [49], pp. 155–156.

small role in human affairs. That is to say, despite the fact that human beings are only partially dominated by reason, and despite the fact that human individual reason is limited and incomplete, he has achieved all that he has. Hayek calls this individualism anti-rationalistic individualism. False individualism assumes that everyone is perfectly equally possessed of Reason (using a capital R to express the word), and that all human achievements are the direct result of (and therefore belong to) the individual's rational control. This view believes too much in the emergence of the power of individual reason and holds that most of the order found in human affairs is the result of conscious design by reason. Hayek calls this individualism rationalistic individualism.[129] It should be said that it makes sense for Hayek to distinguish between these two kinds of individualism. However, it is not accurate for Hayek to call the individualism held by Locke and other people anti-rationalistic individualism. In fact, Locke is an empiricist in terms of epistemology, but in terms of politics and ethics, Locke shows a strong rationalism tendency. In this sense, as He Huaihong, a Chinese scholar, points out, Locke's empiricist epistemology and his rationalist politics and ethics are not logically strict and consistent, and there is a certain break between them.[130] In fact, Hayek himself once divided philosophy into two types. One is constructivist rationalism, and the other is evolutionary rationalism. According to Hayek, constructivist rationalism is a school of philosophy that believes that deductive reasoning can be applied to human affairs. It believes that societies, languages and laws are created by people. It also believes that, since these systems are created by man, man can reconstruct them according to a rational design of human life, and even change them completely. Evolutionary rationalism believes that societies, languages, and laws are developed in an evolutionary fashion, not designed by anyone, and thus cannot be reconstructed in any way that deductive reasoning suggests.[131] Obviously, according to this classification, Locke is an evolutionary rationalist. His individualism is still based on reason, but this reason is not a kind of absolute reason that is omniscient and omnipotent, but a kind of relative reason, or a kind of commonsensible reason, which is deeply influenced by certain intuition and belief that have become prevalent or begin to form in people's daily life.[132]

The classical school of criminology can be said to be based on individual-based values. Beccaria clearly accepts the view of natural law and social contract. He points out that divine enlightenment, natural law and social man-made agreements are the sources of moral and political principles that regulate human behavior. Beccaria believes that these three represent religion, nature and politics, and they should never be in opposition to each other. Beccaria discusses the relationships of the three separately, pointing out that not all conclusions and obligations drawn from one can also be drawn from the other two. Not all that enlightenment requires is required by natural law; not all that natural law requires is required by pure social law. However,

[129] See [51], pp. 3–11.

[130] See [52], p. 270.

[131] See [53], pp. 4, 5 and 8.

[132] See [52], p. 271.

it is of the utmost importance to separate out the things which arise from the human contract, that is, the contract which men affirm or acquiesce in, because its power is enough to properly regulate the relationships between people without shouldering the special mission of God. It seems wrong to accuse those who discuss the social contract and its consequences of talking about violations of natural law and divine enlightenment, since the latter two are not covered in this discussion. In essence, divine justice and natural justice are eternal, because the relationship between two identical objects is always the same. However, human justice, or political justice, is only the relationship between the behavior and the ever-changing social state. It can vary according to the degree to which the behavior becomes necessary or beneficial to society. If people do not analyze the complex and highly variable social relations, it will be difficult to identify this. Once these fundamentally distinct principles are confused, there is no hope of correct interpretation of public issues.[133] Beccaria also discusses the origin and limit of punishments from the perspective of social contract theory. The doctrine of a legally prescribed punishment for a specified crime proposed by Beccaria and further developed by Feuerbach embodies the individual-based values. Its political theoretical basis is the theory of separation of the three powers.[134] Bentham's utilitarian philosophy also has an obvious tendency toward individualism. Sabine, a US scholar, points out that most of the liberal elements in Bentham's philosophy exist on self-evident premises. He is clearly borrowing the principle of equality of natural law when he says "one is worth exactly the same as another", or when calculating maximum happiness, he says each is "only one, and no one is more than one". He is not actually relying solely on the untestable assumption that one's happiness is just like another's. Behind his love of order and efficiency are the prerequisites of true freedom, especially the value of all beings able to live like men, which are not covered by the principle of efficiency or the greatest happiness. It is also a fact that his jurisprudence starts from individualism and has unconscious prejudice.[135]

In the criminal classic school, Kant and Hegel are both philosophers, and it is very significant to analyze the influence of individual-based values in their philosophical thoughts on criminal law thoughts. The social contract, the starting point of Kant's political thought, is an assumed natural state without any legal protection. Before human beings established a social state, there was indeed a barbaric state in which individuals fought against the whole. Kant believes that there is a close relationship between nature, human nature and society. The method by which nature develops the inherent talents of human beings is to make men hostile to each other in society. This hostility arises from the unsocial sociability of men. Unsocial sociability refers to the mixture of sociability (gregarioUSess) and anti-sociability (non-grouping). Kant points out that man has a tendency to socialize, because in this state he feels that he is not only a human being, and he has a little more than developing his natural talents. However, he also has a strong tendency to individuate himself, because at

[133] See [6], pp. 2–3.

[134] See [54], pp. 488–489.

[135] See [55], pp. 756–757.

the same time he has a non-social nature that requires things to be at the mercy of his own wishes, and this finds opposition in all respects.[136] Here Kant expounds the two opposing tendencies of human socialization and individualization. In order to reconcile the two, isolated individuals form the nation-state through a decision, that is, a contract, which Kant calls an original contract. That is to say, the people form themselves into a state according to a statute called an original contract. In this national life, the individual remains free. This freedom is the coexistence of the freedom of each person's will and the freedom of others. In other words, each person has freedom without violating the freedom of others. It should be said that Kant coordinates the relationship between man and society through the social contract, but the purpose itself is still to protect individual freedom. The moral doctrine of retribution advocated by Kant also lays the foundation of criminal responsibility on the morality of the individual. Hegel is a nationalist politically. He profoundly denies the social contract theory, and also criticizes individualism after the French Revolution, which is considered to be politically conservative. It should be said that Hegel's critique is justified and has its historical background. Hegel's critique of individualism targets two distinct concepts. First, he links individualism with the phenomena of regionalism and fragmentation that prevents Germany from realizing its modern nation-state status. He believes that the national character of Germany should be mainly attributed to the influence of Luther. Christian freedom, as Luther points out, is the mysterious independence of the soul free from all secular conditions. Second, Hegel equates individualism with Jacobinism. The latter represents the violence, fanaticism, terrorism and atheism of the French Revolution. Hegel finds that these two errors lie in the separation of man from his position in an organized society, and the separation of man's dependence on society, in which man has a role to play, duties to perform and a status subordinate to his position. If an individual thinks only of himself, he is nothing but a capricious animal governed by a brutal instinct. As Rousseau once says, there is no higher code of conduct than one's own impulses, hobbies and desires, and no higher code of thought than one's own subjective fantasies. One must see an individual as a member of a society to have a correct understanding of man. However, in the modern world, he must also be regarded as a member of the family.[137] Obviously, Hegel places an individual in a society and understands an individual from social relations. Compared with the individualism that regards an individual as an abstract subject separated from society, it has a more profound theoretical value. Of course, Hegel does not completely deny the existence of freedom for individuals. Individuals should be free in society, and this freedom should be guaranteed by national laws. The state is the embodiment of reason. The law is rational. For Hegel, this means that the actions of public authorities should be predictable because they are based on known regulations that limit the power of officials to act arbitrarily; official actions express the authority of the official institution, not the private will or judgment of the person in charge of the institution. The law should treat all people to which it applies equally, because it is universal and cannot

[136] See [31], p. 325.

[137] See [55], pp. 722–723.

take into account the special circumstances of individual people. In this sense, as Sabine, a US scholar, points out, the state in Hegel's mind is what German jurisprudence later calls a state under the rule of law. It wants to achieve high efficiency in domestic administration, especially its judicial system must be able to enforce the protection of property and personal rights. Hegel believes that these rights are essential for civil society to perform its economic functions. Herewith, Hegel's doctrine of constitutional government is consistent with the liberal doctrine in the distinction between legitimate authority and individual power, but it fails to recognize the relationship between governance by law and democratic political procedures.[138] There is no doubt that this opinion held by Sabine is very incisive. Hegel affirms personal value in the sense of the rule of law, which is still the embodiment of individual-based values. In criminal law, Hegel advocates the legal doctrine of retribution, which includes the respect for criminals' reason and the limitation of uncontrolled revenge, all of which have profound individualistic significance.

Individual-based values start with individuals. Although there may be differences in the understanding of an individual, some understand him as an abstract individual, some understand him as a social individual, some understand him as a perceptual individual, and some understand him as a rational individual, they all pay attention to the value of the individuals, which shapes the humanistic character of the classical school of criminology.

References

1. [Japan] H. Ōtsuka, *Basic Problems of Crime Theory* (China University of Political Science and Law Press, Beijing, 1993)
2. [Germany] Kant, *From The Philosophy of Law: An Exposition of the Fundamental Principles of Jurisprudence as the Science of Right* (The Commercial Press, Beijing, 1991)
3. [Germany] Kant, *Critique of Practical Reason* (The Commercial Press, Beijing, 1960)
4. [Germany] Hegel, *Principle of Philosophy of Law* (The Commercial Press, Beijing, 1961)
5. S. Lü, *The Study of Hegel's Legal Thought* (People's Public Security University of China Press, Beijing, 1989)
6. [Italy] Beccaria, *On Crimes and Punishments* (Encyclopedia of China Publishing House, Beijing, 1993)
7. G. Luo, X. Song, *The History of Western Ethic Thoughts*, vol. 2 (China Renmin Publishing House, Beijing, 1988)
8. F. Huang, *Beccaria and His Thoughts of Criminal Law* (China University of Political Science and Law Press, Beijing, 1987)
9. [US] Vold et al., *Theoretical Criminology* (China University of Political Science and Law Press, Beijing, 2005)
10. [US] Q. Richard et al., *The Problem of Crime* (China International Radio Press, Beijing, 1988)
11. [Italy] Ferri, *Positive School of Criminology: Three Lectures* (China University of Political Science and Law Press, Beijing, 1987)
12. [Germany] Marx, Engel, The holy family, in *Marx/Engels Collected Works*, vol. 2 (People's Publishing House, Beijing, 1962)
13. Y. Xie, *Introduction to Study of Criminology* (Hunan Publishing House, Changsha, 1992)

---

[138] See [55], p. 732.

14. [US] T. Hans (Editor-in-Chief), *Legal and Criminal Psychology* (Quzhong Publishing House, Beijing, 1986)
15. [Japan] O. Kiichiro, *Theory of Constitutive Elements of Crimes* (People's Public Security University of China Press, Beijing, 1991)
16. [Soviet Union] A. Gusayinov, Γ. Illitts, *A Brief History of Western Ethics* (China Renmin University Press, Beijing, 1992)
17. [Germany] Kant, *The Metaphysical Principle of Law—The Science of Rights* (The Commercial Press, Beijing, 1991)
18. [Germany] Hegel, *Principles of Legal Philosophy* (The Commercial Press, Beijing, 1961)
19. [Soviet Union] A.H. Trainin, *General Theory of Constitution of a Crime* (Renmin University of China Press, Beijing, 1958)
20. [US] David, On Beccari's thought of criminal law. Transl. Law (5) (1984)
21. [US] David, Cesare Beccaria is utilitarian or retributive. Transl. Law (5) (1985)
22. [Germany] Hegel, *Elements of the Philosophy of Right* (The Commercial Press, Beijing, 1961)
23. *Complete Works of Marx and Engels*, vol. 8 (People's Publishing House, Beijing, 1965)
24. [UK] Hume, *A Treatise of Human Nature*, vol. 1 (The Commercial Press, Beijing, 1980)
25. Y. Gan, P. He, *Foreign Criminal Jurisprudence*, vol. 1 (Peking University Press, Beijing, 1984)
26. [UK] Bentham, *Theory of Legislation: Principles of Penal Code* (People's Public Security University of China Press, Beijing, 1993)
27. [US] David, On Beccaria's criminal law thought. Legal Transl. Ser. (5) (1984)
28. *Selected Materials of the History of Western Legal Thoughts* (Peking University Press, Beijing, 1983)
29. [UK] Bentham, Theoretical basis of penalty, in *Selected Works of Bentham*, English version (1843)
30. [Germany] Filangieri, *Criminal Legislation*, German version (1788)
31. Z. Li, *Criticism on Critique of Philosophy: A Review of Kant* (People's Publishing House, Beijing, 1979)
32. H. Zhang (Editor-in-Chief), *History of Western Legal Thoughts* (Peking University Press, Beijing, 1983)
33. [Japan] K. Kimura (Chief Editor), *Dictionary of Criminal Law* (Shanghai Translation Publishing Company, Shanghai, 1992)
34. [Japan] S. Akasaka, Doctrine of a legally prescribed punishment for a specified crime. Legal Transl. Ser. (1) (1981)
35. Q. Gao, *Philosophical Vision: Metaphysical Meditation* (Jilin University Press, Changchun, 1993)
36. [Germany] Windelband, *Textbook of History of Philosophy* (The Commercial Press, Beijing, 1987)
37. *The Complete Works of Marx and Engels*, vol. 2 (People's Publishing House, Beijing, 1957)
38. [France] Rousseau, *On Social Contract*, 2nd edn. revised (The Commercial Press, Beijing, 1980)
39. [UK] Locke, *Two Treatises of Government, Second Treatise* (The Commercial Press, Beijing, 1964)
40. [UK] W.C. Dampier, *A History of Science*, vol. 1 (The Commercial Press, Beijing, 1975)
41. [UK] S.F. Mason, *A History of the Sciences* (Shanghai Translation Publishing House, Shanghai, 1980)
42. [UK] Russel, *A History of Philosophy*, vol. 2 (The Commercial Press, Beijing, 1976)
43. Compiled by the Teaching and Research Section of the History of Foreign Philosophy, Department of Philosophy, Peking University, *French Philosophy in the 18th Century* (The Commercial Press, Beijing, 1963)
44. [Switzerland] B. Jacob, *The Civilization of the Renaissance in Italy* (The Commercial Press, Beijing, 1979)
45. *Marx/Engels Selected Works*, 2nd edn. (People's Publishing House, Beijing, 1995)
46. [UK] Hobbes, *Leviathan* (The Commercial Press, Beijing, 1985)

47. [UK] S. Peter et al., *Legal Values in Western Society* (People's Public Security University of China Press, Beijing, 1990)
48. [UK] Locke, *Two Treatises of Civil Government, Second Treatise* (The Commercial Press, Beijing, 1961)
49. [France] Montesquieu, *The Spirit of the Laws* (The Commercial Press, Beijing, 1961)
50. G. Zhu, *Restricting Power with Power: A Commentary of Western Decentralization Theory and Decentralization System* (Sichuan People's Publishing House, Chengdu, 1987)
51. [Austria] A. Hayek, *Individualism and Economic Order* (Beijing Institute of Economics Press, Beijing, 1989)
52. H. He, *Contract Ethics and Social Justice* (Renmin University of China Press, Beijing, 1993)
53. [US] Hoey, *Liberal Politics—Hayek's Political Thought* (Sanlian Bookstore, Beijing, 1992)
54. X. Chen, *Philosophy of Criminal Law* (China University of Political Science and Law Press, Beijing, 1992)
55. [US] Sabine, *A History of Political Theory* (The Commercial Press, Beijing, 1986)

Chapter 3
Human Nature Foundation Held by the Positivist School of Criminology

The positivist school of criminology is established upon negating the classical school of criminology. Thus, it contrasts sharply with the classical school in terms of basic criminal issues. The foundation of such contrast differs from the classical school's assumption of human nature.

1 Assumption of Human Nature

The assumption of human nature by the positivist school of criminology is experienced man. The experienced man is an assumption of human nature: all people live in societies, and their behaviors are restricted and impacted by social and natural factors. Essentially, human nature is determined, so free will does not exist.

1.1 Human Nature Analysis of Crime

Starting from the empirical assumption of human nature, the positivist school of criminology holds that the criminal awareness and behavior of criminals are determined. Material and spiritual conditions also determine the reason for humans to commit crimes. The punishment of criminals by criminal laws is based on behavioral determinism rather than free will. Therefore, in essence, criminal liability is a social obligation instead of moral responsibility.

The representatives of the positivist school of criminology are Lombroso, Ferri, and Liszt. Lombroso is the founder of the anthropologist school of criminology, and Ferri and Liszt are the founders of the sociologist school of criminology. Both schools advocate empirical research methods and thus are classified as branches of the positivist school of criminology. More importantly, they hold the same opinion

X. Chen, *Humanistic Foundation of Criminal Law*,
https://doi.org/10.1007/978-981-19-9764-8_3

in terms of the empirical assumption of behavioral determinism of criminals, which is precisely the humanistic foundation of the positivist school of criminology.

The positivist school emerges against the backdrop that the classical school is difficult to adapt to social needs. Although the theories of the classical school are incisive, they lose all merits when facing criminal reality, laying the foreshadowing of collapse. As Ferri mentioned, when the theories of the classical school reached their peak, there was an unprecedentedly large number of criminal behaviors in Italy, which was such a shocking contrast. Accordingly, criminology was powerless to stop crimes. Because of this, the positivist school, like other disciplines, existed naturally. It was laid upon the conditions of our daily life.[1] Lombroso developed his theory against this backdrop and negated the theory of free will by the classical school. He explained crimes with behavioral determinism, arguing that free will was a fabrication by philosophers because a person had no free will in reality at all, and human behaviors were restricted by heredity, race, and other innate factors. Thus, some people were doomed to commit crimes. Lombroso is the first man to advocate behavioral determinism and regard heredity as the only cause for crimes. Although the positivist school of criminology accepted behavioral determinism later, the causes of crimes developed from Lombroso's monism (the biological cause) to pluralism integrating biological, natural, and social causes, from which the anthropological school of criminology developed into the sociologist school. Behavioral determinism can be concluded as follows: every criminal act is unavoidable because the natural and environmental conditions have predetermined it. After Lombroso overthrew the classical school's free will, he proposed the viewpoint of born criminals. As a scientific hypothesis, the theory of born criminals has the ground to exist. However, whether it is correct remains to be verified by science. When Lombroso proposed the theory of born criminals in his book *The Criminal Man* in 1876, he considered this theory evidence-based since it was based on the numerous first-hand information from his observation of thousands of criminals. He was a serious scholar who claimed himself as the "slave of gene". Gene, in this context, referred to the gene that caused people to commit crimes. He held that it was the gene that mattered. He also believed that even though some genes seemed insignificant in that period, they might develop into the foundation of a theory later. As expected, he established the theory of born criminals with these genes. Lombroso was inspired by the anatomy of the head of Vilella, an infamous Italian bandit head, and put forward the concept of born criminals. Viella was especially agile. He was famous for climbing up a steep mountain carrying sheep. He was cynical and shameless, bragging about his criminal acts. After his death, Lombroso anatomized his body. Lombroso, as usual, opened Viella's skull. Suddenly, Lombroso's eyes opened wide. He found an obvious indentation in the occipital bone of Viella's skull. He called it the media occipital fossa which, like that of an inferior animal, was in the middle of the occipital bone, similar to the so-called hypertrophy of the vermis of the cerebellum in birds. In *The Criminal Man*, Lombroso elaborated on Viella's media occipital fossa: the size was special, which was 34 cm long, 23 cm wide, and 11 cm deep. Occipital bones on both sides were hypertrophied,

[1] See [1], p. 3.

and inner occipital pins were completely missing; both sides of occipital bones were obstructed by the protruding bones, and bones were parallel, looking like an irregular quadrilateral, connecting to a small triangle sacral promontory near the hole of the occipital bone. According to this, comparative anatomy and embryology could conclude that it was vermis hypertrophy, the real median cerebellum.[2] Vermis hypertrophy was exactly a symptom of degeneration. The idea of atavism flashed through Lombroso's mind. He asserted that Viella displayed the savage instinct of primitive humanity and inferior animals. Lombroso explained Viella's enormous jawbone, high cheekbones, prominent superciliary arches, solitary lines in the palms, extreme size of orbits, handle-shaped or sessile ears that could only be seen in savages and apes, insensibility to pain, extremely acute sight, tattooing, extreme idleness, love of orgies and the irresistible craving for evil for its own sake, the desire not only to extinguish life in the victim, but to mutilate the corpse, tear its flesh, and drink its blood. Thirty-six years later, in a speech at the Conference of Criminal Anthropology in Turin in 1906, Lombroso described his unusual findings on that gloomy morning in December 1870 in such wordings: in my eyes, these strange deformities were lost in the night but suddenly saw a shining path. In my view, the mysterious curtain between criminals and the truth of crime is uncovered because the characteristics of primitive humanity and inferior animals are bound to be reproduced in the modern period.[3] Born criminals became a core proposition of Lombroso in his early works, and he believed in seeing the same characteristics as savages in criminals. He described born criminals as such: underdeveloped lower legs, tiny skulls, retrofrontal depression, anterior hyperextension, premature suture closure, excessively thick skulls, excessive jawbones and cheekbones, protruding jaws, oblique eye sockets, red skin, big ears, thin beards and hair, over agility, tirelessness, insensitive sense of touch, visual acuity, rapid recover of wounds, weak feelings of love, having lust in early ages, inability to differentiate sex, idleness, easy irritation, keen on gambling, alcoholism, superstition, among others. Once Lombroso's theory of born criminals spread, it was immediately harshly criticized by all walks of society. It was said that the British criminologist Charles Goring's evidence gave Lombroso a devastating blow. When Goring served as a doctor in some prisons in Britain, he led a research plan in which he studied more than 3,000 criminals based on 96 characteristics. Goring himself observed those criminals 1,500 times and made 300 additional observations. After 12 years' work, Goring published a book titled *The British Convict: a statistical study*. According to what he collected in the Parkhurst prison, he tried to eliminate the pernicious influence of old criminology, which made conclusions based on coincidence, biases, and suspicious observations, and established new understandings of criminals on the science-verified facts; these facts and inference led to undoubtful conclusions because of their intrinsic accuracy. Goring asserted that there were no born criminals, and crimes were not heritable. He advocated criminologists placing psychological

[2] See [2], p. 8.

[3] See [3], p. 49.

characteristics, especially mental deficiency, as the causes of criminal acts.[4] Significantly, on the one hand, Goring held that Lombroso's criminology system was a system consisting of confused thinking parallel with astrology, alchemy, and other deceptions. On the other hand, he unconsciously accepted Lombroso's empirical methodology and said that criminals' physiological and psychological factors should be noted in research. In comparison, Sellin, a famous US criminologist, was franker and more impartial, saying that even though he disagreed with every Lombroso's word, Lombroso still enjoyed a critical position in the history of the development of criminological thinking, whose views imposed huge challenges, thus promoting the research on criminals unprecedently. It was unfair to summarize Lombroso's criminology into the only proposition of born criminals. In Lombroso's early works, he did conclude all his criminological theories with the theory of born criminals. However, due to criticism by multiple parties, Lombroso revised his ideas in his later works, where he expanded the impact of heredity and other inherent factors on crime into deprivation and other acquired factors. Moreover, he studied and discussed the causes of crimes from physiological, psychological, environmental and climate aspects, and the ratio of born criminals among the total number of criminals decreased gradually. In the book *Crime, Its Causes and Remedies* published in 1893, Lombroso held that born criminals accounted for 33% of all criminals. The ratio of born criminals among all criminals reduced, illustrating that Lombroso revised his assumptions.

If we say that Lombroso was only satisfied with the observation of human brains and all organs of human bodies in early times, conducted biological research on this basis, and summarized born criminals, then, in the following 20 years, he gradually changed from focusing on physiological factors to considering physiological, psychological and other factors, noticing the anthropological research on criminals while paying more attention to intelligence, emotion, instinct, habits, subconsciousness, language, imitation, and other psychological observations as well as political, economic, demographical, cultural, educational, religious, environmental and other social and natural factors, thus developing a comprehensive theory of the causes of crimes. In *Crime, Its Causes and Remedies*, Lombroso initially specified that many intertwined reasons caused crimes. If we failed to study these reasons case by case, we could not jump to conclusions about the causes of crimes. The complicated situation of the causes of crimes was common to human society. We could never consider these causes isolated, nor could we apply one reason to all. Then, what were the real causes of crimes? Lombroso was overwhelmed with mixed emotion, saying that, frankly speaking, even those best at observation could also not assert the real, special cause for each phenomenon. Thus, Lombroso developed a deeper understanding of the complexity of the causes of crimes in his later ages, changing the simplified opinion that crimes were caused merely by heredity. In this sense, Lombroso is a serious scientist. Lombroso demonstrates rich imagination when understanding objects. He is good at making direct judgments; he is a man of integrity like an intellectual, realizes his shortcomings, and hopes to testify his theories impartially by making comparisons. Undoubtedly, we should connect Lombroso's early times with his later

[4] See [3], pp. 57–58.

times rather than cut them apart. Whether in his early or later times, he had the same experience assumption of criminals and held the idea of behavioral determinism throughout. In his early works, he concluded the causes of crimes completely to biological reasons and proposed born criminals. However, in his elderly age, although still paying much attention to biological reasons, he included other factors apart from the biological ones. Lombroso is a prison doctor and has the condition to measure the physical metrics of criminals. Therefore, he set out his study of crimes from biological factors. As Ferri said, Lombroso ingeniously established a new science of criminal anthropology, which was exactly arising from his research on the physical conditions of criminals when he investigated the causes of crimes. Lombroso started his research on the anatomy of criminals because it was most convenient for him to study skulls in the museum.[5] As one of the reasons for crimes, the biological reason was developed from race and heredity. Regarding the impact of race on crimes, Lombroso explained his opinions on the evolution of human beings. He mentioned that there was no clear opinion of crime for savages; thus, he doubted that there was no opinion of crime for the Pacific Heritage nation. However, each nation has its morality to regulate its people's behaviors, and the violation of morality evolved into crimes. It was even more difficult to determine the impact of race on crimes in civilized societies, but Lombroso did not negate the impact of race on crimes. In particular, he listed a lot of data and information to illustrate the relationship between race and crime. The argument of Lombroso on the relationship between race and crime showed that he paid much attention to the impact of race on crimes, especially seen in his early works, where he emphasized race too much, although changing a little in his elderly times. Ferri, the student of Lombroso, included race into the scope of physical factors and negated the opinion that regarded race and personality as the only reason for crimes. Ferri mentioned that according to the research results on collective society and individuals, society and individual lives were usually comprehensively shaped by anthropological, geographical, and social factors. To this end, even though the race was not a sufficient or the only factor to explain crimes by nations or individuals, it shall not be ignored when national and individual characteristics were studied. For instance, when studying Italian homicide, it was difficult to determine only one factor among situations and status triggering crimes. However, there were many cases of homicide due to the impact of race. Ignoring the impact of race on crimes was the same as denying the existence of daytime.[6] Therefore, Ferri inherited Lombroso's opinion that recognized the impact of race on crimes; however, he disagreed with Lombroso regarding the position of race in the system of the causes of crimes. Apart from the innate factor of race that exerted an impact on crimes, Lombroso also focused on studying the impact of the genetic factors on crimes. Lombroso set out from individual cases in terms of the impact of heredity on crime. He advocated the Atavism theory based on the study of Family Joke. Lombroso particularly stressed the impact of heredity on crimes in his early works and regarded heredity as an important cause of crimes. The relationship

[5] See [1], pp. 28–29.

[6] See [1], p. 30.

between heredity and crime is the core of Lombroso's criminology and an issue that triggers debates most easily. The US criminologist Lawrence Taylor mentioned that it was regretful that their lack of genetic knowledge limited the early advocators of the theory of behavioral nature. As genetics developed, it occupied an important status in modern times. Based on the situation of 1882, some people calculated that the total knowledge of genetics doubled every two years. Therefore, those early scholars who held that heredity was the primary decisive factor of criminal behaviors were greatly limited by their capabilities to answer questions. They merely relied on their observations to make conclusions and proposed their theories only based on the science and knowledge of that time. As per modern standards, knowledge was primary, and so were the theories. Consequently, many of those theories reflect the bare bones but are ridiculous if we look at them now.[7] The criminological theory that pays much attention to the impact of genetics on criminal acts is called the theory of hereditary determination. Indeed, Lombroso's theory that genetics determines crime is primitive, and although he is a positivist, we are amazed at his extraordinary imagination. In his later ages and influenced by Ferri and other people, Lombroso also introduced acquired factors, including geographical and social factors, in addition to innate factors, cored at genetics. Among acquired factors, Lombroso introduced a unique concept—depravity. In his opinion, heredity and depravity were the sources of crimes. There was a tradition of investigating geographical and the environmental impacts on crimes in the West. For instance, Montesquieu, the well-known French enlightenment scholar, is the father of environmental determinism. He believed a country's legal and political regime to be restricted by geography and environment and mentioned that the law should be related to a country's natural conditions, cold, hot and warm climates, the quality, situation and area of the land, and people's lifestyles (including farmers, hunters, and herders). The law shall be related to the degree of freedom to which the political regime tolerated and adapted to citizens' religion, personality, wealth, population, trade, customs, and habits.[8] These relationships constituted the so-called "The Spirit of the Laws". Not only did he investigate laws and political regimes from the perspective of geography and the environment, but also crimes and thus created environmental determinism of crime. In Lombroso's late ages, he gradually realized the geographical and environmental impacts on crimes and elaborated on them in his book *Crime, Its Causes, and Remedies.* He held that climate was the fundamental condition for creatures' activities, among which hotness ranked the top. Physiology and statistics indicated that human functions were affected by hotness. According to Lombroso, humans had stronger fertility in sweltering weather, leading to unfair wealth distribution and political and social power. By contrast, citizens living in tropical areas tended to be lazy and stuck to the status quo. Thus, they tended to be conquered, and less possible to trigger revolutions. However, in a freezing climate, coldness inhibited nervous systems, and citizens living there tended to be calm and kind and had no intention to struggle with evil or trigger revolutions. People living in between, nonetheless, tended to have

[7] See [4], p. 13.

[8] See [5], p. 7.

revolutions and crimes most easily. Lombroso also studied the relationship between crimes and months to prove the impact of climate on crimes. He mentioned that statistics illustrated that most crimes in Britain, France, and Italy happened in hot months. Lombroso argued that the political and economic impacts had increased in recent years, while climate impact had been relegated to second place. On the other hand, Lombroso claimed that climate still exerted influence on crimes. The geographical impact on crimes was also one of the issues Lombroso focused on. For instance, he proved the geographical impact on crimes with the coefficient of correlation by investigating the relationship between the lies of mountains and individual crimes. Among acquired factors of crimes, Lombroso not only illustrated geographical impacts on crimes but also stressed social impacts on crimes. For example, Lombroso discussed how economic conditions affected crimes. He mentioned that it was one-sided to solely conclude the causes of crimes as poverty. Why? Because wealth was also a cause of crimes. The wealth that was easy to acquire was against noble religious and political aspirations and thus was harmful. As a result, poverty and wealth were both the causes of crimes. The poor could not satisfy their basic needs due to poverty, so they were forced to commit thefts to satisfy their desires. At the same time, the poor were addicted to alcohol and even appeased their hunger with alcohol, so their central nervous systems were stimulated by alcohol, and they tended to be impulsive. Coupled with alcohol intoxication and other diseases, they were morally insane. Also, due to poverty, they tended to kill disabled families. Thus, it was common to see relatives and babies killed among the poor. Poverty was also an indirect cause of fornication. The poor could not afford marriage fees, so they solicited prostitutes. If they were unable to pay prostitutes, they were obsessed with lecheroUSess. Factories, where males and females worked together, were also media for fornication. By contrast, the rich were vain and loved to create a sensation, which was a major cause of the crime of property violation. Among the rich, they rarely conducted rape offenses arising from desires; the crimes conducted out of luxurious desires were not due to urgent needs but enjoyed numerous types. Besides, people followed the example of their superiors, leading to more rampant crimes. Some Italian bureaucrats took advantage of crimes to consolidate their positions. Not only was wealth unable to prohibit fornication, but it also increased novel sins, such as sodomy, and catamite, to name a few. To sum up, Lombroso overthrew the theory of free will by the classical school of criminology, revealed the hereditary, geographical, and social reasons that determined criminal acts, and thus created the positivist school of criminology.

We should admit that among scholars of the positivist school of criminology, it was Ferri that criticized the classical school most. First, he negated the theory of free will, positing that the classical school of criminology and the public believed that crimes included moral sins because criminals chose to discard morality and conduct crimes based on their free will, so they should be punished by corresponding penalties, and this has been the most popular crime concept so far. The idea of human free will (the causation relationship was the only significant factor) introduced an assumption: a man could choose between good and evil. Nevertheless, modern psychology, armed with modern positivist methodology, negated the existence of free will and proved that behaviors resulted from the interaction between personality and environment. Then, how would you believe the existence of free will?[9] Ferri argued that the positivist school relied on the evidence from the research of anthropology and environment to make the following conclusion that we could not admit the existence of free will. Because if free will was only an illusion of our mind rather than an actual psychological function of human beings, it should be the power for human beings to make a final selection under the pressure of the environment when human's wills were propelled to decide. It also referred to that according to the law of causation relationship, human will could independently and freely make or not decide on internal and external factors that exerted impacts on the decision. However, Ferri believed this was impossible because the illusion of free will originated from our inner consciousness, which emerged precisely because we were unaware of the psychological motivations and internal and external conditions reflected when we made decisions.[10]

Based on this, Ferri concluded that the positivist school of criminology claimed that crimes were not entirely arising from criminals' wills; to be a criminal, a person must place himself in a material and spiritual state and live in an environment of the causality chain where internal and external factors pushed him to commit crimes. This is his conclusion and the fundamentally different or opposite methodology of our positivist school of criminology from the classical school of criminology in main principles.[11] Therefore, the opposition between the theory of free will and behavioral determinism is the focus of the disagreements between the classical and positivist schools of criminology.

Based on the criticism of the classical school of criminology, Ferri proposed the famous law of criminal saturation. Crime was a social phenomenon arising from the interaction among anthropological, political, natural, and social factors. In other words, each society had crimes brought about by natural and social conditions, the quantity and quality of which were adapted to the development of the social collective. Ferri also quoted Emilyt's ancient proverb, "Crime also has the year-end balance, the increase, and decrease of which is even more regular than the income and expenditure of national economy." Such regularity of the existence of crime is the law of criminal saturation claimed by Ferri.[12] Ferri pointed out that the scientific deduction of the law of criminal saturation led to a series of investigations and research, whose results were satisfying, enabled us to understand things truly, and far outweighed the theory of "a man becoming a criminal because he intended to become a criminal". Ferri held that a man becoming a criminal was not because he intended to do so. However, the seeds of evil could germinate and grow under specific material and social conditions. Therefore, we understood that the interaction of the above factors led to human misfortune, and an abnormal man was a person who failed to adapt to the social environment where he was born. The abnormal men could not lead a social life

---

[9] See [1], p. 9.

[10] See [1], pp. 15 and 16.

[11] See [1], pp. 9–10.

[12] See [1], p. 43.

and were physiologically degenerating. Gradually, they became passive or active abnormal men and criminals in the end.[13]

In terms of the causes of crimes, Ferri established the three types of factors in crime causation, namely, biological, geographical, and societal factors. Ferri pointed out that the anthropological factor that criminals possessed was the primary condition of crime. If we studied from physiological, natural, and social perspectives, we could divide anthropological factors into three sub-types: (1) physiological conditions of criminals, including abnormality of skulls, brains, main organs, sensory and response abilities, appearance, and tattoos. (2) mental conditions of criminals, including the abnormality of intelligence and emotion, especially that of moral emotions and criminal cultures and jargon, among others. (3) individual conditions of criminals, including race, age, gender, and other biological conditions, as well as the biological and sociological conditions like citizen status, occupation, domicile, social class, training, and education. So far, the biological and sociological conditions of criminals have always been regarded as the only subject of the study of crime statistics.[14] Therefore, Ferri inherited Lombroso's opinions, approving the impact of biological factors on crime while denying it as the only decisive factor. Ferri affirmed the concept of born criminals from the perspective of anthropological factors, saying that born or instinctive criminals demonstrated the physiological and psychological features that were determined by criminal anthropology most easily. These people were cruel, peremptory, cunning and lazy and could not distinguish between crimes like murder and robbery, and integrity and diligence. Vregille said, "They are criminals, just like others are good workers." Besides, as Romer Nosi put it, they saw imprisonment as a risk that their occupation must bear, which was the same as masons to falling roofs or miners to biogas. Thus, they were much less impacted by actual punishments than the threat of punishments, or they were not impacted by the threat of punishments at all." They felt no pain in prisons at all. Living in prisons was just like artists articulating a masterpiece in a studio. They were friendly to guards and even knew how to benefit themselves."[15] The second cause of crime referred to by Ferri is the natural factor which, in this context, refers to climate, soil conditions, relative length of day and night, season, average temperature, weather, and agriculture.[16] Ferri paid much attention to the natural factors of crime. He pointed out that the great founder of crime statistics Quetelet found that criminal acts changed as seasons alternated when the number of crimes in winter was less than that of spring and summer in total and he has always agreed with this. Property-related crimes increased in winter, which was the result of climate and social factors because unemployment, lack of food, and domicile aggravated people's hardship, causing them to violate others' properties. However, cold winter decreased sexual and violent crimes. Some people claimed that the frequent socialization in summer exerted some social impact, which made sense. Regarding this,

[13] See [1], pp. 35–36.

[14] See [6], p. 41.

[15] See [6], p. 23.

[16] See [6], p. 41.

Murrow presented the most eloquent facts, who claimed that the pattern of violent crimes, in which warm months saw more crimes than cold days, also adapted to criminals. According to statistics, hot seasons saw the most events of criminals violating disciplines. The environment in prisons was the same in all seasons, so social factors had no impact on prisons, which was an example of how climate affected crimes. In addition, it could also be exemplified that among patients with psychiatric disorders, their incidence rate of psychiatric disorders and epilepsy was higher in summer than in winter. Therefore, we could not negate the impact of natural factors, while social factors could further enhance the impact.[17] From this, we can see that Ferri links up natural and social factors to analyze their impacts on crimes and pays much attention to the social factors of crimes, which was an important feature that differentiated him from Lombroso's early opinions. In this sense, we tend to regard Ferri as a seat warmer from the anthropologist school of criminology to the sociologist school of criminology. The social factors of crime as referred to by Ferri include the density of population, public opinions, public attitudes, religions, family backgrounds, educational systems, industrial conditions, alcoholism, economic and political situations, public administration, judiciary, police, and general legislation, civil and criminal legal systems, among others.[18] Thus, the social factors Ferri understands are extensive; in particular, he dialectically understands the economic and other social impacts of crimes. Ferri mentioned that historical materialism (I'd like to name it economic determinism) indicated that political, moral, and cultural phenomena reflected the economic conditions of certain times and places. Thus, some people tried to explain it narrowly, saying that historical materialism claimed that a country's economic condition was the primary cause, which was free from the impacts of any other causes. Marxism and Darwinism held the same opinion that a country's economic condition determined how other factors interacted and the results.[19] Furthermore, Ferri believed that the social factors on crimes referred to poverty and other conditions such as political, moral, and cultural uncertain factors. Any social condition that leads to deceitfulness and imperfectness in human social life was the social factor that triggered crimes. Ferri focused on discussing the impact of economic factors on crimes and completely utilized Marx's historical materialism method to explain criminal phenomena, which was valuable. He mentioned that human civilization had economic factors that led to crime, and free contention was nothing but cannibalism, which followed the rule of "fighting at the outrance". Within limited occupations, the competition among workers meant that the employment of some people was based on the unemployment of others, which was another way of cannibalism. Unlike primitive humans who ate each other, competitors beat each other through defamation, recommendation, protection, money, and other means, to ensure their positions as the best traders, dragging the most honest, talented, and self-esteemed people into misery of hunger. Additionally, as wealth increased, economic factors also played a role in triggering crimes. Indeed, the current society was a downward stage transiting from

[17] See [1], pp. 33–34.

[18] See [6], p. 42.

[19] See [1], p. 31.

the golden age of human beings in the nineteenth century—the bourgeois civilization, and wealth was a cause of crime. This was because the wealthy did not do physical or mental work, so they became idle and pedantic. They were addicted to the struggle of gambling and money, and their lives were poisoned. Although these people could evade criminal laws, they were trapped in hypocritical lives lacking morality. This way of living caused cavorting crimes. These "parasites" were destined to fraud in gambling. To kill time, they either visited casinos that won by luck or conducted adultery activities. Their examination made them do such things to friends. A British poet has said that the examination of human minds was the birthplace of evilness.[20]

It should be said that Ferri sharply and profoundly revealed the causes of crimes in capitalist societies and the necessity of private ownership for the existence of crimes. In his opinion, the individual, natural and social factors of crimes were not isolated but intertwined, playing a role interactively. Furthermore, the relative interaction among individual, natural, and social factors varied as each crime's psychological and sociological characteristics differed. Thus, Ferri argued that the total number of crimes went up according to crime statistics, but it fluctuated more or less each year. To this end, according to the law of criminal saturation (analogy from chemical phenomena), the number of crimes in each year was co-determined by different natural and social environments, the genetic tendency of humans, and occasional impulses. It was like we noticed that a certain amount of water was dissolved into a certain number of chemical particles under a specific temperature, but the number of atoms did not change. So, in particular natural and social environments, we would find a certain number of crimes.[21]

Among the scholars of the positivist school of criminology, Liszt was noted for his sociologist school's analysis of the causes of crimes, from which we can see that he stressed the sociological explanations of the causes of crimes. Regarding understanding human nature, Liszt favored the experience man as opposed to the rational man with free will. The significance of experience man was enriched by the knowledge of humanities and social sciences and the cause-effect law in social development patterns and laws in natural science. Based on this understanding, Liszt held that humans must be those living in certain societies, so internal and external individual causes of criminals must be studied if we would like to study crimes. Thus, Liszt inherited the monism (one cause theory) of anthropology (hereditism) critically. With the conclusion of human and social causes, he named it dualism (two causes theory). According to him, crime was triggered by the then-current characteristics of the actor who conducted criminal acts, coupled with their surroundings.[22] Admitting the crucial impacts of individual physiological factors on human behaviors, Liszt also stressed the decisive role of social factors, such as unemployment, poverty, alcoholism, cigarettes and drugs, prostitution, high prices, and other social environments.

[20] See [1], pp. 34–35.

[21] See [6], p. 56.

[22] See [7], p. 119.

The positivist school of criminology is based on experience man, the assumption of human nature by behavioral determinism. It understands crime differently from the classical school which is limited to legal concepts and satisfied with the empty preaching of free will and so on. The positivist school develops a theory of the causes of crimes by revealing the causes of crimes based on science, thus creating criminology in the modern sense.

1.2 Human Nature Analysis of Penalty

Since the positivist school of criminology holds that crime is caused by objective reasons that are independent of individual will, the moral responsibility theory of the classical school is unable to be the theoretical foundation of penalty. In this case, the positivist school of criminology proposes the social responsibility theory, which fundamentally changes the understanding of the basis, property, and form of penalty.

The classical school of criminology establishes criminal responsibility on the free will of criminals. Kant and Hegel's retributivism and Beccaria, Bentham, and Feuerbach's utilitarianism are distinct in the essence of penalty but share the same opinion in attributing free will to the basis of responsibility belongingness. Therefore, the classical school of criminology is called the theory of moral responsibility. According to it, behaviors driven by people who have free will and the results thereof should be owed to the actors, who shall hold moral responsibility for their behaviors and consequences. As a behavioral determinist, Lombroso overthrew the legend of free will, arguing that preventing crimes with the classical school's views did fail. He mentioned that crime was inevitable. It was also necessary to cure crimes, as were the punishments on criminals to stop them from doing evil to society. Only in this way was the penalty utilitarian. Lombroso claimed that the penalty had no foundation other than necessity and its rights. Therefore, in his opinion, retributions and deterrence were empty words, and the only reason for the penalty to exist was to defend societies. Ferri expressed this opinion more clearly, saying that the achievements of science and truth changed criminal jurisprudence into a natural function to protect societies from crime and eliminate vestiges of revenge, hatred, and punishment that belonged to uncivilized ages but still existed now.[23] According to the theory of social responsibility, the following conclusions are made: (1) Penalty no longer adapts to the social detriment of criminal acts but the detrimental status of crimes. (2) Criminals are no longer imposed by retributions and deterrence but are deprived of the ability to commit crimes again. (3) Penalty is no longer the only way to deal with crimes, and new methods should be sought to govern crimes.

The detrimental status of the crime is also called physical detriment. Physical detriment is a concept that exists as the positivist school of criminology rises. The classical school of criminology focuses on criminal acts rather than criminals, and only the positivist school extends its theories to criminals, marking the transition

[23] See [1], p. 21.

from criminal acts to criminals. Physical detriment is revealed as a feature of criminals and established on a presupposition that "it is the actors rather than acts that should be punished". In 1910, Prins, one of the founders of the International Association of Penal Law and the advocator of the sociologist school, said, "In this way, we raise a concept, namely the concept of the detrimental social status of criminals that is not understood, to the primary position and replace the exclusive concept of certain prohibitive behaviors with detrimental status. In other words, from an isolated point of view, crimes themselves may be less detrimental than the subject of crimes. If we ignore the inherent characteristics of the subject but punish people who conduct illegal acts, we may be using false methods."[24] The so-called "detrimental social status of criminals" refers to physical detriments, which are sometimes called "social detriments", meaning that penalty laws and regulations stipulate that some behavior should be punished, or that people of no legal competence are free from the penalty but probably conduct behaviors that are stipulated by the laws and regulations repeatedly, and thus impose social detriments.[25] As a physical characteristic of criminals, physical detriments tend to be understood as a tendency towards a type of crime. The famous Italian criminologist Garofalo defined this detrimental status as a person's changeable and inherited tendency to commit crimes in his book *Criteria of Detrimental Status* (1880). Lombroso named such people who tended to commit crimes as born criminals and explained their physical characteristics from the biological perspective, holding that these people had yet committed criminal acts but had the tendency to do so due to their genetic or physical factors. Afterward, Ferri also used the concept of born criminals to represent such people who tended to commit crimes. Ferri held that a born criminal had some innate digression, leading him to tend to commit crimes. Meanwhile, Ferri believed that a person might commit crimes by nature, but if he lived in a good environment, he would be likely to break no criminal laws or moral creeds during his whole life.[26] Obviously, Ferri's born criminals are concerned with the biological factors of crimes. He also discussed the exact difference between born criminals and occasional criminals: for the former, external causes played a minor role than the internal tendency because the tendency had a force to drive actors to commit crimes. For occasional criminals, by contrast, criminal acts were merely the results of actors failing to defend external causes, and external causes triggered most crimes. Among born criminals, the occasional causes of crimes arose from the instinct or tendency that had existed within the actors, which were only an excuse compared to occasional criminals. Furthermore, among occasional criminals, it was the occasional factors that favored the growth of the ever-growing criminal tendency in appropriate environments.[27] If we eliminate pure biological content from the concept of born criminals, the so-called born criminals were nothing but criminals with more physical detriments. Since the anthropologist school of criminology excessively criticized the biological features of criminals, it brought about people's

[24] Traninin [8], pp. 22–23.

[25] See [9], p. 667.

[26] See [1], pp. 40–41.

[27] See [6], pp. 23, 24.

criticism and disapproval. Later, the sociologist school of criminology paid attention to looking for the causes of crimes from social aspects. The representation of physical detriments transformed from pure biology to sociology. For instance, Ferri, in his book *Studies of Criminality in France* (1881), introduced three natural categories to classify all scattered and incomplete causes of crimes, saying that human behavior, whether honest or not, social or anti-social, was the result of the interaction between a person's psychological mechanism and conditions and his living environments.[28] Hence, Ferri revealed the representation of the physical detriments of crimes from personal, natural, and social aspects. To sum up, physical detriments enjoy no position in the classical school of criminology. It is a concept that the positivist school tries its best to advocate, which, in a sense, can be said as the pivot of the positivist school. The meanings of physical detriments are different between the anthropologist and sociologist schools, with the former stressing the biological factors of criminals. Thus, physical detriments are more established on the biological factors of criminals. The sociologist school, however, stresses the sociological factors of criminals, and thus physical detriments are based on the comprehensive analysis of criminals' biological and sociological factors. Even so, both the anthropologist sociologist schools share the same opinion on physical detriments, which fundamentally differentiates them from the classical school. The establishment of physical detriments as the basis of penalty marks the transformation from the generalization of the penalty of the classical school to the individualization of the penalty of the positivist school. The individualization of the penalty requires that penalties should be adaptive to the personalities of criminals so that penalties are substantially impartial, different from the formal impartiality of the generalization of the penalty advocated by the classical school. When analyzing the classical school's generalization of the penalty, Ferri mentioned that the classical school regarded crimes as legal problems, focusing on the names, definitions, and legal analysis of crimes, while putting aside the personalities of criminals formed against certain backgrounds. It only mentioned these exceptionally when legal books explicitly stated them, such as whether criminals were juveniles or deaf or mentally ill, and whether they were drunk when committing crimes, and so on. Only when the above laws had strict stipulations would the classical school theoretically discuss criminals' personalities. Nevertheless, 90% of cases had no or failed to prove the above situations, so criminal jurisprudence was limited to defining facts specifically. Under such circumstances, the classical school held that apart from the cases involving juveniles, deaf, drunk, and mentally ill, every criminal was an abstract, normal person. In fact, the classical school believed that all people committing thefts were thieves and all people killing others were murderers. There was no specific person in legislators' minds, and only judges would value specific people. According to scholars and legislators, criminals were merely live specimens that judges could stick criminal codes on their backs. In addition to exceptions as referred to by penal codes and a few physical conditions, the rest of the cases served only as grounds for judges to select a provision from the penal code applicable to the specimen of the crime. If it was not Article 407 but

[28] See [6], p. 41.

Article 404 that was stuck on criminals' backs, the appellate court would be against any numerical changes. If the living specimen said, "It may be important for you to impose an appropriate article, but if you look closely at all conditions that force me to seize other's property, you will be aware that the importance is schematic." Judges would answer, "It may be like this for the administration of justice in the future, but it is not true to the current one. You break Article 404, so this number will be stuck on your back. When you leave the court and go to jail, you will be changed to another number or other numbers because your personality will vanish in front of the laws representing social justice." This way, the person's personality is erased unreasonably, and he will receive treatment for degeneration in jail. Ferri vividly compared the criminal justice system, which ignored criminals' personalities while dealing with crimes as abstract legal phenomena only, to quacks, believing that this was the same as old-dated medicine science that treated diseases as abstract pathological phenomena and was regardless of the personalities of patients. Doctors in old times did not consider patients' nutrition, age, and physical and neurological conditions. They treated fever as fever and pleurisy as pleurisy. Modern medical science claimed that studying diseases must start from the study of patients. The same disease could be treated with different methods if patients showed diverse situations. Therefore, Ferri concluded, "Criminal behavior is one of the conditions needed for studying criminals. But for the same crime, speaking from anthropology and sociology, since the reasons for crimes are different, we need to take different treatments for criminals with all personalities."[29] This is the basics of the individualization of the penalty.

The retribution and deterrence theories of the classical school have held a dominant position in the West for a long time. However, the crime rate, especially the recidivism rate, in western countries has increased tremendously, so people cast doubt on the deterrence role of the penalty. Meanwhile, positivism philosophy emerged in the Europe continent, which advocated that observation was better than thinking. In comparison, the retribution and deterrence theories in the legal concepts of the classical school featured scholasticism, which made useless comments and thus was empty. Such circumstances gave birth to the special preventionism of the positivist school: first is Lombroso's theory of the deprivation of criminal capacity. Lombroso claimed that according to different situations of born criminals, the following measure should be taken respectively: (1) people who had not committed crimes but had the tendency to do so should be imposed security measures, namely being separated from societies; (2) people who had physiological features of crimes should be treated, namely, through medical measures such as the removal of the forehead and deprivation of reproductive function to eliminate their motives of crimes; (3) people who were highly dangerous should be exiled to remote islands, imprisoned for life and even executed. The common objective of these three measures was to disable criminals' abilities or conditions to commit crimes or re-offend to prevent them from committing crimes. Second is Ferri's theory of equivalents for punishment. Ferri negated that a country enjoyed the penalty power to punish criminals and claimed that penalties were replaced by distinct remedies based on the social situations that

[29] See [1], p. 40.

advocated different personalities of criminals. Third is Liszt's theory of the education penalty. He claimed that the penalty was not an instinct or original retaliation but should set out to reform criminals and protect the whole society. We should not only educate and reform criminals based on their situations so that they could reintegrate into society as quickly as possible but also adapt corresponding penalties based on to what extent the social detriments of criminals violated social interests to defend our society. Liszt's thought is perfectly expressed in the following quote: "correcting the criminals who can be corrected and preventing those who cannot be corrected from doing bad." Guided by the theory of social defense, the positivist school of criminology made adjustments in the following two aspects: (1) the revolution of the penalty itself; and (2) looking for equivalents for punishment.

The positivist school of criminology argued that the classical school's penalty system failed conspicuously. Hence, the penalty must be revolutionized. Lombroso said that the most pivotal revolution of the penalty was its application. The first thing to be changed was the nature of punishment. According to Lombroso, the application of laws should pay attention to social security and peace rather than the possibility of blaming criminals, and criminals rather than evil. Based on the criticism of the traditional penalty mode, Lombroso investigated every penalty specifically and proposed solutions for reformation. His pivotal idea of penalty reformation was to transform the penalty idea of retributing criminals and deterring general people to correcting and treating criminals. Lombroso believed that applying punishments to criminals was not based on retributions but the personality detriments, the purpose of which was defending our society. These opinions of Lombroso laid a theoretical foundation for the establishment of the security punishment system. Ferri explicitly pointed out the failure of the current prison system, holding that the modern penalty system that was established in part based on the assumption that we could measure the moral responsibility of criminals and in part on the fantasy that criminals could generally be reformed, which led to the establishment of imprisonment and single living systems, could never protect our society from crimes.[30] Consequently, Ferri proposed the following measures to reform penalties: (1) an indeterminate sentence system. The classical school of criminology advocated that the punishment was an equivalent to the social detriments of crimes, and thus it was definite. The definiteness of punishments was based on the degree of social detriments of crimes, which completely ignored the physical detriments of criminals. Accordingly, Ferri pointed out sharply and criticized that the classical school's whole penal code served only as a logarithmic table to calculate punishments at the end of its analysis. When a judge sentenced a 19-year-old criminal who was intoxicated and premeditated at the time of the crime, it would be pathetic if the sentence was wrong! It would also be pathetic if the judge mistakenly added or subtracted 1/3, 1/6, or 1/2 according to the mitigating or aggravating circumstances following laws! If due to the miscalculation, the defendant appealed to the appellate court, which would relentlessly say to the judge, "Please re-calculate because your previous calculation was unfair." For the judge, the only issue was: adding the total number, subtracting deducted part, and sentencing

[30] See [6], p. 136.

the criminal to one year, seven months, and 13 days in prison, with no increase or decrease for one day! In this case, the humane observer would ask, "If the criminal fails to be reformed well when his sentence term is due, will you still put him in jail?" The judge would answer, "Then, disregard it. According to the sentence, the criminal would only be imprisoned for one year, seven months, and 13 days." The observer would ask, "But what if the criminal would still be unable to adapt to the social life when his sentence term is due?" The judge would answer as follows, "When the term is due, the prisoner can be released because he has finished the last day of the sentence, which means his debt has been paid off."[31] To reform the deficiency of the definite penalty of the classical school, Ferri noted that for severe crimes committed by genetic or born criminals, or people who tended to do so as a result of habits or mental illness, the positivist school claimed to retain indefinite isolation because it was unreasonable to prescribe terms in advance in cases of dangerous degenerates who committed severe crimes. Ferri held that criminals born to commit crimes or do so due to diseases should not be imprisoned for a period causally. Instead, they should be imprisoned until they could adapt to normal social lives.[32] Whether punishments are definite or not is not a simple issue related to the determination of the prison term but a major one related to the concept of the penalty. The classical school believed that the indefinite sentence system of the criminal law in the pre-capitalist society was a specific illustration of the discretionary principle of the penalty. Under the principle of no penalty without a law, penalties were definite, and even statutory penalties were absolutely definite, let alone sentences. In terms of what crimes should be imposed to what punishments, we should investigate them as accurately as we did for geometry. The positivist school obviously disagreed with this opinion. Setting out from the theory of social defense, Ferri held that for any crime, punishments should not only be allocated to criminals with the dose of medicine equivalent to their moral responsibility but should be limited to the actual situations (violation of laws and damages thereof) and the personal circumstances of criminals (anthropological type of criminals), to determine whether the criminals could return to society and whether it was necessary to isolate these criminals permanently, chronically or temporarily, or whether it was enough to force them to compensate for the damages they had caused strictly. Ferri stated that we established the positivist penalty system on the principle of indefinite isolation of criminals. According to this principle, the penalty should not be retribution for crimes but a necessary result of a theory that it is a method for society to prevent threats of criminals.[33] (2) a compensation system. Among the positivist school of criminology, Garofalo pointed out that this school argued that for many minor criminals, especially petty assaults, it was very useful to replace a few days of imprisonment with an effective method of compensating the defendant's loss. When compensating for the loss was not a legal consequence as today, a right that the civil litigation rules claimed, which the defendant held the inescapable responsibility, could become a real alternative measure for the penalty.

---

[31] See [1], p. 39.

[32] See [1], pp. 50, 51.

[33] See [6], pp. 141, 142.

Ferri further argued for this view, saying that crime, just as it meant the society would respond by segregating criminals indefinitely, should also mean that when an act was serious and the actor was dangerous, the society could respond to them in the form of requiring criminals to compensate (if necessary, it could be imposed along with isolation, or when the act was not too serious and the actor was not too dangerous, it could be used individually). As for petty crimes imposed by occasional criminals, strict compensation, on the one hand, could avoid the defect of applying short-term imprisonment and, on the other hand, would be more efficient and reasonable than criminals staying in national prisons where food and shelter were provided for a few days or weeks. He also proposed that compensation could be in two forms: fines or compensation for states and compensation for victims.[34] Thus, compensation for the loss was a penalty measure against mild criminals, which could overcome the shortcomings of the traditional short-term imprisonment. (3) application of defensive measures against all criminals. This measure was a supplement to the preceding two measures. As Ferri said, just as the indeterminate isolation, which apart from ensuring the specific procedural rules of imprisonment and detention, was a principle of the social defense system proposed by the positivist school, compensation, as a social function, in addition to guaranteeing the procedural rules of implementation, was the second basic principle of the social defense system proposed by the positivist school. These two basic principles proposed by the positivist school would be imperfect if they were not applied according to the general rules of the social defense system; namely, different preventive measures were taken for various crimes. Ferri introduced the defensive measures against all criminals, negated the classical school's opinion of the equivalence of the penalty, and held that scourges of crimes and their treatments must be unified. He quoted Dumaynier's words to express his view, "a criminal, to some extent, is a moral (I would like to add physiological) patient who is treatable, and we must apply main medicine principles to him. We must apply different treatments to different diseases."[35] Ferri's defensive measures established a classification system according to the anthropological features of criminals. Ferri argued for deprivation and forced labor on prisoners and regarded these two as universally applicable rules. He said that we must first notice that isolation was or was not still (because it was common to see) the shelter of lazy criminals but acted as a deprivation. Second, all prisoners (except the ill) should be forced to work. Prisoners should not only be as they were now, paying for alcohol and cigarettes to states, but also for food, clothing, and living, and the rest of the gains through labor should pay for the victims.[36] It should be said that the criminal legislation absorbed Ferri's views in the future, but his draft of the Italian Penal Code, drawn up and published in 1921 and called Ferri's draft, was refused by Congress. Ferri comprehensively and thoroughly implemented the positivist school of criminology ideas, showing up as the mode of "penal code without penalty". Ferri's draft replaced the traditional penalties with a single security punishment and integrated the binary system of punishments

[34] See [6], pp. 148, 150.

[35] See [6], p. 153.

[36] See [6], p. 154.

and security punishments into a concept of security punishments, namely, sanctions (*Sanktion*). Ferri's stipulated sanctions included: (1) sanctions for common crimes on people over 18: 1. fines; 2. local exile; 3. settlement; 4. forced field labor; 5. mild penal servitude in labor places or labor offices; 6. penal servitude in servitude places, and 7. penal servitude for life. (2) sanctions for political or social crimes on people over 18: 1. exile abroad; 2. mild imprisonment; and 3. heavy imprisonment. (3) sanctions on juvenile criminals: 1. supervision; 2. professional correctional institutions; 3. juvenile labor places or farming places; and 4. supervision places. (4) sanctions on mentally ill criminals: 1. supervision places; 2. psychiatric hospitals for mad criminals; and 3. special labor places. (5) additional sanctions: 1. announcement of sentences; 2. good deeds guarantee; 3. suspension of occupations; 4. prohibition from public employment; and 5. expulsion of foreigners. Although Ferri's draft of criminal law was not implemented, it impacted some countries' criminal legislation. Following Ferri's ideas, Liszt proposed the famous "purpose of criminal law" as a part of "The Philipps University of Marburg Outline" in 1882 and particularly stressed social defense, that is, the general purpose of social defense. Liszt believed that one of the ways to defend our society should be to transform criminals into new men who would not commit crimes. For dangerous people who did criminal acts, preventive or defensive measures should be taken in advance to prevent them from conducting anti-social behaviors, which was also an important way to defend society. Based on this "purpose of criminal law", we should put aside the punishments of crimes in the places where they should be convicted and their punishments be announced, and instead announce inclusive security punishments.[37]

The classical school of criminology deals with crimes with punishments, exaggerating the role of penalties. Undeniably, Beccaria and Bentham both proposed thinking and solutions for preventing crimes. For instance, Beccaria introduced the following preventive measures: (1) formulating laws clearly and popularly. (2) brightness accompanying freedom, transmitting knowledge, and eliminating ignorance. (3) ensuring that law enforcement institutions follow laws and do not corrupt. (4) awarding virtue. (5) improving education.[38] If we deem Beccaria's measures of preventing crimes too vague, then Bentham's are much more specific. Bentham divided the methods of preventing crimes into direct and indirect ones. In terms of the direct methods to prevent crimes, Bentham said that before a criminal act was conducted, there might be many omens to illustrate the approaching of crimes. With a series of preparatory events, crimes tended to be prevented before detrimental results were triggered. This preventive method was implemented by all citizens who held liability or by specially authorized people. The capability of all citizens to protect was represented in judicial interference, and thus it might be a judicial preventive method. The following methods were justifiable: fighting against criminals who were committing crimes; preventing suspects; transferring suspects to security officers; asking for aid; detaining items that were believed to be stolen or protecting

[37] See [9], p. 604.

[38] See [10], pp. 104–108.

stolen items that were damaged; requesting the witness to testify; requesting passengers to help transfer criminal suspects to security officers.[39] Direct methods apply to certain timely and specific crimes. But the penalty system will not be perfect, and indirect crime prevention methods are also needed. Bentham posited that the indirect methods that possessed no punishment nature could play a role in people's behaviors and intentions, ensure people follow laws, avoid the lure of evil, and constrain themselves depending on their will and knowledge.[40] Bentham listed 22 indirect methods to prevent crimes and elaborated on them. We should say that these discussions are of great use. Overall, since the classical school of criminology confines the methods of preventing crimes to penalties, mainly through legal intimidation, its prevention of crimes is impractical. The positivist school of criminology is based on the theory of social defense, which states clearly that crime prevention is the primary task of criminal laws, and in particular, Liszt's slogan of "the best social policy is the best criminal policy" enables people to have a broader perspective of crime prevention. Ferri argued that the social environment was the easiest to change, and legislators could control most crimes by altering the natural environment and human physiological and psychological conditions, thus reducing many crimes. We firmly believed that a truly civilized legislator could rely less on criminal codes but on potential social life and legislation remedies to reduce the scourge of crimes.[41] Hence, Ferri believed that sanctions would be in a subordinate position in the future, and various legislation would replace the treatment of diseases with social health treatment so that the latter would be applied every day, through which the theory of crime prevention would be established.

The term "equivalents for punishment" originates from Ferri. The previous penalty systems centered around punishments against liberty, which idolized imprisonment; however, they ignored the effects of imprisonment, especially the defects. Ferri vividly criticized the penalty system that regarded imprisonment as a way to deal with all types of crimes and all forms of criminals, saying that it was like a quark treating diseases, and the quark said to patient A, "Do you have any heart disease? Please take one quart of rhubarb and stay in hospital for 12 days." Patient B said, "My foot is sprained." The quark answered, "Please take a pint of rhubarb and stay in hospital for 17 days." There were differences in the dose of medicine and length of hospitalization only, and this was not prescribing the right medicine. Because Ferri lost confidence in punishments and to defend society, he believed that it was necessary to seek the most effective equivalents. He regarded these indirect defensive methods as the equivalents of punishments, pointing out that when the equivalents of punishments were established among legislators' concepts and methods through the teaching of criminal sociology, they would become a legislative way to erase social factors of crimes. Legislators, through the study of the occurrence, conditions, and results of individual and collective behaviors, gradually learned human psychological and sociological patterns, thus being able to control many factors

---

[39] See [11], p. 27.

[40] See [11], p. 96.

[41] See [1], p. 43.

that triggered crimes, especially social factors, and ensure to exert an indirect but more definite impact on the formation of crimes. That is to say, among legislative, political, economic, administrative, and penalty methods, and from the largest institution to the smallest unit, the social system would be adjusted in a way that human behaviors would not always be deterred by repression and led to a non-criminal track unconsciously and uselessly, so there would be enough room for developing personal abilities and satisfying people's needs while causing the minimum violence and violations of laws.[42] The introduction of Ferri's equivalents for punishment is of great significance in the history of modern criminal law. In Lombroso's later works, he absorbed the thinking of Ferri's equivalents for punishment, saying that now people only curbed crimes and it was not enough, and they must take measures to prevent crimes. Even though we could not curb crimes, we could also figure out ways to reduce the causes of crimes. The so-called ways to reduce the causes of crimes were what Lombroso regarded as the equivalents of punishment. Ferri specifically discussed the following assumptions of the equivalents for punishment: (1) in the economic sector. Free trade (except for specific manufacturing and agriculture that were necessary to be protected temporarily) eliminated many felonies and misdemeanors, especially crimes of violating properties, by preventing starvation and excessive price of food and food tax. (2) in the political sector. The police's arbitrary repression and prevention were of no use for preventing political crimes, including assassinations, rebellions, gang conspiracies, and civil wars. There is no way to prevent this type of crime except to coordinate governmental and national aspirations. (3) in the scientific sector. Science gave birth to weapons, typography, photography, lithography, new poisons, bombs, electricity, hypnotism, and other new criminal tools, and the development of science would surely provide more efficient solutions than repressions by punishments. Printing, measurement, and photography of prisoners, telegram, and railway were effective auxiliary methods to fight against crimes. (4) in the legislative and administrative sectors. The wise testamentary legislation could prevent murders of relatives due to the urgent need to inherit properties. But in the countries where parents permitted marriage, the legislation, which drove fathers to approve their children's marriage and engagement or break the engagement and which stipulated illegitimate children, was the best measure to prevent illegal cohabitation, infanticide, abortion, abandoning infants, indecent rape and murders that were conducted by women who were seduced and abandoned. (5) in the educational sector. The pure knowledge from textbooks was beneficial in decreasing the difficulty of some obvious scams and transmitting legal knowledge, especially in decreasing the lack of foresight, a feature of occasional criminals. To sum up, Ferri mentioned that the examples he had listed, which would become a preventive code if they were complemented with criminal codes, proved that social factors played a role in crimes, especially occasional crimes. Nevertheless, they proved more clearly that legislators could influence the development of crimes within the scope of other anthropological and natural factors by reducing these causes. Therefore, Quetelet said, "Because in each year, crime seems to be a necessity of our society, and if we

[42] See [6], p. 81.

do not reduce the causes of crimes from the preventive perspective, the number of crimes will never decrease. The responsibility of legislators is to admit and try their best to eliminate these causes. They must formulate the budget of crimes like what they do for the national financial budget." This was correct. However, we must keep in mind all the rest of the things apart from formulating criminal codes because history, statistics, and direct observations of criminal phenomena illustrated that criminal laws had minimum effect on preventing crimes, whereas economic, political, and administrative laws and regulations had the best effect. All in all, the observations and conclusions from science teaching should enable legislators to believe that social improvement was more beneficial than penal codes in preventing crimes.[43]

Founded on the experience-man-based assumption of human nature, the positivist school of criminology sets out from behavioral determinism, reveals the limitations of punishments, looks for the equivalents for punishments instead, bases itself on correcting and preventing crimes, and thus makes deductions of penalty theories that are different from those of the classical school that features special prevention.

1.3 Human Nature Analysis of Legislation

The positivist school of criminology holds empirical assumptions about both criminals and legislators. As experience men, legislators are restricted by non-supreme human thinking, so they can formulate a perfect penal code as the classical school of criminology advocates. However, this is a utopian assumption in the positivist school's minds.

When discussing criminal legislation, Ferri stated clearly at the outset that positivist theories reduced the practical significance of penal codes tremendously.[44] This can be seen as the general attitude of the positivist school towards penal codes. The reasons why the positivist school belittles the practical significance of penal codes are as follows:

(1) Change of the view on criminal laws. The classical school of criminology stresses the function of criminal laws in protecting human rights, thus advocating the principle of no penalty without a law and enabling penal codes to be the Magna Carta of citizens' freedom. The positivist school of criminology, by contrast, stresses the social protection function of criminal laws, and the significance of the principle of no penalty without a law is reduced greatly. Of course, the positivist school of criminology pays attention to the role of criminal procedure laws. While arguing that positivist theories significantly reduced the real meaning of penal codes, Ferri also mentioned that those theories increased the importance of the criminal procedure rules designed to have a practical and day-to-day impact on the criminal measures that society used to defend against crimes. If a penal code were a code of the wicked, then a criminal procedure code

[43] See [6], p. 93.

[44] See [6], p. 101.

would be a code of the honest, who had been trialed but not proved guilty.[45] Ferri attaches importance to criminal procedure laws, which we should pay attention to. The classical school of criminology tends to be suspected of emphasizing substance over procedure, and Beccaria harshly criticized the cruel feudal torture system. However, his achievements in criminal procedure laws were far inferior to those in criminal laws. Ferri depended largely on criminal proceedings, believing that criminal proceedings should achieve the effects of punishments. Ferri posited that if the weak deterrent effect that punishments could have on all kinds of criminals depended on the inevitability and immediacy of its application, then other roles just relied on police institutions and criminal proceedings. Putting aside the specialized and technical reforms of the procedure system that even the classical school criminologists requested to represent criminals' interests rather than social interests, we could connect the positivist reform of judicial procedures and the following two rationales: (1) equally admitting the rights and guarantees of the criminals who should be trialed and the societies where the criminals were trialed; (2) the purpose of legitimate judgments was not to determine the indefinite moral responsibility of criminals, nor was it to apply the articles in penal codes to the crime non-individually. Instead, it was to apply the laws that suited criminals most according to the physiologically and psychologically anti-social features that criminals showed more or less.[46] Since the positivist school of criminology claimed that the physical detriments of criminals were the basis of punishments, it could not keep a balance in legislation like the ladder of charges and punishment the classical school of criminology claimed. Therefore, judicial tyranny was easily triggered, and it was necessary to remedy it with criminal procedure rules. From this, we can see that Ferri did not completely ignore the individual interests of criminals but only paid more attention to social interests between individual and social interests. Ferri said, "in terms of criminal law, we think it is necessary to negate the overemphasis on individualism by the classical school for the sake of social defense. Hence, we admit not abolishing individual freedom guaranteed by the old system for criminal procedures. However, I believe it is also necessary to restore the balance between individual and social rights that the classical school's hyperboles have disrupted."[47] In this context, Ferri proposes the principle of keeping a balance between individual and social rights, positing that the positivist school aimed to keep this balance, so it was unsatisfied with supporting society while against individuals. Ferri also agrees with this, but he seems impartial between individual and social interests. Nevertheless, from the following statement by Ferri, we can understand that he prioritizes social interests: Ferri criticizes that the classical school's individualism is indeed incomplete because the guarantee it claims only considers criminals themselves while excluding the victims who are

45 See [6], pp. 101–102.

46 See [6], p. 102.

47 See [6], p. 103.

also individuals and who are worthy of more sympathy and protection.[48] Thus, we can see that Ferri disagrees with the classical school on treating criminal law as the Magna Carter of criminals, and he pays attention to protecting the victims' and social interests. The change in the view of criminal laws is seen as a transformation from a rule-of-law country to a rule-of-culture one. The legitimate core of a rule-of-law country is the principle of no penalty without a law. As time goes by, rule-of-law countries are replaced by rule-of-culture countries, and the principle of no penalty without a law, favored by rule-of-law countries, gradually exits from the position it insists on. For example, according to the principle of no penalty without a law, application by analogy of the criminal law is exclusive, but in many countries, the application by analogy in criminal law is allowed or conditionally allowed; the principle of no penalty without law is against security punishments, but countries not only allow to apply them but also legalize and unify them; the principle of no penalty without law is against the absolute indeterminate penalty, whereas many countries nowadays apply it and it is said to be effective in some countries; the principle of no penalty without law is against suspended sentence (against equality of offense), and parole (changing judgment or undermining res judicata), but international conferences decide to allow suspended sentence and parole, and also relax application conditions. These illustrate clearly that the position that the principle of no penalty without a law insists on has gradually been replaced by the new school, the so-called education punishment of rule-of-culture countries.[49] The principle of no penalty without law is a principle of criminal law by the classical school, whose decadency demonstrates that the role of criminal codes declines with the dominance of the positivist school's theories.

(2) Change of the view on crimes. The classical school of criminology regards crimes as the violation of social contracts, thus focusing on defining crimes from the legal perspective, so the crimes of the classical school are merely crimes within the lens of law. Meanwhile, since the classical school only studies the free will of criminals, it fails to reveal the causes of crimes from a broad social horizon. In response, Ferri pointed out sharply that factually, the criminologists from the classical school saw crimes as a fact that had been done. They analyzed crimes through the lens of professional jurists, regardless of how crimes were conducted and why these criminal facts occurred more or less in all countries yearly. Their theoretical foundation was free will, which excluded the probability of the above science-related problems. Because according to the free will theory, crime was the outcome of human will command. If we admitted this to be the fact, there would be no point in studying the causes of crimes. This was because criminals wanted to kill people, they did so, and that was all about crimes. Once we admitted that free will was a fact, the occurrence of behaviors depended on criminals' commands, namely voluntary choices, then any

[48] See [6], p. 106.

[49] See [7], p. 233.

other reasons would be redundant.[50] However, the positivist school released themselves from this narrow legal concept, regarded crime as a natural and social phenomenon, started from behavioral determinism, and revealed crime's personal and social causes. Therefore, the positivist school broke through the shackles of understanding crimes from the legal form, downplaying the significance of criminal codes.

(3) Change of views on punishments. The classical school of criminology argues for retributivism and deterrence. Hence, punishments are of great significance and serve as the only method to treat the disease of crimes for this school. Nevertheless, the positivist school potently demonstrates the ridiculoUSess of retributivism and the void of deterrence of punishments. As for retributivism, Ferri argued intensely that we could still hear the voice of using "public revenge" to treat criminals, and judicial work was mainly represented by the sword rather than the scabbard. Only when we investigated the causes of crimes that we named chronic diseases from criminals' physiological, psychological, family, and environmental aspects through experimental and scientific methods would the administration of justice, which was under scientific guidance, abandon the bloody judgments on those poor criminals and display the medical function, whose primary aim was to eliminate or reduce the social and personal causes of crimes. Only until then would the law give up all shameless and stupid actions of revenge on criminals through the death penalty and solitary confinement and so on.[51] In terms of deterrence, Ferri tried to demonstrate that punishments had no deterrence, at least not as much as the classical school thought. To start with, deterrence played no role in crimes of passion. Ferri said that people who intended to commit crimes and were dominated by passion or affected by the psychological hurricanes that shook their moral concepts were by no means controlled by punishments or threats because the volcanic-eruption-like passion did not allow them to think anything. As for premeditated crimes, deterrence and threats were ineffective. Ferri said that in the criminal cases where the actor premeditated and prepared, punishments were impotent to stop him from committing it. Because actors hoped to escape punishment after committing crimes, they said unanimously that they were only propelled by one thing when they premeditated crime; that is, hoping to escape legal punishments after committing crimes. If they considered more that they might be found and punished, they would not commit crimes, except those who were triggered by passion and emotion. Ferri also listed a vivid example to explain this issue: if everyone wanted to obtain a persuasive example to demonstrate that legal threats exerted no impact on criminals' minds, that would be the coinage offense. Because for civilized countries, (out of need or convenience) paper notes became the alternatives to metal currencies, and by the nineteenth century, coinage offense was prevalent. People who committed such crimes must be concentrated on imitating the texts on paper notes, including "the law punishes

[50] See [1], p. 25.

[51] See [1], p. 21.

counterfeit", among others. You could imagine what forgers thought when they engraved this sentence on plates. Others could ignore the punishments these forgers would undergo, but they could not. This example was highly persuasive because, under other criminal circumstances, people could assume that even though actors were not extremely impulsive, they would not consider the results of their behaviors. But under the scenario of counterfeiting currency, the criminal fact reminded the actors of legal threats, but they were highly calm when committing the crime.[52] After alleviating the superstition of the retributivism and deterrence of punishments, the positivist school of criminology focuses on the correction nature of punishments, which is the education punishment Liszt advocates: correcting the criminals who can be corrected and preventing those who cannot be corrected from doing bad. Once the deterrence of punishments is no longer advocated, Feuerbach's legislative deterrence loses its audience, and the significance of criminal codes is no longer critical. Above all, the positivist school of criminology reduces the significance of criminal codes.

1.4 Human Nature Analysis of Administration of Justice

If we say that the classical school of criminology stresses legislation while belittling the administration of justice, the positivist school of criminology is precisely the opposite: it belittles legislation while emphasizing the administration of justice. The difference is not a simple issue of dividing the authority of legislation and the administration of justice. However, it originates from the different assumptions of human nature between the two schools. This is because, for the scholars of the positivist school, legislators are determined by the nature of legislation, who are faced with general and abstract criminals, and impossible to regulate all matters in criminal codes; however, judicial officers contact specific cases and criminals and thus can deal with individual cases properly. This insight is precisely established on the assumption that judicial officers are experience men.

The judicial concept of the classical school of criminology means applying articles mechanically and implementing the deduction of judicial syllogism, so it does not consider the personalities of criminals. By contrast, the positivist school of criminology is confronted with criminals and establishes itself on the scientific classification of criminals. Therefore, the classification of criminals holds a vital position in positivist school thinking. Lombroso divided criminals into four categories: (1) people born with criminal nature. Lombroso believed that people born with criminal nature were different from those born evil but carried epilepsy genetics, so many of them had epilepsy. He thought to have seen some identical features as savages in these criminals, such as small cranial capacity, flat foreheads, protrusion of frontal bones, craniosynostosis, curly hair, and large ears, among others. He named this phenomenon devolution or devolution to primitive humans. Lombroso said that he found similarities between patients, savages, and criminals in the later development

52 See [1], p. 26.

of his thoughts. He combined epilepsy and other diseases with devolution to explain born criminals and believed that this disease could cause body changes as those happened to born criminals. (2) insane criminals. Lombroso held that the physical features and status of doing evil of people who were born evil were all shown in insane criminals. Insane criminals potentially had epilepsy, and the manic-prone disease disrupted their minds, so they tended to be impulsive, obscene, and violent. People with neurological disorders, alcoholics, arsonists, thefts, and intermittent madmen, had the same features as people with epilepsy. Therefore, Lombroso concluded that epilepsy was the core of all crimes. (3) lustful criminals. According to Lombroso, this type of criminal had beautiful figures, energetic spirits, sensitive nerves, and emotions, and their motives for crimes were also noble. They committed crimes due to romantic relationships and politics, to name a few. Lustful criminals were different types of criminals who were distinct from born criminals. But such criminals tended to have excessive movements, impulsiveness, a rapid outburst of disease and forgiveness, similar to epilepsy. (4) occasional criminals. Lombroso held that occasional criminals were not real criminals. These people did not seek opportunities to commit crimes. Instead, they were trapped in crimes due to some trivial accidents. He mentioned that only such people had no relationship with epilepsy genetics among all criminals. He also quoted Garofalo that these people were indeed not called criminals. He was the founder of the classification of criminals, significantly promoting applying punishments based on the correct consideration of the personalities of criminals in criminal justice. As the US criminologist V. Fox said, "Although Lombroso's classification fails to stand the test of time, his attitude towards objectivity and scientific methods lay a foundation for adopting a stricter method in criminology."[53]

Ferri and Garafalo were both impacted by Lombroso in the classification of criminals. In Ferri's opinion, crime results from the interaction among physical, geographical, and social factors. Thus, he divided criminals into the following five types: (1) insane criminals. Insane criminals refer to those criminals who are mentally imperfect. Ferri argued that insane criminals should be separated from born criminals to be a unique type. Their organic features, especially physical features, were sometimes the same as or opposite to those of born criminals and occasional criminals, and these features varied largely among different types of mental disorders, despite the same type of crime these people committed. In terms of insane criminals, a further study would find that this type of criminal included those who were completely insane and in the intermediate state between normal and insane. Ferri also criticized the diverse opinions on insane criminals, mentioning that Chorley thought the term insane criminal was self-contradictory as insane criminals held no moral responsibility and were not criminals. Such criticism was disputable. We insisted that social responsibility was the only responsibility applying to all criminals and those mentally imperfect. Chorley and Bianchi advocated insane criminals being divided into the scope of psychiatry rather than criminal anthropology, while such statement was also

[53] Zhao [12], p. 34.

not correct. This was because even though psychiatry was relevant to insane criminals in the sense of psychopathology, this did not exclude the discussions of insane criminals by criminal anthropology and criminal sociology to establish the natural history of criminology and provide remedies for social interests. (2) born criminals. Ferri held that born or instinctive criminals expressed the organic and psychological features that criminal anthropology determined most easily. He said that people had always thought every human behavior was the result of its free will or lack of education instead of innate physiological and psychological ones. The concept of born criminals was, in no doubt, a direct challenge to traditional concepts. Ferri believed that science proved that there was so much scientific evidence of these hereditary criminal tendencies (even different from the clinical status of mental disorders) that there was no need to emphasize them further. (3) habitual criminals. Ferri posited that habitual criminals were those who committed crimes due to bad habits. This type of criminals had yet represented or represented a little of the anthropological features of born criminals. They usually committed crimes at early ages, even during their childhood, and most committed crimes of property violations. Their crimes arose from a weak sense of morality due to sweated environments instead of innate tendencies. Afterward, as Mr. Chorley noticed, failure to be punished when they did the crime for the first time was one of the reasons for them to develop criminal habits, but the decisive reason was that they became physically weaker and mentally corrupted in prison; isolated imprisonment caused them to degenerate; alcoholism made them idle and easy to be irritated. As a result, they returned to the old path of committing crimes and became habitual criminals. (4) occasional criminals. Ferri posited that this type of criminals had no innate or developed criminal tendency at all, and they committed crimes in juvenile times because they could not withstand the lures of individual conditions and natural and social environments. Without these lures, they would not commit crimes or commit crimes again. Hence, they usually committed uncommon crimes or crimes of violations against persons or properties. However, these criminal acts arising from the comprehensive interaction of individual conditions and social environments differed from those committed by born criminals and habitual criminals. (5) passional criminals. Ferri said that passional criminals were not like born criminals or habitual criminals who behaved well, had sanguine temperaments, and tended to be excited and over-sensitive. They were usually nervous or epilepsy-like. Strictly speaking, their crimes might result from their personalities' unconsciousness. Passional criminals, especially female passional criminals, were generally those who suddenly lost self-control driven by anger, injured love or reputation, and other emotions. They were extremely excited before, during, and after committing crimes. They committed crimes, not in a covert but overt manner, and usually used inappropriate methods that exposed themselves from the beginning. Nevertheless, sometimes there were passional criminals who were calm and not impulsive and cunningly committed crimes with premeditations thanks to their preconceptions or sentiments. Finally, Ferri also studied the proportion of these types of criminals, arguing that after the general research conclusions on the classification of criminal anthropology, it seemed necessary to clarify further the proportion of each type of criminals in total criminals. Nonetheless, since there was no absolute division between one type of criminal and another, and because the occurrence rates of some crimes varied as the frequency of the crimes of violations of persons or properties, it was impossible to state the whole picture of crimes clearly. Nevertheless, with similar methods, we could firstly say that the number of insane and passional criminals was the least, accounting for 5–10% only. We also found that born criminals and habitual criminals occupied 40–50% of the total crimes; hence, the proportion of occasional criminals was 40–50%.[54] Ferri's above classification of criminals explicitly displayed the relationship between him and Lombroso as teachers and students, whereas Ferri classified criminals more detailedly.

Garofalo remarkably divided out a so-called "natural crime" (*Natura crime*), saying that "we may conclude that the element of immorality requisite before a harmful act can be regarded as criminal by public opinion, is the injury to so much of the moral sense as is represented by one or the other of the elementary altruistic sentiments of pity and probity. Moreover, the injury must wound these sentiments, not in their superior and finer degrees, but in the average measure in which they are possessed by a community, which is indispensable for the adaption of the individual to society. Given such a violation of either of these sentiments, and we have what may properly be called 'natural crime'.[55]" Garofalo also divided natural crime into two types: the first was the crimes violating pity, including: (1) violation of a person's life and all behaviors intended to cause physical injury, such as imposing physical misery intentionally, intentionally mutating, abusing the ill and weak, triggering diseases, and setting excessive labor on children or other work that might harm their health or development. (2) objective behaviors that immediately caused physical and mental misery, such as the violations against personal rights with the ultimate purpose of benefiting the self, whether it was to satisfy physical pleasure or gain money, and a typical example was the abduction of women or children. (3) behaviors that directly caused mental misery, such as defamation, false accusation, and seduction by the promise of marriage. The second was the crimes violating probity, including: (1) property violations, namely robbery, blackmail with some kind of threat, intentional damage to other's properties, arson, and so on. (2) crimes that were exclusive violence but inclusive of the violation of probity. Such as money scams, violations of others' property, property transfer with the aim of frauding debtors, brokerage (*barqu route*) due to fault or fraud, publishment of professional secret, abuse of power, and all forms of counterfeit aiming to harm the rights of inventors and manufacturers. (3) statements or records leading to the indirect violations of individual property or civil rights made formally or solemnly. This type of crime could also be controlled by the offense of false evidence, counterfeiting or destroying official documents or records, swapping children, and concealing legal identity. Garofalo stated that crime was a moral abnormality, different from physical abnormality. Physical abnormality was a disease, a deviation of humanity, and moral abnormality was a deviation of civilized humans.[56] It is seen that Garofalo's statement on natural crime is based on the

[54] See [6], p. 37.
[55] Garofalo [13], p. 44.
[56] Garofalo [13], p. 100.

quantitative analysis of criminals, which shows a similarity with Lombroso's. Apart from the theory of natural crime, Garofalo also categorized the criminals of natural crimes: murderers, violent criminals, property criminals, and custom criminals. Such categorization of criminals was not as unique as those of Lombroso and Ferri, but it had positive significance because Garofalo proposed different judicial solutions based on this categorization.

Based on the classification of criminals, the positivist school revolutionized the inactive judicial concept of the classical school, vitalized and gave new meanings to criminal justice, and established a judicial concept with subjective initiative. It used scientific knowledge such as anthropology and psychology to effectively correct criminals to defend society, rather than the classical school, which had no subsequent acts after the announcement of sentences to criminals. Ferri stated that if we excluded the moral concept that punishment was the retribution of crime from the perspective of social repression function, and if we believed that the repression function of the society was only a defense power implemented by the law, then criminal justice would not coincide with the precise calculation of the moral responsibility and punishability of criminals. In addition to proving that the defendant was the criminal and that he belonged to what type of criminal, and that the degree of anti-social depravity and degree of re-adaptation to society, criminal justice would lead to no other results.[57] Under this circumstance, the positivist school's criminal justice shows the following features: (1) expansion of judicial authority. As mentioned above, the classical school of criminology featured the limitation of judicial authority, whereas the positivist school argued for expanding judicial authority. Ferri posited that now we had a chance to solve this old issue of the judge's power. Regarding this issue, we moved from one extreme to another and from the arbitrary in the Middle Ages to Bacon's saying that we should respect laws and judges. According to Bacon, the best law was the one that left the minimum room for judges to think, and the best judge was the one who left the minimum room for themselves to make judgments independently. Ferri also criticized the judicial principles of the classical school, saying that if the function of criminal judges was the same as now, which conducted an illusionary quantitative study of the moral responsibility of the defendant based on the Byzantine-like equivalence rule regarding attempted crimes, accomplice and confrontational crimes, namely if the law applied to the object of crimes rather than criminals, then the power of judges should be limited to the number (years, moths and days) of imprisonment stipulated by legal articles, like Chinese laws that precisely regulated the length and thickness of bamboo sticks (this had the same reputation as our single cell in Chinese penalty system). On the other hand, if a criminal trial should be a physiological and psychological investigation of the defendant and crimes relegated to the secondary status, criminals should be raised upfront from the perspective of punishment. Criminal codes obviously should be restricted within some basic rules of the ways of defense and social sanctions and the constituent elements of each felony and delinquency. In contrast, judges should enjoy greater freedom to the extent permitted by scientific and empirical trial data, and thus they

[57] See [6], p. 113.

could use anthropological knowledge to trial the defendant in front.[58] The expansion of the authority of criminal justice did not mean that the judge's power was unlimited. Ferri argued that legal proceedings were a guarantee to prevent judicial errors and accidents for accused citizens. Hence, the judicial power of criminal entities was expanded while criminal procedural rules were stricter to prevent judges from arbitrarily giving sentences, and this was what Ferri imagined. (2) enhancement of the initiative of judges. Natural jurists' legislative theory holds that as long as with reasonable endeavor, jurists would create a perfect code that represented the supreme legislative wisdom and was mechanically applied by the judge.[59] According to this theory, the "automatic application of the law" existed, so it put maximum effort into degrading the role of the administration of justice, viewed judicial activities as a mechanical application of the law, and negated the initiative of judges in judicial activities. Pound, the famous US jurist, wrote that the 19th-century jurists tried to exclude human factors from the administration of justice. They tried to exclude all individualized factors in the application of the law. They believed in establishing and implementing enclosed legal systems strictly, logically, and mechanically. In their views, it was extremely inappropriate to recognize human creative factors in the origination and application and the structuring and the establishment of the system of this enclosed legal system.[60] This view that excluding individualized factors in applying the law would only lead to legal dogmatism, and the law's social effects were hard to achieve. Criminal legislation treated a matter as a case for study, so legal regulations were abstract. However, crimes in judicial activities were specific, with abstract articles applied in specific criminal cases and judges able to take the initiative to individualize punishments. As Ferri said, the character of the judge greatly impacted the quality of the government overall. If good judges did not implement codes, those of the highest academic value and noble ones would have little effect. Nevertheless, if good judges implemented codes, it did not matter much, even if codes or decrees were not perfect. Therefore, Ferri held that judges' initiative could complement legislative defects. The reason why judges played an important role in criminal justice was determined by the features of the administration of justice, according to Ferri. Because for criminal laws, the application of decrees in specific cases was or should not be the same as that for civil laws, which were seen as a legal, abstract logical problem. Instead, it must apply abstract articles from a psychological perspective to people alive. Because judges of criminal law should not separate themselves from their environments and social lives, to become mechanical legal instruments to some extent. The flexible assessment of each criminal judgment on people depends on acts, actors, and the social situations that act on actors rather than statutory law.[61] Hence, the object of criminal justice is not criminal acts simply but criminals with different personalities, so judges are required to suit the remedy to

[58] See [6], pp. 120–121.

[59] See [14], p. 13.

[60] See [14], p. 123.

[61] See [6], p. 120.

the case and apply the right criminal laws according to the personalities of criminals. In this case, judges must be endowed with greater power to take full initiative. (3) application of scientific knowledge in trials. Ferri believed that legal trials should be science-based trials. The positivist criminal procedure system requires that judges adept at anthropology and criminal sociology and that judgments provide the necessary reference to correct criminals based on the personalities of criminals and features of crimes.[62] Therefore, Ferri posited that criminal judges should be those with specific knowledge, including anthropological, psychological, and sociological knowledge, which was significant in criminal justice. Furthermore, Ferri was against jurors participating in criminal judicial activities. He said that even though we put aside a technical-related idea that it was necessary to conduct physiological and psychological trials for each defendant, social justice was obviously not achieved by an inattentive juror's momentary unthinking impression. If a criminal trial was simply an announcement of whether an act was good or bad, then individual moral views were enough. However, criminal trials were a process to determine evidence and examine objective and subjective facts, so it was not enough to rely on moral views simply, and wisdom must be used for each trial.[63] The wisdom Ferri referred to in this context meant the necessary anthropological, psychological, and sociological knowledge that criminal judges must equip. Jurors had no such specific knowledge, so they could not perform their criminal trial functions well.

All in all, the judicial concept of the positivist school of criminology is conscious. According to the positivist school of criminology, criminal justice is not simply about applying criminal laws but, more importantly, individualizing punishments based on the personalities of criminals. Thus, the role of judges must be expanded. In criminal trials, judges utilize anthropological, psychological, and sociological knowledge to analyze criminals and find the most appropriate methods to correct them. Thus, we can see that judges, as administrators of justice, are experienced men.

2 Cultural Background

The positivist school has completely different cultural backgrounds from the classical school, and it is of great significance to deeply understand the positivist school by analyzing their cultural backgrounds.

2.1 *Positivism Methodology*

Positivism is a philosophical school founded by the French philosopher Auguste Comte. Before Comte, rationalism was prevalent in the European continent, which held that real knowledge consisted of entirety and necessity, and the purpose of

[62] See [6], p. 127.

[63] See [6], p. 126.

thinking was to formulate a system of truth where propositions were linked logically. Regarding methodology, rationalism believed in deduction, starting from axioms or self-evident principles to deduct other propositions. If deductions were not wrong, the proposition would be deducted from principles logically which was certain as principles. That is to say; the comprehensive or deductive method was to lead to complex propositions by starting from simple, self-evident ones. Comte named this way of thinking "metaphysics". According to Comte's philosophy, metaphysic (*méta-physi—que*) is not the one we refer to as a methodology opposite to dialectics but a doctrine exploring the ultimate origination and nature of all phenomena.

It is not only idealist philosophy that regards spirits as the origination of the world and ultimate cause of all phenomena but also materialistic philosophy that views matters and objective reality as the origination of the world and the ultimate nature of all phenomena. In contrast to dogmatic metaphysics, Comte proposed positivism. Positivist philosophy (*Philosonhie Positive*) or positivism (*Positivisme*) focuses on the term "positive" (*Positive*). Comte held that his philosophy featured unifying all kinds of knowledge with the positivist spirit of natural science to become positivist knowledge and establishing a positivist philosophical system different from theology and metaphysics. Then, what does Comte mean by "positive"? He discussed its six connotations in the Course on Positive Philosophy comprehensively:

First, "positive" meant "real" (*Ieréel*). All kinds of knowledge must be based on observed facts, and he was against the fantasy of theology and metaphysics, and thus "positive" was opposite to "fanciful" (*chimérique*).

Second, "positive" meant "useful" (*L'utile*). He was against using knowledge to satisfy people's useless and vague curiosity. Knowledge must serve to explore certainty to improve personal and collective lives, and thus "positive" was opposite to "idle" (*oiseux*).

Third, "positive" meant "certain" (*Le certitade*). He was against abstract discussions on those irrelevant and pending questions but instead dedicated to the consistency between personal and human spirits, and thus "positive" was opposite to "doubtful" (*indécision*).

Fourth, "positive" meant "precise" (*Le précis*). He was against discussing things beyond the correctness permitted by the nature of reality but advocated views to be "clear" and "fixed". Therefore, "positive" was opposite to "vague" (*vague*).

Fifth, "positive" also meant "active" (*Le positit*) or "constructive" (*L'organiser*). He was against the destructive tendency of negating reality with the aim of construction by metaphysics, and thus "positive" was opposite to "negative" (*négatif*).

Sixth, "positive" finally meant "relative" (*Le rehtif*). Since our study of phenomena was restricted by internal and external conditions of humans, which was always relative in a sense, we must be against the tendency to pursue absolute knowledge as previous philosophy had, and thus "positive" was opposite to "absolute" (*absolu*).

It should be noted that it was never occasional for Comte to include the above six points as the elements of his positivist spirit of philosophy because they represented the basic features of his philosophical thinking. The reason why Comte stressed "reality" and "precision" as the elements of positivist spirit was that he repeatedly argued that all knowledge must be based on observation experiments and things or phenomena that truly existed, and he was against fantasy or vague arguments that were beyond the nature of things or phenomena, from which Comte's positivist spirit that aimed to detach the supreme authority of pure imagination over previous knowledge was shown. The reason why he included "usefulness", "certainty," and "positiveness" as the elements of positivist spirit was that he stressed reality while belittling blabber. He was unsatisfied with the long unresting society after the French Revolution in 1789 and emphasized that all human knowledge should serve the stability and establishment of a new society. In his view, history left modern society with a great and noble intention that society would be able to use the experience it gained and utilize all materials it collected to construct buildings that suited it best and that it could enjoy. Therefore, Comte stressed repeatedly that knowledge should serve humans, thus treating "usefulness", "certainty," and "positiveness" as the elements of positivism. This illustrated the positivist spirit of Comte's philology to serve to reorganize society and stabilize social orders. Comte included "relativity" as the sixth element of his positivist concept, claiming that the old dogmatism of theology and metaphysics featured absoluteness. In contrast, positivist philosophy featured relativity, demonstrating the phenomenalism, relativism, and agnosticism of Comte's philosophy. Although in Comte's explanations of positivism, "reality" and "usefulness" were fundamental, these connotations were already included in the traditional explanations of positivism, but it was the Comte's uniqueness to have "relativity" as an element of positivist concepts, and he even made it an axis among all other elements. It could be said that the thinking of "all is relative" went through all of Comte's philosophical works. We should note that Comte included "sympathetic" (*sympatique*) as the seventh and the most fundamental element of positivist concepts in later times. This indicated that Comte focused on the knowledge connotation of positivist concepts in the early period while turning to the moral connotation later, namely a change from the positivism of scientific philosophy to that of morality.

To prove that positivism philosophy was advanced, Comte claimed to have discovered the law of three stages of human intellectual development. The law referred to that each branch of our knowledge developed through three theoretical stages: theological or fictitious, metaphysical, or abstract, and scientific or positive. In other words, all studies of the human spirit in each branch passed successively three different or opposite philosophical methods, namely the theological, metaphysical, and positive methods. Comte considered that the theological stage or method, as the primary stage of human intellectual development, had the features that the human spirit always wanted to explore the nature, primary cause, or ultimate cause of its surroundings, but the then-current science failed to explain phenomena, so it initially gave all external things a life-like feature, with Fetishism produced. Later, the theological spirit developed rapidly, and people, by free imagination, endowed illusionary existence with mysterious status; thus, Polytheism was developed, followed by Monotheism. To sum up, the theological spirit intended to attribute all natural phenomena in the universe to the role of supernatural initiators. As the secondary stage of human intellectual development, metaphysics or metaphysical method was merely an extension of the theological stage, which essentially featured the constant pursuit of absolute knowledge, according to Comte. However, it turned to imaginative and fabricated connections as the ultimate cause and nature of phenomena, replaced supernatural creators with abstract concepts to explain all phenomena, and specified ontologies with various phenomena. But this philosophical method was vague and meaningless. Comte held that the positivist stage or philosophical approach thereof, the supreme developmental stage of human intellectual, was utterly different from the previous two stages in a way that it was against the pursuit of absolute knowledge, the exploration of the origination and purpose of the universe, and rejection of understanding the causes of phenomena. In contrast, it was dedicated to exploring the laws of these phenomena; in other words, to discover the continuities and similar relationships of various phenomena. In this way, the positivist philosophical method fundamentally detached the supreme authority of pure imagination in previous knowledge and subordinated knowledge to observation, leading to a normal logical status.

Comte utilized positivism to study social developmental laws and created the discipline of sociology. Comte's sociology was established on the biological theories of human society. Before him, rationalists believed that humans were rational animals. In contrast, Comte disagreed with the definition of human nature and said that the definition by Scholasticism that humans were rational animals was meaningless. In fact, any animal, especially higher animals, were rational to some degree, and there was no difference between human nature and animal nature, except for that of degree. This way, Comte defined humans as a part of the animal world and treated them as a classification of general animals. Hence, Comte held that human society had no undetectable mysteries: regarding positivist biological science, since humans were a part of the general evolution of animals, human society was nothing but a result of biological evolution. In fact, human social development was the ultimate biological evolution that developed constantly and gradually from simple plants and tiny animals to the entire biological world of carnivores and apes. Thus, society was an organism that also followed the rule of biological evolution. Comte aimed to create a naturalistic social science that could explain the historical development of human beings and predict their future process. In addition to establishing a science that could explain the laws of human movement, Comte also intended to clarify the conditions affecting social stability in specific historical periods. He posited that we must use the scientific methods where we studied the natural world to study human society. Although human society was much more complex, it was still the same as the rest of the universe, following the basic laws. Comte held that natural science had successfully determined the laws of natural phenomena and a series of phenomena ranging from free-fall to planetary motion, believing that all obeyed orderly developmental processes. In the natural world, science succeeded in gradually narrowing down the areas that irregular and occasional phenomena relied upon on the surface. The current stage should do the same in social studies. Therefore, Comte applied evolutionism in social studies and affirmed the regularity of social evolution and historical development. In his opinion, all things, including those involving ourselves and society, abided by continuous and similar natural relations. The phenomenon of human life was easy to change compared with other natural phenomena but also followed an unchangeable law, and the main goal of positivism was to find the law. Comte conceived that the theory of the three-stage of human intellectual development applied to the history of human social development. Thus, he proposed the theory of the three-stage of historical development. Comte pointed out that the primary stage of human intellectual development was the theological stage, so the primary stage of historical development must be the military period of theology, in which all theoretical concepts, general or special, were supernatural, whereas all social relations, special or general, were out-and-out military-related, with conquer being the only external purpose of society. In this context, it mainly referred to the slavery period. The second historical period was the metaphysical jurist period, corresponding to the metaphysical period of human intellectual development, featuring in spiritual areas that observation was dominated by imagination, but it was allowed to change imagination within a limit. With the expansion of observation boundaries, it gained the power to study all special theories. This was a period of criticism and discussion. The feature of this period in secular areas represented a further industrial development, which had yet held the dominance, and thus society was not out-and-out military partly or as a whole but was yet industrial. Producers were still enslaved but started to have several rights against militants. The industry moved to a new era, and the progress gradually led to abolishing the individual slavery system. Society had two aims, to conquer and produce concurrently. Jurists held dominance in the political arena. This was a transition from a theological military period to a scientific industrial period. Factually, it referred to the feudal period in West Europe. The third historical period was the scientific industrial period, corresponding to the positivist period of human intellectual development. In this stage, all special and general theories and concepts were positive, with observation dominating imagination. In secular areas, however, the industry dominated. All special social relations were built upon industry, and production was the only external activity in society. This was the capitalist period. Comte held that the social form in this period suited human nature best, where all means for a prosperous society coincided with the soundest development of people and could be enjoyed directly.

The establishment of Comte's positivist philosophy was a revolution in the scientific research methodology. The fundamental feature of Comte's positivist method centered around the important proposition that "observation is better than imagination". According to him, human imagination was a need, and imagination's important and endless role was not terminated even for positivist thinking. However, as in other sciences, only under the dominance of observation would imagination play a completely subordinated role. It was exactly from this point that Comte viewed the establishment of his positivist philosophy as a revolution, which fundamentally featured the transfer of the dominance of imagination to observation, thus moving human's central position in the natural world to the actual position they had in the natural world so that that science could be alleviated from the speculative status to the positivist status. Therefore, one of the fundamental insights of Comte's positivist philosophy was to stress the role of observation as the core of the positivist spirit and to see observed facts as the foundation of scientific knowledge. Comte stressed that there was no real knowledge apart from that based on observed facts. He believed that external objects were human minds' external objects, but they had no nature or internal feature and existed as phenomena only. Our observations aimed not to extract their nature but to describe them only and discuss or judge these objects from themselves or multiple items. Comte's thinking was concluded by a later saying that "the positivist science only studies the ways (how) rather than the reasons (why)." He posited that all science must be built upon observed facts; hence, not only should natural sciences be subordinated to observation but all social sciences and even politics should be. In fact, humans gained scientific knowledge from observation and experiment overall, but it led to no conclusion that all scientific knowledge should be subordinated to observation. This was because not every scientific school was gained from direct observation experiments. Some were based on existing scientific theories and built on wild imagination and strict logical thinking; many scientific theories could not be tested by direct observation experiments but by mathematical methods and logic after they were established. If we said that all knowledge must be subordinated to observation, we would negate the scientific nature of some basic theories and their rights to exist, which imprisoned science in observation experiments and impeded modern science from developing. Therefore, Comte did not correctly figure out the dialectical relationships between perceptual knowledge and rational knowledge regarding epistemology. On the one hand, he considered observation and experiment as the fundamental ways to explore all things and phenomena and the perceptual experience through human observations as the source of understanding, so he placed great emphasis on perception. He held that if humans lost an important sense, they would not sense the entirety of a natural phenomenon, and on the other hand, if they gained a new sense, they would at least perceive a group of facts. It was precisely starting from this perception that Comte inhibited the role of rational thinking and imagination, viewed the perceptual experience as the only factor and parameter to determine the cognitive development, and argued that experience would be the only measure to provide us with power. The recognized tendency of Comte's positivist philosophy toward empiricism was expressed here, which restricted human perception within a given single fact and phenomenon by observation and made knowledge led by perception and experience. This was exactly the reason he stressed that all knowledge must be subordinated to observation. However, Comte was not an empiricist throughout. He posited that studying nature from the positivist perspective was valuable in the way that it provided people with a reasonable foundation. Thus, people needed a kind of realistic and consistent knowledge. If a piece of knowledge was strongly factual but irregular, it was, of course, incomplete to guide human activities. This way, Comte claimed to find out the laws of various phenomena through the combination of deductive reasoning and observation. In other words, to find relationships that were inherited and similar to various phenomena. That is to say, regarding the comprehensive problems of knowledge, Comte again stressed the role of rational thinking, arguing that human perception made humans ask for some theories first in any type of assignment, whether realistic or fantastic, vague or certain. Accordingly, even in any simple research realm, the human spirit tended to be earlier than observation, which was able to establish a certain opinion for corresponding phenomena. In this context, Comte was obviously jumping to the apriorism position. Thus, we can see that Comte, in no doubt, intended to conciliate empiricism and apriorism when dealing with the relationships between perpetual and rational knowledge. When he emphasized the role of experience, he was in the empirical position to suppress rational knowledge and proposed that all knowledge should be subordinated to observation. However, when he stressed the role of reason, he moved to the apriorism position and criticized empiricism, stating that empiricism was completely useless and fundamentally incompatible with human intellectual and claiming that all knowledge to be subordinated to human minds. As a result, Comte's positivism shows a dualism-like comprising feature, representing muddled and contradictory thinking. Overall, we must admit that Comte is an empiricist, or to be more exact, an incomplete or not absolute empiricist.

The positivist school of criminology is a criminal school that claims itself as positivism, especially the criminal school. To this end, Ferri claimed to be a part of the positivist school of criminology, also named criminal sociology. Ferri mentioned that Cesare Lombroso's work in 1872 marked the establishment of the positivist school of criminology. From 1872 to 1876, Lombroso first explored a new path for studying criminal acts by demonstrating that criminals must be understood before studying and understanding crimes. With anthropological views, Lombroso studied criminals in Italian prisons and published the famous book *The Criminal Man* in 1876, which was the embryo of this new school.[64] Lombroso's positivist school of criminology was deeply marked by positivism. Before Lombroso, the classical school of criminology mainly focused on criminal acts, and legal norms primarily restricted their research on criminal acts. Regarding research methods, the classical school pursued rational and dialectical thinking and isolated from individual cases, which limited its study of crimes within empty philosophy. On the other hand, Lombroso believed that crime was the act of human beings, so people who committed crimes must be studied before revealing the nature of crimes. Lombroso completed the transformation from crimes to criminals and from acts to actors. He started from observation, systematically observed and measured ten thousand criminals in Italian prisons and asylums and gathered first-hand information and data. Before Lombroso, quantitative research on crime had been conducted, especially the development of early criminal statistics, which laid a foundation for his study.

When discussing the establishment and development of early criminal statistics, we must mention three people: Quetelet, Lipley, and GoliDe Chapneuve. Quetelet is always considered the first sociologist to deduct criminological theories from crime statistics. His first book about criminal statistics was published in 1827. Although this book was basically narrative, the second criminal book in 1831 raised many variable relationships, including the crime rate between males and females of certain ages among national and social groups; more importantly, he emphasized the necessity to theoretically analyze observed information than narrative reports. In the research works published in 1839, Quetelet treated all kinds of crime rates based on the number of criminals and ordinary people and crimes committed as occasional rates. Generally speaking, his received information only included the number of crimes and features

[64] See [1], p. 6.

of criminals while lacking comparable information applicable to general citizens. To overcome the defect, he utilized the relative ratio. Quetelet has introduced a statistic table of the cross-classification of the French criminal reports in the past two years based on gender and education level. He inferred that criminal act was the outcome of criminal habits formed due to three factors: general criminal tendency, the skill to conduct specific acts, and the opportunity to conduct the act at a particular time. Another critical character that promotes the concept of the social statistical method is Lipley from France, living in the same period as Quetelet. However, unlike Quetelet, Lipley did not focus on official statistics research. He developed highly revolutionary statistics for studying cases, with family being the unit of his analysis. Lipley's methodology consisted of naturalistic observation and record, forming more abstract concepts and propositions from the collected information. The third vital character that promoted social statistics is Goli De Chapneuve, who collected and analyzed Paris's judicial statistics information and applied cartographic methods to explain them in 1829. Conceptually, Goli's research outcomes transcended the social determinism opinions in Quetelet's works which used simple statistics to verify hypotheses. In 1851, Quetelet advocated holding the first International Statistical Conference. The conference was held in 1853 and had ten types of statistics on its agenda, one of which was criminal statistics. The US criminologist Luce Salas and Raymond Surette mentioned in *Origination and Development of Criminal Statistics* that Quetelet, Lipley, and Goli's study showed that they had already deviated from the philosophy of free will while turning to determinism's positivism. The starting point of explaining social behaviors was not an imaginative status of nature but real and known crimes in reality. The analysis of moral statistics did not deduct truths from mutual analysis, nor did it try what things should be. It illustrated what it is now.[65]

The positivist school of criminology that Lombroso established introduced positivist methods and inherited the research achievements of criminal statistics, pushing the research of the science of criminal law, especially the research of criminology, into a scientific stage. Regarding positivist philosophy's impact on the positivist school of criminology, Ferri mentioned that in late-19th-century experimental philosophy, combining human biology, psychology, and natural study of human society, created an academic atmosphere that was especially suitable for real investigations on individual and social criminal phenomena. These general conditions must be studied with the comparisons between over-perfect criminal law and the increase of crimes and between criminal legal theories and numerous studies on the psychological features of criminals. From this point, nothing was more natural than creating a new school (whose objective was to conduct experimental research on sociopaths in terms of criminal symptoms so that theories about crime and punishment can be matched with everyday facts). This new school was the positivist school of criminology, whose primary objective was to study the origination of crime from criminals themselves and the natural and social environments they were living to take the most effective remedies against various causes of crimes. Hence, we not only cared about the explanations of anthropological and psychological theories or a series of criminal statistics,

---

[65] See [15], p. 219.

nor did we only care about establishing abstract legal theories to negate other more abstract theories. Our mission was to certify that every theoretical foundation of the self-defense of society against criminals must be the result of both individual and social observations of criminal acts by criminals. In a word, our mission was to establish criminal sociology.[66] It can be said that the scientific research methods of observation and experiment advocated by the positivist philosophy served as a catalyst for establishing the positivist school of criminology. Lombroso's conclusion of born criminals was biased, but his research work, as Barnes stated in the *International Encyclopedia of the Social Sciences Book*, became the starting point of science. Following Lombroso, Ferri, Garofalo, Liszt, and other scholars insisted on positivist research methods and explained crimes more scientifically, completing the construction of the theoretical system of the positivist school of criminology.

Clearly, naming the criminal law school that was created by Lombroso and developed by Ferri, Garofalo, and Liszt as positivism was precise. The US criminologists Richard Quinney and John Wildman mentioned that there was an obviously dominant genre in the history of criminology in western society which believed in positivism and thus developed positivist methodology. No matter how mixed its theories and research results were, no matter how its sub-schools deepened, and no matter how it succeeded in establishing its knowledge system during accumulation, until now, the history of criminology in western society had been unified by positivism that regarded crime as a reality that existed independently of people's responses to the behavior called crime.[67] So far, in terms of methodology, positivism still dominated western criminology, and the positivist methodology was still widely applied in criminology. This had to date back to Lombroso.

When the positivist school of criminology studied crimes with positivist methodology, it set out from observation, built conclusions upon strict scientific data, and thus ended the metaphysical period that speculated crimes abstractly and created a new era for the study of criminology. Nevertheless, it should not be ignored the same time that Lombroso's study of criminology inevitably brought about the shortcomings of the positivist methodology. Lombroso accepted crimes as reality and was satisfied with the cause-and-effect explanations of crimes but did not take further action to reveal the internal laws for the existence of crimes. Meanwhile, he ignored the limitations of positivist methods, thinking that all criminal problems could be explained by observation and experiments and dealt with complex criminal issues in a simplified manner. Therefore, Lombroso's criminological theory was the outcome of history with historical limitations for sure. As for this point, Ferri, Liszt, and other researchers transformed from the criminal anthropological school to the criminal sociological school, trying their best to explain criminal phenomena from social factors and producing progressive thinking of preventing crimes through social revolutions. However, generally speaking, the positivist methodology still bound the further expansion of thought. The US criminologists Richard Quinney and John Wildman made the following remarks on positivist criminology, which

[66] See [6], pp. 1–2.

[67] See [3], pp. 81–82.

hit the bullseye: the positivist way of thinking believed in the existence of order independent of observators and thus assumed the object; with a certain amount of knowledge by systematic accumulation, scientists could foresee the future and control situations. Positivism posited that all existing orders were good in the same way that positivism had no test on its assumptions of science. The official reality was the foundation for positivism to take effect, and it accepted and supported this foundation. Consequently, positivist criminals supported established systems. Traditionally, positivism focused on the violators of criminal laws instead of the legal systems themselves. The elimination of crimes was usually done through reforming violators but not legal systems.[68] As a result, Lombroso's positivism was a criminal pathology featuring political conservatism. Lombroso's two excellent students Ferri and Garofalo, showed this conservatism explicitly. They followed Mussolini's fascist system of rule in their future career. George B. Wald stated that the overall tendency of positivism was consistent with totalism as Ferri was for fascism in his later life, which clearly illustrated one of the intentions of the positivist theories, namely, it was easy to adapt to totalitarian governments. Ferri's study determined what criminals among the same generation were like and regulated proper treatments without the approval of people (criminals) who were given the diagnosis. There was an obvious similarity in the concept of social power control between positivism and the political reality where governments and bureaucracy had central control over citizens' lives and ignored democratic opinions.[69] Clearly, a specific feature embedded in the positivist methodology is an inherent condition for positivist criminology to become a tool for fascism to strengthen criminal repression. When we study criminal laws, we should not view crimes as an isolated social phenomenon or be satisfied with the pathological explanations of crimes. We should combine crimes and other social phenomena, especially crimes and economic and political systems, to reveal the general law for the existence of crimes and to create conditions for punishing and preventing crimes. Of course, I was not against the pathological study of crimes or the study of criminal law science, particularly the scientific significance of observation, experiment, and other positivist methods in the study of criminology. Instead, we should analyze criminal phenomena scientifically based on many positivist studies of crimes to reveal the general law of crimes. In this sense, positivist methods are still of significance for the current study of criminal law.

2.2 *View of Nature of Evolutionism*

Evolutionism is a scientific concept by the British scientist Darwin. On December 27, 1831, the 26-year-old Darwin started a five-year global voyage on the navy investigation vessel Beagle as a naturalist. In Darwin's later times, when he recalled the glorious risky career at his young age after almost 50 years of peaceful home

[68] See [3], p. 113.

[69] See [15], p. 208.

living, he said emotionally that the voyage on Beagle was the most critical event in his whole life, which determined his research career. Darwin read C. Lyell's works during this global voyage and accepted all his opinions on uniformitarianism. Darwin also collected numerous animal and plant specimens and fossils, observed volcanoes and barbarian Fuegians, and experienced earthquakes. When he was back, he published the Narrative of the surveying voyages of His Majesty's Ships Adventure and Beagle between 1826 and 1836 in 1839, which marked the transformation of Darwin's thinking from species immutability to species mutability. On November 24, 1859, Darwin's well-known work On the Origin of Species was published and sold out immediately. Once Darwin's evolutionism spread, it significantly impacted the development of human thinking. Darwin overthrew the view that treated animal and plant species as unrelated, occasional, divine-made, and unchangeable things, established biology on science totally for the first time, and determined the mutability and continuity of species. In On the Origin of Species, Darwin used numerous facts to prove an indisputable fact that humans originated from animals, which significantly promoted the biological research on humans, pushing anthology, biology, genetics, and other disciplines into a mature stage and laying a foundation for the scientific knowledge to introduce the research on social sciences. The positivist school of criminology was precisely established against this backdrop. Therefore, it was of great significance to deeply analyze evolutionism and the discipline groups it created, to understand the positivist school of criminology and, in particular, Lombroso's anthropological views of criminology.

Anthropology originates from the Latin word *anthropos* (human or humankind) and *logos* (science). Anthropology aims to explore all kinds of human evolution and survival issues, for example, when, where, and how humans landed on the Moon? Why do they have differences in physical features? What are the differences between distinct social traditional concepts and behaviors?[70] Before Darwin, the religious creed that humans were the creation of God held dominance in the European academic community, where there was no scientific, anthropological study at all.

Anthropology is a discipline developing with the existence of evolutionism. In the seventeenth and eighteenth centuries, there were two types of schools of evolutionism[71]: the first was the research of the evolutionism of the lifeless material world and inorganic evolution; the second was the research of the biological evolution or organic evolution. The inorganic evolutionary theory was founded by Kant, who proposed the commonly called nebular hypothesis theory and was developed by Laplace coupled with his mechanics. The theory tried to explain the origin of planets from the interaction between gravity and centrifugal force in rotating Nebula. The organic evolutionary theory was founded by Buffon, who drafted a generally deductive view of organic evolution in the mid-eighteenth century, stating that although species were created at the outset, they experienced occasional mutation and degeneration from generation to generation. Erasmus Darwin (grandfather of Charles Darwin) said that living things underwent different types of progressive changes.

[70] See [16], p. 1.

[71] See [17], pp. 1–117.

As a teacher, biologist and poet, Erasmus Darwin believed in the eternal improvement process in the natural world and held that living things were characterized by the ability to undergo progressive changes in structure, needs, and functions. Erasmus Darwin agreed with Hume, believing that our perceived world was not created but generated. This was a new and comprehensive reinvention of the theory of God creating the heaven and the earth originally preached by the Bible and a new belief in the purpose and progress of the cosmetic scale. After that, Lamarck developed Erasmus Darwin's insights and assumed that living things tended to a certain demand, purpose, and a priori. Lamarck was adept at zoology and botany, carefully studied the different statuses of organics, and created the term biology. Lamarck's theory raised the question of why specific accumulated mutations happened in organisms from generation to generation. Lamarck assumed that organisms had an internal, natural physical response to environmental changes and expounded that the innate response led to the structural change of organisms. When he argued for the issue that those features obtained through the adaption of the environment could be passed down to their offspring, his explanation of the nature of these obtained changes and how innate responses led to them was a bit confusing. Sometimes, he described this as an inherent tendency for organisms to become progressively more complex, and the meaning was clearly consistent with Erasmus Darwin's purposeful direction. Sometimes, he discussed that local conditions completely brought about innate responses and corresponding organism changes. Lamarck's theory included three steps: first, organisms lived in natural environments and dealt with situations with innate responses that adapted to the environment properly. Second, these situations should be compliant and used by an organ. Third, the use of an organ was then being developed until it was inherited by the next generation and became acquired characteristics. Buffon explained variation in the degeneration process or occasional deviations from the original form. At the same time, Lamarck followed Erasmus Darwin, turning over the process and arguing that evolution started from simple, early stages to increasingly complex organic gains. His theory was easily dismissed, but the basic ideas about the role of tension, pressure, desire, purpose, or the role by whatever impulsive and creative factors must be given increasing attention. Not long before Lamarck proposed this theory, there was a debate between Saint-Hilaire and Cuvier. Saint-Hilaire argued for Lamarck's evolutionary theory despite disagreements over its mechanism. However, Cuvier insisted on his theory of catastrophes and refused to accept evolutionary theories on the grounds of lacking evidence. The historical mission to collect evidence to prove the authenticity of evolution and evolutionary mechanisms were assigned to Darwin. Darwin's importance was not because he was the first to think about problems from the evolutionary perspective but because he realized that problems could only be sought by numerous and sorted evidence and methods. Darwin's immortal works made people give up the belief that the world was immutable, and Darwin displayed the cruel, ubiquitous, and unguided changes with facts and information. Darwin's evolutionism is based on the grounds that there was a considerable variation among individuals of the same species, in which an individual might be more suitable or not suitable for environmental requirements. For most species, the total number was stable, although the next generation was more than the previous one. In fish, each pair of ancestors might release hundreds of thousands of eggs, and all but two individuals must be eliminated. This led to the view of survival of the fittest directly. If an organism adapted well to gaining food and defending enemies in an environment, it was the fittest. It must survive and develop till it was able to give birth again. But if there were both the survival of the fittest and the adaption to the environment (this was the necessity for the survival itself), the adaptation to the environment must mean that it was only the best fittest in a certain environment that could survive. If it was the fittest in each generation that could survive, and if the environment changed after several years, the result would be the change in the individual species that could survive. Since it was a continuity that the same species moved to different regions and competed for survival through generations, the individuals that adapted to each region completely would have variations with individuals adapting to other regions; there would be selections in each region if there was an adaptation to the requirements of that area or that adaptive living environment. Darwin's evolutionism scientifically illustrated the dialectical relationships between the adaptation and selection in the origin of species. Darwin's evolutionary theory of natural selection benefited the description of general changes among species and the appearance of new species. Because when different species adapted to distinct environments or lifestyles, they would become more diverse in structure or behavior due to crossbreeding. In other words, they would become separate species. According to Darwin's opinion, the process—the adaption to different environments and situations—illustrated the huge changes in various species observed in the nature.[72]

Evolutionism put forward the development of anthropology remarkably. As Dampier said, among academics restored by Darwin, anthropology benefitted most from the comparative study of humans. As a matter of fact, it was fair enough to say that modern anthropology started from *On the Origin of Species*.[73] Anthropology could be divided into two parts: physical anthropology and cultural anthropology. Physical anthropology tried its best to answer two sets of different questions: the existence and evolution of humans (which the branch of fossil anthropology or paleoanthropology studied) and the variations in biological characteristics of contemporary human inhabitants and why these variations existed (which another branch of the physical anthropology studied).[74] In this context, ethnology was a discipline that studies individual humans and ethnicity with evolutionary theories, whose founder was Francis Galton. In 1869, ten years after the publication of *On the Origin of Species*, Galton published the book *Hereditary Genius* to testify that individual greatness was derived from parentage and the regularity and certainty of this situation were inconsistent with any environment-based interpretation. This study was mostly the investigation of the family trees of genius jurists, scientists, authors, and other characters. The information Galton collected proved that in each case, these characters not only inherited the genuineness from what their numerous ancestors had displayed

[72] See [18], p. 18.

[73] See [16], pp. 5–6.

[74] See [19], p. 381.

but also the specific forms of talents from them. A distinguished jurist or lawyer tended to come from a not-just-ordinary famous family but a prominent family in law. This theory assumed in advance that in a particular past time, there were variations that were likely to be saved in the human lineage. Galton asserted that Darwin's occasional variation principle centering around the average or standard value of a group also applied to humans of average talent and specific talent, just the same way as that to the length of birds' wings or that of polar bear's hair, and these variations tended to retain continually. He also compared the hereditary features of different races and noted that the development of different races resulted from their adaptability to specific environments. Darwin has posted some examples to prove that the skin, limb proportion, and other physical features were adaptable to their lifestyles in certain climate conditions. Galton held that variations did exist among individuals, and what also existed was extensive variations and selection from which new races could develop. Such thinking that was bound to trigger a heated and deep debate would lead to exaggeration. Galton's extremely vital belief in hereditary seemed to be best expressed in the following statements. He further summarized after talking about the study of criminal anthropometry: the lack of conscience among criminals, as indicated by their failure to regret their sins, sincerely surprised all the people who, for the first time, got familiar with the details of prison life. Rarely could be seen the scenario where criminals were frustrated and disappointed. They were never disturbed by nightmares. Galton thought that biological conditions limited all these. Individuals were born with skull and facial features, which were differentiated by talents and retards and equipped with an inherent evil temperament.[75]

Darwin's evolutionism exerted a far-reaching influence on the then-current European academic circle. As a view of nature, it changed people's opinions on society concurrently and thus influenced the development of social sciences. As US scholars Gardner Murphy and Joseph Valachi indicated, evolutionism had been deeply rooted in the understandings and discussions of the social sciences in the nineteenth century. Nevertheless, most of them were evolutionary theories before Darwin. Social scientists explored a new path for transmitting social changes and progressive thinking. People were convinced that from then on, their fates could be improved by themselves. New rules that pursued progress were designed, and people's passion and religiosity in Teleology were no less than their attitudes toward "God creating the heaven and the earth" in early times. However, people had not thoroughly learned from the historical development of Darwin's evolutionism's rationales and evolutionary theories. New combinations of evolutionary thinking did not always estimate the continuous and sophisticated multidimensionality in the random variant natural selection. More importantly, they did not always estimate scientific methods and scientific understanding of nature (including the understanding of human nature and social changes), which was developed by the consistency between thinking and facts, while thinking itself was dominated by gradual evolution.[76] The mid-nineteenth century, when the positivist school of criminology emerged, was exactly

[75] See [17], p. 192.

[76] See [17], pp. 201–202.

a period when natural science that was marked by Darwin's evolutionism developed greatly. Engels has discussed the development of natural science of the nineteenth century incisively in his famous book *Ludwig Feuerbach and the End of Classical German Philosophy* that: until the end of the last century (referring to the eighteenth century; noted by the quoter), natural science was a science that mainly collected information and that was about established things, but in this century (referring to the nineteenth century; noted by the quoter), natural science, in essence, was a science that sorted out information and that was about process and the existence, development, and relationships of these things—the combination of these natural processes into an entirety. The Physiology, which studied the processes of plant and animal organisms; the Embryology, which studied the development of individual organisms from embryos to maturity; and the Geology, which studied the gradual formation of the crust, was all the outcomes of our century. Nonetheless, first of all, the three findings promoted our understanding of the interconnection of the natural process: the first was the finding that cell was such a unit that all plants and animals developed from its reproduction and differentiation. Because of this, not only were we aware that all higher organisms developed and grew based on a common rule, but we noted that a path that enabled organisms to change their species and achieve a higher development than the individual one through the differentiation ability of cells. The second was energy transformation, which showed us that all the forces, namely the mechanical force and its supplements, that acted in the inorganic natural world and the potential energy, heat, radiant energy (luminous energy or thermal radiation), and electrical, magnetic, and chemical energy, were all various forms of universal movement, which transformed from one to another according to some measurement relations. Thus, when a form of energy vanished, another form of energy replaced it with a certain amount, and all movements in the natural world could be concluded into the transformation process from one form to another. Finally, Darwin proved from the first connection that organic naturals, including humans, that existed around us currently were all the outcomes of the long-term development of a minority of original single-cell embryos, which were formed by chemically produced protoplasm or proteins.[77] Undoubtedly, the development of natural science created conditions for the reformation of social sciences. As a sharp-minded scientist, Lombroso absorbed merits from the latest research achievements of natural sciences directly and indirectly. His superior background of being a natural scientist enabled him to handle anything related to natural science proficiently. If we investigated the positivist school of criminology in the mid-nineteenth century unbiased, we could say that the positivist school led the generation in applying natural sciences to study crimes and criminals. One of the representatives of the positivist school, Ferri, discussed the profound impact of scientific development, especially that of Darwin's evolutionism on the positivist school. Ferri mentioned that by annihilating the great fantasy that dominated civilized humans for the last few centuries, we could see the impact of science. The scientific thinking of Copernicus and Galileo had eliminated people's fantasy that the earth was the center of the universe. Reading Cicero's *On Duties* and

[77] See [20], p. 245.

Dante's *Divine Comedy*, you would notice that they believed that the earth was the center of the universe, orbited by countless planets and that humans were the king of animals. This was an earth-centered and human-centered fantasy produced due to lots of far-fetching. Nevertheless, Copernicus and Galileo proved that the earth was not still. It was a particle that shot into the universe, revolved around the sun from ancient times, and was originally countless Nebulas. Galileo was sentenced to death when someone realized that this new theory would overthrow many religious legends and moral creeds. But Galileo told the truth. Nowadays, humans would no longer be addicted to the fantasy that the earth was the center of the universe. Human lives depended on fantasy. However, with scientific development, people had to part reluctantly with what they treasured to do their best to accept the new law produced from the universe (humans were a part of it). Even though the earth-centered theory disappeared, the human-centered theory still existed. People believed that humans were the king of all things on earth and the center of terrestrial creatures. All animals, plants, and minerals were created especially for humans, and since ancient times they had been in the same forms as we saw today. Thus, we could say that any animal and plant that grew on the earth were the same since ancient times. Nonetheless, in 1856, Charles Darwin concluded the research achievements of the century and shattered the illusion that humans were the king and center of all things in the name of science. To fight against the attacks and defamation by the dark sides, he argued that humans were not the king of all things but the last stage of animal evolution merely. The natural world was filled with eternal dynamics, and animals, plants, and minerals (biochemical laws worked even in crystals) evolved from invisible microbes to the highest form—humans. The fantasy of human-centered theory had to vanish in front of scientific achievements, and Darwin's theory has been deeply rooted in our minds nowadays.[78] In our views, the impact of Darwin's evolutionism on Lombroso, the father of the anthropological school of criminologists, can be explained from at least the following two aspects:

From a macro perspective, Darwin's idea that humans originate from animals is another major revolution in understanding human beings following Copernicus. It was the Geocentric model that held dominance before Copernicus, believing that the earth was the center of the universe and humans were the masters of the earth, so was the human-centered theory formed. Since humans were the creations of God, God did exist. Copernicus overthrew the Geocentric model, stating that it was the earth revolving around the sun, not vice versa, and thus proposed Heliocentrism. His Heliocentrism gave a big strike to the human-centered theory and served as a significant challenge to the existence of God. But his Heliocentrism did not overthrow the human-centered theory thoroughly, and considerable people believed in the idea of God creating humans. Darwin explained with many facts that humans were derived from animals and shared the same ancestor as apes, which fundamentally shook the religious concept that God created humans and enabled people to understand their position in nature correctly. As the famous British biologist Huxley said: after the disappearance of passion and biases, we could seek the same result from

[78] See [1], pp. 18–20.

the guidance of naturalists about the great Alps and Andes in the natural world—humans. We did not level down the nobility of humans because they shared the same materials and structures as animals. Because only humans enjoyed the talent to create understandable and reasonable languages, which humans relied upon to gradually accumulated and organized experience when they were alive. These experience was lost when animals were dead. Therefore, humans seemed to stand on the top of a vast mountain, far exceeding their lowly partners' levels, transforming from their barbarian nature, and emitting illumination from the indefinite source of the truth.[79] Hence, we can see that Darwin reduced divinely-coated humans to secular humans. Humans have their weaknesses and wisdom. Humans are humans. It is in this academic atmosphere that the idea of Lombroso attributing crimes to genetically born criminals comes out. Because under the governance of the human-centered theory, humans were considered to be created by God, who was a perfect, free-will, and rational animal. In this case, humans committed crimes because of the devil's haunts or occasional depravation, and the mission of the law was to arise human rationality to be repented. While according to Lombroso's opinions, crimes were the result of genetics, atavistic phenomena and determined by biological features, and there existed born criminals. The argument that deprived of human rationality and dignity with biology imposed the same great challenge on the human-centered theory as Darwin's zoobiquity but was a logical conclusion based on Darwin's evolutionary ideas on crimes.

From a micro perspective, Darwin's evolutionary contents exerted a significant impact on Lombroso as well. Darwin's evolutionism has two core propositions: the origin of species and the origin of adaptation. Based on the proposition of the origin of species, species were mutable, and evolution proceeded with the evolution of species. The currently existing species on the earth were offspring of ever-existing species derived from the same ancestors. The origin of species stresses the historical continuity among species, from which the hereditary concept could be extended. Inheritance was the general term for all biological processes that led to similar traits among parents and children. The core of inheritance was the continuity among species where parents passed down their biological features to the next generation via genes. According to the proposition of the origin of adaptation, various species adapted to a specific living condition respectively through the common origin and divergent developments and displayed colorful adaptation phenomena. The thinking of the origin of adaptation paid much attention to the discontinuity among species, from which proposition extended the concept of differentiation, namely, there were differences in traits between parents and children premised by inheritance. In the proposition of the origin of adaptation, Darwin proposed the selection doctrine of the struggle for survival and survival of the fittest. Lombroso's early works mainly accepted Darwin's first concept—inheritance, thinking that crimes could be transferred to the next generation via genes, and thus, born criminals existed. Many criminologists harshly criticized the theory of born criminals from the beginning. Impacted by Lombroso's students Ferri and other people, in Lombroso's later works, he reduced

[79] See [21], pp. 102–103.

the ratio of born criminals to the total number of criminals and stressed depravation, which in fact marked the acceptance of Darwin's second concept—differentiation, namely, parents had no criminal genes and children committed crimes, not because of inheritance (thus not innated) but depravation (a differentiation).

Lombroso's works show a lot of data and diagrams, showing a totally different style from *On Crimes and Punishments*, a work of the scholar of the classical school of criminology, Beccaria. If we say Beccaria's works are full of the glamor of rationality and wisdom and strict systems composed of logic and reasoning, then Lombroso's works represent the positivist spirit, relying more on data and diagrams as evidence. Hence, Lombroso is the pioneer of introducing natural science, especially biology, into the study of criminology, a qualified doctor and psychiatrist rather than a criminologist. In other words, Lombroso is first a doctor and psychiatrist and then a criminologist. When US criminologists Richard Quinney and John Wildman finally argued why Lombroso's ideas were recognized, they listed the following six reasons: (1) the prestige of natural science, especially biology. Biology was the core of Lombroso's theory. (2) The use of "new" and "positivist" terms brought about prestige and stimulations for the exploration and discussion of criminology, which enabled Lombroso's criminology to lead in the late nineteenth century. (3) The idea of using physical features to represent traits enjoyed a long history in Europe; thus, the idea was easily accepted. (4) The positivist ideas and methods in biological criminology were long accepted and highly reputed by doctors, psychologists, chemists, and local judges. (5) The emphasis on personal inferiority supported national political construction. (6) The tendency to positivism and biology benefitted countries in finding excuses to enhance social control.[80] Among the six reasons mentioned earlier, Quinney and Wildman prioritized applying natural science, especially biology, in criminological theories, which was insightful. For a long time, we were utterly hostile to Lombroso and his methodology since it was considered outrageous to use natural science to study crimes, and thus criminal biology was dismissed as pseudoscience. In my opinion, criminals are humans who display anthropological and biological features. Hence, the study of anthropology and biology is critical, and it is the anthropological school of criminologists founded by Lombroso that moves toward this historically meaningful path.

2.3 *Value of Society as Standard for Education*

If we say that the classical school of criminology is established upon the individual-centered value and stresses the function of criminal laws to guarantee human rights, then the positivist school of criminology is based on the social-centered value and highlights the social protective function of criminal law. The major transformation from the individual-centered value to the social-centered value happened in the late nineteenth century and early twentieth century against the deep social

[80] See [3], pp. 52–53.

backdrop of capitalism transiting from free trade to monopoly. Under this circumstance, the thinking of natural law reflecting the individual-centered value did not suit social demands, whereas various schools of thought reflecting social-centered value emerged constantly. As the representative of the social solidarist school of law, Duguit pointed out, "I have remarked that the individualistic, subjectivist and metaphysical legal systems we brought about from the Roman ages and the Middle Ages where scholasticism was popular are outdated. Such complicated and various relationships arising between individuals and collectives are impossible to be bounded by the old-time scope, and we must completely rule out the metaphysical concept of the substance of the law, subject of rights, and subjective rights, and this metaphysical notion as a source of inconclusive controversy. I have added that only such a rule was and would be indisputable, which must be based on society itself and provide for some positive and negative obligations for people of the same group. However, these obligations did not involve the essence of human will and only took the responses in the group as sanctions when obligations were violated."[81] Once this social-centered value was established, it had a profound impact.

The social-centered value involves understanding society, to be more precise, the understanding of the relationships between people and society. What does society mean? Western classical thinkers have two main explanations of society: first, mixing up society with the nation. For example, Plato replaced the grounds for establishing nations with the needs for establishing society, holding that people's need for living was the only reason for the country's existence. This made people feel that the nation was necessary for their lives. Second, differentiating society from the country. For instance, Aristotle regarded family, village, and city-state (nation) as social groups, and the nation is the supreme and extensive social group and an organization for people to lead a good life.[82] In Greek city-state life, a free man had two identities at the same time: first, he was the city resident of the specific city-state, and in this sense, he belonged to himself and was a private man seeking his interests. Second, he was the citizen of a specific nation, and in this sense, he belonged to the nation and was a public man. Hence, there was a division between city residents and citizens and between society and nation in Greek city-state life. The Romans also differentiated public and private. They named the laws that adjusted the private interest relationships as private laws and that adjusted public interest relationships as public laws. The so-called private interest relationships referred to civil society, and the so-called public interest relationships referred to political nations.[83] Till the Renaissance, a movement for the revival of Roman laws emerged, and private laws prospered because they suited the development of the capitalist commodity economy. Civil society was more and more powerful and became a force balancing political nation. To prevent city residents from the intervention of the nations, the national power was controlled by the constitution to guarantee individual freedom and rights of citizens. In this case, the so-called society is called the civil society, the community of city residents.

[81] See [22], pp. 7–8.

[82] See [23], p. 8.

[83] See [24].

Before capitalism entered the monopoly stage, the nation enhanced its intervention in the social economy; thus, the tendency toward the public law becoming private law existed, with the boundary between the nation and society gradually diminishing till vanishing. In this context, the emphasis on social-centered value meant the supremacy of national interests. Meanwhile, it means that citizens' individual interests should be subordinated to national ones. Therefore, there was a significant change in the relationships between individuals and society. In civil society, social interests were citizens' individual interests. Between individuals and society, emphasis was given to common social interests, which aimed to safeguard citizens' individual interests and thus served as a kind of individual-centered value. However, dominated by the social-centered value, society referred to the nation, had supremacy over individuals, and individuals were required to sacrifice their interests to obey the nation.

The social-centered value led to a re-understanding of society, from which a specific discipline—sociology, was introduced. There were sociologist schools, among which two sociological thinking had a profound impact on the sociologist school of criminology, which was the sociobiological school and the structural sociologist school. The sociobiological school was also named social evolutionism or social organism theory. Social evolutionism was created by the French positivist philosopher Comte, who thought that human society was the ultimate biological evolution and an organism much more complicated and special than common creatures, which must follow biological evolutionary laws. Thus, sociology that aimed to study social phenomena and reveal the laws of social life must be based on evolutionism. Even in Comte's later time, he still emphasized the similarity between sociology and biology and considered this concept the foundation of social sciences. Comte's first argument on introducing evolutionism into sociology was: that social history itself was the same as the natural world, especially the biological world, which was a constant evolutionary process, and not any society or social stage was isolated. All of them were placed in the evolutionary chain of society as a whole and interconnected. Hence, the second critical positivist premise of the sociological study was always regarding the current social status as the necessary result of the entire previous evolution, and every social revolution could be traced back. In Comte's opinion, the change in the human spirit and the progress of scientific knowledge were the decisive factors of social development. Since Comte defined society as a study subject isolated from individuals and determined the evolutionary laws of the development of society itself, society reaped a significant meaning independent of individuals for the first time. As the US sociologist, Lewis A. Coser has mentioned: when Comte dealt with the components of the social system, he never viewed individuals as a unit. Scientific spirits prohibited us from seeing society composed of individuals. The true social unit is family; if necessary, it could be broken down into the couples who were the basis of a family. A family turned into a tribe, and a tribe became a nation. If social sciences viewed individual needs as its starting point, it would fail. It was even more wrong to deduce the social tendency that had been proved to be inherent in human nature from considering human utility. In the early stages of humans, there remained a doubt over whether individual interests in society existed. Obviously, if the reason for society to exist was that people believed to benefit from it, society would never exist.[84] Following Comte, it was the British positivist philosopher Spencer that studied human society from the biological perspective. Spencer proposed the theory of social organism, stating that there was an unknowable eternity of force behind phenomena, which served as the foundation of all phenomena and the source of all experience. It was from the eternity of force that Spencer introduced the all-embracing evolutionary doctrine. In his opinion, from the formation of the celestial body to the origin of species and races, from the inorganic world to the organic world, and from natural areas to human society, they were all dominated by evolutionary laws. Then, what was evolution? Spencer believed that evolution was the synthesis of things. When things were synthesized, they did not move, during which objects evolved from an indeterminate, dispersed homogeneous state to a definite, condensed heterogeneous state. Therefore, evolution was the transition from an indeterminate, dispersed homogenous state to a definite, condensed heterogeneous state. Spencer was also keen on explaining social phenomena from evolutionary laws and introducing biological concepts into social sciences to endow sociology with some biological features. For instance, Spencer introduced his evolutionary doctrines into the field of social history, thinking that social history was as evolutionary as biological organisms. When specifying social evolution, he introduced the principle of natural selection and the survival of the fittest into biology, thinking that the process of social evolution, as a biological evolutionary process, was dominated by the principle of the survival of the fittest. Spencer then proposed the doctrine of the survival of the fittest, explained all relationships among individuals, nationalities, and nations with these biological concepts, and believed there must be competition for survival among them. Spencer posited that society was a "superorganism". This meant that the way for social organizations to become a unity was the same as organs to become a biological unity. Both grew and became mature and declined if organisms were unsound. Therefore, the good status of social organisms was balanced: a balance between individuals, groups, and classes. Social relations, population scale, and the system's nature played a role in this balanced status. For instance, supply and demand were adjusted to satisfy needs, national policies responded to population needs, and population increase was limited by those conditions (especially food supply), as Malthus said. All these adjustments would benefit the integration of the entire society. Nevertheless, the balance was not equal to peaceful coexistence, and it was even so in the early stage of social development. It was an unstable and temporary condition, making a struggle for survival. The sociobiology advocated by Comte and Spencer viewed society as an entirety possessing independent organisms and self-value. This thinking directly impacted the sociologist school of criminology. The theory of social defense claimed by Ferri was established upon this theory. Ferri regarded crimes as social diseases, which drew a demarcation line from the view that crimes were individual moral sins. According to Ferri, crime was the same as poverty, population, and war, which arose from natural and social causes, and only social remedies could be sought to treat social diseases. To survive, society should take all measures against criminals to eliminate the social disease of crime.

[84] See [25], p. 10.

Thus, Ferri established criminal responsibility upon social defense. As US criminologists Richard Quinney and John Wildman have mentioned: the responsibility view that positivists introduced relied upon social needs rather than free will or moral sins. Ferri articulated the positivist claim of the individual's responsibility to society, "Each man should always be responsible for his acts, and the only reason is he lives in this society and did the act." In positivists' views, we should first determine whether the defendant is a criminal before taking measures to prevent criminals from committing crimes again based on criminal sentences. The meaning of positivists' criminal sentence can be seen from Garofalo's penalty theories, which were built upon people's ability to adapt to society.[85]

Structural sociology studies crimes from the perspective of social structure and emphasizes the study of social facts. The main representative of structural sociology is the famous French sociologist Dürkheim (Emile Dürkheim). Dürkheim first investigated what social phenomena were and held that they were behavioral patterns, ways of thinking, and ways of thinking imposed on everyone through a coercive force at the same time. These phenomena differed from those of organisms, and the latter existed through some forms and actions. They were also distinct from psychological phenomena, which existed only in individual consciousness and were expressed through individual consciousness. In a word, these phenomena featured a new nature, and only the term "social" could illustrate its nature and meaning. Because individuals could have "inorganic" and "non-psychological" phenomena, and only society had them. The term "social" would have definite significance only when it expressed a synthetic phenomenon and a phenomenon that was separated from individual phenomena. Such phenomena were specifically possessed by sociology.[86] Dürkheim argued that social phenomena were social facts with unique features and decisive roles and could not stand the test if biological or psychological principles explained them. Social facts did exist for individuals who served as the object of creatures, and when a specific individual passed away or was replaced by others, the facts still exist eternally. Besides, social facts had a coercive force that pushed them to override above all social members and their independent individual will. Whether the coercive force appeared in the form of laws or customs, it always acted when social interests were violated. It overrode individuals, guided individual needs, and affected how individuals think. Therefore, a social fact could be defined as a fixed or non-fixed way with objective constraints on individuals. Hence, Dürkheim was against the social theory of individual tendency, thinking that society could not be produced from individual tendencies that cheated on each other for maximum happiness. Dürkheim proposed the social integration theory, which in this context referred to the process of social members exchanging the moral regulations premised by the existence of unified moral regulations.[87] He also discussed criminal problems from the perspective of social structure, holding that criminals were normal and even had a positive role in society regarding criminal behaviors.

[85] See [3], p. 51.

[86] See [26], p. 5.

[87] See [27], p. 156.

The crime was normal, which meant that society could not compel all its members to object to social orders; otherwise, individual contributions to society would be inhibited. Society should be flexible and adapt to new reforms, which inevitably gave birth to the phenomena that were against social norms. Where there were criminal behaviors, these behaviors tended to influence the collective awareness to choose new forms of social governance flexibly. Indeed, crime merely indicated an expectation of future ethics, which was a step toward the future. Apart from the direct consequences of criminal behaviors, Dürkheim also illustrated the indirect role of crimes of the same significance. He deduced that criminal behaviors could evoke the public emotions toward opposing social regulations, from which social bans were triggered. Therefore, criminal behaviors had unexpected effects that led to and strengthened the common normative consciences to protect public welfare. Crime evoked and attracted a sense of justice. Dürkheim analyzed social phenomena, whose features mainly were as Lewis A. Coser indicated: that we must consider the distinctiveness of social phenomena when we insisted on applying the deduction to the study of society. Dürkheim was against biological or psychological explanations of human social problems but paid attention to the decisive role of social structure.[88] The sociologist school of criminology was a school of criminology that set sociology as its example, and Ferri and Liszt gave much attention to analyzing crimes from the social structure perspective. Ferri mentioned that: in my opinion, general sociology could only make general and common deductions on social lives. Against this backdrop, a few branch disciplines of sociology were all built upon the specific study of different social situations. With this method and studying the special rules of human normal social behaviors after studying the general rules of individual and collective lives, we could establish political sociology, economic sociology, and legal sociology. Therefore, based on this goal and with this method and by studying abnormal or antisocial behaviors in humanity, or to say, by studying crimes and criminals, we could establish criminal sociology.[89] If we say Ferri's thinking includes views of biological sociology, then Liszt can be regarded as a criminologist who mainly absorbed structural sociology's thinking to study crimes. Although differentiating the social and individual factors that produce criminal acts, Liszt emphasized the incomparable importance of social factors over individual factors. He created a formula that limits social factors in the social surroundings of criminals: on the one hand, criminal behaviors are the result of criminals committing crimes; on the other hand, they are the result of the surroundings, especially the economic environment, when criminals committed crimes.[90] Liszt pays much attention to the constraints of social-economic, political, and cultural systems on crimes and claims to reform social systems to eliminate the social roots of crimes.

The social-centered value establishes the independent significance of society, emphasizes the analysis of social functions and structures, and thus shapes the cultural characteristics of the positivist school of criminology.

---

[88] See [25], p. 146.

[89] See [6], p. 2.

[90] See [28], p. 139.

References

1. [Italy] E. Ferri, *Positivist School of Criminology: Three Lectures* (China University of Political Science and Law Press, Beijing, 1987)
2. [Italy] Lombroso, *Criminal Man* (China Legal Publishing House, Beijing, 2000)
3. [US] Q. Richard et al., *The Problem of Crime* (China International Radio Press, Beijing, 1988)
4. [US] T. Lawrence, *Born to Crime: The Genetic Causes of Criminal Behavior* (Quzhong Publishing House, Beijing, 1986)
5. [France] Montesquieu, *The Spirit of the Laws* (The Commercial Press, Beijing, 1961)
6. [Italy] E. Ferri, *Criminal Sociology* (People's Public Security University of China Press, Beijing, 1990)
7. Y. Gan, P. He, *Foreign Criminal Jurisprudence,* vol. 1 (Peking University Press, Beijing, 1984)
8. [Soviet Union] A.H. Traninin, *General Theory of Constitution of a Crime* (Renmin University of China, Beijing, 1985)
9. Y. Gan, P. He, *Foreign Criminal Jurisprudence,* vol. 2 (Peking University Press, Beijing, 1985)
10. [Italy] Beccaria, *On Crimes and Punishments* (Encyclopedia of China Publishing House, Beijing, 1993)
11. [UK] Bentham, *Theory of Legislation* (People's Public Security University of China Press, Beijing, 1993)
12. Compiled and Translated by K. Zhao, *Introduction to Criminology* (China University of Mining and Technology Press, Xuzhou, 1989)
13. [Italy] Garofalo, *Criminology* (Encyclopedia of China Publishing House, Beijing, 1996)
14. [US] Pound, *Interpretation of Legal History* (Huaxia Publishing House, Beijing, 1989)
15. Compiled by The Teaching and Research Section for Legal Practice Studies of China University of Political Sciences and Law, *Introduction to Criminology* (China University of Political Sciences and Law, Beijing, 1985)
16. [US] C. Ember et al., *Cultural Variation: A General Theory of Modern Cultural Anthropology* (Liaoning People's Publishing House, Shenyang, 1988)
17. [US] M. Gardner et al., *Historical Introduction to Modern Psychology* (The Commercial Press, Beijing, 1987)
18. [US] F. Plog et al., *Cultural Anthropology* (Liaoning People's Publishing House, Shenyang, 1988)
19. [UK] W.C. Dampier, *A History of Science,* vol. 2 (The Commercial Press, Beijing, 1975)
20. *Marx-Engels-Gesamtausgabe,* vol. 4, 2nd edn. (People's Publishing House, Beijing, 1995)
21. [UK] Huxley, *Man's Place in Nature* (China Science Publishing & Media, Beijing, 1971)
22. [France] L. Duguit, *Treatise on Constitutional Law* (The Commercial Press, Beijing, 1962)
23. H. Yuan, *A History of Western Social Thought* (Nankai University Press, Tianjin, 1988)
24. G. Xu, Civil society and civil law. J. Legal Stud. (4) (1994)
25. [US] L.A. Coser, *Masters of Sociological Thought* (China Social Sciences Press, Beijing, 1990)
26. [France] Durkheim, *The Rules of Sociological Method* (Huaxia Publishing House, Beijing, 1988)
27. C. Jia (Editor-in-Chief), *History of Foreign Sociology* (Renmin University of China Press, Beijing, 1989)
28. [Germany] H.J. Schneider, *Criminology* (China People's Public Security University of China Press, Beijing, 1990)

Chapter 4
Freedom of Will: A History of Theories

By comparing the assumptions of human nature between the classical school of criminology and the positivist school of criminology, we can find that the key to the differences in understanding human nature between the two schools lies in whether people have free will. The classical school assumes man as a rational person, thereby affirming man's free will, while the positivist school of criminology assumes man as an experienced man, thereby denying man's free will. Therefore, an in-depth investigation of the criminal law thinking of the classical school and the positivist school of criminology is impossible to exclude the issue of free will. There is no doubt that free will is first and foremost a philosophical problem, but it is closely related to law, especially criminal law, and can be said to be a prerequisite basis for criminal law theories. Engels pointed out, "It is hard to deal with morality and law without coming up against the question of so-called free will, of man's mental responsibility, of the relation between necessity and freedom."[1]

With the awakening of human self-awareness, the issue of free will began to arouse the thinking of philosophers of all ages. This thinking led to disputes between schools and confrontations between various points of view, which lasted for thousands of years. However, it still maintains its attractiveness. Plekhanov once put it, "The old but eternally new question of freedom and necessity rose up before the idealists of the nineteenth century, just as it had arisen before the metaphysicians of the preceding century, and as it arose before absolutely all the philosophers who had concerned themselves with questions of the relationship of being and thought. Like a sphinx it said to each such thinker: unravel me, or I shall devour your system!"[2] Free will is such a Sphinx myth that has devoured the system of countless thinkers. The historical investigation of theories on the issue of free will is undoubtedly a prerequisite for solving this Sphinx myth.

The famous British philosopher Russell wrote, "The contradiction between free will and determinism is one of those that run through philosophy from early times

[1] See [1], p. 454.

[2] Plekhanov[2], p. 87.

X. Chen, *Humanistic Foundation of Criminal Law*,
https://doi.org/10.1007/978-981-19-9764-8_4

to our own day, taking different forms at different times."[3] Next, we will separately investigate the theories of free will at various times.

1 Theory of Free Will in Ancient Philosophy

The Russian philosopher Lossky said that the discussion of free will in European philosophy began at the time of Aristotle.[4] This statement is generally correct but not exact. In fact, before Aristotle, there was already a debate about whether free will existed in ancient Greek philosophy.

1.1 Democritus

The ancient Greek materialist philosopher Democritus believes that everything subject to causation is a necessity. Therefore, everything has a reason, and everything is necessary and determined. In this case, there is no free will at all. Democritus is the father of ethical naturalism. The so-called ethical naturalism is a doctrine that studies the moral and ethical thoughts from the materialistic cosmology and epistemology of the view of nature and real-life human experience, especially from human nature.[5] Therefore, naturalistic ethics emphasizes human nature and deduces human morality from the demands of the so-called eternal and unchanging biological nature that all humans possess. Determined by natural ontology, Democritus negates man's free will, believing that man, as a part of nature, like everything else in nature, is determined by necessity.

1.2 Plato

The ancient Greek idealist philosopher Plato holds that freedom is innate in its highest form, so people pursue actual purposes and obey personal choices. Meanwhile, a man is free throughout his actions because he is the owner of his actions. Although Plato also emphasizes the natural ontology of humans, he argues that people who conform to nature should pursue a rational life. There are two parts of human nature: rationality and lust. Only under the control of the virtue of "moderation" can one lead a rational life. The moderation mentioned by Plato in this context undoubtedly includes people's control over their lust and actions. It is at this point that it shows that human actions are selective. Therefore, it incorporates the content of free will.

[3] Russell [3], p. 337.

[4] Lossky [4], p. 1.

[5] See [5], pp. 129–130.

1.3 Aristotle

Aristotle inherits Plato's ideas and further develops the view of the selectivity of actions, discussing the voluntary nature of human actions. Aristotle distinguishes two types of actions: voluntary and involuntary. As Aristotle put it, "Since virtue is concerned with passions and actions, and on voluntary passions and actions praise and blame are bestowed, on those that are involuntary pardon, and sometimes also pity, to distinguish the voluntary and the involuntary is presumably necessary for those who are studying the nature of virtue, and useful also for legislators with a view to the assigning both of honors and of punishments."[6] It can be seen that Aristotle differentiates voluntary actions from involuntary ones from the perspective of ethical evaluation, which is of great significance for determining human responsibilities. Then, what are voluntary and involuntary actions? Here involves the distinction between the two. According to Aristotle, involuntary actions are done under compulsion or by reason of ignorance. By contrast, the starting point of voluntary actions is in the person who has cognition and who understands the things that he lives in one by one. Regarding the voluntary nature of actions, Aristotle also discusses choice, arguing that it is obviously voluntary, but the two are not equivalent, and the connotation of voluntariness is broader. The reason why a specific action is voluntary is that humans make a choice in this action. It can be seen that regarding the distinction between voluntary and involuntary actions, two groups of categories corresponding to each other can be listed in Aristotle's discussion, namely, knowledge and ignorance, choice and compulsion.

Knowledge and ignorance are the first criteria for distinguishing voluntary actions from involuntary ones, and these are the criteria of cognition. Knowledge is knowledge of things, while ignorance is ignorance of everything. Aristotle said, "Everything done by reason of ignorance is not voluntary." Aristotle also distinguished ignorance into the ignorance of the universe and ignorance of particulars. He mentioned, "...it is not mistaken purpose that causes involuntary action (it leads rather to wickedness), nor ignorance of the universal (for that men are blamed), but ignorance of particulars, i.e., of the circumstances of the action and the objects with which it is concerned. For it is on these that both pity and pardon depend, since the person who is ignorant of any of these acts involuntarily."[7] Therefore, ignorance of the universe is reprehensible ignorance, while only ignorance of particulars is involuntary ignorance.

Choice and compulsion are the second criteria for distinguishing voluntary actions from involuntary ones, which is the standard of will. Aristotle believes that choice is the most distinct characteristic inherent in virtue, which is voluntary and cannot be equated with desire, passion, intention, or opinion. The choice is not shared with irrational things. It always has a purpose to achieve and is always achievable. It has good and evil ones. The choice can be named a kind of pre-existing thinking. The so-called pre-existing thought means that choice is always composed of reasoning and thinking, and the name of choice means claiming things before they exist (*Proairesis*).

[6] Aristotle [6], p. 41.
[7] Aristotle [6], p. 43.

In Aristotle's view, choice shows the voluntariness of actions, a decision made based on one's free will, so one's actions should be praised or blamed. Therefore, Aristotle argued, "...the vices that are blamed must be in our power."[8] The so-called "vices in our power" are avoidable; in other words, they are vices based on voluntary choices. Then, what are compulsory actions? Aristotle said, "We answer that without qualification actions are so when the cause is in the external circumstances, and the agent contributes nothing."[9] It can be seen that the fundamental difference between compulsion and choice is that the reason for the former lies beyond the actor, while the reason for the latter lies within the actor.

In terms of the voluntariness of the choice of actions, Aristotle emphasizes the choice of evil and good. According to Aristotle, "The end, then, being what we wish for, the means what we deliberate about and choose, actions concerning means must be according to choice and voluntary. Now the exercise of the virtues is concerned with means. Therefore, virtue also is in our power, and so too vice. For where it is in our power to act, it is also in our power not to act, and vice versa; so that, if to act, where this is noble, is in our power, not to act, which will be base, will also be in our power, and if not to act, where this is noble, is in our power, to act, which will be base, will also be in our power. Now, if it is in our power to do noble or base acts, and likewise in our power not to do them, and this was what being good or bad meant, then it is in our power to be virtuous or vicious."[10] We can see that Aristotle believes that people have the freedom to choose to do noble or base acts and thus demonstrated personal responsibility. Aristotle posits that a person should be responsible for his voluntary actions and be praised or blamed for them. The character of the evil is developed due to their slack and debauched lifestyles. Because they commit crimes and do certain behaviors repeatedly, they develop special habits and characters that make them unjust or indulgent. Such people should be responsible for their habits and should be condemned. Even if doing evil due to ignorance can sometimes not be morally accountable, some ignorance is the root cause of crimes, such as crimes due to alcoholism. Drinking is the reason for his ignorance, but he could have stopped drinking. Besides, everyone should be aware of social norms. Still, he does not know or neglects them, so if he does evil and commits a crime, he should also bear moral and legal responsibilities and be condemned and punished because he can rely on his efforts to avoid this kind of ignorance and negligence and make an appropriate choice. In short, Aristotle believes it is up to one's decision what moral purpose he determines, what means he chooses, and how to create his character and morality. It is natural for a person to be condemned for committing evil deeds without cultivating the habit of virtue. Aristotle's discussion based on human responsibility shows that he advocates free will. Moreover, in his thinking, we can find the origin of the early modern theory of moral responsibility.

[8] Aristotle [6], p. 51.

[9] Aristotle [6], p. 42.

[10] Aristotle [6], p. 50.

1.4 The Stoics

In ancient Greece, the Stoics (*School of Citium*) also discussed the issue of free will. On this issue, the Stoics have a profound contradiction between their cosmology and ethics. As the US philosopher Thilly mentioned, "In metaphysics, the Stoics advocate determinism, whereas, in ethics, they advocate free will."[11] In the view of the Stoics, fire, and God, as primitive matter, are identical. God is the soul fire of the universe. It is inseparable from the universe and the soul of the universe, which permeates everything in the universe and determines their life and death. The same is true of human beings who cannot be separated from God; everyone contains a part of the divine fire and is endowed with the soul of the divine fire, so they must obey God's arrangement. In the philosophy of the Stoics, God, soul, fate, and universe are all the same thing, and they possess omnipresent and omnipotent power and the law of necessity, which is rationality. This rationality is universal, and the order of things it manifests results from a particular purpose governed by absolute law and necessity. Therefore, they deny that people have free will. In their view, the universe is an absolute unity, and man, like the universe, is a small universe and an inseparable part of the absolute unity of the universe. The entire universe is a unity whose unified order is produced by the highest rationality and Logos. The law of nature is the bond or coercive force that connects all people into a vast unity. At the same time, morality is the power of humans to maintain consistency with the highest rationality in their minds. As a result, the ethics of the Stoics combines the law of nature with moral requirements. According to the requirements of the law of nature, the root of goodness and badness lies only in the ability to adapt to external laws and rational principles to suppress one's desires. Starting from the concept that the law of nature determines fate, the Stoics believe that the existence and development of the individual are consistent and coordinated with the law of nature, consistent with the highest rationality. The relationship between man and the universe, the soul and God, is like the relationship between water droplets and the ocean, parts and the whole. Every life is connected with the universe and is determined by the law of the nature of the universe. Therefore, individuals have no chance of opportunity or free will. In short, in the philosophy of the Stoics, man, as a part of nature and as a natural thing, is like a tree whose acts result from the necessity of nature and who has no freedom.[12] At the same time, the Stoics emphasize that whether the choice of actions is rational remains in whether one correctly recognizes the actions of his mind, highlighting that the law of people's lives lies in knowing one's mind. In this case, the Stoics also acknowledge that man has free will. Of course, this is free will within a specific limit. As the British philosopher Russell pointed out when commenting on the Stoics, when the sacred part of a person could morally embody his will, this will was part of God's free will, so in this case, the human will was free. When a Stoic persuaded people to adopt a tolerant attitude towards criminals, he argued that the guilty will resulted from the reasons above. In his opinion, it seemed that only the virtuous will

[11] Thilly [7], p. 131.

[12] See [5], p. 272.

was free.[13] The Stoics' contradiction between cosmology and ethics regarding free will stems from their understanding of the world and people. The Stoics make a clear distinction between the material world and the rational world and between man's nature. They divide the nature of man into two types: one is as a natural person, and the other as a rational person. Man has no freedom in nature; the only freedom is spiritual freedom. It should be said that the contradiction between the Stoics on the issue of free will is profound, and it has important implications for us to solve the problems of free will scientifically.

2 Theory of Free Will in Medieval Philosophy

Entering the Middle Ages, free will became a theological proposition. Among them, the discussions of Augustine and Aquinas are the most famous.

2.1 Augustine

Aurelius Augustine is the leading representative of the patristic philosophy. He has written the book *On Free Will*, which made a unique explanation of the issue of free will. Augustine's doctrine of free will was gradually completed in polemics in AD 411, the same year as the early Christian theologian Pelagius (approximately AD 360–430). In his missionary activities, Pelagius repeatedly emphasized that the crimes committed by the personal depravity of the ancestors of mankind, Adam and Eve, should not call their descendants, human beings, to account. Therefore, people were born innocent, and doing good or evil depended on everyone's free will; he also pointed out that good human deeds did not come from the grace of God, and the behavior of Christ was only a model of doing good for human beings. Pelagius believed that people had enough will and the ability to control themselves from committing crimes. However, Augustine argued that these theological ideas of Pelagius were heresy. He pointed out sharply that Adam was pure and of good character when God created him. If Adam could maintain this state of innocence at that time, God would give him grace and let him inherit a kind character. He and his descendants would inevitably enjoy the honor and happiness of the angels, nor would they know what pain and death were, the tragic encounters that happened in everyone's life. However, the fact was that Adam fell. He abused the trust given by God and went from good to evil. The evil tendency driven by the evil consequences of this crime (*dura necessitas peccatum habendi*) destroyed not only himself but also brought the original sin inherited from generation to generation to his descendants (*in quo orrnes peccaverunt*). Even a baby who was just born could not escape the guilt of original sin, because it had been a degenerate person since it was born (*massa*

[13] Russell [3], p. 338.

perditionis). It inherited the depraved nature of the ancestor, and its various desires would exceed rationality. When it reached a certain age, it would commit its own crimes (the Catholic Church referred to people's own crimes as their own crimes) and commit the crime it was bound to do. Although this kind of sin became almost a certainty in everyone's life, it could not be exempted from punishment due to this nature. Therefore, Augustine stressed that human crimes were not a fault forced by external forces but voluntary. This was because a person tempted by the devil showed his tendency to act evil, and this freedom to do evil was a manifestation of human free will.[14]

2.2 *Aquinas*

Medieval theologian Thomas Aquinas' discussion of the issue of free will began with an understanding of human nature. Aquinas said that man was the only being who could realize the purpose and means between heaven and earth. Since the purpose was associated with the concept of good, man was the only thing that good things and concepts could promote. The characteristics of human actions were voluntary, which must meet two prerequisites: (1) the inner principle of the activities of the actor (person) (self-discipline); (2) understanding of the goals pursued. Human will determined the former; rationality provided good and evil judgments to the will, thereby determining the consequences. Aquinas believed that man had a rational soul and free will. In this way, he could choose and be responsible for his actions. People could draw correct concepts about good and evil, make conscious choices and practice kindness. Aquinas recognized man's freedom and the freedom to choose his actions, which is crucial because only in this way could we explain why people should be responsible for their acts and why they should be punished for criminal acts. As Aquinas mentioned, people had free will; otherwise, consultation, advice, orders, prohibitions, rewards, and punishments were all in vain. People acted as per their judgments, and based on their comprehensive abilities, they could judge whether certain things should be avoided or pursued. Nevertheless, in the case of specific special actions, the judgment did not originate from instinct but the comparative activities of reason. As a result, they acted according to their free will and retained the ability to do different things. People needed to have free will because they were reasonable. The actions completed by people were unique and appropriately called human actions, which were unique to people as human beings. Humans were different from irrational animals in that they were the masters of their acts. In those unique acts that were aptly called human actions, humans were the masters. Now, humans became the masters of their actions because of their rationality and will, and because of this, free will was called the instinct of will and reason. In this way, those actions were appropriately called human actions, which arose from a deliberate will. If any other actions were suitable for humans, then they could be named the actions of a

[14] See [8], pp. 24–25.

man but could not be generally referred to be human actions because they were not actions of humans as humans. It was now clear that all actions came from a power that was produced according to the nature of its purpose. Nonetheless, the purpose of will was to produce results and kindness. Thus, all human actions must be for a purpose.[15] Of course, limited by the times, Aquinas' doctrine of free will is still religious, which argues that although people can make their own choices, complete freedom of will only exists when God supports it.

3 Theory of Free Will in Early Modern Philosophy

The subject's self-awareness awakened through the intermediary of Renaissance humanism, and the religious theory of free will was abandoned. The issue of free will has attracted more attention from early modern philosophers based on humanism.

3.1 Descartes

René Descartes, the pioneer of modern philosophy, affirms that man has free will. Descartes is a dualist philosophically. He opposes the spirit and the body, believing that the body is a passive machine while the spirit is active and free. As an attribute of the spirit, human free will is self-evident in Descartes' view. Descartes pointed out that we also had free will, which we could agree or disagree with at will. This truth could be attributed to the first and most ordinary thoughts we were born with.[16] Descartes advocated Innatism and believed that the human ability to have free will was also gifted. With this free will, humans could disagree with suspicious things and thus avoid mistakes. As Descartes put it, the kind of thing we called conscience or rationality was naturally equal for everyone.[17] Descartes regarded human free will as a highly perfect quality. Moreover, humans acted freely by free will, and they should be responsible for the consequences of their actions, so human actions should be praised or punished. At the same time, freedom was also the difference between humans and things. Descartes has elaborately discussed this. He posited that if there was a machine that looked like a monkey or organs of other irrational animals, we could not explain how their nature differed from these animals. But if there was a machine similar to our body and imitating our movements as much as possible, we still had two ways to show that they were not real people. The first was that they would never use language or other signals as we did when expressing our thoughts to others. But it was entirely possible to imagine that a machine that could speak should be made, which could even articulate events related to changes in one of its components.

[15] See [9], pp. 74–75.

[16] See [10], p. 15.

[17] See [11], p. 103.

For example, when a part of it was triggered, it would cry and say it was injured. But humans could not make such a machine that could arrange different words to reply according to the meanings of the conversations, which even the dumbest person could make. The second was that although this kind of machine could do many things and did as well as us, or even better than us, they would fail in other ways, despite that such failure was not due to their fault, thus revealing the secret that their actions did not come from rationality but the arrangement of their components; a machine must tolerate such changeable arrangements so that it behaved in all life events like the way rationality instructed us to act, which was simply impossible.[18] It can be seen that Descartes believes that the only difference between humans and animals is that the former possesses rationality, which contains the connotation of free will. In other words: although machines can imitate human actions, they can never have human rationality. As Descartes pointed out, "For self-acting machines are not commended because they perform with exactness all the movements for which they were adapted, seeing their motions are carried on necessarily; but the maker of them is praised on account of the exactness with which they were framed, because he did not act of necessity, but freely; and, on the same principle, we must attribute to ourselves something more on this account, that when we embrace truth, we do so not of necessity, but freely."[19] Here, Descartes, for the first time, proposed the contradiction between necessity and freedom in free will. He mentioned, "But because what we have already discovered of God, gives us the assurance that his power is so immense that we would sin in thinking ourselves capable of ever doing anything which he had not ordained beforehand, we should soon be embarrassed in great difficulties if we undertook to harmonize the pre-ordination of God with the freedom of our will, and endeavored to comprehend both truths at once."[20] It can be seen that Descartes advocates free will but has no intention to blaspheme God. His way out of the predicament is to restrict human freedom properly and reconcile it with the Divine pre-ordination. To this end, Descartes said, "our mind is limited, while the power of God is infinite." In this context, God actually refers to necessity. In Descartes' view, human free will is ultimately subject to the restrictions of necessity and is within the limit of necessity. Although Descartes adopts a reconciling attitude towards freedom and necessity, its elaboration of the relationship between the two, especially the view of the relativity of free will, is enlightening to some extent.

3.2 Hobbes

The British philosopher Hobbes is a typical mechanical materialist. He uses the principles of mechanics and geometry to explain and demonstrate the nature of matter and the regularity of movement. Furthermore, he also regards man as a machine

[18] See [9], p. 83.
[19] See [10], p. 14.
[20] See [10], p. 15.

that moves in accordance with mechanical properties. Hence, his analysis of human nature is also completely based on mechanical materialism, which leads to the denial of human free will. According to him, all things in the real world are objects, and the events that occur in these objects are movements. Therefore, the entire natural world is actually a combination of moving objects. In his view, man is also a part of nature, nothing more than a special object, and human physiological and psychological processes are also governed by the general mechanical laws of object movement. In this sense, there is not much difference between the structure of the human skeleton and the machine, the human body's activity, and the machine's operation. Therefore, the method of studying man is not fundamentally different from the method of studying physics. In the book *Leviathan*, Hobbes compared man, the most refined object in nature, to a clock, thinking that the human heart was like the spring of a needle; the human nerves were like the gossamer of a clock; the human bones were like the gears of a clock. Therefore, the entire activity of man was no different from the operation of clocks. Then, how can human nature be seen from human activities? Hobbes believed that human activities could generally be divided into two categories, one was innate and consistent with the organism's vital motion, such as blood circulation, breathing, digestion, excretion, etc.; the other was animal motion, also known as free motion, such as walking, talking, etc. In Hobbes' view, these two activities had both differences and commonalities. The former was a purely biological function that was exempted from being obtained through imagination and external stimulation, while the latter was a conscious activity that required the help of imagination and external stimulation. But both were for the maintenance and continuation of life, and they were both necessary conditions for the preservation of mankind. Hobbes analyzed autonomous human activities in particular and believed that autonomous human activities were rooted in the effect of the movement of foreign objects on human senses. This effect could lead to two results—happiness or misery. Because of this, the initial impulse of desire that appeared in autonomous human activities was correspondingly manifested as two tendencies: one was to enable people to pursue objects that led to happiness, which was manifested as the desire at this time; the other was to avoid objects that caused misery, which was manifested as hatred at this time. Hobbes believed that the feeling of happiness could lead to happiness by promoting the movement of life, while hindering the movement of life would cause misery. Therefore, desire and hatred were based on whether the movement of life was promoted or hindered, that is, on happiness and misery. In Hobbes' view, with desire and hatred, there was also love and hate. The so-called love was desire, and the so-called hate was hatred. All human emotions could be attributed to the desire and hatred for different objects under different circumstances. Hobbes believed that desire and hatred could be either instinctive or acquired. The root of acquired desire and hatred was that humans wanted to obtain objects that experience showed to bring them happiness and avoid objects that experience showed to bring them misery. Therefore, for people, whether it was conditioned instinctive reflex activities or planned autonomous activities, they were all for the pleasure and against suffering, which substantially lied in the self-preservation of life. Hobbes believed that people's determination and choice of good and evil must go through their inner thoughts. The decision of desire or disgust obtained after thinking was the will. Will was the final desire after the process of thinking. An act made according to a certain will was a voluntary act. Therefore, will resulted from emotional domination by desire or aversion, which had no freedom. In Hobbes' view, the so-called free will only meant that the behavior had not encountered external obstacles. Hobbes pointed out, "Liberty, or Freedom, signifieth (properly) the absence of Opposition; (by Opposition, I mean external Impediments of motion)"[21] As far as the subject's interior was concerned, due to the dominant effect of desire and aversion on the will, the will could not be free. All in all, for all voluntary human actions, there must be a reason for the will that arises from it, and there is a reason above the reason. The ultimate end of the chain of this reason should be in the hand of God. God is the last cause of all causes. Therefore, all human actions are not so much out of free will as out of necessity. It should be pointed out that Hobbes' discussion of free will is based on the scientific analysis of human nature. Although he comes to a negative conclusion about free will, Hobbes' analysis of the mechanism of human activity is still significant for us to understand the inner mechanism of human actions and connect free will with the law of behavior for investigation.

3.3 Locke

The British philosopher John Locke has a unique insight into the issue of free will. Before Locke, although Bacon talked about freedom, he did not fully explain it theoretically. Hobbes negated human free will because he was confined to the principles of mechanical materialism. Locke realized the narrowness of the idea of absolute mechanics and tried to correct it. Locke argued, "A great part of men are so far from finding any such innate moral principles in themselves, that, by denying freedom to mankind, and thereby making men no other than bare machines, they take away not only innate but all moral rules."[22] In Locke's view, Descartes set out from innatism and regarded human free will as an attribute of talent, which was illusory. However, Hobbes used the perspective of mechanics to see through the illusory nature of innatism, but at the same time, unfortunately, negated the freedom of human subjectivity, bringing about difficulties in explaining how the subject of human activities applied moral principles, which was equivalent to abolishing moral principles. To eliminate the contradiction of mechanism, Locke emphasized the role of freedom and will in morality. Nevertheless, Locke rejected the traditional theory of free will and replaced it with the issue of human freedom. Locke's understanding of freedom is different from the general views of other early modern thinkers. Before and after Locke, when people discussed freedom, they always linked it to human will. This was not the case with Locke. Locke believed that whether freedom belonged to will was a difficult question that had been debated for a long time, but people failed to

[21] Hobbes [12], p. 97.

[22] Locke [13], pp. 37–38.

figure it out. The key was that people confused will and freedom and did not see their true nature. According to Locke, will and freedom were two distinct human power, both belonging to the subject of man and being attributes of the entity of man. Consequently, we could not connect them. Locke said, "…to ask, whether the will has freedom, is to ask whether one power has another power…"[23] This confused the relationship between power (attributes) and entity (humans). Attributes could only belong to entities, power could only belong to the subject of humans, and attributes could not belong to attributes. Thus, freedom could only be attributed to humans, not to will. Because will, like freedom, was a power. Locke pointed out, "Liberty being as little applicable to the will, as swiftness of motion is to sleep, or squareness to virtue."[24] Locke posited that will was a selection ability or special function of the human mind, a functional attribute. It was subject to the dominance of willing and guidance of thinking within the subject, which must be based on psychological choices to make will decisions; beyond the subject, it must be dominated by the external world, and under the action of external conditions, the motivation and will were determined by the then-current feeling of happiness or bitterness, which was manifested as the certainty of pursuing happiness and avoiding suffering. Meanwhile, Locke asserted that will was not free. The arguments about free will in traditional ethics were all the result of confusing the ability of the human minds and humans. They were only discussing the freedom of the human mind controlling the will or the freedom of thinking; that is, it was only the freedom of the human mind instead of free will. In Locke's view, freedom was a human ability, not an attribute or power of will that belonged only to human functions. As rational beings, humans had the right to determine their physical and mental activities (movements). They could choose to think or not to think and exercise or not to exercise according to their psychological choices and guidance, and this was the freedom of the subject. Of course, freedom also had its scope and was bound by necessity. One could not do whatever he wanted. Locke mentioned, "If to break loose from the conduct of reason, and to want that restraint of examination and judgment which keeps us from choosing or doing the worse, be liberty, true liberty, madmen and fools are the only freemen."[25] In other words, freedom is based on choices and actions under rational guidance and correct judgment. Whether this judgment is correct depends on whether it recognizes the necessity, which is the pursuit of happiness. Therefore, Locke believed that the goal of freedom was achieving the happiness that people chose. If one could act or not act as per what he had chosen, he was a free man. Freedom belonged to human beings, and the so-called freedom was free from the domination of others. Locke distinguished will from freedom, arguing that will itself had no freedom, and freedom was a human attribute. This solution of free will theory is unique. In fact, Locke's view that the will itself was not free was influenced by Hobbes' mechanical determinism. But Locke did not deny the freedom that man himself had, and at the same time, believed that this freedom was subject to rational domination and guidance and

[23] Locke [13], p. 212.

[24] Locke [13], p. 211.

[25] Locke [13], p. 235.

only meant that it was not subject to the domination of others. It should be said that Locke's discussion of free will is intriguing.

3.4 Spinoza

The Dutch philosopher Spinoza disagreed with the view of free will, an inevitable conclusion drawn from his pantheistic materialist philosophy. According to him, the universe is a material substance that moves by itself. All existences in the universe reflect the essence of the substance in a certain special pattern, and at the same time, they are interconnected and interact with each other to form an infinitely complex and unified substance. The substance Spinoza refers to (*substantia*), is something that is known within and through oneself. In other words, the concept of forming the substance is independent of other things.[26] The substance is governed by necessity. There is nothing accidental in nature. Everything is determined by natural necessity and exists and moves in a certain way. Everything happens for a reason, and only the divine or God is the free cause that must exist. Although Spinoza's view of substance overcomes Descartes' dualism and draws a strict line with religious mysticism, if this substance theory of absolute necessity is implemented in ethics, it inevitably brings mechanical determinism to its ethics. One of the significant reasons for Spinoza to emphasize the necessity and "the necessity of divine nature" is to negate the theological theory of free will. Spinoza believed that human "free will" was a "concept passed down through generations" of Scholasticism's philosophy. According to this concept, the spirit was not created by natural reasons but by God, nor was it transferred by other things, and it had the right to absolute freedom. Spinoza believed that this so-called "free will" was fundamentally non-existence. The idea of free will only come from the imaginary arbitrariness of people's actions, from the arbitrariness of people who were aware of their actions but did not know the reason for the decision to act. A child believed that he was free to find milk to drink, an angry child believed that he was free to take revenge, a coward believed that he was free to escape, a drunk believed that he could say at his will that he would drink heavily after waking up, etc., which were all under this case. Spinoza put forward the following proposition: will could not be said to be a free cause but only a necessity. It was proved that will, like reason, was a style of thinking, so every will could only exist and act if it was determined by another reason, which was again determined by another reason, so the recursion was infinite. If the will was infinite, its existence must be determined by God as much as the action, not because God was an absolutely infinite entity, but because it had the attributes that could express the eternal and infinite essence of thinking. Therefore, no matter how we understood the will, whether finite or infinite, there were reasons to determine its existence and action. The will could not be said to be a free cause but only a necessity or coercion.[27] Spinoza once vividly described

[26] See [14], p. 3.
[27] See [14], p. 31.

that those who believed that man had free will were like a stone that gained a certain amount of movement and continued to move in a specified direction, which believed itself to be free. A man was conscious of its movement like a stone but was ignorant of the causes and believed himself free. In fact, man was impossible to have free will. This meant that in the sense that will, as a desire, was always determined by a certain cause, Spinoza believed that man had no free will. Although Spinoza denied free will, he tried keenly to reveal the dialectical relationship between necessity and freedom. Spinoza asserted that freedom did not lie in doing whatever you wanted but in the necessity of freedom. He emphasized that necessity and coercion should not be confused, and the latter should be opposed to freedom. He pointed out that people did not see any difference between necessity and coercion (or violence). A person had the pursuit of life and love, etc., but his pursuit was never driven by violence but a necessity. Spinoza wrote, "That thing is called free, which exists solely by the necessity of its nature, and of which the action is determined by itself alone. On the other hand, that thing is necessary, or rather constrained, which is determined by something external to itself to a fixed and definite method of existence or action." The greater the possibility that all activities we achieved beyond ourselves would be combined with us, the more perfect they would be so that they could share the same nature as us. In other words, the more a person's actions conformed to his nature, the fuller and more comprehensive his freedom would be. In short, freedom was to act following the necessity of human nature.[28] It can be seen that Spinoza starts from mechanical determinism, arguing that everything is necessary, denying the existence of chance in the material world and the existence of free will in the spiritual world. As Engels criticized, recognizing this necessity means we still haven't moved out of the theological view of nature.[29]

3.5 Leibniz

The German philosopher Leibniz absorbed atomism in ancient Greek philosophy and constructed a monastic system following the rationalist principles established by Descartes. From Monadology, Leibniz held that a monad did not allow anything to pass through and enter it to force its ions and was not subject to external decisions. In this sense, the human will is free because it is also a monad. The mind determines its behavior based on its nature, desires, and concepts. Leibniz's thinking on the issue of free will begins with the analysis of human abilities, which is the same as Locke's, despite that the two understand abilities differently. Locke regarded ability as the choice of human beings to start or not to start, continue or terminate the activities of the soul and the movements of the body. It determined whether a certain special activity of human beings started or not started, continued, or terminated. This ability was the human will, whose practical usage was desire. Freedom meant that

[28] See [15], p. 13.

[29] See [16], p. 561.

people were able to move unhindered according to their desires. Oppositely, Leibniz understood human abilities from the perspective of movement changes, emphasizing that ability was only a possibility of change divided into active and passive ones. The active ability was called function, and the passive ability was called receptivity. Therefore, in Leibniz's view, free will did not refer to the ability of man to do whatever he wanted, but to whether man's will itself was independent sufficiently, not to ask whether man's limbs could move freely, but to ask whether the human mind was free and what this freedom lied in. If freedom was understood as unhindered movement, then once a ball moved on a plane, it could become a free motor. This was not correct. Because to say that a certain activity was free meant not only that it was automatic but also that it was rationally and carefully thought out. Therefore, Leibniz emphasized that freedom must be rational, reasonable, deliberate, and linked to necessity. Leibniz also analyzed the concept of freedom, arguing that freedom was a polysemy, with de jure freedom and de facto freedom, freedom of thought, and freedom of action. According to the de jure freedom, slaves had no freedom, and ordinary subjects were not completely free. But if de facto freedom was freedom in any term, it could be said that everyone had the same freedom. But there were limits to this kind of freedom. People in different situations did things differently, and there was different freedom between what people wanted to do and what they could do. If freedom was only understood as the freedom to do things within a certain range of rights, then if a person was physically sick or imprisoned, his freedom would be hindered, or he had no freedom at all. According to Leibniz, this kind of freedom did not belong to ethical freedom. Ethical freedom had two meanings: one was in terms of the relationship between rationality and emotion. When a person lost his independence due to the imperfection of rationality and the coercion of overwhelming emotions, he could not be free. Because under this circumstance, people could not think as they should, nor could they do as they should, or even completely lost the guidance of rationality and became emotional slaves. Only when they got rid of emotional servitude could they gain a certain degree of freedom. The other was in terms of the relationship between will and external necessity. Whether this kind of will was free or not depended on whether the cause for the reason of desire presented in front of the will was powerful. That is to say, free will lied in the sufficient causes provided by rationality. Nothing happened for no reason. There was also order and connection in the concept. The freedom of the mind remained in the completeness of this connection and order, and it had sufficient reasons to maintain the independence of the will. Influenced or interfered with by other forces, the mind would immediately perceive them, tell them to stop, and catch them. If they were good, advance them; otherwise, control them. This showed human ability and free will. Therefore, what Leibniz emphasized was the freedom that was guided by rationality and linked to necessity. However, Leibniz did not treat free will as something controlled by absolute necessity but recognized the chance of will activity. According to his understanding, rationality or reason could determine the will according to the dominant perception and rationality. Even if this way of the decision was unmistakable, it only led the will to what it tended to do instead of making it do something for sure. Namely, the sufficient causes provided by rationality for the will only determine the tendency of the will's activities, not the necessity. In this sense, good and evil only produced a certain tendency for the activity of thinking, not force it to move in a certain way. As a result, the consequences of morality were not necessary, and this was the so-called probability of morality. Moral probability is one of the most popular issues discussed in German ethics in the seventeenth century. The so-called probability is that the rationality that guides the activities of the will provides a certain number of causes, which are conducive to promoting the will to have a certain tendency to be good and to act ethically. Still, this kind of cause does not determine whether the will and actions will be good or whether acts will be ethical for sure. In this context, there is the relationship between freedom and necessity, chance and opportunity, spontaneity and coercion. Leibniz believed that there were two types of necessity: logical necessity, also known as the metaphysical or mathematical necessity, and moral necessity. Logical necessity was due to the contradictions implied in the opposites. In contrast, moral necessity was manifested by the tendency of the wise to choose the best and make the mind follow the maximum goodness. This necessity did not hinder the freedom of choice because it was complete freedom to do the best thing without hindrance. In other words, moral necessity was the necessity of will and actions under the control of motivation and rationality, governed by the law of sufficient reasons. It was a kind of rational guidance and promotion that contained the contradiction between necessity and chance, the relationship between chance and opportunity, and spontaneous and coercive factors. The situation was complex, so it was a kind of probability, not an absolute necessity. It was in this sense that moral necessity and free will were not diametrically opposed. Leibniz's view of free will, especially the distinction between logical necessity and moral necessity, which limits the free will to the moral realm, is profound.

3.6 Hume

The British philosopher Hume detailedly analyzed the issue of free will in his writings. The era of Hume's theories saw heated debates between the British school of emotionalist ethics and the school of rationalist ethics. Emotionalist ethics is represented by Hobbes, Locke, etc., and Cudworth represents rationalist ethics. The debate centered around an important issue: free will and necessity. Hobbes was negative towards free will, believing that previous causes determined any event, and the same was true of human will. In this sense, human actions were free, equaling those resulting from the actor's own will. Locke believed that will and freedom were both forces of the mind, which were different, and we should not confuse these two forces by asking the question "whether the will is free". On the other hand, Cudworth posited that we needed the free will to be the basis of our moral life. We could experience within ourselves that we had free will. The will was inherently inclined to goodness, and when there was no distinction between good and evil behaviors, our will had the freedom to choose behaviors. Hume pointed out that the reason for having these two views was due to the ambiguity of rhetoric and concepts so that both sides could not understand and accept each other. To this end, Hume defined the concepts of necessity and free will separately. He believed that necessity was composed of two factors: the eternal combination and the inference of the mind. When we experienced the connection, combination, and eternity between action and motivation, character and environment repeatedly, that is, when similar personalities, motivations, and environments always brought about similar actions, we felt a sense of necessity in our minds, from which we could make inferences and predictions about some actions of a person. From this point of view, there was no freedom in mind. The activity of will and behavior performance were all caused by necessity; that is, people's behavior must have some connection with their then-current character, motivation, and the environment. They must be caused by each other in a certain way, and they could all be inferred and expected by bystanders. Hume posited that will was the inner impression we sensed and conceived when we consciously initiated any movement of our body or any new perception of our mind.[30] The so-called freedom referred to the ability to act or not according to the decision of the will; that is to say, we could stay tight or act at our will.[31] Therefore, according to the principle of causation, Hume held that various causes predestined human will in a specific way. Freedom was the possibility of activity based on the decision of the will. He believed it was not the freedom of will but the freedom of action. According to this concept, everyone, except prisoners, was free. But this freedom was conditional. We wanted to rest before we would rest, and we wanted to walk before we would walk. In short, Hume used determinism to solve the problem, shifting the focus of the problem from free will to freedom of action. In Hume's view, freedom was not the opposite of necessity but coercion. On this basis, Hume affirmed the importance of the theory of will necessity and freedom to moral sciences. Hume pointed out, "The doctrines, both of necessity and of liberty, as above explained, are not only consistent with morality but are absolutely essential to its support."[32] Why is the doctrine of necessity an essential condition for morality? Hume discussed distinctly that if there was no necessary connection between cause and effect in human actions, not only was the punishment impossible to be just and morally fair, but it was impossible for any rational being to think of punishing others. The eternal and universal object of hatred or anger was a person or animal with thoughts and consciousness; when any sinful or infringing behavior stimulated that kind of hatred, it was only because the behavior was related to that person. However, according to the doctrine of freedom or opportunity, this kind of relation became non-existent, and people were not responsible for intentional and premeditated behaviors, just as they were for occasional and accidental behaviors. Behaviors were short-lived and perishable by their nature. If these behaviors did not happen for certain reasons in the character and temperament of the person who committed them, they could not be fixed on the person. If it was a good deed, glory could not be endowed; if it was an evil deed, notoriety could also not be given. The behavior itself might be reprehensible. It might be a violation

[30] See [17], p. 437.

[31] See [18], p. 85.

[32] Hume [18], p. 87.

of all the rules of morality and religion, but the person was not responsible for it; since the behavior was not a lasting or constant property happening in his character and did not leave traces of this property afterward, he couldn't become the object of punishment or revenge as a result. Therefore, according to the hypothesis of freedom, after a person committed an extremely evil crime, he was as pure and unblemished as he was when he was born, and his character had nothing to do with his behavior. Because his behavior did not occur due to his character, the bad behavior must not be used as proof of the corruption of his character. According to the principle of necessity, a person would have merit due to his behavior, no matter how general opinions tended to the opposite.[33] While affirming the importance of necessity to morality, Hume also recognized the necessity of freedom to morality. Hume pointed out that freedom was also an essential condition for morality, and if human actions were not free, they had no moral nature and therefore could not be the object of appreciation or disgust. Various behaviors could become the object of our moral interests (such as likes and dislikes) because they were some signs of the inner character and revealed emotions. Therefore, if they did not come from these roots but only from external forces, then they could not arouse our praise or condemnation.[34] Hume unifies the necessity of will and the freedom of will in his moral doctrine and can justify it, which is of historical significance.

3.7 Holbach

The French philosopher Holbach is a typical mechanical determinist with a negative attitude toward free will. Holbach believed that everything in the world was necessary, and there was neither chance nor human freedom. Holbach criticized the libertarians, mentioning that these people advocated that the soul was different from the body and was immaterial. These people believed that the soul was the master of its fate, could regulate its activities and determine its own will based on its abilities. In short, they advocated that people were free. Holbach believed this was a wrong view. Philosophers' mistakes regarding human freedom originated from their view of human will as the driving force of their actions. Moreover, because they did not investigate it further, they did not see at all that the intricate reasons that drove the will move by itself, or arranged and changed the mind, were independent of man who, in the impression he accepted, was purely passive.[35] Accordingly, in Holbach's view, human beings, like other beings, followed the law of absolute necessity, and nothing could be changed. Humans had no freedom. Holbach said that any human action was illiberal; it was not difficult to understand that even according to the concepts of theologians, human free will was also a pure illusion. Anyone who considered himself free was nothing more than a fly who conceived itself as the ruler of the universe.

[33] See [17], pp. 449–450.

[34] See [18], p. 89.

[35] See [19], pp. 163, 175.

Although the fly was, in fact, utterly subject to the laws of the universe, it was unaware of this.[36] Since necessity was irresistible, every moment of human existence was a passive tool in the grasp of necessity. Therefore, Holbach publicly stated that there was no moment in a person's life when he was free. Since this, he could only obey the mercy of necessity, namely, fate. Holbach pointed out that predetermination was the eternal and necessary order established in nature or the unavoidable connection of various causes that used their results to act. The necessity of the multiple movements that dominated the physical world also dominated the various movements of the moral world, so everything in the moral world was subject to fate.[37] Setting out from mechanical determinism, Holbach emphasized the necessity of objectivity and denied the freedom of human will, thus concluding fatalism. Holbach even believed that people were not free when they made choices. They took it for granted that they chose what they thought was good for them or made them happy. When they did not make a choice, they were still not free; before they did not know or thought that they did not know the attributes of an object they chose, or before they did not consider the results of their actions, they had to give up the choice. You would say that people always did what was knowingly harmful to them and sometimes committed suicides, and it was wrong to say they were free. Was it free for people to make correct or incorrect inferences? Was it not people's rationality and wisdom dependent on the beliefs formed in them or on the traits of their organisms? And since neither human belief nor organisms were beyond people's control, this could not be evidence that man had free will.[38]

3.8 Diderot

The French philosopher Diderot did not wholly deny human free will like Holbach. He believed that human will was both free and not free. Freedom embodied the choice of wisdom and the decision of the will. Diderot said, "The will is always born of internal or external motivation, a current impression, a memory of the past, a desire, or a future plan. After saying these, I will only use one sentence to talk to you about freedom, that is, our closest action is the necessary result of a single reason: this reason is ourselves, which is very complicated but also single."[39] This meant that a person's will to do something was not produced for no reason but both subjective and objective reasons. Objectively speaking, firstly, the stimulation of foreign objects created an impression, and then introspection was carried out based on the ideas obtained via the impression. After introspection, wishes and plans were generated, and actions were taken. In this way, people were not free. But directly speaking, human actions were only the result of a single reason: ourselves. In this

[36] See [20], pp. 76, 78.

[37] See [19], p. 191.

[38] See [20], p. 78.

[39] Diderot [21], p. 184.

sense, Diderot recognized that humans were free. In the moral realm, on the one hand, Diderot affirmed that people were not free as they were influenced by society. He pointed out, "Virtue should be said to be an act of doing good, and sin should be said to be an act of doing evil. Some men are born to be lucky while some are not; men are irresistibly drawn by the general trend, which glorifies one person and humiliates another."[40] Thus, the social environment could lead people to good and be respected, but it could also make people do evil and be despised. Therefore, a person's moral behavior depended on the social environment. On the other hand, Diderot recognized that people could decide their actions and had free will, which was the key to judging moral behaviors. Diderot believed that if man was not free to do good or evil, he held no liability, just as the engine was driven by external forces and was not responsible for its movement. If there was no freedom, the compensation was ridiculous, and the punishment was unfair. Neither compensation nor punishment was meaningful. Therefore, freedom was the basis for implementing compensation or punishment, and it was also a necessary condition for judging moral behaviors. Diderot's discussion of free will has a hint of dialectics and shows progress compared with the absolute determinism of will by mechanical determinism.

3.9 Kant

The exploration of free will reaches its peak in German classical philosophy. Kant's theory of free will, the founder of classical German philosophy, begins with the understanding of man. Kant believed that human beings, as rational beings, had dual attributes, namely sensibility, and rationality. Relative to these two attributes, man existed in a "dual world". The first world was the world of sensual phenomena, that is, the natural world, including man's natural existence. People perceived this world through their senses, and the law of natural causation was applied in this world. The other world was the super-emotional ontological world, which was the rational existence of man. This world must be thought about and speculated through human rationality. There existed a law of free causation utterly different from the law of natural causation. Compared with such a dual world, man was an existence that spanned the dual world. Obviously, as rational animals, men had free will. The reason why human will was free is that it was rational. In Kant's system, will was the practical ability of rationality, which was the practical rationality. Therefore, will was the starting point of Kantian ethics. Kant believed that practical rationality must obey categorical imperative. Therefore, the categorical imperative was the fundamental law of practical rationality. Categorical imperative refers to: "Act only according to that maxim by which you can at the same time will that it should become a universal law."[41] According to Kant, as a sensual being, man had sensory desires, which were part of nature, and could not get rid of the control of nature, so he was not free.

[40] Diderot [21], p. 184.

[41] Kant [22], p. 30.

However, as a rational being, man could be completely independent of all emotional conditions and therefore had absolute free will.

Kant introduced free will into ethics, whose crucial purpose was to clarify human moral responsibilities. In Kant's eyes, as a rational being, a person had free will and could legislate and enforce the law for himself; that is, he had self-discipline of will; therefore, he should be responsible for his actions. The will of a rational being could only be his will when he acted under the control of the concept of freedom. Therefore, this concept must be attributed to all rational beings within the scope of practice. According to the view of determinism of will, the human will was subject to the same necessary law of causation, so we could conclude that all things, including morality and law, were meaningless. Because blaming an unethical behavior was tantamount to blaming a stone for why it landed and hurt others. Kant pointed out that if this was the case, anyone who committed a crime could defend himself by claiming that the law of causation dominated his behaviors; that is, his behaviors arose from objective reasons. All immorality or crimes were bound to be determined by the environment, conditions, character, and habits, and people held no liability; thus, there was no need for all penalties and censure. This meant that morality was meaningful only if free will was recognized. Morality was the expression of freedom; otherwise, morality was meaningless. If a person's actions were entirely controlled by necessity with no freedom, how could he still behave morally and take moral responsibility for his actions? Therefore, the concept of freedom was the key to understanding the self-discipline of the will.

Kant believed that freedom could have two meanings: one was negative; that is, it was an unrecognizable free thing that existed beyond the necessary law of natural causation. The other was positive, as practical rationality, that is, it was a kind of will self-discipline of morality. Kant believed that the will of all rational people was free, which was not governed by the causality of the sensual world but obeyed the laws prescribed by itself. Therefore, rationality must consider itself the one who established the principles of its behavior and was completely free from external manipulation. Rationality, whether it was considered practical rationality or the will of the rational person, must consider itself free.[42] Kant posited that pure rationality legislated for nature, which was the necessity of nature, and practical rationality legislated for one's moral behavior, which was human freedom. Therefore, freedom was the keystone of the entire building of the practical rationality system and the basis for all other moral concepts. So, how to understand Kant's self-discipline of will? Kant believed that human behavior possessed a willed process and an effect process. Will was practical human rationality, and the willed process was the process of motivation to decide to do a certain act. Based on the mechanism of this process, the norms of behavior were established and conformed to certain universal laws. The effect process of behavior was the process by which behavior produced results and functions. According to Kant, the only thing that had moral significance was the motivational process of behavior. The only motivation was the basis for judging behavior. The effect process of behavior was within the determination of the law of

[42] See [23], p. 62.

natural causation. From at least three aspects, the result of behavior was uncertain and could not be used as a basis for judgment: (1) behavioral results were established within the scope of subjective perceptual perception; (2) the generation of these results was determined by the law of natural causation and had nothing to do with choices; (3) they could only have beneficial or harmful effects relative to human sensibility. It can be seen that the process of behavioral effects has no universal and necessary nature. The only thing that can be evaluated is the motivation for behavior. And motivation is precisely dominated by human will, and the willed process is the process of motivation selection. As for self-discipline, it is relative to others-discipline. Others-discipline means that the will is determined by other factors, including the laws of the outside world or the will of God. By contrast, self-discipline refers to acting for the principles set by oneself. Kant held that human self-disciplined will was neither a slave to lust (animal nature) nor a tool of God. It was neither driven by pleasure, happiness, and desire nor governed by God's will, destiny, and conscience. Man was not a thing (who only knew obedience), nor was he a god (who only knew legislation), but a master who obeyed his legislation. The moral law was absolute obedience, with the law established by oneself; it was generally effective for the purpose.[43] Therefore, Kant's so-called self-discipline of will is essentially free will. It is worth noting that although Kant emphasized that behavior should come from rational norms, he emphasized free will. However, on the other hand, he did not deny that behavior was deterministic at the empirical level and was affected by factors such as environment and education. To sum up, Kant argued that behavior was the unity of rational character and empirical character: on the one hand, man belonged to the world of perceptual phenomena, so his behavior was governed by empirical environmental conditions in this regard, obeying the laws of nature and being deterministic, or in short, it was necessary; on the other hand, man was subordinate to the rational ontological world, so his behavior was also governed by his own will, this rational condition of self-determination was atemporal, eternal, and beyond the influence of sensibility, and therefore free. Kant pointed out this dual opposing character of the same behavior and, at the same time, tried to combine them, emphasizing the decisiveness of rational character to empirical character, unifying necessity and freedom in behavior. Kant gave an example to illustrate that if the actor was held accountable for an act that used malicious rumors to impose social chaos. However, from the empirical character of this act, we could find some reasons, such as the adverse effects on the environment, lack of education, defects in personal qualities, etc.; we did not forgive his behavior because of the necessary influence of these natural factors. This was because we believed that his own rational decision was a fundamental cause, which could stipulate the actor to make or not to make such behavior, that is to say, because the rational ability of the actor had the possibility of making decisions freely, it could have been got rid of the impact of these experience. However, as the ultimate basis for the behavior, it failed to do this, so the actor should be responsible for his behavior and be sanctioned by law.[44] It can be seen that Kant

---

[43] See [24], p. 284.

[44] See [25], p. 222.

affirmed the determinism of behavior and the theory of free will from the two aspects of phenomenon and ontology and tried to unify the two.

3.10 Hegel

Hegel inherited Kant's doctrine of free will and, at the same time, pointed out that Kant did not truly unify freedom and necessity. Hegel opposed the metaphysical view that opposed freedom and necessity and drew on Kant's view that freedom was rational self-determination, arguing that freedom was inherently specific and always decided itself by itself, so it was necessary simultaneously. In particular, Hegel held that freedom was historic and manifested in understanding necessity. When necessity changed from "self-being" to "self-making", it was transformed into freedom. Knowing the necessity, one could avoid blind spontaneity and conform his actions to the objective logic of the development, which was also manifested in the subjective logic of thought. Therefore, freedom was to consciously follow objective necessity, that is, the objective logic of the development of absolute ideas. As Engels commented, "Hegel was the first to state the relation between freedom and necessity correctly. To him, freedom is the insight into necessity."[45] In the book *Philosophy of Right*, Hegel wrote, "The territory of right is, in general, the spiritual, and its more definite place and origin is the will. Will is free; thus, freedom constitutes the substance and essential character of the will."[46] Hegel considered that will and freedom were closely linked, which could not be separated even for a moment. Freedom was the fundamental provision of the will, just as weight was the fundamental provision of objects. The thing that was free was will. Will had no freedom, and it was just an empty talk; at the same time, freedom was only realistic as the will and the subject. Hegel divided the development of free will into three stages: (1) the direct abstract stage. The concept of free will at this stage is a direct and abstract character. Its existence is direct external things. This belongs to the realm of abstract or formal law. (2) the inner law stage of subjective will. Will at this stage is set from the outside existence, and after reflection on itself (that is, "prescribing the truth with the relationship of thought"), it is stipulated as a subjective singularity as opposed to the universal. This "universal" as an inner thing is good, and as an outer thing is the existing world. These are the two aspects of the ideas, and these two aspects are intermediaries between each other. This is the idea in its division or its unique reality. Here there is the law of subjective will, which is opposed to the law of the world and the law of ideas, and this is the moral realm. (3) the unification stage of the previous two links. At this stage, the concept of goodness is realized in the reflective will and the external world. Freedom exists not only as subjective will but also as reality and necessity, which is the ethical realm. Hegel also distinguished free will from impulse, thus distinguishing humans from animals. Hegel said animals

[45] Engels [26], p. 455.

[46] See [27], p. 10.

also had impulses, desires, and tendencies but no will. If there was nothing external to stop them, they could only obey impulses. Only man, as something that followed no rules, overrode impulse, who could also prescribe and set it as his own thing. Impulse was a natural thing, but he put it in this self, and this thing depended on his will. Therefore, his will failed to justify himself under the pretext that impulse was natural.[47] It should be said that Hegel's discussion of free will, especially the view of the dialectical unification of freedom and necessity, has reached a very high level of understanding. Of course, since Hegel started from the concept of objective idealism, the actual subject of freedom was the absolute concept, so he did not fundamentally get rid of fatalism.

4 Theory of Free Will in Modern Philosophy

In modern philosophy, there is still a debate between positive and negative views on the issue of free will, but some scientific and technological content has been introduced in the debate, thus making it modern.

4.1 Green

The British philosopher Green considered that the primary characteristic of the motivation for moral behavior was the characteristic of "self-reflection" it represented. Man was the subject of consciousness, and moral behavior was the realization of self-awareness. Its motivation was not simply the satisfaction of needs but the motivation to participate in a realistic concept of goodness. The special composition of this motivation determined that human moral behavior had a different nature from ordinary natural events, and it also showed that the good and evil values of moral behavior relied on the character of the actor himself. Character determined the characteristics of motivation.[48] Green believed that human character had a history of formation, which was not achieved overnight. Therefore, the behavioral motivation determined by this character could not be isolated but was a complex organic entirety. Human behavior was the outcome of the combination of character and environment. The environment was the external factor that affected behavior, and character was the internal reason that determined behavior. A kind of moral behavior always represented the actor's character. Green pointed out that if a person's behavior did not represent his character, but was just an arbitrary, some kind of motiveless grotesque behavior dominated by the unexplained power of will, then why should people be ashamed of their behaviors and blame themselves for them? Conversely, human beings' moral

---

47 See [27], p. 23.

48 See [UK] Green: *Prolegomena to Ethics*, English version, p. 99. The following Green's views are all from this book, see [28], pp. 230–237.

awareness of their behaviors precisely proved that human moral behavior was motivational and determined by their character. More thoroughly, the subject will and purpose of the person who was the "free cause" were the ultimate causes of moral behavior. Accordingly, the issue of morality eventually became the subject of human will, and free will was the highest noumenon of morality. Green held that free will was the essential prerequisite for human morality to become possible, and it was also the foundation of ethics. Green expounded the psychological basis of the theory of free will from the relationship between desire, rationality, and will. In the past, ethicists often regarded desire and rationality as the root causes of people's common moral behavior and will as the arbiter of actions based on rational desire and opposed desire, rationality, and will. Green considered that desire, rationality, and will coexist in a self-conscious subject. There was a subject or mind which, in general, desired the experience of a person's desires, desired all its rational abilities and all the will in the action of its will, and the essential characteristics of its desires depended on all the desires of its subjects which were precisely the same and being understood; the essential characteristics of its rationality depended on the activities of its subjects which were the same and also being desired; the essential characteristics of its will also relied on the utterly same will arising from the will being desired and understood. This meant that the individual's performance of desire, rationality, and will was a unified and inseparable entirety, and any of these factors could not be regarded as inferior to the others in isolation. Among them, the will had a particularly critical significance. If people considered will the same ability as other abilities that a person possessed—those thoughts, emotions, desires, etc.—it must be a mistake. This was because the will had unique privileges independent of other abilities, so, at any time, a person's established character was the result of the direction taken by those other abilities. On the other hand, the will retained something different, which might produce something different from that stimulated by emotions in action. Therefore, Green determined the central position of the will in the various constituent elements of the subject's self, regarded the will as the origin of morality, and then took free will as the theoretical starting point of ethics.

4.2 Bradley

In his ethical writings, the British philosopher Bradley dabbled in the issue of free will. Bradley first critically analyzed two traditional misconceptions: one was traditional determinism, and the other was abstract non-determinism. Bradley believed that the most popular view in existing ethics was simply to assimilate free will and necessity. This was to talk about the relationship between free will and moral responsibility from the perspective of determinism. To analyze the gains and losses of this view, we must consider the following issues: (1) determining the general meaning of the concept of responsibility in a general sense; (2) discerning the inconsistency (namely contradiction) between the two concepts of free will and necessity; (3) exploring the connotation of the relationship between moral responsibility and freedom and necessity. In Bradley's view, the so-called moral responsibility was a moral attribute possessed by human autonomous behavior. There must be three conditions for the existence of moral responsibility: first, any responsibility must have an actor as its bearer. In other words, my responsibility must be based on two prerequisites. On the one hand, I must be the owner of the behavior, that is, the owner of a certain behavior; on the other hand, the behavior must belong to me—it must be my behavior. The two aspects complemented each other. The former was the same relationship between me and the behavior, and the latter was the same relationship between my will and the behavior. In other words, behavior with the attribute of moral responsibility belonged to me and was based on my will's self-discipline. Its essence was that behavior must come from my will. Second, the actor's conscious awareness (necessary rationality) was the second condition of responsibility. Bradley pointed out that the actor must be rational and know the unique environment of the facts. If this person was at a loss and ignorant and did not understand his obligations, then this kind of behavior was not his behavior. Therefore, a certain amount of rationality or sensation was a condition of responsibility. Third, the actor must possess the necessary moral abilities; that is to say, he could fully realize and judge the nature of his moral behaviors to be able to be responsible for his behaviors. Because responsibility refers to a moral agent and anyone who did not know the moral nature of his behavior could not explain the moral nature of his behavior, he could not assume the moral responsibility for his behavior, such as children, mentally ill people, among others. The actor's existence was the carrier of moral responsibility, and rationality and moral ability were necessary conditions for the generation of moral responsibility. Without rationality and moral ability, responsibility could not exist.[49] Recognizing and determining these conditions had nothing in common with simple determinism. Bradley wrote that determinism or necessitarianism completely negated the subject of the will, negated the subject's rationality and moral ability, and therefore negated the self-independent personality of the actor. The result was to make all behaviors the same, essentially denying both the self as the will and the identity as the self—same. Therefore, determinism could not gain insight into the essence of moral responsibility. Bradley dismissed determinism as a type of psychology, arguing that it forgot the sameness of individuals and behaviors, lost the subject of responsibility and therefore lost the necessary conditions for confirming responsibility. Bradley also disagreed with the doctrine of abstract non-determinism because this doctrine also put aside human rationality, character, and the environment that generated human character, making the will a certain kind of accidental behavior opportunity, treating it as an irrational connection, and simply failing to explain human free behavior and moral responsibility. Bradley argued that the doctrine of non-determinism advocated that behavior was not the result of an established character in any situation and an established position. It was free because it was neutral. People named it cleverly "a will willing none". Therefore, Bradley regarded the two

[49] See [UK] Bradley: *Ethical Studies*, English version, pp. 5–6. The following Bradley's views are all from this book. Quoted from [28], pp. 256–261.

ostensibly opposing views of determinism and abstract non-determinism as fallacies that went the same way. Determinism negated the willpower of the conscious subject of behavior. The relationship between the personality of the abstract non-deterministic actor and its environment was different in form. Still, the essence of the two lied in the failure to recognize the character composition of the actor itself, so that the subject's consciousness was empty, or limited in determinism, or transcended rationality, and became unexplainable arbitrary serendipity, which led to the polar division of behavior and responsibility. Bradley argued that the key to explaining human free will and moral responsibility still remained in understanding human character. He agreed with Green's view that only human character fully contained the subjective inner temperament of the subject and its relationship with the external objective environment, the dual significance of the unification of subjectivity and objectivity (internal and external). Personality displayed the existence of the subjectivity of behavior and integrated the subject's rationality and moral ability. It enjoyed the basic conditions for explaining human will and moral responsibility. As a result, understanding the individual character was the key to answering the relationship between free will and moral responsibility. According to Bradley, the character was an inner character formed by the person (subject) in the connection and interaction with the external environment. The human character was not created by others but self-created. It originated from human temperament and environment. In other words, the character was the self-creation of the subject, but this kind of self-creation had a necessary relationship with a certain objective environment, and its composition reflected a kind of subject-object connection and unity. Explaining the relationship between free will and moral responsibility by character could not only avoid the purely subjective prediction (non-determinism) but also support people's free will (behavior) and moral responsibility by the subject, thus overcoming the mistakes of determinism. Bradley also analyzed the subjectivity basis of moral responsibility from the relationship between coercion and responsibility and believed that if we considered will from a very low-level perspective, it could indeed be considered that human will was also relatively coercive. However, this did not mean the will was passive; otherwise, there was no responsibility. Absolute coercion would completely negate human will and make human behavior non-self obedience. It was the product of the human spirit or physical state without a person's actual will and the will he was against or pre-assumed. The opposite was true of relative coercion. It was not just a warning or just a request but also a threat because coercion stemmed directly or indirectly from a person's will. In other words, absolute coercion completely exceeded the will of the actor, while relative coercion was still related to the will of the actor. The former had no responsibility, while the latter had. Determinism was tantamount to an absolute compulsion, but non-determinism did not see the objectivity of relative compulsion in the subject's behavior. Bradley specifically analyzed the composition of character and believed that human character was neither innate, immutable, or fickle but relatively fixed. Human character reflected a human as a whole, gradually systematized and immobilized in the interaction between human temperament and the environment. But the fixity was only relative because it always had the possibility of change. The reasons were: (1) we could not exhaust all possible external conditions; (2) we could never systematize the entire self. Everyone's understanding and grasp of the external environment they faced or were involved in was always relative, just as the understanding and shaping of the self itself could not be thorough. Consequently, it was impossible for the character caused by the inner temperament and the external environment to achieve absolute stability and solidification. It was always in the process of being created. Even so, the character did not lose its relative stability. Therefore, human personality could be called human's "second nature". It depended on a processing material of temperament and a self-personality that had not yet been fully systematized and solidified. In short, human free will exists, and human freedom is an out-and-out "not-must". It is a kind of pure denial and an "ought". But it has an inherent personality foundation and is an explicable and rational behavior of the subject's will. Only by understanding in this way can it be explained that man is both the subject of behavior and the bearer of moral responsibility. It should be said that Bradley is negative towards determinism, but he is not simply affirming the theory of free will. He is based on the human character to explain the relative freedom of human will.

4.3 Sartre

The French existentialist philosopher Sartre advocated the absoluteness of human freedom and emphasized the relationship between freedom and responsibility. Sartre argued from the a priori structure of consciousness that man was free, and consciousness was the revelation and manifestation of the world, so consciousness was nothingness and negation. Negation led people to freedom because consciousness constantly made people forever choose themselves through negation.[50] Therefore, Sartre held that human freedom preceded human nature, which was obtained through human free choice, and human life was free. Since man was the subject of freedom, the free choice was the only way for him to realize the value of the subject. Sartre pointed out that we could not distinguish freedom from choice; that is to say, we could not distinguish freedom from the individual self. The freedom that Sartre referred to was not the same as the freedom that people usually referred to. It did not mean that people achieved their goals in practice, but it only meant that people could independently make choices. Therefore, even if people could not choose their position, they could still choose how to recognize, treat, and take what attitudes and actions for this position. Moreover, Sartre's so-called "being free" was not equal to "getting what you want"; on the contrary, it meant "it's up to you to decide (in the broad sense of choice) and to request". Success or failure was irrelevant to freedom. In addition, Sartre believed there was no law, standard, or basis for human choice to follow and fall back on. It was unconditional, unfounded, and absolutely accidental. Sartre held that freedom was freedom only because the choice was always unconditional and unfounded, which was only motivated by itself. In this way, the subjective inner

[50] See [29], p. 233.

certainty of individual moral freedom as the content became the only criterion for the rationality of people's free choices. The result of choice was equal to responsibility. Responsibility referred to "the indisputable author(s) consciousness of an event or an object".[51] To this end, Sartre posited that responsibility was an inevitable consequence of free choice. Just as people had to choose freely, he had to bear moral responsibility for it.

4.4 James

The US pragmatist philosopher James believed that the casuistic question was important in ethics. It explored the measurement scales of various good and evil. People recognized this scale so philosophers could set the true order of human obligations. Therefore, the fundamental problem of morality was our free will. Suppose we confirmed that the issue of free will was the key to explaining the problem of determinism in ethics. In that case, we must not only oppose the abstract principle theory of rationalism but also transcend the mechanical determinism of universal materialism. According to the former, people were often accustomed to regarding ethics as a code of merit, that is, as a system of abstract evaluation principles or norms, which was doubtful. Because all principles were established and fixed, whereas human moral life was empirical and constantly changing. Their psychology, sensations, consciousness, concepts, and actions were all under exceptional circumstances, and no wholly fixed moral principle could be entirely suitable for explaining these unique moral phenomena. According to the latter, traditional determinism absolutely obliterated human ethical issues themselves. According to the interpretation of determinism, it would never be possible to explain the value and responsibility of people's behavior. Therefore, we faced the ancient ethical dilemma of free will or non-determinism and the law of causation or determinism. Free will supporters argued that if our behavior was determined in advance if we could only pass on the driving force of the entire past, what could we be praised or blamed for? We were not the main parties concerned but just agents. So, where was there any valuable blame and responsibility at all? In contrast, determinists retorted that if we had free will, where was the accountability and responsibility? If the act of freedom was a completely new thing, it did not come from self, the previous self, but out of nowhere, then how could self, the previous self, be responsible? How could self have a permanent, stable character long enough to accept praise and criticism? Life was like a string of beads; the inevitable internal lines were drawn away by the absurd non-determinism and scattered into disconnected beads.[52] Therefore, neither determinism nor free will theory could explain the source of human moral responsibility. James posited that traditional determinism must be abandoned, but this did not mean that it must lead to purely arbitrary subjectivity. On the contrary, we could choose a new determinism to eliminate difficulties.

[51] Sartre [30], p. 708.

[52] See [31], p. 63.

James called traditional determinism "hard determinism", and his new determinism was a kind of "soft determinism", that is, a kind of free will theory with new pragmatism. The fundamental difference between soft and hard determinism was that it was no longer confined to concepts such as "destiny, will, restraint, and necessity", but focused on the creation of new things in the future and the choice of opportunities or possibilities. Therefore, fundamentally speaking, James still advocated non-determinism or free will. According to James, the pragmatist meaning of free will meant that there were new things in the world. In terms of its most profound essence and superficial phenomena, people hoped they would not repeat or imitate the past in the future. If there was indeed a particular necessity, then freedom was the only necessity that could be understood, while the highest restraint was the same as true freedom. Therefore, James believed that there were the following differences and opposites between non-determinism and determinism[53]:

Determinism	Non-determinism
Monism	Pluralism
Necessity	Possibility (contingency, opportunity)
Pessimism	Optimism
Fatalism	Free will
Totality	Individuality
Justifiability	Emotion or perceptuality

James also discussed free will from a psychological perspective. He wrote, "The question of fact in the free-will controversy is thus extremely simple. It relates solely to the amount of effort of attention or consent which we can at any time put forth." He believed that will or effort of will was the effort of attention that consciousness (or object) gave to an idea. "If the amount of effort be not indeterminate, but be related in a fixed manner to the objects themselves, in such wise that whatever object at any time fills our consciousness was from eternity bound to fill it then and there, and compel from us the exact effort, neither more nor less, which we bestow upon it, —then our wills are not free, and all our acts are foreordained." According to this principle, James defined free will: "If it be really indeterminate, our future acts are ambiguous or unpredestinate: in common parlance, our wills are free."[54] That is to say, the so-called freedom is "unpredestinate or ambiguous", thus, free will refers to that the amount of effort of attention (or object) that the human "mind" or consciousness can at any time put forth is unpredestinate or ambiguous. James continued, "the question of free will, on strictly psychological grounds, was insoluble. After a certain amount of effort of attention has been given to an idea, it is manifestly impossible to tell whether either more or less of it might have been given or not. To tell that, we should have to ascend to the antecedents of the effort, and defining them with mathematical exactitude, prove, by laws of which we have not at present

[53] See [US] James: *The Will to Believe*, English version, p. 149. Quoted from [32], p. 272.

[54] James [33], p. 390.

even an inkling, that the only amount of sequent effort which could possibly comport with them was the precise amount which actually came. Measurements, whether of psychic or of neural quantities, and deductive reasonings such as this method of proof implies, will surely be forever beyond human reach." Further, he argued, "The most that any argument can do for determinism is to make it a clear and seductive conception, which a man is foolish not to espouse, so long as he stands by the great scientific postulate that the world must be one unbroken fact, and that prediction of all things without exception must be ideally, even if not actually, possible. It is a moral postulate about the Universe, the postulate that what ought to be can be, and that bad acts cannot be fated, but that good ones must be possible in their place, which would lead one to espouse the contrary view. But when scientific and moral postulates war thus with each other and objective proof is not to be had, the only course is voluntary choice."[55] James himself chose to believe in the view of free will. His reason is ethical, not psychological, because free will is the ethical basis for rewarding good and punishing evil, and holding moral responsibility.

4.5 Brightman

The US humanist philosopher Brightman is unique for his intense focus on value personality. He believed the world was twofold, including the empirical world of phenomena and the ideal world of ontology. From the perspective of value-personality ethics, it was divided into the natural or material world and the value or personality world. Brightman investigated nature and value separately. Nature referred to the totality of material reality other than the mind and spirit, or "what it is". The value referred to something inherent beyond the natural world and had a transcendent permanent spiritual meaning. The essence of value lied in its "ought to be" nature as the inner pursuit of the purpose of human beings, and this was the fundamental difference between "to be" and nature. Brightman believed that the meaning of personality was the foundation of the world of value. Then, what is personality? According to Brightman, "A personality is a complex but self-identifying, active, selective, feeling, sensing, developing experience, which remembers its past (in part), plans for its future, interacts with its subconscious processes, its bodily organism, and its natural and social environment and can judge and guide itself and its objects by rational and ideal standards." Or, more specifically, a personality is a variety of complex changes in consciousness, including the unity of all its experiences—its various memories, various purposes, various values, various abilities, various activities, and the various interactions it experiences with its environment.[56] Brightman regarded spiritual freedom as one of the principles of the philosophy of personalism, holding that more important than spiritual freedom was the freedom of spiritual

---

[55] James [33], p. 392.

[56] See [US] Brightman: *Nature and Values*, English version, pp. 53, 56. The following Brightman's views are all from this book, see [32], p. 381.

personality. The entire history of humanity is the history of the struggle for human freedom. The true personality is an independent spiritual personality, confined to nothing and subject to no one. Everyone has an independent personality. Without spiritual freedom, it is impossible to have an actual personality. Freedom is the right given to everyone by God, and it is also the foundation of its existence, development, and improvement.

4.6 Skinner

The US behaviorist philosopher Skinner posited that man's absolute freedom did not exist. Everyone was under various control of the environment all the time, and his behavior must be restricted by multiple stimuli and affected by behavioral consequences. In other words, human behavior must rely on certain environmental stimuli and strengthening effects, and they were connected by objectivity. Skinner proposed the concept of "inner man" and "outer man". When people could not explain human behaviors, they utilized the term "inner man" to explain. They stated that people were divided into inner man and outer man, with the outer man being dominated and constrained by the inner man. The outer man is very similar to the inner man, and the inner man is a fictional model of the outer man. The psychologism interpretation by Skinner explains the behaviors of the outer man based on those of the inner man. Skinner stated that the inner man's function provided an interpretation, but the interpretation could not be explained, so the explanation ended with the inner man. Inner man was not the intermediary between the past behaviors and actual behaviors but a center where behaviors emerged.[57] Behavioral science thoroughly abandons the interpretation of psychologism. Rather than seeking interpretations from the inner mind of humans, it turns to the external environment. This is the idea that the external environment determines human behaviors, which is also one of the most important propositions of behavioral science.

Behavioral science is against seeking reasons for behaviors within organisms. According to Skinner, seeking explanations for behaviors within organisms usually covers some variables that can be directly used for scientific analysis. These variables exist outside organisms in the present and past environments of organisms, which have a physical state suitable for general scientific approaches so that our explanations of behaviors are as scientific as possible.[58] Thus, human behaviors can only be interpreted from the outside environment. Skinner argued that for a long time, people had not been clearly aware of the role of the environment on behavior. It was Descartes who first reminded us that perhaps the environment played an active role in determining behavior. The stimulating effect of the environment was called "stimulus" (the word came from Latin and was initially referred to as a thorn stick), and the impact on organisms was called "response". "Stimulus" and "response"

[57] See [34], p. 12.

[58] See [35], p. 29.

together were considered to form a "reflex". The environment not only stimulated or spurred but also made choices. When considering the effects of the environment on organisms, not only should we consider its effect before the responses of organisms, but also the impact after the responses. Behaviors were formed and maintained by effects. Once we realize this fact, we could set forth the interactions between organisms and the environment from a broader perspective. This way, two crucial results were produced. One of them involved fundamental analysis. Behaviors that acted on the environment and produced results ("operant" behavior) could be studied by arranging certain environmental conditions, where the specific results "depended on" the particular behavior. As the dependency became more and more complex, these results could perform their explanatory functions of behaviors. Another result was practical, that is, we could control the environment. Indeed, human genetic talents could only be changed slowly, while the change in individual environments was rapid and dramatic. We would see that there would be considerable progress in operational behavior technologies, and it might be possible to demonstrate that operational behavior technologies might be applied to address our issues.[59]

Skinner believed that people and their behaviors could not transcend the constraints of the social environment and therefore were not free and determined. According to the interpretation of behavioral science, freedom was nothing more than the reinforcement of dependent connections, not the feelings generated by these dependent connections. Therefore, man's pursuit of freedom was not because he had the so-called free will but because of a tendency he displayed in the process of behavior to escape or evade the so-called unfavorable factors in the environment. Therefore, Skinner opposed using free will, an inherent imaginary factor, to explain human value behavior, insisting that any behavior occurred based on specific external rules of behavior.

When using behavioral science to explain human behavior, a difficult issue will be proposed: how to understand human responsibilities. Skinner posited that in the traditional concept, a person was free, and external reasons did not cause his behavior. In this regard, he was autonomous. If he deviated from the rules, he would take responsibility for it and be punished fairly. When scientific analysis revealed the unexpected restrictive relationship between behavior and the environment, it was necessary to re-understand this concept and corresponding practice.[60] The question raised by Skinner is profound, and its conclusion denies free will and human responsibility. According to Skinner, when behavior was attributed to the role of human genetic endowments, the concept of responsibility was even weaker. For example, Skinner pointed out that the sexual behavior of different individuals varied in degree, and the degree of influence of sexual enhancement was not the same. So, should they be equally responsible for controlling their aggressiveness or sexual behavior? Moreover, was it fair to impose the same punishment on them? As a result, Skinner clearly put forward the concept of responsibility denial, arguing that the idea of responsibility was of no benefit to this problem because the core of the problem was manifested

[59] See [34], pp. 15–17.

[60] See [34], p. 18.

in human controllability. The use of punishment failed to change genetic defects, and this change could only be achieved through long-term genetic engineering work. What must be changed was not the owner's responsibility but the environmental conditions or genetic effects. Human behavior was nothing more than the product of these conditions or influences.

Through the historical investigation of the theory of free will, we can find that free will is indeed a chaotic issue and has puzzled people for thousands of years. A critical reason for this situation is that there is no distinction between free will in the sense of existentialism and that in the sense of value. The famous German philosopher Paulsen said: "Let us first distinguish between the two meanings of freedom: free will in the psychological sense and freed will in the metaphysical sense. The former means being able to make decisions and take actions according to one's own will (freedom of choice), while the latter means there is no reason for the will or special decision itself."[61] I believe that the free will in the metaphysical sense mentioned by Paulsen is the free will in the sense of existentialism, while that in the psychological sense is the one in the sense of value. These two issues are indeed related to a certain extent, but they are not problems of the same nature at the same level. Throughout the entire history of philosophy, these two issues have always been more or less confused, resulting in unnecessary entanglements and contradictions. To scientifically explain the issue of free will, it is necessary to distinguish between the two issues of free will in the sense of existentialism and the sense of value.

References

1. *Marx-Engels-Gesamtausgabe*, vol. 3, 2nd edn. (People's Publishing House, Beijing, 1995)
2. [Russia] Plekhanov, *Research on Plekhanov's Conception of History* (Sanlian Bookstore, Beijing, 1961)
3. [UK] Russell, *A History of Western Philosophy*, vol. 1 (The Commercial Press, Beijing, 1963)
4. [Russia] Lossky, *Freedom of Will* (Culture Life Press, Beijing, 1992)
5. G. Luo, X. Song, *The History of Western Ethic Thoughts*, vol. 1 (Renmin University of China Press, Beijing, 1985)
6. [Ancient Greece] Aristotle, *The Nicomachean Ethics* (China Social Sciences Press, Beijing, 1990)
7. [US] Thilly, *A History of Philosophy*, vol. 1 (The Commercial Press, Beijing, 1979)
8. S. Zhang, *The Culture of "God" in the Middle Ages: A History of the Christian Church in the Middle Ages* (Zhejiang People's Publishing House, Hangzhou, 1987)
9. [Britain] S. Leslie, *The Study of Human Nature* (Renmin University of China Press, Beijing, 1992)
10. [France] Descartes, *Principles of Philosophy* (The Commercial Press, Beijing, 1958)
11. Compiled and translated by the Teaching and Research Section of the History of Foreign Philosophy of Department of Philosophy of Peking University, *Philosophy of Western European Countries in the 16th–18th Centuries* (Sanlian Bookstore, Beijing, 1958)
12. [Britain] Hobbes, *Leviathan* (The Commercial Press, Beijing, 1985)
13. [Britain] Locke, *An Essay Concerning Human Understanding*, vol. 1 (The Commercial Press, Beijing, 1959)

[61] See [36], p. 385.

14. [Holland] Spinoza, *Ethics* (The Commercial Press, Beijing, 1983)
15. [Soviet Union] B.JI. Golubenko, *Necessity and Freedom* (Peking University Press, Beijing, 1984)
16. *Marx-Engels-Gesamtausgabe*, vol. 20 (People's Publishing House, Beijing, 1971)
17. [Britain] Hume, *A Treatise of Human Nature*, vol. 2 (The Commercial Press, Beijing, 1980)
18. [Britain] Hume, *An Enquiry Concerning Human Understanding* (The Commercial Press, Beijing, 1957)
19. [France] Holbach, *The System of Nature*, vol. 1 (The Commercial Press, Beijing, 1964)
20. [France] Holbach, *Good Sense: Natural Ideas Opposed to Supernatural* (The Commercial Press, Beijing, 1966)
21. [France] Diderot, *Diderot: Selected Philosophical Writings* (Shanghai Sanlian Bookstore, Shanghai, 1956)
22. [Germany] Kant, *Critique of Practical Reason* (The Commercial Press, Beijing, 1960)
23. [Germany] Kant, *Kant's Groundwork of the Metaphysics of Moral* (The Commercial Press, Beijing, 1957)
24. Z. Li, *Criticism on Critique of Philosophy: A Review of Kant* (People's Publishing House, Beijing, 1979)
25. J. Chen, *Construction and Guidance: The Methodology of Kant's Philosophy* (Social Science Academic Press, Beijing, 1992)
26. Engels, Anti-Dühring, in *Marx-Engels-Gesamtausgabe*, vol. 3, 2nd edn. (People's Publishing House, Beijing, 1995)
27. [Germany] Hegel, *Elements of the Philosophy of Right* (The Commercial Press, Beijing, 1961)
28. J. Wan, *History of Modern Western Ethics*, vol. 1 (Peking University Press, Beijing, 1990)
29. C. Xu (Editor-in-Chief), *Existentialism* (China Social Sciences Press, Beijing, 1988)
30. [France] Sartre, *Being and Nothingness* (Joint Publishing, Beijing, 1987)
31. [US] James, *Pragmatism: A New Name for Some Old Ways of Thinking* (The Commercial Press, Beijing, 1979)
32. J. Wan, *History of Modern Western Ethics*, vol. 2 (Peking University Press, Beijing, 1992)
33. [US] James, *The Principles of Psychology* (The Commercial Press, Beijing, 1963)
34. [US] Skinner, *Beyond Freedom and Dignity* (Guizhou People's Publishing House, Guiyang, 1987)
35. [US] Skinner, *Science and Human Behavior* (Huaxia Publishing House, Beijing, 1989)
36. [Germany] Paulsen, *A System of Ethics* (China Social Science Press, Beijing, 1988)

Chapter 5
Freedom of Will: Ontology

In the sense of ontology, freedom of will refers to the question of whether there is a cause for will. If there is a cause for will, the will is determined, or the will is free. So, freedom here means freedom in the sense opposite of necessity. The freedom of will in ontology involves the basic issues of philosophy.

1 Will and Existence

The relation between will and existence is also the relationship between thinking and existence, and the subject and object. What needs to be solved here is the question that which is the principal and which is the secondary of will and existence, that is, who decides who.

1.1 Ontological Study

Hegel said, the opposition between thinking and existence is the starting point of philosophy, which constitutes the whole point of philosophy.[1] In his point of view, the relation between thinking and existence is the central problem of all modern philosophy. On this basis, Engels put forward the basic problem of philosophy in a clear form. He said, the major fundamental problem of all philosophies, especially modern philosophy, referred to the relation between thinking and existence.[2] The relation between thinking and existence, is also the relation between spirit and matter. Obviously, the spirit here includes a human will. The highest expression of the basic problem of philosophy is that which of thinking and existence, spirit and

[1] Hegel [1], p. 292.
[2] See [2], p. 223.

X. Chen, *Humanistic Foundation of Criminal Law*,
https://doi.org/10.1007/978-981-19-9764-8_5

matter, is the principle? Is the world created by thinking or spirit or has it always existed naturally? Is the nature and basis of the world thinking, spirit or matter? The answer to the question is the theory of existence and the nature of existence, which belongs to the so-called ontological problem in the history of philosophy. It is the foundation and fundamental starting point for the establishment and development of all philosophical systems. Engels pointed out that, according to how they answered this question, philosophers were divided into two camps. Those who concluded that the spirit was the principle for nature, and thus ultimately believed in creationism (which is often far more complex and absurd for philosophers, such as Hegel, than for Christian), formed the idealist camp. Instead, those who regarded nature as the principle formed the schools of materialism.[3] It's the unique criterion and basis for dividing materialism and idealism in philosophy. Contemporary western philosophy strives to negate the basic philosophical question that, which of thinking and existence, spirit and matter, is principle? It believes that the question is meaningless, false and metaphysical, claiming that if we give up the question, we can transcend the opposition between materialism and idealism. In fact, the question about thinking and existence is inescapable, and philosophers are still answering this question in different ways.

Investigating the question of free will from the perspective of ontology, we are faced with the following two answers to the relation between will and existence: materialists hold that existence determines will and therefore advocate volitional determinism, while idealists hold that the will determines the existence and therefore advocate libertarianism.[4]

In the early ancient Greek philosophy, there was a dispute between Democritus' materialism and Plato's idealism. Democritus advocated atomism, arguing that everything in nature was made up of the smallest, indivisible particles of a substance, which were known as atoms. The atoms and the place where atoms move—the void constituted the principle of all things. There were countless atoms without any qualitative differences, except in size, shape, location and order. It was these differences that made things different. For Democritus, the motion of atoms was obvious. It drove the unite and separation of atoms, making all things in the constant process of formation and destruction. Democritus believed that atoms were the principle of the world, and that feelings and thoughts were generated by images of external objects acting on our senses and souls, thus affirming that human consciousness was the reflection of external objects. Based on this, Democritus denied the freedom of will and believed that human will was determined. Plato advocated the idealist theory that when we gave the same name to certain individual things, we assumed there must be a concept. Everything has a corresponding concept, which is independent, and is the idea that produces things. All the concepts constitute an independent world, which is the so-called world of ideas. The real world is just a projection of this idea world. Plato believed that objective and fickle things are unreal and illusory, and only the world

---

[3] See [2], p. 224.

[4] In the sense corresponding to determinism, libertarianism is often referred to as indeterminism. This book uniformly adopts libertarianism for clarity.

of ideas is real and eternal. His idealist theory reverses the relationships between the subject and object, as well as thinking and existence, and is therefore a kind of primitive idealism. Based on this theory, Plato emphasized the selectability of man, advocated the moderation of rationality over behavior, and, in a word, advocated the freedom of will.

The ancient Greek philosopher Aristotle swayed between Democritus' materialism and Plato's idealism on the basic problem of philosophy, showing the tendency of eclecticism. The core of his philosophical thought is the so-called theory of substance. According to this, the material world is objective, and the natural world is the sum of objects, which moves and changes perpetually. So what causes things to move and change? To deal with it, Aristotle proposed the so-called Doctrine of Four Causes, which were the material cause, the formal cause, the moving cause and the final cause. The material cause shows what things are made of; the formal cause explains how things develop based on the structure and relationship; the moving cause explains the reason why things can change; and the final cause describes the tendency and purpose of things to move and change. According to Aristotle, these four causes coexisted with the development of things, and all man-made things and natural things contained four causes. To adhere to the theory of substance, Aristotle attributed the four causes to two causes, namely the material cause and the formal cause, and believed that the relationship between the two was about the relationship between the individual and general. The form consists of matters and cannot be separated from matters. This kind of thought is referred to as materialism. However, Aristotle did not carry through materialism to the end. While explaining the relationships among and the development of the four causes, he often attributed the formal cause, the final cause and the moving cause to the formal cause, and held that the form was the essence of existence, the purpose of matters, and also the driving force that pushed matters to change from possibility to reality. The form is positive, active, and is the principle that exists prior to matters. In this regard, Aristotle was inclined to Plato's idealism. In addition to this, Aristotle also acknowledged the existence of the so-called pure form for all forms, that was, the god, which was the "prime booster" that drove the whole world to move with purpose. So, Aristotle fell back into idealist views in terms of substantial issues. In epistemology, Aristotle admitted that nature and the objective material world were the objects of cognition and the source of all experience and feelings on one hand, but on the other hand, he also exaggerated the role of rationality, thinking that rationality could be separated from the body. According to Aristotle, there were two roles for human rationality, or there were two different kinds of rationalities. One is straightforward and active, which can be called cognitive rationality; while the other is indirect and passive, which can be called value rationality. The task of the former is to know the truth; the function of the latter is to judge what is right. The former is the function of pure thinking separated from the body, while the latter is the function of feelings and the mind that cannot be separated from the body. Therefore, in terms of free will, Aristotle advocated dualism, that was, the objects for cognitive rationality were necessities, while value rationality referred to introspective calculation, and its objects were accidental things. As these accidental things could be elective by man, he regarded choice as the cause of human behaviors. However, in his point of view, the purpose of behavior was only the object of desire, not the object of choice, only the methods and means to achieve the purpose were the object of choice. Thus, his conclusion was that morality or vice is within our power. It can be seen that Aristotle acknowledged the freedom of choice to a certain extent, and he also connected choice with human cognition. But his limitation for freedom was not only within the scope of ethics, but also limited to the selection of means and methods to achieve the purpose. As a result, Aristotle's theory of free will is closely related to his ontology. As some philosophers have pointed out that Aristotle's ontology was indeed infused with the essence of human nature. His way of thinking here was to project all the contradictions of human nature into the essence of things in advance, and then turned around to explain human beings according to them, so that the materialized essence of human beings became the highest noumenon that rules everything. This is the theory that human nature is represented in an inhuman, or more exactly superhuman, form, which obviously has double essences and significances. On the one hand, it is a formal affirmation of the action of soul, that is, the affirmation of dominance of people and the nature of mobility, for only people alone possess the highest essence of the soul. On the other hand, people are also confused with things here at the same time, and since human nature is compared to the essence of things by the object, it not only elevates the object, but also puts human beings under the control of it's own materialized nature. It was in this way that Aristotle split the essence of human beings into the contradiction between subjectivity and objectivity. People's initiative is not only manifested in cognitive rationality, but also in the pursuit of value. In essence, human activity belongs to the activity of realizing human purpose targeting object. The value rationality materializes into the highest noumenon and forms the supreme good god, while the grasp of the noumenon by cognitive rationality is the highest task of philosophy. Aristotle seemed to unify man and nature, and realize some coordination and even integration for subjectivity and objectivity, thinking and existence, human nature and material nature, subjective logic and objective logic, but the combination was completely fantasy, without objective and realistic nature.[5] It can be seen that Aristotle didn't acknowledge the free will of human beings from the principle of natural substance, but in the sense of ethics, Aristotle affirmed that man has the freedom to choose his own behaviors. It should be said that Aristotle's dualism about free will is rooted in his ontological dualism, which swings between materialism and idealism, but also has certain dialectical thinking inside. In particular, the view that man has freedom of will in the scope of ethics is actually affirming the freedom of will in the sense of axiology, which has important reference significance for us to explain the problem of free will scientifically.

Throughout the Middle Ages, orthodox scholastics proclaimed that everything in the material world was created by God, and that all human rationality and consciousness came from God. In scholasticism, there were conflicts between realism and nominalism, which to some extent involved ontological problems. Realism holds that the general concept, and the universal are real, and that the concept of God is the

[5] See [3], pp. 212–213.

greatest and most perfect concept of being. Thus, God should exist in reality. This is the so-called ontological argument that deduces the existence of God from the concept of God. Nominalism, on the contrary, is opposed to the view of realism that the general substance is real, thinking that only sensible objects are real, instead of the general substance. Thus, it can be seen that realism belongs to the pure idealism, while nominalism is closer to materialism. Under the domination of medieval theological worldview, God must be recognized as the principle, and as a result, only God has the freedom of will. The saying that only God has the freedom of will is actually a kind of divine determinism, which means that man is subject to God, and has no freedom fundamentally speaking. Yet completely denying the free will of people, their sins should be in the charge of God, which contradicts to the saying that God has the nicest look. Therefore, the scholastics in the Middle Ages were faced with the contradiction between divine determinism and people's free will, and tried to coordinate with it. For example, Augustine affirmed the free will of God on the one hand, and also believed that God endowed people with freedom while creating them on the other hand. But they lost freedom because of the original sin. It was by the grace of God that people could regain the freedom, which was about getting rid of various desires, and freeing from the bondage of the body to do good things. Aquinas believed that divine providence did not exclude free will, and people's will was free, they had the freedom to choose behaviors. People's free will relied on the fact that man was rational, and the rationality and will could determine each other. Rationality can drive will, as it enables will to get to know its own objects, allowing it to make decisions in accordance with rational purposes. Yet it is not compulsion, compulsion means that things can be determined inevitably by external causes. Therefore, people's will is free. It can be seen that based on the idealist standpoint, the scholastics in the Middle Ages advocated divine determinism in ontology, while still acknowledging that man has certain freedom of will in axiology.

As the ancestor of modern philosophy, Descartes was a dualist in the ontology. He believed that matter and soul were two independent substances. The essence of matter was an extension, which was divisible and passive, while the essence of the soul was thinking, which was indivisible and active. The matter couldn't think, while the soul couldn't be extensive, so they were independent of each other, and also the highest substances which were created by God. As a result, the dualism of Descartes ultimately leads to objective idealism. As for the problem of free will, Descartes denied the freedom of will in ontology, thinking that the laws of nature were objective.[6] But in terms of axiology, Descartes advocated the freedom of will.

After Descartes, Hobbes, Locke, Holbach, Diderot and other philosophers inherited his theory in the aspect of materialism, and tended to deny people's free will from ontology. For instance, Hobbes criticized Descartes' claim that the soul was an immaterial substance. He pointed out that the thing under thinking was still a kind of substance, because in his point of view, all subjects of activities could only be conceived as something tangible or substantial. We couldn't separate thinking from the thing under thinking. For Hobbes, there was only one kind of substance, which he

[6] See [4], p. 64.

called the object. He thought that the object was independent of our thoughts, which could be consistent with some parts of the space or maintain the same extensive property as well.[7] Thus, Hobbes thought it was quite clear that matter was independent of human consciousness, and human consciousness was the product of matters. Seeing from the mechanistic materialism, Hobbes denied people's free will straightforwardly. Locke built on Hobbes' mechanistic materialism, thinking that matter had two kinds of properties. The first one referred to the extension, shape, motion, stand still, etc. of an object, and the second one referred to the ability of an object to produce the feeling of sound, color, taste and so on by acting on our sense organs with its properties of the first kind. The first kind of properties could not be separated from the object under any circumstances, while the second kind of properties depended on the first kind. Both two kinds could produce concepts by means of imperceptible objects acting on our sense organs. From the materialistic ontology, Locke denies the freedom of will. But in the meantime, he also acknowledged the freedom of human subjectivity and linked it with rationality, which to some extent confirmed the freedom of will in the sense of axiology. Spinoza conquered Descartes' dualism of substance and thinking and moved towards materialism. Spinoza regarded nature as the only substance, and believed that nature was objective, unique, eternal and infinite, emphasizing that the substance was something known for its own sake.[8] Spinoza affirmed the movement of objects, yet also believed that this kind of movement is mainly referred to as mechanical movement. Thus, Spinoza's theory reveals obvious mechanical characteristics. Based on mechanistic materialism, Spinoza denied people's free will. Holbach believed that the so-called soul referred to the function of feeling and thinking of the brain when the human body was alive. Holbach pointed out that, the brain was a common center through which all the nerves scattered in all parts of the human body passed and converged here. All the functions attributed to the soul were carried out by means of this inner organ, and it was the impressions, the changes, as well as the movements conducting on the nerves that change the brain. Therefore, the brain would react by letting all the organs of the body move, or by acting upon itself so that it could be able to produce a great many different movements inside, namely the intelligent movements.[9] Since the human soul is only the function of the brain, and the brain, as a kind of substance, is governed by inevitability, there is no such thing as free will. As a materialist, Diderot emphasized that consciousness was a reflection of external things and he thought that people were like musical instruments endowed with feelings and memories. The senses were the keyboard, which was constantly tapped by the surrounding nature, as well as people themselves, thus forming the impressions and concepts. Therefore, Diderot believed that man was not free fundamentally. But on the other hand, Diderot conquered the bias of mechanical materialism to a certain extent, believing that as the subject of behaviors, man had freedom. Therefore, Diderot's analysis of free will is dialectical to a certain extent,

[7] See [5], p. 20.

[8] See [6], p. 3.

[9] See [7], p. 93.

which means man is not free and is passive from the ontological point of view, while axiologically speaking, man is free.

After Descartes, philosophers such as Leibniz and Hume inherited his theory in the aspects of idealism and agnosticism. Leibniz was an objective idealist. He believed that the substances that form everything should be dynamic and holistic, without any qualitative differences. Therefore, such substances could not be objects, but only spiritual things, which he called monads. The monad was dynamic. It had the power to move as pure matters, and also had the consciousness and desire like the soul. Leibniz fundamentally negated Locke's idea of the possibility that matters were capable of thinking. For it seemed to him that by mechanical motions, the completely passive matters could not produce rationalities, and also sensations. Leibniz pointed out that all the thoughts and actions of our souls came from within themselves, instead of given by sensations.[10] From objective idealism, Leibniz acknowledged people's free will. Hume was an agnostic, he believed that all knowledge came from perceptual impressions. So where did these impressions come from? Hume argued that it was unknowable, asking by what arguments could we prove that the hallucinations in the mind must be caused by something similar to these (if possible) but quite different from them? By what arguments could we prove that they could not be caused by the suggestion of a spirit which was invisible and unknowable, or by some other cause that was hard to understand? It was acknowledged that in fact, much of these perceptions were not derived from external things, as in dreaming, madness, or other diseases.[11] Therefore, Hume regarded the objects of perception as impossible to be proven, and he was also skeptical of the existence of either material or spiritual substance. As for the problem of free will, Hume also tried to solve it with a skeptical view. Hume believed that admitting objective necessity and considering freedom as an escape from necessity, then the problem cannot be solved. So Hume approached this problem in two ways. On the one hand, Hume denied the inevitability of the material world, arguing that inevitability was not inherent in objective things, but a habitual association in our thinking or imaginations. On the other hand, he also aimed to revise the concept of freedom as it was commonly understood. Hume pointed out that freedom was nothing else but an opportunity when it was opposed to necessity and not to limitations, which was nonexistent for human beings. On the contrary, the so-called freedom was merely the power to act or not to act as will, that was, we could choose to stand still, or take actions.[12] For Hume, this freedom was completely possible, because there was no such an objective inevitability for will to oppose it, so that it could make decisions. It can be seen that Hume's skepticism still cannot solve the problem of free will scientifically.

Modern German classical philosophy related the problem of free will to ontology. Kant was a dualist in philosophy. He divided the unified world into two distinct realms, namely the phenomenon and the thing-in-itself, and held that there were impassable gulfs between the two. Kant's so-called phenomenon referred to the sum

[10] See [8], p. 36.

[11] See [9], p. 135.

[12] See [9], pp. 85 and 86.

of all attributes of natural objects, which was constituted by the sensory representation of the thing-in-itself acting on our senses. The thing-in-itself was something that existed outside of us and acted on our senses. From this point of view, Kant tried to conquer the opposition between determinism and libertarianism, and he regarded these two fundamentally opposite views as the antinomy arising from rationality understanding the concepts of the world. The positive view said there were reasons out of freedom in this world. While the converse was that all things were referred to as nature without freedom. Kant argued that the contradiction between freedom and necessity in rationality was false and could be resolved if the two concepts were applied separately to the thing-in-itself and the phenomenal world. For Kant, everything in the phenomenal world was governed by the inexorable laws of cause and effect. Everything that happened in a time had its own causes, and every cause would presuppose another cause. Therefore, there couldn't be an absolute, causeless and spontaneous cause, which meant there won't be any causes with absolute freedom. However, seeing from the perspective of the world as a whole, we had to admit that the whole phenomenal world arose from a free and spontaneous cause. The cause of freedom neither existed in time, nor belonged to experience. It was the thing-in-itself beyond experience. Kant believed that man, as a part of nature, also exists in the causality series of natural phenomena, so his behavior is necessarily under the condition of things that existed in a previous time. As the past time is no longer under man's control, every act of it is necessary by certain grounds which are not included in its control, that is to say, man is not free in the nature of experience. However, as a rational being, man is free. This kind of freedom cannot be understood by rational knowledge and can only be a priori. It is the result of practical reason. Kant thought there were two meanings for freedom, one was negative, namely it was the thing-in-itself that existed outside the inexorable laws of natural causality, which was unrecognizable. The other was positive, which meant freedom was a kind of will autonomy of morality, as the practical reason. Kant's differentiation for freedom here was actually a division of free will into ontological and axiological freedom of will. Hegel was an objective idealist who regarded the whole universe as the dialectical development process of the self-movement of absolute ideas, and regarded the material world as the external form of the alienation of absolute ideas. Hegel believed that the unification process of thinking and existence is a dialectical development process of self-consciousness. As a result, Hegel acknowledged the freedom of man's self-consciousness. Under the unity of substance and subject, Hegel united the view of freedom and epistemology with ontology, making it a different expression of the same spiritual essence or absolute objects, and thus freedom was attributed to the absolute being or spirit. Freedom, and the development and realization, as well as understanding of freedom were regarded as the nature, process, and end of the absolute essence of spirit.[13] It can be seen that Hegel affirmed man's free will in the sense of ontology based on his philosophy of objective idealism. Feuerbach made a materialistic explanation and argument for the relation between matters and consciousness. He believed that man is a part of nature and nature is the

[13] See [10], p. 97.

foundation of man. Man is the unity of body and soul, namely the unity of matter and consciousness. Feuerbach regarded nature as the sum of all things and attributes, and believed that objective things are entities that can be felt in time and space. Therefore, the matter was primary and spirit was secondary. Spirit and consciousness are the highest products of matters, namely the function of the brain. Consciousness is the reflection of objective things and depends on interpersonal communication. From the perspective of materialist ontology, Feuerbach affirmed the inevitability of human activities and criticized the libertarianism of idealism. He pointed out that libertarians believed that will was independent of any natural laws and causes, and so of any compulsions. But virtually there wasn't a single word in history that affirmed the fanciful and supernatural freedom of will.

In modern western philosophy, there was still a trend of thought which negated the traditional ontological model fundamentally. For example, the pragmatic philosopher James believed that traditional philosophy debated whether the world was monistic or pluralistic, deterministic or free, material or spiritual, which were all meaningless and metaphysical. These insights may or may not be right for the world, and the arguments on them never end. In such cases, the pragmatic approach is to try to find the practical consequences of every insight to illustrate it.[14] Nevertheless, the question of the relationship between thinking and existence, spirit and matter, has not, of course, been eliminated. As for those philosophers who advocated abandoning metaphysics or ontology, nature contained the premise and basis of ontology. They thought the same way in terms of the problem of free will.

Generally speaking, in terms of ontology, when it comes to the relationship between will and being, namely the problem of which is the principle, materialists hold that existence determines will and therefore affirm volitional determinism, while idealists hold that the will determines the existence and therefore affirm libertarianism. Of course, due to the different theoretical starting points of each school, their specific views are also different.

1.2 Materialistic Determinism

Ontologically speaking, we advocate materialist determinism and deny the free will of man. In other words, man's will is essentially determined by existence. In this sense, and only in this sense, man has no freedom of will, which is an inevitable conclusion of Marxist materialism. As Marx said, "The production mode of material life restricts the whole process of social, political and spiritual life. It's not the consciousness of men that determines their existence, but rather their social existence that determines their consciousness."[15] According to Marxism, materialist determinism is manifested mainly in the following aspects:

[14] See [3], p. 245.

[15] See [11], p. 32.

1.2.1 The Conclusiveness of Nature over Man

In the relation between will and existence, the will refers to the will of man, while the being refers to the being of things. Thus, people are the subjects and things are the objects. People as the subjects should firstly affirm the natural premise of their existence, which is the so-called preexistence of nature to human beings. Man is not a supernatural subject, which surpasses nature or descended from another world. Man is divided from the material nature and evolves from the natural history premise of the general life process of it. Although man is divided from the material nature, he still belongs to it, and his existence and activities still depend on it and submit to its laws. As Marx said, "Man is the natural being frankly. Man as the natural being with life has the natural forces and vitality that exist in man as gifts, talents and desires, and can be dynamic on the one hand. On the other hand, man as the natural, physical, emotional and objective being, is passive, conditioned and restricted just like animals and plants. That is, the objects of man's desire are independent of him and can exist without him, while on the contrary, these objects are exactly what he needs, which are indispensable and necessary for the expression and confirmation of his essential power. To say that man is physical, natural, vital, realistic, emotional and objective, that is to say there are realistic and emotional objects for man's essence, namely the expression of his life; or in other words, a man can only express his life by means of realistic and emotional objects."[16] As a natural being with life, man is a part of the material nature on the one hand. His body organs, natural forces, vitality and life processes, all belong to the material nature and are governed by natural law. On the other hand, human existence and activities depend on other natural beings, which are indispensable for these. That's why it is necessary and possible for a man to interact with the objects materially with a realistic, emotional and objective material force, and reflect the objects in his mind on this basis.

The conclusiveness of nature over man reflects the relationship between man and objects, which usually refers to the relationship between heaven and man in ancient Chinese philosophy. There is no doubt that the relationship between man and objects is not immutable, but with the deepening of man's understanding of nature, a man gains more and more freedom. As for the evolution of human history, people have experienced changes from chaotic unity to sharp opposition and then to harmonious unity of man and objects. In primitive society, due to the low level of human practice, man could rarely interfere with nature, thus the active status of the human in nature and the superiority of humans to other species could not be fully manifested. It seemed that man was just a natural thing, the same as other beings of nature. In consciousness, it meant that people could not consciously separate themselves from nature, and also regarded themselves as the homogeneous things of natural beings, which were the unity of chaos. They not only compared some of their characteristics (such as emotions, movements and cognitions) with natural beings,

[16] See [12], pp. 167–168.

but also explained human life with certain conditions (such as mutations) of nature.[17] In this case, man depended on nature to a considerable extent, which can be direct conclusive for him. With the development of productivity and the improvement of people's practical ability, people have entered a state of man-object opposition, which was manifested in the establishment of the ancient Greek philosophy of ontology. In essence, ontology is a way to understand and grasp things in a certain relation. However, the ancient philosophy first put forward the relation of things to things only, it has not figured out that the relations of things to people, and of people to things were the ones mainly manifested here. Even so, the ancient philosophers did not completely get rid of the relationship between men and things while exploring the existence of all things. The difference was that this relationship was completely projected to that of things to things, and was understood as an essential part of that relationship. And just because of that, their understanding of noumena would inevitably exist two fundamentally opposite views of matter and soul.[18] In modern times, with the development of science and technology and the further improvement of productivity, human beings continued to make use of and conquer nature, which seemed that man has won the battle against nature. But as Engels said, we should not be over intoxicated with our victory over nature. For every such victory, nature would take revenge on us. Thus, we should always keep in mind at every step that our governance over nature never seems like a conqueror ruling another race, and we do not seem like being outside nature. On the contrary, we belong to and exist in nature, along with our flesh, blood and brains. Our dominion over nature lies in that we are better than all other creatures, and are able to understand and apply nature law correctly.[19] It can be seen that in terms of the relationship between man and nature, although man can conquer, transform and humanize nature, and also become the master of nature, he is still determined by nature fundamentally.

1.2.2 The Conclusiveness of Society over Man

Man is not merely a natural being, which is determined by nature, moreover, he is also a social being and is determined by society. Man exists in a certain social relationship, and is the product of society. Although man is the product of long-term development of nature and evolved from anthropoid apes, they can only form certain social relations through social labor to be produced. Moreover, every human being born into the world has to inherit the productive forces as well as relations of the existing society, and accept various behavior habits and moral norms. In this way, individuals can interact with others, as well as society, and can become real people. And that all human activities are social activities, and human transformation of nature and society can only be carried out by forming social relations with others. Marx

[17] See [13], p. 66.

[18] See [3], p. 165.

[19] See [14], pp. 383–384.

said that individuals were social beings. The expression of their lives, even if it did not take the immediate form of a common life expression accomplished with others, was also the expression and confirmation of social life.[20] In this sense, Marx held that the essence of man was the sum of all social relations in reality.

To define human essence with social relations is a scientific revelation of it. So what are social relations? They are closely related to society. Society has a broad and narrow sense. In the narrow sense, society is a system in which people interact with each other, and it's a form of social relations. In this sense, social relations are those things that can exist for their own sake in society, which define the nature of society and constitute its basic contents, and which integrate society into a system as a whole. Therefore, there wouldn't be society itself without social relations. Losing the relations would be like abolishing society and taking its life away. Thus, society in the narrow sense is not revealed as the totality of its elements and components, the nature of society is explained through its essence, and social relations, which are the most important thing. In the broad sense, society is the product of human interaction, the completed essential unity of human and nature, as well as the totality of the forms and consequences formed historically by people's common activities. In this sense, the social concept juxtaposed with social relations is revealed as the whole system of people's whole life activities and development. Thus, society in the broad sense refers to the sum of people's all kinds of practical activities. The practical activities here first refer to the activities of material production, and also the activities of spiritual production. Whether they are products of material or spiritual labor, or the results of history or people's present activities, social relations always form some kind of related objects that are people's activity results. Thus they are irrevocably (like the activity itself and any variants thereof) have the nature of objects. The nature of objects here does not refer to the reflection of social relations as such, or the material form of existing objects, but to the social relations subject to a certain object. There won't be any relations without objects. Just as every social relation presupposes its own objects, the object itself is also a social relation.[21] Marx and Engels elaborated on the close relationship between the material objects as the fruits of labor and people's social relations. He pointed out that the material object is the existence of human beings, the physical existence of human beings, as well as the eternal existence of human beings for others, the human relationship for him with others, and the social relationship between human beings.[22] As a part of society, individuals do not live in a vacuum, but in a real society and are determined by social relations. The famous German philosopher Poulsen once described the conclusive role of society on individuals like how does a person or a person's will come into being? As far as we know, a person's life begins in time. Aren't there any reason for the beginning? Or was it the result of his own choices? All of these seem impossible. A man, like animals, is born by his parents. He is physically and spiritually similar to them, inheriting their temperaments, desires, senses, and intellectual faculties, as

[20] See [12], pp. 122–123.

[21] See [15], p. 23.

[22] See [16], p. 52.

well as their body features. He also accepts the physical and spiritual properties of his nationality as a natural gift. As for gender, which has a potential influence over a person's life, is also determined. While the reasons are unknown, no one would assert that it is the result of their own choices. Thus, when it comes to the beginning of people, nothing can indicate that it constitutes an exception, an enclave in the realm of nature, that is free from any natural laws. These qualities or tendencies then develop under the conclusive influence of the natural environment, especially the social environment. Kids are educated by their families in the peculiar forms of life of their nationalities. They acquire their languages, as well as a complete set of concepts and judgments more or less. They learn about the customs of their nationalities, by which the actions and judgments of most of them are governed throughout their lives. They would be sent to schools, where they can learn the general culture of the times; or to the churches, where they can receive further training, which may continuously influence their inner life in both positive and negative ways. At last, when they are finally able to leave their homes and schools, they are immediately exposed to a new educational force, society. Individuals are born in society. They usually don't have much choice. They are born into a certain class and cannot choose their own lives. Society is constantly influencing them, telling them if the words and actions are proper, decent, or attractive. It assigns people tasks in accordance with the laws of supply and demand. Everyone takes guidance from his time. The architect does not choose buildings according to his own standards, but to the standards of the times: the buildings in the fourteenth century are gothic; in the sixteenth century are in the style of cultural revival; and in the eighteenth century are in the style of rococo. Nor did the classicists decide their scientific tasks on their own, the times would choose it for them: in the fourteenth century it was a special logical topic about substances and chances; in the sixteenth century it was the Latin poem modeled on Virgil; in the eighteenth century it was the mathematical or physical discussion, or the commentary on the dangers of superstition. And the classicists of our time are engaged in a kind of historical investigation of a lost Greek writer or in the excavation of prehistoric ruins. There seems to be no break or crack in the chain: nationality and age, parents and teachers, as well as environment and society determine the temperament and development, identity and life issues of every person. Man is the product of the collective that derived him. Just as the branches of a tree attribute their shapes and functions not to their will, but to the whole body from which they grow, it can be said that a man is inexistent before his birth, and he cannot determine the manner and fate of his future life by his own will. He comes into the world and acts as a member of a collective. His life forms a part of the collective, a part of the general historical life of mankind, as well as a part of the universal nature ultimately.[23] Thus, it is not practical to deny the conclusive role of society on human beings.

The conclusiveness of society over man reflects the relationship between man and the environment. In the eighteenth century, French materialists once put forward the proposition that man creates the environment, or the environment creates man, but they could not dialectically understand the relationship between man and the

[23] See [17], pp. 389–390.

social environment, especially the practical nature of social life. As a result, they could not get out of the vicious circle of who creates whom between man and the environment, and eventually fall into the idealism in which opinions dominate the world. As for me, I think in the relationship between man and the environment, man is the subject, while the environment is the object. Therefore, there are two kinds of movement between man as the subject and the environment as the object, which are opposite but unified internally, namely, the movement of the man as the subject towards the environment as the object, as well as the movement of the environment as the object towards man as the subject. The former one refers to people's understanding and transformation of the environment, that is, the objectification of the subject. The latter one refers to the generation of the environment for people, which is the subjectification and non-objectification of the object. The dialectical and unified movement of subject objectification versus object subjectification, and objectification versus non-objectification between man and the environment consists of the dynamic internal operation mechanism. Specifically, objectification is the condensation and embodiment of the activity of the subject and the essential power of man on the environment, which is the product of man's objective activities, so that the effectiveness of the subject becomes the attribute of the object, that is, the environment. As a result, the initiative of subject activities acquires its object form, so that the essential power of man is reflected in the transformed new environment, and the environment as the object lies in the stipulation produced and revealed by subject activities. When the initiative of subject activities becomes objectified, human activities are transformed from indefinite to definite, from moving to static. Objectification reveals the environmental change caused by human activities. The objectification of man's essential power is essentially the process that endows the object with subject characteristics, or endows the environment with human features. As for non-objectification, it refers to the process in which the stipulation, regularity and logic of the object environment are changed into those of subject activities, behaviors and thinking by the practical activities of the subject. Non-objectification is the essential power to reveal the object to the subject and enlighten people with the logic of the existence of the object. Non-objectification illustrates the development of man, the subject, caused by objective activities. And this kind of development transforms the essence of the environment and various stipulations into the essential power, wisdom, talent and skill of the subject, and various forms of human activities, revealing the state changing process of the environment from free to self-determined, and then to produced by man under the impact of human activities.[24] Therefore, objectification refers to man creating the environment, while non-objectification refers to the environment creating man. Man creating the environment means objectification features initiative. People's understanding and transformation of environment and the impact of their essential power on environment are a dynamic process full of initiative and creativity, which fully demonstrates the characteristics of human life activities. Objectification activities go beyond all animal activities. They are free and conscious activities of human beings, and are the vivid embodiment of the powerful material and spiritual shaping

[24] See [18], pp. 123–124.

capability of the environment. As for the environment that creates man, the characteristic of non-objectification mainly lies in its passivity, that is, the subject is subject to restriction. If objectification refers to endow the environment as the object with the natural and social forces, creativity and initiative of man as the subject, then non-objectification is to restrict the scope and mode of human activities with the objectivity and social historical existence of the object environment, and to limit the nature of human activities and the formation of man's essential power by the nature and various forms of regulation of the object environment, as well as the connection among these natures—objective law. In terms of the relationship between man and the environment, the conclusive role of the environment on man is the most fundamental.

1.2.3 The Conclusiveness of History over Man

Human existence is not only a concept of space, but also a concept of time. Time can be divided into past and future. Past time refers to history. Although history is created by human beings, it is conclusive for people today. Marx and Engels once pointed out, "In every stage of history, there are certain material consequences, and a number of productive forces. Man and nature, as well as interpersonal relationships formed in history, show that huge amounts of productivity, capital and circumstances are passed from one generation to the next. Although, on the one hand, this productivity, capital and circumstances are transformed by the new generation, on the other hand, they predestine the living conditions of the new generation, enabling them to realize a certain development and obtain special qualities."[25] It can be seen that history is a continuous process, and people always live under certain historical conditions; as a result, history presupposes people's living conditions, and thus has a conclusive role on people. As the subject of history, man has initiative. In this sense, man has a certain ability to make historical choices. The so-called historical choice here refers to the activity and process in which the subject of history discriminates, selects, acts on and creates the object (nature, society and even itself) with initiative according to the unity of internal and external scales.[26] The essence of historical choice activities is: the creative activity or ability of the historical subject to point to definite objects consciously in the possibility space with certain social ways. It should be pointed out that although man has the ability to make historical choices, they are all under the conclusive premise of history, and cannot go beyond the scope provided by history fundamentally. Just as Marx said, "Are people free to choose a certain form of society? The answer is never... Men are never free to choose their productivity, which is the basis of their whole history, for any productivity is a given force, the product of past activities. As we can see, productivity is of course the result of men's applying ability, it, however, depends on men's living conditions; on the productivity

---

[25] See [19], p. 43.

[26] See [20], p. 69.

previously acquired; on the forms of society which have existed before, not created by them, but by the generation before them."[27] Thus, historical conclusiveness is fundamental in comparison with historical choice, which is derivative. As historical conditions predetermine the way people act, each generation cannot make history as their wishes. "People make their own history, but so far they do not make their history according to a common will, to the same plan, or even within an established society with clear boundaries," said Marx.[28]

In conclusion, in terms of the relationship between will and existence, will, as an attribute of man, is essentially determined by the existence of nature, society, and history. Since the will are meant to be determined, the freedom of will is nonexistent. Only idealist views insist on libertarianism in the relationship between will and existence. This libertarianism, in fact, holds that human will can transcend nature, society and history, and is not restricted or determined by the latter at all.

2 Freedom and Necessity

As mentioned above, in the relationship between will and existence, materialistic views believe that existence determines will, instead of in reverse, so we advocate materialist determinism and deny the freedom of will. But the determination here does not mean that one side denies the other, or the object denies the subject. It's just a kind of constraint. Instead of turning one side to nothing, constraint regulates the relationship between the two sides on the premise that both sides exist and cannot determine each other.[29] In this sense, we advocate dialectical determinism instead of mechanical determinism. Therefore, it is necessary to further discuss the dialectical relationship between freedom and necessity.

2.1 Methodology Study

In philosophy, methodology is unified with ontology and epistemology. Methodology is of great significance for solving basic philosophical problems. In the history of philosophy, there exists a contradiction between metaphysics and dialectics. When comparing dialectical methods with metaphysical methods, Engels pointed out that dialectic, in contrast to metaphysics, knew nothing of absolute and distinct boundaries, as well as unconditional and universally valid "either/or". It transformed metaphysical differences, recognized "both and" where appropriate apart from "either/or", and mediated opposites. Then Engels came to the following conclusion that dialectic was the only thinking method that suited this stage of the development of nature

[27] See [2], p. 532.

[28] See [2], pp. 732–733.

[29] See [21], p. 35.

views. As for the daily application and scientific exchange of nature, metaphysical category remained valid. Engels believed that the methodological significance of dialectic was that it taught people the ability to think with flexible concepts.[30]

On the relationship between freedom and necessity, from the perspective of methodology, there are differences between metaphysics and dialectics. The former puts freedom and necessity in opposite positions, while the latter dialectically unites them. Thus, clarifying the distinctions between them is of great significance for correctly defining freedom and necessity.

In early Greek philosophy, Democritus advocated causal determinism, which denied human freedom to a certain extent. Democritus believed that everything subject to causality was necessary, i.e., he equated necessity with causality. Since everything was for a reason, everything was inevitable. Democritus tried to classify necessity, dividing it into external necessity and internal necessity, and held that internal necessity was not the one placed into things and processes by man, but naturally produced and developed under the influence of certain conditions, while external necessity was formed by agreements between men. According to Democritus, the power of necessity depended on how solid the atomic bonds were. As Democritus denied the chance and attributed everything to necessity, he turned to fatalism. As a result, there was no freedom for him. While Plato held that it was not necessity that ruled the world, but the order fit for purpose. Everything in the world was in pursuit of a certain goal, i.e., to achieve good. Plato asserted that there were three principles in every human soul, that were rational, passionate, and irrational or erotic principles. According to him, now that everything was related to concepts and ideas, the rational principle of human soul was also related to concepts. Therefore, human freedom is impossible without human soul participating in the world of concepts. The task of man was to subordinate the irrational part of his soul to the rational part and to suppress his evil desires. For Plato, therefore, freedom lied in the determination of will by goodness, rather than arbitrary choice. Determined by evil, people's will and choice were enslaved; otherwise, if determined by the greatest goodness, they were free. It can be seen that Plato emphasized man's choice of freedom, thereby denying necessity. In terms of necessity and freedom, Democritus and Plato metaphysically split the relationship between them, and failed to realize dialectical unity. Aristotle's understanding of necessity and freedom contains contradictory ideas. He divided rationality into cognitive rationality and value rationality. Among them, cognitive rationality took necessity as its object, while value rationality took contingency as its object. Within the scope of cognitive rationality, man is not free; only in the range of value rationality, one can has the freedom of choice. Compared with Democritus and Plato, who unilaterally emphasized one side and resolutely denied the other side, Aristotle acknowledged the opposition between freedom and necessity, which was of historical significance. The Stoicism did not consider freedom and necessity to be entirely opposed, and the idea of modern philosophers Spinoza and Hegel that freedom was the understanding of necessity had already been incubated in the Stoicism. The Stoicism in the late Greece period believed that all changes in nature,

[30] See [22], pp. 56–57.

no matter how small were they, were absolutely determined. Likewise, man's will was absolutely determined, too. The whole universe was like a continuous chain of causes and effects, and the outset of the chain is the first driver. Everything came from the will of God and was under the will of God. From this point of view, Stoicism scholars were extreme determinists, but they still acknowledged human freedom while insisting on determinism. Stoicism believed that man was different from animals: animals had no rationalities, while the man had rationalities and the ability to use concepts to think. Man was capable of thinking and choosing actions that rationality approved of. So they believed that as long as one obeyed rationality and fate, and acted in accordance with the eternal laws of nature, he was free. The Stoicism even believed that philosophers, when fully aware of fate or law, could be as free as God. Thus it can be seen that the Stoicism's understanding of freedom and necessity has certain dialectical factors.

From the perspective of Christian theology, scholastics in the Middle Ages recognized that God was absolutely free, and all things in the world, including people, were created by God, and all their movements and changes were arranged by God. That was to say, all man's actions were under the control of God. Man had no freedom at all. However, they also believed that God's precognition did not contradict man's free will. God foresaw all events because some were going to happen, and some did not as God already knew them. God's precognition could be compared to human memory, and the fact that a person remembered an event did not mean that it was inevitable or arbitrary. Likewise, just because God foresaw something didn't mean it was true. It can be seen that medieval theologians were faced with the contradiction between god's free will and man's free will, and the so-called god's free will referred to necessity. Under the bondage of religious theology, it was impossible for scholastics to dialectically understand the relationship between freedom and necessity.

In modern western philosophy, there were still differences between metaphysics and dialectics on the relationship between freedom and necessity.

Descartes elaborated his theory of freedom and necessity on the basis of dualism. He believed that the physical world was governed by necessity, while man's actions were governed by the will, and the freedom of will should not be doubted just like anything that was clearly understood. Just because of their freedom of will, people had the problem of right and wrong in cognition, and the problem of being praised and punished in behavior. Thus, seeing from dualism, Descartes metaphysically split the relationship between necessity and freedom.

Hobbes affirmed the objective necessity of things, saying that both natural phenomena and individual behaviors were subject to the necessity of things. In this sense, Hobbes clearly differed from Descartes, whose necessity rested in the physical world, whereas Hobbes applied it to human behaviors. But He went to the other extreme, fundamentally denying the existence of freedom, and claiming that there was no such thing as free will. Freedom, according to Hobbes, lied in finding no obstacles in doing what he would, expected or tended to do. Obstacles came from the outside world, as well as the actors themselves. When one person was doing something without both two obstacles, the person was free. But as a matter of fact, such freedom without any obstacles was impossible. As a result, Hobbes, who regarded freedom and necessity as mutually exclusive, still fell into the trap of metaphysics.

Locke inherited Hobbes' ideas, and affirmed that human behaviors were governed by objective necessity. According to him, such being without thinking or intention was governed by necessity and was not a free subject in every respect. Although man had ideas, intentions and wills, he was incapable of preventing such movements and events from happening, thus in this sense, man was not free. However, Locke also regarded freedom as the power to choose whether to execute or not, which was free within the limits of one's ability. The so-called freedom here was not the freedom corresponding to necessity in the ontological sense, but the freedom in the axiological sense. Locke acknowledged man's freedom of choice, but denied the freedom of will. Thus in the scope of ontology, it can be seen that Locke still put necessity and freedom in opposite positions and held a metaphysical view.

Spinoza criticized Descartes' dualism, and his separation of freedom and necessity. He realized that freedom and necessity were not absolutely incompatible. He pointed out that freedom did not lie in following one's heart, but in the necessity of freedom. That was to say, God simply did not have the kind of will that belonged to the man. There was nothing arbitrary for God at all, everything occurred with the same necessity. God himself existed because of the necessity of his own nature, so he was both necessary and free. According to Spinoza, the thing existed only from the necessity of its own nature, and its behaviors were determined only by itself, which was called Libera (freedom). It can be seen from his discussion on freedom that he actually saw the internal connection between freedom and necessity, and even expressed such scientific views as freedom lied in the understanding of necessity. But the freedom mentioned by Spinoza was only sought from the inside, not applied to the outside. Freedom did not refer to transforming the outside world through the understanding of the necessity to achieve the purpose of human beings, but to making the inner world to adapt to the outside world negatively, so it was still a kind of freedom within the subjective scope. Therefore, Spinoza still regarded necessity as everything, and it dissolved freedom in the same sense as freedom, which was still a metaphysical view.

Holbach was a typical mechanical materialist, who emphasized the objective necessity to an extreme degree and fundamentally denied human freedom. Holbach declared that the necessity which governed the movements of the physical world governed that of the moral world as well. Thus, in the moral world, everything is subject to destiny.[31] The so-called destiny was nothing but man's rationality, and the natural law derived from the human intention of self-improvement, as well as from human desires and demands. Therefore, Holbach believed that human acted according to rationality and natural laws. One acted in the world according to his nature, and his behaviors would cause some other behaviors of people around him. Thus, the concepts of good and evil, virtue and vice would come into being in his consciousness, which were completely based on the natural relationship among people. In Holbach's view, there was only biological natural relationship among

[31] See [7], pp. 191–192.

people. Because on the one hand, society is a natural product, and the necessity of society is generated from human's original nature. While nature created society by letting people be born in it, the social life is not only in line with human's natural interests, but also in line with human benefits. In a word, the society was created in accordance with people and their original nature. On the other hand, the natural laws derived from human nature, defined our social relations and the basic principles of our social behaviors. Man is always in the state of nature; he can never go beyond the bounds of his own nature, and is always compelled to obey its laws. It can be seen that Holbach equated human society with nature, and thus permeated the necessity of nature throughout the human society, and negated human freedom, which is obviously a metaphysical method of thinking.

Kant tried to conquer the opposition between materialist determinism and idealist libertarianism by thinking that necessity belonged to the thing-in-itself and freedom belonged to the phenomenal world. Kant not only denied the objectivity and knowability of necessity, but also interpreted freedom as the freedom of subjective will, which actually put necessity and freedom in complete opposite positions. It was a dualistic view, and its essence was still metaphysics.

As a master of German classical philosophy and modern philosophy, Hegel comprehensively and profoundly revealed the dialectical relationship between necessity and freedom on the basis of idealism. Hegel neither agreed with voluntarism necessity, nor agreed with fatalism freedom, or various dualism ideas that split necessity and freedom, arguing that necessity and freedom are dialectically unified. Hegel criticized the dualists and metaphysicians before him for placing necessity and freedom against each other. He pointed out that the metaphysical philosophers before Kant always thought that natural phenomena were governed by inexorable laws, while the spirit was free. This distinction was undoubtedly important, and was grounded in the innermost demands of the spirit itself. But considering freedom and necessity as abstractly opposed to each other only belonged to and was valid in the finite world. The freedom without necessity, or the simple necessity without freedom, was just an abstract and untrue idea. Freedom was essentially concrete; it was always self-determining, and therefore was necessary in the meantime. Speaking of necessity, general people always thought it to be determined only from without; however, it was just an external necessity, and not the truly inner necessity, for the inner necessity was freedom.[32] So Hegel believed that freedom and necessity were not completely separate and opposed to each other; on the contrary, they were different parts of a whole, which were interdependent, interrelated, and could transform into each other. He pointed out that necessity was not yet freedom with no doubt; but freedom presupposes necessity, and contains necessity in itself as something sublated. Hegel clearly put forward the proposition that the truth of necessity was freedom.[33] In other words, freedom was the knowledge of necessity. Moreover, this freedom was not negative and abstract, but positive and concrete. According to him, a virtuous man himself

---

[32] See [23], p. 105.

[33] See [23], p. 322.

was aware of the necessity of his actions and the obligation of freedom and self-determination. Just because of this, not only did he not feel that his freedom was being interfered with, but it was by virtue of this sense of necessity and obligation that drove him to achieve freedom with truly substantial content first, as opposed to the plain freedom with mere possibility, which came from obstinacy.[34] Engels once praised Hegel's dialectical thought on necessity and freedom by saying that Hegel was the first to correctly describe the relationship between freedom and necessity. According to him, freedom was the knowledge of necessity.[35] It should be noted that Hegel, despite making important contributions to the dialectical thought of freedom and necessity, still did not get rid of intuition and fatalism. The intuition of his objective idealism was that his real subject of freedom was actually the absolute ideas rather than realistic human beings. As for him, the understanding of necessity was actually the understanding of the unalterable historical destiny of human beings, who were nothing but negative materials of absolute ideas; as a result, he got trapped in fatalism.

Through the methodological investigation of the relationship between freedom and necessity, we can see that the metaphysical method of thinking is to split and put freedom and necessity in opposite positions, which may either fall into mechanical determinism or voluntarism, so that it is not able to correctly explain the relationship between them. Only with dialectical thinking can we understand the relationship between freedom and necessity scientifically.

2.2 *Dialectical Determinism*

Methodologically speaking, I advocate dialectical determinism and reject mechanical determinism and voluntarism; in other words, existence determines will, and there is no absolute freedom of will in essence. But it does not necessarily lead to the conclusion of mechanical determinism or even fatalism, and does not prevent us from dialectically understanding the relationship between freedom and necessity. We recognize relative freedom of will, as Engels pointed out that freedom did not consist in the illusion of independence breaking away from natural laws, but in understanding these laws and thus being able to systematically make the laws serve certain purposes. Whether they were external natural laws, or the laws governing man's physical and spiritual existence, it was all the same. These two kinds of laws could only be separated from each other in concepts rather than in reality. Therefore, freedom of will was simply the ability to make decisions according to the knowledge of things. The freer a man felt in judging certain questions, the greater the inevitability of its content; indecision, on the other hand, was because of ignorance. It seemed like an arbitrary choice among many different and contradictory possible decisions, which just proved that it was governed by what ought to be governed by it, so that

[34] See [23], p. 323.

[35] See [14], p. 455.

it was not free. Freedom, therefore, consisted in governing ourselves and external nature according to the knowledge of the inevitability of nature, which meant it was the product of historical development with no doubt.[36] According to Marxism, dialectical determinism can be explained as follows:

2.2.1 Definition of Necessity

Necessity is an attribute of existence, which means an objective inevitability. Inevitability, regularity and causality belong to the same level of category.

By object, inevitability can be divided into material inevitability (natural inevitability) and spiritual Inevitability (social inevitability). Material and natural inevitability refer to objective inevitability. The objective inevitability is not transferred by man's subjective will, but appears in the form of laws. While laws refer to the essential, universal and inevitable connection inherent between objective things. When ancient Greek philosophers were examining the principle of the universe, they began to feel vaguely the objective regularity of natural beings. For example, ancient Greek philosophers regarded the relationship between numbers as universal laws, and called it fate, believing that fate was the source of universal order. Heraclitus further referred to fate as logos, and he pointed out that everything followed by fate, which was inevitable. He declared that the essence of fate was the 'logos' that ran through the universal entity. It was an etheric object, the seed that created the world, as well as the scale that determined the period.[37] Democritus regarded atoms as the principle of all things, he revealed the inevitability of atomic motion, and equated causality with inevitability. Therefore, ancient Greek philosophy mainly focused on the inevitability of the universe itself, which is based on the simple views of matter and nature. With the development of natural science in modern western countries, people's understanding of the motion laws of matters has been further deepened. Materialist philosophers in the eighteenth century revealed the motion laws of matters. For example, Holbach systematically studied the regularity of the motion of natural things, believing that all the motions in nature were subject to some invariable and inevitable laws. It can be seen that people's understanding of objective inevitability is a developing process. If material inevitability is easily understood, while spiritual and social inevitabilities will not be easily grasped. Spiritual and social inevitabilities refer to the regularity of human spiritual and social activities. In the history of western philosophy, some philosophers tended to admit the inevitability of the motion of matters, while denying the inevitability of spiritual and social activities. Descartes, for example, thought that the physical world was governed by inevitability. The actions of animals were inevitable because they had no thoughts. While man had thoughts, and exerting will was one of the thinking methods, so that spiritual activities were not governed by inevitability. In this sense, Descartes acknowledged

[36] See [14], pp. 455–456.

[37] See [24], p. 17.

man's freedom of will. However, there were still many philosophers who introduced inevitability into the realm of spiritual and social activities. Democritus, for example, believed that all phenomena in nature were inevitable, and everything in the present world was arranged by fate. Moreover, Leibniz divided inevitability into absolute inevitability and hypothetical inevitability, or into metaphysical inevitability and moral inevitability. According to him, hypothetical inevitability was the inevitability that imposed the foreknowledge and prearrangement of God upon contingent things, while moral inevitability referred to the inevitability which led the wise to choose the best, conforming all minds to the greatest tendency. Therefore, inevitability also existed in the field of human moral activities, which did no harm to man's freedom. Leibniz pointed out that if the inevitability was interpreted as man's exact decisions, so that the comprehensive understanding of all situations internally and externally could enable a perfect mind to anticipate, then all the thinking and actions represented by them were decided, and all the free activities were inevitable for sure.[38] As far as I'm concerned, both material (natural) inevitability and spiritual (social) inevitability exist objectively. Inevitability exists not only in the material (natural) field, but also in the spiritual (social) field. In social activities, active individuals are thoughtful and goal-directed; while in society as a whole, their activities are still based on rules, which mainly refer to statistical rules. It is an objective fact that the development of human history follows the law of its own development, which is also the basis and premise of the existence of social science. Just as Engels said that history was made in such a way that the final result always arose from the conflicts of many individual wills, each of which was formed by virtue of a number of particular living conditions. Thus, there were innumerable interlocking forces, like the forces of parallelograms which formed a resultant force, and that was the historical result. This result could be regarded as the product of a holistic force acting unconsciously and involuntarily. However, each one's will all wished himself to obtain the things his constitution, and external and, after all, economic circumstances (either of his own, or the society in general) appealed him to. Although nobody was able to fulfill their desires, instead their forces merged into a mean value, a resultant force, it must not be concluded from the fact that these wills were making no sense. On the contrary, every will contributed to the resultant force, and was therefore included in it.[39] In consequence, the wills of each person involved in social activities vary, and are seemingly with no rules to follow. However, the interaction of numerous individual wills constitutes the historical resultant force, which thus forms the law of social development that is independent of individual wills.

It should be pointed out that although material (natural) inevitability and spiritual (social) inevitability are both objective existences, they are both consistent and discrepant. Generally speaking, there are three kinds of determinism: one is strict determinism, which understands causality as singled, strictly corresponding and predetermined. Laplace summarized the thinking mode of strict determinism, so it was also called Laplace determinism. He pointed out that we should regard

---

[38] Leibniz [25], p. 167.

[39] See [2], p. 697.

the present state of the universe as the result of its previous state and the cause of its subsequent state. Assume that at some point, there was a kind of wisdom that could master the specific conditions of all natural forces, as well as everything that made up nature, which was profound enough to analyze the information available, so that it could encapsulate all the movements of the universe from the largest objects to the tiniest atoms in the same formula. Nothing was uncertain for it, and the future, like the past, also lay before it.[40] In strict determinism, the only law of nature is the strictly established and inevitable causality. Each stage in the causal sequence is singly determined by the previous stage beforehand. The second is statistical determinism, which holds that not everything in nature follows the strict and single causality (or the limited and single causality), and all things can be described strictly and definitively by differential equations. There are things in nature that can only be described by probabilities. That is to say, there is no pure and ideal single causality in nature, as numerous accidental factors are destroying the established causality, making the individual behaviors in the group with uncertainties. Although statistical determinism holds that the causality views cannot account for all natural phenomena, and should be supplemented by means of probability views, it still admits that natural phenomena have laws to follow, which are statistical laws. If strict determinism deals with individual causality, statistical determinism then deals with group causality. Statistical determinism considers the causality of a set of individuals and behaviors whose appearance and movement direction are random and irregular. However, when considered as a whole, their appearance and movement direction are certain, inevitable and regular. The third is systematic determinism. A group is a collective of independent and discrete random events or individuals. While different from a group, a system is a complex of interacting elements. That is to say, it is an organic whole with particular functions that are composed of interacting and interdependent components, and the system itself is still part of a larger system. The system is featured with integrity, the coherence of elements, the hierarchy of structures, the specificity of the structure functions, and the intentionality of system evolution. Causality takes a new form in systems. Systematic things possess not only the mechanical certainty of individual things, but also the statistical randomness of group things. In addition, they are also equipped with the fuzziness of the new nature of the system, which is caused by the correlation of elements, and is not possessed by individuals and groups. The interaction between the elements of the system forms the non-linear causality, which adjusts the internal structure and influences the function of the system. And when the external environment acts on one or several elements of a specific system, the elements react to each other, which then causes the fluctuation of the system, and reveals certain changes. The new nature of the system is determined by the sum of the coherence relations between the elements. The law systematic things follow is neither strictly determined causality nor statistically determined causality, but the systemically determining causality. Systematic determinism is an advanced form of determinism, which sublates strict determinism and statistical determinism, retains their advantages and conquers their limitations.

[40] Chen [26], p. 7.

The causality shown by the movements of individual things is linear, concise and definite, but as long as individual things are related to each other randomly, people must admit the randomness of individual movements when talking about causality. This randomness does not deny that group things can reveal certain rules of motion as a whole. The two cases mentioned above can be described by strict determinism equations and statistical determinism equations respectively. However, if the system, a group of things with coherent relations, needs to be studied, it is impossible to explain the new nature of the system caused by coherent relations with these two kinds of equations. Therefore, the most complex causality in the system must be explained by systematic determinism. In the three deterministic models, strict determinism is obviously inapplicable for explaining social causality, as social beings are more complex, variable and random when compared with natural beings. While statistical determinism and systematic determinism can be applied to the social field, because the society is collective or systematic, and the social and historical laws are characterized by statistical determinism and systematic determinism.

Inevitability can be divided into absolute inevitability and relative Inevitability in degree. Absolute inevitability is a naked and mechanical inevitability, and is therefore a kind of fatalism. Mechanical inevitability asserts that freedom is incompatible with universal causality in any sense. Now that everything is caused by others, the cause of human behaviors will eventually break up with man and go beyond his control. Holbach, for example, believed that everything in the world was inevitable, and there was neither contingency nor human freedom. The relative inevitability is opposed to the absolute inevitability. It acknowledges the existence of freedom and contingency. As far as I'm concerned, the absolutization of inevitability is against science. Inevitability can only be defined correctly on the basis of the unity of necessity and chance. Engels once criticized the view of absolute inevitability by saying that according to this view, what reigned in nature was the simple and forthright inevitability. There were five peas in the peasecod, instead of four or six; the dog's tail was exactly five inches long, which was neither longer nor shorter; this alfalfa flower has been pollinated by a bee this year, while that one has not, and this flower has been pollinated by the particular bee at the particular time; the particular dandelion seed blown by the wind sprouted, while that one did not; this morning a flea bit me at exactly 4 o'clock, not 3 or 5 o'clock, and it bit me on the right shoulder, instead of the left leg…All of these were the facts caused by unalterable causal chains, as well as an unshakable inevitability, and the air masses that gave rise to the solar system were already arranged so that these things could only happen in this way instead of other ways. In acknowledging such an inevitability, we were still constrained by the theological view of nature.[41] Therefore, we reject absolute inevitability and stand for relative inevitability.

[41] See [14], pp. 324–325.

2.2.2 Definition of Freedom

Freedom is an attribute of will, which means subjective initiative. The word "freedom" comes from the Liberas in Latin, meaning to be freed from bondage, and to cast off restrictions. Freedom, choice and subjective initiative belong to the same level of categories.

Freedom is a unique attribute of human beings. There only exists inevitability and no freedom in nature. As for animals, according to Engels, if an animal constantly affects its surroundings, then it is unintentional and accidental for the animal itself. But when people increasingly transcend animals, their influence on nature becomes more thoughtful, systematic, and goal-oriented. In other words, animals only use the external nature and simply cause changes in nature by their own existence; while man dominates nature by making changes to allow nature to serve his own purposes.[42] Animal activities are essentially the same as those general activities in the natural world, as they do not have consciousness, or the unique human mental activities of human beings. Therefore, although animal activities are controlled by the animal itself, this control is only a kind of unconscious self-control. It seems like an automaton, and its control procedures come either from the innate physiological inheritance, or from acquired learning and experience accumulation, but this kind of learning and accumulation is still just an unconscious process. In this way, though animal activities are controlled by the animal itself, unlike the activities of other natural beings, since the law of this control is unconscious and does not originate from the animal itself, the animal activities are just a kind of heteronomy, a process governed by the inevitability of natural laws outside itself. It can be seen that one of the important differences between man and animal is that man has freedom, which is mainly manifested in his subjective initiative. Man is a kind of active natural being, and his initiative is mainly manifested in the following aspects: (1) self-making. Self-making is corresponding to freedom, thereinto, freedom indicates that the existence of something is completely governed by objective inevitability, while self-making means a man getting rid of instincts. It means to understand inevitability to some extent and use it to improve its own living environment and conditions. (2) Self-consciousness. As a kind of self-making existence, man is also a kind of conscientious, intentional and goal-oriented existence. Man can not only realize the existence of the external world, but also realize his own existence, so that he can distinguish himself as the subject from the objective external existence. Man can not only realize the existence of the outside world and the man himself, but also conceptually grasp the existing attributes and development laws of the object world through the cognitive activities of thinking, so that these attributes and laws can be adopted purposefully and systematically to serve the man himself. Moreover, man can not only realize the existence of people and objects, as well as their existence properties and development laws, but also be able to realize self-control and self-regulation of their inner activities and behavioral activities. As man shows active consciousness everywhere,

[42] See [14], pp. 382 and 383.

he is a conscious being. (3) Autonomy. Autonomy means self-determination. Man is essentially independent of external forces; he is neither the slave of external things and their forces, nor an idle puppet at the mercy of external forces. Man has the power of autonomy: man is the subject of the world around and himself; man constructs objective relations with external things on his own initiative; man always occupies a dominant position in the relationship between people and surrounding things, i.e. man dominates things instead of the other way around; man can select and evaluate external objects and their own behaviors independently; man is the master of himself and his own life. (4) Self-discipline. Self-discipline is relative to heteronomy, which is constrained by the external natural environment, while self-discipline refers to self-restraint and self-regulation. Man's self-discipline shows that he can direct his own behaviors according to objective inevitability, and correct his behavior in time to conform to inevitability.

2.2.3 Dialectical Unity of Necessity and Freedom

In the history of western philosophy, some philosophers' understanding of the relationship between necessity and freedom has approached the scientific level. For example, Hegel regarded freedom as the understanding of necessity, thus dialectically expounding the relationship between necessity and freedom. However, Hegel established this kind of relationship based on objective idealism, only Marxism dialectically discussed the relationship between necessity and freedom on the basis of practice for the first time. It can be seen that only on the basis of practice, can we scientifically understand the relationships between will and existence, freedom and necessity.

Marxist philosophy holds that practice is the philosophical category that marks the relationship of transformation between the subject and object. It is a physical social activity in which the subject can actively transform the object, while the subject itself is transformed, too. First of all, practice is a kind of human social activity. Activity is a fargoing concept, including human activities, animal activities and various material movements in nature. Practice is a kind of activity whose subject is human beings. Moreover, practice must be carried out under certain social and historical conditions and certain social relations with others. Second, practice is a kind of human social activity in which the subject can transform the object, while the subject itself is transformed, too. Practice refers to the transformation of the subject to the object, which may change the external morphology, the structure and nature, or the information state of the object. The realization of any aspect means the achievement of the direct purpose of transforming the object. When the subject acts on and changes the object, it also changes itself. Because in the process of practice, the subject first obtains the knowledge about the object and the experience and lessons of transforming the object, and then realizes the possession of the object in a form useful to itself. Every success in practice improves the practical ability of the subject and makes the subject stride forward a step towards freedom. When the subject transforms the object through practice and produces a world that meets its needs, it also changes and thus produces itself. Third, practice is a relational category. Like cognition, practice is still a basic aspect of the subject-object relation. Cognition marks the reflectional relationship between the subject and object, while practice marks the transformational relationship between them.

Practice presupposes objective necessity, without which there is no human practice. As the bridge that connects the subject and object, there exists an object subjectification problem in practice. The subjectification of the object refers to the process of the practice object that corresponds to and actually interacts with the practice subject, reversely affecting and influencing the practice subject, and transforming the objective things into the subjective things through various ways and forms.[43] During practical activities, the role of the object to the subject is mainly reflected in providing the practice subject with life materials to maintain its life and physical strength, with the objects and tools of activities, and with the objects of cognition. The existence and development of the objective world around people have their own objective laws. Objective things not only have their internal structure, and organic interrelation, but also have intricate laws of motion. Both natural objects and man-made objects are essentially the products of the interaction of various objective laws, and it is these objective laws that restrict people's practical activities. Only with dialectical thinking can we understand the relationship between freedom and necessity scientifically.

Practice is also based on subjective initiative. According to Marx, only when things related to man in the way that a man did, could a man relate to things in the way man did in practice.[44] It shows that practical activities are inseparable from the initiative of the subject, which means there exists a subject objectification problem. The so-called objectification of subject, from the perspective of the practice subject, is the process of the subject positively effecting, influencing and transforming the practice object through active and realistic practical and conceptual means, actively realizing the objectification of all kinds of essential strengths and subjective structure of the subject itself, and infiltrating and merging into the object, so as to make it a humanized being, an organic part of the subject structure, the embodiment and projection of the subject, as well as the work that confirms and embodies the subjectivity of human beings. Through the realistic objectification of the subject, the essential power of the subject and the subjective structure of man appear on the object, and the subject can reflect on, get to know, and realize itself from the object. Generally speaking, the objectification of the subject is the process of the regulation and function of the subject to the object, the objectification of the subject's subjective structure to an objectified being, and the realization of the subject's essential power into the objective structure, so that the object is more and more endowed with the nature and structure of the subject, more and more expresses the essential power of the subject,

[43] See [27], p. 126.

[44] See [28], p. 124.

and is more and more humanized.[45] Therefore, the objectification of subject fully displays man's subjective initiative.

Practice is a process that never ends, and the subject-object relation is also a constantly changing process. Similarly, the relationship between necessity and freedom is also in dynamic change. In the primitive society, due to the low level of human practice, man's ability to interfere with nature is very limited, thus their active position in nature is not obvious, and they are largely dominated by nature. In this case, human freedom is very limited. With the development of social productivity, people's level of practice is constantly improving. More and more objective laws are recognized and mastered by people in practice, and are utilized to transform society. In this case, human freedom is increased. Therefore, both necessity and freedom are relative, not eternal. The development of human society is a continuous process from the kingdom of necessity to the kingdom of freedom.

References

1. [Germany] Hegel, *Lectures on the History of Philosophy*, vol. 3 (The Commercial Press, Beijing, 1959)
2. *Marx/Engels Selected Works*, vol. 4, 2nd edn. (People's Publishing House, Beijing, 1995)
3. Q. Gao, *Philosophical Vision: Metaphysical Meditation* (Jilin University Press, Changchun, 1993)
4. P. Yao, *Descartes's Theory of Innate Ideas* (Qiushi Press, Beijing, 1986)
5. [Soviet Union] Weitzman, *Thomas Hobbes* (The Commercial Press, Beijing, 1962)
6. [Holland] Spinoza, *Ethics* (The Commercial Press, Beijing, 1983)
7. [France] Holbach, *The System of Nature*, vol. 1 (The Commercial Press, Beijing, 1964)
8. [Germany] Leibniz, *New Essays on Human Understanding*, vol. 1 (The Commercial Press, Beijing, 1982)
9. [Britain] Hume, *An Enquiry Concerning Human Understanding* (The Commercial Press, Beijing, 1957)
10. H. Xue, *Development of Freedom Consciousness* (China Social Science Press, Beijing, 1983)
11. *Marx/Engels Selected Works*, vol. 2, 2nd edn. (People's Publishing House, Beijing, 1995)
12. *Marx/Engels Collected Works*, vol. 42 (People's Publishing House, Beijing, 1979)
13. S. Shan, *Critique of Subject and Object Theory* (Renmin University of China Press, Beijing, 1989)
14. *Marx/Engels Selected Works*, vol. 3, 2nd edn. (People's Publishing House, Beijing, 1995)
15. [Soviet Union] Л.A. Rachkov (Editor-in-Chief), *Social Relations: General Theoretical Issues* (People's Oriental Publishing & Media, Beijing, 1991)
16. *Marx/Engels Collected Works*, vol. 2 (People's Publishing House, Beijing, 1957)
17. [Germany] Paulsen, *A System of Ethics* (China Social Science Press, Beijing, 1988)
18. J. Zhao, Discussion on the unity of "man creates environment" and "environment creates man", in *Further Discussion on Materialist Dialectics: Proceedings of the Second Sino-Japanese Symposium on Materialist Dialectics* (People's Publishing House, Beijing, 1993)
19. *Marx/Engels Collected Works*, vol. 3 (People's Publishing House, Beijing, 1960)
20. L. Hao, *Historical Choice Theory* (Renmin University of China Press, Beijing, 1992)
21. N. Wang, *Guide to Human Activity Theory* (Nankai University Press, Tianjin, 1993)
22. [Soviet Union] B.Г. Ivanov (Editor-in-Chief), *Subjective Dialectics* (People's Oriental Publishing & Media, Beijing, 1988)

[45] See [27], p. 139.

23. [Germany] Hegel, *Lesser Logic* (The Commercial Press, Beijing, 1980)
24. Compiled and translated by the Teaching and Research Section of the Section of Foreign Philosophy of the Department of Philosophy of Peking University, *Ancient Greek and Roman Philosophy* (Joint Publishing, Beijing, 1957)
25. [Germany] Leibniz, *New Essays on Human Understanding* (The Commercial Press, Beijing, 1982)
26. K. Chen, *How Does God Play Dice* (Sichuan People's Publishing House, Chengdu, 1987)
27. Y. Wang, *Theory of Practical Activities* (Renmin University of China Press, Beijing, 1992)
28. [Germany] Marx, Economic and philosophic manuscripts of 1844, in *Marx/Engels Collected Works*, vol. 42 (People's Publishing House, Beijing, 1979)

Chapter 6
Freedom of Will: Axiology

Freedom of will means that the will can dominate one's actions in the sense of axiology. If one's actions are dominated by his will, or, resulted from his choices, the will is free; if not, the will is not free. The actions carried out with free will are valuable for the actor, which can be imputed to him; but if the actions carried out without free will are unworthiness for the actor, which can't be imputed to him. Therefore, the freedom of will here is a precondition of responsibility, and it is a kind of ethical freedom of choice.

1 Will and Value

The relationship between the will and value means value evaluation to will. In the sense of axiology, the will only refers to the thinking corresponding to existence and the subject corresponding to object, which is a philosophical analysis. But in the sense of axiology, will not only is corresponding to behavior, but also refers to the internal mechanism of behavior, which is a psychological analysis. Therefore, the relationship between will and value is that whether the behavior is controlled by will, which is the basis for value judgment on will.

1.1 Psychological Analysis of Will

Will is an attribute of the subject, which is presented as a mental activity of man. The investigation of the psychological mechanism of will is of great significance to the understanding of axiological freedom of will.

In the history of western philosophy, mechanical determinism holds that human being is the product of nature, existing in nature, subject to its laws, and can't transcend nature, or take a step beyond nature, even by thinking. So, in the perspective of

X. Chen, *Humanistic Foundation of Criminal Law*,
https://doi.org/10.1007/978-981-19-9764-8_6

mechanical determinist, will is a change in our minds, by which it plots its actions, in other words, it prepares its body organs to take something influential to it in a reasonable manner, and to turn away from those harmful to it. Intention means to prepare for action. Those external objects or internal ideas made us give rise to this intention in our minds are called motives, for which are the key or power that determines man's actions and activates body organs. All the actions of one's own accords are physical activities determined by mind changes.[1] It follows that what the mechanistic determinist calls will is entirely passive, and merely a conditioned reflex of external action. Kant, an idealist libertarian, believed that will has two meanings: Wille which refers to practical reason itself and Willkün which refers to the conscious will to act. The former is the will of common legislation, and the latter is the will of individual to implement. With Wille but Willkün, it means we legislate without enforcement; on the contrary, With Willkün but Wille, it loses its moral significance and is untenable. Only when these two are accepted and executed as law, can will be true.[2] Thus, in Kant's view, the will is pretersensual and transcendental, for which the will of human being is free. It is free is because it is rational. In Kant's philosophy, will is the practical faculty of reason, and the reason of practice. He also ascribed will to good will. According to Kant, will, as the starting point, must be both a special will from the moral life of ordinary people and a special will beyond ordinary people. The result of Kant's rumination was a good will which was universal and beyond the special will of ordinary people. In Kant's view, what of universal moral value does not come from the will of God, nor from man's natural nature and the authority of the world, but only from the good will of human reason itself. Such good will is not good for pleasure, good for happiness, or good for utility, but is moral good for good itself. Only which kind of good will is unconditional. Kant thought that in the world, in general, it is impossible to conceive of anything unconditionally good except good will, even outside of the world.[3] It can be seen that Kant only logically demonstrated the ethics of will, without touching the psychological reason of will at all. With an equal emphasis on the logical analysis of the will, Hegel was opposed to empirical analysis of it. He pointed out that speaking of freedom of the will, it reminded the former method of understanding—presupposing the representation of the will, from which the attempt is made to define and confirm it. And then, in accordance with the methods of the empirical psychology before, from the search for the sensations and phenomena of consciousness, like repentance and guilt, to infer the so-called proof to prove that the will is free, and to assert that these things above can only be explained by the free will. But it would be more convenient to directly dismiss freedom as an existing fact of consciousness that we have to believe, rather than take this approach. Hegel argued that this proposition of free will and the nature of will and freedom can only be deduced in relation to the whole. The basic features of this premise are: mind is intelligence first; The various determinations which the intelligence experiences in its development from feeling through presentation to thought are the means by

[1] See [1], p. 634.

[2] See [2], p. 287.

[3] See [3], p. 42.

which it produces itself as a will, and this will, as a general practical spirit, is close to the truth of the intelligence.[4] Thus, in Hegel's view, it is self-evident that will is an attribute of thought, and that as long as human being has thought, he must have a will. Hegel even held that the thought and will is intrinsically identical. Hegel pointed out: generally, the spirit is thinking, human being is different from animals because of the ability of thought. But we cannot suppose that human being is thought on the one hand and will on the other, or that he carries thought in one pocket and will in the other, for it is unrealistic. According to Hegel, the difference between thought and will is nothing more than that between theoretical and practical attitudes. They are not two faculties: the will is only a peculiar mode of thought which transforms itself into being, and as an impulse to be there. Hegel also discussed the relationship between intelligence and will concretely. He pointed out that we cannot have will if no intelligence. On the contrary, the will contains in itself something theoretical. The will prescribes itself, which is an internal thing at first, because when what I desire appears in my imagination, it is an object for me. Animals act by instinct, motivated by something within, and thus they are also practical. But animal does not have a will, because it does not visualize what it desires. In the same way, human cannot act or think theoretically without will, because he is acting when thinking.[5] It should be said that Hegel's exposition of the relationship between thought and will was reasonable, but he did not reveal the psychological mechanism of will in depth. In his analysis of the content of will, it was also speculative. Hegel pointed out that the will contains (a) the elements of pure indeterminacy or pure reflection of the ego in itself. In this reflection, all the limitations immediately existing from nature, needs, desires, impulses, or anything made ready and determined by whatever means, are removed. It is the unbounded infinity of an absolute abstraction or universality, the pure thought of itself. (b) The ego is the transition from the undifferentiated indeterminacy to a determinacy that is differentiable, defined and establishing as a content and an object. Such content is either given by nature or arises from the notion of spirit. The ego enters into the general Dasein by positing itself as the particular, which is the absolute element of finiteness or specialization of the ego. (c) The will is the unity of these two elements, the specificity which, reflected in itself, returns to the universal—the singularity. It is self-definition of the ego.[6] It shows that Hegel merely discussed the thought process of the will.

It is James, a famous US psychologist, who analyzed the will of human from the perspective of psychology. The neurophysiological mechanism on which James's theory of will is based is the principle of the reflex arc. James pointed out that the pathways of the nervous system are all in one direction, namely from "sensory" cells to "motor" cells, and from motor cells to muscles—never in the opposite direction. For example, a motor cell never stimulates a sensory cell directly, but only through the afferent nerve currents caused by its excretion. And a sensory cell always excretes to the motor area, or generally tends to do so. This direction is called the "forward

[4] See [4], pp. 10–11.

[5] See [4], pp. 12–13.

[6] See [4], pp. 13–17.

direction". In other words, this principle is: all neural currents through the brain initially, i.e., by birth, flow to the Rolandic region, from which it goes out, and never going back. From this point of view, the distinction between sensory and motor cells has no fundamental significance, because all cells are moving, but we call the cells in the Rolando area, in the nearest "funnel", the special motor cells.[7] It means that the basic direction of all nerve impulses is from sensory cells to motor cells to muscles—the neural activity of motor cells can only be stimulated by the "nerve current" of sensory cells, and the neural activity of sensory cells must also be "excreted" to motor cells, so the "nerve current" does not terminate in sensory areas. Therefore, the "ideas" caused by the neural activity of the sensory area of the cerebral cortex are, in principle, all the change or movement of a certain body organ by vigor. What's more, the physical movement can only be induced by the sensory activity in principle. James first studied the relation between idea and action, and put forward the following theorem: every idea of an action can somewhat induce the actual action of its objects, and that no such idea can at the same time be affected by a hostile idea in the mind. When this idea is prevented and cannot be induced in this way, it will cause the actual action to the greatest extent.[8] James argued this theorem from the following aspects: (1) Generally speaking, the nature of consciousness (i.e., mental conceptual activities) is impulsive (but consciousness must reach a certain intensity before its impulsivity can be fully effective). As James said, the action is not performed before we have a feeling or a thought first, and then add some impetus to it. All our fluctuations in consciousness are linked to a kind of neural activity that is triggering some actions. Our feelings and thoughts are only "cross-sections" (say) of neural current whose primary outcome is action, and which flows into one nerve and flows out of another at once.[9] (2) In the case that people immediately do something as soon as they think of it, the idea of the action (i.e., the action presentation) alone can initiate their corresponding action. All the actions come out without hesitation or immediately following the idea of the action in the mind are the ideologically motivated actions. But sometimes people's ideas don't act, which James explained, without exception, it is because other ideas present at the same time deprived the acting power of those ideas.[10] He cited an example of people who, on a cold morning, think about getting up for a thousand times, but actually not. It's the feeling of warmth in the quilt combined with the image of the cold weather against the idea of getting up. The thought of getting up to do something immediately induces the action of getting up, only when people happen to forget about the cold for a while. As soon as the idea of inhibition ceases, the idea of action immediately realizes its effect. (3) When there are hostile ideas in the mind, it is necessary to issue a clear instruction, if the hostile inhibition idea is to be eliminated, that is, to agree to execute a certain action. Regarding the essence of the "command" of this kind of action, James made the analysis: the secular concept is that consciousness alone is not the precursor of

[7] See [5], pp. 344, 400.

[8] See [5], p. 344.

[9] See [5], p. 345.

[10] See [5], p. 343.

activity at all, but a kind of "willpower" must be added in order to have activity; it is a natural impulse of the exceptional cases where we think about for a long time without actually doing it. These are not ordinary cases, however, and are examples of hostile thought suppression. When the suppression relaxes, we feel as if an internal spring has loosened, an additional impulse, a command, which makes the action successful.[11] That is to say, the action "command" in the ideological struggle is not a special "willpower", but is the automatic withdrawal of the hostile inhibitory idea. In fact, this psychological process can be experienced by people themselves. James also pointed out that the suppression of an action is the same as the execution of an action. In the absence of hostile ideas, only an idea in the mind can induce an action, and only another idea can suppress it from happening. The behavior of a conscious person is the reconciliation of two opposing neuricities at any time. (4) Regarding the behavior after deliberation. James said, deliberate behavior means that there are a lot of ideas in the mind with hostile or benign the relationship of each. One of these ideas is the one of an action, which, if alone, would induce action. But there are other considerations in consciousness that block motor nerve currents, conversely, other considerations would make this current turn out. The result is a particular upset, called "indecision." In the continuous state, when all objects being noticed all the time, we can say, we are deliberating; and at last the original cue may prevail, making an action take place, or it may be decisively overwhelmed by hostile action, we can say, we have decided. In other words, we gave the instruction that we intend to do one action. Those ideas that aid or inhibit are the reasons or motives for the so-called determination.[12] That is to say, the so-called deliberate will choices are actually just a series of mutual "aid" or "inhibit" activities among a series of ideas. (5) According to the relationship between ideas and actions, James believed that the motives of actions are only pain and pleasure. Objects and thoughts about them induce our behaviors, and the pleasures and pains brought about by behavior influence the course of the behavior and restraint it. If an action makes us comfortable, we would do it again and again as long as the pleasure continues. If an action causes us pain, our muscle contractions stop immediately. There are so many pleasures that, once we have experienced them, we almost have to continue the activities. The influence of pleasure and pain on our actions is so extensive and profound that a precocious philosophy asserted that only pain and pleasure are the power to provoke action, and thought that whenever there seems to be no pain or pleasure in action, it is simply because pain and pleasure are ignored for they are far away in the "remote" images that give rise to the action. However, it is a big mistake. Although pain and pleasure play an important role in the influence on our actions, pain and pleasure are not its exclusive stimuli, for consciousness is impulsive, and action is the natural and immediate result of consciousness, whatever its nature may be. This is true in reflex actions, emotional expressions, and will life. As soon as this idea occupies consciousness, and no other idea can take its place, the result of all action naturally belongs to it has to take place. In short, its impulses are in a good wicket and would

[11] See [5], p. 345.

[12] See [5], pp. 346–347.

manifest naturally. This is what we see in instinct, emotion, ordinary ideas, hypnotic suggestion, pathological impulses, and involuntary aspirations—push ideas are that occupy our attention.[13] After making the above argument, James concluded that the will is a relationship between the mind and its "ideas". We have come to the heart of our study on the will when we question that by what process the idea of a certain object can stably occupy the mind. In a word, the main achievement of the will, when it is most "intentional," is to observe a difficult object and fix it in the mind. It is an instruction, as soon as the object is noticed, the actions take place, which are only incidental incidents. James indicated that the essence of the function of the will is how to make the relevant ideas occupy the center of our attention, and once the condition of promoting the idea to occupy the mind is realized, the psychology of the will should end. The subsequent actions are only a physiological phenomenon, following the neural events corresponding to this idea, according to the laws of physiology. As soon as the idea prevails, the action of the will ceases; whether there follow actions or not, as far as the action of the will is concerned, it is entirely irrelevant. The above is the basic content of James's theory of the will, whose main spirit of is to explain the so-called willed process—actually the activity process of ideas. In the willed process, apart from the conceptual activity and its corresponding neural processes (including the associated physical movements), there is no need to assume any impetus of the "willpower" in this concept. It should be said that James's analysis of the psychological mechanism of will activity can be established in theory, which is of great significance for us to correctly understand the psychological connotation of the will.[14]

In psychology, the will is a psychological process in which people consciously determine the purpose and governance their behavior to achieve the anticipated purpose. In my opinion, to explore the psychological mechanism of the will, the following issues are worth studying: (1) The problem of body and mind. "Mind" refers to the psychological attributes of the will, and "body" is the physiological mechanism of the will. Will is the category of mind, but contains certain physiological mechanism. Will, like cognitive and emotional processes, is a function of brain. There is still not complete and sufficient study on the physiological mechanism of complex willed processes, but we have a clear understanding of the mechanism of voluntary movement. Voluntary movement is regulated by consciousness, which people can stop, accelerate or slow down, strengthen or weaken at will. Human's volitional activities are realized by a series of voluntary movements. Revealing the physiological mechanism of voluntary movement contributes to understand the physiological nature of the willed process. Physiological researches show that human voluntary movement is dependent on the nervous system, first of which are the certain morphological and functional activities of the brain organs. No matter how complex and ingenious one's voluntary movement is, and no matter how smoothly and freely one moves, it always depends on a certain anatomical and physiological

[13] See [5], p. 378.

[14] See [5], pp. 379–380.

basis. It's evident that human's volitional action is restricted by internal physiological conditions.[15] Therefore, it is contradictory to the science that regarding the will as a pure psychological activity, or even attributing it to the result of the mysterious force of human function. For example, Mo Gu, a British psychologist in the late 19th and the early twentieth centuries, asserted that human behavior is determined by an internal "drive", which is based on the body's mysterious instincts. The famous contemporary Australian neurophysiologist J. C. Eccles also regarded the human consciousness and the brain as two independent entities. He believed that the brain receives a volitional action from the conscious mind, and the brain transmits the conscious experience to the mind in turn. In short, they held that the will is a primary reality, while everything else is a derivative, a secondary reality. Since the will is a primary reality, the freedom of the will is of course not restricted by any material element.[16] Obviously, the above assertion has been proved wrong by physiology. So, the will, with a physiological mechanism, in other words, is restricted by the physiological function, can it deny the freedom of the will? Our answer is no. Therefore, human's body and mind are unified, and both mental and physical are the phenomena of human beings. Psychology and physiology are originally a unified function, which are separated for the convenience of scientific research. Therefore, the will not only refers to the psychological process, but also includes the physiological process. From the point of view of the unity of body and mind, we have to recognize the autonomy of human will activities. (2) Regarding the problem of matter and me. The relationship between matter and me actually refers to the relationship between object and subject, existence and thinking. "Me" refers to the subject, and "matter" refers to the object. The attribute of subject is will, which itself can be cultivated. That is to say, the will is not completely voluntary, it is gradually learned in the long-term social life with a certain operating mode, and then forms a certain psychological structure. The reflection of the will to the external world is restricted by its psychological structure. At the same time, the will is not empty, but guided by one's goals and motivated by motives; but the goals and motives are determined by one's needs, which themselves are a reflection of objective reality and are subject to natural laws and social living conditions. In this sense, freedom of will is simply the ability to make choices by knowledge of things. Since the human will is limited by objective conditions, can the freedom of the will be denied? Our answer is also negative, because the human will reflects the objective world not in a mechanical way, but an active one. Therefore, the autonomy of the will cannot be denied for above-mentioned limitation. (3) Concerning the question of cognitive consciousness. "Cognition" refers to the cognitive process, and "consciousness" refers to the willed process. There is also an inseparable relationship between cognition and will, which is what Hegel called the relationship between thinking and will. It should be said that Hegel made a correct exposition on the relationship between knowledge and will. Cognition is the premise of the will. When realizing each specific volitional action, in order to establish the purpose and choose the means, it is usually necessary to examine objective

[15] See [6], pp. 82–89.

[16] See [6], p. 79.

situation, analyze actual conditions, review experiences, imagine consequences, and make various programs, formulate action plans, and weigh and ponder all of them repeatedly, which must relies on the process of perception, memory, imagination, and thinking. These processes actually constitute the intellectual component of volitional activity. Therefore, without the cognitive process, there would be no volitional activity. At the same time, the will also has a great influence on the cognitive process. First of all, people's understanding of the external world is a process with purpose, plan and various difficulties needed to be overcome. The processes like organizing observation activities, maintaining random attention, conducting a random memory, realizing creative imagination, and developing thinking activities to solve problems, are inseparable from will efforts, namely, the willed process. Secondly, people's understanding of the objective world is completed in the process of changing things, and all practical activities for changing the reality are volitional actions, which must be controlled and regulated by the willed process. Therefore, without the will, there is no deep and complete cognitive activity. (4) On the question of knowledge and action. The relationship between knowledge and action refers to that between thought and action, where knowledge includes cognition, and more importantly, the will. Will and action are also closely related, for action is the externalization of will and is governed by will. Will has a regulating effect on action, which mainly occurs in two aspects: one is initiation, which means to promote someone to act necessarily to achieve the predetermined end; the other is stop, which means to stop the actions that do not meet the predetermined end. Therefore, for human's external action, the will is the motive, and there is a causal relationship between the will and the action.

1.2 Value Evaluation of Will

Before evaluating the value of will, it is necessary to define the concept of value correctly. In philosophy, value refers to the existence, function of objects and a certain suitability, closeness or consistency to a certain subject's needs and development of their changes.[17] The concept of value reflects the relationship between subject and object. From the perspective of human nature, the nature of value is manifested in the following two aspects: (1) Value is the objectification of human nature or subjectivity. There is a value relationship only between the subject and the object. Any value relationship between the subject and the object means that this thing has become the being of objectification of people. It means that people "occupy" things, through their relationship with things and their own objective relationship. If things have nothing to do with people, their natural attributes would not become the objects of people; if there is no corresponding subjectivity and essential power of people, the natural attributes of things cannot become value attributes either. Value, from the perspective of its generation, is essentially the objectification of human essential power in the object, whose value attribute is essentially the human's subject attribute

[17] See [7], p. 13.

embodied and condensed in the object. (2) Value is the function and significance of the object to enhance the essential power or subjectivity of human beings. It means that as an object, something or someone can directly or indirectly help and improve the human body strength to get rid of the shackles of nature, society and self, further establishing and expanding freedom of human beings.[18] One of the core issues of value is evaluation, namely value evaluation. Evaluation shows that in a certain value relationship between subject and object, whether the object can or has satisfied the subject's needs and desires, whether the object fits the subject's needs and makes the subject aware of this fitness. Therefore, there are two basic outcomes in evaluation: positive and negative. As the Czech philosopher V. Brozik pointed out that evaluation is a process in which the objective value objectivity is manifested in the form prescribed by the norms chosen by the subject.[19] Thus, evaluation endows objective value objectivity in a subjective form. Therefore, value objectivity is presented to us as moral, aesthetic, political and other values. Value evaluation is of great significance in the field of morality and law, both of which involve the evaluation of human behavior, and human behavior is governed by the will. As a consequence, there is a question of the value evaluation of the will.

People are social people and always live in a certain society. People are not only in contact with nature, but also with other people. This relationship between people is what we usually called social relations. People in a certain social relationship are bound to be restricted by certain social norms, and morality and law are the main manifestation of such social norms. When talking about moral evaluation, Soviet ethicists indicated that the process of social development is subject to historical inevitability, which is manifested in various forms. In the field of morality, the contradictory nature of inevitability and its various possibilities as manifestations of inevitability are embodied in the mutual relations between people. The way to resolve these situations depends first and foremost on the objective conditions that make certain possibilities become reality. It can be seen that people's moral consciousness plays a great role in this regard. The objective inevitability of history not only does not exclude people's conscious actions, on the contrary, it must be premised on people's conscious actions. People either promote new and progressive things or keep old and decadent things, depending on their class status and level of consciousness. It leads to the moral evaluation of people's behavior: behavior that contributes to progress (the welfare benefiting to society) is moral, otherwise, is immoral. People's activities can be evaluated from various standpoints. Moral awareness evaluates people's activities in terms of moral claims and moral norms, which are external inevitability to the individual. Being aware of these claims, accepting them subjectively, and organically combining the individual will of conscious actions with beliefs and emotions, all of these are the so-called moral freedom. Therefore, moral freedom is a certain moral standard system with awareness and acceptance as moral necessity, and the voluntary compliance with these moral norms in practical

[18] See [8], pp. 63–65.

[19] See [9], p. 64.

activities.[20] It shows that in a certain society, people's will is not arbitrary, but is constrained by certain moral and legal norms, which exists as the value evaluation object of morality and law.

The value evaluation of morality and law is based on a basic concept—ought. Henry Sidgwick, famous British ethicists come straight to the point in the book *Methods of Ethics* that if we interpret a method of ethics as a reasonable procedure enabling us to determine a man what "should" do, or what is "fair" to do for them, or something they "should" strive to realize through act of will, then, for the purpose of this book, perhaps the boundary of ethics needs to be fully defined at the beginning.[21] In explaining the concept of ought, Henry Sidgwick pointed out that in the narrowest sense of ethics, we always regard what we judge to be "ought" as the action out of the will by anyone making the judgment. It is impossible for me to think that I "ought" to do something that I am incapable of doing. However, in a broader sense—which people can't optionally exclude—sometimes I would judge that I "should" know the things a more intelligent people may know, or "should" feel the emotions a better man in my situation might feel, although I may know that I can't generate this knowledge or feeling directly within myself by any willpower. In this case, the word "ought" refers only to an ideal or paradigm which I ought, in its strict sense, to imitate as far as possible. This broad sense seems to be that we usually carry with in artistic norms and political judgments. When I judge that the laws and constitution of my country "ought" to be something else, it does not mean, of course, that I or anyone else can change the existing laws and constitution by will alone, but both in the narrow and broad sense, it means that ought is a possible cognitive object; In other words, what I judge as "ought" must the same as that by any reasonable man who is really judging the question, unless I misjudge it.[22] Henry Sidgwick's distinction between the narrow and the broad of "ought" is important to us. In the narrow sense, "ought" means possible, which is premised on possibility. The possibility here refers to both the objective and the subjective possibility. Objective possibility, of course, refers to that in the scope where objective condition allows. And the subjective may be related to the will, that is to say, it may subjectively refer to what can be done from one's will, or within the will. This is also the basic requirement for the object of moral evaluation. As Tilly, an US philosopher, pointed out that moral judgment takes behavior as the object, but we must supplement that not all behavior is suitable for moral judgment. Only the actions of conscious beings like us human can be judged like this. Generally speaking, we hope there is a spiritual or psychological basis for this action, and we make moral judgments about actions only if they are manifested by a conscious person. If we know the actor cannot control his action, it is not of his own will, or he cannot reason, feel and judge in a sound way when he does it, we do not judge. We do not commend the actions of men in epileptic seizures, in hypnotic trance or in sleep, or the purely reflexive action taken in the absence of self-control, nor do we condemn the actions of a psychopath. But if the action in question

---

[20] See [10], pp. 45–46.

[21] See [11], p. 25.

[22] See [11], pp. 56–57.

is the necessary consequence of some previous actions of the actor, which could have been avoided, we make moral judgments about the actions, or at least about the actor. Wherever we are convinced the actions are purely mechanical, namely, they are biologically determined and not accompanied by consciousness, and we do not judge them morally. Similarly, whenever and wherever it is performed consciously, we can try to judge it.[23] Therefore, what Henry Sidgwick called "ought" refers to the premise of moral judgment of will in a narrow sense—without consciousness, it is impossible to put forward moral claims for a person. "Ought", in a broad sense, and perhaps more importantly, refers to the moral claims of the will itself, and also to the setting of moral values, which directs the will to achieve such a moral value. In this case, as Henry Sidgwick pointed out, the knowledge or judgment that "something ought to be done" is actually discussed as an "order" or a "commandment" of rationality to the individual concerned.[24]

Distinguishing between ought and reality is the distinction between value and fact, which involves the understanding of moral law and natural law. German philosopher Paulsen pointed out that the natural law is a formula that represents the eternal unity of natural phenomena, which means the absolute unity that does not recognize any exceptions in a narrow sense. So, physics firmly believes that the law of universal gravitation is an accurate mathematical expression for the unified interaction of all masses in the universe. In this sense, the law of causality is understood as a strict universal law of nature. However, in a broader sense, we can also label the unified, not absolute but quite persistent phenomenon in nature as the law of nature. Most of the laws of biology belong to this natural law, like the laws that represent the unity of the structure and function of an animal or plant species. In the same sense, we can the propositions of ethics as the natural laws, which also show the permanent relationship between the types of behavior and their effects on life. The possible opposition is that ethical propositions or moral laws claim something ought to be, rather than natural laws claim something is. "Don't lie" is a moral law and a universally correct proposition that allows no exceptions in reality. Moral imperatives are considered to be closely related to the laws and decrees in legal books rather than natural laws. They are indeed linked to the law; Moreover, we may say that law represents only part of moral laws. However, it does not prevent them from being connected with the natural laws. It is no doubt that law shows what it should be, and there are exceptions in practical practice. But this is only an exception, because usually, the law shows the actual behavior of citizens, we do shouldn't cavil a legal provision not been generally observed in the national law. It is a real law, not because it is printed on some paper, but for it is a manifestation of the unity of behavior, even if not absolute. In addition, although the national law is rooted in people's will, in the final analysis, it is based on the nature of things and the causal connection between the types of behavior and their effects on life. Don't commit forgery, theft, arson, or as stipulated in the law: Whoever commits forgery, theft or arson will be punished like this. These laws are rooted in the fact that such actions will damage society. Theft tends to subvert

[23] See [12], p. 7.

[24] See [13], p. 58.

property rights, while forgery tends to undermine credit, disrupting the production and distribution of goods. This natural law is the ultimate basis of the law. The law is a regulation of the conduct set for the members of a group, which aims to ensure the conditions of social life.[25] Paulsen here explained the moral law with the natural law, only to show that what the moral law wants to express is the objective law in human society. Therefore, for the individuals with action, it is also an external natural law. Paulson revealed the factual basis of moral law, which also shows that there are internal relations between fact and value. Of course, it does not mean to deny the difference between fact and value, because value is not what the fact is, but puts forward a value standard that what it should be, which can guide people's behavior. People's volitional activity is autonomous, and this autonomy is not arbitrary, but an activity according to a certain value orientation. A certain value standard elevating to moral and legal norms is an "absolute command" for individual will, which makes the will subject to a certain value standard through self-discipline and heteronomy.

2 Freedom and Responsibility

Responsibility is a core issue in morality and law, which is closely related to freedom of will. Responsibility is based on the freedom of will, namely there is no responsibility without freedom of will. Therefore, it is of great significance to both morality and law for studying responsibility in freedom of will.

2.1 Choice Mechanism of Freedom

In the sense of ontology, freedom is associated with necessity, and is dominated by necessity, which is determinism. But this determinism is not inflexible, because inflexible determinism negates human freedom actually; it is dialectical determinism, therefore, human can control necessity on the basis of understanding of necessity, and in the extent permitted by necessity, human has a certain degree of freedom in turn. From the perspective of axiology, human freedom means a choice that is corresponding to compulsion. Therefore, choice is the core of freedom.

Freedom is a complex concept with various understandings in the world. The British philosopher Berlin has divided his understanding of freedom into negative and positive view of freedom.[26] The negative view of freedom consists of three propositions: (1) Freedom is not being interfered by others. Berlin indicated that negative freedom refers to the matter of the range of choices and activities that individuals can make independently without the control of others, or to the matter of the range of control. As long as no one interferes with my activities, I am usually

[25] See [14], pp. 17–18.

[26] See [15], p. 211.

free. In this sense, political freedom is a matter of the extent to which a person can act been unimpeded. If I am prevented from doing what I could have done, I am not free; if the range of my uninterrupted activities is reduced to be narrower than the minimum by others, I may be coerced, or be enslaved. (2) Freedom is restricted because there is a value equal to or higher than that of freedom. Berlin pointed out that although the classical political philosophers disagreed on how wide freedom could or should be, they all believed that freedom could not be unlimited. If no limit, there will be a state where all people can interfere with others limitlessly. This kind of natural freedom either leads to social chaos, making people's minimum requirements unable to be met, or causes the freedom of weak to be suppressed or deprived by the strong. Classical political philosophers realized that freedom is not the sole goal of human beings, nor the highest value. Other goals and values, such as justice, happiness, culture, security, and equality, are either of equal or higher value than freedom. Therefore, for other goals and values, but also for freedom itself, the range of freedom must be limited by law. As Locke said, where there is no law, there can be no such freedom, for freedom means exemption from bondage and rape by others, and there can be no such freedom where there is no law. But freedom, as we are told, is not a matter of doing as they please.[27] And as Montesquieu said, in a society with laws, freedom only means "one can do what he should do, and not be compelled to do what he should not do". Freedom is the right to do everything permitted by the law; if a citizen can do something prohibited by the law, he is no longer free, because other people have the same right.[28] (3) A minimum freedom must be preserved. Berlin pointed out that classical thinker also believed that although freedom should be restricted, such restriction should not be too rigid, and a certain absolute and inviolable free area should be reserved for individuals. For if the range of freedom is violated excessively, the individual would feel that his life was extremely circumscribed, unable to develop his most basic natural abilities, which are necessary for the individual to pursue his ideals. So, a line must be defined between the sphere of private life and public power. And it is a worthwhile matter about where exactly that line is, with a bargain indeed. Freedomists advocate that a larger free range of mobility should be reserved for individuals, while conservatives believe that the scope of centralized control should be expanded. But whatever the principle of division may be, whether it be the principle of natural law and natural rights, the principle of utility, the principle of absolute imperative, or some other principles, freedom here means "freedom from something", requiring no intervention should cross a variable but always determinable edge. In a word, the individual cannot have unrestricted freedom; freedom cannot be unrestricted; and the restriction of freedom itself cannot be unrestricted. This is the basic idea of the negative view of freedom. The positive view of freedom is different from that of negative. Berlin pointed out that positive liberty involves controlling or interfering with the origin of people's action, namely, it is self-control or controlled by others? Positive view of freedom comes from the subject's desire to become his own master. I want to be an instrument of my own act of

[27] See [16], p. 36.

[28] See [17], p. 154.

will, not that of someone else. I want to be a subject, not an object, driven by my own self-consciousness and rationality, and not be dominated by external factors; I want to be famous more or less, not insignificant. I want to be active and make decisions by myself, instead of by others. In conclusion, I want to realize that I am thoughtful, wishful and active who can take responsibility for my own choices and explain the reason according to my own concepts and purposes. I feel free when I believe these to be true, otherwise enslaved. It can be seen that there is a difference between these two views of freedom, the former is to get rid of foreign objects, while the latter is to promote oneself. The US scholar Sartori talked about two basic meanings of freedom: I can and I am able to. Obviously, the freedom of "I can" is negative, while the freedom of "being able to" is positive. Sartori pointed out that the freedom of "I can" means a permission, but the freedom of "being able to" means a capacity. They are interrelated, because the permission without capacity is as empty as capacity without permission. The difference between "I can" and "I am able to" correspond to the difference between the objective and subjective categories of freedom. If we are interested in the objectification of freedom—that is, in the actions of freedom—freedom takes the form of permission. If it does not involve objective freedom, we are concerned with the freedom to express capacity. Terms such as "independence" "protection" and "action" are mostly used to refer to objective freedom, while "autonomy" "self-realization" and "will" often involve the freedom inherent in human nature.[29] Despite the above differences in the understanding of freedom, choice is always the meaning should be in freedom. It is fair to say that there is no freedom without choice.

In theory, selection is a unique ability and activity of human beings. We can summarize it as the subject, according to his own needs and subjective and objective conditions, consciously starts from the internal relationship of various objects and possible dynamic development process, and judges and strives for the activity of the object or the mode of subject-object interaction that can satisfies his own needs to the utmost extent and most comprehensively first.[30] Therefore, the concept of selection is generally associated with human's subjectivity, which is a term to express subjectivity capacity and condition. But in western history, the concept of selection had a very broad meaning, and the term of natural selection has a great influence in particular. In 1859, Darwin published the book *On the Origin of Species* and put forward the famous theory of natural selection, with which explained the evolutionary mechanism of organisms. Darwin believed that under natural conditions, organisms would increase in geometric progression with an extremely high reproductive rate. In order to compete for food and space, in addition to fighting against inorganic natural conditions, living beings also carry out a severe struggle for survival with other individuals of the same species and with the creatures of their close species. So the result was that the variations beneficial for survival were preserved, while others harmful were eliminated. Darwin called this process of survival of the fittest as natural selection. It should be said that in this process of natural selection, even if animals have the ability or action to select the environment, it is only based on

---

[29] See [18], pp. 302–303.

[30] See [19].

instinct. Because in nature, there is no distinction between subject and object, there is no conscious action of choice by subject. Any activity of living things is nothing more than a concrete form of movement in nature. Therefore, from the perspective of the human subject, the nature is a world without choices. In pure nature, there is no distinction between subject and object, and matter is the subject of all changes, which is only the undertaker of motion and variation, and is a subject without object, so it can only be understood as a noumenon. All biological species with sensory properties can only instinctively adapt to the natural environment around and are governed by natural inevitability blindly. For example, animals treat nature with mechanical, rigid and innate forms that satisfy their own needs. These forms are determined by the structure and physiological function of animals, and constitute a strictly fixed type of activity. It is impossible for them to treat the species they belong to as a class, or treat the surrounding purposefully and consciously, which means they cannot grasp the external things to change the existing natural existence according to the internal measure of their own needs. Therefore, for a certain biological species, natural selection is essentially a dominated process, rather than an autonomous process. Corresponding to natural selection, in the sense of freedom, selection is a social selection, whose emergence must be premised on the differentiation of subject and object, and the emergence of man as the subject. As a product of long-term development of nature to a certain stage, human development is not mainly carried out by natural selection. The emergence of human beings is inseparable from the ability to get rid of the instinct of animals and obtain some kind of ability to choice freely. As Fromm describes in *Escape from Freedom*, humans emerged when instinct becomes beyond a certain point of inability to fix behavior, when adaptation to nature loses its feature of compulsivity, when inherited innate function can no longer fixed their way of behavior. In other words, existence of human beings and freedom of choice are inseparable from the very beginning. In a certain social connection, people use concepts and practices to grasp nature and society in activities of their actions. The world presented to people is the result of human subjects transforming nature, society and humans according to their own internal measures (needs, concepts, purposes, etc.) and external measures (objective laws) inherent in the objective material world. In natural selection, animals are absolutely obedient to nature. In social selection, people make purposeful and creative choices in the external world for that suit their own needs. In man's choice of nature, subject and object undergo material transformation, creating a natural environment suitable for their own survival and development. In people's choice of society, the subject is constantly remolding and creating a social environment suitable for his own survival and development. What's more, while consciously adjusting the relationship between human beings and the surrounding, human beings would continue to choose new target modes to shape and improve their own quality. This process of actively treating and remolding nature, society and human bodies in social history is the process called Social Selection.

Not only is social selection different from natural selection, but there is also a significant difference between individual selection as a social member and history selection as a whole. Society is made up of countless individuals, in which there is no thoughts and consciousness, while individuals as members of in it are thoughtful and conscious. Therefore, the choice of the society is the result of countless individuals, but the laws of the two are different. Engels once pointed out, "What are active in the field of social history are humans who are conscious, thoughtful or passionate, and pursue a certain end; nothing happens without a conscious intention or an expected purpose. However, no matter how important this distinction may be to historical study, especially to that of epochs and events, it in no way changes the fact that the course of history is governed by internal general laws. For in this area, although every individual has consciously anticipated ends, it seems that been dominated by the contingency on the surface by and large. What people anticipate seldom comes true, and in most cases, many anticipated ends interfere, conflict with each other, or they are never going to, or lack of the means to achieve. Thus, the conflict of countless individual wishes and individual actions creates a situation completely identical to the domination by unconscious nature in the field of history. The purpose of the action is expected, but the actual result of the action is not, or the result seems to be consistent with the expected purpose at first, but out of the result in the end. In this way, historical events seem to be governed by contingency in general. But something playing a part outwardly is always governed by hidden laws within, and what we need to do is only to discover these laws." "Whatever the outcome of history, humans always make their history by each purpose of them to pursue their self-consciously anticipated. And these desires to move in different directions and the resultant of their various effects on the external world is history."[31] Here, Engels profoundly pointed out the regularity of historical development, so can we draw a conclusion and understand his point as historical determinism? It cannot be simply understood in this way. As pointed out by Chinese scholars, it is impossible to scientifically understand the nature of social history purely from the object or the subject. In his conception of history, Marx took a two-way perspective in the study of the essence of history: based on historical activities of practice, the relationship between man and history is examined from the subject's selection activities, and the influence of natural and social factors on people is investigated from the restriction of the object on the subject. In other words, from the bidirectional unification of the two-way action of subject and object, Marx revealed that social history is essentially a process of unification of subject selection and object restriction. Marx's conception of history was not indeterminism, but it fully affirmed the objective causal relationship or objective regularity in the social and historical processes, and transcended traditional determinism at the same time, which is manifested in that it is based on human historical activities, or more precisely, on human history as a logical starting point, seeking historical law or historical inevitability from the subject-object relationship reflected in historical selection activities, and understanding the essence of historical process as the unity of selectivity and determinism. Only by explaining this two-way perspective can we truly grasp the profound dialectics of Marx's historical determinism.[32] It was on the basis of this understanding that the theory of historical

[31] See [20], pp. 247–248.

[32] See [21], p. 15.

selection is put forward. The proposition of this point was profound, but this historical selection theory can only be a supplement to historical determinism, rather than another conception of history opposed to historical determinism.

If historical choice reflects the selection of the whole society, it is a symbol of social freedom; then, individual selection reflects the choice of some individuals as members of society. Although it is in the double limitation of laws of nature and society, it still embodies human's subjective initiative with its impressive content, also called subject choice, embodying a kind of personal freedom. In the sense of epistemology, subject choice is a manifestation of human's subjective initiative, in which freedom is realized in such conscious choice. Active choice runs through a series of activities in the cognition and practice of subject. From the principle of theory of reflection, feeling is the beginning of all conscious activities. Science has proved, however, that the human receptors have certain functions of selection, adjustment and integration when receiving the stimulation of external information to form feelings. In human perceptual activities, facing the complex phenomenal world, the subject's attention is always directed to some aspects related to its own will. It is because subject's will is selective in perceptual activities, that is to say, the subject's will is selected and rejected for countless objective phenomena when people are in perceptual activities. In the stage of rational cognition, the object of thinking is of course the perceptual materials obtained in perceptual activities, and it is impossible to form a rational cognition without such perceptual materials. However, rational cognition is not a direct cognition of objective things, but an indirect one after abstracting and generalizing to the perceptual materials by human brain—the processing factory. In the stage of rational cognition, if cognition of the subject wants to reflect the entire attributes of the target, the essence of things and their internal regularity, the rich sense data should be turned to transformations of discarding the dross and selecting the essential, eliminating the false and retaining the true, proceeding from the one to the other, and from the outside to the inside. There is a series of active selection processes inside, for some of the rich perceptual materials are false or real; partial or unilateral; integral or global; superficial or essential; and are inevitable or occasional factors for reflecting the development and movement of things. Therefore, the subject's choice is inseparable, when it processes and transforms the perceptual materials to form an abstract rational cognition. The first is to choose the authenticity of perceptual materials, for only reliable and real materials can be the basis of rational processing. However, even if it is a real material, some reflect the essence and comprehensiveness, and some reflect the appearance or partial situation only, it must be a choice too. When the cognitive subject gets the real and essential material to forms a concept and theoretical system, there is also a problem of how to choose the correct and scientific expression. This selectivity of rational cognition is manifested in people's various rational thinking. In the process of cognition, the concept of the object is the result of the subject construction, which manifests the function of subject selection in rational cognition. Human cognition is a selection process, so is human practice. Practical activity is first and foremost characterized by the immediacy of its purpose, which is always carried out for some actual interests of the subject. It would never arise from a purposeless simple occasional interest, but is firmly conditioned by immediate purposiveness. In this sense, with strong subjectivity, practical activity always regards the target as something available, and treats things from the needs of the subject. The purposiveness of human activities just reflects the subjective selectivity of human beings. There is no conscious choice without conscious purpose, and the vested purposiveness must be realized through choice. In human life, all kinds of freedom objectively existing are generally the result of the subject's choice.

As a manifestation of human freedom, subjective selectivity is characterized by: (1) Subject selection is a conscious value selection. There is an extremely important value of freedom to the subject, which provides the necessary conditions for free existence, free activities and self-development to the subject. As an object being, there will be a value problem of freedom-related when it is relation to the subject. In terms of the nature of its action, this value can be positive and negative; in terms of the nature of the needs to be satisfied, it can be material and spiritual; in terms of the time range of its action, it can be long-term and short-term; and in terms of the role of its action, it can be main and secondary. It is expressed as a value relationship between the object and the objective world, when the subject chooses. The value attributes of object beings can better or optimally satisfy the subject's wishes and needs to freedom, and people always use and transform these attributes through their own practical activities to serve their own free purposes. Values are a measurement for human beings examine things and carry out practical activities. From the perspective of the subject's activities, selection is an activity under the control of the subject's value needs. Selection is to absorb the things valuable to the subject, and eliminate those of little or no value to the subject, whose process is the combination of the subject's values and external things. The selection of the subject is the application and performance of the subject's values in the process of cognition and practice. (2) Subject selection is a concrete form to realize the unity of subject and object, whose fundamental way to realize it lies in humans' practical activities. Because of the close relationship between choice and the practical activities, and the characteristics of selectivity of the practice the unity of the subject and the object is realized through the specific humans' select activities. To realize the unity of subject and object, the activities of the subject must follow certain objective laws. However, people also have active selectivity in dealing with objective laws. Although from the overall of human activities, as long as been recognized, the various laws existing objectively are always beneficial to people, but under some specific circumstances, the effects of the specific laws are not equivalent for each specific subject activity, but there are differences between benefits and harms, as well as different degrees of benefits. People would always choose those laws beneficial to them to serve their own purposes when applying laws; at the same time, they always try to prevent those unfavorable to them from acting, or make them change the direction of their effects. When people realize the unity of subject and object in selection, they do not violate the objective laws, but consciously seek profit and avoid loss through selection to achieve their own goals on the premise of following certain laws. (3) Subject selection is a vivid manifestation of subjective initiative. From the relationship between human and objective inevitability, freedom lies in the degree to which people recognize and utilize objective inevitability; and from the perspective of human's initiative, freedom lies in the autonomy and creativity of his choice, which is an autonomous activity. When a person is in practical activities, he has consciously and actively conceived a blueprint for implementation through thinking activities. As Marx said, the ability of bees to build houses makes the architects of the world feel ashamed, but the worst architect is better than bees because he has had an idea in his mind before building. Human's choice activities clearly reflect that they are in the active position of the subject and show the autonomy of the subject. Human choice is also a creative activity. Creation is a transcendence of reality. If there is no creative spirit in selection activities, it is extremely low-level selection, and does not really reflect the characteristics of human selection. The ingestion of subject to the object is a creative transformation process of the object to make it fit the subject's requirements. The object selected by the subject is no longer that of the original shape and characteristics, but the processed one. Therefore, the choice of the subject is full of creativity.

As the selectivity of the subject, freedom is a voluntary behavior. Therefore, selectivity can also be understood as voluntary. Human have a voluntary choice of behavior, but in real life, not every behavior can be chosen according to the actor's desire, but may be forced by the outside. External compulsion often makes people lose their freedom of choice and fall into an unfree situation. Coercion means that effort is out of the reach, whereas freedom is within the reach. In other words, compulsion is what it cannot be, and freedom is what it can be. Moore, the British ethicist, pointed out that whenever a prescribed act is really the actor could have taken if he had chosen beforehand, it can simply said the act was the actor could have done, even though he did not do it. Similarly, when we say that the actor can do something, or something is possible, we always only mean the possible situation if the actor made such a choice. Therefore, Moore argued that what could have been is a prerequisite for moral judgments: because our theory holds that if a person could have acted in some other way if he had made another choice in advance, it gives us the right to judge the actor's actions as actually right or wrong. What's more, what could have been is also should be in the freedom of the will, as Moore pointed out, the statement that we have free will is, of course, generally understood to that in fact, we do sometimes have the capacity to act in a way that is different from the way we actually act. Therefore, if someone tells us that we have freedom of the will, but wants to deny that we have the above capability at the same time, he is simply leading us astray. If we can't actually act in any sense other than what we have already done, we obviously have no freedom of will in general.[33] It is in this sense that Aristotle said that we are to blame for every evil from our voluntary subjectively.[34] Under the external force, where a person is originally cannot, namely the result is not his wish, but cannot avoid either, or perhaps cannot avoid originally, there is no freedom of choice for the actor, which is a kind of involuntary behavior.

---

[33] See [22], pp. 98–100.

[34] See [23], p. 51.

2.2 Responsibility Definition of Freedom

Freedom can lead to good or evil. Hegel pointed out that the root of evil generally exists in the mystery of freedom, namely the speculative thinking of freedom. According to this mystery, freedom must come out of from the naturalness of the will and become an internal thing in contrast with it.[35] When explaining Hegel's words, Japanese ethicists point out that, in other words, freedom is the basis of good and evil, which is a bifurcating point to both good and evil. The separation of naturalness and immanence of the will marks the "distinction between the irrational animals and human beings", and features the rational human symbolized by Adam and Eve. Hegel pointed out that "the individual subjectivity that reversed the ethical order, of course, is responsible for evil" (*"die Schuld des Bosen"*). Hegel critically inherited Kant's ultimate evil recognized as an act of reason, and re-understand it as the limitation of human responsibility. Freedom is the choice of good and evil, which is based on the individual's decision, therefore it is he who is responsible for his own actions.[36] So according to the logic that freedom is the root of evil, the question of responsibility arises from freedom, and any evil is to be blamed on the person. In this sense, it can be said that responsibility is a consequence of freedom, which also means a definition of freedom.

Freedom is defined by responsibility because of the nature of freedom. Freedom is social and is the attribute of people living in society, so it is not unrestrained. In real life, any action of freedom contains due responsibility. Freedom and responsibility are two sides of the same coin.[37] Classical Marxist writers greatly emphasize the inseparability of freedom and responsibility, and definitely believe that the responsibility of individual's actions to others is the boundary mark of freedom. Marx pointed out that freedom is the right to engage in all activities that do no harm to others. The boundaries of activities what everyone can do that do no harm to others are defined by tradition, just as the boundaries of land are defined by landmarks.[38] Therefore, freedom and responsibility are closely related, so responsibility is the definition of freedom.

The definition of freedom by responsibility is mainly reflected in the connection between law and freedom. In western history, despite significant differences in the understanding of freedom, not even the most radical freedomists have argued that freedom is free from the law, but only the extent of it is restricted. In ancient Greece, Aristotle was the first to make scientific argument on the relationship between freedom and law. Aristotle pointed out that the citizens were living by the rules of a state, and that which should not be regarded as a slavery (opposed to freedom) but rather as salvation.[39] It shows that Aristotle saw the identity of freedom and law, and citizens can enjoy freedom only within the boundaries of law. "Law should not be

[35] See [4], p. 143.
[36] See [24], p. 99.
[37] See [25], p. 166.
[38] See [26], p. 438.
[39] See [27], p. 276.

regarded as a slavery (opposed to freedom) but rather as salvation" became Aristotle's famous saying on the relationship between freedom and law, which profound influenced on later generations. Cicero, an ancient Roman philosopher, also said a famous saying about the relationship between freedom and law—"In order to obtain freedom, we are the servants of law." Of course, Cicero understood law in the sense of natural law, pointing out that the law is the highest rationality, and it is rooted in nature, which governs what should be done and forbids what should not be done. When this highest rationality is firmly established and fully developed in human understanding, it is law. Law is intelligence, whose natural function is to govern what is right and to forbid what is wrong. Law is a natural power, the spirit and rationality of intelligent people, and the standard for measuring justice and injustice.[40] Although what Cicero talking about is natural law, in his opinion, the positive law under the republic at that time is the embodiment of natural law, so the acquisition of freedom is not only means subjecting to natural law, but also to the positive law. Locke, a modern western philosopher, made a wonderful discussion of the relationship between freedom and law. Locke divided freedom into two natural freedom and social freedom. The so-called natural freedom is the freedom that one can enjoy in the natural condition. According to Locke, the state of nature is free and equal. Firstly, it is a state of complete freedom in which men, within the sphere of natural law, can decide their actions and dispose of their possessions and persons as they think fit, without the permission of or under the orders of anyone. Secondly, it is also a state of equality, in which all powers and jurisdictions are mutual, no one has more power than the others, and there is no subordination or control. Locke believes that although human beings enjoy a wide range of freedom in the state of nature, it is unstable and unsafe, so it is flawed. Because in the state of nature, people can only use their own power to exercise and defend their free rights according to their own judgments, so it is difficult to ensure that their own judgments are correct, and that they do not conflict with that of others. Therefore, it is difficult to ensure their natural rights are not to be violated by others, especially when others are stronger than them. In order to get out of this state, people established countries and made laws by social contracts to enjoy social freedom. Therefore, in Locke's view, social freedom is higher than natural freedom, and human beings can obtain it in a social state. This so-called social freedom is freedom within the limits of the law. Social freedom is clearly stipulated by the laws of the country, establishing well-known standards of right and wrong, and ensuring the realization of the law with the coercive force of the country. Locke believed that in this case, people still enjoy the original freedom, and it is more stable and more secure, but which is premised on the state and the law. Therefore, Locke pointed out that the freedom in society is not subject to any legislative power except those established in the state by the consent of people; it is not governed by any will or to any law, except law made by a legislature in accordance with its mandate. So, freedom is not, as Sir Robert Firmer said that the freedom is that we do as we please, and to live as we please, without being bound by any law. Locke pinpointed that the freedom of people under the government should have

[40] See [28], p. 64.

long-term effective rules as the criterion of life, which are jointly observed by all members of the society and formulated by the legislature established by the society. This is the freedom that we can do all the things not stipulated by the rules with my own will, and not be subject to another capricious, unknowable, and arbitrary will, just as natural freedom is not subject to any other restrictions except natural law.[41] Therefore, "where there is no law, there is no freedom" became Locke's famous saying about the relationship between freedom and law. After Locke, Montesquieu also made a profound discussion on the relationship between freedom and law, who believed that real freedom is inseparable from real law, and political freedom can only be obtained in a society with a rule of law. Therefore, the main meaning of freedom is that a person is not compelled to do things not stipulated by the law, who is free only when he is governed by the civil law (i.e., the positive law). So, we are free because we live under civil law.[42] Montesquieu clarified various misconceptions in the understanding of freedom, especially criticized the theory of freedom that people can do almost what they want to do, and tried his best to advocate freedom, especially emphasizing that political freedom can exist only if connected with the law. In a democratic country, freedom exists precisely because of laws. With the law, there is order, and anarchy with chaos can be avoided, and unreasonable interference and violation of my freedom, that is, my legitimate rights, can be prevented, and the true personal independence can be maintained to do what I should do. So, freedom is nothing else, not unlimited as most people understand, but the right to do what is not prohibited by the law. Montesquieu pointed out that in democracies, it is true that people seem do what they want to do; however, political freedom does not mean to do what they want. In a country, e.g. in a society with laws, freedom is simply that one can do what he ought to do, and not be compelled to do what he ought not to do.[43] Therefore, Montesquieu put forward the following famous statement on the relationship between liberty and law—"Freedom is the right to do all that the law permits; if a citizen can do what the law forbids, he is no longer free, because other people also have the same right."[44] The British philosopher Mill wrote *On Liberty*, which also discussed the relationship between freedom and law. Mill held that there are two kinds of freedom: freedom of will and social freedom. Mill mainly discussed social liberty, that is, the nature and limits of the power that society can legitimately exercise over individuals. Therefore, in this sense, freedom is actually a division of power between individuals and society, and it is the power that society or rulers should give to individuals. Accordingly, Mill defined freedom as that the only veritable freedom is the one that to pursue what is beneficial to us in our own way, so long as we do not try to deprive this freedom of others, and do not try to impede them or hinder their efforts to obtain it.[45] So Mill believes that as long as the individual's behavior does not harm others, there is complete freedom, and others

---

[41] See [16], p. 16.

[42] See [29], p. 194.

[43] See [30], p. 154.

[44] See [30], p. 154.

[45] See [31], p. 13.

and society have no right to interfere; only when others' interests are violated, the society can restrict his behavior, and the law can prevent it and punishment. Therefore, the law does not limit freedom, but only actions beyond the scope of freedom. The above-mentioned thinkers' discourses on freedom are closely related to the law. It can be seen that in a law-based society, the law is the landmark of freedom, which can only be in the legal sense.

The legal provisions of freedom are mainly realized through the relationship between rights and obligations, which is that between freedom and responsibility. In legal theory, there are different opinions on the nature of rights, which can be summarized as follows[46]: (1) The theory of freedom, namely the theory of natural rights, holds that right is freedom, and any behavior within the scope of freedom is right. (2) The theory of scope, which means that rights are the scope of human behavior permitted by law, according to which all legal behavior are rights. (3) The theory of meaning, namely the will theory, which is mainly advocated by Savigny Wind-scheid, a French jurist, that right is willensmacht or willensherrschaft endowed by law; there is no right where there is no willensmacht of claim. (4) Interessentheorie, which was mainly created by French jurist Jhering, holds that rights are interests protected by law. The interests referred to by Jhering are in a broad sense, including not only the material interests of the subject of rights, but also all the interests related to the subject of rights, on body and spirit. In other words, all utilitarian things that can be enjoyed by people are rights. But in fact, this statement is criticized because some interests are not expressed as legal rights, and interests are only the ends of the exercise of rights. Afterwards, Jhering modified this theory, regarding the protection of individual specific interests within the scope of rights as the essential element of the existence of rights, considering rights as the protection of interest self-discipline. (5) The compromise theory of between willensmacht and interest, which was mainly proposed by German scholars Burke and Jerunek, thought that the theory of willensmacht and interest are biased, if the two compromised, it was appropriate, that is, right is the willensmacht to protect interests, or the interest to protect according to the willensmacht. (6) The theory of validity, which was proposed by German scholars Michael and Regelsberg, holds that right is the validity in law and that can be claimed by law, namely the sphere of influence, but the right is not boundless and must be aimed at enjoying specific life interests. (7) The theory of law and power holds that rights are the powers and functions of law, that is, actions within the scope of law. (8) The theory of dependency-domination, initiated by French scholar Par Jean Darbin, holds that the essence of rights is the relationship of dependency and domination, or possession and disposition, in which the reason of domination is determined by domination. The so-called dependency refers to the inseparability between personality and the subject of rights; and the so-called domination refers to the disposal of the things of the subject of rights. The right arises from the dependency, and its dependency is accomplished by the domination, in which the two links constitute the whole process of a right. (9) The theory of choice, proposed by the British jurist Herberf Hart, holds that rights mean that in a

[46] See [32], pp. 6–8.

specific interpersonal relationship, the law recognizes the choice of one person (the owner of the right) over that of others (the obligor). A man has rights because the law recognizes his superior choices.

Maybe It should be said that the above views reveal the nature of rights from various aspects, but each of them inevitably be biased. In fact, the concept of right is substantial in content, and should be comprehensively understand. Pound, an US jurist, summed up the following six meanings of rights: (1) Interests. Rights mean things that should be recognized or guaranteed based on ethical grounds, or recognized, delimited and guaranteed interests. (2) Right is a legally recognized and delimited interests, which may be called a broad legal right plus the legal instruments for securing them. (3) The ability, through politically organized social force, to compel another or all others to engage in certain acts or not to engage in certain acts. (4) The ability to create, change, or deprive various narrow legal rights to create or alter obligations. (5) Some certain situations which are not subject to law, that is, that are not legally restricted to the natural ability, here mainly refers to the right of freedom. (6) Justice in the sense of ethics.[47] Rights have many meanings, but it is mutual that they are limited by social structures. Because human nature is the summation of all social relations, the acquisition and exercise of human rights cannot exist without the restraints of social structure for a moment. At the same time, rights are also restrained by corresponding obligations. Freedom implies rights as well as obligations, which exists as the counterpart of right, and acts as a restraint to right. Obligation has the following three characteristics[48]: (1) obligation is a kind of personal responsibility for others, the collective, or a nation of collective and the country generated from interpersonal relationships, and the need to complete a task or mission; after fulfilling its obligations, an individual or a collective will have a sense of satisfaction, that is, the feeling of obligation in mind and psychology. The demand and satisfaction of obligation is a sense of obligation of the subject. (2) Obligation, as a mission and task, is also a value goal and ideal and pursuit of the subject. (3) The fulfillment of obligations are always with the enjoyment of rights. Even moral rights will objectively enjoy some rights more or less in the process of fulfillment. From the perspective of the characteristics of obligations, it is the same with rights, just as Marx said: there is no right without obligation and no obligation without right.[49] The inseparability of right and obligation shows that obligation objectively restrains the choice of individual behavior and the exercise of rights given by society. However, this restraint is not a denial of freedom, but an affirmation of it. As Hegel puts it that a binding obligation is a restraint only from subjectivity without stipulation or abstract freedom, and from the impulse of natural or moral will (which arbitrarily prescribes the good without stipulation). But in obligation, the individual is liberated actually. Obligation restrains only subjective capricioUSess, not freedom, but if there is only an abstract freedom, that is, non-free. Obligation is the freedom to attain the essence and gain

[47] See [33], pp. 46–48.

[48] See [34], pp. 90–91.

[49] See [35], p. 610.

affirmation.[50] It may be said that Hegel's argument is very profound and of great significance for our understanding of the nature of obligation.

Obligation is the premise of responsibility, breach of duty will inevitably lead to responsibility, from which the concept of responsibility is extracted. In fact, freedom itself is an ambiguous concept. When discussing moral responsibility, US ethicist Frankena pointed out that according to our moral judgment, moral responsibility should be attributed to a specific actor. We do this in at least three cases: (1) when introducing X, we sometimes say he is responsible, or a person with a sense of responsibility. That is to say, he has good moral character. (2) Assuming Y is a past act or sin by X, we say X was and is responsible for Y. (3) If Y is an action to be taken, we may say that X is responsible for Y, which means that X is responsible for doing Y. Frankena pointed out that here, there is roughly similar meaning between saying that X is responsible in the first sense and that X is expected to bear its responsibility in the third sense. The first type of responsibility is another second-order quality that we should strive to cultivate. To say that X has some responsibility in the third sense is simply to mean that he has an obligation—either because of his office or he has made a promise to do it in the past—which is a direct normative judgment of obligation. Frankena is most interested in the second responsibility. If X is responsible for Y, under what circumstances is this judgment correct or justified? To say that X is responsible for Y, Frankena argues, is, first of all, a causal, not a moral judgment; So when someone says "X is responsible for Y", it may simply means "X is the cause of Y" and may also have the qualification of X does Y voluntarily and intentionally. However, if X is responsible for Y is not merely a special causal explanation, nor a simply meaning that X can do Y, as the suffix (*ible*) of "responsible" implies. Because suffixes meaning "be able to" like "ible" and "able" don't always represent an ability, but may have a normative meaning.[51] Here, Frankena is talking about the question of the condition of responsibility, in other words—it is fairly to ascribe responsibility to the actor under what conditions—which also exists in legal liability. Frankena quotes Aristotle as saying that one is actually responsible for his actions if and only if (1) the cause of the action is internal, e.g., he is not compelled by someone or something external to him; (2) the action he took was not the result of blindness without his own pre-selection. Then, and only then, may his action be considered voluntary.[52] Obviously, Aristotle is right in his analysis of the grounds or the conditions of moral responsibility, but he did not mention the point of obligation, which was perhaps self-evident for moral obligation, and so he left it out. For legal liability, this particular obligation is very important. Therefore, the three conditions of imputation should be as follows: (1) The objective obligation of preexistence. Obligation is the premise of responsibility, there is no obligation will not lead to certain responsibility. So, illegality, is actually a breach of obligation. Obligation is imposed on the individual by society, manifested as a kind of external compulsion, which indicates the limitation of rights and the limit of freedom, therefore. (2) The

[50] See [4], pp. 167, 168.

[51] See [36], pp. 148–150.

[52] See [36], p. 150.

preexistent subjective ability. Ability is a kind of potential initiative of the subject, that is, freedom of the will. Marx pointed out that one can he be fully responsible for his actions only when he has the complete freedom to act with his will.[53] (3) Voluntary when present. This kind of voluntary means that there is no external compulsion to one, whose behavior is the result of the subject's choice. The above three conditions can be called responsibility in an independent sense. According to the view of US jurist Hart, responsibility (1) can be role responsibility; (2) is ability responsibility; (3) is responsibility to be blame. In addition, Hart mentioned causal responsibility, which is not covered here. To illustrate the concept of responsibility, Hart creates a fictitious shipwreck[54]: Robinson is the captain of a cruise ship. As a captain, he is responsible to the crew and passengers. But on his last voyage he indulged in excessive drinking every night and was responsible for the ship. It was said that he was mental confusion, but doctors determined that he was sane and held him responsible for his actions. He behaved rather irresponsibly throughout the voyage, as showed by his events of his life. Robinson argued that the shipwreck was caused by an unusual snowstorm. However, in the legal proceedings against him, the court found a direct link between the sinking of the ship and his negligence, holding him criminally responsible for it therefore. The civil action against him was brought in a separate case. In the trial the court held that he was legally responsible for the loss of life and property. Robinson is still alive and morally responsible for the deaths of women and children. Hart said that as can be seen from the above statement, the word responsibility has many meanings, for which he mainly analyzed the following four meanings: (1) Role obligation. The captain is responsible for the safety of the ship, which is from his role or duty (post). Every legal role has a responsibility. In a social organization, the obligation of providing welfare to others or promoting it to realize the goals is always attributed to a certain status or position, namely a certain role. Whenever one occupies a position, it is appropriate to say that he is responsible for the fulfillment of those obligations, or to do what is necessary for the fulfillment of those obligations. This obligation is one's role responsibility that plays a decisive role in determining some criminal and civil liabilities. In administrative legal system, legal responsibility is almost role obligation. (2) Causal responsibility. The fault of the captain caused the shipwreck, or the negligence of the captain caused the wreck, or the fault of the captain has a causal relationship with the wreck, these different statements are related to the causal responsibility. Not only can the actions of a man be the cause of certain effects, but also the movements of nature. The causal responsibility a person can bear is the responsibility caused by his actions (action or nonfeasance). (3) Legally liable. It is often said that when a rule of law requires or inhibits a certain action, the offender should be punished for his or her action, or be forced to compensate the victim under other rules of law. In many cases, he was both punished and forced to pay compensation. In this sense, someone who is legally responsible for something (an action or injury) is that someone who is legally liable or forced to pay for his or her action or injury, i.e., liability equals

[53] See [37], p. 93.

[54] See [15], pp. 1–165.

legally liable. Strictly speaking, however, these two statements mean different. The question that whether someone should be punished by the law because of his behavior, is lies on that whether all the requirements of legal responsibility have been met, in other words, and whether he is legally responsible for his behavior is usually only associated with such a problem, namely, in a series of elements, a certain one (about the spiritual elements people often asked) meets. (4) Capacity responsibility. On many occasions, the statement that someone should be responsible for a certain behavior is an assertion that there was a man who had some normal ability, namely the ability of thinking, understanding and controlling behavior, (legally)—that is, the ability to understanding what law rules require, careful thinking and to make a decision about these requirements, as well as the ability to acted on the decision after his decision. Hart's correct analysis of various meanings of responsibility is helpful for us to fully understand the concept of responsibility. Although the concept of responsibility is ambiguous, obligation is an essential content of responsibility, which can be the basic meaning of responsibility, and other meanings of it are based on obligations. We cannot discuss the responsibility without the content of obligation, as the saying goes that catch fish in a tree—a useless search.

Responsibility is a limitation of freedom mainly because the undertaking of responsibility means the deprivation of certain benefits. To impose certain responsibilities on those who overstep the boundaries of freedom defined by law and violate certain obligations is not only the due result of their actions, but also a certain deterrence effect to them, so that people will not overstep the boundaries of freedom. Since freedom is a right in a certain sense, responsibility and right are also closely related. Just as The British scholar Lamont said that the definition of human includes the concepts of right and responsibility. Right and responsibility are necessarily linked in a sense, for A's right (or responsibility) always implies B's responsibility (or right). But the concept of right features a "logical priority", as we discovered in the theory of value judgment that "the utility of a marginal unit" concept and the concept of "the balance marginal unit" are interrelated and complementary. But in condition that the former can only be regulated according to the latter, it also features a "logical priority". Therefore, although the concepts of right and responsibility are interrelated and complementary, responsibility can only be defined in terms of right. Right is the sphere of freedom which the law defines to a man, within which he may act or restrain himself according to his own conception of good; Liability is a legal requirement, namely, a claim on other individuals or people (who are related to the rights granted to a particular individual by law).[55] Therefore, only from the relationship between right and obligation can we deeply understand the nature of responsibility.

---

[55] See [38], p. 336.

References

1. Compiled and Translated by the Teaching and Research Section of the Section of Foreign Philosophy of the Department of Philosophy of Peking University, *French Philosophy in 18th Century* (Joint Publishing, Beijing, 1963)
2. Z. Li, *Criticism on Critique of Philosophy: A Review of Kant* (People's Publishing House, Beijing, 1979)
3. [Germany] Kant, *Fundamental Principles of the Metaphysic of Morals* (Shanghai People's Publishing House, Shanghai, 1986)
4. [Germany] Hegel, *Elements of the Philosophy of Right* (The Commercial Press, Beijing, 1961)
5. [US] James, *The Principles of Psychology* (The Commercial Press, Beijing, 1963)
6. R. Cao (Chief Editor), *Normal Psychology*, vol. 2 (People's Education Press, Beijing, 1980)
7. D. Li, *Axiology* (Renmin University of China Press, Beijing, 1987)
8. G. Yuan, *Introduction to Axiology* (Beijing Normal University Publishing House, Beijing, 1991)
9. [Czech Republic] V. Brozik, *Value and Valuation* (Knowledge Publishing House, Beijing, 1988)
10. [Soviet Union] A.X. Shishkin et al., *The Principles of Ethics* (Peking University Press, Beijing, 1981)
11. [UK] H. Sidgwick, *Methods of Ethics* (China Social Science Press, Beijing, 1993)
12. [US] Thilly, *Introduction to Ethics* (Renmin University of China Press, Beijing, 1987)
13. [UK] Sidgwick, *Methods of Ethics* (China Social Science Press, Beijing, 1993)
14. [Germany] Paulsen, *A System of Ethics* (China Social Sciences Press, Beijing, 1988)
15. W. Zhang, *Contemporary Western Legal Philosophy* (Jilin University Press, Changchun, 1987)
16. [UK] Locke, *Two Treatises of Government*, The Second Treatise (The Commercial Press, Beijing, 1964)
17. [France] Montesquieu, *The Spirit of the Laws*, vol. 1 (The Commercial Press, Beijing, 1961)
18. [US] G. Sartori, *The Theory of Democracy Revisited* (People's Oriental Publishing & Media, Beijing, 1993)
19. J. Guo, On Marxist ideology of choice. Jianghan Trib. (11) (1987)
20. *Marx/Engels Selected Works*, vol. 4, 2nd edn. (People's Publishing House, Beijing, 1995)
21. L. Hao, *Historical Choice Theory* (Renmin University of China Press, Beijing, 1992)
22. [UK] Moore, *Ethics* (China Renmin University Press, Beijing, 1985)
23. [Ancient Greece] Aristotle, *The Nicomachean Ethics* (China Social Sciences Press, Beijing, 1990)
24. [Japanese] O. Yukiyoshi (Chief Editor), *Introduction of Ethic* (China Social Sciences Press, Beijing, 1990)
25. H. Zhang (Chief Editor), *On Freedom* (Shanghai People's Publishing House, Shanghai, 1990)
26. *Marx/Engels Collected Works*, vol. 1 (People's Publishing House, Beijing, 1965)
27. [Ancient Greece] Aristotle, *The Politics* (The Commercial Press, Beijing, 1965)
28. *Selected Materials on the History of Western Legal Theory* (Peking University Press, Beijing, 1983)
29. [French] Montesquieu, *The Spirit of the Laws*, vol. 2 (The Commercial Press, Beijing, 1961)
30. [French] Montesquieu, *The Spirit of the Laws*, vol. 1 (The Commercial Press, Beijing, 1961)
31. [UK] Mill, *On Liberty* (The Commercial Press, Beijing, 1982)
32. Y. Chen, *Relativity of Rights* (People's Publishing House, Beijing, 1994)
33. [US] Pound, *Social Control Through Law* (The Commercial Press, Beijing, 1984)
34. Z. Bao et al., *On Rights* (Shanghai Sanlian Bookstore, Shanghai, 1993)
35. *Marx/Engels Selected Works*, vol. 2, 2nd edn. (People's Publishing House, Beijing, 1995)
36. [US] Frankena, *Ethics* (Sanlian Bookstore, Beijing, 1987)
37. *Marx/Engels Collected Works*, vol. 21 (People's Publishing House, Beijing, 1965)
38. [UK] Lamont, *Value Judgement* (China Remin University Press, Beijing, 1992)

Chapter 7
Human Nature Foundation of Crime

Through the philosophical investigation on free will, a conclusion is summarized that from the perspective of ontology, the human will is not free; however, from the perspective of axiology, the human will is free. This conclusion is of great significance to the study of crime because crime can also be analyzed from the perspectives of ontology and axiology. The ontology of crime regards crime as a social phenomenon, and it belongs to the research of criminology. The mission of criminology is to reveal the general law of criminal phenomena, especially the causes of committing crimes. Therefore, the study of criminology only exists when it is researched from the perspective of behavioral determinism. The axiology of crime regards crime as an individual behavior, and it is the study of criminal law. The mission of the study of criminal law is to determine whether human behaviors constitute crimes and hence to provide the factual basis for the investigation on criminal responsibilities. Accordingly, the study of criminal law exists only when it is researched through the lens of free will. Ontology and axiology provide analytical frameworks for us to reveal the humanistic foundation of crime, and also serve as a foundation to clarify the arguments between the classical school and the positivist school of criminology.

1 Theory of Crime Ontology

The crime ontology, which exists based on criminal phenomena, reveals the social and individual causes of committing crimes. Therefore, it is an empirical analysis of crime, the core of which is causality analysis. Consequently, crime ontology could only be studied based on behavioral determinism.

X. Chen, *Humanistic Foundation of Criminal Law*,
https://doi.org/10.1007/978-981-19-9764-8_7

1.1 Theoretical Foundation of Crime Ontology

As a social phenomenon, crime has bothered human beings since human beings lived in civilized societies. Since crime existed, explanations of criminal phenomena have emerged. It is these explanations that constitute the sources of thoughts and theoretical resources of criminology.

The explanations of crime in western countries originated from ancient Greek philosophers. Ancient Greek philosophy set out to explore the origin of the world. Primarily, it was interested in nature, so natural philosophy, represented by the Milesian School, was established. Hence, early ancient Greek philosophers did not study crime. Later, philosophy turned to study human beings and society, which featured humanism in nature, represented by Plato, who established Moral philosophy. Starting from Plato, philosophy has explored politics, ethics, and law, and crime became one of its study topics. Plato believed that human nature consisted of "goodness" and "wickedness". If a person's "goodness" could control "wickedness", the person would be praised. Otherwise, the person would be blamed. If a person's "goodness" took the upper hand and was in a dominant position, then justice took place, so there was no need for the law. But if a person indulged malevolence, the brutish nature would become active. At this point, laws were established to prohibit human beings from indulging their lust. People who had unjust acts must be punished once such acts were uncovered, and their evil deeds would be inhibited.[1] Consequently, Plato interpreted crimes from the perspective of human nature who attributed crimes to wickedness rooted in human nature. This theory was profound under the historical conditions at that time. Apart from this, Plato also interpreted crimes from social and economic aspects. He believed that unhealthy education and environment spurred human beings' wickedness to hold preponderance and thus they did bad. In addition, Plato pinpointed that people's greed for money was the cause of many crimes. It was not rare to see that the greed for money caused crimes, and Plato made a preliminary conclusion about this. Following Plato, Aristotle argued that crime stemmed from poverty, sexual desire, and excess. He pointed out that in addition to the major problems such as internal disorder, we should also consider the criminal offenses that happened in ordinary lives. (1) Some crimes originated from the lack of clothes and food. To remedy this, Phaleas came up with the equalization of property, through which everyone could get access to necessities. Hence, thefts stemming from hunger and coldness would be prevented. (2) Clothes and food, nevertheless, were not the sole cause of crime. People, with food to eat and clothes to wear, were bothered by their sexual desires. They relieved some vexation through pleasures, and therefore breached criminal law. (3) Furthermore, people committed crimes not just for getting rid of the vexation arising from their sexual desires. People, who had wealth and fame with sexual desires satisfied, still cherished limitless desires. They pursued endless authority and finally committed crimes due to their unrestrained pleasures.[2] Aristotle ranged the three causes of crime based on the classification of social class, with

[1] See [1], p. 382.

[2] See [2], p. 71.

the poor who were in the lower-class committing crimes due to the lack of clothes and food. The middle-class people had clothes and food, so they committed crimes because of their sexual desires. The wealthy who were in the upper class had enough clothes and food, and their sexual desires were satisfied as well. They committed crimes because of their excesses. Aristotle said with emotion that the greatest crimes in the world were caused by excess, not by lack of necessities.[3] It should be noted that the ancient Greek philosophers are not jurists and they didn't specialize in crime. Therefore, their discussions on crime are superficial. They only summed up some phenomena but with no scientific understanding of crime. However, the discussions of Plato and Aristotle on crime reflect the highest level of people's understanding of crime at that time, so we do not necessarily demand perfection. Additionally, it is praiseworthy that ancient Greek philosophers, setting about from simple philosophical concepts, have connected crime with socio-economic, political, human nature, and other factors, and explored the causes of crime from society and human nature. In the Middle Ages, religious theology prevailed among western countries, so the explanations of crime were attributed to theology. For example, Augustine advocated the original sin. He believed that human beings were born sinful, which was inherited from their ancestors, and he attributed the reasons for committing crimes to the human's evil will. He pointed out that bad will caused bad behaviors but it came from nothing. Only such evil will, which had not been deteriorated by any other will and was bad will per se, could be considered the first bad will.[4] This is an analysis of the causes of crime from the perspective of theology. Aquinas explained the causes of crime from the perspective of human temperament. He said that some young people, who were kind in nature or well-brought-up or were helped by God, volunteered to lead a virtuous life. For such young people, guidance and advice from their fathers were enough. But other young people who were sullen in nature tended to do evil, and could barely be moved by earnest advice. So pressure and threats should be in place to prevent them from doing bad. If these methods were introduced to prevent them from doing evil, the rest of the people in society would enjoy peaceful lives. These young people would be guided by habits and volunteered to do things that they were scared to do in the past and eventually got used to doing good.[5] Up to modern times, crime was explained based on secular explanations. The classical school of criminology, Beccaria in particular, also explored the causes of crime. As the Chinese scholar Xie Yong mentioned, it was not factual nor reasonable to say that the classical school explained the causes of crime based on free will, and thus accused it of hindering the discussion of such causes. This was because first, Beccaria discussed the causes of crime from social, economic, customary, and other aspects. His analysis inherited Aristotle's materialism and his opinions were even not inferior to those of the positivist school in later times. Second, the historical mission of the classical school of criminology was not to explore the causes of crime. Rather, it was to create principles

[3] See [2], p. 71.

[4] See [3], p. 353.

[5] See [4], pp. 115–116.

of criminal penalty that were needed by Europe at that time and to provide a theoretical basis for these principles.[6] It can be said that among theories within the classical school of criminology, the theory of normative criminal law holds predominance, whereas the exploration of the causes of crime was not as theoretically profound as it was supposed to be. The person and school starting to conduct scientific research on crime and separate criminology from criminal law studies to make it an independent subject are Cesare Lombroso and the school of anthropology of crime established by him, and the school of sociology of crime developed later. The positivist school of criminology examines criminal phenomena scientifically and thus starts a new era of criminological research. I believe that the contributions of the positivist school of criminology to criminology are mainly as follows: (1) It is based on behavioral determinism. As discussed earlier, the study of criminology is based on criminal ontology. The study is impossible to go deeper if behavioral determinism is not considered. In terms of the classical school, retributivism represented by Kant and Hegel ends its study in free will and fails to go deeper. Of course, as Kant and Hegel are philosophers, they only have had a light touch on crime. Their fundamental contributions lie in the study of theoretical criminal law. We cannot require them to conduct special research on crime. As for the utilitarianism represented by Beccaria and Bentham, it does discuss the causes of crime and undeniably its discussions on the causes of the crime impress people with behavioral determinism. However, Beccaria and Bentham focus on how to deter people with criminal penalties, so as to achieve utilitarian effects that crimes would be prevented. Hence, their theories focus on criminal law, and free will is the necessary logical presupposition of their theories on criminal law. Restrained by free will, Beccaria and Bentham's explanations of the causes of crime are superficial. They have occasionally mentioned the causes when discussing the problems of criminal law, rather than conducting special criminal research like the positivist school of criminology. The positivist school of criminology denies free will expressly, publicly advocates behavioral determinism and stretches out its theories to explain the causes of crime, from which criminological research becomes an individual system. (2) It is based on empirical methodology. Criminology is an empirical discipline, and only by adopting empirical methods can this research be scientific. The positivist school of criminology introduces the empirical methodology when studying crime. What it focuses on is a variety of crimes that happen in society. It has investigated the causes of crimes and explained them theoretically. Although the explanations may be wrong or even ridiculous, the research method introduced by the positivist school of criminology becomes the theoretical paradigm of criminology. This is why even though Cesare Lombroso's "born criminal" theory is no longer recognized, he still holds a firm position in the history of criminology. The famous Austrian psychologist Sigmund Freud once said that real scientific activities began with the description of phenomena, followed by the grouping and classification of the phenomena to find out their relationships. It was in this way that Freud made psychoanalysis a science. This was Freud's experience. Cesare Lombroso also

[6] See [5], p. 85.

conducted his research on crime by describing the criminal phenomena. He systematically observed and measured the differences in soldiers' physics and noticed that they had the habit of tattooing their skin. Later, he connected this habit with criminals. He also dissected a number of criminals' bodies and found out the statistics of crimes and prisons in Italy. All of these have provided empirical materials and data for the establishment of criminology. On the contrary, the classical school of criminology primarily adopts a metaphysical speculative research method. Metaphysics is needed in the research of crime but empirical analysis is more important. Accordingly, the metaphysical speculative research method has hindered the criminal research of the classical school of criminology to a certain extent. (3) It is based on criminal phenomena, especially criminals. The classical school of criminology fundamentally studies the crimes defined in criminal law. A crime of such type is a legally abstract concept and based on criminal acts. Hence, as a social phenomenon, crime fails to be truly studied by the classical school of criminology. By contrast, the positivist school of criminology studies crime as a social phenomenon rather than a legal one. It particularly focuses on the people who commit crimes. Therefore, the transformation of theoretical perspectives from criminal acts to criminals has been completed. The first criminological work of Cesare Lombroso is named *Criminal Man*. It is not a coincidence but the result of the criminological research. To sum up, I believe that before the positivist school of criminology, people have already paid attention and tried their best to explain crimes in a reasonable manner, especially the classical school of criminology whose explanations have reached the new historical height. However, it was the contributions of the positivist school of criminology that enabled criminology to become an independent discipline. The main contribution of the positivist school is its insistence on using behavioral determinism to study crime. Of course, the introduction of empirical methodology and the transformation of the theoretical perspectives are also of great significance.

It has been over two centuries since the positivist school of criminology was established, and the study of criminology has made great progress. Among the study of criminology, there are a number of schools, opinions, works and researchers. Criminological study shows prosperity. Nonetheless, the study of criminology is still far from what society has required it to be. The Chinese study of criminology, in particular, was tightly restrained by politics, so it started late and low. Overall, much improvement should be made regarding the research level. I believe that a key problem here is to establish the study of criminology on the basis of scientific theories. Then what is the theoretical basis for the criminological study? To answer it, we should regard crime as a social phenomenon, which involves the definition of the system, object, and method of the study.

1.1.1 Criminological Systematology

Originating from the Latin word "Criminic", criminology refers to the study of crime, which was firstly proposed by the French anthropologist Paul Topinard in 1879, and the term criminology was firstly used by the Italian criminologist Raffaele Garofalo, who published a book on the study of crime in 1885, the title of which was *Criminology*. Since the emergence of criminology, there have been diverse understandings of it. The first one is narrow criminology, which studies crimes and criminals as a whole and explore the causes and laws of crimes. There are two sub-divisions within it: criminal biology and criminal sociology. The second one is general criminology, which not only studies the causes and laws of crime but also pursue appropriate solutions to preventing crime. That is to say, general criminology includes the theory of the causes of crime and that of the solutions. Criminology in China refers to general criminology, whose recognized definition is that under the guidance of Marxism, it reveals the laws and characteristics of the occurrence and development of crime in the primary stage of socialism in the country, explores the causes and conditions of crime, and studies the scientific measures and ways to prevent, reduce and even eliminate crime.[7] Hence, the prevailing criminological system in China includes the theory of the criminal phenomenon, the theory of causation of crime, and the theory of crime prevention. The issue involved is whether crime prevention should be included in the system, namely whether criminology should be classified into general criminology and narrow criminology. It is usually considered that the countries with the civil law system adopt narrow criminology, while those with the common law system adopt general criminology. The Japanese professor Nishimura said that the so-called criminology in the US and British legal academia primarily studied the cause of crime. Apart from this, the solutions to dealing with criminals and other issues are included as well. Therefore, criminal law and criminal policy are integrated. It is completely different from the German school, which distinguishes *Kriminologie* from *Kriminalpolitik* strictly.[8] Criminology has the same meaning as *Kriminoligie*, while *Kriminalpolitik* refers to criminal policy. Next, let us take a look at the use of these concepts in different countries.

In France, criminologists are used to studying criminology and penology as a whole and naming them collectively. French scholars believe that criminology is to study the causes and any other issues of crime and criminals specifically. However, penology is designed to study the composition and operation of penalties, different prison systems, new property penalties, penalties to deprive one's rights, and other types of reeducation measures. Even though criminology and penology study different things, they share close relationships. On the one hand, criminology serves penology because the efficacy of penalties depends largely on how the organizations and personnel which carry out criminal penalties understand the composition and causes of crime as well as criminals. Also, it depends on the achievements of criminological research. On the other hand, penology helps achieve the research objectives of criminology because the research achievements of criminology will be reflected as anti-crime measures through legal procedures, the most important of which are criminal penalties. In France, the concept of criminal policy is adopted as well. For instance, French Professor Christine Lazerges, a well-known criminal

---

[7] See [6], p. 4.

[8] See [7], pp. 5–6.

policy scientist, believes that from the perspective of epistemology, a criminal policy is a comprehensive analysis of criminal phenomena, and an interpretation of the measures to fight against criminal phenomena and illegal acts. It is also a social and legal strategy that aims to crack down on and prevent crimes based on theories.[9] Therefore, criminology and penology are two parallel empirical sciences in France, in order to distinguish them from the study of criminal law that serves as a normative science, while criminal policy is a science of decision-making. Even though the research objects of the three disciplines are overlapping, they are independent basically.

In Germany, Schneider believes that the object and mission of criminology are to analyze the processes of criminalization and decriminalization. Criminal acts are recognized through the processes of social criminalization and decriminalization, and what belongs to this process includes the criminal legislation in a narrow sense, as well as the social reality basis, and the actual social effects of criminal legislation. Schneider points out that as a criminal science, criminology (ontology) has close relationships with criminal law (deontology). Criminology is an empirical humanitarian and social science (Jean Pinatel, 1971) and the mission of the science of criminal law is to systemically develop and interpret the norms of criminal law within their intrinsic connections (Hans Göppinger, 1980). It distinguishes the boundaries among the norms of criminal law and attributes the cases in real life to the norms of criminal law. Then it interprets and applies these norms, and pays attention to observing the principles of a country ruled by law when interpreting criminal law. Because criminal law is a guarantee to criminals in a way that criminals will only be punished for an act, and before committing crimes, they have been threatened to be punished by criminal law (*Great Charter of Criminals*). If subjective thoughts prevailed in criminal law, then criminology pursued the analysis that were as free as possible from the influence of values and scientific objectivity (Gunter Kaiser, 1980).[10] Schneider clarified criminology as ontology and distinguished it from the science of criminal law which served as deontology. Accordingly, the research object of criminology was limited to the interpretation of criminal phenomena, excluding criminal policy, and not to mention crime prevention. Again, the German criminologist Kaiser argued that the concept of criminology referred to the facts that were observed and subjectively verified within a certain scope. Criminology was an empirical science. The term "empirical" was a research method, the foundation of which was observations rather than arguments or evaluations. In criminology, nevertheless, evaluations and explanations were included as well. However, the solid foundation of criminology was the result of facts and observations. Any assumption or theory should be verified by them. Therefore, the empirical method forced researchers to focus more on facts instead of evaluations. Furthermore, even though facts contradicted one's expectations and views, one should be subject to facts first.[11]

---

[9] See [8], pp. 13, 15.

[10] See [9], p. 99.

[11] See [10], pp. 16, 19.

In US, criminology is divided into general criminology and narrow criminology. General criminology posits that criminology is a science that studies criminal phenomena and the social responses to them. However, narrow criminology only studies the causes of crime. General criminology includes crime prevention. Crime prevention is divided into conventional prevention and unconventional prevention. Conventional prevention refers to such functional judicial activities as investigation, trial, and correction engaged in by judicial departments including the police, courts, and correctional institutions within their respective competencies. Unconventional prevention refers to the crime prevention activities excluding the functional judicial activities performed by the above-mentioned functional agencies. Generally speaking, more attention is paid to conventional prevention than unconventional one in US.[12] In fact, works of criminology in US are mainly about conventional prevention, as seen in *Criminology* (Qunzhong Publishing House, 1988) by the US criminologists D. Stanley Eitzen and Doug A. Timmer, in which special chapters of the criminal justice system include police service, criminal court, criminal punishment, and prison. The US criminologists Harold J. Vetter and Wright Jack Jr.'s book *Introduction to Criminology* (Knowledge Publishing House, 1992) includes special chapters about the implementation of the law, criminal trials, and criminal offenders, as well as the conventional prevention of crime.

In Japan, the British term criminology is translated into the "science of crime", while the German term "Kriminalpolil" is translated into "criminal policy", and the French term "Sciences pnaies" is rendered into "criminalistics". However, Japanese scholars tend to use the three terms in a mixed way. Criminology (criminalistics and criminal policy) fundamentally studies crimes, criminals, and penalties, overlapping and interactive with criminal law, and is thus included in the study of criminal law in Japanese academia.[13] Therefore, criminology in Japan includes criminal policy. For instance, the book titled *Criminology* (Qunzhong Publishing House, the 1989 edition) by Koichi Kikuta, a Japanese criminologist, contains two chapters that discuss criminal policies, including criminal justice policies and situations of criminals.

In the Soviet Union, criminology studies criminal phenomena and causes, features of criminals, and measures to prevent criminal phenomena. Crime prevention, nevertheless, is a system that accommodates all national and social measures to eliminate the causes and conditions of crime or to reduce (limit) the effects of causes and conditions, and to ensure that crime will be reduced and eliminated in the future.[14] Crime prevention in Soviet Union's criminology mainly refers to social prevention, equivalent to the comprehensive governance in China. It can be seen that although British and US scholars study crime prevention in criminology, they primarily refer to conventional, functional, and judicial prevention, whereas the

[12] See [11], p. 6.

[13] See [12], p. 140.

[14] See [13], p. 130.

Soviet Union researchers refer to social prevention, which does not involve judicial prevention. This is a huge difference, the reason for which lies in the difference in the understanding of the concepts of social system and crime.

Obviously, the system of criminology in China was introduced from the Soviet Union, so it is a general concept that includes the theory of criminal phenomena, the causes of crime, and crime prevention. Then, does criminology integrate crime prevention and social prevention in particular? My answer is negative. The reasons are as follows: (1) Criminology is crime ontology, which should first study criminal phenomena. If crime prevention is integrated into the criminological system, it will exceed the boundary of crime ontology, while the integration of the response to crime will broaden the scope of the concept of criminology. (2) Crime prevention, especially social prevention, is an activity that merely utilizes the principles of criminology. Crime prevention is not a theory but an application of the theory. Thus, criminology will lack its scientific and theoretical characteristics if the application of a theory and the theory itself are confused. It is undeniable that Liszt has said that "the best criminal policy is the best social policy". However, social policy is not criminal policy. If all social policies are accepted by the criminological system, criminology will lose its professionalism and become a hodgepodge. (3) Undoubtedly, the concept of crime prevention is correct, but prevention can only reduce the occurrence of crime rather than eliminate it. The advocates of crime prevention tend to eliminate crimes as the goal of prevention, which is certainly unrealistic. As for this, I will also discuss it in the following parts. As a consequence, I claim that criminology should only study the causes of crime.

1.1.2 Object Theory of Criminology

When the scientific foundation of the criminological theory is established, another issue is the research object, which is closely related to the criminological system. As its name indicates, crime is the research object of criminology. This presupposition per se is not wrong, but it is nearly a paraphrase, thus failing to reveal the substance of the research object of criminology. Therefore, it is necessary to further define the concept of crime. Two issues are involved concerning this: (1) There is a distinction between legal and non-legal concepts of crime. The non-legal concept is referred to as the sociological concept of crime. The concept of crime studied by criminology is not limited to legal concepts but originated exactly from the deviation of legal and non-legal concepts. Regarding this, Raffaele Garofalo, a distinguished Italian criminologist, one of the founders of criminology and a representative of the positivist school of criminology, posits seriously in his book titled *Criminology* that criminology must give up the definition of crime by criminal law because the crimes described in criminal law are solely behaviors that are prohibited by the law; however, this definition does not reveal the nature of the crime. As a result, the crime prescribed by the criminal law is formal. Garofalo believes that criminology should study substantial crime, so he proposes the concept of "natural crime". "Natural" means non-formal. It is a social being that is independent of the environment of a certain period and that needs urgently to be separated from the specific concept of lawmakers. "Natural crime" refers to the acts that are regarded as crimes and will be punished by all civilized societies.[15] The concept of "natural crime" raised by Garofalo may not be scientific, but this ingenious concept was raised with profound intention. It is because he noticed the different research objects between criminology and criminal law that he has made great theoretical contributions to the establishment of criminology. The classical school makes little contributions to criminology mainly because it discusses the crimes within the concept of the crime defined by criminal law, thus lacking a distinctive theoretical perspective. However, the positivist school tends to deviate excessively from criminal law by integrating all mental diseases into the scope of crimes. This may be an hyperreaction. This idea is undesirable because we should correctly understand the relationship between the legal and non-legal concepts of crime. In response, the German criminologist Schneider said that "social deviance" that was located at the frontier and interior of the legislation of criminal law was of significance. Social deviance, which changes over time and space, and depends on the social tolerance ability, plays an important role in society to some degree since it promotes social unity (such as the comparison role). This is a behavior that is considered a breach of behavioral norms by the majority of people in society, and that arises and disappears during societal processes. Deviant behaviors per se have no properties. They depend primarily on informal social reactions and the repercussions of these reactions. The social definition of socially deviant behaviors is a social supervision method. Criminology has special interests in the interaction between criminal behaviors and deviant behaviors. Through criminalization (legislation of criminal law), criminal behaviors arise from socially deviant behaviors. Meanwhile, criminal behaviors may be downgraded to deviant behaviors by the action of lawmakers (decriminalization). Criminal behaviors arise and disappear through individual criminalization and decriminalization.[16] It is of great significance that Schneider defines the concept of crime from the dynamic relationship between criminalization and decriminalization. In this sense, I agree with the Chinese scholar Xie Yong's following arguments that criminology should adopt the definition of the crime prescribed in criminal law. But a realistic, flexible attitude should be taken when this definition is applied, to avoid the rigidity of the concept of crime. There are two specific solutions. First, between objective detriments and formal illegality, the two established legal standards for crime, choosing the former as the primary, absolute standard so that legal, moral, religious, cultural, or political crime standards have a common standard to refer to. Second, based on the above-mentioned comparisons, criminology should make a historical and specific analysis of the relationships between the definition of the crime prescribed by criminal law and other types of definitions, to reveal the condition that enables them to unify or to explain the reason that causes the split of the unity. In this way, the dynamic

[15] See [5], pp. 29–30.

[16] See [9], p. 95.

process of the connection and communication between the two will be displayed.[17] (2) There is a distinction between abstract and concrete crimes. Crime in the abstract sense refers to holistic crime, while that in the concrete sense refers to individual crime. The holism analysis and individualism analysis of the crime are involved. The analysis by the classical school is not limited to the concept of criminal law but a holistic approach. Thus, crime is always an abstract concept stipulated by law as a whole. Within the positivist school, the anthropological school of crime adopts the individualism approach and has transformed its perspective from criminal behaviors to criminals. Although the sociological school of crime adopts the holism approach, it also has transformed its perspective from legal analysis to social analysis. It is the two perspective transformations that mark the launching of criminological research. Since then, both holism and individualism theories have proved their merits, with holism theory focusing on sociological research and individualism theory on the biological and psychological research of crime. The Chinese scholar Xie Yong said that the contradiction between holism and individualism marked one of the deepest disagreements among modern criminological theories. First of all, they touch upon the definition of the object of criminology. Criminology studies criminal phenomena, or crimes or individual criminal behaviors. According to the different answers, criminological theories lay particular stress on the level of interpretation. According to Xie Yong, criminology should pay attention to the causes of crime at the macro level. Therefore, he concludes that criminology is a sub-division of sociology.[18] However, I disagree with him on this point. I believe that crime is an integration of abstractness and concreteness, holism and individualism, and society and individuals. Based on this, the causes of crime are divided into social and individual reasons, and a basic clue to analyze the causes of crime is formed.

1.1.3 Methodology of Criminology

The last issue involving the scientific foundation of criminological theory is the methodology, which is mainly related to the standpoints of researchers. It is the "value-free" problem. Pi Yijun, a Chinese scholar, mentioned that it was quite common that the subject of criminological study relied heavily on "emotional logic" and "value involvement". The inappropriateness of this method has become the crux of the problem of the stagnation of criminological study in China. The so-called "emotional logic" means that researchers have been conducting their studies with their indignation against criminal phenomena, and brought their emotions to the process of thinking logic and judgment. As the research object is overflown with emotions, the rational and scientific components are weakened, and the true nature of the object is covered up. The so-called "value involvement" means that researchers directly injected their values and moral tendencies throughout the study, in a way that

[17] See [5], pp. 61–62.

[18] See [5], pp. 18, 110.

observers understand and study the object with bias. Before the object is fully understood, it has been assumed subjectively. The value involvement hinders the incisive observation of the research object and obstructs the objectivity of the research to a large extent. Based on the deep analysis of value involvement, Pi Yijun proposes that the principle of value-free should be adhered to in criminological research. The "value-free" refers to that the attitudes of the observation subjects are excluded when subjects collect and analyze materials and observe the characteristics of the object.[19] I completely agree with this opinion. Value-free is determined by the positivism of criminology. Value-free originated from Max Weber, who proposed a methodological principle, namely "value neutrality". Weber believed that value judgment arose entirely from individual emotions. Values were only related to individual freedom, decisions, and choices. They had no logical or ontological relationships with facts, so values were not the research object of empirical science. Empirical science aims to study the phenomena of "is", so metaphysics should be discarded to retain the "value neutrality" of sociology.[20] It is obvious to see that criminology is an empirical study that studies the social existence of criminal phenomena. As a result, it should adopt the "value-free" methodology, and the descriptive rather than evaluative theoretical expression. The classical school of criminology values evaluation, mainly legal evaluation, and classifies the crime as evil, so it fails to separate criminology from criminal law. The positivist school abandons the evaluation opinions in the criminal study. It does not treat crime as evil but as a social disease and observes and analyzes it in an objective manner, thus establishing criminology. Accordingly, value-free is a fundamental methodological principle for criminological study, which should be fully affirmed.

1.2 Social Interpretation of Criminal Existence

To begin with, criminal existence is a social existence, the social interpretation of which aims to discuss the social reasons for crime. The social interpretation of crime dates to the sociological school of crime, and Franz von Liszt is one of the founders of the social interpretation of the causes of crime. The later social interpretation falls into two situations, namely the interpretation by criminologists and the interpretation by sociologists. In this section, I take the social analytical framework established by sociologists as the foundation to interpret the criminal existence from a social perspective.

The social interpretation of criminal existence sets out from society. Sociology is different from biology or psychology which sets out to study individuals. Oppositely, it bases on how individuals are impacted, restricted, adjusted, bound or determined by their social relationships with others and social organizations. According to the opinions of sociology, individual behaviors can be interpreted most reasonably based

[19] See [14].

[20] See [15], pp. 267–268.

on the social environments and conditions.[21] Since the interpretation of sociology is based on the social explanations towards criminal existence, different opinions on social nature lead to different interpretations of crime. In sociology, the interpretation of crime by the social structure theory stands out most and has been accepted by many criminologists. The structure theory posits that society is an organic entirety composed of diverse components. In this entirety, a change of any component has a significant influence on the others. A complete and unified society is stable, whose members have a common understanding of social norms, objectives, principles, and values because they have common interests. The structure theory emphasizes the comparative analysis of behaviors, so it is also called structural functionalism. One basic concept of the structural theory is the social structure, but sociologists have diverse understandings of social structure. As the US sociologist Jonathan H. Turner says, sociologists frequently use the concept of social structure, but the concept is still ambiguous. In my opinion, many structure-related concepts are metaphors to describe social interaction and relationship in the long term; however, apart from this, there is no accurate conclusion about structure. We have encountered concepts similar to structure-related ones, such as "social system", "coercive cooperative group", "system", "integration tendency", and "network", among others. These concepts as well as others stress that human social relationships have been shaped into a pattern and remain stable for a long time. Most theories in sociology merely try to figure out how and why this phenomenon arises.[22] Among sociologists who advocate structure theory, the well-known one is the French sociologist Émile Dürkheim. Dürkheim argues that the individual phenomenon is different from the social phenomenon, so individual consciousness cannot explain social phenomena, the explanation of which is based on the nature of society. Social phenomena exceed far beyond individual phenomena in both time and space. It has the authority to force the ways individuals behave and think, and enables individuals to feel its pressure. It influences each individual by the holistic role of society, and this is the special mark of social phenomena.[23] Based on the social structure theory, Dürkheim established the anomie theory to explain crimes. Anomie (also translated into normlessness) is a social condition in which social norms lack, mix or vary so that it fails to provide guidance for social members to follow.[24] Dürkheim explains the criminal phenomena from the social structure theory and anomie theory, from which he concludes that crime is a normal phenomenon that exists inevitably in any society. He does not agree with the idea that treating crime is a pathological phenomenon. He said, "People regarded crime as a pathological phenomenon, and this seemed to be uncontroversial. Previous criminologists accepted this although they explained it in different ways. However, they unanimously regarded crime as a pathological phenomenon. However, I think crime should be analyzed carefully." Dürkheim concludes from his analysis that crime not only exists in certain societies but all societies. A society

---

[21] See [16], p. 3.

[22] See [17], p. 497.

[23] See [18], p. 81.

[24] See [19], p. 53.

exempt from crime is utterly impossible. The forms and behaviors of crimes are displayed differently in diverse societies as well as within the same society. It can be said, however, that in any society and at any time, there are some people whose acts should be punished. If through the evolution from a more primitive society to a civilized society, the annual crime rate, namely the ratio of the criminals to the population, reduces gradually, then though a normal phenomenon as a crime is, it is losing this characteristic. Nonetheless, no evidence shows that crimes reduce gradually during the evolution from a more primitive society to a civilized society. On the contrary, during this process, crimes showed a tendency to increase. The reason why crime is regarded as a normal phenomenon lies in the following points: (1) Crime exists in every society. Dürkheim mentions that there cannot be a society in which the individuals do not differ more or less from the collective type. Therefore, behaviors of criminal nature inevitably appear among a number of individuals. The criminal nature is not the nature of an individual but the one defined by public awareness. As a result, crime is a phenomenon that cannot be eliminated in society. (2) Crime is necessary for society. Dürkheim believes that crime is normal and even has a positive role in society in terms of the occurrence of behaviors. The crime is normal, meaning that society can not compel all its members to object to social orders; otherwise, individual contributions to society will be inhibited. Society should be flexible and adapt to new reforms, which inevitably give birth to phenomena that are against social norms. Where there are criminal behaviors, they tend to influence the collective awareness to flexibly choose new forms of social governance. Indeed, crime merely indicates an expectation of future ethics and it is a step towards the future. (3) Crime directly helps the evolution of society. Dürkheim has a saying that "reforms and crimes are two terms of an inseparable pair. One is as indispensable as the other." This is because, in order that the originality of progressive thinkers whose thoughts transcend their country may find expression, it is necessary that the originality of crime, which is below the level of their time, shall be possible. According to Dürkheim, crime triggers the need for society to reform and directly make preparations for reforms under certain circumstances. Crime enables old-fashioned collective awareness and methods to be changed into new ones and guides some old-fashioned ways of thinking to evolve into new ones. Some criminal behaviors seem to breach the morals of that time. In fact, they have predicted what morals will be in the future. In *The Division of Labor in Society*, Dürkheim mentions that crime evokes and attracts justice consciousness.[25] Because criminal behaviors can evoke the public emotions to object to the violations of social norms, from which social bans are introduced. Therefore, criminal behaviors have unexpected effects which lead to and strengthen the common normative consciences to protect public welfare. It can be said that Dürkheim's functional analysis of crime is unique, and his conclusions are purely objective judgments. He relates crime with social structure and views crime as an inevitable product of social structure. Also, the form of crime changes with the vicissitudes of social structure. Dürkheim's theory is inherited and developed by the US sociologist Robert King Merton. Merton believes that social structure comprises

---

[25] See [20], p. 160.

many parts, of which the most important two aspects are: first, culturally defined goals. All people in society strive to achieve culturally recognized goals. Second, formulating the standard for regulations as acceptable modes of achieving these goals. He presupposes that deviant behaviors are perceived by sociology as a manifestation of the deviance between the aspirations stipulated by culture and methods provided by society to achieve these aspirations.[26] Accordingly, Merton's theory has two basic concepts and one logical judgment. The two basic concepts are cultural structure and social structure. One logical judgment is that crime is the product of the inconsistency between cultural and social structures. The cultural structure proposed by Merton refers to the normative value objectives prevailing in society, which define the normative purpose of life for various social groups and classes of social members. Social structure refers to the social relations comprised of people of different roles, identities, and statuses. Merton reckons that social members achieve their life objectives stipulated by cultural structure through a certain social structure, that is to say, the social structure is a method to achieve value objectives. Since society has stipulated value objectives for its members, and provided methods to achieve these objectives, the objective and method should be consistent and harmonious. Only in this way can all social members achieve their value objectives through lawful methods. However, if a society's cultural structure contradicts its social structure, then although cultural structure stipulates clear value objectives for people, social structure fails to provide lawful methods to achieve the objective, or, people feel that though there are laws to seek, they still have no idea what the value objective they pursue will be. Thus, Merton summarizes that the contradiction between the objective and method, and the discrepancy between cultural and social structures is the social cause of crime. The structure theory provides us with a new sociological perspective to analyze the causes of crime, which is convincing. The social structure theory helps to explain the overall crime existence in China scientifically. The following issues should be considered when the current crime existence in China is interpreted from a social perspective.

1.2.1 Issues on the Anomie Effect

China is experiencing the transformation from a planned economy to a market-oriented economy. During this change, the existence of both new and old laws causes the conflict of law contents, and the time gap due to the disconnection of new and old laws leads to a number of anomic behaviors. In the economic sector, due to the conflicts and clashes between the planned economy system and the market-oriented economic system, as well as the contradictions and conflicts of the economic operation plans compatible with both economic systems, anomic behaviors surge. Anomic behaviors refer to behaviors without norms or hard to regulate due to the anomic status. Norm and anomie are a pair of contradictions. Norms determine

[26] See [21], p. 79.

which behaviors are recognized, appropriate, desirable, and elegant, which may be an important legal right. Norms refer to those behaviors that are perceived as normal in a general sense, namely the behaviors and responses that can be expected and approved by people. Norms play a role in a way that social group members can eliminate estrangement and keep normal relationships.[27] Norms are divided into social norms and legal norms, and legal norms are also a kind of social norm. In other words, legal norms are social norms that are elevated to law and enforced by coercive force, and criminal law is the sternest sanction among legal norms. The violation of the norm is anomie, the antonym of the norm. According to sociology, anomie is also referred to as deviance. Deviance describes any thoughts, feelings, or actions that are judged by the members of a social group as violating social norms or values. It should be said that deviance is a broad concept. The US sociologist Douglas has listed ten deviant behaviors as follows: (1) the feeling that something is not right, strange, and peculiar; (2) the feeling of disgust and revulsion; (3) the feeling of something violating norms or values; (4) the feeling of something violating moral norms and values; (5) the feeling of something violating norms or moral values; (6) the judgment of something violating moral norms or values; (7) the judgment of something violating orthodox moral misdemeanor laws; (8) the feeling of something violating orthodox moral felony laws; (9) the judgment of something violating human nature; and (10) the judgment of something that is absolute evil. Douglas says that criminologists have applied the seventh and eighth levels of definition when they study deviant behaviors. Nevertheless, criminologists limit themselves to legal problems and rarely discuss the forms of deviance that are not mentioned formally in the law.[28] Therefore, the concept of deviance is broader than that of anomie. Anomie is better applied for the study of criminology. Normal behaviors are not crimes, but severe anomic behaviors are. The interaction between normalization and denormalization is the realistic status of a nation's legal existence. Because as long as there are norms, anomic behaviors that violate norms exist definitely. In this sense, as Dürkheim says, anomic behaviors are normal phenomena. In China, however, especially in the economic sector, anomic phenomena are excessive, due to the transformation of the Chinese economic system.

The anomic behaviors in China are classified into the following three categories: (1) behaviors lacking norms. This type of anomic behavior refers to the behavior that is not provided for by existing laws and, therefore, has no law to abide by. As the market-oriented economy has been established, all value standards for and legal principles of the planned economy model lose their merits. Under this circumstance, the legal blind spots that appear due to the lagging legislation are expanding quickly. A lot of economic behaviors in the market-oriented economy are not bound by old laws, nor are they regulated by new ones, so they are in the legal void. Their legal nature is hard to define, and thus uncontrolled. (2) behaviors conflicting norms. This type of anomic behavior refers to those that are difficult to choose legal basis due to the existence of both new and old laws whose contents are conflicting. China's reform of its economic system is a transformation from the old system to the new one.

---

27 See [21], p. 5.

28 See [22], pp. 12, 13.

In other words, it is a revolution from one economic pattern to another. However, the transformation cannot be completed overnight. It needs quite a long time. Although the old system has drawbacks, it has been there for decades and cannot be eliminated immediately due to its huge historical inertia. Meanwhile, the new system has great power, but it must be established with all subjective and objective conditions in place. It is impossible to be in place immediately. In this way, when the economic system reform develops to a certain degree, a period is inevitable to exist when a dual system co-exists. A dual system is not the ultimate goal of economic system reform but a necessary stage during the transformation of the new and old systems. Therefore, the dual system per se causes severe results in a way that the co-existence of the dual system leads to the dualization of the decision-making behaviors in the micro sense and the control behaviors in the macro sense, bringing about conflicts in the economic life. When it comes to the law, first is reflected as the conflicts between new laws and old ones. This is a temporal conflict of the law. Certain economic behavior is prohibited by the old law but advocated by the new law and vice versa. Since the old law has not been abolished and the new law has been published, the two contradictory laws have legal effects concurrently, leading to the opposite determinations of the legal nature of the same economic behavior. Objectively, it causes some economic behaviors to be free from the regulation of laws. The second is reflected in the legal conflicts among different functional authorities. This is a spatial conflict of the law. As each department and jurisdiction establishes its own law, people are at a loss when confronted with a number of laws. (3) behaviors that are hard to regulate. This type of anomic behavior refers to those that violate the existing laws and regulations but since some provisions of the existing law are outdated, they are inappropriate to apply, and the new law has not yet been introduced, so legal norms are difficult to regulate these anomic behaviors. On the surface, anomic behaviors are caused by the untimely enactment and denormalization of laws. That is to say, the lack of norms and the difficulty of their application is caused by lagging legislation. Factually, this is a cultural phenomenon arising from the change of social structure.

After deep investigations of the anomic behaviors in China's current economic sector, a conclusion is summarized that the occurrence and increase of anomic behaviors are inevitable legal and cultural phenomena resulting from the transformation of China's economic system. According to Merton's analytical paradigm, the breakage between the cultural structure and social structure is inevitable during the specific period of economic transformation in China. After the economic system reform, the specific interests of various economic bodies are fully affirmed, and the pursuit of interests has increasingly become the value objective that is recognized by the mainstream ideology. However, social norms lag severely. They fail to provide effective ways for people to achieve their interest objectives, which triggers the comprehensive anomic effect. As a result, there are mainly three causes for anomie as follows: (1) the increase in material temptation. It is human nature to pursue material interests. The planned economy system has stifled individual interests and regarded the pursuit of material interests as heinous. Thus, human materialistic desires have been severely suppressed and human nature has been distorted. But after the reform of the economic system, the planned economy system that suppresses human nature has been demolished, and suddenly human materialistic desires explodes like a volcanic eruption. The commodity economy, in particular, stimulates and brings about human selfishness. Because the special economic interests of producers are the origin and destination of the commodity economy movement. In a commodity economy, the law of value and market mechanism force every producer to exchange their products motivated by the achievement of self-interests. When the commodities are exchanged, there is an objective interconnection between the subjects; however, no one cares about it at all. In other words, the subjects are not motivated by the interconnection or common interest. Their behavior motivations are merely their own interests. Consequently, the commodity economy generates human's strong selfish motivations. Selfish motivation promotes social and historical progress to an extent, but the excessive expansion of it inevitably brings about negative results and anomic behaviors. As Dürkheim says, "The intense changes in social life spurs desires naturally. The more prosperous a society is, the stronger desires people have. As traditional constraints lose their authority, there are greater expected rewards and stronger stimulation. Desires reduce though. Unconstrained passions intensify this unruled, chaotic state."[29] Anomic behaviors are necessarily the products of this chaotic state. (2) the weakening of social integration. Society is the product of a balance of various political, economic, cultural, and other social factors. Under normal circumstances, social dispersal exists but social integration holds the dominant position overall. Therefore, society is in a stable, balanced state. Nonetheless, social balance is not eternal because the imbalance in the development of social factors disrupts the old balance to achieve the new one. During this transformation, society experiences a temporary unbalanced period, when social integration is greatly weakened. As Dürkheim has said, "As long as the uncontrolled social motivation does not achieve a new balance, all values of this period are unstable, and there are no rules or standards. The boundary between possibility and impossibility is blurry, so it is difficult for people to distinguish between justice and injustice, and between reasonable demands and inordinate ambitions. People's desires thus lose constraints."[30] China's economic system reform has broken the planned economic system, whereas the market-oriented economic system fails to be established immediately. Thus, there are some gaps in people's economic lives. It is fundamentally represented as the lack of economic orders. In this case, economic activities are not regulated and people from all walks of life lose their confidence in the future of economic activities. People feel they are conducting economic activities in an environment of great uncertainty, and there is no guarantee for their expected interests and even properties. Therefore, there are bound to be short-term behaviors. This not only illustrates the short-term behaviors of enterprise, but also those of individuals, governments, and society. When social orders lack, economic chaos and even social upheavals are inevitable.[31] Therefore, reforms will certainly bring about social unrest. As conflicting interests, ideas, and psychological imbalance abate the social control power, a great number of anomic behaviors appear. (3) the blockage

---

[29] See [23], p. 212.

[30] See [23], p. 212.

[31] See [24], p. 186.

of norms from being internalized. In every society, there are social norms, including laws, customs, morals, religions, and disciplines. They are the rules to regulate and guide behaviors and constitute the normative system of a society. But social norms play a role not relying on external coercion but the internalization of norms so that social norms are transformed from external social control to the internal control of the social members. The premise of the internalization of norms is that the norms should reflect the common interests of the social members. Based on Dürkheim, "Only when people regard a norm as just and volunteer to be bound by it does the norm come into effect. If it is maintained only by habitual power and suppression, then peace and harmony are just an illusion, and disorder and discontent grow secretly. Desires that seemingly have been controlled will erupt at any time."[32] Currently, China's economic system reform deepens and promotes the alternation of the old laws by new laws. This is not an individual phenomenon as it involves the whole legal system. There are even situations where the law needs to be transplanted on a large scale, so the clash between the new and old laws becomes more intense. In this case, it is inevitable that the internalization of norms is blocked and triggers legal absence. Legal absence falls into three situations: first, outdated laws fail to be replaced by new laws in time, and this leads to the absence. Second, the application conditions of certain laws are not in place due to the over-advanced legislation, and this leads to the absence. Third, after laws are transplanted, they do not suit the local conditions and fail to be localized, and this leads to the absence. Under the above-mentioned circumstances, though complete norms exist, they cannot be internalized into the behavioral patterns of social members, thus they exist in name only. More severely, it is better to have no law to follow rather than have the law but no one follows. The is because not investigating violations of law erodes the authority of the law and disseminates the law-absent thought. As a result, the blockage of legal norms from being internalized leads to the surge of anomic behaviors.

1.2.2 Issues on Transformation Effects

China is experiencing a period of social transformation. Therefore, the social explanation of crime cannot isolate the specific historical environment of social transformation. Theoretically, transformation refers to the transitional process from one movement pattern to another. It includes the transformation of the structure and also that of the movement mechanism. Social transformation refers to the conversion process of social structure and social operation mechanism from one pattern to another.[33] The core of social transformation is the change from traditional society to modern society. As a consequence, the concept of social transformation includes the following three-level stipulations: (1) Social transformation refers to that "the Chinese society changes and develops from a traditional society to a modern society,

[32] See [23], p. 210.

[33] See [25], p. 306.

from an agricultural society to an industrialized society, and from a closed society to an open society", and this is the factual stipulation. (2) Social transformation refers to "the social change and development under the tension between tradition and modernity", and this is the substantive stipulation. (3) Social transformation is "the conversion from China's 'traditional social structure' to the 'modern social structure'", and "the change of the specific structural and developmental forms of social life" at the level of social formation. This is the structural hierarchy regulation.[34] Social transformation brings about the transformation effect, which refers to a special effect on the transformed society due to the asynchrony of social structural changes and the latecomer effect. The special effect of social transformation is expressed as the structural deficiency of society. Social transformation, first, is the change of social structure. Social structure is a stable structure, which refers to a balanced, stable state of all components because of the interaction between all components of a system. However, the system deviates from this state due to the disturbance of the outside environment, while the interaction between systems still brings it back to this state. A stable structure is what things tend to move towards, and the unstable structure in the intermediate state tends to be a certain stable structure.[35] Nonetheless, during social transformation, the old social structure has been deconstructed but the new social structure has not been established. Social structural deficiency appears during the alteration of the old and new social structures. In sociology, the structural deficiency is vividly described as the "bunches-of-grapes effect", which means that all components of a social system are connected as a whole, so the change of any component leads to the change of other components and the whole system. A society in transformation is a transitional society with its social structure being adjusted, and the change of one structure causes the change of other structures and the whole social system. This is a domino effect that brings about conflicts and problems one after another, just as bunches of grapes. The old conflicts and problems have not been addressed, whereas new ones emerge constantly. People call this phenomenon the "bunch-of-grapes effect".[36] Thus, when a society transforms, social issues including crimes exist frequently.

China's current social transformation, in essence, is a change from a traditional society towards a modern society, and this is a modernized process. The US scholar Black has described modernization as the process by which a society obtains modernity. Modernity refers to the common characteristics shared by countries that are at the most advanced level of technological, political, economic, and social development. Therefore, modernization refers to a dynamic pattern, which is the result of the explosive growth of knowledge in the modern world during the time-honored reform process. Its special meaning originates from its dynamic characteristics and universality of the impact on human affairs. Modernization originates from people's eagerness to change and the belief that society can and should change. If a definition is needed, modernization may be defined as a process, during which the function of

---

[34] See [26], p. 23.

[35] See [27], p. 4.

[36] See [25], pp. 320–321.

the system formed throughout history changes rapidly. It is born with the advent of the scientific revolution, which reflects the unprecedented growth of human knowledge so that human beings can control the environment.[37] China's modernization starts in 1840, but it is only the recent decade that witnesses the rapid change of modernization in China, so there is the latecomer effect. The core of this effect is latecomer, which is established based on the two theoretical premises as follows: (1) Modernization is deemed as a global social phenomenon that, with tremendous power, links all countries or regions that enter modernization into a whole in which they are mutually affected and bound. (2) Modernization with different starting types faces distinct development-related issues. Thus, the latecomer effect of modernization means a special effect produced by the influence and constraints of the developing countries in the development process against the international backdrop where some western developed countries have realized modernization.[38] The latecomer brings about social issues, especially the soar of criminal phenomena. Louise Shelley, an US criminologist who has deeply studied the relations between modernization and crime, says that modernization has obvious and universal effects on the rate and methods of crime as proved by a huge amount of evidence. From this, Louise Shelley concludes that the social development process elevates the effects of crime from an isolated social issue affecting urban centers to the main problem of modern society. As urbanization penetrates society increasingly, what is once a local problem affecting the lives of urban dwellers becomes a problem that affects people's survival in the modern world, and hinders the future development of many countries. Crime has been one of the most obvious and fundamental costs of modernization.[39] In Chinese criminal academia, a detailed analysis has been made on the general evolutionary law of the criminal phenomena during modernization: (1) During the primary stage of the modernization of society, new social revolutions weaken the old system swiftly and violently, and introduce and develop the factors of the new system, so the new and old systems clash and repel each other. This way, a pattern in which a dual system exists and mixes is formed, featuring institutional gaps, institutional inversions, and institutional reversals. The contradictions, clashes, and confrontation between the new and old institutions, systems, and social structures trigger drastic changes in the social environment and lead to significant variations in public security. The change is reflected in the different growth degrees of the crimes (primarily the number of registered criminal cases and registration rate), whose growth accelerates gradually, by the obvious change of crime structure (primarily the ratio of all criminal cases) and increasing damages of crimes to society. (2) During the middle stage of the modernization of society, social reforms develop, and clashes from all areas of society even act as a counterweight to each other in an all-around manner. During this time, the number of criminal cases (including the absolute and relative numbers) continues to increase, showing an upward trend. The crime structure changes continuously and the damages of criminal phenomena to society reach an extremely serious peak. (3)

---

[37] See [28], pp. 5, 6.

[38] See [25], pp. 316, 325.

[39] See [29], pp. 1, 158.

When the modernization of society enters the mature stage, new institutions and social structures break through and get rid of the influences from the old institutions, systems, and social structures. They start to steadily and permanently constrain developments and changes in all areas of society. On the premise of this, the scale and level of social development become steady, with the speed of development slowing down in a reasonable manner and thus in the state of virtuous development. In the social environment in which social developments and changes tend to be steady, the growth rate of criminal phenomena slows down relatively and even displays a downward trend under certain circumstances. There are fewer public security-related issues and the social security order becomes stable and even improves.[40] In my opinion, this analysis reveals the relationship between the process of modernization and changes in crimes, which is insightful for the analysis of China's current and future crime development tendency. To some degree, the significant increase of China's crimes is the inevitable cost of the social transformation towards modernization.

1.3 Individual Interpretation of Criminal Existence

Criminal existence is not only a social existence but also an individual existence. Of course, the individual referred to in this context is a social member, who cannot be separated from the biological environment, namely society. But the social interpretation of crimes should not replace the individual interpretation. The individual interpretation of crimes, however, is vital as well. The Chinese scholar Xie Yong believes that criminology should focus on the causes of crime at the macro-level. He categorizes criminology into sociology, holding the view that criminology should be a sub-division of sociology. Based on this, criminology is divided from criminal psychology because criminology studies crimes at the macro-level whose object is criminal phenomena specifically, whereas criminal psychology studies crimes at the micro-level whose object is individual criminal behaviors specifically. Therefore, both have their specific objects to study and they are independent, parallel disciplines. Xie Yong says that many researchers consider that the relationship between criminology and criminal psychology is not parallel but subordinate. Criminal psychology, criminal anthropology, and criminal sociology constitute the main divisions of criminology; however, criminology claims to be a kind of "synthesis" of the findings of these sub-disciplines. However, an obvious fact is that there is no other factual reason for "synthetic" criminology to exist apart from its significance as "an encyclopedia of criminal research".[41] I believe that criminology is an independent discipline, which is somewhere in between jurisprudence (mainly criminal law), sociology, anthropology, and psychology, but it does not belong to the sub-division of any discipline. In short, criminology is not the sub-discipline of other disciplines. However, crime,

---

[40] See [30], pp. 273–274.

[41] See [5], pp. 4, 19.

the research object of criminology, possesses the elements of jurisprudence, sociology, psychology, anthropology, and other subjects, so criminology is closely related to these disciplines. In the research on criminology, the analytical frameworks and methodologies established by these disciplines may be learned from. Thus, the criminal phenomenon, which serves as the research object of criminology, is not only a social phenomenon but also an individual phenomenon. Cesare Lombroso, the founder of criminology, started his research on criminals. In this way, I think criminology includes both the social interpretation of criminal existence which, from the macro level, answers why crimes exist in a society, and the individual interpretation of criminal existence which, from the micro level, answers why individuals commit crimes in a society.

The individual interpretation of criminal existence sets out from individuals. It is no doubt that individuals are the subjects in social relations because the individual interpretation of criminal existence can only be made scientifically within the overall framework of social interpretation. Individual interpretation remains the most controversial part of criminology. There are three tendencies towards the individual interpretation of crime: (1) Anthropological interpretation, which is also called biological interpretation. The German criminologist Schneider pointed out that the modern biological theory of crime was linked up to positivism and its predecessors. These theories no longer claimed that crime was only or mainly caused by heredity. But according to this theory, the nature-nurture scheme has fundamental significance and the theory is supplemented with the third factor, namely the personality of the criminal. Personality is not only shaped by genetic talents and social influences but also actively shapes talents and environments. In this scheme, only offenders and their social environments are investigated and compared to the control group of non-criminals, so it is called the criminal-centered scheme. According to the modern biological theory of crime, there is an interaction between genetic factors and environmental factors. A person's environment not only refers to the space in the narrow sense (such as plants, animals, and buildings) but also the sum of all social external factors in the broad sense, which depend on an individual's choice of the environment to some extent. Nonetheless, social environmental factors influence an individual's personality greatly. Personality is more or less reflected by the previous environments. Hence, environmental factors play dual roles in the causes of crime. In the mid-to-long term, the environment shapes the personality of criminals, while in the short term, it triggers criminal behaviors. Heredity and environment are mutually affected in a dynamic way. Additionally, the nature-nurture paradox is a dichotomy of unfortunate choices. Personality is a reasonable entirety that could not be broken down into talents or environmental impacts. Talent, environment, and personality are intertwined so closely that they are inseparable and cannot be proved as independent genetic factors.[42] Thus, the modern biological theory of crime is based on the interpretation of the personality of criminals. Though it does not regard heredity as the sole factor to determine crimes, it still pays much attention to the

[42] See [9], p. 397.

impacts of genetic factors on the personality of criminals. As modern scientific technologies develop, criminal biology gradually appears as a science. For instance, the US criminologist Taylor, based on the opinion of E. O. Wilson in *Sociobiology*, studied the relationships among identical twins, XYY chromosome abnormality, premenstrual syndrome, the relationships between androgen and violent offenders, the biological factors of schizophrenia and alcoholism, the biochemical reasons of hostile behaviors, and other issues, and interpreted human behaviors and criminal behaviors particularly based on biochemical reasons. Taylor quoted a scientist who said that it was feasible to decompose social behaviors. This method decomposes human social behaviors into independent parts, and its significance and results are determined from the relations of behaviors. This method is justified by the evolution of genetic neural structures. In addition, the "hormone-determines-behaviors theory" can be used to establish functional relations among hormones, brain biochemistry, and behaviors, while aggression can be considered the most interesting area to connect all problems.[43] It should be said that as human behaviors, criminal behaviors possess a biological foundation. Particularly the natural crimes that are closely related to human nature, such as rape, murder, harm, and other crimes, which have certain relationships with human biological factors. But criminal biology highlights the status of biological factors when interpreting crimes, so it is hard to be affirmed before solid scientific evidence is found.

(2) Behavioral interpretation. Behavioral studies, also called behavioral science, was originally a school of psychology but has been separated from traditional psychology and became an independent discipline. Skinner, a well-known US psychologist, proposed the concept of "inner man" and "outer man". When people cannot explain human behaviors, they utilize the term "inner man" to explain. They state that people are divided into inner man and outer man, with the outer man dominated and constrained by the inner man. The outer man is very similar to the inner man, the latter being a fictional model of the former. Explaining the behaviors of the outer man based on those of the inner man is called the psychologism interpretation by Skinner. Skinner states that the function of the inner man does provide an interpretation, but the interpretation cannot be explained, so it ends with the inner man. Inner man is not the intermediary between the past behaviors and behaviors in reality but a center where behaviors emerge.[44] Behavioral science thoroughly abandons the interpretation of psychologism. Rather than seeking interpretations from the inner mind of humans, it turns to the external environment. This is the opinion that the external environment determines human behaviors, which is also one of the most important propositions of behavioral science. Behavioral science is against seeking reasons for behaviors within organisms. According to Skinner, seeking reasons for behaviors within organisms usually covers some variables that can be directly used for scientific analysis. These variables that exist outside organisms are in the present and past environments of organisms, which feature a physical state suitable for general scientific approaches so that our explanations of behaviors

[43] See [31], p. 62.

[44] See [32], p. 12.

are as scientific as possible.[45] Thus, human behaviors can only be interpreted from the outside environment. Skinner pointed out that humans failed to realize the environment's influence on behaviors for a long time. It was Descartes who reminded us for the first time that maybe environment played an active role in determining behaviors, and the stimulating effect of the environment was also named "stimulus" (originating from Latin, referring to "goad"). The effect that acts on organisms is called "response". "Stimulus" and "response" together are considered to form a "reflex". The environment not only stimulates or spurs but also makes choices. When considering the effects of the environment on organisms, not only should we consider its effect before the responses of organisms, but also the effect after the responses. Behaviors are formed and maintained by effects. Once realizing this fact, we could set forth the interactions between organisms and the environment from a broader sense. In this way, two crucial results will be produced. One of them involves basic analysis. Behaviors that act on the environment and produce results ("operant" behavior) could be studied by arranging certain environmental conditions, where the specific results "depend on" the specific behavior. As the dependency becomes more and more complex, these results can perform their explanatory functions of behaviors. Another result is practical. That is, we can control the environment. Indeed, human's genetic talents could only be changed slowly, while the change of individual environment is rapid and dramatic. We will see that there will be considerable progress in operational behavior technologies, and it might be possible to demonstrate that operational behavior technologies might be applied to address our issues.[46] As for the interpretation of criminal behaviors, I believe that crime is an act, which is an antisocial and illegal behavior as defined by criminal law, but it still has the same generation mechanism as general human behaviors. Thus, the explanation of the causes of crime by behavioral science has certain merits. The famous US criminologist Edwin Hardin Sutherland proposed the theory of differential association based on his studies of criminal phenomena and behavioral science. He believed that crimes were always related to bad interactions, and like other complicated behaviors, people would learn to commit crimes before implementing them. Individuals can differentiate the stimulus that act on them. After multiple tries of a certain stimulus that has been differentiated, the stimulus will establish an association with a certain response of the organisms and thus form a differential response. So, the learning process of criminal behaviors is the process of a certain response an individual has established with certain stimulus. The learning of criminal behaviors only relies on the temporal and spatial proximity of the stimulus and responses. On the basis of this, Anthony Burgess and Hans Jürgen Eysenck further apply Skinner's operant conditioning theory and believe that criminal behaviors happen in such an environment where criminal behaviors have been reinforced so that people won't control or inhibit their responses to commit criminal behaviors. Furthermore, human behavior is not only a response to a stimulus. The operant behavior plays a reinforcement role for individuals to set up the stimulus–response association of the behavior, namely

[45] See [33], p. 29.

[46] See [32], pp. 15–17.

strengthening the association between a stimulus and the behavioral response of the organism, thus affecting the frequency of the behavior to happen in the future. This is the differential association-reinforcement theory developed on the basis of Sutherland's theory of differential association.[47] It should be noted that Sutherland and other criminologists have applied behavioral science to explain the origin of criminal behaviors and helped us to have a deeper understanding of the generation mechanism of criminal behaviors, which is meaningful because it isn't limited to the simple statement that the social environment determines criminal behaviors but explores the internal mechanism of how the social environment interacts with and trigger criminal behaviors.

(3) Psychological interpretation. The psychological interpretation of criminal existence explains the causes of crime based on the psychological factors of criminals. The psychological interpretation of crime has different opinions, among which a famous theory is a psychoanalysis by the Austrian psychologist Sigmund Freud. Psychoanalysis is a kind of depth psychology, which does not limit itself to the surface value of psychological phenomena. Rather, it believes that behind any psychological phenomenon there are other more important and far-reaching spiritual effects, so it aims to thoroughly reveal these deeply hidden spiritual effects through psychoanalysis. Freud denied in clarity the theory of free will and said that every person had a rooted belief in spiritual freedom and the role of will. Such belief is absolutely against science, which is bound to surrender to the determinism that also controls the spiritual life. Freud began his study from absolute determinism and argued that human spiritual lives covered from trivial things in daily life to sleep and dreams, from occasional mistakes by normal people to symptoms of the psychopath, all of which had far-reaching and complicated significance.[48] He believed that every human had a personality, which was composed of three parts, namely Id, ego, and superego. Id is composed of all instinctive impulses that have existed at birth. It is the most inaccessible and primitive part, only dominated by pleasure and pursuing satisfaction blindly. Ego is the realistic Id, modified from Id through the direct influence of reality. This part that has divided from Id becomes reasonable under the influence of reality. It no longer blindly pursues satisfaction that is dominated by the pleasure principle. By contrast, it seeks satisfaction while avoiding pains under the guidance of the principle of facts or reality. Ego is responsible for contacting facts and monitors and regulates Id's activities guided by the superego. Superego is the moralized ego, which is formed along with personality. It is the most civilized part. Freud was a psychoanalyst who, at first, was not completely aware of, and later only in principle recognized the significance of his psychoanalysis on criminology. In 1915, Freud laid a psychoanalytic foundation for criminology in a thesis titled *Conscious Criminals*. However, he did not develop it further. Freud believes that the reason for criminals to commit crimes is that criminal behaviors are banned and committing crimes bring criminals pleasure feelings spiritually. A long-held, unidentified sense of negligence that actually originated from the Oedipus Complex is associated with a certain behavior through

---

[47] See [34], pp. 207–208.

[48] See [35], pp. 346, 347.

crimes, and it has a conscious and tolerable form. Committing crimes actually relates the innate sense of negligence that originates from the Oedipus Complex to the act of commission, and the sense of negligence can be relieved by punishment. The obvious criminal behaviors cover up the original Oedipus complex.[49] Accordingly, Freud's psychoanalysis states that committing crimes is a manifestation of abnormal personalities, within which the inner control (ego and superego) fails to suppress the primitive instinct of the ego that deviates from society. The above-mentioned individual interpretations of crime have some merits and can be referred to. But crime is the result of the interaction among biology, environment, and psychology. Thus, I advocate taking criminal personality as a basic analytical framework to interpret crimes from the individual perspective in a comprehensive way.

Among scholars of the classical school of criminology, Beccaria has occasionally interpreted crimes from a social perspective. However, no one has ever interpreted crimes from the individual perspective. The classical school posited that criminal behaviors were the outcome of free will. It did not delve into the psychology of criminals and the external environment. The school of anthropology of crime started to focus on criminals and tried to interpret crimes from the individual perspective, but its interpretations were basically biological. The school of sociology of crime, on the contrary, paid attention to the social interpretation of crimes, not much to the individual interpretation. The development of modern biological, behavioral and psychological theories provides a scientific foundation for us to interpret an individual's criminal behaviors correctly.

The term "Personality" dates back to the Latin word "Persona", which refers to mask. Mask is a special covering worn by the character on the stage to show the identity of the character in the play. By defining mask as personality, two implications are indicated: (1) the behaviors by a person on his or her life stage; and (2) a real self. Likening personality to covering illustrates that personality is the outer self to be presented in public. What we show to the world are our personalities. This statement exactly shows that people have something hidden and, for some reason, they do not show it. After the term mask was applied and developed by the psychology community and other industries, the Swiss psychologist Carl Gustav Jung coined it for his school, endowing it with the meaning of the extension of self.[50] Personality is a concept that is widely used in philosophy, psychology, sociology, and jurisprudence, among which the personality concept in psychology has a deeper significance. With the efforts of Jung and other scholars, personality psychology has been created. Personality psychology is of great significance for us to explain the causes of individual crimes because personality can be described with a series of invariable behavioral patterns. In other words, personality is a consistent behavioral pattern. Crime is human behavior, but is it isolated? The classical school of criminology gave a positive answer. They believe that it is the behavior that should be punished. However, the positivist school does not agree and argues that criminal behavior is an external manifestation of physical detriment. Thus, they believe that it

---

[49] See [9], pp. 500–501.

[50] See [36], pp. 1–2.

is the person who conducts behaviors rather than behaviors themselves that should be punished. The idea of the positivist school makes sense from the perspective of Jung's personality psychology. Since it reveals the internal correlations between behaviors and people who conduct behaviors. In a certain sense, the objective foundation of physical detriment is criminal personality. The psychologist Gordon Willard Allport said in *Personality: A Psychological Interpretation* (1937) that personality was "what a man really is". It means that personality is what men have set and done, existing after the action and inside individuals. In order to avoid viewing personality as a mere hypothetical entity, Allport put forward that personality was definitely real and existed in men. Thus, in Allport's system, men are alive, complete and functional. Therefore, personality is the dynamic organization within the individual of those psycho-physical systems that determine the characteristics of a person's behaviors and thoughts. The following analysis can be made regarding the meaning of this definition: (1) Dynamic organization refers to the organizational structure in which personality is ever-changing. Allport believes that personality is never something that has been formed but something that is becoming. Although a man maintains his identity from one experience to another, he is never the same man in case of a special experience. Thus, personality is organizational, constant, and changing all the time, or to say, constantly changing into different things. (2) Psycho-physical systems refer to the psycho-physiological systems, which means that personality is not completely psychological nor neurotic. This organization shares the functions of body and mind, both of which cannot be separated and become a totality of an individual. (3) Determine. According to Allport, personality is not an abstraction or a fiction but does exist. It is and does certain things. Allport was deeply convinced that humans were absolutely not simple negative responders to the environment and human behaviors stemmed from the inner personality structure. When personality tendency is triggered by an appropriate stimulus, human nature will be reflected in their behaviors. (4) Characteristic behavior and thought refer to that personality are of great importance to individuality. Allport stressed the study of individuals rather than the laws that regulated human beings. There are no same men. Thus, the way to understand a man is to conduct specific research on this man.[51] Based on the theory of personality psychology, we can make the individual interpretation of crime as below:

Criminal behavior is not an occasional, isolated behavior of criminals, and it is true for those who occasionally commit crimes according to criminology. However, the latter do not develop stable criminal personalities, so they are impacted by the external environment more. Thus, offenders who occasionally commit crimes are also called occasional criminals. Habitual offenders, by contrast, have stable criminal personalities, so their criminal behaviors are the inevitable outcomes of their criminal personalities. If their criminal personalities are not corrected, their criminal behaviors cannot be eliminated. Apart from the two extremes of occasional offenders and habitual offenders, most criminals have certain criminal personalities,

---

[51] See [36], pp. 61–62.

which only differ in the degree of stability. Hence, the individual interpretation of criminal existence should start from the formation of the criminal personality.

Criminal personality, also named criminal characteristic, is a severe antisocial personality. The formation of a criminal personality is a complex interaction between physiology and psychology, and society and individuals. When personality is formed, the physiological or to say, biological factors are important. Because personality is premised on biological humans, so the biological nature of man has an undeniable role in the formation of personality. The biological nature is an innate factor of humans, which is also called talent. The US psychologist Hergenhahn mentioned that a lot of brilliant personality theorists attributed the constant behavioral pattern to genetic factors. Almost all personality theories are premised on certain innate factors, including the theory of physiological needs (Freud, Skinner, Maslow, etc.), the theory of self-actualization tendency (Jung, Rogers, Maslow, etc.), or the theory of social interest (Adler, etc.). In this way, the problem is not whether genes influence personality but to what degree and in which way.[52] I believe that it is wrong to deny the biological effect on personality. However, biological determinism is not desirable. The biological nature is one of the factors that determine personality, and it is true to the formation of criminal personality as well. For instance, violent attacking offence, especially sexual assaults, has a close relationship with human physiology; however, it is not the only cause of the formation of the criminal personality. In addition to biological factors, the environment plays a more important role. The environment is referred to as the external social environment. The absolute environmental determinism treats human as an organism that mechanically reflects the environment, which belittles the subjective initiative of humans. In my opinion, the environment does not act on humans automatically. On the contrary, humans take active in absorbing the environment, during which the criminal psychological structure is formed and leads to the formation of the criminal personality. Hence, the formation of personality relies on the interaction between humans (subject) and the environment (object). When the subject correlates with the external environment, it is profoundly restricted by the object. Among the things that often influence the subject, some are suitable for subjective needs and willingness, while some are not and bring difficulty for the subject to carry out practices. To sum up, objective things penetrate the living experiences of the subject constantly and influence the activities of the subject. The influences of the objective things are saved and fixed in the subject's reflection organ through cognitive, emotional, and volitional activities. They constitute a subject attitude system and are reflected in subject behaviors in certain forms. Thus, they constitute the specific behavioral pattern of each subject so that the behavioral pattern is consistent and constant. Once the subject's psychological structure is formed, it not only plays a decisive role in behaviors but also a selective role in the impacts of the external environment in a way that any behaviors which coincide with the subject's willingness are absorbed and which go against are rejected. As this process develops, a stable psychological structure is formed, and personality is exactly the comprehensive manifestation of this psychological

[52] See [37], p. 3.

structure. For criminal offenders, the formation of criminal personalities is the same complex psychological process. Besides, the formation of personality is also a socialization process. In sociology, the process in which the subject and object interact to obtain the social attribute of the subject is called socialization. During socialization, society enables humans to gradually accept cultures, traditions, and norms of group life, and to obtain abilities for living in society. In other words, socialization is a process in which certain social characteristics extend and develop among individuals who are interacted. Therefore, socialization is the consistency of individuals and society, in which individuals are assimilated by society. Socialization is a standard evaluation and remolding, that is, to request and correct human behavioral patterns according to the unified regulations of the whole society or social groups. This is the standard principle of socialization.[53] It is, nevertheless, impossible to shape everyone based on social norms. Hence, society itself is a complicated complex, in which not only does the dominant culture with the mainstream ideology as its core exist, but also various sub-cultures whose ideology deviate from the mainstream one co-exist. Socialization is the process in which individuals accept the dominant culture and some sub-cultures that share the same ideology with the dominant culture. Meanwhile, individuals may accept some sub-cultures or anti-cultures that deviate from the dominant one. Individuals may deviate from or rebel against society. Thereinto, the process of accepting some sub-cultural traits and patterns that deviate from the dominant culture of the society is called incomplete socialization, while the process of accepting anti-cultures is anti-socialization. The process of anti-socialization, in essence, reflects the discontinuity and failure in the process of socialization. Thus, it is also called the deficiency of subject socialization. The deficiency is reflected as (1) the deviation of individual cognitive mode (especially mode of thinking), which leads to the deficiency in individual consciousness and self-consciousness; (2) the change of value orientation, which leads to the deterioration or worsening of moral consciousness; and (3) the deficiency in individual legal consciousness. Individuals always distinguish between rightness and wrongness through their understandings and regulate, control their minds and behaviors through value orientation, moral consciousness, and legal consciousness. The above-mentioned three aspects constitute the dominant aspects of personality psychology. The deficiencies will affect the other adverse effects of personality structure and result in deficiencies in minds and behaviors. Because the three aspects are the core of individual social psychology whose deficiency may cause personality disorder.[54] Anti-socialization deeply influences the formation of the criminal personality. Anti-social consciousness or antagonism consciousness plays a key role in criminal personality.

Criminal personality is a stable psychological structure that moves towards crimes under the constraint of biological and social factors. It is the source of criminal behaviors. Specific criminal behaviors, dominated by such criminal personality, are reflected through a series of subjective and objective conditions, in which the subjective condition is primarily expressed as the criminal motive, while the objective

[53] See [38], p. 459.

[54] See [39], p. 111.

condition is mainly expressed as the criminal situation. Criminal motive arises from human needs, and it is an antisocial negative need that appears under the influence of the negative factors and conditions in the social environment. First, the original need structure of individuals is changed, so that it changes negatively, and gradually tends to adapt to the badness of the outside world. The change of need results in the evolution of individual behavioral motives, the formation of the antisocial demand structure, and the generation of criminal motives. Criminal motives further produce criminal objectives which are reflected as criminal behaviors in certain social situations. Before criminal personality is corrected, the development process from criminal motive to criminal behavior continues and further influences criminal personality, which will form a more stable criminal psychological structure.

When using criminal personality to interpret the causes of crimes that are committed by individuals, two issues should be noticed: (1) the relationship between criminal personality and normal personality. The essence of this issue is whether criminals possess different, special personalities from normal people. There remain different opinions among criminological theories. The German criminologist Schneider mentioned that someone had tried to use psychological testing to identify the personality of lawbreakers and criminals, and compared them to that of law-abiding people and non-criminals. Karl F. Schuessler and Donald R. Cressey (1950) discovered that there was no connection between committing crimes and personality. They analyzed 133 criminal psychological surveys and only determined the difference between criminals and non-criminals in 42% of the surveys, which was a kind of specificity in terms of the criminal personality. But the result has drawbacks regarding the methodology because all criminal samples came from prisons, the environment of which may affect the personality. Gordon P. Waldo and Simon Dinitz (1967) reviewed 94 empirical criminal psychological surveys. In 76 out of the 94 surveys, they discovered statistically significant differences between the criminal and non-criminal control groups. All 94 comparison investigations were conducted with modernized, reliable personality testing method. Among them, 56 investigations applied objective psychological testing method, in which 51 proved that there was a statistically significant difference between delinquents and non-delinquents.[55] I posit that a criminal personality is not another personality independent of the normal one. There are similarities and differences between criminal and normal personalities. Even though having committed crimes and possessing a personality that deviates from the normal one, criminals still share similar personalities with normal people, but with the special attributes of crime in the normal personality. Relatively speaking, the personality of natural criminals deviates more from the normal personality, while that of statutory criminals deviates less. Of course, criminals may have alternated personalities as well. According to psychology, alternation personality refers to that two or three distinctive and separate personalities appearing alternatively in the same person.[56] Alternation personality does not mean that a person has several different personalities but different personality surfaces. Criminals who have

[55] See [9], p. 423.

[56] See [40], p. 204.

alternation personalities tend to hide their criminal personalities by disguising normal personalities, which makes people feel that their behavioral patterns are inconsistent, but it is not so in reality. (2) The relationships between criminal and abnormal personalities. The second issue related to the above-mentioned issue is whether a criminal personality is an abnormal personality. Abnormal personality is one type of personality disorder, which refers to the personality adaption deficit without psychiatric symptoms. The development of behavioral tendencies of people who develop the personality disorder does not have a definite start and end date. Personality disorder develops slowly and is extremely difficult to treat, but it is not uncorrectable. These behavioral tendencies consist of undesirable behavioral patterns that are not allowed by society.[57] There is antisocial personality disorder among personality disorders, which relates to the criminal personality to some degree. Criminals who have this type of abnormal personality are the "insane criminals" according to Cesare Lombroso and Ferri. Ferri mentioned that further study of insane criminals found that this type of criminal included people who were completely insane and who were in the intermediate state between normal and insane.[58] Therefore, "insane criminals" coined by Ferri is a broad concept. There are criminals with abnormal personalities among criminals. They are inclined to conduct anti-social behaviors due to their personality disorder, and they have different personality characteristics from normal people. However, criminal personality is not equal to abnormal personality because most criminals still have normal personalities and it's just that such personalities have criminal psychological features. As a result, we cannot draw a sharp line between criminals and normal people.

2 Theory of Crime Axiology

If crime ontology is based on behavioral determinism, crime axiology is premised on free will. Crime ontology focuses on the descriptive analysis of criminal phenomena that do exist, while crime axiology pays attention to the value-based judgments of criminals and their criminal behaviors. Crime axiology is one of the important contents of criminal law, the study of which is of great significance for the development of criminal law studies.

---

[57] See [36], p. 416.

[58] See [41], p. 23.

2.1 Theoretical Foundation of Crime Axiology

Crime is a social phenomenon, while at the same time, it is a legal phenomenon. As a legal phenomenon, crime is the recognized outcome of the negative legal evaluation of harmful behaviors by legislators. Hence, crime axiology should make negative evaluations of criminal behaviors based on criminal law. Then, since crime is both a social and legal phenomenon, what relationship do the two shares? This is a vital question that involves both the social and legal nature of the crime, as well as the objective foundation of the evaluation of criminal law, so it is necessary to be discussed theoretically.

Criminal law is one of the most important expressions of law. Thus, the incomplete understanding of the nature of law restricts the understanding of the nature of criminal law. Concerning the nature of law, there remain different understandings throughout history. In conclusion, two famous understandings are (1) the concept of objective law. For instance, Montesquieu said that in the broadest sense, a law was the necessary relations arising from the nature of things. In this sense, all beings have their laws. Therefore, fundamental rationality does exist. Law is the relationship between the fundamental rationality and beings, as well as that between beings.[59] This is the "general law" mentioned by Montesquieu. It is applied in the sense of objective law, so Montesquieu regarded law and regular pattern as an integral whole. This is the typical concept of objective law. (2) the concept of subjective law. For example, Hegel brought up that the base of law, generally speaking, was something spiritual, whose definite status and the starting point was will. Will is free, so freedom constitutes the substance and definitive property of law. The legal system is a kingdom that has already achieved freedom, and a spiritual (a second nature) world arising from spirit.[60] Therefore, what Hegel stressed was the subjective will of the law, so it was the typical concept of subjective law. I believe that the law is the unity of objective law and subjective will. First, the law reflects objective law. That is to say. The law is not the subjective assumption of legislators nor the fantasy of jurists but is presupposed on the objective law in reality. According to materialism's opinions, the law reflects the social material conditions. It only determines or records certain economic relations, while it cannot dictate such economic relations. Second, law enjoys the property of subjective will. Since the law is expressed through legislation and legislators turn it into legal norms through their understandings of objective laws, the legal norms reflect the subjective will of legislators. Last, there is a dialectical unity between the objectivity and subjectivity of law. The subjective will of legislators can play a role in social life only when it follows the objective law. If it contradicts the objective law, even though it has been made, it will still be invalid objectively. Meanwhile, only through legislation can objective law be turned into legal norms and behavioral regulations that are universally abided by society. Then, it will change from self-being to self-making and play a bigger role in social life. As a division

[59] See [42], p. 1.

[60] See [43], p. 10.

of law, criminal law also enjoys subjectivity and objectivity and is reflected by its relationship with crime.

Crime is a social phenomenon that exists before the law. It emerges from the same material living conditions as the law. At the same time, crime is a legal phenomenon that is established by legislators through the law, so it possesses the property of illegality. As Marx said, illegal behavior was the result of the economic factor that did not depend on the will of the legislators. However, as proved by the implementation of the *Juvenile Justice Act*, determining whether a breach of an officially enacted law is criminal or negligent depends to some extent on the official authority. Distinguishing these terms is crucial because it decides the fate of thousands of people and the morality of society. The law could not only punish criminal behaviors but also fabricate them. It even plays a greater role when the law is taken into the hands of professional lawyers in particular. For example, an excellent historian mentioned that in Middle Ages, the Catholic monks had dark opinions on human nature, so they transferred their opinions to the enactment of criminal law with their influences, and formulated even more criminal behaviors than forgiveness of faults.[61] Marx profoundly pointed out the duality of crime. The crime was determined by the material living conditions of society, so it enjoyed objectivity. Also, it was determined by legislators in the form of law, so it enjoyed subjectivity. When legislators did not reflect the objective law correctly, they tended to fabricate crime. Hence, according to Marx's views, the legal evaluations by legislatures and even law enforcement authorities could turn wrongful conduct into those that should be punished by criminal law. They could even fabricate crimes. The problem is to determine to what extent should this freedom of legislators be extended?[62]

The objectivity of criminal existence is the objective foundation of the prohibition of criminal law. The objective standard of criminal behaviors can only reflect the objective damages of the behaviors to society. The prohibited evaluation of criminal law only determines the actual social damages imposed by the infringement on social order and social relationships. Hence, the Soviet Union criminologist Spiridonov mentions that criminal activities (and criminal phenomena) exist objectively, which are not changed by the evaluations of legislators. The objective social substance is that it can do actual harm to society. Therefore, the nature of the law that can cause harmful behaviors corresponding to this nature makes it necessary and possible to prohibit the official law as criminal activities, administrative negligence, and illegal conduct of citizens. The actual requirement of social organs in the prohibition of law is reflected by the objective attitudes of society on behaviors. The "true law", termed by Marx, is established. This type of law is formed through the development of history, which only needs legislators to reveal and formulate it by establishing specific laws.[63] Therefore, the opinions of "brand theory of crime" or "labeling theory" in criminological theories are merely pseudo propositions. By contrast, this theory pays attention to responses, highlighting that human beings are the social targets that are passively

[61] See [44], p. 552.

[62] See [45], p. 84.

[63] See [45], p. 85.

determined by the external world. A radical theory of social structure comes out as social psychology develops. It mixes the interaction theory and power conflict theory and argues that deviant behavior is defined by society, and the definition is decided by the power within capitalist societies. To safeguard the power of the ruling class, the supervision authority sanctions the lower class selectively, and thus illegal behaviors and crimes emerge.[64] According to this theory, crime is the outcome of criminal law, and criminals are those who are imprinted by crime. The term "imprint" dates back to ancient Greece, referring to the mark on criminals, runaway slaves, or people working for the church. The basis of the imprinting theory is the social interaction theory, which believes that society is the result of people's interaction. To maintain the balance between the environment and themselves ("homeostasis"), people, as a group, stipulate behavioral norms and expect these norms will be followed forever. If these expectations are proved invalid, sanctions take place. This is a new form of "interaction". Hence, the imprinting theory is also called the way of interaction.[65] It can be said that the imprinting theory has a certain significance to uncover the subjectivity of the prohibitive evaluation in criminal law in the capitalist society, from which the conclusion is made that it is revolutionary and radical to say that the criminal phenomena cannot be eliminated without the elimination of the capitalist law. Thus, this theory is a relatively thorough criminological theory of liberalism. It categorizes the cause of the definition of statutory crime into the study of the cause of crime.[66] However, the imprinting theory exaggerates the role of evaluation on legislation, categorizes crime completely into the subjective scope, and denies the objectivity of crime as a social existence, so it is one-sided.

The subjectivity of criminal existence refers to that although crime is a social phenomenon, prohibitive evaluation can only be carried out through legislation, so illegality is also an important characteristic of crime. Among criminological theories, critical criminology denies the legal concept of crime but advocates the sociological concept of crime. For instance, the US criminologist Quinney and Wildeman says that sticking to the traditional criminal concept, at least, enables some criminologists to study the role of existing legal systems. Nonetheless, critical criminology, not bound by the official authority or existing definitions of crime, is still needed. Critical criminology is required to serve all people's needs rather than the interests of a few people in our society. A few people refer to the upper members who have the controlling power over national policies and legislation. Critical criminology not only does not serve a few people but is required to reveal the contradictions in our fundamental system. It is these contradictions that have existed and continued to produce an uncivilized social structure with crime genes in this country (US, note from the quoter). Critical criminology is grounded on the most basic sense of human dignity and it satisfies our basic needs. Hence, it defines crime as the behavior that harm society and violate human basic rights.[67] Critical criminology insists on the

[64] See [9], p. 571.

[65] See [45], p. 81.

[66] See [46], p. 91.

[67] See [47], pp. 6, 11.

sociological concept of crime and is not limited to the legal concept, so it is of significance for the study of social criminal phenomena. But it completely gets rid of the legal concept of crime, excessively stresses the objectivity of crime, and denies the role of the prohibitive evaluation by legislators to a certain extent, which is also one-sided.

I believe that crime is the unity of objectivity and subjectivity, so the concept of crime is also the unity of the concept of sociology and that of criminal law. This is true to criminological study as well as the research of criminal law. Crime axiology examines the role of legislators in evaluating crime, and the evaluation is based on the criminal phenomena that do exist in reality. Any view that unilaterally emphasizes or completely denies the evaluation role of law on crime is not desirable. This can be seen through the analysis of natural crimes and statutory crimes. The Roman law distinguishes "malainse" and "mala prohibita". "Malainese" means that some illegal behaviors are evil in themselves. The malignancy is innate, which has already existed in behaviors even before being regulated by the law. However, the malignancy of some illegal behaviors originates from the prohibitive regulations of the law. It is not born with behaviors or inherent to the behaviors. Hence, although some illegal behaviors are not regulated, they are still to blame according to moral views. By contrast, some illegal behaviors are not against morality. However, the reason why they are prohibited as illegal behaviors is purely due to legal regulations. So far, this theory has been used to interpret the difference between criminal illegality (natural crime) and administrative illegality (statutory crime).[68] Natural crime is a "malainse", which is strongly ethical. It exists before legal evaluation and is subjective and universal. But whether natural crime is included in the scope of criminal law needs the provisions by criminal law. Only when the blameworthiness of ethics is raised to the prohibitive evaluation of criminal law can natural crime be officially determined as a crime by criminal law. Therefore, the evaluation role of criminal law is dispensable for natural crimes. It should be admitted that the evaluation of criminal law on natural crimes plays a minor role compared to statutory crimes. Statutory crime is "mala prohibita". A behavior is recognized as a crime only because it is prohibited by law. But the objectivity of statutory crimes should not be denied, and statutory crimes should not be purely regarded as the outcome of will. The reason why legislators recognize one behavior rather than another as a crime is determined by the social living conditions. Only when legislators are based on social reality can the objectivity of statutory crime be truly revealed.

The objectivity and subjectivity of crime introduce the substantive and formal concepts in criminal law. There are differences between substantive and formal concepts in civil law criminal theories. The substantive concept of crime is actually a sociological concept of crime, while the formal concept of crime is the legal concept of crime. The former highlights the social substance of the crime and the latter reveals the legal formal characteristics of crime. For example, Hitoshi Otsuka, a Japanese specialist on criminal jurisprudence, mentioned that crime is divided into

---

68 See [48], p. 112.

substantive crime and formal crime. Substantive crime refers to anti-social behaviors in the broad sense. It means those human behaviors that infringe on the interests of social life (legal interests). Crimes based on this definition can be generously understood as human behaviors that encroach on the common orders of social life no matter they are murders by psychotics or arsons by children. Formal crime refers to the blameworthy behaviors in the substantive crime, namely, the behaviors punished by the law.[69] Theories of criminal law involve the concept of crime in the substantive sense but they are mainly in the formal sense. In criminal legislation, countries with civil law systems provide for the formal concept of crime, namely, defining crime as an act punishable by criminal penalties for violating the law. However, scholars of criminal law from the Soviet Union indiscriminately regard the concept of the form of crime in the criminal code of the civil law system as formalist jurisprudence and argue to adopt the substantive concept of crime in the criminal code. This claim is represented in 1919s *Guiding Principles of the Criminal Law of the Russian Federation*, 1922s *Criminal law of the Russian Federation*, and 1926s *Criminal law of the Russian Federation.* For instance, the Soviet Union's criminal jurist M. A. Cherizov-Bebutov says that the capitalist criminal code stipulates the definition of crime in form, and crime should be prohibited by the law when it is committed and should be punished. The Soviet's legislation is different. It defines crime in terms of its damages and harms to the legal order. Additionally, Г. И. Volkov even claims that since Soviet criminal legislation studies crime from its essence, it is inevitable to come to the conclusion that the criminal responsibility system for specific criminal acts should not be stipulated.[70] It shows a view of legal nihilism, which prevails in the 1920s in the Soviet Union. It sets the form of law against society. For instance, then well-known jurist Pashukanis asserts that the form of the law never belongs to society, so he advocates replacing the law with administrative regulations. Legal nihilism imposes great damage on legality, which leads to tens of thousands of deaths during the "Great Purge". US jurists have made the best comment on Pashikanis's opinions. They say, "this professor has left us". With the establishment of the Russian government plan, the theory needs to be changed. But he has no time to adapt his teaching to the new change of order. If there is law rather than administrative orders in Russia, he may lose his job but not his life.[71] Given the lesson paid for with blood, the Soviet jurist Durmanov first begins to study the substantive and formal characteristics of crime, which is affirmed by other Soviet jurists. The 1958's *Basic Principles of Criminal Legislation of the USSR and the Union republics* determines the definition of the crime formulated by Soviet scholars after years of creative discussion from the legislation. The Item Seven of the *Basic Principles* reflects two fundamental characteristics of crime: social detriment and criminal illegality.[72] This concept of crime is considered as the unity of the substantive and formal concepts. I believe that the concept of the form of law in the criminal code is developed from the

[69] See [49], p. 98.

[70] See [50], pp. 19–21.

[71] See [51], p. 285.

[72] See [50], pp. 22, 24.

doctrine of a legally prescribed punishment for a specified crime. According to it, crime is expressly stipulated in the criminal law, and there is to be no penalty without a written law. Therefore, the legalization of crime is expressed by the establishment of the form of law in criminal law. The substantive concept of law denies the formal characteristic of crime, which inevitably leads to damage to the legal system, denial of the principle of a legally prescribed punishment for a specified crime, as well as encouragement of judicial tyranny. On the surface, the unity of the substantive and formal concepts of crime seems to be sound; however, when the substantive characteristic conflicts with the formal characteristic, which one should be the standard for determining crime? If the substantive characteristic is the standard, it still results in judicial tyranny. If the formal characteristic is set as the standard, the substantive concept of law is superfluous. Therefore, I claim that the formal concept should be established in criminal legislation setting out from the doctrine of a legally prescribed punishment for a specified crime.

The substantive concept of crime has positive significance in the study of the theories of criminal law. The study of the theories of criminal law not only mechanically annotates legal regulations but also contains value assessments of legal norms, so it does not satisfy the concept of the form of crime. The understanding of the nature of the crime is involved here. The Japanese criminal jurist Hitoshi Otsuka mentions that there remain contradictions between the behaviorism and objectivism of the classical school and behaviorism and subjectivism of the modern school. This is common sense. The classical school argues that crime is an objective expression of the specific behaviors of criminals, while the modern school holds a different position. As its slogan "it is the actors rather than behaviors that shall be punished" shows, the modern school posits that what should be punished is the social detriments of actors. The above contradictions lead to the antagonism between realism and representativism in the sense of criminal behavior. Realism is based on the classical school and objectivism, which holds that the behaviors of criminals manifested in the outside world are crimes, whereas representativism is premised on the subjectivism of the modern school and holds that the social detriments of the actors are expressed by what they have done. The modern school proposes the view of actors' detriments, but it is an extremely demanding problem to define detriments. It is even not possible to fully understand the criminal detriments of actors with today's advanced science, so it is even more impossible to explain the reasons over a century ago. Therefore, modern school scholars have to explain that the criminal behaviors by criminals are the representations of the detriments possessed by criminals themselves, and criminal behaviors are the basis to understand the detriments of actors.[73] Where the antagonism between the classical school and positivist school is displayed as that between social detriment and physical detriment. The classical school posits that social behaviors, which do harm to society and are conducted by criminals based on their free will, should blame on criminals. This is the theory of moral obligation. Oppositely, the positivist school argues that criminals have no free will and their criminal behaviors are shaped by physiological, social, and psychological factors.

[73] See [52], pp. 1–2.

Physical detriment is the fundamental characteristic of criminals, so criminals should be punished in order to defense society. This is the theory of social obligation. In the *Philosophy of Criminal Law*, I have proposed the dualism on criminal essence, in which I mention that social detriment and physical detriment are parallel, and both are the fundamental characteristics of crime.[74] Based on the dualism on criminal essence, a further point should be mentioned that the behavioral determinism of the positivist school has a positive role in the study of criminology because criminology is the theory of criminal existence. However, the criminal theory of criminal law is not based on behavioral determinism but only on free will that is proposed by the classical school. This is because it is the theory of crime axiology, mainly concerned with the evaluation of criminal law. Nevertheless, the research achievements of the positivist school should be drawn from during the study of criminal law. For instance, the theory of physical detriment should be studied to make up for the shortcomings and enrich the theories of the classical school.

2.2 Social Evaluation of Criminal Existence

The social evaluation of criminal existence evaluates crime in the social sense and interprets the social detriment of crime to provide a social foundation for the criminal obligation. The social evaluation of criminal existence is different from the social interpretation of criminal existence.

Based on the social interpretation of criminal existence, there are certain social causes for crime, which is a social phenomenon, to exist. The social causes do not depend on the will of legislators but on some social living conditions. While the social evaluation of criminal existence uncovers the social significance of criminal behaviors based on the correct understanding of the social causes of crime. Although crime is an individual behavior, all individuals live in society, so their behaviors are of social significance. The social significance of crime is reflected as a social detriment.

The evaluation of social detriment is based on history. In the beginning, there was no strict boundary between criminal behaviors and civil trespass. However, as the national power strengthened, crime became an independent domain. The British criminal jurist Turner said that in ancient laws, there was no apparent distinction between criminal illegal acts and civil illegal acts according to the books on the legal system in Britain. Both were called "binders". Any behavior that harmed individuals would do harm to society when it developed to a certain degree since society was composed of individuals. Therefore, it was not wrong to say that committing crimes was an illegal behavior that harmed society; however, this saying failed to distinguish crimes from torts. The difference between the two lies only in the degree. The ancient history of common law indicated the true difference from what we discussed today, namely, why it was not used as a scientific classification term but as a sign of emotion. Hence, the term "felony" referred to things that were cruel, fierce, evil,

[74] See [53], p. 152.

or contemptible. Turner also discussed the original state of crime. He said that the term "crime" dated back to the fourteenth century whose meaning could be found exactly from the original meaning of felony. It gave people an impression of disrepute, evilness, or contemptibility. Any behavior, as long as it was felt as harmful to the interests of a powerful authority in a specific society, such as endangering the security, stability, or comfort of the authority, would be regarded as particularly evil and cracked down with strict measures by the authority. Furthermore, if possible, the authority would ensure the coercive power at the disposal of state sovereignty could be used to prevent detriment or punish anyone who caused it. These harmful behaviors were called crimes.[75] Thus, crime was provided with a strong feature of ethical blameworthiness, but the reason why a behavior was defined as a crime was whether the behaviors violated social interests and were of social detriments.

The concept of social detriment is firstly proposed by Beccaria who holds that the harm of crime on society is the true parameter to measure crime. According to the nature of the harm of crime to society, Beccaria also categorizes crimes into three aspects: some crimes that directly do harm to society or the representatives of society; some crimes that violate the citizen's security in terms of life, property, or reputation, and some crimes that are contrary to what the public interest requires every citizen to do and not to do.[76] Here, Beccaria classifies the social detriment of crime into three types, with the first type on the violation of national interests, the second on the violation of individuals, and the third on the violation of social interests. Beccaria conducts social evaluations of crime from the national, individual, and social perspectives, and has revealed the in-depth meaning of social detriment, which is of great significance. Later, the German criminal jurist Feuerbach proposes the theory of violating rights, believing that the nature of crime and the violation aspects of crime are detriments to subjective rights, and the mission of criminal law is to protect subjective rights and guarantee the freedom of citizens. It should be mentioned that Feuerbach's theory of violating rights is developed from the doctrine of a legally prescribed punishment for a specified crime, which plays a role in limiting the expansion of the crime concept. Moreover, his theory abandons the criminal view of the Middle Ages when committing crimes was regarded as evil, and moral and legal obligations were mixed. His theory strictly defines the scope of crime from the legal perspective, which is historically progressive. His theory has shortcomings as well. It only covers the crimes that violate individual interests, while excluding those which violate national and social interests.

As the Japanese criminal jurist Hitoshi Otsuka says, the theory considers one aspect of crime, but there are a lot of parts in crime that are hard to clarify whether they belong to the violations of rights.[77] Hence, Feuerbach's theory of violating rights is soon replaced by Birnbaum's theory of violating legal interests. Birnbaum advocates the "gut theory", which posits that some "guts" are endowed by nature and some are the fruits of the development of human society and unity of citizens. States should

---

[75] See [54], pp. 1–2.

[76] See [55], p. 69.

[77] See [52], p. 4.

use their power to indiscriminately safeguard all people living in them. The concept of crime is based on reason, and Birnbaum becomes the pioneer of the theory of legal interests. The theory of legal interests holds that crime violates sundry "guts" that replace rights as the object of crime. Therefore, from the perspective of the nature of things, crime should be punished because "guts", which are safeguarded by national power, are violated or endangered in a way that is attributable to human intent.[78] After the notion of legal interest is proposed, its content evolves from materialization to spiritualization. Birnbaum agrees that legal interests share the features with specific, tangible objects based on the relationships between the "guts" protected by law and the concept of violation, and believes that legal interests include all opinions on life, reputation, freedom of personality, property, religion, and ethic. With regard to the nature of the crime, apart from the theory of violating legal interests, Schaffstein also proposes the theory of the breach of obligation, arguing that the nature of the crime is not the violation of legal interests but the breach of obligation. But the concept of the breach of obligation, as evaluated by the Japanese criminal jurist Hitoshi Otsuka, has considered all universal natures of crimes at the first glimpse, but it is so ambiguous that it is not specific and thus can not help understand all specific natures of crimes compared to the theory of violating legal interests. Only when criminal law sentences people whose behaviors breach the obligation and who are given special evaluations by criminal law do we have to admit the role of the concept of the breach of obligation. Therefore, he believes that the nature of the crime should be based on the theory of violating legal interests. Additionally, the forms and patterns of the violations of legal interests in all types of crimes should be considered. Nevertheless, for crimes whose central element is the breach of obligation of the behavioral subject, to supplement the theory of violating legal interests, the theory of the breach of obligation should be used together. Also, the crimes, which are able to recognize the nature of crime only when the breach of obligation of actors is considered, are called obligation crimes.[79] Currently, among the civil law criminal theories, the theory of violating legal interests is a universal theory that reveals the essential characteristic of crime from the perspective of the violation of legal interests, thus providing the foundation for the social evaluation of crime.

Legal interest is protected by the law, in which a subject has the value of an object or state related to it. Therefore, legal interest per se is a concept of value judgment. Legal interest is divided into three types: (1) National legal interest. It refers to the legal interest that belongs to the state exclusively, so it is different from social or individual legal interest. Since the evaluation of crime is expressed by national legislation, a state must announce the behaviors that violate national legal interests as crimes, in order to safeguard its basis for survival. National legal interests are guaranteed by sacrificing individual freedom. But in modern society, a state is a fundamental social organization, where all political and economic activities are conducted. Hence, it is of great significance to ensure the safe performance of national power. (2) Social legal interest. It is a public interest, which differs

78 See [56], p. 62.

79 See [52], p. 7.

from the national and individual legal interests but is closely related to them. In terms of the relationship between social legal interests and national legal interests, safeguarding social order is one of the important functions of the state, and without a stable social order, there will be no stable state ruling in that state ruling is built on social order. With regards to the relationship between social and individual legal interests, social interests can be transformed into individual ones. The Japanese criminal jurist Haruo Nishihara says that social interest is separated from individual interest and becomes an independent interest in a way different from national interest. Societal moral order becomes an independent interest to be protected. Citizens have the obligation to abide by this moral order. Thus, the breach of this obligation is deemed illegality. Based on the above-mentioned views, such behaviors as issuing, selling, and displaying obscene books and pictures are illegal and constitute a crime because these behaviors breach the moral order. Even though playing pornographic movies to adults inside a secret chamber is criminal since it breaches the sexual moral order.[80] (3) Individual legal interest. Why does the violation of individual interest have social significance? This question is concerned with the understanding of the nature and value of crime. According to ancient Roman law, crime (*delitto*) refers to all illegal behaviors that will be punished. As with illegal behaviors in general, two elements are required to constitute a crime, which is the violation of a certain right and subjective will (offense). The result is serious because criminal behaviors impose such serious results on the social order that criminals are not only liable for compensation but also penalties. Crime is divided into public crime (*delicta publica*) and private crime (*delicta privata*). The punishment of the former enjoys the public feature, namely public crime is punished by the state (*poena publica*) no matter whether it is initiated by public litigation. The latter crime, which is discussed in this book, punishes individuals. In early times, people expiated their guilt with money to avoid punishment.[81] Even though private crime is within the scope of the crime, it is distinct from public crime (the crime in the real sense). The Chinese jurist of Roman law Zhou Liang has said that private crime violates private proper or body which, in ancient Rome, is not regarded as an influential behavior on the impact of the public order. Actors only hold damage liability and pay money to the victim. In principle, only the victim has the right to litigate. The victim can also waive their rights to claim compensation. Therefore, the private crime in Rome is different from the torts in modern civil law, but both share the same nature.[82] According to the classification in the book titled *The Institutes of Justinian*, there are four types of private crime, which are (1) theft; (2) robbery; (3) property damage; and (4) physical injury.[83] Maine, a well-known British jurist, responds that "The civil wrongs acknowledged by Roman law starts with thefts (*Furtum*). We tend to believe that the exclusively criminal offences are completely illegal behaviors, not only including thefts but also rapes and robbery. Jurists relate them with infestations, literary slanders, and oral

---

[80] See [57], pp. 46–47.

[81] See [58], p. 401.

[82] See [59], p. 781.

[83] See [60], p. 190.

slanders. All of these produce 'gut' or legal locks, which can be compensated by money."[84] The classification of illegal acts by Roman law indicates that the crime concept in ancient Rome includes the contents of the damages to the state or social community.[85] The detriment of crime is viewed as the damage to the state or society, and the violation of individuals is private, which can be addressed through civil litigation. It reflects the superficial understanding of crime value by early Romans. As society develops, the Romans have deeper understandings of the crime detriments, when a change from "illegal acts" to "crime" called by Maine emerges. At first, the Roman legislature did not abolish civil reliefs for fierce crimes and it still provided the victim with compensation that would be definitely accepted by them. However, even when Augustus completed his legislation, there were a few offences that were still viewed as "illegal acts", whereas these offences should be deemed as criminal in modern society. It was not until later, in an uncertain period, when the law began to pay attention to a new crime called "extraordinary crime" (*crime extraordinaria*) in the "compilation of jurisprudence", that they became criminally punishable crimes. Undoubtedly, there is a certain type of behavior that is purely deemed as illegal acts by the Roman jurisprudence theory; however, as the sense of dignity increases in society, people are against that offenders are only punished financially without additional serious penalties. This way, such offences are approved to be litigated as extraordinary (*extraordinem*) crimes under the willingness of the victim, that is, crimes are litigated through a relief that is different from the ordinary procedure. Since the first time when these extraordinary crimes are admitted, Roman's list of crimes should be as long as that of all societies in the modern world.[86] It is since then that the illegal acts which violate individual legal interests are called crimes in the social sense.

As the foundation of the social evaluation of crime, social detriment should be understood from the legal perspective and more importantly, from the social perspective. In terms of sociology, the social detriment is centrally reflected as the violation of certain social relations. It can be said that social relations are the key to uncover the nature of the crime. Hence, a sociological analysis of the concept of social relations is needed. The Soviet Union criminal jurist Spiridonov says that social relations are the relationships between social members rather than those between human beings as a species (*homo sapiens*). All social characteristics of individuals are obtained from society, and social relations feature non-individuality because what is important for society is not so much the individual's description of fantasy but a certain social status as the ability to perform social functions. Individual behaviors are nothing but social functions. A conclusion is thus made that apart from people who are the embodiments of social functions and the direct participators of social relations, society is another most authoritative party that is a part of social relations. This means that social relations are never a connection between two social roles which are established based on the "Robinson-Friday" pattern. As the relationship of the entirety in

[84] Maine [61], p. 208.

[85] See [61], p. 217.

[86] See [61], p. 222.

two parts, society always exists in the relationships among people who have social characteristics.[87] The social relations theory provides a sociological standard for us to evaluate individual behaviors. The encroachment of crime on social relations is usually achieved through humans and things. Humans are the subject of social relations, and this indicates that humans are not an isolated existence; rather, they are a part of the network of the social relations who enjoy their positions in the division of social labor, so they are organically connected with other social members. Thus, when criminals do harm to individuals, they are damaging society. This way, crimes that cause damages to some social members become social phenomena that are of social significance. In addition, the different positions of individuals in social relations determine the degree of social detriments of the criminal acts against them. In some societies, although everybody is equal before the law, people are in different positions in social relations, so the social relations embodied by them remain different. It is the different natures of the social relations encroached by law that determine the degree of social detriments of crimes. Things are the object of certain social relations, so social relations disappear when human beings are excluded. Similarly, there will be no social relations without things. However, where human beings and things constitute relationships, all those relationships reflect those between human beings. Marx has mentioned that theft of woods is criminal behavior, however, the criminal nature is not the violation of woods, but the violation of the ownership, which is the nerve of a state.[88] The great importance of social relations on evaluating social detriments can not only be seen from the subject and object, but social relations also play a key role in determining the meaning of behaviors. According to criminal law theories, there is a difference between the theory of spontaneous behavior and that of social behavior. The former is the mainstream of criminal law thoughts in the nineteenth century, which looks upon the behaviors defined by criminal law the same as those defined by natural science, especially by physics. Active actions that are expressed in the outside world and are part of human physical activities, such as punching others' heads, which leads to the swollen of the victim's head, are behaviors. This can be said as an easily understood behavioral theory. The example that falls into the category of the theory of spontaneous behavior can be cited from Liszt, who holds that behaviors will cause changes in the outside world through intentional (*wilkürlich*) actions. Hence, the theory of spontaneous behavior focuses on the physical nature of behaviors, centering on the physical activities initiated in the outside world and the consequent changes in the outside world. The theory of social behavior, which is based on the denial of the theory of spontaneous behavior, is firstly proposed by the German criminologist Carl Schmitt. The theory argues that the behavioral value is not about the unscrupulous behaviors of individuals but the normalization of society. The human being's behavioral elements are first, to note down the arbitrariness of the elements and second, to normalize the social nature of elements. Arbitrariness should be regulated by social nature. Since social elements feature

[87] See [62], pp. 27–28.

[88] See [63], p. 168.

normalization, which is the outcome of the millions of individual arbitrary behaviors under the constraints of the normalization of the social element, and through the dramatic adjustment, are condensed into a large purposeful behavior as a whole. The infinite expansion of such an entirety becomes a purposeful universe. Therefore, purposeful behaviors are not important in the arbitrariness of individuals, and their importance lies in the normalization of society, that is, every arbitrary behavior of individuals must be regulated by the law of social norms. The arbitrary behaviors of social members are various, so if the law of social norms does not exist, there will be no social history and no civilization history of human beings. In face of the serious reality, the importance of social norms is highlighted; meanwhile, the necessity of legal compulsion is displayed. Legal compulsory norms are based on social norms. Human behaviors have been evaluated by social norms before being evaluated by criminal law. Hence, human behaviors are ultimately socially meaningful and valuable under the law of social norms. According to criminal law theories, the opinion that crimes constitute neutral, colorless behavioral facts is not all-inclusive in that before the evaluation of legal regulations, all behaviors have already been evaluated by social norms. Criminal behaviors that have been recorded by written articles are not neutral or colorless. The theory of social behavior is based on social nature and has uncovered the essential characteristic of criminal behaviors. Compared with the theory of social behavior, the theory of spontaneous behavior is hard to describe the behavioral nature of omission based on its physical nature. The behavioral nature of omission can only be explained through the social nature of the theory of social behavior. The behavioral nature of omission must and can only be seen insightfully through certain social relations. Likewise, the usefulness of the opinion of value can only be found in social relations. The fundamental reason why behaviors are of social detriments is that they violate certain social relations. Thus, the negative value of commission or omission can only be explained in certain social relations. In some societies, humans form certain social relations, which are established through the law, through which legal relations that are at the core of the relationship between rights and obligations are formed. Rights and obligations are two different aspects of the same legal relationship, which are interdependent and changeable. Holding certain legal obligations, in fact, is the premise of the fulfillment of others' rights, and one's rights are performed before he or she holds the obligation. Therefore, the behavior of openly violating others' rights (commission) has social detriments. Meanwhile, failing to hold one's obligation that one should and can hold (omission) is also a violation of the rights of others, so it is also a socially harmful behavior. In this sense, the omission is equal to the commission in terms of its negative value. The equivalence is decided by the natural social relations they have violated. Based on certain social relations, the behavioral nature of omission can be explained definitely.

As the social evaluation of criminal existence, the social detriment is enriched with social and political content and is closely related to social life. Therefore, as an evaluation standard, the social detriment is the objective social property of criminal behaviors. Meanwhile, the social detriment is determined by legislation, so criminal behaviors feature illegality. It is of great significance to understand the relationships between the objectivity and subjectivity of social detriments in the right way. The

Soviet Union jurist Spiridonov mentions that the behavioral diversity against the social order and the historical variability of the degree of damage objectively caused by each behavior brings the issue of the criteria for evaluating the social detriment of a crime to the forefront. Without such criteria, society cannot respond to crimes consciously or fairly. From a sociological theoretical point of view, the degree of the adaptation of behaviors to the objective law of social development is the criterion for evaluating human behaviors.[89] The objective law of social development mentions here is the ultimate criterion for the evaluation of human behaviors. Both laws and criminals should be evaluated based on this criterion. Only the behaviors that contradict the law of social development are viewed as social detriments in the ultimate sense and the negative evaluation of prohibition should thus be given in criminal law. However, the objective law of social development does not depend on human will nor will it take the initiative to evaluate human behaviors. Only after the objective law of social development is recognized and recorded in the provisions of the law will it be the evaluation criterion of human behaviors. But whether legal criteria truly reflect the objective law of social development, and the quality of the reflection is another question to be judged. Under such circumstances, the formation of the criteria of criminal law is of significance. The Soviet Union jurist Spiridonov mentions that the law of social development, including the possibility of laws on which the development of legal forms depends, determines that law is influenced by many other factors throughout its formation. The law exists in this way, instead of other such forms as normative or legal relations. This is the outcome of the interactions among economic, political, and socio-cultural factors. When we illustrate the nature of transforming social relations into legal relations, a situation cannot be ignored. It is that the reflection of the law on economic systems is not a negative "mirror" reflection of the existing social systems. By contrast, the superstructure, which includes the law, is positive. It not only impacts the things that it reflects but also its formation and development. This enables the law to be a relatively independent social phenomenon. As a relatively and special social phenomenon, the law further evolves, and thus consolidates and develops its independence.[90] The relative independence of law becomes an independent value criterion when social detriments are identified. But the value criterion of law is constrained and supplemented by social evaluation criteria when it was applied in reality. In the criminal law theory of the civil law system, there is a theory of social correspondence. The Japanese criminal jurist Taira Fukuda has said that the terms "social correspondence" and "social correspondence behavior" are frequently used in criminal law studies. One of the main advocators Hans Welzel makes a definition and says that "social correspondence behaviors refer to the behaviors that are allowed by the ethical order in society, which is formed throughout history in social life." According to his saying, if the behaviors that infringe on all rights and interests of the social life are deemed as illegal and thus prohibited, we should do nothing in our social living environment. Therefore, in order to live in all the laws and rituals of social life, we do not

[89] See [62], p. 48.

[90] See [62], pp. 66–67.

deem the infringement on all rights and interests as illegal and thus prohibit it. An orderly social life should play its role actively, so only when the infringement on legal interests exceeds a certain degree will it be prohibited as a breach of law. Accordingly, within the scope which is formed through the history of social life, motorized activity behavior, or social correspondence behavior is not illegal unless it exceeds social correspondence.[91] The theory of social correspondence is of significance to the judgment of social detriment.

2.3 *Individual Evaluation of Criminal Existence*

The individual evaluation of criminal existence evaluates crimes and clarifies the physical detriment of crime based on the social evaluation of criminal existence, and it provides a theoretical foundation for the criminal obligation.

The individual evaluation of criminal existence is different from the individual interpretation of criminal existence. The individual interpretation of criminal existence holds that committing crimes is a behavior of human beings. It is grounded on personality. Criminal behavior, which is restricted by criminal personality, enjoys the consistency of the behavioral pattern. But the individual evaluation of criminal existence is based on the individual interpretation of criminal existence to determine the obligation of the subject. The individual evaluation of criminal existence is also distinct from the social evaluation of criminal existence. The social evaluation of criminal existence is the foundation and presupposition of individual evaluation, which evaluates the social detriment of crime from the social perspective. However, individual evaluation is a subjective evaluation of criminals, which aims to study the obligation of the subject. The obligation is held by individuals. Although regarding the emergence of crime, the obligation has close relationships with society, society is impossible to hold the obligation directly. It is undeniable that what we mention is the legal obligation. Society should also pay for the crime. Paulsen, a German philosopher mentions, "We find a dual obligation. We insist that individuals hold obligations. Then, the community including the family, social class, nation, and even mankind that shapes individuals also have obligations. Finally, society has responsibility. The following situation, where we judge a group's value by the goodness and evilness of its individual members, happens all the time. But this does not mean that evaluating individuals is unnecessary. On the contrary, the evaluation of individuals is still the fundamental premise of other larger-scale evaluations. An individual is a point. Our feelings and judgments extend from this point to the entirety to which a person belongs." He also argues that "theorists constantly trap into strange confusions and questions owing to that they steadily ponder on the issue of metaphysical freedom or stare at statistics, such as whether society has the right of punishment, and whether society itself is guilty and shall hold responsibility. Similarly, the ratio of crimes, such

[91] See [64], pp. 177–178.

as false oaths, murders, and other immoral sins, repeatedly recur in a way as the regularity of a natural event. A necessity seems to function, and those special criminals are selected and sacrificed to fulfill the criminal indicator of society. We answer that this phenomenon is very real. Society is guilty, so it shall be punished. Society gives birth to individuals who tend to commit crimes and also provides temptations and opportunities for crimes. But is society not punished? Is crime per se a punishment to society? The infringed people, like criminals, are social members as well. The feeling of fear and anxiety arising from crime is a further punishment on society. And the punishment of criminals is another punishment. Criminals are punished as a member of society because society has committed crimes through its member. At last, as a totality, society is punished by itself. Isn't it a punishment that a nation spends a lot of money on prisons and indoctrination centers, providing guards, supporting and recruiting a number of people?[92] It should be said that the consideration of such a question is profound. Crime is not only an issue of individual obligation but also a social issue. But speaking from the law, only individual (including legal person, hereinafter as the same) responsibility is held accountable.

Then, what is the basis for an individual to hold criminal liability? The classical school of criminology and the positivist school of criminology have different answers. The classical school is noted for the theory of moral responsibility. The theory posits that the basis of criminal responsibility exists in the theory of moral blameworthiness. The theory is grounded on free will, which believes that people who have free will are able to conduct legal behaviors based on it; however, when their behaviors break the law, there remains a possibility of moral blameworthiness. That is to say, if a mentally competent person (the responsible person), who is aware of the moral norm and can decide his or her action as per that awareness, conducts the act even though he or she is aware of its illegality (intent), or at least may be aware of it but conducts the act through inattention (negligence), then the moral blameworthiness imposed on this person is the core of responsibility. Since the theory is premised on free will, actors are not the factor of the subject of free will. The core of the issue is the responsibility of each behavior (individual responsibility for behavior). The theory holds that the bad will in each behavior shows the sign of blameworthiness (responsibility for will). Thus, in terms of the punishment on behaviors that are expressed externally, the theory reflects the view of objectivism and thus is developed into the theory of moral responsibility of the classical school. The theory of moral responsibility is proposed on the basis of the opposition against the arbitrary judgment of crime and punishment in feudal criminal law. At the same time, it regards responsibility as moral blameworthiness and takes free will as the premise of imputation, which is scientific. Of course, the theory of moral responsibility has shortcomings. It sets out from the abstract rational man and studies free will metaphysically. It does not notice the social constraints on human behaviors, so ignores the social nature of the criminal obligation. Additionally, it breaks down human behaviors from actors and identifies the liability of behaviors unilaterally. The positivist school of criminology advocates the theory of social responsibility which, based on behavioral determinism, holds that

[92] See [65], pp. 393–395.

crime necessarily depends on the quality and environment of actors. It criticizes the opinions of the theory of moral responsibility which advocates that crime is caused by the free judgment of the people who have free will. It believes that such opinion is meaningless, and denies the theory of free will which is based on the theory of moral responsibility. The theory of social responsibility points out that it is completely meaningless to morally blame actors based on specific behaviors. This is because the criminal behaviors of criminals are determined by the person's quality and environment. However, criminals are usually those who have dangerous personalities and impose dangerous acts on society, and society must get rid of the violations from such people to protect itself. Society should protect itself from violations, so it should understand the importance of punishment in the right way, and the status that must bear punishment is called criminal responsibility. According to this theory, it is not the specific behaviors that constitute responsibility but the personality of the actors who impose dangers on society. Then, whether specific behaviors are completely ignored by the theory of social responsibility? In fact, it is not. The theory of social responsibility holds that responsibility should be discussed based on the personality of endangering society (social detriment) reflected in each specific behavior. In other words, each behavior is only to justify the detriments of the actor's personality. This theory studies the issue of criminal responsibility from a social perspective. It argues that the nature of criminal responsibility is to defend society, and particularly to notice the physical detriments of criminals. It stresses the individualization of the penalty, which is scientific. But this theory fundamentally denies human free will and illustrates the basis of responsibility from behavioral determinism, which denies the blameworthiness of responsibility to some extent. As Hitoshi Otsuka has mentioned, the theory of social obligation advocated by the modern school believes that the criminals who have social detriments should be punished for social defense, and status is responsibility. The modern school uses "social blameworthiness" and other terms as well. However, since it is grounded on the determinism that crime is produced by heredity and environment, it cannot blame criminals in the real sense. This is because if there are no other possibilities except for crime, and if the existence of freedom is not admitted, there will be nothing to blame. Doctor Hideichi Makino says straightforwardly that it is better to call it "theory of social measures" than the theory of social responsibility.[93] This indicates the nature of the theory of social responsibility in an extreme manner.[94] I believe that the crime by a criminal is not completely determined. It is chosen according to the criminal's will, while the will itself is not isolated from the material living conditions in society. Therefore, criminals should hold criminal responsibility for their behaviors that damage society. At the same time, human behaviors are not isolated. They enjoy the morality and consistency of behavioral patterns, the foundation of which is criminal personality. Therefore, the basis for criminal responsibility is not only expressed as the social detriment through behaviors but also the criminal personality that dominates these behaviors. This way, criminal responsibility is based on the unity of the social detriment and

[93] Hideichi [66], p. 509.

[94] See [52], p. 169.

physical detriment of criminals. Only in this way will the nature of criminal responsibility be revealed. And it is in this sense that we agree with the theory of personality responsibility. The theory of personality responsibility originates before the Second World War in Germany, where the "lifestyle-guilt" theory by Edmund Mczger and the "lifestyle-decision-guilt" theory by Paul Bockelmann are proposed. In Japan, the theory is first adopted by Doctor Yasuhira Masakichi and Doctor Takeo Fuwa, and it is Doctor Dando Shigemitsu that tries to develop this theory after the war. Human beings are constrained by quality and environment, but they still enjoy the freedom to act and meanwhile, they can dominate the constraints to some extent. This is the humanistic foundation of the theory of personality responsibility. The theory holds that the foundation of responsibility is not only the specific acts but also the personality of actors. The theory of personality responsibility holds that criminal behavior is the concretization of the personality of actors and that of the subject. That is to say, criminal behaviors do not necessarily reveal the personality of the actors but selectively exclude other possibilities to conduct behaviors according to the personality characteristics of actors under internal and external conditions. Therefore, behavior is only one aspect of personality dynamics. Through this aspect, we must first admit that behavior itself is the foundation of criminal responsibility. Accordingly, the issue of the personality and attitude of the actors on specific criminal behaviors is raised. In this sense, the theory of personality responsibility is equal to the lifestyle-guilt theory. However, as a potential personality system can be predicted from criminal behaviors, it is not possible to discuss behaviors without considering them. Additionally, the potential personality is formed under the constraints of quality and environment. Hence, within a scope that the actor can commit a behavior independently and autonomously, the person may be subjected to criticism of the formation of his or her personality. The behavioral responsibility and personality formation responsibility can be differentiated from their concepts. The former is mainly primary, while the latter is subordinate. However, behavioral responsibility also interprets and responsibly judges the personality and attitude reflected in behaviors. In addition, the personality when the crime happens cannot be understood in a true sense if the process of the formation of the previous personality is detached. Hence, to understand the personality and attitude in behaviors, we must understand the formation of the previous personality. In other words, we should consider both. The behavioral responsibility and personality formation responsibility are collectively called personality liability. Taira Fukuda, a Japanese criminal jurist, holds that the practical meaning of the theory of personality liability in the criminal law theory is as follows: first, it is the basis for enhancing the responsibility of habitual criminals. This theory believes that habituation is the foundation for aggravating punishment in sentencing. But according to the views of the moral liability theory which stresses individual behavioral responsibility, the basis for aggravating penalty is normative consciousness. This way, habitual criminals who have weak consciousnesses of illegality bear minor liability. If according to the view of personality responsibility theory, actors are to blame in the formation of this habitual personality, they can be identified as having great liability. Second, the issue of the understanding of illegality. This theory believes that intentionality is established as long as there is a possibility of the understanding of illegality. The theory of personality liability holds that since the essence of intentional responsibility can be understood from the direct normativity of personality attitudes, from which the facts are known, there is no essential difference at all between knowing illegality and possibly knowing it, owing to that the actors are confronted with the problem of the norm. Moreover, since actors know and admit facts, even though they do not understand illegality. If there is such a possibility, we still affirm that they have anti-normative personality attitudes. Therefore, intentionality exists when there is the possibility that actors have understandings of illegality. As the core of negligence liability, unintentionality (unconsciousness of dangers and insufficient tension) reflects the personality attitudes of unconsciousness. Hence, due to the theory of personality liability, negligence liability has a right basis. Furthermore, the theory of personality liability helps establish the standard of determining what punishment to give and sentencing.[95] Therefore, behavior is not isolated but dominated by the personality of the behavior. The repetition and regularity of behavior can find a logical basis in the personality system. The same opinion should be given to criminal behaviors as well. Based on the theory of personality liability, the moral liability of one's behaviors shall be affirmed, so does the possibility of blame exist. Additionally, it analyzes the behavior from the personality subject to the social environment, so it includes the content of physical detriment.

The theory of personality liability learns from the blameworthiness concept of the theory of moral liability based on free will and integrates the physical detriment concept of the theory of social liability which regards behaviors as the expression of the personality of the criminal. It is a comprehensive theory of liability. The theory of personality liability does not deny human free will. The Japanese criminal jurist Hitoshi Otsuka has argued that the relatively free will thought is not only widely supported in the philosophy academia but also has been empirically demonstrated in the field of criminology, so it should be adopted as the basis of criminal law. Only from this standpoint could we blame the responsibility of the actor who implements illegal acts as a subjective existence for the individual illegal acts that meet the constitutive elements.[96] Based on free will, the blameworthiness of liability will be illustrated. The blameworthiness of behavior has close relationships with subjective faults, objective behaviors, and subjective characteristics. First, the human subjective fault is grounded on free will. Criminal psychology includes the cognitive and will factor of humans. The cognitive factor refers to the subjective cognition of humans, which is the basis of free will. The will factor refers to a subjective tendency of people to the harmful results caused by their acts. It is obvious that the anti-social tendency of the subject is reflected only when the subject has free will. If an actor's behavior is completely determined, there is nothing about human free will at all. Criminals understand illegality when they intentionally commit crimes, but they still decide to conduct these behaviors. Hence, criminals have free will to commit crimes. It is the theory of free will that explains why criminals have anticipated possibility, and it provides a theoretical basis for criminal responsibility. Then, how to explain criminal

[95] See [64], pp. 222–223.

[96] See [52], p. 170.

negligence by using free will? For instance, Ferri argues that free will cannot explain why negligence, especially that due to carelessness, should bear criminal liability.[97] In the common law system, some jurists believe that the state of mind of a purely negligent and careless person does not seem to be evil at all, and no retribution theory provides a foundation to blame the person.[98] In my opinion, the view is not true. In the case of negligent crimes, actors conduct criminal acts when their will is not free, that is to say, they are unconscious to do so. However, the lack of freedom is grounded on the capability to achieve freedom. Because in the case of negligent crimes, there are sufficient conditions of the necessary relationships between the understanding of behavior and the result. Whether people have an objective understanding of objectivity totally depends on their willingness to play the role of subjective initiative that they already possess.[99] In this sense, the lack of freedom, when the negligent criminals conduct criminal behaviors, is merely a phenomenon, behind which free choices of the actors are included, even though choices are unconsciously made. As Hart has mentioned, the decisive factors when we punish negligent criminals are that the people we punish should have had, at the time of their conducts, the normal physical and mental capacity to commit legal acts and to refrain from committing acts prohibited by law, as well as a fair opportunity to exercise those capacities.[100] Therefore, free will can fully explain the subjective basis of criminal liability for negligent crimes. Moreover, human objective behaviors are conducted by free will, so the behaviors, which are conducted when free will is lack, are not considered as the behaviors defined by criminal law. According to this criterion, the following behaviors are not determined by the will of the actors, so these behaviors are non-criminal concepts: (1) reflex acts without the participation of consciousness; (2) mechanical acts that are under the direct coercion of another person's violence, in which the actor is completely unable to resist and exercise his or her will; (3) acts or inactions during sleep or those that are conducted unconsciously; (4) convulsions due to disease, electric shock or nerve reflex; and (5) inactions when hands and feet are bound, so that people are impossible to act. The following acts are still determined by human will, so they are acts defined by criminal law: (1) automatic acts in daily life; (2) impulsive behaviors; and (3) specific behaviors under the indirect coercion of another person's violence, so that the will of the actor is impacted.[101] Therefore, whether an act is defined by criminal law is based on whether these behaviors are controlled by subjective wills. In the case of force majeure, although the actors have recognized the occurrence of harmful results, due to external forces, they lose free will, so their behaviors cannot be regarded as harmful acts as defined by criminal law, and the actors do not hold criminal responsibility as criminals. Finally, the establishment of the subject of crime is based on human free will. The core of the subject of crime is criminal liability ability. The Chinese criminal law includes criminal liability ability,

---

[97] See [67], p. 12.

[98] See [68], p. 126.

[99] See [69].

[100] See [68], p. 145.

[101] See [70], p. 74.

which refers to the capabilities of the actors to recognize and control their own behaviors as defined in criminal law, which is necessary for the actors to commit crimes and bear criminal responsibility. It is composed of cognitive ability and volitional ability. Cognitive ability refers to the ability of the actors to distinguish the meaning, nature, role, and consequences of their behaviors as defined in criminal law, while volitional ability refers to the ability of the actors to control whether to commit the behaviors prohibited by criminal law. If the cognitive ability is the ability to tell rightness or wrongness, then the volitional ability is the ability to choose rightness or wrongness. Thus, the essence of criminal liability ability is the existence of the actor's relative free will capacity when he or she causes social detriment. Hence, criminal liability ability can be regarded as free will ability in some sense. Humans are not born with free will but gain it as they grow up. The law prescribes a certain age, before which actors are presumed not to have free will, so actors are not the subject of crime. The legal age is the age for criminal responsibility. Meanwhile, humans are not born with free will, and they may lose free will due to some mental diseases. In this case, if actors lose their free will, they are not the subject of crime. In conclusion, free will is the premise of the subject of crime.

The theory of personality liability affirms the position of physical detriment in the essence of criminal liability. Then, does physical detriment contradict free will? Our answer is negative. Physical detriment is on the basis of the criminal personality. Especially as the criminal psychology of habitual criminals has been strengthened gradually in criminal activities, they develop criminal personalities, dominating criminal acts, and getting used to commit crimes. It is difficult to control their criminal desires. This way, criminals seem to lose free will. However, according to Aristotle, actors should be responsible for their habituation because it is developed due to the indulgence of their desires. The habituation is premised on free will. This is the formation of personality. Among Japanese criminal jurists, Professor Ryuichi Hirano denies the personality formation liability and argues that not only is it not clear whether the quality and environment behind the behavior makes liability greater or lighter, but it is also realistically (and maybe theoretically) impossible to specify what exists behind the personality formation process that can take liability for it. In response, the Japanese criminal jurist Hitoshi Otsuka mentions that it is impossible, at least at this moment, to accurately measure the specific significance and degree of personality formation. However, based on the quality and environment of the actor, his or her personality and the process of personality formation so far can be evaluated correctly by the existing scientific theories. Even though the evaluation is not complete, it is undoubtedly necessary to take it as the reference for liability judgment through efforts. We should not discuss the significance of the actor's personality regardless of his or her personality formation in the past.[102] I think Hitoshi Otsuka's view is correct. Regarding whether the liability is greater or lighter due to the formation of a criminal personality, I think we cannot simply generalize it. Compared to occasional criminals, habitual criminals develop the habit to commit crimes due to their criminal personalities. They tend to repeatedly commit crimes and are difficult

[102] See [52], pp. 170–171.

to rectify. So, they should be punished harshly. However, when criminals have the same criminal personality, the formation process of the criminal personality should be specifically analyzed. As long as the criminal personality is impacted greater by the external environment and less by the subjective will, it has less liability for the formation of criminal personality and otherwise, greater liability.

References

1. [Ancient Greece] Plato, *The Republic* (The Commercial Press, Beijing, 1986)
2. [Ancient Greece] Aristotle, *Politics* (The Commercial Press, Beijing, 1965)
3. *Selected Works of Western Ethics*, vol. 1 (The Commercial Press, Beijing, 1964)
4. [Italy] Aquinas, *Aquinas Political Writings* (The Commercial Press, Beijing, 1963)
5. Y. Xie, *Introduction to Study of Criminology* (Hunan Publishing House, Changsha, 1992)
6. S. Kang (Chief Editor), *An Introduction to Criminology* (Peking University Press, Beijing, 1992)
7. [Japan] K. Koichi, *Criminology* (Quzhong Publishing House, Beijing, 1989)
8. *Comparative Criminology* (People's Public Security University of China Press, Beijing, 1992)
9. [Germany] Schneider, *Criminology* (People's Public Security University of China Press, Beijing, 1990)
10. [Germany] Kaiser, *Criminology* (Northwest University of Political Science and Law, Xi'an, 1985)
11. J. Guo, *A Few Basic Issues about the US Criminology* (People's Public Security University of China Press, Beijing, 1992)
12. Q. He, *Legal Studies in Contemporary Japan: Humans and Works* (Shanghai Academy of Social Sciences, Shanghai, 1991)
13. [Soviet Union] B.K. Tverbly et al. (Chief Editors), *Criminology* (Quzhong Publishing House, Beijing, 1986)
14. Y. Pi, The "value free principle" of the study of criminology. Polit. Sci. Law Trib. (3) (1993)
15. G. Su, *Rationality and Its Limitation: Introduction to Weber's Thoughts* (Shanghai People's Press, Shanghai, 1988)
16. D· Stanley Eitzen et al., *Criminology* (Quzhong Publishing House, Beijing, 1988)
17. Turner, *The Structure of Sociological Theory* (Hangzhou Publishing Group, Hangzhou, 1987)
18. [France] Durkheim, *The Rules of Sociological Method* (Huaxia Publishing House, Beijing, 1988)
19. [US] Douglas et al., *Sociology of Deviant Behavior* (Hebei People's Publishing House, Shijiazhuang, 1988)
20. [US] Coser, *Masters of Sociological Thought* (China Social Sciences Press, Beijing, 1990)
21. [US] H.J. Vetter et al., *Introduction to Criminology* (Knowledge Publishing House, Beijing, 1992)
22. Douglas et al., *Sociology of Deviant Behavior* (Hebei People's Publishing House, Shijiazhuang, 1987)
23. [France] Durkheim, *Suicide: A Study in Sociology* (Zhejiang People's Publishing House, Hangzhou, 1988)
24. Y. Li, *The Unbalanced Chinese Economy* (The Economic Daily Press, Beijing, 1991)
25. H. Zheng et al., *Introduction to Social Operation* (China Renmin University Press, Beijing, 1993)
26. X. Lu et al., *China Society in Transformation* (Heilongjiang People's Publishing House, Harbin, 1994)
27. J. Xiong, *Social Change and Structural Deficiencies* (Law Press, Beijing, 1991)
28. [US] Black, *Dynamics of Modernization: A Study in Comparative History* (Zhejiang People's Publishing House, Hangzhou, 1989)

29. [US] S. Louise, *Crime and Modernization: The Impact of Industrialization and Urbanization on Crime* (Quzhong Publishing House, Beijing, 1986)
30. Z. Wang, J. Huang, *Economic Development and Crime Change* (China Renmin University Press, Beijing, 1993)
31. [US] L. Taylor, *Born to Crime* (Qunzhong Publishing House, Beijing, 1986)
32. [US] B.F. Skinner, *Beyond Freedom and Dignity* (Guizhou People's Publishing House, Guiyang, 1987)
33. [US] B.F. Skinner, *Science and Human Behavior* (Huaxia Publishing House, Beijing, 1989)
34. Z. Shen (Editor-in-Chief), *Legal Psychology* (Peking University Press, Beijing, 1986)
35. Q. Yang, *Main Schools of Modern Western Psychology* (Liaoning People's Publishing House, Shenyang, 1980)
36. Z. Chen et al., *Personality Psychology* (Liaoning People's Publishing House, Shenyang, 1986)
37. [US] B.R. Hergenhahn, *An Introduction to the History of Psychology* (Hebei People's Publishing House, Shijiazhuang, 1988)
38. L. Song, *Modern Sociology* (Shanghai People's Publishing House, Shanghai, 1987)
39. H. Gao (Editor-in-Chief), *Criminal Psychology* (Nanjing University Press, Nanjing, 1993)
40. D. Luo (Editor-in-Chief), *Dictionary of Legal Psychology* (Quzhong Publishing House, Beijing, 1989)
41. [Italy] E. Ferri, *Criminal Sociology* (People's Public Security University of China Press, Beijing, 1990)
42. [France] Montesquieu, *The Spirit of the Laws*, vol. 1 (The Commercial Press, Beijing, 1961)
43. [Germany] Hegel, *Elements of the Philosophy of Right* (The Commercial Press, Beijing, 1961)
44. *Marx-Engels-Gesamtausgabe*, vol. 13 (People's Publishing House, Beijing, 1962)
45. [The Soviet Union] Л.И. Spiridonov, *Criminal Sociology* (Quzhong Publishing House, Beijing, 1993)
46. J. Bai, *Principles of Criminology* (China Modern Publishing House, Beijing, 1992)
47. [US] Q. Richard et al., *The Problem of Crime* (China International Radio Press, Beijing, 1988)
48. S. Lin, *Economic Crimes and Criminal Law of Economy* (San Min Book, Taipei, 1980)
49. [Japan] K. Kameji (ed.), *Dictionary of Criminal Law* (Shanghai Translation Publishing Corporation, Shanghai, 1991)
50. [The Soviet Union] A.A. Piontkowski et al., *History of the Criminal Law Sciences of the Soviet Union* (Law Press China, Beijing, 1984)
51. [US] S. Bernard, *The Law in US: A History* (China University of Political Science and Law Press, Beijing, 1989)
52. [Japan] O. Hitoshi, *Basic Problems of Crime Theory* (China University of Political Science and Law Press, Beijing, 1993)
53. X. Chen, *Philosophy of Criminal Law* (China University of Political Science and Law Press, Beijing, 1992)
54. [UK] Turner, *Kenny's Outlines of Criminal Law* (Huaxia Publishing House, Beijing, 1989)
55. [Italy] Beccaria, *On Crimes and Punishments* (Encyclopedia of China Publishing House, Beijing, 1993)
56. P. Chen, *Special Research on Criminal Law* (San Min Book, Taipei, 1988)
57. [Japan] N. Haruo, *The Basis and Philosophy of Criminal Law* (Shanghai Sanlian Bookstore, Shanghai, 1991)
58. [Italy] B. Peng, *Roman Law Textbook* (China University of Political Science and Law Press, Beijing, 1992)
59. L. Zhou, *Original Theory of Roman Law*, vol. 2 (Commercial Press, Beijing, 1994)
60. [Ancient Rome] Justinian, *The Institutes of Justinian* (Commercial Press, Beijing, 1989)
61. [UK] Maine, *Ancient Law* (Commercial Press, Beijing, 1959)
62. [The Soviet Union] Л.И. Spiridonov, *Criminal Sociology* (Quzhong Publishing House, Beijing, 1989)
63. *Marx-Engels-Gesamtausgabe*, vol. 1 (People's Publishing House, Beijing, 1965)
64. [Japan] K. Kameji (ed.), *Dictionary of Criminal Law* (Shanghai, Shanghai Translation Publishing Corporation, Shanghai, 1992)

65. [Germany] Paulsen, *A System of Ethics* (China Social Science Press, Beijing, 1988)
66. [Japan] M. Hideichi, *General Theory of Criminal Law*, vol. 2, Full edn. (1959)
67. [Italy] E. Ferri, *Positive School of Criminology: Three Lectures* (China University of Political Science and Law Press, Beijing, 1987)
68. [UK] H. Hart, *Punishment and Responsibility* (Huaxia Publishing House, Beijing, 1989)
69. Z. Zhang, On the theoretical basis of criminal responsibility for negligent crime. Chin. J. Law (2) (1982)
70. S. Lin, *General Principles of Criminal Law* (San Min Book, Taipei, 1986)

Chapter 8
Human Nature Foundation of Punishment

Punishment is a social response to crimes. Crimes can be analyzed from both ontological and axiological perspectives, in the same way, punishments can also take these two perspectives as frameworks to analyze human nature. The ontology of punishment, premised on the ontology of crime, studies punishment as a phenomenon of social control, and it is the study of penology. The mission of penology study is to reveal the social basis of the existence of the punishment phenomenon and provide the basis for scientific decisions on crime control. The axiology of punishment is based on the axiology of crime, which examines the functions and purposes of punishments, and it is the study of criminal law. The humanistic foundation of punishment is closely related to the humanistic foundation of crime but has its unique theoretical perspective and therefore deserves in-depth studies.

1 Theory of Punishment Ontology

The punishment ontology, based on the existence of punishments, reveals the social foundation of punishments, and provides an empirical analysis of punishments. In the sense of the theory of punishment ontology, the existence of punishment is not subject to human will, so it is a theory of penology grounded on behavioral determinism.

1.1 Theoretical Foundation of Punishment Ontology

Punishment, which exists as the counterpart to crime, is a social repercussion of crimes. Through a considerable period of history, the punishment has been seen as the only way to deal with crimes. With the emergence of the classical school of criminology, punishment issues gradually come to the forefront of society. However, the classical school mainly focuses on mitigating punishments. For instance, Cesare

X. Chen, *Humanistic Foundation of Criminal Law*,
https://doi.org/10.1007/978-981-19-9764-8_8

Beccaria attacks the harsh punishments in feudal society based on the principle of humanitarianism of punishment, saying that "who does not shudder with horror reading in the history of the barbaric and useless torments that are coolly invented and executed by men who are called wise? Who does not tremble at the thoughts of thousands of wretches, whose misery, either caused or tolerated by the laws that favor the few and outraged the many, have forced in despair to return to a state of nature; who does not shudder seeing people who share the same senses and therefore desires to tease the frantic public by accusing of impossible crimes, the fabric of ignorance and superstition; or guilty only of having been faithful to their own principles?"[1] Although he criticizes the feudal punishments, and, in particular, famously advocates the abolition of the death penalty, the centerpiece of Beccaria's criminal policy is the prevention of crime through the psychological deterrent effect of punishment. "Scholars of the classical school have written several volumes on the death penalty and torture, but only a few pages on crime prevention", Ferri quotes Elio as saying. Ferri comments further that the historical mission of the classical school of criminology is to mitigate punishments since it was born on the eve of the French Revolution, which represents individualism and natural rights. The classical school is a protest against the barbaric punishments in the Middle Ages. The brilliance of the classical school, therefore, lies in its propaganda to abolish the most barbaric medieval punishments, such as the death penalty, torture, and mutilation.[2] The positivist school of criminology begins to study the causes of crimes and base penalties on the prevention and control of crimes. In the beginning, Cesare Lombroso proposes a new method to punish criminals, arguing that crime is inherited and has an innate predisposition that is almost irredeemable. Neither education nor prisons are sufficient to remedy the situation. As Lombroso calls it, the new methods of punishment are those which, while abolishing the traditional system of repressive penalties and replacing it with a purely preventive one, seeks alternatives to penalties and advocates a revolutionary change in the traditional penalty system. Ferri, on the other hand, refers to the mission of the reform by the classical school as the alleviation of penal suffering, while defining the mission of the penal reform by the positivist school as the reduction of the number of crimes. Ferri points out that we will take over the realistic and scientific mission of the classical school and undertake the more noble and fruitful task of reducing crimes while mitigating punishments. Ferri argues that the classical school focuses solely on punishment and the repressive measures after crimes are committed, through a variety of mental and material dire consequences. The positivist school, on the other hand, focuses on the correction of criminals. Ferri mentions that in the most barbaric state of mankind, it is a historical rule that the penal codes only provide for punishments but not for the correction of the criminals; as human civilization progresses, the opposite idea that there are only corrections but not punishments emerge.[3] The positivist school of criminology thus pioneers a new epoch in the study of punishment. Although the positivist school

[1] See [1], p. 42.

[2] See [2], pp. 45–46.

[3] See [2], pp. 5 and 46.

does not find a discipline known as penology, Ferri develops it within the scope of criminology or criminal sociology and names it "countermeasures of crimes". The development of criminal policy science and the social defense movement have their origins in the positivist school. As the US criminologist John L. Gillin remarks, "In an aspect of penalties, Ferri accomplishes the same course for the Italian school or positivist school. He brings together materials equivalent to or in place of the penalty and developed a judicial theory that does not adopt the classical doctrine of the free will of criminals. This theory is the responsibility of society. In his outline of the penology, the equivalence of penalties, or what we call the preventive method, plays an important role."[4] I believe that the contributions of the positivist school of criminology to penology are the following: (1) Evolution of the ideas of punishment. In the classical school of criminology, Kant and Hegel's doctrine of retribution considers punishment exclusively as a form of retribution and thus is not deemed as a specialized study of punishment. The utilitarianism of Beccaria, Bentham, and Feuerbach, while posing the problem of crime prevention, is centered on the psychological coercion effect through the hierarchical, timely and inevitable nature of punishment. In Beccaria's book *On Crimes and Punishments*, the issue of how to prevent crimes is specifically addressed, but it is vague, unprofessional, and impractical. In general, the classical school still emphasizes the punitive nature of punishment. The positivist school of criminology moves from the punitive nature to the corrective character of punishment, focusing on the crime prevention of criminals and preventing them from further committing crimes through corrective measures. In other words, the positivist school of criminology evolves from general prevention to individual prevention. As criminals are specific, the corrective function of punishment can be implemented, which allows punishment to develop from unspecified psychological coercion to a specific corrective measure, thus providing a theoretical foundation for penology. (2) The introduction of scientific methods. Concerning the study of punishment, the classical school focuses on the speculative method, especially Kant and Hegel, and is obsessed with the causal relationship between crimes and punishments, rather than scientific arguments of the function of punishment. The positivist school of criminology introduces scientific methods into criminal law, not only for the study of crime but also for that of punishment, greatly expanding the scope of the study of punishment and making it an independent discipline to be studied. When discussing the historical development of criminal policy, a Taiwanese scholar Kan-mei Chang divides it into two stages: first, the humanitarian stage of the classical school, which is the early stage of the germination of criminal policy thinking, whose ideas and theories were mainly philosophical based on life experience or humanitarianism, thus not scientific. The theory of criminal policy is in the humanitarian phase, which is based on justice or humanitarianism, thus lacking a scientific basis. This is the scientific stage in which the criminal positivism school is situated. In the nineteenth century, the development of the research of positive science on crime lays a scientific foundation for the study of criminal policy, which evolves from metaphysical to scientific in the modern sense. Among the most important contributors to the science

[4] See [3], p. 503.

of criminal policy are the Italian criminologists, represented by Cesare Lombroso, Enrico Ferri and, Baron Raffaele Garofalo, and the German criminologists, represented by Franz von Liszt, Franz Exner, Edmund Mezger, and Gustav Aschaffenburg, who, from the standpoint of their respective positive sciences, such as anthropology, sociology, psychology, psychiatry, and biology, elucidate the reasons why criminals are involved in crimes and provide a scientific basis for criminal policy. In particular, Liszt emphasizes the scientific nature of criminal policy, arguing that criminal policy without a scientific basis will make the criminal policymaker a mere do-gooder (*Dlettant*).[5] In my opinion, the study of penology should adhere to humanitarianism but more importantly, introduce scientific principles to provide a theoretical basis for the prevention of crime through the empirical analysis of penalties. (3) The establishment of a unique perspective. In the study of punishment, the classical school has merely studied the penalties prescribed by criminal laws, thus it belongs to a normative study. The classical school regards punishment as the only way to suppress crimes, and relegates it simply to imprisonment, focusing on the length of imprisonment. Depending on the legal responsibility of criminals, punishments are imposed based on the degrees set in advance. As Ferri has said, the entire penal code is, in its final analysis, a mere logarithmic table for calculating penalties.[6] The positivist school of criminology, on the other hand, breaks away from the narrow normative perspective by studying punishment as a corrective measure through the lens of crime prevention. In this case, punishment is no longer a simple legal stipulation, but a means of combating crimes, especially correcting criminals, thus bringing the study of punishment into a broad social perspective.

The empirical study of punishment has progressed considerably since it was strongly advocated by the positivist school of criminology. However, because penology has not been as self-contained as criminology, which has been studied under the rubric of criminology or criminal policy, it is a highly immature discipline in comparison to criminology. In China, the study of criminal law emphasizes the theory of crime over the theory of punishment, which also affects the study of criminal law. In this regard, it is necessary to establish the theoretical foundation of penology and enable it to be an independent discipline. Then, what are the theoretical foundations of the study of penology? To answer it, we should study the existence of punishment as a social phenomenon, and define the system, object, and method of the study of penology.

1.1.1 Penological Systematology

Penology is a term that is closer to the meaning of the criminal policy. Criminal policy originates in France, where it is first coined by the German criminologist Feuerbach in his textbook on criminal law. The term is then popularized by scholars such as Franz Liszt before being adopted by the countries using the civil law system and

---

[5] See [4], pp. 12, 15–17.

[6] See [2], p. 39.

eventually becoming a science: criminal policy. The term does not exist in the countries adopting the common law system, and now a British translation of the French expression "Kriminal Politik" is used, but it is not widespread and has not been an independent discipline. Strictly speaking, the content of what is called criminal policy by common law countries is different from that of criminology in the civil law system. The criminology of the common law system is mainly concerned with the trial of crimes and the treatment of criminals in criminal justice. It is generally true that in common law countries, the term criminal policy is closer to the term penology used among civil law countries. *The Oxford Companion to Law*, for example, does not contain the term criminal policy, but has an entry for *Penology*, stating that penology is a discipline that studies the principles and approaches used by different countries at different times to punish and dispose of criminals, the strengths and weaknesses of these approaches, and which ones are still in use and which ones are worth promoting.[7] In addition, the US scholar John Lewis Gillin has written a book entitled *Criminology and Penology*, in which criminology is the study of the causes of crimes, and penology is the study of the treatments of crimes. Although Germany is the birthplace of the term criminal policy, we have not seen any translations of German works on criminal policy, but Schneider's book *Criminology* does not include the content of the criminal policy. In Japan, criminology and criminal policy are used interchangeably, and the Japanese criminologist Kikuta Koichi advocates the establishment of criminology that includes criminology and criminal policy in a narrow sense. Kikuta Kouichi points out that, even though the content of such wording is extremely broad, what used to be called *Criminology* or *Criminal Policy* in Japan is centered on the views of jurists. These jurists are the metaphysical criminal jurists who are based on traditional German concepts of jurisprudence and normative jurisprudence, and who also teaches Criminology and Criminal Policy in universities. Kikuta, therefore, highlights the need to free the study of criminology from the confines of the categories of Criminology and Criminal Policy that are deeply connected to the Japanese tradition of interpreting jurisprudence.[8] In the Soviet Union, no discipline is dedicated to criminal policy. The only component of criminology is crime prevention, which is not the study of criminal policy. In Taiwan, the concepts of criminology, criminal policy and penology are used in parallel. The Taiwanese scholar Kan-mei Chang proposes to limit the scope of criminological research to the study of the causes of crimes, namely criminology in a narrow sense, and to place the study of crime prevention measures within the scope of criminal policy.[9] Thus, Kan-mei Chang's two books, *Original Theory of Criminology* and *Criminal Policy*, are essentially based on the above classification. However, according to Taiwanese scholar Chi-tung Lin, criminal policy can be divided into broad and narrow senses. In the broad sense, criminal policy is considered to be the investigation of the causes of crimes to develop measures to deal with them. In the narrow sense, it is considered to be the exploration of the causes of crimes and the criticism of the existing

[7] See [5], p. 684.

[8] See [6], p. 6.

[9] See [4], p. 2.

punishment system and related systems, to improve or apply the existing punishment system and related systems to prevent crimes. The contrast between these two standpoints illustrates that these two senses share similarities in exploring the causes of crimes as the starting point of criminal policy, and preventing crimes as the ultimate goal of criminal policy; the difference is that the narrow sense is within the range of improving or applying the existing punishment system, whereas the broader sense is not limited to this range. Chi-tung Lin advocates the narrow sense, whose criminal policy includes the following: (1) The study of the causes of crimes. (2) Critiques of the existing penal and related systems. (3) The study of how existing penal systems can be improved or applied. (4) The study of how penal systems can be improved or applied. (5) The ultimate goal is the prevention of crime.[10] Thus, the content of Chi-tung Lin's theory of criminal policy is identical to that of the Japanese criminologist Kikuta Koichi. The Taiwanese scholar Shan-tien Lin has written a book entitled *Penology*, in which he states that "penology is the science that studies the theory of criminal punishment and the theory of security measures, as well as the norms and experience of the criminal punishment system and the security measures system from the perspectives of criminal jurisprudence, criminal policy and criminology."[11] Thus, for Shan-tien Lin, penology is a discipline distinct from criminology and criminal policy. Penology is better distinguished from criminology (the study of the causes of crimes in the narrow sense), but how can it be distinguished from criminal policy? According to Shan-tien Lin, criminal policy (*Kriminal Politik*) is the theoretical and empirical study of the anti-crime effect of criminal law norms taking into account the achievements of criminological research to summarize the anti-crime principles before reviewing the current criminal policies according to these principles, so as to comprehensively plan in criminal legislation, criminal justice and social policy and combat crimes in the most effective manner. Criminal penalties and security sanctions are the most concrete means of combating crimes among criminal policies, and the study of penology should therefore be discussed from the perspective of criminal policy.[12] However, based on the above definitions, it is still difficult to distinguish between penology and criminal policy. In China, criminology is essentially the same as in the Soviet Union, and the term penology is also used specifically, for example, Qiu Xinglong and Xu Zhangrun's book *Penology* defines penology as the study of the philosophy of punishment and its implementation in criminal practices. It argues that criminology, even according to the criminological theory in the broad sense, is not a study of punishment in general, but limits the field of study to the preventive role of punishment in crime and its relationship to other crime prevention measures.[13] It is therefore advocating the distinction between penology and criminology. In recent years, the concept of criminal policy has been introduced in China, and the study of criminal policy has been carried out, with monographs on criminal policy having been published. The criminal policy of China, according to Professor Ma Kechang,

---

[10] See [7], pp. 3–4.

[11] See [8], p. 2.

[12] See [8], p. 4.

[13] See [9], pp. 3 and 5.

refers to the guidelines and countermeasures formulated by the Communist Party of China and the people's democratic regime, guided by Marxism and Maoism, to prevent, reduce and even eliminate crimes following China's national conditions and the situation of a certain period.[14] The specific content of these criminal policies mainly refers to China's fundamental criminal policies, namely the policy of combining punishment and leniency, the policy of education, probation and rescue for juvenile criminals; the policy of "less arrest or death penalty and more leniency" for crimes committed by ethnic minorities, and the policy of comprehensive treatment. As another example, Professor Yang Chunxi points out that criminal policy is the strategy of the country or the ruling party to apply penalties and related measures to criminal behaviors and criminals as per criminal situations, to effectively achieve the purpose of punishment and crime prevention. China's criminal policy refers to the policy and strategy of the Communist Party of China and the country to apply penalties or other means of treatment to criminal behaviors and criminals according to the criminal situation and the causes of crimes in China, to effectively punish criminals and prevent crimes.[15] Accordingly, the main content of criminal policy is also to elaborate on the policy of comprehensive management of social security, the policy of combining punishment and leniency, the policy of reforming criminals, and the policy of dealing with juvenile delinquents. Hence, there is a significant difference in the content of criminal policy in China when we compare it with that of civil law countries. This is mainly because the term policy is widely used in China's politics, which usually refers to the policies of the Communist Party of China. The policy refers to the action guidelines set by political parties to achieve the objectives and missions across a certain historical period. In China's previous studies of criminal law, we have discussed relevant criminal policies that are of guiding significance to criminal law, such as the criminal policy of combining punishment with leniency. At present, the criminal policy study in China is an exegesis and interpretation of these existing criminal policies. Under such circumstances, the so-called criminal policy is at best an interpretation of existing criminal policies, which cannot be called an independent theoretical discipline. Considering the specific political meaning of "criminal policy" in China, the term would not be in line with the international academic community even if it were to be adopted. Therefore, I prefer to use the terminology of "penology", which corresponds to criminology.

1.1.2 Object Theory of Penology

What does penology study? This is where the understanding of the term penalty comes into play. Penalty in a broad sense refers to all legal effects with a penal character, including criminal punishment (*Kriminalstrafe*) and security measures, as well as administrative, order and disciplinary penalties, among others, whereas in a narrow sense, it refers only to the criminal penalties that enjoy penalty characteristics

[14] See [10], p. 5.

[15] See [11], p. 7.

most. In an eclectic sense, it refers to the two primary legal effects of criminal behaviors, which are criminal penalties and security measures.[16] The penalties in the study of criminal law generally refer to statutory penalties that are primarily the normative analysis of statutory penalties. Penology, as an empirical discipline, is not limited to statutory penalties; rather, it is the study of penalties in a broad sense, i.e., the criminal measures that are the legal effects of crimes. The study of penology is inseparable from statutory penalties, but statutory penalties are not absolute. The dialectical movement of penalization and depenalization is a general rule of penal development. Historically, the death penalty was a major form of punishment, but as civilization progressed and developed, the cruelty of the death penalty became increasingly at odds with social civilization, creating a worldwide trend towards the abolition and restriction of the death penalty, and some countries have already abolished the death penalty. It is foreseeable that the death penalty will disappear from the criminal law system. Oppositely, some new measures to punish crimes will become penalties and be stressed by people increasingly. Throughout history, the concept of punishment is always changing. In ancient times and the Middle Ages, the concern was with the punitive nature of punishment, whereas in modern times, the concern was with the corrective nature of punishment. One theoretical view is that punishment is a punitive concept and therefore advocates its abolition and replaces it with neutral terms such as social defense, sanctions, or disposal. However, the name is changed, and it is difficult to erase the distinctive character of punishment, a method of dealing with crimes. In penology, punishment is analyzed from a factual and empirical point of view, primarily from the perspective of the criminal policy concept of crime prevention. In describing the tasks of criminal science, Liszt distinguishes between criminal law and penology as follows: criminal law is to train criminal law specialists to find out crimes in practice; penology is to explain the causes of punishments.[17] Although Liszt fails to go further with the interpretation of penology, the well-thought references to explain the causes of punishment are worth considering. Criminology, like criminal law, is the study of crime, however, criminology is a separate discipline whose object is to study the causes of crimes, whereas criminal law is to study the legal characteristics of crimes, which is different from criminology, so both exists in parallel are complementary. Likewise, penology, like criminal law, is the study of punishment, then is there any difference in contents? According to Liszt, penology is the study of the causes of punishments, which corresponds precisely to the causes of crimes. But while the causes of crimes are easy to understand, those of punishments are not easy to explain. In my view, the causes of punishments are the reasons why punishment is called punishment. It is an examination, setting out to prevent crimes, of what kind of disposals can be punishments in the light of a certain criminal policy. The study of penalties in criminal law, on the other hand, takes statutory penalties as the starting point for normative interpretation. Thus, penology differs from criminal law in that it has a special study object different from that of criminal law. Thus, criminal law is a normative study of penalties, whereas penology is a reactive study

[16] See [8], p. 1.

[17] See [9], p. 4.

of penalties. In this sense, there are some similarities between penology and criminal policy. It is noteworthy that in criminological studies, criminal responses are often incorporated and considered criminal policies. For example, according to Professor Wang Mu, criminal policy refers to criminal countermeasure. Criminal policy instruments can be divided into criminal punitive policies and social preventive policies. Criminal punitive policies refer to all the means, approaches, and measures used by state authorities to combat crimes with the adoption of criminal law. The main elements of the criminal punitive policies are: the policy principles of criminal legislation and legislative practices, the disclosure of criminal facts and criminals, the prosecution and punishment of crimes and the enforcement of punishments. Social preventive policy, on contrary, refers to the social activities of preventing, reducing, and eliminating crimes by eliminating and weakening the causes, conditions and factors that give rise to negative human personalities.[18] Given the misunderstanding of the term policy in China, I believe that the term criminal policy reveals the true meaning of criminal policy in civil law countries more. However, the inclusion of the social preventive policy in criminal policy remains a question. I have already mentioned that criminology should not include crime prevention, especially social prevention. Likewise, there should be no social prevention in criminal policy, or in what we call penology. Liszt has a famous saying that the best social policy is the best criminal policy. Therefore, there is a difference between criminal policy and social policy. It is difficult to understand the criminal policy if we are based on a too broad sense. As Taiwanese scholar Kan-mei Chang points out, "theoretically, crime is not only a criminal problem but also a serious social problem. If we intend to prevent crimes effectively, we should combine with various social policies related to crimes. In reality, however, if we take a broad sense, the scope of criminal policy will be too broad that we have difficulties in specialized and insightful research and practical activities, leading to no real achievements. Thus, books on criminal policy are not necessarily concerned with social policy generally.[19] More importantly, crimes always occur in a society where the social ecology is a constraint on the legal punishments. For example, improving the social environment, developing the economy and reducing unemployment all contribute to crime prevention, but society will never improve the social environment, develop the economy or reduce unemployment to prevent crimes. Another example is that the transition from a planned economy to a market-oriented economy will inevitably bring about the economic crimes that are unique to a market-oriented economy. Particularly during the transition period, due to the dual-track system of the economy and a certain degree of economic and social disruption, the crime of all kinds will proliferate, and criminal waves will emerge at the cost of economic take-off and social development; nonetheless, economy and society will never fail to progress because of crime waves. Thus, in certain social conditions, the criminal policy is a measure to deter crimes, while other social preventive policies are virtually invisible and resistant to the occurrence of crimes. For example, the US scholar Professor James Q. Wilson has argued that

---

[18] See [12], pp. 383 and 391.

[19] See [4], p. 3.

whatever causes of crimes we have discovered or may discover are never, or hardly ever, of any value to policymakers. Much of the knowledge gained from studying the complex causes of crimes rarely converses into social policy because the conditions to which it draws attention are not easily changed at will. In short, Wilson argues that policies to reduce the disadvantages of social structures and improve social conditions should pursue their inherent goals without regard to their potential to reduce crimes. Wilson advocates greater reliance on specialized anti-crime measures because, even if crime preventive tools barely emerge from these studies, changes affecting crime rates, in the long run, can only rely on broad and slow social processes. We cannot wait for the causes to be revealed but should take administrative measures as soon as possible. Wilson points out that the analysis of crime causation leads to a neglect of practical and concrete measures to change people's behaviors. Wilson, therefore, insists that we should approach this from the views of the policy analysts, and must focus on the concrete implementation of control instruments—rewards and punishments—based on objective conditions. In short, this means that enforcement and sanctions have greater inevitability and effectiveness.[20] I posit, therefore, that the criminal policy can be understood as a response to crimes, and that the response can only be a criminal response to crimes in a narrow sense, i.e., a variety of measures specifically designed to deal with crimes in criminal justice, measures which in a broad sense are called penalties. Thus, criminal policy can be reduced to the study of penology. In the system of penology, there is both the macro study of penal control modes and micro study of penal correction measures: the former is the constructive exploration of the criminal control modes (the system and severity of punishments), and the latter is the study of the specific roles of criminal measures in the correction of criminals, both of which are the specialized study objects of criminal policy.

1.1.3 Methodology of Penology

When we investigate the theoretical foundation of penological studies, the methodologies of penology are also worth studying. According to the Taiwanese scholar Shan-tien Lin, penological studies are targeting the theories and systems of penalties and security measures, and therefore both normative methods (normative Methoden) and empirical methods (*empirische Methoden*) should be adopted collectively to study penology. On the one hand, the juristic theories of penalties and security sanctions and the relevant legal provisions are studied deductively and inductively from the view of normative science; on the other hand, the functions of penal methods and security measures in criminal policy should be studied empirically from the perspective of empirical science (*elnpirische Wissenschaft oder Grfahrung swlssenschaft*).[21] In my view, Lin's approach to the study of penology is both normative and empirical, and it is therefore difficult to distinguish his approach from that of the science of criminal law. The study of punishment in penology is an entirely normative

[20] See [13], pp. 34–36.

[21] See [8], p. 9.

and analytical approach. Therefore, if penology is to be an independent discipline rather than a comprehensive study of punishment, it should have distinctive research methods that differ from the normative approach of penology. The answer is the empirical method of analysis, that is, the empirical method. Accordingly, I believe that penology is an empirical discipline, as opposed to the science of criminal law, which is a normative discipline. The study of penology is primarily concerned with the study of countermeasures and methods of criminal treatment of crimes, based on the scientific foundations provided by criminology.

1.2 Theory of Criminal Control

Every society is under the pressure of crimes, and punishment is a legal instrument designed to curb crimes. The criminal system and criminal facilities constitute a country's criminal control models and undertake the mission of controlling crimes.

As for the criminal control model, there has been a succession of the models of punishment deterrence and social defense throughout history. The utilitarianism of the classical school of criminology advocates the punishment deterrence model, especially Feuerbach, who is known for his theory of psychological coercion. The punishment deterrence model is premised on the criminals' free will and therefore, according to the utilitarian principle of harm avoidance, punishment deterrence is sufficient to curb crimes and psychological coercion is declared to be the only legitimate means to curb crimes. The criminal sociological school of the positivist school advocates the social defense model, such as the social prevention rules proposed by Ferri, who contrasts social prevention with social defense. Ferri states that legislators should apply social defense rules to eliminate the root causes of crimes. This, however, requires legislators to be committed to legislative reforms of individuals and social lives in economic, moral, political, and cultural contexts in their daily lives.[22] It should be noted that these two models of criminal control are not contradictory as each has its strengths and weaknesses. The punishment deterrence model is a relatively old model of crime control and has been used by rulers throughout history. But the mere punishment deterrence does not help. As Marx has said, "Generally speaking, punishment should be a means of probation or deterrence. But what right is there to punish a man to inspire and deter others? Moreover, history and statistical science have proved clearly that the use of punishment to inspire or deter the world has never succeeded since Cain (the firstborn son of Adam in the Christian Bible, who killed his brother Abel—A note from the citer)."[23] Crimes have their roots in society and to eliminate them, the transformation of society is required. It is in this sense that Lenin points out that it is far more important to change the social and political systems to prevent crimes than to adopt punitive measures.[24] It is in this sense that the

[22] See [2], p. 48.
[23] See [14], p. 578.
[24] See [15], p. 360.

criminal sociological school while denying the criminal deterrence model, proposes the social defense model, and, in a broader sense, social measures to combat crimes, which is true of significance. It is under the influence of the criminal sociological school that the social defense movement is launched in the modern West. One of the advocates of the social defense movement, the famous French criminologist Mare Ancel, points out in his book titled *Social Defense: A Modern Approach to Criminal Problems* that the term "social defense" is so widespread and its use is becoming more frequent, which inevitably leads to many different meanings.

In its original sense, "social defense" refers to the protection of society from the violation of crimes. For a long time, social defense has been based on a harsh penal system against crimes and often referred to as the "necessity of social defense". People referred to as such only because they intended to create the basis and justify establishing a complete criminal system. In this way, however, "social defense" lost its true value. In the nineteenth century, and particularly in the late nineteenth century, with the development of the humanities and the emergence of criminology and penology, the purpose and rationality of the penal system began to be questioned. It became clear then that social protection (social defense in the strict sense) was not only embedded in the group of "penalty–punishment", that criminals were not homogeneous but diverse, and that there were many other highly valuable and not necessarily response (feedback) approaches, in addition to the penal codes that defined what was illegal and what was punishable. It was at this point that the term "social defense" took on a new meaning, obtained a new value and a certain autonomy over criminal law and the punishment system. What followed was a great intellectual movement which, on the one hand, attacked the traditional, purely retaliatory legal provisions and, on the other hand, actively sought new ways to protect society as a whole and individuals. This movement, which was unsatisfied with the status quo, determined to reform it and advocated humanity, was the social defense movement in the modern sense, and the meaning of "social defense" contained therein.[25] As Ancel has said, the social defense movement emerging in the late nineteenth century is a product of the thought of the criminal sociological school. The criminal sociological school believes that the purpose of punishment is to defend society. Thus, social defense in its original sense refers to the protection of society from crimes. Lombroso states that crime is inevitable, and society needs to eradicate and punish crimes so that they do not impose harm to society. Only then does punishment fulfil its utilitarian purpose. Lombroso also asserts that there is no basis for punishment other than natural necessity and the right to self-defense. He further explains in layman's terms that there is no need to ask whether it is the nature of the beast to eat people. Therefore, whenever a beast is seen to eat a man, it is to be killed. The same principle of self-defense applies to the confinement of the mentally ill. Punishment must be based on self-defense, and there is no room for objection.[26] Ferri also considers social defense as the most important and immediate task of criminal justice. He is a fierce critic of the traditional penal system, arguing that it cannot effectively

[25] See [16], pp. 5–6.

[26] See [17], p. 94.

punish crimes to defend society and cannot effectively assume the responsibility of social defense. Later in 1889, Liszt, Prince and Hamel founded the International Society of Penal Law, which strongly advocated the theory of social defense. After the Second World War, the protection of human dignity and respect for individuals arose a widespread concern. In 1945, Gramatica founded the Center of Studies on Social Defense in Genes, which held its first international conference in San Remo in 1947 and its second in Liége in 1949 and established the International Society for Social Defense, of which Gramatica was the president. Gramatica was heavily influenced by the positivist school and in 1961 published *The Principles of Social Defense*, reflecting a view of social defense that Ancel considered being extreme. Gramatica recommended that criminal law be consigned to the dustbin of history and advocated to replace criminal law with a social defense law whose ultimate purpose, he believed, was to adapt individuals to the social order, not to sanction their behaviors. Gramatica also called for abolishing the basic concepts of criminal law, such as crimes, punishments, and responsibilities, and replacing them with concepts such as physical detriments, security measures and anti-sociability; and replacing judges with experts. Gramatica argued that crime was predetermined, and the state had no right to punish criminals. He advocated that criminals should not be punished but re-socialized and improved through medical and preventive methods. Gramatica's theory of the social defense has been criticized from all sides as being too extreme. In this case, Ancel's new theory of social defense emerged. Ancel summarized the three basic ideas of social defense movement as follows: (1) The theory of social defense begins with the critical research, or even the questioning, of the existing system that fight against crimes. From the point of view of historical development, this is how the theory of social defense arises. People also remember that the social defense theory evolves directly from the "rise of positivism" at the end of the last century. The blunt criticism of the existing system is one of the most solid elements of social defense theory. (2) Social defense theory has always advocated the unification of all human sciences and the multidisciplinary study of the phenomenon of crime. From the very beginning, it rejected the traditional notion of emphasizing the study of the phenomenon of crime only through criminal law and jurists, and the traditional idea that solving problems through the exclusive right. From the outset, the theory of social defense established the necessary links with the study of criminology and the development of crime. (3) The theory of social defense hopes to utilize its scientific critique of the existing system and its cooperation with the humanities to build a new system of criminal policy based on the following two complementary guiding ideologies: on the one hand, strong rejection of the traditional retaliatory punishment system. The social defense movement has therefore been an anti-criminal or at least non-criminal (i.e., excluding criminal) movement from the very beginning. On the other hand, it is determined to protect rights, defend human and improve human values. This is what one might call the humanism of the social defense movement.[27] Ancel claimed it as a new theory of social defense, and the "new" was mainly reflected in the following aspects: (1) It is distinct from the classical school of criminology. Ancel opposes

[27] See [16], pp. 30–31.

the classical school's views on criminal responsibility and punishment, arguing that the classical school's theory, which requires punishment to be adapted to the criminal behaviors, fails to regard the individual characteristics of the criminals, and is wrong to regard that the criminal behaviors are absolutely retaliatory. According to Ancel, the basis and measurement of criminal responsibility is not the behavior but the actor, who should be treated humanely, namely, the actor should not be subjected to compensatory, retaliatory punishment, but rather non-retaliatory sanctions and non-punitive methods whose ultimate goal is to prevent crimes and thus reintegrates the actor into society. (2) It is different from the criminal sociological school. Ancel is against the determinism of the positivist school but recognizes to a large extent the freedom of the human will, so he disagrees with the traditional social defense theory that opposes the theory of moral responsibility and instead embraces it. Ancel retains the concept of responsibility ability and empowers it in a more important position than that in the traditional institution. Ancel regards the responsibility ability as everyone's intrinsic feeling of taking responsibility, including criminals, and such psychological factor is a necessary basis for anti-criminal struggles to reintegrate criminals into society; at the same time, he strongly opposes the positivist theory of born criminals, arguing that criminal policy influenced by this concept is to primarily isolate dangerous criminals. Ancel askes to provide criminals opportunities to repent during the process of re-socializing criminals. Ancel also disagrees with the positivist view that signs of crimes can be found among future or potential criminals, arguing that crime is, first and foremost, a manifestation of the criminals' personalities and that the focus should be on studying their personalities. He advocates a dynamic theory of crime, which explores the diverse causes of criminal behaviors the moment when criminals are determined to commit crimes. The traditional theory of social defense is negative in the sense that it focuses on sanctioning and treating crimes to defend society. Ancel holds that education rather than punishment should be the first consideration for all kinds of abnormal people or criminals. The view is positive in the sense that it expresses the characteristics of the policy centered on the right of rehabilitation. (3) It is distinct from Gramatica's social defense theory. Ancel opposes Gramatica's argument for the abandonment of penology, firmly upholding the doctrine of a legally prescribed punishment for a specified crime, and the revision of penal codes based on the various conceptions of a sound criminal policy, so that this movement can be unified into penal codes to guarantee the freedom and rights of those who should be reintegrated into society. At the same time, Ancel also disagrees with Gramatica's monism of security measures and advocates reforming the existing penal system (abolishing the death penalty and improving the treatment of criminals) by merging penalties and security measures into a single system of criminal sanctions and choosing penalties or security measures based on the adaption to the type of act or the necessity of the actor. To sum up, the new social defense theory advocated by Ancel is centered on the humanitarian criminal policy movement, which recognizes the right of criminals to be reintegrated into society, the obligation of society to reintegrate criminals into society, and the highest form of humanitarian is reforming criminals into new people to reintegrate into society through education and rehabilitation. To this end, Ancel proposes a new attitude to criminals: on the one hand, considering the personality of criminals and, at the same time, revising the system of sanctions, to modernize the system of penalties and the content of statutory sentences so that they play a better role in educating criminals and especially preventing crimes than it currently does.[28] It should be noted that the introduction of the theory of social defense, which gets rid of a purely punitive concept of punishment, is of significance for the improvement of the penal system. In civil law countries, the theory of social defense also has profound influences. However, the social defense movement did not achieve the expected results. Since the 1970s, changes in the crime itself have been in opposition to this movement that humanizes and decriminalizes the criminal justice system. Over the past 20 years, crime has increased significantly and existed in new forms. Criminals have become younger, and crimes have been more organized and internationalized. Meanwhile, crimes have become increasingly violent. In this context, there has been a loss of confidence in the social defense movement, which has been severely criticized, and in some countries, there has been a return to harsh legal sanctions on crimes.[29] Thus, the theory of social defense, while novel and attractive, is very difficult to put into practice. An empirical approach that views crime as a "pathological-related" and "public health problem" is being overly optimistic because it has enormous impacts on the extensive, varied and culturally deep-rooted phenomena.[30] Therefore, I believe that the model of criminal control should be a combination of penal deterrence and social defense.

China also has to choose a model of criminal control. The transition from a planned economic system to a market-oriented economic system has brought about drastic changes in the economic relations of society and has triggered changes in all aspects of society. To adapt to this situation, the model of criminal control should be reconstructed, and the basic idea is to change from an ideal model of criminal control to a realistic model. Under the planned economy system, the single economic property relations characterized by "large and public" (first, people's commune enjoys large scale; second, people's commune enjoys a high degree of public ownership) have shaped a sluggish social landscape. Based on the proposition that private ownership of the means of production is the general root cause of crimes, it is hoped that the establishment of a system of public ownership of the means of production will eradicate the root causes of crimes and lead to an ideal crime-free world. This is expressed in criminal law in the form of the elimination of crimes as the goal model of criminal control. In China's jurisprudence academia, the ideas of eliminating crimes are often found in various theoretical works on criminology and criminal policy. For example, when discussing the aims of criminal policy, Chinese scholars point out that there is a difference between capitalist and socialist scholars as to the specific aims of criminal policy, and even completely opposite in terms of nature. According to capitalist scholars, criminal policy aims to reduce crimes and minimize the scope of their existence. Scholars in socialist countries, nevertheless, hold that the aim of criminal policy is to gradually reduce and finally eliminate crimes from society. This difference

[28] See [18], pp. 591–592.

[29] See [11], p. 4.

[30] See [13], p. 36.

is based on a different understanding of the nature of the crime. Capitalist scholars, drawing on the well-known views of sociology in capitalist countries, consider crimes to be eternal and inevitable phenomena that cannot be eliminated from society, while scholars in socialist countries consider crimes to be historical phenomena that do not always exist and are not eternal. Crimes begin to appear in slave societies and will be eliminated in communist societies, and they are phenomena specific to class societies. These scholars also believe that the phenomenon of crime in socialist societies will gradually decrease and be eliminated in communist societies. Thus, in the view of scholars of socialist countries, the criminal policy has two goals: one is the immediate and regular goal of gradually reducing crimes, and the other is the long-term goal of gradually reducing crimes and eventually eliminating them from society.[31] The overall purpose of Chinese criminal policy is also considered to be the ultimate goal of crime elimination. For example, Chinese scholars have pointed out that China's criminal policy is formulated on the basis of the purpose of crime prevention, crime reduction and even crime elimination, and thus in implementation, whether it is conducive to crime prevention, crime reduction and even crime elimination becomes an important criterion for evaluating whether a certain criminal policy or the implementation of criminal policy is appropriate.[32] Since the goal of criminal control is to eliminate crimes, penalties are over-invested at the cost of achieving this goal. This ideal model of criminal control has not proved to be successful, mainly because the crime rate has not been reduced as much as desired and the number of major cases remains high, not to mention the elimination of crimes. The excessive use of particularly heavy penalties has led to an invisible devaluation of their effects. There are two issues worth considering: (1) the social function of crime. In the past, we used to regard crime only as a manifestation of class struggle, define crime in a political sense and negatively evaluate it in the political sense; or regard crime as an evil, interpret crime in the ethical sense and give it a negative moral evaluation. In fact, this view may not be comprehensive. As a social phenomenon, crime is a product of the interaction of social, psychological, and physical factors, and its existence has a certain social inevitability. Therefore, until this social inevitability disappears, the elimination of crime is only a fantasy. Moreover, in the sense of functional analysis, the existence of crime has its rationality as crime provides a certain social tension for society to leap in the alternating changes between order and disorder, and crime and non-crime. As the famous French sociologist Dürkheim has said, crime is normal in the sense of the generation of criminal behaviors, that is, society cannot force all social members to obey its orders unanimously; otherwise, society will inhibit individual contributions to society. If society is to remain flexible and adapt to new changes, violations of social norms are bound to occur.[33] Especially when social institutions or value norms lag behind social life, crimes, as a violation of social institutions or value norms, often become a precursor for social changes, in its unique form influence the development of society, and eventually cause changes

[31] See [12], p. 381.

[32] See [10], p. 68.

[33] See [19], p. 160.

in the concept of crime. Crime will lift themselves from the shackles of crimes in the sense of legal norms and complete the historical leap from crime to non-crime. For example, under the planned economy, long-distance trafficking and the opening of private factories are regarded as a crime of speculation; the receipt of remuneration for part-time work by scientific and technical personnel is regarded as a crime of bribery and should be sanctioned by law. It is a large number of such so-called criminal acts that constantly impact the system of planned economy and play a catalytic role in the process of the transition from a planned economic system to a market-oriented economic system. Therefore, to correctly evaluate the social function of crime, we should get rid of the wrong ideology of taking class struggle as the key link, insist on understanding and analyzing crimes under the guidance of dialectical materialism, and establish the concept of relativity of crimes. (2) the social cost of punishment. As a means of punishing crimes, punishment requires material support: the operation of the criminal system (including legislation and justice) requires a large amount of human and material resources, and the maintenance of criminal facilities is inseparable from material conditions. Prisons, for example, are a physical manifestation of the power of the state (primarily the power to impose penalties). Therefore, although penalties can produce positive social benefits (let us not talk about the negative effects of penalties) as they inhibit crimes, the achievement of social benefits of penalties is not costless, and it requires social costs. There is a problem with the effective allocation of penal resources. US scholars Robert Court and Thomas Yolen point out through their economic analysis of punishment that the optimal deterrent effect is not to eradicate all crimes because the cost of doing so is high and the social benefits will continue to decline. Policymakers need to allocate limited resources. The goal of deterrence is sought to be achieved at the lowest cost, that is, the goal is achieved in an efficient manner. Thus, in penology, we aim to minimize the direct and indirect costs of crimes and the costs of operating the criminal justice system.[34] The US scholar Gary S. Becker analyzes that the total social cost of punishment is the cost of criminals adds the cost of others or subtracts the gains of other members. Fines are equal to the gains of other members in addition to the costs of collection, and thus, as a transfer payment, the social cost of fines is approximately equal to zero, because other costs are also compromised. Therefore, the social cost of probation, imprisonment and other punishments usually exceeds the cost of criminals. For ease of calculation, Becker writes the social cost according to the cost criminals as: $f' = bf$. Here, f' denotes the social cost and b denotes the conversion factor from f to f'. The value of b varies considerably for various penalties. For fines, $b \approx 0$; for interrogation, probation, parole, imprisonment, and most other punishments, $b > 1$; for borstals and adult incarceration, the value of b is extremely high, and for interrogation or adult parole, b is very close to 1.[35] In the United States, the debate over drug legalization versus illegalization is instructive for us to understand the social cost of punishment. Advocates of drug legalization argue that anti-drug laws have even more negative effects than the drugs themselves: because the law prohibits the supply and sale of

[34] See [20], p. 755.

[35] See [21], p. 68.

drugs, but it does not prevent the demand and purchase of drugs. The price of drugs is staggeringly high, and the lucrative drug trade is seductive for people. According to the economist Milton Friedmann, "Much of the damage to society by drugs is caused by the perception of drugs as illegal." Legalization can eradicate this social cancer. If drugs were legal, the government could control the drug market and lower drug prices. Drug addicts could get their share of drugs through normal channels, and drug sellers would give up drug selling or turn to other businesses because they would not make much profit from drugs. Just as the repeal of prohibition law led to the disappearance of bootleggers, so the elimination of drug law would lead to the disappearance of drug dealers. The Princeton University professor Ethan A. Nadelmann estimates that in a single year, the US federal and local governments spend about $8 billion directly on drug control, and much more indirectly. Not only would legalizing drugs save huge amounts of money, but the government could increase state revenues by imposing heavy taxes on legal drugs and use the savings to publicize the benefits of drug rehabilitation and treat addicts. Professor Dershwitz of Harvard Law School says, "If we already consider the sale of alcohol and tobacco to be sinless, why should we consider the production of drugs to be sinful?" Democrat congressman Engel asks the advocates that if drugs were legalized, what types of drugs could be included on the legal list? By what means would drugs be sold? Would be there an age limit for drug users? What doses of drugs would drug users be allowed to buy? If these questions were not answered satisfactorily, then talking of drug legalization was just bullshit. Opponents of drug legalization suspect that legalization will eliminate drug-related crimes. This is because a flat tax administered by the government does not mean that the entire black-market trade will be eliminated. Because drug users will gradually be unable to work, they may not even be able to pay the low prices stipulated by the government, and theft, robbery and prostitution will be inevitable to get the money to buy drugs. In today's society, there is a natural link between drugs and crimes. The legalization of drugs will wipe out previous achievements in banning drugs. It is not possible to admit that drugs cause crimes and at the same time declare them legal. The legalization of drugs will jeopardize the dignity, sanctity, and consistency of the law.[36] In the United States, the debate on the legalization of drugs is far from over. Whether the benefits of legalization outweigh the disadvantages, or the disadvantages outweigh the benefits cannot be tested by social experiments because the costs borne by society are too high. As far as I am aware, the arguments in favor of legalization are difficult to sustain, but the economic costs raised by legalization advocates are a matter of concern. The analysis of the social causes of punishment is therefore vital, and this is where the economic analysis of the law is applied in the study of punishment. As the Chinese scholar Sun Lin says, the study of legal economics will provide us with a new way of thinking to reconceptualize and evaluate the functions of laws. In fact, every law and every legal act has a problem concerning economic evaluation. The law itself is the most concentrated, specific, and comprehensive reflection of economic issues. In a sense, all legal issues are, in the final analysis, a reflection and requirement of economic relations, and every law

[36] See [22], pp. 212–213.

reflects the basic laws and principles of economics.[37] Although penalties are strongly political, they are also economic in nature. Of course, the economic perspective is not the only one; political analysis, the concept of justice and humanitarianism also matter. But the economic analysis of penalties remains instructive in that it leads us to recognize that penalties have a social cost and that a scientific model of criminal control maximizes the suppression of crimes with minimal criminal costs. In the past, when penalties were seen as a mere tool of dictatorship, the emphasis was on their political functions and thus little consideration was given to social costs, which could easily lead to incorrect applications and even the abuse of heavy penalties. In conclusion, as a social investment, penalties are not only productive but also expendable, and therefore the economic concept of penalty should be established. Based on these two considerations, it is logical to conclude that criminal law is incomplete and the last resort. In other words, as a social control instrument, criminal law has limited functions and the task of maintaining social order cannot be left entirely to criminal law. In my view, the criminal control model should be based on the concept of the relativity of crime and the economy of punishment. The aim is not to eliminate crimes but to control them within the bounds of social tolerance to the maximum extent with the minimum social cost. It is therefore necessary to break away from the notion of heavy penalties and pan-criminalization and to establish a criminal control model that achieves the optimized allocation of penal resources and the best results in suppressing crimes.

In the context of criminal control, the issue of criminal policy deserves careful study. The criminal policy is the soul and core of criminal law, and criminal law is the ordinance and boilerplate of criminal policy. Therefore, criminal policy has a direct guiding role in the formulation and application of criminal law. The criminal policy is always based on a certain crime situation and is adjusted and amended promptly according to the situation of social development and changes in crime and there is no such thing as a criminal policy that is set in stone. Then, what is the main criminal policy we are currently using in fighting against crimes? Obviously, it is the policy of "enforcing the law severely and quickly", which is introduced in the early 1980s. It should be said that this criminal policy was proposed against a specific historical background and was justified by the historical conditions of the time. In the early 1980s, after the end of a long period of political turmoil, China entered a new historical period in which democracy and the rule of law were strengthened. However, due to the relative weakening of social control, criminal activities such as murders, arson, explosions, rapes and robberies, which seriously endangered social security, were rampant in some places. Under such circumstances, the Political and Legal Affairs Committee of the Central Committee of the Communist Party of China held a national symposium on political and legal work in five major cities in May 1981, establishing the basic policy of comprehensive management of social security and putting forward the criminal policy of severely and speedily punishing a very small number of criminals who seriously endangered social security, such as murders, arson, explosions, rapes and robberies, following the law. In

[37] See [23], p. 2.

August 1983, following the deployment of the Central Committee of the Communist Party of China and the Standing Committee of the National People's Congress Decision on Severe Punishment of Criminals Seriously Endangering Social Security, a nationwide campaign was launched to crack down on crimes seriously endangering social security as per the law and in a strict and expeditious manner. This criminal policy was later extended to apply to all crimes, including economic crimes. It should be said that the introduction and implementation of the criminal policy of dealing with crimes with severity and speed following the law had a positive effect on the maintenance of social security at that time, resulting in a decrease in the incidence of criminal offenses. However, after that, the number of criminal offenses has increased significantly, and the momentum was still developing. In particular, cases of bombing, murder, robbery, and theft, which posed great threats to public security, continued to occur, seriously threatening the lives and property of the people. Particularly noteworthy was the resurgence of gang crimes. Some criminal gangs were running rampant in the countryside, playing the tyrant in a locality, committing the crime and acting with arrogance, and some have become organizations of a triad nature. These criminal activities seriously endangered social stability and economic development.[38] The same was true of economic crimes, which show a tendency to grow constantly. Therefore, severe crackdowns could only temporarily curb crimes, and criminal crackdowns were only a solution to treat the symptoms but not the root causes. Moreover, the objective of achieving fundamental improvements in social security, as proposed at the time, was also worth reflecting on in retrospect. In fact, social security should pursue a dynamic balance. As long as criminal activities did not cause social unrest, and social change and development-maintained vitality, social security should be regarded as basically normal. Likewise, the lack of specific quantifiable indicators to achieve radical improvements was at the same time unrealistic and only a wish. The criminal policy of "enforcing the law severely and quickly" has been put in place for more than a decade, and it is time to theoretically rethink the criminal policy and consider appropriate adjustments to criminal policy. First of all, we should have a scientific understanding of the current social situation in China and correctly analyze the crime situation. It should be said that the current sharp rise in crime is an abnormal phenomenon, but it is a by-product of the economic system reform currently underway in China. This is because reform is a profound social change, and in this process of social change and the advancement of the old and new systems, it is inevitably accompanied by social shocks, from economic to political, from the economic base to the superstructure, and from ideology to the psychological bearing. In the economic sphere, in particular, the transformation of the old and new systems cannot be achieved overnight; rather, it requires a rather long conversion process. Therefore, when the reform of the economic system reaches a certain level, there is bound to be a period when the two systems coexist. During this period, the two systems co-exist and influence each other, with elements of the new system appearing more and more in the economic operation, but it is not possible to replace the old system completely and immediately; a considerable part of the

[38] See [24], p. 98.

old system cannot but to exist and operate for a certain period. This dictates that problems and contradictions will inevitably arise from the reforms, and that a certain degree of disorder will occur in economic activities. As a result, crimes of all types will increase. To a certain extent, the current massive increase in crimes in China is a necessary price for the transition of the system and the transformation of society. The development of crime has its own laws and does not depend on human will. Although penalties can influence and restrain the development of crimes to a certain extent, it cannot be expected that the negative impact of crimes on society can be fundamentally eliminated through severe penalties. Therefore, I agree with the view that there should be a greater psychological tolerance for the problem of crimes, that tolerance should be greater, and that the standard of normal social security should be set more broadly. It is a normal situation as long as criminal activities do not reach an uncontrollable level and thus seriously affect economic development and social progress.[39] Firstly, from the perspective of the law of crime evolution, the role of severe and speedy punishments is limited and can only be used as a specific guideline for dealing with crimes for a while but cannot be regarded as a permanent and foolproof solution to the problem of social security and crimes. Secondly, the deterrent effect of penalties should be correctly understood. According to the law, severity refers to the severity of the penalty, and speed refers to the timeliness of the penalty. The implementation of severe and speedy penalties is still mainly dependent on the deterrent effect of penalties to curb crimes. The question of the perception of the deterrent effect of penalties is involved herein. I believe that penalties do have a certain deterrent effect, but it is limited and should not be overly relied upon. The conclusion that punishment is limited in its effectiveness is imposed by the fact, and as the Italian penologist Ferri pointed out, it was exactly because of the failure of every previous application of punitive statutes in preventing crimes that the success of the application of every punitive statute proved this point as what Jeremy Bentham mentioned. However, this conclusion was in direct opposition to public opinion, and even to the views of judges and legislators. When criminal phenomena arose and developed, legislators, jurists and the public only thought of simple and illusory remedies, thinking of penal codes or new repressive laws and orders. But even if such an approach was effective (doubtful), it inevitably enabled people to ignore more effective, albeit more difficult, preventive, and societal remedies. Ferri stressed that punishment was only a secondary means of social self-defense and that the treatment for crimes should be adapted to the actual factors that led to them. Furthermore, since the social factors that lead to crime are the easiest to eliminate and ameliorate, we agree with Princeton that "For social ills, we should seek for social cures".[40] At the same time, the severity of punishment is not unlimited but is bounded by ethical factors. Generally speaking, punishment and morality should be consistent; punishment supports and backs morality, that is, criminal law has a moral mission. Likewise, morality also underpins punishment and serves as its moral foundation, but only moderate punishment can be reconciled with morality. Excessive and abusive

[39] See [25].

[40] Ferri [26], pp. 70 and 71.

punishment not only does not support morality but even corrupts social morality. It is in this sense that I agree with the Soviet penologist A.Л. Lemmenson's assertion that punishment, however brutal the method, undermines the moral foundations of society and causes serious damage to society which cannot be remedied by harsher menaces to some wobblers.[41] It is generally accepted that the criminal policy of "severity and speed" following the law has a limited applicable object and does not apply to all crimes. It applies mainly to criminals who have committed serious offenses against the public order such as murders, arson, robberies, rapes, explosions, poisoning and hooligan gangs. Other common criminals are not included in the list of offenses to be dealt with seriously and speedily.[42] However, crimes are interrelated, and the application of penalties is also interlinked, and there is a question of boats going up with the level of the water. The imposition of severer and speeder penalties for criminals who seriously endanger social security will inevitably influence the application of the whole penalties towards heavier sentences. This can be seen from the development of criminal legislation and criminal justice in China after the implementation of the heavy criminal policy. In terms of criminal legislation, the number of offenses for which the death penalty can be applied is increasing. According to statistics, the number of offenses punishable by death under the Criminal Law in 1979 was 28, whereas from June 1981 to the time of publication of this book (December 1995), 38 offenses punishable by death has been added by separate criminal laws, which already exceeds the number of offenses punishable by death prescribed in the Criminal Law. It is no wonder that alarms were raised about the "rapidly expanding death penalty legislation" and that it was seen as a "dangerous trend".[43] In criminal justice, the severity of penalties has generally increased, particularly the application of the death penalty. Short-term liberty penalties are applied less frequently, and probation is applied even less frequently. In stark contrast, the number of criminal offenses, especially major cases, remains high and the social security situation remains critical. Based on the above analysis of the crime situation and the effectiveness of penalties, I believe that the criminal policy of punishing crimes "severely and quickly" following the law has been implemented for more than 10 years and, although it has achieved some results, it was under the expected social effect of fighting against crimes and thus should be considered for appropriate adjustments. We should discard the ancient maxim of "heavy-handedness in troubled times" and replace it with a scientific criminal policy. In particular, China is currently in the process of modernization amid institutional and social transformation, it is even more important to start from the objective laws of crime evolution and adhere to the criminal policy of combining punishment and leniency on the premise of implementing comprehensive treatment of crimes. By comprehensive management, it means that prevention and punishment are required, with particular emphasis on the prevention of crimes. At present, if China is to fundamentally curb the surge in crimes, the way out lies in furthering the reform of the economic system, accelerating the process of social modernization,

[41] See [27], p. 356.

[42] See [28], p. 246.

[43] Bao [29].

improving social integration, tiding over the period of social imbalance, and creating a favorable social environment for reducing and controlling crimes. At the same time, in punishing crimes, we must, on the one hand, strictly adhere to the principle of equality before the law and effectively grasp the scope of criminal punishment; on the other hand, we must make specific analyses, treat people differently, impose appropriate sentences, pay attention to the full implementation of the policy of leniency and severity, minimize the application of death penalty and pay attention to overcoming the tendency towards heavier sentences. Through effective penal activities, efforts should be made to keep crimes within the tolerable range of society.

1.3 Theory of Criminal Correction

In a society, the criminal phenomenon is inevitable. Where there is a crime, there are criminals. Therefore, the attitude towards criminals marks the civilization degree of society. In penology, criminal correction enjoys an important position.

The idea of criminal correction originates from the positivist school of criminology, and neither retributivism nor utilitarianism has a concept of correction for criminals. Retributivism sees punishment as retribution and criminals deserve to be punished. According to retributivism, criminals should be punished because they have only themselves to blame. This view that criminals "earn" the punishment themselves determines an obligation, a debt owed to criminals that must be repaid. At the same time, it is a social debt. This contains moral obligation. Because all law-abiding citizens are threatened by crimes, the debt (the obligation to punish) must be recovered. In short, the fundamental punishment theory of retributivism is based on the principle that criminals deserve to be punished, and they have earned the punishments for their previous transgressions. Just as rightful punishment is seen as a way of achieving equality—a fair balance between criminals and society—by eliminating the illicit gains (the criminal behaviors) through a mandatory cost (punishment). This standpoint is based on moral judgement.[44] It follows that retributivism sees the criminal punishments of criminals as the payment of social debts and has no idea of correcting criminals. Utilitarianism, on the other hand, emphasizes primarily the deterrence of criminals, and although Beccaria and Feuerbach advocate both general and individual prevention, general prevention holds the dominant position of their thinking, and it is not even too much to classify the two scholars as general precautionalists. According to Beccaria, penalties should primarily be proportionate to the social harms of acts. Thus, only the difference of behavior, not the difference of the actor, is considered. As the Chinese scholar Huang Feng puts it, Beccaria argues that by establishing a ladder of crimes and punishments and symmetrizing them, the motives that induce people to commit crimes can be effectively curbed. In fact, it is not so simple. to prevent criminals from committing crimes again, it is necessary to take different corrective measures according to each individual's personality traits

[44] See [30], p. 94.

and degree of antisocial tendencies, rather than focusing solely on the harmful consequences of criminal behaviors.[45] Clearly, the concept of correction is absent from Beccaria's theory. The positivist school of criminology introduces criminal correction into the theory by shifting the focus from the behavior to the actor. The object of correction is the actor, and since the positivist school stresses the criminal, the idea of criminal correction can only be found in the positivist school. In the positivist school, Lombroso introduces the idea of deprivation of criminal ability based on the theory of born criminal. Deprivation of criminal ability means incarcerating criminals, isolating them from society to prevent them from committing crimes. It should be said that the deprivation of criminal ability is an integral part of individual prevention, but it is negative and does not contain the positive part of criminal correction. Although Ferri has also emphasized the deprivation of criminal ability and even suggested that criminals who were born criminals or committed crimes due to illness should not be incarcerated for a while, but until they were able to adapt to normal social life. This is the idea of indeterminacy. But Ferri began to propose the concept of correction, which came from treatment because Ferri often compared crimes to diseases, viewing social prevention of crimes as public health and the individual prevention of criminals as personal health. Moreover, according to Ferri, some criminals were mentally ill, and punishment for these criminals would not help, and they should be treated. For criminals, this was a criminal correction, as opposed to general treatment. Therefore, Ferri pointed out that the segregation of felons should be managed scientifically the same as psychiatric hospitals. The management of such institutions must be scientific, and the correction of criminals must also be scientific because felonies often manifested the pathology of the individual criminals.[46] By the time of Liszt, a clearer philosophy of correction was developed, which was reflected in a Liszt famous statement that "correct the criminal who can be corrected and prevent criminal who cannot be corrected from doing badly".

The introduction of the concept of criminal correction brings about a fundamental change in the way prison is viewed, which leads to the prison reform movement. The history of prisons as an adjunct to punishment is as long as the history of punishment. In the early days, the main forms of punishment were death penalty and corporal punishment, supplemented by banishment. The dominance of these punishments dictated that prisons were not yet as important as they are in modern society. For example, exile, also known as banishment, was the expulsion of the criminal from a tribe, nation or country. Banishment became a way of dealing with many social problems: beggars, vagrants and other poor people were expelled from villages, and criminals and potential criminals were expelled from their communities. Exile embraced the idea of individual prevention for the purification of society, but it could not yet be described as a form of correction. It was not until the eighteenth century that imprisonment became a major form of punishment in Europe. Before this, imprisonment was only for the purpose of detention. The original prison was

---

[45] See [31], p. 125.

[46] See [32], pp. 51 and 52.

a simple, chained place of detention where prisoners awaited their public punishments. Modern imprisonment was documented to appear in the mid to late sixteenth century. This was because of the sharp rise in the number of imprisonments during this period, and the widespread of reformist ideas (concern for the relief of the poor). Both phenomena, together with the influence of religious schools (especially Calvinism), led to increasingly strong criticism of corporal sentences and the death penalty. The consequence was that temporary custodial sentence (initially out of mercy and later fixed in law) began to replace the corporal sentence and death penalty, and the idea of changing criminals from bad to good began to replace the idea of retribution, a shift in penal thinking that was made possible partly due to the relief of the poor in Britain and the Netherlands, but mostly due to the worrying social development of the time: namely, beggars, and vagrants surged, and, in Britain, there was a shift from farming to animal husbandry, which left many previously employed in agriculture unemployed. In Europe, it was mainly due to the Crusades. After the end of the Crusades, in almost all European countries there were a large number of ex-warriors who became vagabonds, thieves, and beggars. The above-mentioned developments in Britain led to the recognition of the fact that social problems could no longer be solved by the corporal punishment and death penalty alone, but more primarily by what we today call labor-employment schemes. Thus, in 1555, King Edward VI of Britain, at the instigation of the Church, set up a workhouse (later called the "House of Correction") in his castle, where vagrants, beggars, prostitutes, and some thieves should be firstly accustomed to working to be better reintegrated into society in this way. Thus, the idea of punishment for the sake of punishment took a back seat. In the following years, the reformatory developed into a model for many other places of reeducation through labor. Influenced by the British model, a man's reformatory was built in Amsterdam in 1595. These institutions were called "reformatories" because people hoped that those who lacked upbringing would be accommodated and accustomed to normal life through strict discipline. Accordingly, a number of workhouses were set up in the reformatory, as in the detention center. The staff consisted of several workplace supervisors, a teacher, and a doctor. Also, a labor bonus was specifically established for the criminals of longer terms of imprisonment to encourage them. In 1603, with the introduction of the "solitary confinement" system, the size of the prison was increased.[47] However, throughout the eighteenth century, the rapid development of society facilitated by the commodity economy led to an increase in the number of crimes and a surge in the prison population, while the material conditions did not allow for a simultaneous improvement and increase in prison facilities. This situation resulted in overcrowding, poor living conditions, poor hygiene, the epidemic of diseases, intermingling of prisoners, and serious cross-contamination. The initiator of prison reform is John Howard, an British penologist. Given the poor condition of prisons at that time, Howard made the first comprehensive survey of prisons in Britain, and examined many prisons in France, Germany, Netherlands, and Belgium, and wrote a book *The State of the Prisons* in 1777, exposing the darkness of prisons, calling for and proposing the idea of prison reform. As the US scholars Richard

[47] See [33], pp. 2–4.

Hawkins and Geoffrey P. Alpert put it, Howard's work went viral. Two years later, his ideas were reflected in the Penitentiary Act in 1779. Howard's goals were reflected in one of his most famous mottos: "Mere penalties can hardly control criminals. Only strict discipline can discipline them." Howard's works and their impacts on Britain, Europe, and the United States led to the rehabilitation of criminals (what today might be called "correction").[48] In terms of the classical school of criminology, Beccaria delivered a powerful attack on the darkness of the feudal prison system, noting that as punishment became lenient, as misery and hunger were removed from the prison, as mercy and humanity blew through the doors and dominated the hard-hearted law enforcement officials, the law would be content to arrest on suspicion.[49] But Beccaria did not see prisons as places of correction. Bentham made a unique contribution to the development of modern prisons. In Bentham's time, prisoners were generally not held in prisons, but were mistreated or placed on prison ships (ships used as prisons) or transported to colonies and islands where they were held. Bentham opposed this practice, arguing that prisons should be placed in urban centers so that they would serve as a warning of the consequences of crime. Those lazy customs should be eliminated, and prisoners should learn to choose good occupations. Thus, Bentham designed a circular prison, believing that the shape of the prison building would make the inmates feel the moral restraint and the requirement of order. The term circular prison is derived from two Greek terms: "mortal" and "place of observation". It was originally conceived as a kind of factory for organizing labor. The main idea was that all workers would work under the supervision of a central supervisor, who sought omnipresent surveillance of workers' work. A circular building with outer walls linking the rooms and a surveillance tower in the middle would serve this purpose. The main function of the circular prison was to guide the prisoners to be aware of their situations as they were constantly visible, to ensure that power worked automatically. Thus, the circle prison played a role in supervising uninterruptedly, even during intermittent work. A perfect power should be inclined to abstain from the exercise of unnecessary acts. The instrument of construction should be a machine that created and ensured the use of a relationship of independent power. In short, prisoners must be under the control of a situation of power that they bear. To achieve this, simultaneous and uninterrupted surveillance by a single supervisor was inadequate and redundant: it was inadequate because prisoners knew they were under surveillance; it was redundant because the supervisor in fact needed not to supervise. In view of this situation, Bentham devised the principle that power must be visible and unverifiable. Visibility meant that prisoners' eyes were always filled with the tall shadow of the tower, the source of surveillance. Non-verifiability meant that prisoners could not prove with certainty that they were under surveillance at any given moment, yet they were certain that they were always supervised. The goal of Bentham to design the circular surveillance architecture was not to achieve the maximum human surveillance effect, but to achieve an effect that transcended the human and created

[48] See [30], p. 33.

[49] See [34], p. 17.

an illusion for prisoners that the supervisor was present everywhere (all the time).[50] While not widely accepted as a design per se, Bentham's philosophy was widely welcomed by prison administrators. Since Bentham was essentially a comfort-chair thinker, he did not know much about prisons, so his vision was not practical. All in all, Bentham was only an advocate of a new type of prison management system but not a practical contributor to the prison correctional system. In the positivist school of criminology, Lombroso focused on the practical investigation of prisons, on the basis of which he proposed a vision of prison reform. He argued that while the compartmentalized prison could segregate convicts and reduce the opportunities for contact among them, it was also very expensive and had a big disadvantage of creating inertia among convicts, making them automatic machines and erasing their human nature. Lombroso quoted Burins' saying that the purpose of compartmentalized prisons was to cut off the opportunity for inmates to learn from each other's misdeeds and to be influenced by the beneficial influence of good men. But the guards themselves, coming from the same place as the criminals, were only able to make a living in the prison, who were not different from prisoners, and seldom fulfilled their duties as guards. This led Lombroso to conclude that our conception of prison should be changed. Lombroso pointed out that the Irish system was the most praised by all the penologists who have been working on improving prisons. Lombroso described in detail the hierarchical prison system: the first time a person was imprisoned, he or she was given a life of deprivation for no more than nine months and no less than eight months. The person was given vulgar clothes and coarse food and should put the messy linen in order. The second level was common work, which was supervised extremely strictly. Prisoners were divided into four shifts, the suffering of which decreased according to the shift, and only those who worked hard and had good conduct could be promoted. Those who worked in the first class were paid nothing for their work but were only given some pocket money. Those who had 54 merit scores could gradually move up, with their pay increasing, and they became closer to reintegrating into society. Moving up from this level, the most liberal level was reached. The prisoner might work in the wilderness, wear his or her usual clothes, receive his or her salary, take several days off and has regular contacts with the outside world. At the end of his or her imprisonment, he or she could be temporarily liberal but should be supervised by the police constantly and would have to return to prison if mistakes were made. This graded system was highly appreciated by Lombroso, who believed that this method of gradual emancipation was suitable for criminals psychologically and economically because the restoration of freedom was like a dream for prisoners, and freedom was obtained through disciplinary methods so that society did not despise those who were released from prison, and the prisoners had a sense of self-confidence after being released from prisons. For Lombroso, the prison was not simply a place of retribution and punishment for criminals, but more importantly, a place of salvation for them. Therefore, Lombroso opposed the old-style prisons where criminals were locked up, and advocated education and reformation of prisoners in prisons so that prisons could gradually shift from closed style to open or

[50] See [30], pp. 38–39.

semi-open style, thus transforming prisons into a hospital for the treatment of criminals. Ferri also pointed out that the criminal system, based on the criminal theory and prison rules of the classical school, had the following defects: the establishment of absurd standards of moral responsibility; total disregard or neglect of the physio-psychological type of criminals; a gap between verdict and sentence on the one hand, and that between sentence and execution on the other hand, resulting in the abuse of amnesty; the serious outcome due to the degradation of prisoners in prisons and their interactions; millions of people sentenced to stupid and absurdly short prison terms; and the unstoppable increase in recidivism. Thus, Ferri pointed to the urgency of replacing the current penal system with one that was appropriate to the primary causes of crime, more effective in social defense, and at the same time mitigating the unwarranted harm caused to those it dealt with.[51] It was with the strong advocacy of the positivist school that prisons were transformed from the places where prisoners were passively held into the institutions for the correctional treatment of prisoners.

The term correction refers to the imprisonment of convicted persons by those legally entitled to do so, or to the monitoring institutions and the measures of treatment they impose.[52] The purpose of correction is to re-educate, retrain and treat the behavior of prisoners and to re-socialize them. The possibilities of correction are based on science. Correction is mainly the change of criminal personality, although the criminal personality is a stable psychological structure, it does not mean that the psychological structure is unchanged. In fact, it can be changed. The Chinese scholar Jiao Ke has discussed the scientific basis of the criminals to be reformed: (1) philosophical basis. The reformation of criminals, from the perspective of philosophical understanding, is essentially a process to change and correct the wrong and distorted understanding of the objective outside world in the minds of criminals for them to obtain the correct understanding. (2) physiological basis. In the criminal consciousness and psychological activity of criminals, although the unconditioned reflexes of criminals, based on innate genetics, play a role, and this role is considerable for some criminals (this more fixed neural connection can also still be improved and controlled by means of supervised education, drug treatment and social supervision), the decisive role in the criminal consciousness and psychological activity is played by conditioned reflex, namely the temporary neural connection built into the criminal's cerebral cortex. The conditioned reflex, or the temporary neural connection, is not, firstly, innate, but is formed during the life activities of criminals; secondly, it is not fixed, but is changed in response to changes in external conditions or environments, i.e., in response to external stimuli (first and second signals) and in response to changes in the intensity and frequency of the stimuli. Thus, according to Pavlov's doctrine, under certain conditions, this socially harmful temporary neural connection in the criminal's mind can be changed; and it is also modifiable and flexible. (3) psychological basis. The psychology of criminals can be reformed in principle, that is to say, the criminal mind can be eliminated, and a new, healthy psychological

---

[51] See [35], pp. 137 and 138.

[52] See [36], p. 27.

structure can be built on this basis. The criminal minds can be reformed and eliminated because most of their factors or components are formed under the influence and effect of many related factors, so they can be eliminated under the influence and effect of many related factors.[53] Furthermore, the correctability of human behaviors is based on the conclusion of the intrinsic mechanisms of human behavior revealed by behavioral science. The understanding of human behaviors is one of the most important elements of the understanding of human nature, and it can be argued that human nature can only be understood scientifically when the inner mechanisms of human behaviors are correctly revealed. There is no doubt that behavioral science is a historical milestone in the history of understanding human behaviors. Before this, behaviors were seen only as a human instinct, and there was no scientific revelation of the way people behaved. Some philosophers already had some intuitive understandings of the behavioral mechanisms. For example, in the sixteenth century, the well-known French philosopher Descartes argued that some spontaneous behaviors of living beings were explicit, and behaviors were sometimes related to explicit activities. Descartes had already postulated that behaviors were externally controllable.[54] In the nineteenth century, behaviorism emerged in the West as a trend and school of psychology conducted a great deal of research into the mechanisms underlying human behaviors, mainly from a physiological perspective. Modern research into human behaviors began at the turn of the century, represented by the experiments of the famous Russian physiologist Pavlov, who developed the theory of conditioned reflexes through extensive experiments on dogs. Pavlov studied the effects of the time interval between stimulus and reinforcer, the extent to which the multiple properties of the stimulus could be controlled, and the process by which conditioned stimuli lost their power to elicit a response when not reinforced, the process of which was called "fading."[55] It was the US psychologist Watson who truly developed behavioral research into an influential school of thought. Watson popularized Pavlov's "stimulus–response" principle, which held that all human behaviors were the result of conditioned reflexes that were learned later in life. In addition, he proposed that human learning behavior exhibited two main laws: the law of recurrent causes and the law of proximate causes. The former meant that the more frequently a response to a stimulus occurs, the more likely it was that the stimulus would occur again; the latter meant that the more recently a response to a stimulus occurred, the more likely it was that the stimulus would occur again. Watson's theory was known as the learning theory or psychology of learning. On this basis, the famous US psychologist Skinner proposed the operant behavior theory. He was not satisfied with the simple model of "stimulus–response" to explain all human behaviors. In his view, human behaviors could be divided into two categories, one being reflexive behaviors triggered by specific stimuli, which he called response behaviors. Most human behaviors, however, did not fall into this category, but into complex operant behaviors triggered by the environment. Operant behaviors were triggered by a variety of

[53] See [37], pp. 201–216.

[54] See [38], p. 45.

[55] See [38], p. 51.

stimuli present in the environment, and these stimuli were so numerous and complex that it was difficult to determine which ones triggered the behaviors. However, we could see that different environments produced different behaviors, and that changes in the environment caused changes in behaviors. Skinner argued that human behaviors were conditioned not only by the environment but also by reinforcement, namely by the consequences of the behaviors. Through extensive experiments with animals, Skinner found that there were three main types of reinforcement: (1) positive reinforcement, i.e., if a behavior brought about something that made the actor feel happy and satisfied, such as food, money, praise, love, etc., the actor would tend to repeat the behavior; (2) negative reinforcement, i.e., if a behavior removed something that made the actor feel unpleasant and disgusted, such as noise, cold, heat, electric shocks, scolding, etc., the actor would also tend to repeat the behavior; and (3) punishment, i.e., if a behavior resulted in something that made the actor unpleasant or removed something that made the actor pleasant, the actor would tend to terminate or avoid repeating the behavior; in other words, punishment was exactly the opposite of positive and negative reinforcement. Based on these findings, Skinner proposed that since human behaviors depended on the environment and reinforcers, human behaviors could be modified and controlled by changing the environment and using various reinforcers. Skinner therefore introduced the concept of "cultural design". Culture in this context refers to the social environment that shapes and sustains the behaviors of the people who live in it.[56] The cultural design is thus the selection and creation of a certain social environment following certain values, based on the principles of behavioral science. Clearly, in this sense, Skinner's behavioral science introduces a social field in which people can produce benefits. The findings of behavioral science have greatly enriched the understanding of the mechanisms inherent in human behaviors and have provided a scientific basis for the social control of human behaviors. Laws, including criminal laws, are an instrument of social control. As the famous US jurist Pound put it, "in the modern world, the law has become the principal instrument of social control".[57] The control of society by law, and in particular the control of society by criminal law, is achieved through the regulation of human behaviors, in which criminal correction plays an important role. The basic principles of behavioral science can therefore be used to reinterpret criminal behaviors and the correction as a means of controlling such behaviors, which enlighten us in a new way.

In Western countries, there are two main models of criminal correction: (1) the reintegration model. This model emphasizes the economic and social conditions that are the causes of crimes, arguing that the lack of appropriate life skills and lack of regular employment opportunities for criminals facilitate criminal behaviors. As such, the reintegration model revolves around planned reintegration training and a reintegration system that includes pre-release training, labor release, educational release, return to leave, halfway houses and social support systems. However, the reintegration model is difficult to implement because it requires job skills to enable

[56] See [39], p. 12.

[57] See [40], p. 10.

prisoners to compete in the labor market and some efforts to help them secure regular employment after release. But all this is difficult or beyond the control of the prison. As US scholars have argued: the rehabilitation of prisoners requires prisoners to be taught the basic skills, knowledge, and expertise (not just the right way of thinking) to ensure that they do not engage in criminal activities after release and that they are able to support themselves. For many prisoners, this will represent their first opportunity to live according to laws. Even after recognizing the need for correction, the concept of prisoner rehabilitation poses a second dilemma: how do we determine what work opportunities have been offered? When in-prison programs provide qualifications for some prisoners and rehabilitative education for others, it is not certain whether prisoners will be successfully reintegrated into society upon release. Clearly, prisoners should have access to decent jobs—which they often lack at the best of times—and they should have the opportunity not to be discriminated against because of their criminal records. However, even the best in-prison programs rarely change the level of unemployment, employment discrimination or the social acceptance of those leaving prison. The key elements of correctional success are often outside the control of correctional personnel.[58] For this reason, the return-to-society model has been a considerable failure in the United States. (2) the rehabilitation model. This model is based on the idea that criminals are fundamentally different from law-abiding citizens, that they may be sick, and their antisocial personalities should be treated for reasons that are intrinsic to the criminals themselves. Among most correctional facilities in the United States, there are many forms and treatments such as psychodrama, psychotherapy, communication analysis, reality therapy, behavior modification therapy, therapy groups, among others. Of interest is the extensive use of behavior therapy in criminal correction. The rationale that behaviors are treatable is that if all behaviors are subject to learned laws, then abnormal behaviors are learned as well, and this is what behavioral psychology insists on. Abnormal behaviors are not pathological; they are learned in the same way as so-called normal behaviors; they differ from the latter only in that they are non-adaptive.[59] In criminal correction, the main methods of behavioral treatment are cross-inhibition and systematic desensitization. Cross-inhibition, sometimes referred to as counterconditioning, is the weakening of the link between the stimulus and the discomfort response if a normal response that is incompatible with the discomfort response is induced by the stimulus that trigger the former. Systematic desensitization involves the gradual weakening of behavioral stimuli that cause discomfort until they are eliminated, so as to form a new response to counter stimuli. This behavioral therapy can be used in executive practice. Behavior modification, sometimes referred to as therapy or contingency treatment, uses a variety of methods to reinforce positive behaviors and eliminate negative behaviors of prisoners. Systematic desensitization, elimination of adverse reactions, conditioned responses, and symbolism are the basic methods of behavior modification.[60] Behavior modification is mainly used to correct criminals

[58] See [30], p. 218.

[59] See [41], p. 65.

[60] See [36], p. 251.

with certain behavioral problems, such as correcting sexual inversions. In the United States, Bech (1971) has carried out behavior modification on pedophilias, using a systematic method of desensitization, whereby the intensity of sexual inversions is gradually reduced by the negative effects of electrical stimulation so that the sexual deviants are no longer sexually attracted to sexual objects such as children. This was done by having the sexual deviants sit in a laboratory and watch a slide show on a screen. Whenever a child or other inverted sexual objects appeared, a simultaneous electric shock was given; conversely, when an image of an adult female appeared on the screen, no electric shock but a reward was given. Barlon and Agras (1973) have used the fading method successfully to treat homosexuals. A naked man first appeared on the screen, at which point the homosexual person experienced inverted sexual thoughts, but the image of the man on the screen soon faded to that of a naked woman. In this way, the inverted sexual thoughts were transformed into normal sexual thoughts.[61] A rehabilitation model centered on individualized treatment is appropriate for the prison environment. Symptoms are identified through individuals, classification is used to determine the appropriate program, treatment is used to solve the problem (correctional program) and the degree of cure is used to determine whether the person is to be released (parole). The medical terminology denotes a shift from punishment to treatment, expressing the humanitarian motivation for treating prisoners, with correction becoming treatment.[62] Of course, the correctional model is not a panacea; it should be combined with the social reintegration model. Although the results of these correctional models have so far been unsatisfactory, the idea of starting to rehabilitate prisoners in this way is sound and points the way to the development of criminal correction.

China's criminal correctional system is based on a reform-through-labor model and adheres to the combination of punishment and education. This is a model of criminal correction with Chinese characteristics and in line with China's national conditions. In past practice, China has achieved significant results in the rehabilitation of criminals. However, with the development of society and economy, this correctional model has also revealed some problems, and the correctional effect has declined, mainly manifested in the prominent problem of recidivism, especially after 1986, when the recidivism rate of released prisoners was on the rise.[63] For this reason, it is necessary to further improve criminal correction in China. With the promulgation of China's Prison Law, the criminal correction system has gradually been based on the law, and prison management has been governed by law, thus improving the quality of criminal correction.

---

[61] See [42], pp. 379–380.

[62] See [30], p. 226.

[63] See [43], p. 84.

2 Theory of Punishment Axiology

The theory of punishment axiology is based on the theory of the value of crime, which examines the value of punishment, thus providing a scientific basis for the creation and application of punishment.

2.1 Theoretical Foundation of Punishment Axiology

Punishment is a special sanction established by the state and applied to criminals, which deprives criminals of a certain benefit and expresses the state's negative evaluation of criminals and their behaviors. Therefore, the state is the subject of evaluating the value of punishment. In establishing the theory of the value of punishment, it first involves the problem of the penalty power, that is to say, the nature of penalty is discussed from its relationship with the state.

The penalty power is the power of the state to impose criminal sanctions on criminals based on independent sovereignty, which is one of the external manifestations of state power and therefore belongs to the category of state power. The existence of the penalty power is premised on state power, and in this sense, the penalty power belongs to the power of the public penalty and is distinguished from the power of the private penalty. Marx pointed out, "Public punishment is the reconciliation of crime with the reason of the state. It is therefore a right of the state, and a right which the state cannot transfer to an individual, just as a man cannot transfer his conscience to another. Any right of the state against the prisoners is at the same time a right of the prisoners against the state. No intermediary links can turn the prisoner's relation with the state into a relationship with an individual. Even we assume that the state would renounce its rights, i.e., suicide, it would be not merely an act of indulgence, but a crime, for the state to renounce its obligations."[64] By public punishment as a right of the state, Marx here means that the state has the power to punish crimes, that is, the penalty power. The penalty power is not abstract or inane, it must be expressed in a certain way and has different expressions at different stages of criminal activities, which are the types of penalty power. The penalty power can be divided into the following categories: (1) the power to create sentences. The penalty power, as a state power, first manifests itself as the power to create sentences. In a broad sense, the power to create sentences includes: 1. abolition, i.e., the power to abolish the penal system following the objective needs of social development; 2. modification, i.e., the power to modify the penal system following the objective needs of social development; 3. establishment, i.e., the power to establish the penal system following the objective needs of social development. The abolition, modification, and establishment of the penal system constitute the power to create sentences. The power to create sentences is one of the important manifestations of the penalty power, and it is of great significance as it is exercised directly by the organs of state power in the

[64] See [44], p. 169.

name of the state. (2) The right to suggest sentences. When a sentence arises, it is to be applied to certain criminals. The question is who, through what ways, requests that the sentence be applied to the criminal, and this right to request that the criminal be punished is the right to suggest sentences, also known as the right to prosecute. In ancient societies, the right to suggest sentences was often in the hands of the victim. As state power expanded, the right to suggest sentences was brought into state ownership and granted to the public prosecution in the name of the state and the form of public prosecution, thus becoming an important part of state power. In a few cases, however, the right to suggest sentences is still exercised by the individual (generally the victim) in the form of private prosecution. The right to suggest sentences in private prosecution cases is an individual right granted by the state to citizens in the form of a law, and therefore does not fall within the scope of the state's penalty power. (3) The power to sentence. After criminal proceedings have been instituted, there is the question of sentencing. The power to decide whether to impose a sentence and what sentence to impose is the power to sentence. The power to sentence includes both the question of whether to impose a sentence and the question of what sentence to impose. Whether to impose a sentence means deciding whether or not to impose a sentence to the defendant based on a finding that he or she has committed a crime. The sentence imposed is the determination of the specific amount of the sentence to be imposed on the basis of the determination that the criminal should be sentenced. (4) The power to execute sentences. The power to sentence only addresses the issue of the quantum of the sentence. The sentence determined by the written judgment has yet been executed, which raises the question of the execution of the sentence. The power to execute sentences refers to the power to execute the sentence on the criminal, is a natural extension of the power to suggest sentences, but it is not a negative dependency of the power to sentence. It has positive content and should therefore be given great importance. It should be said that the aforementioned powers to create, impose and execute sentences, and the right to suggest sentences is an organic entity, which together constitutes the complete content of the state's penalty power.

The penalty power is the power of the state to use punishment to punish crimes and therefore falls within the realm of state power. How, then, does the penalty power come into being? On this point, the divine-given theory and the contract theory in criminal law theories are controversial. The divine-given theory, based on the theory of the divine right of kings, holds that the penalty power is also divinely given. It should be said that it had a wide influence. The thought of criminal law in ancient China was replete with the content of punishment given by the divine. For example, according to ancient historical records, the idea of divine right arose in the Xia dynasty, which deified its rule and glorified the laws of the time as the manifestation of the will of the gods. As a result, the rule of the Xia dynasty was described as "commanded by heaven" and the suppression of rebellions against its rule was described as "the execution of heaven's punishment".[65] This is the idea of "Heaven Punishment" based on the "Order of Heaven", which is the embodiment of the theology of divine right in ancient Chinese criminal law. In the Middle Ages

65 *The Book of History: Tang Oath.*

in the West, due to the influence of religious theology, the doctrine of the divine right of punishment was also prevalent for a while. For example, the ancient Roman theologian Augustine argued from the doctrine that human ancestors who committed sins and remained on earth would be punished by God.[66] Thus, the penalty power originated from God. Till modern times, there were still some Western criminal lawyers who followed this idea, for example, the German criminologist Stahl, when discussing the penalty power of the state, stated, "God's order, as found in the secular world, means the state. The integrity of the body, the protection of property, the order of the family, the existence of the state, the survival of the monastery, are all foundations of the divine order, and whoever breaks this order commits a crime. The gods command the representatives of secular power (i.e., the state) to punish the perpetrators of this disruption, and this is the origin of the penalty power of the state."[67] The contract theory was advocated by Enlightenment thinkers. The British philosopher Locke, for example, believed that in the state of nature, all men were equal and independent, and no one should violate the life, health, liberty, or property of another. To restrain all men from violating the rights of others and violating each other and to keep all men observing the natural law, which was designed to preserve peace and to defend all mankind, the natural law was given to all men to enforce in that state so that each man had the right to punish those who violated it, to the extent that the violation of the natural law was stopped.[68] In the state of nature, however, there were obstacles to human existence. For this reason, according to the French philosopher Rousseau, it was necessary to find a form of union which would guard and secure the physical security and property of each of the united persons with all its joint power, and by which each individual united to the whole would be merely subordinate to himself or herself and still free as before. This was the fundamental problem that the theory of social contract sought to solve.[69] In other words, state power comes from the creator of the social contract. The penalty power comes from the same source. Beccaria used the theory of social contract to explain the origin of the penalty power, arguing that the social contract was the true and fundamental starting point of the monarch's power to punish crimes.[70] Obviously, the divine-given theory and contract theory offer quite different explanations of the origin of the penalty power. The divine-given theory, with its strong religious and theological overtones, has become unbelievable in the modern times when civilization has been baptized although it had its justification in the ancient times when intelligence was not yet developed. As for the contract theory, it is historically progressive in attacking the divine-given theory and secularizing the penalty power. However, this argument was based on the assumption of the state of nature and lacks a solid scientific basis.

In my view, the penalty power, as an important element of state power, cannot arise without certain social and material conditions. In primitive societies where

[66] See [45], p. 84.

[67] See [46], p. 3.

[68] See [47], pp. 6 and 7.

[69] See [48], p. 23.

[70] See [34], p. 8.

modes of production were primitive and productivity was low, it was difficult to meet the minimum needs of human beings for survival. Under such historical conditions, to make human beings survive, only the primitive communal system of equal distribution of products could be implemented. In the primitive communal society, there was no interpersonal deceit, and the customs passed down from generation to generation were sufficient to regulate interpersonal relations. Therefore, there was neither state nor law in primitive societies, and certainly there was no punishment as one of the important symbols of state and law. In primitive societies, the security of the individual depended on the clan, and the ancient custom of revenge by blood relatives prevailed. As Morgan, a leading US anthropologist has pointed out: since there was human society, there have been murders; and since there were murders, there has been kinship revenge to punish murders. Among the Iroquois and other Indian tribes, it was a recognized obligation to avenge a murdered relative. However, it was the obligation of the clans of both the murderer and the murdered to try to reconcile the crime before resorting to unusual approaches. Members of both clans met separately and offered terms of leniency for the murderer's actions, usually in the form of a gift of considerable value and an apology. If the crime was justified or the conditions for mitigation were present, mediation was usually agreed upon; but if the relatives of the murdered clan refused to reconcile, the clan appointed one or more avengers from among its members, who were responsible for tracking down the murderer until the one was found and killed. If they completed this act of revenge, no member of the avenged clan would have any reason to be indignant about it. Now that the murderer has paid for his or her life, the demands of justice were satisfied.[71] Thus, in primitive societies, to make up for the lack of individual self-defense, the formation of the original social organization of human society was based on blood relations (clan). In the clan society where blood was the natural bond that maintained the relationship between people, whoever hurt an individual hurt the whole clan. Thus, from the blood relations of the clan arose the obligation of blood-revenge recognized by all members. In the initial stage of the clan system, any harm done to a member of a clan by a foreigner was regarded as an insult to the clan in which the member lived, and the aggrieved clan thus committed the collective killing of the clan that imposed harm. Later, with the development of private ownership, the clan system gradually disintegrated, and blood ties became looser so that the target of revenge was narrowed from all members of the aggressor's clan to the aggressor. The subject of revenge was narrowed from all members of the clan of the aggressor to the family members of the aggressor, and the revenge of blood relatives evolved into private revenge. In this case, the clan was no longer able to protect the individual, and the clan had finally come to its end. If the practice of revenge was adapted to the productive state of primitive society, the penalty power of the state was based on the emergence of private ownership resulting from the further development of productive forces. As a result of the great division of labor, a need arose in society that a minority of individual members should be vested with certain powers to carry out social functions that had existed from the beginning of

[71] See [49], p. 75.

primitive society for the common interest, and these functions were the germ of the state power. As the division of labor expanded, society was divided into different classes and based on irreconcilable class conflicts, the state emerged to safeguard the common interests of society. The power of the state to manage the common affairs of society is the state power. It is the supreme power of all social powers and the public power that performs the social function, with a series of material appendages such as the army, police, courts, and prisons. The emergence of the state puts an end to the history of revenge and replaces it with the exercise of the penalty power. It is clear that punishment is metamorphosed out of revenge, and Engels described the intrinsic link between punishment and revenge in the most eloquent terms when he said, "The death penalty of today is only the civilized form of revenge."[72] Not only the death penalty, but all penalties are civilized forms of revenge. In a state, crime is no longer a mere violation of individual rights, but a violation of the interests of society as a whole. As Hegel puts it: a certain kind of coercion, as an act of violence, committed by a free man, violates the existence of freedom in the concrete sense, violates the law as law, and this is a crime, that is, an infinite judgment of negation in the full sense of the word.[73] Consequently, the punishment of crimes is not of the nature of private punishment either. The penalty power is based on and subject to certain material conditions in society. In this sense, punishment is no more than a means of self-defense for society against the violation of its conditions of existence, whatever they may be.[74] Thus, the penalty power is essentially a social power of defense, which has its origin in the material conditions in society.

After the elaboration on the origins of the penalty power, it is appropriate to examine further the question of the basis of the penalty power, i.e., why does the state have the power to punish crimes? It should be said that this question is of greater theoretical significance for the understanding of the penalty power.

The penalty power, as a state power, is manifested as a dominant force over individuals, backed by national violence and therefore coercive. This does not mean, however, that the state can do whatever it wants by virtue of this power. From the standpoint of necessity, the exercise of the penalty power should be expressed as a form of social self-discipline. In ethnics, there is a distinction between self-discipline and others-discipline. Self-discipline is self-restraint, self-control, and therefore such restraint and control are determined by free will. Others-discipline, on the other hand, is to be disciplined and controlled, so such discipline and control are imposed by external forces, and the actor loses free will. The exercise of the penalty power on an individual criminal is a law for the criminal. In other words, the actor does not want to be punished. The punishment is imposed by the state beyond the will of the criminal. Since crime is the result of a free choice based on the will of the criminal, the imposition of the penalty should also be a socially deserved retribution for the criminal. Fundamentally, the penalty is always imposed on the criminal and is a form of others-discipline. However, in society as a whole, the exercise of the penalty power

[72] See [50], p. 95.

[73] See [51], p. 98.

[74] See [52], p. 579.

is socially self-disciplinary. As the Japanese criminologist Haruo Nishihara puts it: when an act is convicted as a crime, the actor is forced to accept the punishment. This means that the freedom of the nationals is limited. Therefore, if a penal code is enacted directly by the sovereign without the participation of the nationals, the state is not free in this regard. However, if this unfreedom is determined by the state itself, it still maintains freedom in the sense of self-discipline.[75] Here, Haruo Nishihara only discussed the social self-discipline of criminal law from the perspective of the power to create sentences, but it was more important to examine the self-discipline of criminal law in terms of the content and scope of the exercise of the penalty power. In this sense, the exercise of the penalty power is socially self-disciplinary only when it promotes and facilitates social development and reflects the objective laws of social development. Social self-discipline reflects the self-restraint and self-control of society, which is obviously different from individual self-discipline. Individual self-discipline is based on the premise of individual initiative and free will, reflecting the autonomy of the individual. Society is made up of countless individuals, and people do not all have the same perception of things. They have different perceptions based on their different social positions. However, individuals share a common interest, and to realize the common interest, public power comes into being, which becomes an effective guarantee for the realization of the common interest of society. To this end, society imposes coercion on individual members who act against the common interests of society, demonstrating the self-regulation of society. This can be seen in the taboos of ancient societies. Taboo is a Polynesian word that is translated almost as "sacred, untouchable fear". Sigmund Freud (1940) emphasized the double meanings of the word, that is, it meant, on the one hand, something sacred and holy, and the other hand, something eerie, dangerous, forbidden, and impure. Taboo has the effect of limiting and prohibiting the asking of certain questions and the expression of certain opinions. It tries to make people unreasonably accept intuitive aversions, the reasons for which may be traced back to the fear of supernatural forces.[76] In ancient times when mankind was in a pre-civilized stage, due to low productivity and unenlightened intelligence, certain impermissible acts, such as marriage between blood relatives, were found to be detrimental to the common good of the clan and were prohibited through the common experience of generations over time. Violators were subject to certain penalties. Clearly, such primitive taboos are an expression of the self-discipline of primitive societies. In the age of civilization, men became more sensible about their material conditions of life and the violations of the social conditions of existence were criminalized and punished. Thus, according to the French sociologist David Émile Dürkheim, crime was simply an act that was forbidden by the collective consciousness. For Dürkheim, therefore, criminal laws could reveal the power of people's collective emotions, the outgrowth and character of these emotions.[77] In modern society, therefore, the exercise of the penalty power is socially self-disciplinary.

[75] See [53], p. 2.

[76] See [54], p. 5.

[77] See [55], p. 348.

While social self-discipline explains one aspect of the basis of the existence of the penalty power, this power is relative because although its exercise fundamentally protects the interests of society as a whole, it does so at the expense of the freedom of individual citizens. As the Japanese criminologist Haruo Nishihara has said, penalties, while protecting the interests of the state, also narrows the scope of freedom and infringes on the vital interests of the actor. In this respect, the exercise of the penalty power must enjoy the nature of social others-discipline. The nature of social others-discipline means that the exercise of the penalty power is subject to certain restrictions and that it is not subordinate to the will of the sovereign. In a sense, crime is a violation by an individual against society, and the penalty is a sanction imposed by society on the actor to preserve its conditions of existence. It is therefore up to the legislators to decide what is a crime and what punishment should be imposed. However, there are limits to the power of the legislators since crime is usually the result of economic factors and does not depend on the will of the legislators. Similarly, punishment as a response to crime depends to some extent on the crime itself, and the exercise of the penalty power is subject to social and other factors. The death penalty, for example, was widely used in the Middle Ages, and the right of the state to impose the death penalty on criminals was considered natural and never questioned. Beccaria first enlightening raised the abolition of the death penalty. Beccaria argued that when people first entered into social contracts, they gave the public authorities a minimum of freedom, which certainly did not include the power to dispose of their lives. Beccaria made it clear that the death penalty could not be a right, and therefore was not a right. Once the death penalty abolition was put forward, it triggered a profound reflection on the power of the state to impose the death penalty, sparking a debate on the existence and abolition of the death penalty and at the same time giving impetus to the world collation against the death penalty. Whether a country abolishes or does not abolish the death penalty depends on various factors such as the political, economic, cultural, and historical factors of the society, and the death penalty cannot be simply judged as barbaric or civilized. However, it can at least show that with the development of civilized societies and the widespread dissemination of human rights, the power of death penalty has been excluded from the penalty power in some countries. It is thus clear that the penalty power is not absolute and that its existence and scope are limited by the material conditions in a given society. It is in this respect that the exercise of the penalty power exhibits the nature of social others-discipline.

The exercise of the penalty power is a unity between social self-discipline, which justifies the exercise of the penalty power, and social others-discipline, which points to the appropriate limits of the exercise of the power. The duality of social self-discipline and social others-discipline in the exercise of the penalty power is the basis of the penalty power.

The distinguished Italian criminologist Beccaria quoted Montesquieu, the famous French Enlightenment scholar whom he admired, as saying that any penalty that was not absolutely necessary was autocratic. It is clear that the exercise of the penalty power should be limited to what is absolutely necessary. Otherwise, the penalties established to defend society will be alienated into instruments that harm society.

The question is: how can the reasonable limits of penalty power be determined? On this issue, retributivism and utilitarianism in the theories of criminal law are in dispute. Retributivism holds that punishment is essentially a form of retribution for crime, and therefore the exercise of the penalty power can only be limited to achieving social retribution, otherwise it is an abuse of penalty power. Hegel, for example, has suggested that the concept and measure of punishment should be sought in the behaviors of criminals. Hegel concluded that punishment should be diverted from existing crimes and the exercise of the penalty power should be limited to retribution. This view of Hegel influenced Marx in early times. Marx states that "if the concept of crime is to have a punishment, then actual crimes must have a certain scale of punishment. There is a limit to actual crimes. Therefore, for punishment to be practiced, it should also have limits for it to be legitimate, and punishment should be limited by legal principles. Our task is to make the punishment a real consequence of the crime. In the criminals' view, punishment should be a necessary consequence of their actions, and therefore their own actions."[78] This statement from Marx bears traces of the exposition of Hegel's theory of criminal law. In short, retributivism seeks reasonable limits to the penalty power in terms of the crimes committed and is concerned with social justice in the exercise of the penalty power. Utilitarianism holds that punishment is not retribution for a crime, but a means to achieve certain social ends. Thus, the penalty power should be exercised to achieve socially beneficial values. For example, Jeremy Bentham states that "every punishment is a harm, and all punishments are evil. According to utilitarian principles, if punishment is considered necessary, the only reason is that punishment is thought to serve as a guarantee against greater evil". As a corollary to this, Bentham argues that the following situations should be exempt: I. No basis: there is no preventable harm, and the act is not harmful to society as a whole. II. No effect: the harm cannot be prevented by punishment. III. No help or the cost is too expensive: if the punishment causes more harm than it is intended to prevent. IV. No necessity: if the harm would have been prevented, or stopped on its own even without the punishment, and this is the cost of less use.[79] If Bentham advocates normative utilitarianism, then Lombroso advocates behavioral utilitarianism. Behavioral utilitarianism places more emphasis on the correction of criminals. For example, Lombroso advocates the doctrine of depriving criminal ability. Behavioral utilitarianism therefore sees the reasonable limits of the penalty power in terms of, for example, the correction of criminals. Clearly, behavioral utilitarianism is socially oriented and places greater emphasis on protecting the interests of society at the expense of the individual interests of criminals, and even tolerating the abuse of punishment. It is unlike normative utilitarianism, which is individually oriented and emphasizes the safeguarding of individual freedom. Nevertheless, normative utilitarianism and behavioral utilitarianism have one thing in common: they both seek the reasonable limits of the penalty power from unaccomplished crimes and are concerned with the social utility of the exercise of the penalty power. In my opinion, retributivism and utilitarianism, which pursue social justice and social utilitarianism

[78] See [44], pp. 140–141.

[79] See [56], pp. 493–494.

as values respectively, are one-sided. It should be said that social justice and social utilitarianism are opposed in form, but in substance, they are related in content, and therefore, they should be unified on a certain basis. In other words, the reasonable limits of the penalty power are governed by social justice and social utilitarianism respectively. Social justice cannot be ignored in the exercise of the penalty power because social justice represents the evaluation standard of society, and only when social justice is satisfied does the exercise of the penalty power have a solid social basis and is following the psychological state of society. However, the standard of social justice is not immutable; it changes dramatically from clan to clan and from stage to stage and changes dramatically as the material conditions in society change. In this regard, Hegel notes that "the crimes committed in society seem to be more serious, but the penalties are less severe. This appears at first sight to be a contradiction. But society cannot indulge in crime with impunity, for this would make crime legitimate; but because society has confidence in itself, crime is always an individual value directed against society, which is not assumed and isolated. Because society is stable, crime acquires the status of purely subjective. The subjectivity does not seem to be the product of a deliberate will but of natural impulses. In this view, crime acquires a less position and the punishment become less severe. If the society itself is not stable, it is necessary to set an example through punishment, because punishment itself is an example against crime. But in a stable society, crime is less likely to happen, and therefore the punishment for crime must also be measured against that likeliness. Severe penalties are therefore not arbitrary injustices but are linked to the circumstances of the time. A penal code cannot be suitable for all times."[80] It is in the changing nature of social justice that we can glimpse its connection to social utility. Thus, social justice does not exist independent of social utilitarianism. In a sense, social utilitarianism is the basis for the existence of social justice and has a constraining effect on social justice. Because social utilitarianism is the measure of the value of a certain society, all social beings must have their utilitarian basis for their existence, although the content of utilitarianism can vary. If something has no utilitarian significance, then its existence is not justified. The same is true of the exercise of the penalty power, which is a legal tool for maintaining the stability of social relations, protecting the interests of society and safeguarding individual freedom. Of course, although the exercise of the penalty power has obvious social utilitarian value, social justice cannot be ignored in achieving this social utility. In short, in determining the reasonable limits of the penalty power, the dual criteria of social justice and social utility should be taken into account penalty power.

2.2 *Generalization of Punishment*

As opposed to the individualization of punishment, the generalization of punishment is mainly the value evaluation of the criminal's behaviors in terms of the general

[80] Hegel [51], p. 229.

notion of social retribution and social justice, which claims that the punishment is balanced against the social detriments of criminal behaviors, thus generalizing the punishment.

The basic idea of the generalization of punishment is social justice, so the generalization of punishment has a long history. The generalization of punishment manifests itself in two ideological forms. First, retributivism. The concept of retribution can be traced back to homeopathic revenge in primitive societies. Homeopathic revenge reflects the simple and vulgar idea of fairness in primitive societies. In ancient societies, the custom of homeopathic revenge survived and was recognized by the law, further strengthening the concept of retribution. The ancient Greek philosopher Aristotle pointed out that "if a man hits another and another is hit, and a man kills another and another is killed, there arises an inequality between the sufferings and the acts, so punishments are put in place to equalize the sufferings or deprive the benefits."[81] Aristotle therefore argued that there was a relationship of justice between people, which crime destroyed, and which punishment restored. Therefore, the limits of punishment should also be within the scope of restoring the original relationship of the justice for equality. Aristotle stated that injustice was the opposite of this justice, and a violation of proportionality. Justice in interaction was equality, while injustice was inequality. The measurement was not according to the geometric proportion, but the arithmetical one. It made no difference whether good people caused harm to bad people or vice versa. The law treated all people equally, paying attention only to the magnitude of the harm inflicted. Who has done injustice, who has been treated unjustly, who has done harm and who has been harmed were situations that were concerned with injustice and inequality, so the judge tried to equalize them as much as possible.[82] Thus, the principle of justice, which in effect means the principle of retribution, is a general requirement of social justice. In the modern retributivist thought of Kant and Hegel, social justice has always been taken as the basis of retribution. Kant explicitly sees retribution as a norm of justice, and Hegel as a necessity of justice. Retributivism establishes a general standard of justice against which criminal acts are measured and made deserving of punishment. Although according to retributivism, there is an individualized process when the general standard of justice to criminal acts is applied, it presupposes the generalization of punishment, and individual results should also conform to the requirements of general justice, with the obvious effect that the same crime is punished in the same way, referring to accomplished criminal acts. Retributivism involves two aspects of empiricism: (1) The conditions to prove whether the criminal is eligible for the applicable penalty. (2) The proportionality of the penalty to the criminal acts. US scholars have noted that in practice these two empirical areas, namely responsibility and proportionality, intersect, and both require a certain level of severity of criminal acts, including criminal harm and culpability. However, there is also the important issue of determining the detriment of the act, and difficult questions about the degree of criminal detriment (for example, is robbery more harmful than theft?) and determining the

---

[81] Aristotle [57], pp. 95–96.

[82] See [57], p. 95.

degree of culpability may make it highly impractical to base sentencing standards on an assessment of the degree of harm caused by the crime. Despite these empirical obstacles, we can still notice its merits in the opinions of the punitive-based penalties by Kleinberg (1973), proportionate penalties by Von Hirsch, and Von Hirsch and Hanrahan's revised penal model. These new retributivist ideas attempt to put into practice the moral foundations of the retributivist theory of penology. Some comments on these new ideas include: (1) The punishment for a particular crime is measured according to the criminal act and its severity. (2) The length all criminals should serve in prison should be reduced to a range corresponding to the severity of the crime. (For example, Von Hirsch suggests that imprisonment should not exceed five years and most sentences should be less than three years). (3) Definite or fixed sentences should be imposed. A system of sentence reductions for prisoners in prison may be allowed, but the aim is to abolish indefinite sentences. (4) Parole should be abolished, or at least significantly modified to reduce the discretion of those applying it. (5) Prison conditions should be improved to create a just and equal environment for the serving of sentences, such as Fogel's model of justice. (6) Imprisonment should not be used primarily to achieve other objectives, such as crime prevention, correction or general detention.[83] Therefore, new retributivism, while no longer insisting on an absolute notion of retribution, still prioritizes "measuring the punishment for a given crime according to its severity". Second, utilitarianism, which refers to normative utilitarianism in this case. In ethnics, there is a distinction between normative utilitarianism and behavioral utilitarianism. Behavioral utilitarianism (also called action utilitarianism) determines the rightness or wrongness of an action based on the good or bad effects of the action; normative utilitarianism (also called rule utilitarianism or standard utilitarianism) determines the rightness or wrongness of an action based on the good or bad effects of the norm that each person's action should follow in the same specific situation.[84] Thus, normative utilitarianism focuses on the overall utilitarian effect, while behavioral utilitarianism focuses on the individual utilitarian effect. In the theory of criminal law, all schools of utilitarianism are against retributivism and advocate the application of punishment pursuing utilitarian effects. For normative utilitarianism, the utilitarian effect mainly refers to general prevention, while for behavioral utilitarianism, the utilitarian effect mainly refers to individual prevention. Both Beccaria and Bentham are normative utilitarians. The US scholar Clemens Butlers have summarized Beccaria's theory as follows: (1) The basis of all social behaviors must be the utilitarian concept of bringing the greatest happiness to the most majority of people. (2) Crime must be seen as a detriment to society and the only correct criterion for judging crimes is the degree of detriment of crimes. (3) The prevention of crime is more important than the punishment of crime. Factually, punishment is only justified when it helps to prevent crimes. To prevent crimes, it is necessary to improve and enact laws to gain the understanding and support of nationals. Good moral character should be rewarded, and public education should be improved in terms of legislation and life. (4) In criminal proceedings, secret trials

[83] See [30], p. 95.

[84] See [58], p. 9.

and torture should be abolished. Trials should be conducted promptly. Defendants should be treated humanely in court and be entitled and empowered to promote the production of evidence in their favor. Treason is not much different from the so-called crime of treachery and must be abolished. (5) The purpose of punishment is to deter people from committing crimes, not cause people conduct social revenge. It is not the severity of the penalty, but the certainty and promptness, that best ensures the achievement of this purpose. Punishment must be certain and timely, and the sentence imposed must be strictly proportionate to the social detriment caused by the crime. Property offenses should be punished by a fine or by imprisonment if a person could not afford to pay a fine. Exile is the best penalty to apply to those who have violated the interests of the state. There should be no death penalty. Life imprisonment is the best deterrence. The death penalty is a method of punishment which, once carried out, does not bring the life of the deceased back, i.e., it cannot prevent possible wrongs once carried out, nor can it be corrected afterwards. (6) Imprisonment should be widely used, but the manner of its application should be greatly improved by providing better material conditions and the segregating and classifying prisoners according to age, sex, and degree of criminality. Butlers also discussed Bentham's calculation of pleasure and pain, stating that Bentham believed that a rational person should base his or her behaviors on the greatest enjoyment and the greatest suffering. If the penalty is appropriate to the crime, it prevents crimes. Thus, punishment has four purposes: (1) preventing all crimes, if possible. (2) dissuading a person from committing a more moderate offense than a more serious one, if the person is determined to do so. (3) dissuading a person from causing more harm than is necessary to achieve the purpose of the offense when the person is determined to committing an offence. (4) deterring crimes to the lowest possible level of incidence.[85] It can be seen that both Beccaria and Bentham take normative utilitarianism as their philosophical basis, measuring the utilitarian effect of one's actions according to certain norms, and generalizing the utilitarian standard. This is reflected in the generalization of penalties. It should be noted that retributivism and normative utilitarianism both advocate the generalization of punishment, both take the social detriment of crime as the general standard for measuring punishment, but the content of the generalization of punishment is different. Retributivism advocates that crimes should be punished, and therefore penalties are established solely on the basis of the accomplished crimes and no other factors should be taken into account. Normative utilitarianism, on the other hand, advocates universal prevention, and although the understanding of the nature of the crime still emphasizes the socially harmful nature of the existing offense, the penalties prescribed in the legislation are necessary to deter the general population from committing crimes from the perspective of prevention. In this context, the penalties applied to specific offenses are no longer retaliatory but preventive. Retributivism and normative utilitarianism do have some common ground. This is why there has been a tendency of the merging of retributivism and normative utilitarianism. In recent years in the United States, for example, some awareness of the uncontrollable nature of utilitarian punishment has led to a return to

[85] See [59], pp. 9–10.

the retributivist position. Another reason for this return is that the idea of correction was no longer trusted, that is, it was no longer seen as valid on the basis of the denial of utilitarianism. It was also criticized on moral grounds as being arbitrary and coercive in its application. The retreat to retributivism does not represent a total rejection of utilitarian goals such as the prevention or imprisonment to deprive criminals of the ability to commit crimes. Instead, attempts have been made to bring these objectives under control. In particular, restrictions based on just punishment have been used to accommodate the utilitarian goal that the demands of justice should include the aim of preventing crimes. This mandatory requirement is achieved by allowing deserved punishment to override other criminal law doctrines. This proposal is based on the rights-oriented of the individual. Andep von Herb (1976) has outlined the internal logic of this view of rights that "this hypothesis of the fundamental-rights-oriented of the individual, rather than the utilitarian justification of punishment and prevention, can stand on its own. When the theory of prevention is applied to explain why the existence of punishment is necessary for the interests of the majority, its benefit to many people does not lie in the fact that it has a just basis in itself for depriving the criminal of liberty and honor, but in the fact that other reasons are needed to explain the punishment of the criminal. Such a justification is retribution. Because the criminal has engaged in wrongdoing, caused harm, or existed which is prohibited by the law, the criminal may be subject to some deprivation. Punishment is therefore not only a means of preventing crimes, but also a response to the criminal's crime and an expression of what Cantinas calls the restoration of balance and the moral negation of wrongs. In other words, when prevention is used to explain the social role of punishment, it is necessary to use punishment to explain why the utilitarianism that causes the criminal's suffering is just." As this argument suggests, justice may well require that the goal of utilitarianism be diminished through the control of punishment based on retaliatory theory. Some combination of the two main theories sketched here is needed if justice is to be achieved.[86] This is the theory of the so-called neoclassical school, a theory that is compatible with retributivism and normative utilitarianism as one of the main antagonists to the correction-centered theory of punishment that is advocated by behavioral utilitarianism as an alternative. The main point of the neoclassical school remains the generalization of punishment whose grounding is in social justice thought.

The generalization of punishment reveals the value of the existence of punishment to some extent. Retribution is an integral part of punishment. Retribution suggests that punishment is a response to crime, that this response presupposes the existence of crime, and that punishment is not punishment without retribution. Retribution also limits the scope of the existence of punishment, and the initiation and application of punishment should be limited by retribution. Retribution is therefore necessary to explain the basis for the existence of punishment. Stephen, a famous British criminologist, said, "Retribution is to punishment what sexual desire is to marriage." Thus, in Stephen's view, retribution is the satisfaction of a sense of social justice. Although Stephen's words are somewhat exaggerated, they are by no means alarmist.

[86] See [30], pp. 100–101.

Of course, it is undesirable to advocate retaliatory punishment alone. Because punishment is, after all, an instrument of social control that has its own utilitarian purpose of preventing crimes. It has also long been thought that by punishing those who have already committed crimes, the aim of preventing the recurrence of crimes can be achieved. However, the utilitarian nature of this punishment must be based on retribution, otherwise it may lead to injustice. The potential injustice of utilitarianism is a problem that requires constant vigilance and prevention, an example of which is given by H. J. McCloskey in his article *A Commentary on Utilitarian Punishment* that a small-town judge can prevent a serious riot by only "framing" one innocent person as the scapegoat and thus hundreds of people will be killed in the riot. In such case, action utilitarians usually endorse the daily moral sentiment of the matter. They may point out that the dishonesty of the judge is likely to be discovered, with the consequence of weakening loyalty and respect for community law and order, an effect even worse than the painful deaths of hundreds of people. However, McCloskey might immediately point out that he could present an example in which none of these objections to the judge's conduct would be appropriate. For example, it was conceivable that this judge had the best facts to prove that he would not be found. The objection to the judge's behavior (i.e., that although he knew that the person he "framed" would be killed, he still insisted that if the person had not been framed, the riot would have happened) was therefore not credible. The result of the ability of some people like McCloskey to keep revising his story was that we had to admit that if utilitarianism was correct, judges must frame innocent people. While utilitarians could argue that such situations as those cited by McCloskey were never empirically possible, McCloskey might point out that they were logically possible. If action utilitarians opposed such unjust actions (or systems), they had clearly abandoned utilitarianism.[87] The situation cited by McCloskey is highly unlikely to occur in reality, but it makes the potential injustice of utilitarianism clear all the same. As US scholars have pointed out: determining the justice of punishment by future goals often hurts our sense of justice, and to accept utilitarian goals as the basis for determining punishment is to open Pandora's box.[88] Utilitarianism can therefore only prevent its potential injustice within the context of retributivism and establish a general standard of criminal justice.

2.3 *Individualization of Punishment*

The individualization of punishment, as opposed to the generalization of punishment, refers mainly to evaluating the value of punishment on the criminal's personality, and asserting that penalty is adapted to the personal detriment of the criminal, thus individualizing punishment.

---

[87] See [58], p. 67.

[88] See [30], p. 100.

According to the US scholar Zirin, the rise of the individualization of punishment can be traced back to Roman canon law. According to Zirin, the theory of individualized sentencing by judges was initiated by the Roman ecclesiastical tribunals. In another aspect, we must not forget that, in addition to the humanitarian treatment of criminals, there was the obvious notion that the purpose of criminal law and the use of criminal law by judges, was to warn people from committing crimes and thus secularized society. Furthermore, it must be remembered that legislators and judges are responsible for the enactment and enforcement of laws, not only on the basis of free will and theories of responsibility prevalent in society at a given time, but also with regard for the real anger of society at a given detriment. Since the punishment of criminals was believed at the time to be dealt with based on whether criminals committed crimes of their own free will, in practical application the decision should not be made at the time based on the psychology of the time, but on the basis of the environments where criminals committed crimes. There was no other criterion on which judges could base their decisions than the inference of free will and responsibility of the environments of the time.[89] It should be said that the individualization of punishment that Zirin refers to is only the individualization of punishment in the sense of individual responsibility, and not the individualization of punishment based on personal detriment as advocated by the criminal positivists. The individualization of punishment proposed by the criminal positivists is based on behavioral determinism, which holds that crime is the product of the interaction between the physical and psychological conditions of the actors and their surroundings, not free will, let alone the same free will for all. Therefore, the penalty should be determined following the physical detriments of actors It should be said that the behavior determinism advocated by the criminal positivists is not valid, and the theory of free will advocated by the classical school is also too vague, especially that the denial of the impact of the personal detriment of the criminal on the penalty in the name of will free is also unscientific. Human behavior is not isolated but is governed by personality. Consequently, criminal behavior is also an external manifestation of the criminal personality and the determination of a penalty based on isolated external behavioral characteristics without taking the personality of the criminal into account is clearly insufficient to reflect a comprehensive evaluation of the crime in the law.

The individualization of punishment is not a negation of the generalization of punishment, but an individualization of punishment under the premise of the generalization of punishment. Therefore, the relationship between the individualization of punishment and the generalization of punishment must be properly understood. The generalization of punishment means the establishment of a just ladder of crimes and penalties, focusing on the balance and symmetry of crimes and penalties at the macro level. Generalization of punishment also means that the determination of the penalty for the criminal is based on the social detriment of the crime. The individualization of penalties is an individualization based on the generalization of punishment, which cannot be separated from the objective structure of crimes and penalties provided for by legislation. Also, in determining penalties for criminals, we should be based

[89] See [3], pp. 476–477.

on the social detriment of the crime and take the personal detriment of the criminal into account. Thus, both are not contradictory but unified. Some scholars of the positivist school advocate completely abandoning the concept of the social detriment of the crime and replacing it by the personal detriments of the criminal. Obviously, we cannot agree with such a polarized view. What we call the individualization of punishment is based on the dualistic nature of crime and the dualism of the aim of punishment and presupposed on the generalization of punishment, which is therefore not contradictory to the generalization of punishment.

The most demanding part of the individualization of punishment is the determination of physical detriment. Physical detriment is not as easy to grasp as social detriment. Failure to correctly determine physical detriment can lead to bias in the application of penalties. As a result, the personality investigation system, which aims to identify the physical detriment of the criminal, has been widely used in countries. The personality investigation system, also known as the pre-sentence investigation system, is a system established to enable the court to carry out a scientific analysis of the qualities and circumstances of the defendant during the pre-sentence hearing, to select the appropriate treatment for each criminal in the criminal proceedings.[90] The establishment of the personality investigation system has resulted in a significant change in the traditional concept of trials. Traditionally, trials were divided into two organically linked phases: conviction and sentencing. Conviction was merely a finding of the facts constituting the offense, whereas sentencing was the mechanical imposition of punishment based on the facts that were found to constitute the offense based on a conviction. The establishment of the personality investigation system has added a more complex element to the trial because judges not only found out the constitutive facts of the offense, but also conduct meticulous investigations into the personality characteristics of the criminal, making it the first prescription for dealing with the criminal. In discussing the significant impact and role of the personality investigation system on criminal justice activities, the Japanese scholar Makiko Kikuta has said that originally, in our criminal justice, conviction and sentencing were not separated. The judge's work was mainly focused on the determination of facts before sentencing. Sentencing was based solely on previous precedents and trial intuition, so information about the circumstances was mainly to clarify the moral and normative significance of specific criminal acts, so that it could be a necessary basis for deciding on other legal responsibilities. However, it was nothing but limited to the motive, purpose, method, and result of the criminal act. In such a state, there was no necessity to investigate specific circumstances. However, if we consider reprieval, protective observation, punishment of prostitutes and the suspended sentencing issue now under discussion without thorough understanding, investigation and identification of the criminal's qualities, characters, mental states, level of knowledge, state of health and remorseful attitude, especially with regard to the criminal's reproductive history, family, neighbor, school, classmate and work, then we cannot assess the

[90] See [6], p. 178.

personality detriment correctly.[91] It is thus clear that the personality investigation system is crucial to the individualization of punishment.

As the idea of individualization of punishment has taken root, the personality investigation system has received increasing attention. This system has been introduced in the United States, Germany, Belgium, Japan, and other countries. Among juvenile laws in different countries, there is often an explicit provision for the investigation of the personality of the criminal as the basis for trial. When the International Penal and Prison Congress held its twelfth session in The Hague in 1950, it included the question of pre-sentence investigation of the personality of the criminal as one of the issues to be discussed and the topic was whether it was appropriate to investigate the criminal before the sentence was pronounced to assist the magistrate in making the necessary and appropriate treatment of the criminal's conduct. In the description of this issue, it was stated that the penalty was not only intended to punish the prisoner, but also to prevent recidivism and correct the prisoner as far as possible so that he or she can return to a normal social life, and this is now generally accepted as the purpose of the execution of the penalty. This fundamental principle had a revolutionary impact on previous execution procedures. It was therefore not enough to establish the specific facts of the offense, assess its subjective and objective importance and thus pronounce a heavier or lighter sentence, and it was necessary to understand the prisoner's personality and environment, anticipate the impact of the punishment he or she would receive in prison and choose the most effective treatment, i.e., investigating the personality of the accused before pronouncing the sentence. Furthermore, the prison authorities were often unaware of the reasons for the magistrate to impose a sentence, which led to no link between the sentence and its execution. To remedy this shortcoming, it was also necessary to carry out a pre-investigation of the prisoner before sentencing and to bring unduly delayed sentences to the point of general prevention. After discussion, the following resolutions were made: (1) In modern criminal justice, in addition to the situations of the offense, it was highly desirable that a report on the prisoner's physical, identity, character, and socio-educational background be investigated prior to sentencing as the basis for sentencing, corrective treatment, release, among others. (2) Among the Latin US law countries, a personal investigation was not mandatory when the defendant was allowed to prepare for release, but it was mandatory when the law did not allow the defendant to prepare for release. (3) The scope and extent of the investigation should enable the magistrate to obtain sufficient information and take reasonable action in relation to the matter. (4) With regard to the above-mentioned investigations, it was hoped that states would pay attention to the study of prognosis (e.g., forecasting tables) to corroborate each other. (5) It was also hoped that education in criminology would be provided in the training of magistrates working in criminal correction. Furthermore, when the United Nation Congresses on the Prevention of Crime and the Treatment of Criminals was held in Geneva in August 1955 to discuss the principles of treatment in penal institutions, delegates and experts agreed that "the rules of life in penal institutions should, as far as possible, resemble those of

[91] See [6], p. 178.

social life, be adapted to the needs of the sentenced person, and provide individualized treatment."[92] This shows that the international community is very concerned about personality investigations.

The content of the personality investigation should generally be matters that can prove the physical detriment of the criminal. According to the Japanese scholar Makiko Kikuta, the matters to be investigated under the personality investigation system are as follows: (1) investigation of crimes and illegal acts. Crimes and illegal acts are reflected in the environment in which the person is placed. Therefore, the investigation of not only existing crimes but also previous crimes and illegal acts is an indispensable tool for discovering and selecting the appropriate treatment for the defendant. (2) social investigation. This should be obtained primarily from meetings (interviews) with the person concerned. The following investigations are carried out by means of interviews: 1. family relations and reproductive history, parents and siblings, the protector's address, occupation, property, state of health, the parents' characters and degree of harmony, family atmosphere, lifestyle, family ideals, the defendant's attitude to and relationship with his or her parents and couple; 2. educational level, academic performance, subjects he or she likes or dislikes, attitude to school and teachers, reasons for leaving school, aspiration for further education, and relationship with classmates; 3. residence and surroundings, trust and affection of neighbors on the defendant, as well as family relocation and past and present friendships; 4. work history, reasons for changing jobs, attendance, job performance, hopes and attitudes towards work, and relations with colleagues; 5. past and present income and expenditure, assets, reasons for debts, repayment plans and repayment; 6. medical history, past and present physical condition; 7. oral qualities, religious beliefs, recreation, habits, and interests; 8. marriage and sexual life. (3) Confirm investigation. Investigators learn about the surroundings of the defendant to check and confirm the authenticity of the statement through visiting defendant's home, neighborhood, schools and meeting their families, neighbors, employers, colleagues, teachers, or using telephone, letters, and other means. (4) Physical and mental identification. The identification must be carried out by expertise in relative fields. At present, the trial standard is that, as long as the defendant seems to be mentally and physically normal, the investigation should stop. However, there are many cases of crimes arising from physical and mental defects. Therefore, a comprehensive personality investigation of the defendant remains necessary.[93] In China, the personality investigation system has yet been implemented. Of course, in the case of probation imposed on defendants or crimes against juveniles, the necessary on-site investigation is often carried out, but not institutionalized. Chinese scholars have proposed the theory that the personal situation of the criminal should be investigated to make a correct assessment of the physical detriment of the criminal and provide a reliable basis for the correct punishment. Personal situation of the criminal is mainly sorted into four categories: (1) basic information of the criminal. It primarily refers to the criminal' s age, psychological condition, physiological condition, living condition,

---

[92] Lin [60], pp. 88–90.

[93] See [6], pp. 181–183.

working condition, moral concept, education, and other basic information; (2) the performance of the criminal before the crime. Considering the various behaviors of the criminal before the crime not only helps to understand why he or she commits the crime, but also helps to evaluate the possibility of the criminal to commit the crime again; (3) the situation of the criminal in the crime; and (4) the attitude of the criminal after the crime. The basic information of the criminal, the performance before the crime, the situation in the crime and the attitude after the crime only determine and indicate whether the physical detriment of the criminal exists or whether it is severe or not, rather than all situations of the criminal. In addition, the subjective and objective reasons for the criminal to commit a crime, the criminal 's political beliefs, religious beliefs, outlook on life and world, and other aspects also affect the severity of the criminal's physical detriment. Therefore, attention should be paid to the overall situation in evaluating the existence and severity of the physical detriment of the criminal.[94] On the basis of information, the content of personality investigation should be analyzed and identified to provide accurate basis for the individualization of punishment.

Based on the personality investigation, correctly evaluating the physical detriment of the criminal, and then punishing the criminal with appropriate penalties which are adapted to his or her personality and the circumstance of the crime is the main content of the individualization of punishment. At this stage, the first is to determine whether the penalty is applicable according to the criminal facts and the personality of the criminal; if the penalty is applicable, what kind of penalty and its procedure should be considered. As the concept of correction spreads, countries tend to test those criminals who are less guilty and less physically detrimental by setting them for free and monitoring them. In the United States, this is called pretrial diversion, which is sorted into three types: adjustment, deferred prosecution (or suspended prosecution) and alternative measures to tackle street crimes.[95] In addition, other measures including probation are suitable for those less physically detrimental criminals.

References

1. [Italy] B. Cesare, *An Essay on Crimes and Punishments* (Encyclopedia of China Publishing House, Beijing, 1993)
2. [Italy] Ferri, *Positive School of Criminology: Three Lectures* (China University of Political Science and Law Press, Beijing, 1987)
3. [US] Gillin, *Criminology and Penology* (The Commercial Press, Shanghai, 1937)
4. K. Chang, *Criminal Policy* (San Min Book, Taipei, 1979)
5. [Britain] D.M. Walker, *The Oxford Companion to Law* (Guangming Daily Publishing House, Beijing, 1988)
6. [Japan] K. Makiko, *Criminology* (Quzhong Publishing House, Beijing, 1989)
7. C. Lin, *Criminal Policy* (Cheng Chung Book, Taipei, 1969)
8. S. Lin, *Penology* (The Commercial Press, Taipei, 1983)

[94] See [28], pp. 195–197.

[95] See [36], p. 103.

9. X. Qiu et al., *Penology* (Qunzhong Publishing House, Beijing, 1988)
10. K. Ma (Editor-in-Chief), *Chinese Criminal Policy* (Wuhan University Press, Wuhan, 1992)
11. C. Yang (Editor-in-Chief), *A Treatise on Criminal Policy* (Peking University Press, Beijing, 1994)
12. M. Wang, *Criminology* (Jilin University Press, Changchun, 1992)
13. *Contemporary Studies in Foreign Criminology* (1st Collection) (Quzhong Publishing House, Beijing, 1991)
14. *Marx-Engels-Gesamtausgabe*, vol. 8 (People's Publishing House, Beijing, 1972)
15. *Vladimir Lenin Bibliography*, vol. 4, 2nd edn. (People's Publishing House, Beijing, 1984)
16. [France] Ancel, *The New Theory of Penology* (Cosmos Books Ltd., Hong Kong, 1990)
17. X. Chen, *Genetics and Crime* (Qunzhong Publishing House, Beijing, 1992)
18. K. Ma (Editor-in-Chief), *The Complete Book of Penology* (Shanghai Scientific and Technological Literature Press, Shanghai, 1993)
19. [US] L.A. Coser, *Masters of Sociological Thought* (China Social Sciences Press, Beijing, 1990)
20. [US] C. Robert, Y. Thomas, *Law and Economics* (Shanghai Sanlian Bookstore, Shanghai, 1991)
21. [US] G.S. Becker, *The Economic Approach to Human Behavior* (Shanghai Sanlian Bookstore, Shanghai, 1993)
22. S. Ni et al., *Drug Crimes in All Their Aspects* (People's Oriental Publishing & Media, Beijing, 1992)
23. L. Sun, *The Economics of Law* (China University of Political Science and Law Press, Beijing, 1993)
24. S. Kang (Editor-in-Chief), *General Theory of Criminology* (Peking University Press, Beijing, 1992)
25. Z. Zhang, Reflections on the "strike-hard" criminal policy. Public Secur. Stud. (1) (1992)
26. [Italy] Ferri, *The Sociology of Crime* (China University of Political Science and Law Press, Beijing, 1990)
27. [Soviet Union] Л.B. Bagri-Shakhmatov, *Criminal Responsibility and Penalties* (Law Press China, Beijing, 1984)
28. Z. Zhou, *A Treatise on the Application of Punishment* (Law Press China, Beijing, 1990)
29. S. Bao, Deeper reflections on the death penalty in China. Sci. Law (1) (1993)
30. [US] H. Richard et al., *US Prison Systems: Punishment and Justice* (People's Public Security University of China Press, Beijing, 1991)
31. F. Huang, *Beccaria and His Thought on Penology* (China University of Political Science and Law Press, Beijing, 1987)
32. [Italy] Ferri, *Positivist Criminology* (China University of Political Science and Law Press, Beijing, 1987)
33. J. Xu et al., *The German Prison System: Execution of Penalties in Practice* (People's Public Security University of China Press, Beijing, 1993)
34. [Italy] Beccaria, *On Crimes and Punishments* (Encyclopedia of China Publishing House, Beijing, 1993)
35. [Italy] Ferri, *Criminal Sociology* (People's Public Security University of China Press, Beijing, 1990)
36. [US] B. Clemens, *An Introduction to Corrections* (People's Public Security University of China Press, Beijing, 1991)
37. K. Jiao, *On the Reformability of Criminals and its Conditions, in A New Research into the Juristic Theory of Reform Through Labor* (People's Public Security University of China Press, Beijing, 1991)
38. [US] Skinner, *Science and Human Behavior* (Huaxia Publishing House, Beijing, 1989)
39. US] Skinner, *Beyond Freedom and Dignity* (Guizhou People's Publishing House, Guiyang, 1987)
40. [US] Pound, *Social Control Through Law* (The Commercial Press, Beijing, 1984)
41. [US] B. Adelaide, *A Primer of Behavioral Psychology* (Sichuan People's Publishing House, Chengdu, 1987)

42. Z. Shen (Editor-in-Chief) *Legal Psychology* (Peking University Press, Beijing, 1986)
43. J. Li (Editor-in-Chief), *Studies on Recidivism in China* (Law Press China, Beijing, 1992)
44. *Marx-Engels-Gesamtausgabe*, vol. 1 (People's Publishing House, Beijing, 1965)
45. H. Zhang (Editor-in-Chief), *History of Western Legal Thoughts* (Peking University Press, Beijing, 1983)
46. J. Wang, *A Treatise on Chinese Penology* (Zhonghua Book Company, Beijing, 1933)
47. [Britain] Locke, *Two Treatises of Government. Second Treatise* (The Commercial Press, Beijing, 1964)
48. [France] Rousseau, *The Social Contract or Principles of Political Right* (The Commercial Press, Beijing, 1980)
49. [US] Morgan, *Ancient Society* (The Commercial Press, Beijing, 1977)
50. *Marx-Engels-Gesamtausgabe*, vol. 4, 2nd edn. (People's Publishing House, Beijing, 1995)
51. [Germany] Hegel, *Philosophy of Law* (The Commercial Press, Beijing, 1961)
52. *Marx-Engels-Gesamtausgabe*, vol. 8 (People's Publishing House, Beijing, 1965)
53. [Japan] N. Haruo, *The Roots and Philosophy of Penology* (Shanghai Sanlian Bookstore, Shanghai, 1991)
54. [Germany] H.J. Schneider, *Criminology* (China People's Public Security University of China Press, Beijing, 1990)
55. [France] A. Raymond, *Main Currents in Sociological Thought* (Shanghai Translation Publishing House, Shanghai, 1988)
56. *Selected Sources on the History of Western Legal Thought* (Peking University Press, Beijing, 1983)
57. [Ancient Greece] Aristotle, *The Nicomachean Ethics* (China Social Sciences Press, Beijing, 1990)
58. [Australia] J.J.C. Smart et al., *Utilitarianism: For and Against* (China Social Sciences Press, Beijing, 1992)
59. [US] C. Butlers, *A Brief Introduction to Corrections* (People's Public Security University of China Press, Beijing, 1991)
60. C. Lin, *Criminal Policy* (Taipei, Cheng Chung Book, 1969)

Chapter 9
Human Nature Foundation of Legislation

The legislation refers to the activities of making and enacting criminal law. Criminal legislation enjoys a time-honored history, as shown by the famous British scholar Maine's saying that the older a code is, the more detailed and complete its criminal legislation is.[1] In this sense, criminal law is the earliest law from which other laws derive and separate. Until now, criminal law still enjoys the highest level of education among other laws, and its nature determines it as such. Criminal law relates to citizens' life and death, so penalties should be legalized to safeguard citizens' freedom. The previous discussions on criminal legislation laid particular stress on the legislation technique while paying no attention to the nature of criminal law. Therefore, research on the nature of law and the humanistic foundation of statutory law and case law should be conducted from human nature.

1 Legislative Concept

Criminal legislation is a practical activity of human beings, which should be guided by theories. Only when we establish the legislative concept based on science can we correctly define the nature of legislation and direct criminal legislative activities.

1.1 Theory of the Origin of Law

Legislation is the making and enacting of law, so it is of great significance to understand the origin of law. Our understanding of the law, including the origin of criminal law, has evolved from divinity to humanity through human history.

[1] See [1], p. 207.

X. Chen, *Humanistic Foundation of Criminal Law*,
https://doi.org/10.1007/978-981-19-9764-8_9

In ancient societies, as impacted by Theology, people did not understand the law based on science, so they regarded it as divine law. The divine-origin concept of law had profound influences on the legislation in ancient times. The concept was the outcome of the thoughts of the divine right of kings. There are different academic opinions on whether the concepts of divine law existed in ancient China. Derk Bodde, a US sinologist, believed that there were no concepts of divine law in ancient China.

He said that Chinese theories of history and philosophy had one feature, namely, paying attention to real social lives, which was shown in early China. Generally speaking, when interpreting secular phenomena, Chinese theorists would rather adopt rationalism (rational as they thought) than supernatural doctrines. The fate of Chinese myths, as shown in early Chinese documents, illustrates it well. There are some scattered historical data among these documents, which indicates that according to the principle that "myth is history", people realized gods, semi-gods, and monsters into the wise kings, heroes, or rebellions who did exist. Therefore, we won't be surprised at the law possessing the secular feature.[2] The British scholar Maine has shared similar opinions. He believed that human society had a period when legal norms were not separated from religious norms, whereas China had transcended this period. However, the well-known Chinese scholar Teng Tsu Chu disagreed with him. Chu said, "On the surface, we barely see the status of religion in China's legal history. We do not have divine-right laws like Hammurabi, Manu, or Moses codes according to historical data. Our ancestors had no such ideology as the Greeks that each law was a concept formulated by gods. Meanwhile, our laws were never maintained by the power of sorcery or religion. All laws had no curses. It was not the people who knew witchcraft or divine power that held judicial power. In China, legal sanctions and religious or ritual sanctions were separated. If we study it more deeply, however, we can see a close functional relationship between witchcraft and religion, and the law."[3] As Teng Tsu Chu said, although China's ancient concept of law became secular earlier, the thought of religious authority did exist. Zhang Guohua, a historian of Chinese legal thought, has summarized the existence, development, and evolution of religious authority in ancient China: existing in the Xia dynasty, peaking in the Shang dynasty, and starting to fade in the Western Zhou dynasty.[4] The thought of religious authority of the Xia, Shang, and Western Zhou dynasties is manifested in that the law reflecting the ruling will is said to be the embodiment of God's will in order to legalize the rule. The noble, led by the King, unanimously claimed that they ruled people because God or Heaven willed it (Heaven's decree). For instance, they quoted, "the existence of the Xia dynasty is by Heaven's mandate," "the existence of the Shang dynasty is under Heaven's decree," "the great and wise King Wen of Zhou undertook the great mission of Heaven," among others. The "Heaven's decree" thought of "receiving instructions from Heaven" helped the rulers legitimize their ruling and empowered them with sacred, absolute authority. Hence, only they had the right to issue orders, and no one was allowed to disobey. Their repressions of slaves

[2] See [2], p. 8.

[3] See [3], p. 250.

[4] See [4], p. 19.

and civilians and punitive expeditions against the feudal princes were portrayed as the "Heaven punishment," and they always "killed people by Heaven's decree." Based on the thought of the religious authority, the origin of law is God's will, which sanctifies the law. Therefore, the legal concept and the concept of the divine right have close relationships in ancient China. The original divine right was the direct basis of the legal authority and even legal contents. As time went by, the fundamental function of divine right was to justify the rationality of legal systems.[5] The thought of the divine origin of law was even more popular among ancient western societies. The prologue of *Code of Hammurabi* claimed straightforward, "Then Anu and Bel (God and Lord respectively; a note from the citer) called by name me, Hammurabi, the exalted prince, who feared God, to bring about the rule of righteousness in the land, to destroy the wicked and the evil-doers; so that the strong should not harm the weak; so that I should rule over the black-headed people like Shamash (Sungod; a note from the citer), and enlighten the land, to further the well-being of humankind."[6] The prologue directly indicates that the monarchical power comes from God, so the law is also God's will. The divine origin of law is an inevitable process of the legal and cultural origin of humans. The world outlook of the ancient tribes, including the Greeks, was of mythological feature in early development when political opinions and legal views were not independent and were a part of the mythical world outlook. According to the mythical views, the world's order was an integral part of the world (universe) order provided with the origin and will of God. The mythical statement of the origin of the universe (Theory of the Origin of the Universe) and origin of God (Theogony) is not only a joint of the formation of thoughts but also a principle to interpret thoughts (the key for interpretation). By this joint and principle and within the range, people's secular lives, social, political, and legal systems, relationships with God, relationships among themselves, and other issues are explained by myths. The Theory of the Origin of the Universe and Theogony is the mythical narrative of events rather than a simple illustration of past events. They are the views of things that everyone should follow. As a unique form to explain the past, myth is also the origin of norms and rules that have binding force and that must be observed unconditionally at present and in the future.[7]

The evolution from the divine origin of the law to the human origin of the law has seen a long history. In the West, the classification of divine law and human law originated from ancient Greece. Two concepts run through the history of the law and philosophy of ancient Greece: the concept of natural law and the concept of the law established and formulated by humans, or natural law and positive law.[8] Natural law evolves from divine law, which represents the divine or God's will, whereas positive law is enacted by human beings, which represents human will. Natural law overrides positive law. The existence of the concept of positive law marks the beginning of the change of the origin of law from divinity to humanity. The US scholar Bodenheimer

[5] See [5].

[6] Diakonov et al. [6], p. 152.

[7] See [7], pp. 5–6.

[8] See [7], p. 15.

introduced that the change started in the fifth century B.C., when a profound shift in the Greek philosophy and thoughts happened where philosophy was separated from religion. The ancient, traditional lifestyle of Greece was blistered. People no longer regarded the law as an unchangeable decree by God but a creation of humans, which was formulated for convenience and could be changed arbitrarily.[9] Apart from positive law, the concept of natural law existed, both of which constituted the dualism of the concept of the law. Dualism did not exist in the thought of divine authority in ancient China. Since the idea of divine authority in the Western Zhou dynasty was abolished, the law has been developed into family law or ethical law. As rituals were integrated into the law, the origin of law was the monism of rituals. Rituals in this context were human rituals rather than divine rituals, so they were the monism of the human origin of the law. Therefore, the dualism of natural law and positive law in the West greatly influenced the development of its legal culture. In the Middle Ages, Theology still dominated the concept of the law when divine law and human law co-existed. For example, Aquinas mentioned that the law was merely an order of practical rationality "embodied by the King" who ruled an entire society. However, if the world was ruled by God, as discussed in the first chapter, the entire society of the universe was dominated by divine rationality. So, God's reasonable ruling of creations enjoyed the legal nature as the King of the universe…the law of such was called eternal law.[10] He clarified that human law was nothing but an embodiment of eternal law. This concept has been fully reflected in ancient Roman law. The famous ancient Roman jurist Justinian said that natural law, by which all states abided, was enacted by God's will, remaining unchanged forever. On the other hand, the laws formulated by each country frequently changed, which was due to the implied consent of citizens or other later-prepared laws.[11] Until the Enlightenment when humanism thrived, the human origin of law was finally established. The legal concept in *On Social Contract* was most apparent. For instance, according to Rousseau, people must voluntarily unite to establish a state, and enact the law based on the complete equality principle for protecting everyone's natural rights, namely freedom, life, and property. To achieve this, they must pursue a combined form so that the form could defend and protect the life and wealth of all combiners with its power. Still, at the same time, individuals who united with the entirety were only subject to themselves and were as free as ever. This is the fundamental problem that the social contract addresses.[12] Based on Rousseau's ideas, the social contract is still a combined action between people, bringing about the state and law. Therefore, Rousseau viewed the law as the product of people's agreement and said that people had combined their will into a single will in all social relations. Hence, all agreements that illustrated the single will become the fundamental laws binding to every state member. These basic laws constrained and regulated the designation and power of the officials who bore the responsibility to supervise and implement other laws. The power might include all

[9] See [8], p. 3.

[10] See [9], p. 106.

[11] See [10], p. 11.

[12] See [11], p. 20.

functions and powers necessary to maintain the constitution but exclude the change of the constitution.[13] Rousseau regarded the law as people's will explicitly, thus secularizing the law thoroughly.

1.2 Ontology of Law

Based on the human origin of law, the origin of the law is human will. But where does the will originate from, and what is its basis? In a broad sense, whether the basis of the law is material or spiritual is concerned with the contradiction between materialism and idealism of the law, which is also the ontological issue of the law.

The idealism of the ontology of law is represented by Hegel, who believes that the bases of law, generally speaking, are spiritual things, whose determined position and starting point is will. As will is free, freedom constitutes the substantive and prescriptive nature of the law, and the legal system is the realm of freedom that has been attained. Hegel said, "Any existence, as long as it is the existence of the free will, is called the law. Hence, the law is freedom as an idea."[14]

In other words, the law is the existence of the free will and the fulfillment of freedom. According to Hegel, during the development, the will experiences three stages: the absolute will, the specialized will, and finally, the true will. The legal system is therefore divided into three components. First is the law of objective will, which is the realm of abstract law in which free will is achieved through external things and possession of property. Second is the law of subjective will, which belongs to the realm of moral law. The fulfillment of the free will in the mind is represented by the inner belief of goodness and badness of the subjects conducting acts. Third is the unity of the law of objective will and subjective will, which belongs to the realm of ethical law, the fulfillment of the free will in a more perfect and higher form, which is expressed through the state, the highest stage of the realization of ethical ideas. This way, free will moves from simple to complicated, from one-sided to comprehensive, and from lower level to higher level in an orderly, logical manner. Free will contains abstract law, moral law, and ethical law, enriching itself as a comprehensive proposition of a variety of prescriptions.[15] Thus, Hegel set out from the idealistic philosophy and defined the law as the existence of the free will, thus denying the decisive role of social material conditions to the law and concluding that it was the law that determined society, not vice versa.

Based on the criticism of Hegel's idealism of the ontology of law, Marx created the materialism of the ontology of law. Marx's materialism is summarized in the following conclusion: legal relations are the same as the states' form, which cannot be understood from themselves or the general development of the human spirit.

[13] See [12], p. 138.

[14] See [13], p. 36.

[15] See [14], p. 15.

Oppositely, they are rooted in the relations of material life.[16] This opinion can be explained from the generation and enactment of the law. In terms of the generation of the law, it comes from the needs of social and economic life. Engels has vividly described the general rule of how the law existed, who said that in a very early stage of the development of society, a need was generated that the production, distribution, and exchange of goods were bound by a common rule, by which individuals are subject to the common conditions of production and exchange. The rule was first expressed as a custom and later as the law. As the law existed, the organ which bore the responsibility to safeguard the law was produced, and it was the public power, namely, the state. As society developed further, the law was developed into extensive legislation, more or less. The more complex the legislation was, the more its expression would be distant from what economic living conditions of daily social life wanted to display.[17] Therefore, the law was produced mainly by the development of economic relations. In terms of establishing the law, Marx has clarified that legislators did not invent but express the law. He said that only those who had no idea of history were unaware of that the King had to obey economic conditions all the time and could never issue orders to these conditions. Both political legislation and civil legislation merely indicated and recorded the requirements of economic relations.[18] Marx even believed that legislators should view themselves as natural scientists. Legislators were not making or inventing the law but only expressing it, and they expressed the inherent law of spiritual relations in the conscious existing laws. If legislators replaced the nature of things with their imagination, we should blame them for extreme waywardness. Likewise, when individuals wanted to run counter to the nature of things and behaved capriciously, legislators had the right to regard them as extreme waywardness.[19] However, Marx's inherent law of spiritual relations was not what Hegel mentioned as a subjective idea; instead, it should be understood as the objective law. Therefore, legislators should take the inherent law of objective things as their cognitive object, which was not changed by the legislator's will.

Legislators could not replace the nature of things by their subjective will; otherwise, they were extremely wayward in legislation. Of course, the materialism of the ontology of law was not the denial of the role of legislation. When legislators expressed the law, there remained an issue on how to express it accurately. Engels pointed out that if civil codes just expressed the social, economic, and living conditions through the form of the law, these codes could express these conditions well or badly depending on different situations.[20] Whether the standard is good or bad only depends on whether the law coincides with economic development, meaning that good laws promote economic development, whereas bad laws hinder economic development. Hence, legislation is a complicated process in which subjectivity and objectivity interact. In conclusion, according to Marx's ideas, legislative activities are

[16] See [15], p. 32.

[17] See [16], p. 211.

[18] See [17], pp. 121–122.

[19] See [18], p. 183.

[20] See [19], p. 253.

subjective, purposeful creative activities. Legislative activities are the processes in which legislators (the subject) consciously express the law through their purposeful objective activities. As the subject of legislative activities, legislators do not directly view and adapt to the object but reform and humanize the object following the interests and needs of their class. Accordingly, legislative activities are purposeful and conscious activities, which belongs to subjective activities. Nevertheless, legislative activities are not common conscious activities; rather, they are special conscious activities. As a special conscious activity, legislation is a crucial representation of the ruling class's conscious initiative of legal practices. The establishment of the law expresses the distinctiveness by the ruling class to provide the legal basis for the establishment, maintenance, and development of the social relations and social orders that benefit its class. The subjective purposefulness of legislative activities never satisfies its subjectivity, nor is it limited within the subjective consciousness. It has a strong intention to transform from subjectivity towards objectivity and from the materialization or objectification of specific concepts of the law towards the reality that creates the law. Undoubtedly, if legislators do not take the initiative to create laws, the subjective purpose will only exist as a wish of all people, an ideal thing that should exist, and a thing that may exist in reality. Only through the legislator's conscious and active practices of creating the law can the legislative purpose be changed from the subjectively set object to the real object.[21] Marx's materialism of the ontology law is vital for us to understand the nature of law and the general rule of the dialectical movement of the law.

Setting out from the materialism of the ontology of law, we should understand and grasp the general rule of socio-economic development when creating laws for legislation to be grounded on society and reflects society, and promotes social development. There involves an issue on how to understand legislative conditions correctly. That is, how to coordinate the relationship between the stability of the law and social changes. Roscoe Pound, an US jurist, said that the law must be stable and static. Therefore, all legal thoughts tried to coordinate the contradictory needs for maintaining stability and pursuing changes. The social interest in general security urged people to seek a definite basis for the absolute order of human behaviors to guarantee a solid and stable social order. However, the constant changes in the social living environment required the law to consistently adjust itself based on other pressures of social interests and the new forms endangering security. As a result, legal orders must be stable and flexible concurrently. People must check and revise the law according to the changes in real life that the law should adjust to. If we probe the principle, we should explore both the principle of stability and change. Therefore, the primary problem that legal thinkers are committed to solving is the ways to coordinate the fixed thoughts (individual waywardness is not allowed) in the law with the thought of change, development, and formulation of the new law, to unify legal theories with legislation theories, and to unify the judicial system with the law enforcement by judicial personnel.[22] China is in a period of social transformation, and the relations

[21] See [14], p. 125.

[22] See [20], p. 1.

between legal stability and social changes are particularly vital. China is reforming its economic system, and the development of market-oriented development has brought about social changes in an all-around manner. Thus, we need to change laws, which makes legislation a weighty mission. In this case, we should timely enact laws based on the changes in our social life and keep in mind that the law is stable to prevent laws from frequently changing. A key issue is that legislation should timely and accurately reflect the changes in social life.

1.3 Epistemology of Law

The law is the subjective expression of the inherent rule of objective things by humans; then, is this reflection of objective things expressed by legislators rational or empirical? This is a crucial question worth studying. There has been a disagreement regarding this question between the rationalist concept of law and the empirical concept of law.

The rationalist concept of law regards the law as the representation of human reason and calls it rational law. The concept of rational law dated back to the thought of natural law in ancient Greece, where it was the Stoics who first promoted the thought of natural law. For example, one of the founders of the Stoics Zeno of Elea posited that the entire universe was composed of a substance, which was the reason. In his opinion, therefore, natural law was rational law. As a part of the universe and nature, humans were rational animals who obeyed the order of reason and arranged their lives based on their natural law. Cicero, an ancient Greek philosopher, was similar to the Stoics, who tended to determine nature and natural reason, and imagined reason as the dominant power of the universe. He mentioned that there was a real law—right reason—adaptive to nature and all humans, which was unchanged and external. The law called for people to perform their obligations through the decrees of the real law; people would not do unjust things through the prohibitions of the real law. Decrees and prohibitions influenced kind people constantly but had no impacts on bad people. It was never morally justified to offset the right reason with human legislation. It was never allowed to try to abolish a component of the right reason, and it was impossible to abolish it altogether…the right reason would not establish a law in Rome while establishing another in Athens, nor would it change every day. What we had was an externally unchanged law, which every state should observe at all times. Humans only had a joint master and governor—God, because God was the law's creator, promulgator, and implementer.[23] According to the thoughts of the natural law by ancient Greek and Roman philosophers, natural law represents national reason. Oppositely, positive law is formulated based on natural law, so it expresses human reason. Modern Enlightenment scholars further promoted the thoughts of reason, and the concept of rational law became the dominant legal theory of that time. According to the US jurist Pound, the concept of reason proposed then was to

[23] See [8], pp. 13–14.

counterbalance the Middle Ages' authority and to establish a new authority, which was the reason. These jurists held that the law was a manifestation of reason, which achieved justice through the authoritative declaration of reason, and justice was the ideal relationship among people.[24]

The empirical concept of law regards the law as the representation of human experience, and the law is the organized experience. Customary law is accumulated through the long life of humankind, which is the accumulation and crystallization of human legal experience, so empiricism stresses customary law. The historical school of jurisprudence advocates the empirical concept of the law. The founder of the historical school Friedrich Carl von Savigny, a German jurist, was against the rationalist concept of law by the natural school of jurisprudence. He denied the existence of natural law and negated that positive law was the creation of legislators. Savigny held that natural law was an unfounded supra-empirical a priori hypothesis, and could not be the origin of the law. Positive law was not formed due to legislation, and it was formed beyond the scope of legislators' activities. So, the rationalism's opinion on the legislation that formulating a universally applicable code of human beings through the universal reason of human beings was a ridiculous fantasy.

Savigny believed that the law was only born and bred within a state and developed capriciously, which was not established by formal, rational legislative means. While against natural law, he claimed that the law represented national spirit or national consciousness. Only national spirit or common national consciousness were the actual creators of positive law. Setting out from the legal ontology of national spirit, Savigny insisted that common law be the basis of the law. He believed that the best source of law was not legislation but customs. The only rational law should be alive among people. Customary law was most vital, and its position was far exceeding legislation; only customary law could easily achieve the fixity and clarity of legal norms.[25] He advocated national spirit and safeguarded customary law, contending with rationalism's concept of legal rationalism, from which his empirical philosophical thoughts were revealed.

Whether the law expresses reason or experience is directly related to legislation. In my view, reason and experience are inseparable during the legislation. Legislation is the rational understanding of the inherent law of objective things, and legislative activities can only be conducted scientifically based on reason. However, legislative activities should depend on experience because rational understanding originates from the reflection of objective things. The rationalist concept of law stresses the importance of reason in legislative activities, which is undoubtedly correct. Nevertheless, if the empirical understanding is thoroughly excluded, human reason will be water without a source and a tree without roots, inevitably becoming a fantasy. The empirical concept of law denies the role of reason in legislative activities. It depends on experience excessively, and even takes the experience as the reason to negate statute law, which is very biased. Statute law and customary law are not always

[24] See [20], pp. 5, 110.

[25] See [21], pp. 367–372.

contradictory. The legislation includes two circumstances: enactment and recognition. Apart from legislative activities that directly creates the law, customary law is formulated into the law through the legislature's recognition. Recognition refers to the recognition of customary law. Hence, reason and experience are united in legislative activities. In a sense, the legislation promotes human experience and human's understanding of objective things to the law through rational processing.

The epistemology of law can only be illustrated correctly when reason and experience are dialectically unified. As the US jurist Pound has said, the philosophical school of jurists paid attention to reason, whereas the historical school of jurists focused on experience. Both made sense. Only the law that passed the test by reason could persist, and only the rational declaration based on experience or tested by experience could become a permanent part of the law. The experience was formed by reason, and the reason was tested by experience. Apart from them, nothing was valid in the legal system. The law was the experience organized and developed by reason, which was officially published by law-making or law-promulgating organs in a politically organized society and supported by social force.[26]

Among China's current legislative activities, there is an argument about whether legislation can be advanced, which involves the relationship between reason and experience to a large extent. There are three opinions in China's legal academia[27]: first, the lagging perspective. It holds that the following law should be established when the preceding one becomes mature. Some people even state that the following article should be established when the preceding article becomes mature. Their fundamental reason is that China is in reform, and we have no experience, so we should gain experience from social practices first. When the experimental things become mature, we will then fix the mature and definite experience in the form of law. So, the law should be lagging. This is a traditional fundamental principle of legislation, which has dominated the previous legislative practices. Second is the synchronization perspective, which believes that legislation should not be in advance or lagging but be synchronous with social development. The fundamental reason is that lagging legislation fails to play the full role of the law and is not conducive to the development of legal systems; however, legislation in advance does not coincide with the reality, which is difficult for the law to be implemented. Third is the advance perspective, which posits that legislation should be based on the objective conditions when the law is formulated and should make predictions on society.

Legislators should take the predictions on future social conditions as their basis, reflect the social conditions during the implementation of the law, and make some advance provisions. The fundamental reason is that social development has a regular pattern, which is knowable. So advance legislation is possible. Meanwhile, the law does not act on the society where it is formulated but the later society, so it should be based on the future social conditions. This indicates that advance legislation is necessary. According to the three arguments mentioned above, the following issues are worth studying:

---

[26] See [22], p. 110.

[27] See [23], pp. 91–92.

The first issue is how we see the law's role in society. Some negative understandings of the law's role holds that the law only reflects or establishes some social relations. Now, people have considerably changed their understandings of the law's role. They believe that the law reflects social life, which leads and promotes the development of social life. In this sense, the law is merely a tool for social development, especially in times of social change, the law's role for social development is more prominent. Modern social science holds that the repetitive interactions among social members define the society. The change of a society is the change of these repetitive interactions. Thus, social change is defined as the change of repetitive behavioral modes, and development is a form of social change. Repetitive behavioral mode is limited by regulations and supported by sanctions, which expresses the expected behaviors of social members. Hence, the law promotes social change through changing repetitive behavioral modes. The US scholar Ann Seidman and Robert B. Seidman mentioned that the law participates in the social developmental process through two methods. First, a state always promotes social reforms step by step and purposefully. Usually, only states have enough capabilities, resources, and legality to fulfill this intimidating task. States change the rules that prescribe repetitive behavioral modes to make officials perform in a new way, that is, to change legal orders and promote social development. The need for development is the need for new laws: the right of land use, market commission, planning machine, electoral politics, educational system, monetary system, tax system, and other new rules. Second, a state promotes social changes in a violent and turbulent manner.

Under this circumstance, revolution, war, harvest, and inflation may appear. Society is changed under the force of legal orders, and new behavioral modes are produced through legal reforms. Rather than introducing reforms into another static society, the production of new behavioral modes is to urge the existing change process. To sum up, in the twentieth century, governments discussed social issues through legal orders. They used a tool earnestly to change behaviors and even systems. From the perspective of an instrumentalist, the purpose of the state and law was to influence the behavioral modes of society, to consolidate all essential social systems directly and indirectly.[28] Therefore, both the views of lagging legislation and synchronization legislation ignore the promotion role of the law and understand the role of law negatively.

The second issue is whether the law is predictable. To be precise, the issue is whether human reason can predict social development. Our answer is positive because advance legislation is not entirely independent of social reality. The comrades who negate advance legislation believe that the meaning of "advance" surpasses reality; nonetheless, the law should not surpass reality. The objective reality is the starting point of all legislation work.[29] I believe that advance legislation does not contradict the dependence on reality. Advance legislation must be based on reality. In this sense, the advance nature and actuality of the law are unified. The advance nature, the legislative principle, should not be independent of reality. It must have

[28] See [24], pp. 20–23.

[29] See [25].

both "should" and "may" in reality. As science develops, we can correctly understand and predict the trends and rules of social development and transform them into explicit legal norms to lead and regulate people's behavioral activities. As people have mentioned, advance legislation is the topic of the fundamental social contradictions and social functions of legal norms, the component of the legislative activities, one of the operation rules of the law, and the necessary demand for the development of the contemporary information society.[30]

The third issue is the epistemological basis of legislation, that is, does the law reflect reason or experience? Undoubtedly, the idea of lagging legislation has a strong tendency towards empiricism.[31] Then, can we say advance legislation denies the role of experience in legislation, and is purely based on reason? The answer is no because I have mentioned that advance legislation is not independent of social reality; it foresees social development based on social reality. I also disagree with the advance nature that is wholly divorced from reality. Thus, advance legislation has boundaries. Some Chinese jurists have pointed out the changes in legislative ideas and the difference with early legislative ideas. Legislation has no longer been limited to the conclusions of experience or direct descriptions of reality of social management. The legislative idea, which is consistent with the lagging social development, limited economic form, simple interpersonal relationship and single social management in the early stage, is so weak in today when society develops rapidly, economic forms diversify, complex interpersonal relationship increases, and social management integrates. If people do not define the law and provide litigation methods before the behaviors that have not been conducted but will be conducted, they will meet countless dilemmas when implementing the law. History calls for a more profound intervention of the law. Social development needs to be directed by stable laws, and legal norms also pursue a long, relative unification. To do this, advance legislation is added into the empirical legislation and conclusive legislation, and the proportion of advance legislation in social legislation has increased considerably. From the advance content of some articles to the advance setting of the whole law, and from focusing on the past and the present to the present and the future, the practicability of law has been expanded historically. As the supplements of empirical legislative concepts, the concepts of advance legislation and transplanted legislation have been shown in contemporary legislative practices.[32]

Therefore, legislation has changed from reviewing the past, notably recognizing and recording the experience and facts in the past, to facing the future, particularly understanding future social changes rationally. As a result, legislation will play a more prominent role in promoting social development.

---

[30] See [26].

[31] See [23], p. 93.

[32] See [27].

2 Legislative Mode (1): Statutory Law

Statutory law has become the primary form of the contemporary law all over the world.[33] Statutory law means that the law has been codified, and that code is the best carrier of the legal spirit. Statutory law has been a representation of the rule of law, which impacts and penetrates all aspects of social life. Generally, legislation first reminds people of the enactment of statutory law. Then, what is the fate of statutory law? It is necessary to probe the humanistic foundation of statutory law to understand the value of statutory law more profoundly.

2.1 Historical Investigation of Statutory Law

Statutory law does not exist simultaneously with the law. It is the outcome of the law that has developed to a mature stage. Thus, the transformation from unwritten law (mainly customary law) to statutory law is a legal revolution in human history.

The revolution of statutory law in ancient China emerged in the Spring and Autumn and the Warring States. Some scholars inferred that there were Yu, Tang, and Jiu punishments before the Spring and Autumn and the Warring States. Although they were in different periods and their contents and forms were diverse, all of them might be statutory laws. Through the investigation of historical documents, it is believed that the ancient statutory law has already taken shape as late as the Zhou Dynasty.[34] In the Spring and Autumn Period and the Warring States Period, statutory laws were promulgated on a large scale, which was closely related to the social revolutions at those times. The Spring and Autumn Period and the Warring States Period was a period of social revolution from slave society to feudal society. Since the Spring and Autumn Period, the slavery system has declined, and feudalism has risen when the emerging landlord class continually launched reform movements to change the slavery system into feudalism. The reform movements marked the start of the statutory law. There was a fierce struggle around the publication of statutory law. Zichan and Deng Xi of Zheng, and later Xunzi and Legalists advocated publishing and implementing statutory law, whereas Confucius disagreed with publishing it. Publishing statutory law was the prominent need of the mass of the Spring and Autumn Period, particularly the emerging landlord class who were not nobles. In the past, the slave-owner nobles did whatever they wanted to do with the slaves in their fiefs and arbitrarily persecuted civilians, including landlords who were not nobles. To abuse punishment, they refused to publish the punishment book on what behavior was a crime and what punishment should be imposed for what crime. They did so primarily because they wanted to put people in an extreme horror where "if the law is not promulgated; it has unlimited power" (*Zuo Zhuan*) and could be arbitrary and domineering. This was the convention of the slave society and special

[33] See [27].

[34] See [28], pp. 41, 42.

power empowered to the slave-owner nobles. In the Spring and Autumn Period, as private ownership developed, people gained more power, and the emerging landlords who were not nobles, merchants, and the working masses pressed for formulating and publishing the statutory law that limited the nobles and protected their private property, physical security, and other rights. As society was experiencing a huge change, some feudal princes and aristocrats in power, especially the aristocrats who were transforming into feudal landlords, promulgated statutory laws step by step to adapt to new changes and strived for the support of the landlord class who were not nobles and other civilians. In 536 B.C., Zichan of Zheng's "Casting Penal Book" was published; in 513 B.C., Zhao Yang of Jin's "Casting Penal Pot" was published, and later Deng Xi of Zheng's "Bamboo Penal" was made. The publication of statutory law was strongly opposed by the conservatives who safeguarded the etiquette system. According to the *Zuo Zhuan: the Sixth Year of Duke Zhao of Jin*, "In March, Zheng cast the penal book on a tripod. Shu Xiang wrote to Zichan, 'I placed my hope on you, but now it is over. The former Duke measured the severity of an event and decided the punishment. There was no penalty because he was afraid of people fighting over each other. However, crime could not be prevented. Therefore, he had morality to prevent crimes, political orders to constrain crimes, and rituals, credits, and kindness to avoid crimes. He also set up official rank and salaries to encourage obedient people and severely convicted crimes to threaten indulgent people. He was still afraid these would not work, so he taught people with loyalty, rewarded people according to their behaviors, taught people with professional knowledge and skills, asked people to work with a pleasant attitude, treated people seriously, supervised people with dignity, and judged crimes with a firm attitude. He would also visit smart and capable ministers, sensible officials, loyal and trustworthy township heads, and kind teachers. Only by these means could the people be used, and no disaster would be triggered. If people knew the law, they would not respect the Duke and wanted to fight over each other. People take the law as the basis, and if they avoided punishments successfully, the Duke could no longer control them. The Xia dynasty had some people who breached the law, so it published *Yu Punishment*; the Shang dynasty had the people who breached the law, so it formulated *Tang Punishment*, and the Zhou dynasty promulgated *Jiu Punishment*. When these laws were published, these dynasties were on the verge of extinction. You are the minister of Zheng. You designate the boundary of fields and ditches, set up regulations for people who slander political affairs, formulate laws and regulations, and cast penalties on the tripod. Is it not difficult to stabilize people in these ways…If people knew the basis of the competition, they would abandon the etiquette and refer to the punishment book. People would have each word and sentence of the punishment book out. There would be more crimes and bribery. I'm afraid Zheng will decline when you live! I heard that when a state was going extinct, it would make more laws and regulations. I am afraid this is the case.'" Confucius was even more distressed and disgusted at Jin's casting the punishment on the tripod and rebuked it, "Jin will extinct because it has lost all moral standards. Previously, Shu Yu of Tang of Jin formulated laws to restrict people. The nobles would observe laws according to their levels of official rank. Therefore, the people respected nobles, and nobles could defend their industries.

There was no chaos between the upper class and lower class, and this was the moral standard...Now, the moral standard is abandoned and replaced by the punishment cast on the tripod. People can see the law on the tripod, and who will respect nobles? How do nobles maintain their industries? Since there is no order between the nobles and people, how does the Duke govern the state? Also, Fan Xuanzi's penal book was made when he inspected barbarian areas. It violated the old rituals of Jin. How could it be a law?" Confucius' criticism first is that the content of the statutory law violates the old rituals of Jin, so the statutory law should not be defined as a law. More importantly, Confucius's attitude towards statutory law can be seen. Confucius believes that according to the traditions of nobles, criminal law is not published to the public so that nobles can arbitrarily punish civilians and slaves. Therefore, the statutory law should not be punished from an institutional point of view. Until the late Warring States period, statutory law has become a consensus for people. Legalism in particular, advocated that laws and regulations must be "made known to the public." Legalists held that after legislation, if people are to abide by it, it must be published to the people in a written form and strive to be well-known to all households. The purpose of publishing statutory law is not only "making people behave according to the law" but also "deterring officials from browbeating people in the beach of the law, and people from breaking the law to provoke officials." It can prevent officials from arbitrarily deciding the crimes and punishments while preventing criminals from pleading or purposefully making difficulties. Legalism's claim effectively attacked the tyranny of nobles and officials at all levels, and the secret law tradition that "if punishment is unknown, its power is unpredictable."[35] Even the Xun Kuang of Confucianism advocated to formulate and promulgate statutory law. He did much propaganda to inform "all people that theft makes no one wealth; robbery and murder make no one longevity; violation of King's prohibitions makes no one peace...hiding and fleeing after committing crimes makes no one get away with punishment."[36] It could be seen that people agreed to publish statutory law mainly because they had new understandings of the role of statutory law, having found its threatening effect, so they changed their concept that "if punishment is unknown, its power is unpredictable." From the perspective of psychology, whether the threatening effect of law comes from its indefiniteness and unpredictability or its definiteness and predictability is worth researching. Anyway, statutory law is better than customary law, and this is uncontroversial. Starting from the Spring and Autumn Period and the Warring States Period and from *The Canon of Laws* to *Qin Law*, *Han Law* and *Tang Law*, China's legal tradition of statutory law was traced to the same origin, and China's magnificent legal system featuring statutory law was thus formed. The legal system stood its own feet in the world legal system until the end of the Qing dynasty. The revolution in the late Qing dynasty introduced the civil law system that was expressed by statutory law rather than the common law system that was expressed by case law. The reason was that the former shared close relationships with China's cultural background of the law and that statutory law could be transplanted.

---

[35] See [4], p. 122.

[36] *Xunzi Junzi*.

The civil law system is noted for statutory law, whose legal tradition originates from ancient Roman Law. The British historian Edward Gibbon classified Roman Law into four periods: customary law, statutory law, developed period of statutory law, and codification. He also defined them temporally based on legislative techniques. The customary law period covered from the Italian city of Rome to the formulation and publication of *The Twelve Decemviral Tables*. The statutory law covered from *The Twelve Decemviral Tables* to the Late Republic. The developed period of statutory law experienced from the early Roman Empire to the reign of Alexander Severus in the early third century. The codification was from the reign of Alexander Severus to Emperor Justinian.[37] In the ancient period of ancient Rome, there was no statutory law. Its customary law was composed of old habits and traditions of the state, general social customs of that time, and judicial precedents, which were approved by the state and empowered with legal validity. Early Rome had no laws but only customs, so it had no specific judicial organs or judicial system to hear cases. The administrative organ performed the judicial function. Until the early Republic, legal concepts and judicial concepts were integrated closely into state organs. Early in the sixth century B.C., when Servius Tullius conducted his revolution, the social class struggle in Rome made its first appearance. When the Roman monarchy was overthrown and the Republic was established, the struggle further intensified. As for the law, civilians were extremely dissatisfied with the legislative tyranny of senior officials, particularly revolting against their arbitrary behaviors in judicial activities. It was said that in 462 B.C., when tribunes suggested formulating the law to limit the power of supreme administrative officials, nobles were against it immediately. They had struggled around this issue for several years, and finally, nobles compromised. Under this circumstance, Roman Senate decided to delegate a committee of three people to investigate the legal system of Greece, especially to study Solon's law. Two years later, in 452 B.C., the investigation group returned to Rome and established a ten-man legislation committee (the Decemvirate) led by Claudius, making ten tables of statutory law strictly according to the coordination principle in 451 B.C. A year later, a new ten-man committee continued to add two tables, which produced *The Twelve Decemviral Tables*. *The Twelve Decemviral Tables* included proceedings preliminary to trial, trial, execution of judgment, paternal power, inheritance and guardianship, ownership and possession, real property, torts or delicts, public law, sacred law, supplementary laws of the first five tables, and supplementary laws of the last five tables. *The Twelve Decemviral Tables*, consisting of old habits and new orders, mostly including the acknowledgment of old habits, which became the developmental basis of Roman law later.[38] Although it acknowledged old habits, it was codified, which exerted profound impacts on the formation of the civil law system. The formation of *The Twelve Decemviral Tables* shows that it is the result of the struggle between nobles and civilians, which motivates legislation socially. The famous Italian scholar Giuseppe Grosso has an excellent comment regarding this: it was the episode of the struggle between nobles and civilians in Roman history

---

[37] See [29], p. 13.

[38] See [30], pp. 30–31.

that was so special that people interpreted *The Twelve Decemviral Tables* as the 'unique' milestone through Roman history. The development of habits is independent of legislative intervention. As we will see, it is a natural process of legal (*iut*) development. The legal theory, as the source, is also involved. During the earliest period of this process, an important legislative activity emerged, which was attributed to historical requirements that promoted the development of law externally. This is the great struggle between nobles and civilians. Precisely, this is the struggle emerged in the intensification stage before civilians succeeded and were incorporated into the city-state.[39] After *The Twelve Decemviral Tables*, another grand occasion in Roman history is the Justinian's codification. Codification is one of the marks of advance legislative techniques and legislative activities for legal norms to be systematic. The ancient Roman codification started from the compilation of laws and regulations. Early in the third century, the supreme slave governor began to monopolize legislative power, formulate and supplement sacred law through enacting decrees, and allow jurists to compile decrees. Jurists started to compile the emperor's decrees, of which the most noted was the *Gregorian Code* (*Codex Gregorianus*), which was compiled by the jurist Gregorius appointed by the Roman emperor Theodosianus. The Code was promulgated in 295, covering all laws from Emperor Valerianus in the mid-third century to 294. Another was the *Hermogenian Code* (*Codex Hermogenianus*), which was compiled by the jurist Hermogenian during the late reign of Emperor Justinian. It was promulgated in 324, covering the 30-year laws since 294. Sooner after that, the official authority started to compile codes. The *Theodosian Code* formulated in the fifth century was the earliest official code. This was a codification of decrees led by Emperor Theodosius II, which was promulgated in 438. It had 16 books, and each was sequenced by the production of the laws, covering extensive themes and contents. Additionally, it clarified the legal effect of the codification of the previous two sacred codes. In 527, Justinian became the emperor and appointed the jurist Tribonianus to establish a ten-man committee and compile legal codes on February 13, 528. In 529, twelve books of the *Code of Justinian Law* were compiled, and 50 books of *Digest* were compiled in 530. The completion of the *Code of Justinian* and *Digest* marked the systematization of the Roman law and the fulfillment of the reformation of old Roman law. In 533, Gaius's *Institutes* no longer adapted to the objective social needs, so Justinian suggested that Tribonianus compile new legal textbooks based on *Institutes*. After the book was sent to Justinian for approval, Justinian empowered it with the force of decrees and promulgated it across the country. This was known as Justinian's *Institutes*. After the huge compilation of codes, Justinian believed that the three codes which he had put all efforts into had covered all existing social relations, so there was no need for new legislation. Hence, he prohibited all jurists' works in the administration of justice and only allowed the three legal documents he participated in compiling. He also ordered to burn all works and manuscripts of jurists that had not been collected in his *Institutes*. Furthermore, he prohibited all comments on his codes. He held that his codes could address all legal problems and there was no need for the comments and notes from jurists. His codes had been perfect, and

[39] See [31], p. 82.

any commentary on them would only undermine their glory. However, the reality smashed his fantasy cruelly. New social relations were not included in the codes, forcing him to publish new decrees for adjustment. During the 31 years from 534 to 565, Justinian has promulgated 165 decrees, which jurists compiled after his death, and this was *Justinian's Novels*. The four legal documents of the *Code of Justinian*, *Digest*, *Institutes*, and *Justinian's Novels* were later known as the *Body of Civil Law*, the most systematic and comprehensive Roman law.[40] As the Roman Empire perished, Roman law lost its force. Until the twelfth century, the Revival of Roman Law started in Europe, and the thirteenth century's civil law system was gradually formed based on Roman law. In particular, the systematic codification, unified scattered laws into a unified national legal system. Strictly speaking, codification began in France as the outcome of the French Revolution. The US scholar Ehrmann has discussed the codification movement in the early nineteenth century in Europe deeply and mentioned that the codification, which began in the early nineteenth century and spread over the whole European continent from the Atlantic to the Ural Mountains, was due to the region's different political climate from that of Britain and its colonies, where, under the efforts of royal judges, common law has unified a lot of diverse habits. The French Revolution and the newly-established German Empire had to be confronted with disorderly and complicated common laws and local laws. The French emperor's requirement of unifying moderate requirements of the existing laws came to a failure due to the boycott of local courts. The fact, however, was that these courts were the judicial organizations of feudal lords and local nobles who tried to utilize the laws to serve their interests. The chaos and injustice caused by them made the judiciary the most corrupted part of the kingdom, which the Revolution destroyed. "Do you want good laws?" shouted Voltaire, "Burn those you have and make new ones!" Combining the positive belief for novelty and the positivist idea that all laws needed to be reformed effectively formed an idea consistent with the Enlightenment Spirit, which set the tone for all important codification. The law had no relations with politics on the surface, so it was not utilized by the latter. However, only when social elites unanimously believed that codes benefited the establishment of norms and systems would the effect of laws be guaranteed.[41] The French revolution was comparatively thoroughgoing. During Napoleon's reign, the *Civil Code of the French*, *Code of Civil Procedure*, *Penal Code*, *Code of Criminal Procedure*, and *Commercial Code* have been completed, marking the successful completion of codification. In Germany, however, the feudalistic influence was powerful, so the revolution was not thoroughgoing, and conservatives obstructed the codification movement. In the late eighteenth century, Germany was the most economically and politically left-behind country in western Europe and was very feudal in the legal system. Even though it was still named "Holy Roman Empire", there was no unified imperial law, and states' laws were in utter disorder. Prussia had a state law; nonetheless, the content was so complicated that the law only had the supplementary effect in many cases. Other state laws were not a quarter as good as Prussia's. To change the situation, in

[40] See [32].

[41] See [33], pp. 51–52.

the early nineteenth century when Napoleon I was defeated, Thibaut, a law professor from the University of Heidelberg, felt it was time for Germany to seek independence, so he published the pamphlet titled *On the Necessity of a General Civil Law for Germany* to initiate the promulgation of a unified code across the country. In the pamphlet, Thibaut appealed for all state governments to abolish old bad habits by virtue of this opportunity and work together to formulate a code universal across Germany, which covered the civil code, penal code, and litigation. Otherwise, the Federal Republic of Germany would not be prosperous because state laws were full of contradictions, which only divided the Federal Republic of Germany and hindered judges and administrative officials from understanding laws. Also, state laws were fragmentary, so there was a need to formulate a concise code that was made by itself and suitable for the needs of the people and national conditions. The author held that laws must be unified before the nation was unified. The foundation of the independence of the Federal Republic of Germany was the formulation of codes prevailing in all states so that nationalities within the country observed the same law and enjoyed the same rights. Thibaut's claim to formulate a unified code across Germany was completely suitable for the situation and was of historical significance. However, under the historical conditions of Germany, the bourgeoisie was very weak, and it was the feudal nobles that held the dominant position. Therefore, Thibaut's claim was opposed by the majority of Prussia's political and legal communities. The vanguard of opposition was Savigny, the representative of the German Historical School of Jurisprudence. Savigny specifically wrote the book titled *Of the Vocation of Our Age for Legislation and Legal Science* to oppose Thibaut. In his pamphlet, Savigny strongly advocated the customary law representing the interests of decadent feudal governors, regarded it as the foundation of legislation, and opposed the formation of a unified code across Germany. Savigny said that the law could be established but not fabricated. For instance, language was developed naturally during the nation's development, and we must not compile a dictionary as the universal language for all nations. Similarly, the law was the manifestation of the national spirit produced from the "legal concept" of nationals, so we must not require a unified law by compiling a general code. If we hope to compile a code to unify nations, it is as ridiculous as compiling a dictionary to unify language. Therefore, Savigny insisted that customary law was the foundation. In his opinion, customary law became a law not because of customs. Rather, it became a custom because it was a law. Although obstructed by conservatives, codification was completed in Germany later. *The Penal Code of the German Empire* of 1871 and *The Civil Code of Germany* of 1900 became the most representative codes in the civil law system and exerted a huge influence on the codification of other countries.

Britain primarily adopts case law, but it does not mean there is no statutory law in Britain. Opposite to case law, statutory law is generally called statute law in Britain, where early statute law could not even be distinguished from common law. The Normans and the early House of Anjou promulgated charters, imperial edicts, and decrees, but these were far from statute law in the modern sense because independent legislatures have yet been formed. These governmental laws and regulations were not seen as the supreme authority, but many had the validity of statute law. These legislative documents, which were less authoritative than statute law, vanished from the scene since the late Middle Ages. Even today, many statute laws fail to enjoy the absolute authority they should have. Till the nineteenth century, the weaknesses of the British law started to reveal. The indefiniteness and rigidity of the litigation procedure of the common law brought about criticism, the representative of which was Bentham. Based on the utilitarian philosophy, Bentham reviewed the British law, concluding that the common law was the product of occasional historical events rather than reasonable design. The old concept, complex court organizations, and cumbersome litigation procedures did not ensure people's safety or promote their happiness. Instead, they were the main barriers to social reforms. Bentham strongly advocated reforms on British law, mainly through codification, in order to implement codification comprehensively. He also drafted the constitution, criminal code, and civil code. Although Bentham's proposals on reform were opposed by judges and lawyers and were not accepted directly, they exerted profound influences on the reforms of the 19th British law, from which the status of the British statute law improved gradually. The British scholar Walker mentioned that statute law was the third primary historical origin of the British law, following the common law and equity. Now, it has been the leading force of legal reforms, and with the uprising of codification, it was becoming the most fundamental origin of British law. In addition, all the rules of modern court organizations, jurisdiction, and litigation procedures originated from statute law. Common law and equity were the historical origins of the fundamentals of British law, while statute law was the manifestation. This was an accurate description. Walker even believed that the nineteenth century would greet the codification of codes and judicial judgment, when statute law leaped from a completely subordinated legal origin that aimed to develop the common law to a primary legal origin that outmatched common law and equity.[42] US law was developed based on the adoption of common law, and the basis of US law was British common law. By the mid-nineteenth century, the status of common law among US laws was determined preliminarily. During the determination of common law, some people criticized the case-featured common law and launched the codification movement, which started in the 1930s, represented by Field, a lawyer from New York state. Advocated by him, New York state established the first codification committee in 1847. Five codes were drafted by 1865 with efforts: *Code of Civil Procedure*, *Code of Criminal Procedure*, *Penal Code*, *Civil Code*, and *Political Code*, collectively referred to as "*Field Code*". Schwartz, an US scholar, said that when he evaluated the 19th-century codification movement, David Dudley Field acted as an activist, and this movement was always linked with his name. During a half of the century, Field led the tough attempt to codify common law, when he urged New York state to adopt a comprehensive substantive law code several times. However, he did not achieve all objectives, failing him to become the "US's Justinian". More importantly, the failure of Field defined the relative role of judges and legislatures in the development of law in the nineteenth century and ensured that US laws would develop according to the

[42] See [34], pp. 71–72.

direction of common law.[43] Nonetheless, US statute law still possessed important positions. In particular, in criminal law, by 1980, 24 states have codified common law crimes. The *Model Penal Code* drawn out by US Law Institute has imposed significant influence on the criminal legislation of states.[44] Despite this, the statute law of the common law system compared nothing to the codes of the civil law system. The French scholar David said, "the key difference between British law and French law appears. In France, we have codes, whereas, in Britain, code is nothing important. The crux is that Britain cannot have French codes as long as it maintains its traditional legal concept, insists on following the doctrine of precedents, continues to use its techniques of interpretation rather than the broad concept of the civil law system, or uses the interpretation techniques of the civil law system."[45]

The historical investigation of statutory law shows that statutory law is the outcome of the law that develops to a certain stage, with profound socio-historical reasons. As Chinese scholars have said, throughout the world's history of law, the emergence of statutory law is premised on certain cultural development, such as the popularization of characters and complex social relations. However, the specific reasons and social significance are different.[46] If we do not understand the historical background, it is difficult to understand the natures and significance of statutory law in different countries.

2.2 *Value Analysis of Statutory Law*

As a specific legal culture of human beings, statutory law is universally accepted by countries around the globe and has become one of the most fundamental carriers of law, so it must have its unique cultural value. The cultural value includes the positive value as well as the negative one and the analysis is as follows.

2.2.1 Definiteness of Statutory Law

Definiteness is one of the main values of statutory law, which has been the consensus of legal scholars. The definiteness of statutory law refers to the nature of law that provides the predictable result of behavior for the actor before the behavior is conducted. Based on the definiteness, the law should prescribe a stable causal relationship between a behavior and a result to provide people with fixed, legalized behavioral patterns. Therefore, before people conduct behaviors, they can predict the legal outcomes and act following the law. A law with no definiteness does not allow people to predict the legal outcomes of their behaviors, so people feel at a loss and

[43] See [35], p. 78.

[44] See [36], pp. 21–22.

[45] See [37], p. 23.

[46] See [28], p. 40.

do not know if their behaviors are safe. The law should integrate as many behavioral rules in all aspects of social life as possible for people to follow the rules and achieve freedom within the boundary of law. Meanwhile, laws and regulations must be clear and indefinite regulations should be removed. This is because the predictability of law is grounded on clarity; otherwise, even though ambiguous provisions exist, people are still at a loss since they do not understand the objective of the law, and their safety still is not ensured. Definiteness means that the law is a rule-based system that cannot be changed frequently. Once the law sets a scheme for the relations between rights and obligations, it should try to avoid frequent revisions and breakage of the scheme. Otherwise, the law will lose its authority, and people will cast doubts due to the law's frequent changes.[47] This statement has generalized the connotation of the definiteness of statutory law. The definiteness is represented by clarity, stability, and predictability.

The definiteness of statutory law first requires clear content. Clarity means thoroughly understood, and definiteness means strictly definite. The clarity of statutory law should first ensure citizens' freedom to be free from illegal violation. Particularly in criminal legislation, the doctrine of no penalty without a law gave born to the doctrine of definiteness. US criminologists proposed the "Void-for-vagueness doctrine" in the early twentieth century. Based on this doctrine, although the penalty is defined by law, it fails to prevent the abuse of the power of penalty if it is vague, and the doctrine of no penalty without a law cannot ensure citizens' freedom. The solution is that criminal norms must be clear, and vague criminal norms should be deemed unconstitutional and void. The doctrine of definiteness is the derived doctrine of no penalty without a law and is the key to it.[48] Regarding the definiteness of statutory law, the French Enlightenment thinker Montesquieu said that "after the law has prescribed all concepts very clearly, we should not use any vague or ambiguous wording. Louis XIV's *Criminal Ordinance* precisely lists lawsuits directly related to the King and added, 'all lawsuits that the king's judges have heard'. People just got rid of arbitrary; however, they were pushed back by this sentence."[49] Thus, citizen's right of freedom cannot be guaranteed without the definiteness of law. It should be noted that the definiteness of statutory law is reflected by language, so it is a vital issue to treat legal language correctly. US scholars Nonet and Selznick divided legal order into three modes: repressive, autonomous, and responsive. The authors held that the autonomous law featured Legal Formalism, centered around judges, and was bound by principles. The judges rather than police and legislators represented legal order, so their elaborate preparations of legal rules endowed the law of this stage with a unique style and spiritual temperament. In terms of the objective, a "rule" was a scope-definite and applicable norm. It involved more on the function and aspiration rather than the logic or form. Any abstract norm was impossible to determine a specific judgment or a behavior process.

[47] See [38].

[48] See [39], p. 498.

[49] See [40], p. 297.

However, autonomous law covered the tense relations between generality and particularity, and abstractness and concreteness. It tried to explain every norm as if it was or should be extremely accurate and clear. It achieved this by seriously treating every word and phrase. One mark of autonomous law was the careful investigation of meaning.[50] Thus, the definiteness of legal language is vital. Liang Qichao, a thinker in the late Qing dynasty, said, "Legal language has three elements. First is clarity; second is definiteness, and third is elasticity. Clarity is related to legal language, and elasticity is related to meaning. If obscure wording is used and not understood by women and children, it is unclear. It was always used in ancient times to fool people, so it should not be adopted today. Using clear wording is correct. Bacon said, 'the best nature of law is its correctness,' and this is true. Elasticity means the law contains so much that there is space for explanation. Clarity and elasticity seem to contradict. However, they do not. Elasticity is at the meaning level, while clarity is at the language level. Bacon also said, 'The best law has minimum space for judges to give free rein to, and it has some elasticity. However, if a law has clarity and elasticity at the same time, it is definite.'"[51] China's legislation unilaterally pursues the popularization of legal language, but the popularized language is at the expense of the rigorousness and accuracy of legal rules, which vulgarizes the law,[52] and is undesirable.

The stability of statutory law refers to that law can adapt to the social changes because it is elastic and effective for a long time without a revision. Stability is one of the characteristics of statutory law. If laws are changed frequently, the authority of law will lose.

The stability of statutory law is also the necessary condition of the safety value of the law. If a law is not stable, it will not be safe. The US scholar Bodenheimer said that the safety objective of the law focused on protecting primary needs and interests rather than forming orderly legal techniques. It tried to reduce the frequency of arbitrary changes insofar as the frequency jeopardized the implementation of socially necessary tasks.[53]

The predictability of statutory law refers to that a clear, stable law provides people with a repetitive behavior pattern and guides people's behaviors to predict the legal consequences of their behaviors and thus people draw on advantages while avoiding disadvantages. Therefore, there will be a win–win situation for individuals and society. The Canadian jurist Crépeau said, "Codification—especially when a country's guiding ideology is to formulate popular codes rather than obscure ones—makes the law to be predictable to the greatest extent. When codes allow citizens to know how to behave in advance with specific rules or even general standards, there exists the predictability of the law. The legal system by legislation becomes more and more important for adjusting the increasingly complicated relations among social

[50] See [41], p. 67.

[51] Liang [42], pp. 59–60.

[52] See [43].

[53] See [8], p. 290.

members.[54] The predictability of law represents the justice value for citizens. In the criminal field that has the power of life and death over many people, predictability even matters. The unpredictability of law may increase the deterrence of law, which resonates with an ancient Chinese saying that "if a law is not published, it has unlimited power." However, this is an injustice to citizens, which is called punishment without teaching. A just law teaches people before imposing punishment. It provides citizens with clear lists of penalties, so citizens choose between crimes and non-crimes, and justice and injustice. The predictability of law requires the effect of law to be not retrospective. In the civil law system, non-retroactivity has been a doctrine, especially in criminal law.

To sum up, the definiteness of statutory law requires the law to be clear, stable, and predictable.

It should be noted that definiteness is not held by the civil law system only, but the definiteness of the common law system has huge differences with that of the civil law system. The US scholar Merryman has compared them and said that each legal system pursued definiteness, but definiteness was more valuable in the civil law system because it was the undoubtful basic creed and the most fundamental objective. In the civil law system, definiteness arose mainly from the distrust of judges. Based on the requirements of definiteness, judges should not create laws; legislation should be complete, clear, and logical; the interpretation and applicability of the law should be the "automatic" process to achieve "definiteness". In this sense, definiteness reflected the aspiration of preventing judges from creating laws. The definiteness of law was generally recognized among the countries of the common law system. The definiteness of the common law system had three characteristics: first, it was understood based on more practical concepts and had not been elevated as a must-followed creed. Second, the common law countries achieved definiteness through endowing judicial cases with legal force, while it was not allowed by the civil law system. Finally, the common law countries (especially the United States) generally believed that definiteness was only one of the essential legal principles that sometimes conflicted with other legal principles. In the common law system, definiteness existed as an opposite legal principle of flexibility, and both restricted each other. In the civil law system, definiteness was the most vital legal principle, whereas flexibility was among complicated procedures that would occasionally address problems such as preventing judges from creating laws. To illustrate the crucial position of definiteness in the civil law system, Merryman mentioned that definiteness was an abstract, crucial legal concept, and it was like a queen in a chess game that could move unrestrictedly.[55]

Even though the definiteness of statutory law has positive values, it has adverse effects as well. The modern Chinese scholar Xue Siguang has said that the law had two essential natures: justice and definiteness. These two natures were opposite.

Because if laws were to be followed by people, they had to be permanent to a considerable degree. If they were changed frequently, they would lose authority, causing people to have no laws to follow. If people recognized the existence of laws,

[54] See [44], p. 100.

[55] See [45], pp.49–50.

they had to admit that laws were permanent to a considerable degree. If laws were changed frequently, they would lose authority and cause people to have nothing to abide by. If people recognized the existence of laws, they had to admit that laws were definitive. However, society was either advancing or regressing. Whatever, it was not static. As laws were published for a long time, their justice was utterly or mostly lost for the sake of definiteness. Definiteness was the definiteness of justice, and if laws lost their justice, definiteness would be completely valueless. Under this condition, laws could only exert validity on an applicable case, being overwhelmed, and people did not trust or respect laws anymore. Codes had to change to maintain justice.[56] There remained a discussion on Xue Siguang setting justice against definiteness because the definiteness of law is the prerequisite of justice and frequent changes of laws made them difficult to maintain justice. Xue Siguang argued the limit of the definiteness of laws—it was hard to maintain the justice of laws if definiteness was so highlighted that laws were not changed timely—which was entirely correct. The Canadian scholar Crépeau vividly described the rigid definiteness of laws as the "crystallization of law" and said that one of the drawbacks of codification was the extreme tendency that I referred to as "crystallization", which always "froze" policies. This led to the potential danger of a "crack" between the legislative policies, which were considered valuable and thus collected in codes, and the social reality that codes aimed to adjust. Undoubtedly, when legal norms were disjointed with social reality and customs, the best result of the inconsistency was the disrespect of laws, and the worst result was the violation of laws.[57]

Therefore, we should comprehensively and dialectically understand the value of the definiteness of statutory law.

2.2.2 Universality of Statutory Law

Universality is one of the critical features of statutory law. Bodenheimer, an US scholar, has discussed the elements of the universality of laws, in which he quoted some arguments on the universality of laws by philosophers and jurists throughout history. For instance, Aristotle said, "Law is always a general statement." Also, Cicero stressed that law was a standard, and according to this standard, justice and injustice could be measured. The ancient Roman jurist Papinianus described the law as "a kind of general order." Ulpianus said that laws and regulations were not formulated for individuals. Oppositely, they were universally applicable. Paul recognized that laws and rules were only applicable for situations that were uncertain in quantity and said, "Legislators ignore the situations which happen occasionally." St. Thomas Aquinas regarded the law as a "standard and norm on behaviors." However, Jean-Jacques Rousseau commented, "the object of the law is always universal."[58]

[56] See [46].

[57] See [44], p. 100.

[58] See [8], pp. 225–226.

Therefore, philosophers share a consensus that the law should be universal. Nonetheless, the universality of law is not born with the law. The development of law evolved from individuality to universality through history. For countries in the contemporary world, the primary task of laws is general adjustments, so law enjoys universality. The universality is represented as generality, institutionality, and transplantability.

The generality of statutory law refers to a type of social relationship that is adjusted rather than a social relationship. The generality requires "equal treatment for same things" or "same law applying to the same case" to show the value of the justice of the law. The generality of the law means to abandon the specialty and individuality of things, and it is a high abstraction and generalization of the commonness of the social relations it adjusts. Regarding generality, Hegel has mentioned, "Setting a thing as a general thing means to make it known by consciousness, which is the thought as we know. When the content is reduced to its simplest form, it is empowered the prescriptive nature by the thought. If a law-related thing becomes a law, it must obtain a universal form and real prescriptive nature. Therefore, if we intend to legislate, we should not just see one link—treating a thing as a behavioral rule valid to all people—but realize a more important, intrinsic, and substantial link, that is, the universal content that has been prescribed."[59] Hegel advocated that legislation should be based on universality, represented as the adjustment of general things.

The institutionality of statutory law refers to legal norms that are not only generally applicable but repeatedly applicable. "Repeatedly applicable" means institutionality. Because institution refers to a rule that can be duplicated, the rule can be applied repeatedly as a behavioral pattern. Thus, institutionality contains a temporal dimension of permanency rather than provisionality. Discussing institutions when problems crop up is not an institution. Setting laws in advance and making them into rules is what the institution is.

The transplantability of statutory law means that since statutory law features generality and institutionality, it can be thoroughly transplanted from one country to another.

There are considerable disagreements between the scholars of the civil law system and those of the common law system on whether laws can be transplanted. Scholars of the common law system tend to disagree with it. For instance, the US scholar Ann Seidman and Robert B. Seidman clarified that the law was not transplantable and mentioned that in Africa, even though British law was adopted, the institution that provided the British economy and society did not appear. Concerning this, the African colonies that spoke British had the same experience as those of different periods and places. Turkey copied French laws, Ethiopia copied Swiss laws, French-speaking African colonies copied French laws, and Indonesia copied Dutch laws. These laws failed to trigger the same behaviors as those that appeared in their original countries. We tried to explain this. Through our explanations, we concluded that laws could not be transplanted and institutions were repetitive. Institutions determined the repetitive modes of human behaviors. People said that legal transplantation was rarely practicable because, in a new environment, legal transplantation rarely triggered the

[59] See [13], p. 218.

same behavioral model as that in the original country. The same legal rules and their binding force did not trigger the same behavior for different roles at different times and places and in different material and institutional environments.[60] The scholars of the civil law system tend to show a positive attitude. For example, Japan has transplanted more laws from other laws than any other country, and the Japanese scholar Takeshi Kojima said that Japanese law had integrated foreign laws, such as British law, French law, and German law, thus forming a unified legal system. Therefore, foreign laws and domestic laws became colorful and intertwined knitting formed under a special atmosphere. Takeshi Kojima clarified that it was certain to say that the transplanted western laws had taken root in the Japanese society, and this was a typical, successful example of the comprehensive transplantation of laws.[61]

Chinese scholars have also studied legal transplantation and shown positive attitudes generally. However, they advocated using the terms "reference" and "absorption", who said, "We applied transplantation, relocation, influence, and absorption indiscriminately. If we apply these terms in the sense of introducing a part or entire law or system into another legal system, the connotations of these terms are not different fundamentally, and they only differ in terms of degree. In terms of the term 'transplantation', it is not a legal term but one used in botany and medical science. When people introduce it into jurisprudence, they fail to differentiate it properly. From the perspective of botany, transplantation means transplanting the whole plant and thus contains the meaning of the transplantation of the whole rather than part of it. Nonetheless, from the perspective of medical science, the transplantation of organs means transplanting a part rather than the whole. Moreover, the transplantation of organs reminds people of a series of complex physiological activities such as the exclusivity of the human body. In this way, if the term is used in the sense of botany, people will easily notice that the term is over-simplified, while they have no such impression or understanding if the term is used from the perspective of medical science." The author agrees with using the term; nevertheless, we must explicit its meaning when using it to avoid any misunderstanding. From the perspective of customs, it is more convenient and accurate to coin "reference" and "absorption" that we are acquainted with, and the two terms represent the complex process of introducing foreign laws and adapting these laws to national conditions.[62] In my opinion, understanding transplantation as imitation is wrong, but even the terms "absorption" and "reference" do not reflect the essential characteristics of the specific phenomenon of legal transplantation. Scholars of the civil law system and the common law system have different understandings because of their different legal and cultural backgrounds. The civil law system implements statutory law, which features universality and reflects the commonality of legal phenomena, so it is easier to transplant laws even though there have been several failures. By contrast, the common law system implements case law, which features individuality, and since its

60 See [24], pp. 90, 91.

61 See [47], p. 52.

62 See [48], p. 217.

judicial proceeding and court system is complex, it has greater difficulties to transplant laws. I believe that transplantability is one characteristic brought about by the universality of statutory law. Every country has its special circumstances, so legal transplantation should be localized. When transplanting laws, we should prevent ignoring the specific circumstances.

All in all, the universality of statutory law is represented as generality, institutionality, and transplantability. The universality of statutory law indicates that the application of statutory law is a deductive process from generality to individuality. Since the legal articles are general and abstract, and cases are individual, specific, and diverse, it is difficult to ensure that each case is fairly treated because flexibility is insufficient in the judicial application. More importantly, the universality of statutory law requires covering all situations so that all cases find a basis in statutory law. However, the law is incomplete and relative, so it always has loopholes and blind zones.

2.3 Rational Foundation of Statutory Law

The German well-known scholar Weber has proposed an important concept—rationality, which is different from but related to "reason" used in the philosophical context. Weber's rationality originally referred to the essential nature of the western legal system in modern times that was based on practical reason. In his opinion, every legal system was a legal order composed of decrees and regulations. These decrees usually include two components: imperative component and traditional component. The former is created by legislators, guided by a specific philosophical ideology, while the latter is the outcome of the experience. In ancient Rome, the traditional component was produced by the experience of jurists when they answered the issues of lawsuits in the courts. It came from judges' experience in ruling cases and the principles that solve judicial problems in modern times. Specifically, in a legal system, where the imperative component held the majority, such as Europe, statute law was adopted; by contrast, where the traditional component held the majority, such as Britain, common law was applied. Nevertheless, no matter which legal system was taken, it was dominated by an ideal when it pursued just laws. Weber held that since the nineteenth century, natural law has lost its position as ideal universal legislation and was replaced by the emergence of formal legal theories based on practice rationality. As Weber referred to, the formal legal theory was the modern western law developed from Roman law's formalism principle, which had four characteristics: (1) the rationalization of judicial procedure, which meant that all formal laws should be relatively reasonable in form. In a reasonable legal order, an individual's rights and obligations were determined by a universal, unverifiable principle. This must be certain. The decisions to abolish legitimate orders, or the legitimacy that made these decisions only apply to special occasions and recognition, which was decided based on the specified verifiable principle, were regarded as irrational. (2) the systematization of legal relations. According to Weber, the systematization of legal relations appeared when legal thoughts became mature. It symbolized the integration of legal judgments that were made through analysis. These legal judgments constituted logically clear, inherently consistent, and at least theoretically strict legal systems through integration. All imaginable situations must be logically included so that their orders had an effective guarantee. The concept of this legal system was a special mode of legal ideology, which specifically referred to the modern western legal system under the influence of the formal legal principle of Roman law. (3) the legal analysis method in the sense of logical analysis. The law was "formal", meaning that the law would be considered only when facts were of a conclusive general nature in both substantive and procedural aspects. Formalism can be divided into two types. The tangibility that could be perceived like sensory data was likely to be the characteristic of the things related to the law.

The practice of insisting on the external characteristics of facts, such as the expression of specific words, the signing on documents, and special symbolic behaviors, represented rigorous legal formalism. Another type of formalism was displayed as that the characteristics of the law-related facts were revealed by logical analysis and that clearly-defined legal concepts were constituted and applied in the form of highly-abstract laws and regulations. This meant that only those legal concepts that were logically analyzed and interpreted could become the legal norms in the systematic form. (4) reason controlling. Weber believed that original laws enjoyed two obvious characteristics that differed them from modern laws; that is, they were formally rigid and irrational.[63] The formal legal system in modern western countries, which Weber argued, referred to the common law system, but I believe that it was targeting the civil law system. It summarized four characteristics of formal law, which could be regarded as the characteristics of statutory law. Marx Weber held that European laws featured logically formal rationality. D. M. Truberk interpreted this notion as that "The rationality of legal thinking is established based on transcending the rationality of specific issues to a formal extent that the internal factor of the legal system is the decisive scale; to a logical extent that legal norms and principles are built into the special mode of legal thinking consciously. The thinking is highly logic and systematic that judgments on specific issues can only be made in the specific logical deductive procedure of the pre-set legal norms and principles."

Therefore, the legal norms developed from a single legal source and set in advance were the basis for court decisions. The formal rationality of the law revealed by Marx Weber only existed in German law and vanished in British law.[64] German law could be extended to the civil law system featuring statutory law, while British law could be understood as the common law system featuring case law. In the view of Weber, statutory law had formal rationality. Formal rationality was also referred to as instrumental rationality, a crucial notion for Weber to analyze the social structure. The opposite term was substantial rationality or value rationality. According to Weber, formal rationality was factual, which was the judgment of causal relationship between facts.

---

[63] See [49], pp. 218–222.

[64] See [50], p. 29.

On the other hand, substantial rationality was of the value nature, which was the judgment of the logical relationship between values. Formal rationality was concluded as the calculability of methods and facts, which was objective rationality; substantial rationality was the value of purpose and result, which was subjective rationality. From the perspective of the maximum calculability of purely formal and objective action, Weber posited that science, technology, capitalism, modern legal systems, and administration (bureaucracy) were highly reasonable. However, the rationality was purely formal, and it was always in a tense and antagonistic relationship with substantial rationality—meaning rationality, belief, or value commitment from a substantial special purpose.[65] Weber's notion on formal rationality and substantial rationality was a useful analytical framework for statutory law, although it was to analyze the social structure.

According to Kant's philosophy, reason integrates the concepts provided by intelligence through the governing principle. Kant named the reason that provided transcendental principles as pure reason and distinguished it from the practical reason relevant to actions. Applying Kant's concepts of pure and practical reason, Weber has argued the juristic evolution from natural jurisprudence to formal jurisprudence. Weber held that in the 18th and early nineteenth century in the West, natural law theories had provided an ideal for legislature and jurists. Natural law referred to the joint rights or just systems of human beings, which embodied the eternity and harmony of nature in the field of state and law. As a set of ideal legal theories that was effective at all times, among all nationalities and in all areas, natural law originated from pure reason; as a set of principles that was universally recognized as reasonable behaviors, natural law corresponded to the statutory law formally promulgated by the state and implemented by certain decrees. However, since the nineteenth century, natural law theories have been challenged greatly by all aspects of social practices. In conclusion, these challenges were in the following aspects: (1) Natural law theories originated from the deductive reasoning of transcendental assumptions, which could not address the complicated social problems of class polarization and increasingly acute social class contradictions, which existed after capitalist countries were established; (2) The French Revolution and the European social upheaval in 1840 announced the bankruptcy of social contract theory that was based on the eternal harmony of the nature; (3) The French Revolution, under the banner and guided by the theoretical rationality of Enlightenment thinkers, led to the "terrorist rule" of the dictatorship of the Jacobin Club, and excessive consequences; and (4) The practice-based legal reforms brought more effective results to society. From the standpoint of pure jurisprudence, natural law could not make itself an effective tool for promulgating and discovering laws. When natural law was said to be ideal (valuable) and universal that originated from universal reason, it was the natural law about positivity rather than the one about "nature". It was an idealized reproduction of the law in a specific time and space. It provided a premise for the law to criticize itself.

Against such social background, since the nineteenth century, natural law has lost its position as ideal universal legislation and was replaced by the emergence of

[65] See [49], p. 227.

formal legal theories based on practice rationality.[66] What we refer to in this context is the evolution from natural jurisprudence to formal jurisprudence, which indicates the reformation of natural law during its transformation towards positive law. Natural law is premised on pure reason, which displays the Enlightenment scholars' "transcendental illusions" of the law. When Kant described pure reason, he proposed the notion of "transcendental illusions" and believed that it came from human nature. He mentioned that human nature was unsatisfied with intellectual, scientific knowledge or conditional things. It required to grasp absolute, unconditional, all-inclusive, the most complete, and the most unified entirety. That is to say; it did not satisfy with the previous two integrations: the first was the integration of sensory data by time and space in a priori form, and the second was the integration of perceptual knowledge by pure intellectual concept in a priori form. The results remained in the phenomenal world and within the intellectual, scientific knowledge. However, human nature called for a third integration of knowledge to transcend the phenomenal world and grasp infinite "thing-in-itself". The "thing-in-itself" referred to the entirety independent of our understanding, which was all-inclusive and was explained by itself. Then, what tool should be used for a third integration? According to Kant, the tool was nothing but the intellectual notion because people naturally depended on it. Nonetheless, the intellectual notion was only effective in the phenomenal world, which could only be applied to intuitive, temporal, and spatial things. It could not be applied to essentiality or to prescribe the super-empirical "thing-in-itself". The "thing-in-itself" was not provided by sensory experience. If the "thing-in-itself" were specified transcending the phenomenal world to pursue the completeness and unity of all experience—to specify unconditional, limitless absolute entirety with limited things—there would be self-contradictions and fallacious inferences, in which an illusionary object was formed, which mistakenly regarded the concepts in mind as objective existence, and regarded the subjective pursuit as the object of objective existence.[67] The natural law thought that Enlightenment scholars advocated was the legal transcendental illusion. The eternal, absolute just, equal and free law required by natural law was only a subjective aspiration rooted in human nature. For Enlightenment scholars, however, such a law was set as an objective existence, and these scholars described the natural state in ancient times by talking about the present from experience. For example, the British Enlightenment scholar Locke quoted what the wise Hooke had mentioned in Chapter 10 of Volume 1 of *Laws of Ecclesiastical Polity* as the response to those people who believed that humans were never in a state of nature. He said, "The above laws—natural law—are binding on human beings, even a group of people, although the group never had fixed organizations or signed solemn agreements on what should do or not. Nevertheless, since we cannot live as what our nature asks for on our own, that is, the necessary materials for humans to live with dignity, we naturally lead a common life with others to make up for the shortcomings and defects that must be produced when we live alone, and this is the primary reason for people to unify to constitute a political society". Locke further said, "I assert further that all human

[66] See [49], p. 219.

[67] See [51], p. 197.

beings are in this state and have been in this state before they agreed to become a member of a political society."[68] This statement reflected the persistence and arbitrariness of thinkers, who completely replaced objective existence with subjective imagination. As the US scholar Bodenheimer has mentioned, "these philosophers (referring to Locke, Montesquieu, and other Enlightenment scholars; a note from the citer) addressed legal issues in a properly and logically arranged manner but their manner was often characterized by old-fashion, simplification, and arbitrary assumptions. For example, they held no ground that reason could design all the legal system's universally effective details." However, what can we accuse them of? Bodenheimer answered this question well, "Even if in this aspect, classical natural jurists should not be blamed excessively.

They ignored history and focused on discovering an ideal legal and justice system through which they completed a social task, and the significance exceeded the scholars who purely studied legal history. Through the efforts of thinkers of several generations, the classical natural jurists laid the cornerstones which were used in erecting the legal edifice of modern Western civilization."[69] Undoubtedly, the natural legal thoughts of Enlightenment thinkers represented the unremitting pursuit of the rationality of legal value. However, substantial rationality was merely a moral ideal. It required to supply and satisfy the needs of all social members equally, guarantee the substantial equality of everyone's rights, obligations, property, and distribution, which was ideal equalitarianism. In this sense, substantial rationality was incompatible with formal rationality. Formal rationality was not equal to substantial rationality, at least in a way that its sufficient supply of needs did not satisfy the requirements of substantial rationality.[70] The same was true in the legal field. As a transcendental illusion, natural law provided a facsimile for legislation. However, the value rationality of law should be represented by formal rationality, during which something was lost. The codes that were promulgated completely based on natural law thoughts tended to be inoperative. For instance, the change from the *Penal Code* of 1791 to the one of 1810 illustrated this. After the French Revolution, the National Constituent Assembly promulgated the first penal code of modern France on October 6, 1791. The penal code embodied the classical natural law thoughts comprehensively, especially in its insistence on the doctrine of no penalty without a law and harsh provisions of the penalties of crimes without distinguishing the maximum level and minimum level. The function of judges was to determine crimes, and if a behavior constituted a crime, judges would impose the penalties prescribed by the code upon criminals. This was exactly the legislation of judicial syllogism by Beccaria, the representative of the classical school of criminology. The legislation of absolute statutory sentence prohibited arbitrary judgment of crimes and penalties, but the absence of judges led penalties to be entitled to punish criminals of different culpabilities. This caused the situation to move from one extreme to another, and the rigidness of the code, so the code was hard to satisfy judicial needs. Until the establishment of Napoleon's

[68] See [52], pp. 11–12.

[69] See [8], pp. 66–67.

[70] See [49], p. 231.

dictatorship, the government has started to codify codes systematically. Recognizing the deficiencies of the *Penal Code* of 1791, the government established a committee to reform criminal laws. It was criticized when the draft of the *Penal Code* of 1801 was sent to the supreme court, the appellate court, and the criminal trial court for soliciting opinions. To further discuss and revise the draft, Napoleon ordered to list all problems during the opinion solicitation, and an important question among them was whether judges should be empowered the right of discretion between the minimum level of penalties and the maximum level. The legislative procedure of the code was completed in 1810, and the code came to effective since January 1, 1811. Although the *Penal Code* of 1810 observed the doctrine of no penalty without a law, it empowered judges with some right of discretion. The Chapter 3 of the *Code* concretized the doctrine of no penalty without a law, but it did not stipulate only one penalty for one crime like the *Code* of 1791. Rather, it stipulated the maximum and minimum level of penalties and even two different penalties for the same crimes (i.e., deprivation of liberty or fine). Judges could determine the penalties between the range of the maximum and minimum level of the deprivation of freedom and choose one to implement. This way, the *Code* observed the doctrine of no penalty without a law and overcame the inflexibility of the *Code* of 1791. The *Penal Code* of 1810 represented the method and style of Napoleon's codification in legislative technique. The general provisions of the *Code* were far less advance than specific provisions. This was partly because it observed the doctrine of no penalty without a law (because every crime must be stipulated in clarity) and also because the *Code* paid attention to practice. It did not pursue to generalize the criminal law principles theoretically but to stipulate the application of these principles. The *Code* was concise because the provisions of similar crimes were arranged in adjacent provisions regardless of their severity and penalties so that judges could cite them more easily. The change from the *Penal Code* of 1791 to the *Penal Code* of 1810 illustrated the revision of the doctrine of no penalty without a law, which the classical school of criminology advocated in legislation.

There is a distance between legal thoughts and legal forms, the same as between value and instrument.

Therefore, when statutory law fulfills its formal rationality, the value of rationality is lacking for sure. Nevertheless, formal rationality is necessary to guarantee the fulfillment of the maximum (not all) value of rationality. The US scholar Alan Watson discussed the formal rationality of the civil law system and said that formal rationality meant that the law existed in the form of a reasonable system, but the law itself was not an end. Legal procedures and legal norms were merely social instruments, which were closely related to the internal objective of the law. The distinct characteristic of the law was that, in case of disputes, the law increased the possibility to deal with these disputes based on normative procedures, and the objective of these normative procedures was to prevent the conflicts that were free from the adjustment of norms. When people thought about legal issues, they were easy to misunderstand that legal procedures were nothing important compared to justice, freedom, or social norms and thus stressed the feasibility of the procedure, which evaded the crucial point. Methods to achieve justice, freedom, or social norms, however, still existed.

Standards were deemed as legal norms because they were implemented through legal procedures. Accordingly, we must keep in mind that legal, as an instrument, has its limits.[71] Watson indicated that the formal rationality of law was instrumental rationality, by which the limits of legal instrumentalism and the law as an instrument were highlighted. It should be noted that legal instrumentality and legal instrumentalism are not equal. Chinese scholars have mentioned that legal instrumentalism is a legal outlook and epistemology on the nature and function of the law. Legal instrumentalism stresses that the law is a mere instrument and method to achieve social objectives in the social system.[72] The definition of legal instrumentalism by these scholars fails to distinguish legal instrumentalism from legal instrumentality but only affirms legal instrumentality. The law is of instrumentality, and this is correct. However, the vital problem of legal instrumentalism is that it ignores the value of law which serves as an instrument, resulting in the negation of the distinctive value of the law on the grounds of substantive values such as justice, equality, and freedom.

While these scholars criticize legal instrumentalism, they propose the objective of the law. The objective means that the law is a fundamental expression of the value demands of a country and its people. The law is both the guideline for the journey of a country and society and a lighthouse for a country and society to achieve their goals.[73] The objective of the law in this sense refers to the value rationality of the law. However, legal instrumentalism gives up or negates the formal rationality of the law to pursue the value of rationality. Therefore, in my opinion, the view on the unification of legal instrumentalism and the objective of the law is correct, and China does need to reflect on legal instrumentalism because only in this way will the authority of the rule of law be established. Nonetheless, when reflecting on legal instrumentalism, we should highlight the value of the formal rationality of the law. In the primary stage of developing the rule of law in China, a formal legal system should be established through legal enlightenment. When we advocate the formal rationality of the law, we should not ignore the limitations of the law that serves as an instrument. As the primary manifestation of the law, statutory law tends to satisfy general justice while ignoring individual justice due to its normative characteristic. In particular, the excessive, rigid articles lack necessary flexibility and thus damage value rationality. To solve it, we should combine formal rationality and value rationality organically so that formal rationality penetrates and reflects value rationality for it to be transformed. For statutory law, nothing is more important than this.

3 Legislative Mode (2): Case Law

Case law enjoys long prosperity in legal history because of its distinctive glamour and thus becomes a legislative mode comparable to statutory law. Common law is expressed in the form of case law. Apart from this, even the civil law countries

[71] See [50], p. 30.

[72] See [53].

[73] See [53].

advocating statutory law also stress the role of legal precedents and make them a necessary supplement of statutory law. Thus, we should further explore the humanistic foundation of case law to deeply understand its value.

3.1 Historical Investigation of Case Law

We should differentiate case law from legal precedents. Case law depends on legal precedents, but the collection of legal precedents by no means is equal to case law. Since case law develops based on legal precedents, we should set out from legal precedents to explore and discuss the formation of case law.

Laws in ancient China were represented by statutory laws, but legal precedents still played a vital role. In the *Legal Questions and Answers* in the Shuihudi Qin Bamboo Texts unearthed in Yunmeng in 1975, "*Ting Xing Shi*" (precedent of adjudication) was referred to as the basis. This indicated that in the Qin dynasty, there was a system to hear cases based on legal precedents in judicial activities. Additionally, "*Feng Zhen Shi*" (procedures of judicial interrogation) collected many cases, including stealing cattle, horses, money, clothes; fleeing from home, escaping from the conscripting, killing and harming people, for relevant officials to learn and refer to when dealing with these cases.[74] For instance, in *Legal Questions and Answers*, there is such a case and its answers as follows: "Person A and Person B did not know each other. When Person A arrived at Person C's and wanted to steal from Person C, Person B arrived as well. Person B talked with Person A, and the two stole things worth 400 qian (currency unit) respectively and were caught after leaving Person C's. If the two have planned the plot, they would be sentenced based on the combination of the stolen goods; if not, they would be sentenced separately." Through the case, the difference between common crimes and concurrent crimes was illustrated. This shows that people understood the close relationship between general laws and individual cases in the Qin dynasty, and it was more vivid to discuss laws through cases. More importantly, legal precedents reflect the monarch's will in due time to compensate for the shortcomings of statutory law.

As Professor Ning Hanlin has mentioned, "'*Ting Xing Shi*' means determining the penalties of some crimes according to the monarch's orders. The cases represent monarch's decrees, which become precedents, so if similar cases happen later, these precedents are the standards for deciding crimes and penalties. As time goes by, even though there are provisions in criminal law, monarchs can decide crimes and punishments of certain crimes based on their decrees. As long as they are defined as legal precedents, these decrees will be applied as the standard for deciding crimes and penalties. On the one hand, this is to maintain the monarch's power of penalty since crimes and penalties are decided only based on monarchs' criminal laws and decrees to strengthen the autocratic ruling of monarchs. On the other hand, with situations combined, it is easier to crack down on the crimes endangering feudal governance.

[74] See [54], pp. 149, 244.

Since there is '*Ting Xing Shi*' to decide crimes, legislation beyond laws maintains the rule of the feudal landlord class more effectively."[75] In the Han dynasty, legal precedents were called exemplary cases of judgment, referring to the legal precedents or collections of legal precedents for hearing cases. The exemplary cases of judgment in the Han dynasty originated in the early Western Han dynasty when, if a case could not be settled because there were no provisions, it could be compared to similar articles and reported to the emperor for a final decision. The legal precedents of this kind, which were collected, edited, and approved by the emperor, were called exemplary cases of judgment. They were effective as laws and decrees and became the basis for future cases. Until Emperor Wu of Han, as many as 13,472 *Exemplary Cases of the Death Penalty Judgment* have been formulated in this way. The most well-known one in the Han dynasty was the exemplary cases of the Spring and Autumn Period judgment, which was also named *Legal Judgments by Reference to Classics*. During the reign of the Emperor Wu of Han, Dong Zhongshu attached the *Spring and Autumn Annals* to the laws of the Western Han dynasty to judge cases and decide penalties. Dong Zhongshu compiled 232 cases into a book as the basis for the judicial organ to adjudicate cases. According to *The Book of Later Han: Stories of Ying Shao*, "The prime minister of Jiaodong Dong Zhongshu has resigned due to his old age; however, when the imperial court discussed political affairs, the emperor delegated Zhang Tang, a senior official, to visit Dong's shabby house and ask him opinions. Therefore, Dong Zhongshu compiled 232 cases into a book for reference. One example is that Person A has no child but picks up an abandoned baby B by the side of the road and raises the baby as his son. When B grows up, B kills a person and A hides B. Others brought a suit against A, then what is A's crime?" This was one example of the *Legal Judgments by Reference to Classics*, and it expanded the doctrine that the concealment of certain statutory crimes between fathers and sons did not constitute a crime to that between foster fathers and sons.

In the Tang dynasty, where laws were complete, there were four legal sources: codes, decrees, rules, and procedures, and "all should be decided by codes." Decrees, rules, and procedures were detailed and specific, and *Tang Law* was a penal code. Behaviors that seriously violated decrees, rules, and procedures were stipulated in *Tang Law*, with the charges and penalties established. Behaviors that slightly violated decrees, rules, and procedures were punished as general violations of decrees, rules, and procedures.[76] Therefore, the Tang dynasty had advance statutory law, so legal precedents played a minor role in judicial activities, and Tang dynasty shows high degree of centralization. The promulgation of *Tang Law* has exerted a huge influence on later laws, and *Tang Law* has become an example for imitation. The study of specific provisions of criminal laws after the Tang dynasty indicated that many provisions were the same as *Tang Law*. Taking *The Great Qing Legal Code as* an example, a scholar estimated that around 30–40% of the provisions of *The Great Qing Legal Code* were directly copied from the *Tang Law* of 653 without any changes, and

[75] See [55], pp. 535–536.

[76] See [56], p. 54.

there were many other provisions only changed in words and sentences. US sinologists Bodde and Morris commented, "Chinese people believe that as the collection of moral regulations, the law transcends the temporal and spatial limit and enjoys permanent effect. The inheritance of the above legal provisions reflects the Chinese people's view of the law. This view of the law cannot be fully achieved. For instance, even though 30–40% of the provisions in *The Great Qing Legal Code* copied the *Tang Law*, 60–70% of the provisions were invented by the Qing dynasty or revised based on relevant provisions of the *Tang Law*. During the long history, some old legal provisions have been deleted while some new ones have been established. Also, some have been revised with different degrees to adapt to the changing social conditions. Among those that have remained unchanged, a part of them was retained in the codes as meaningless character symbols, and very few or none of them have been implemented."[77] In this case, emperors could revise laws based on their decrees and even abolish the validity of laws.

The emperor's decrees might only be effective for some litigation cases, but some might be effective over a long time, and some might even be codified and thus had the universal validity as laws and regulations. If the function of codes was to maintain continuity and stability of the law, the handling of individual cases by decrees enabled the law to be flexible and adaptable. In the Ming dynasty, a complete system was generally formed to tackle the change of laws specifically, and this legal form was called the "precedent rule". Generally, precedent rule contained the meaning of principle, formula, concept, or example. In the legal system of the Ming dynasty, precedent rules have the meaning of legal precedents. Specifically, precedent rules are the judgment made in previous litigation cases that can be referred to for later cases. US sinologists Bodde and Morris held that as a specific legal term, the real name of a precedent rule should be "sub-statute" or "quasi-law". As one type of legal norms, precedent rules supplement codes—the basic legal norm. There are two primary sources of precedent rules. The first is the emperor's decrees, and the second is the judgments made by the Ministry of Justice on specific cases and approved by the emperor. The latter is more common. According to *The History of Ming: Treatises of Criminal Law*, in 1492, the Minister of Justice reported to the emperor for compiling scattered precedent rules into a book. In 1500, the book was finished and named *Wenxing tiaoli* (clauses and precedent rules for judicial interrogation), which contained 297 clauses. Emperors formulated precedent rules to address specific situations that the formulators had not expected in the *Ming Code*, and their function was to supplement codes and make up for the shortcomings of codes rather than abandon them. In real life, it was not rare and even serious that precedent rules replaced laws. Since *Wenxing tiaoli* was compiled, it has become a supplement to the *Ming Code*, and both enjoyed validity. When new precedent rules were produced, they were supplemented promptly into the *Wenxing tiaoli*. By 1549, the number of precedent rules in *Wenxing tiaoli* has been added from 297 to 349 with this supplementation method. In 1585, the codification method of the

[77] See [2], p. 59.

Ming dynasty's laws changed significantly. The precedent rules in *Wenxing tiaoli*—which has increased to 382 sections—have been codified into the *Ming Code*, and the *Wenxing tiaoli* and *Ming Code* merged into an independent code that contained codes and precedent rules, which was *The Great Ming Legal Code*. The code form, which combined codes and precedent rules, was inherited by the Qing dynasty, which created *The Great Qing Legal Code*. Thus, in the Ming and Qing dynasties, codes and precedent rules were two fundamental legal forms. US sinologists Bodde and Morris pointed out that in a long-standing legal system, since it had the first codification, it needed an auxiliary legal form to supplement formal legal provisions to adapt to the changing social environment. The precedent rules whose contents are emperor's decrees or court decisions originally aimed at very specific matters, so they were much narrower than the laws they were attached to. In the Qing dynasty, people observed such a principle that where both codes and precedent rules applied to a case, it was usually the precedent rules rather than codes that were referred to for judgment; where precedent rules were inconsistent or even conflicted with codes, rules prioritized. The advantage of precedent rules was that rules could address the special incidents that failed to be expected by code formulators. However, the existence of precedent rules arose chaos and difficulty in the application of the law. On the one hand, precedent rules were only applicable to some matters and would lose their significance when they exceeded this scope; on the other hand, once they were codified, they became stable as codes. As a result, sometimes precedent rules remained in the code even if their pertinence has been lost. According to *The Draft History of Qing: Criminal Annals*, "Precedent rules are used while codes are not, leading to that codes become dead letters and precedent rules become more and more complicated and trifling, during which codes and precedent rules are contradictory; punishments are enhanced regardless of precedent rules; precedent rules violate codes; a precedent rule is set for only one case; different localities apply different precedent rules; or even a precedent rules gives rise to another rule."[78] Thus, precedent rules have a place in the legal system of ancient China. Some Chinese scholars even name the laws from the Western Han dynasty to modern China as "mixed law", which is not completely statutory law or case law. It is the combination of the two and thus has a style of its own.[79] By "mixed law", it means the unification of statutory law and case law. When statutory law is suitable for reality, people tend to advocate statutory law while excluding the creation and application of precedents; if statutory law has not existed or the current laws are not suitable for society, people will create and apply precedents to guide the judicial activities throughout the country. As precedent rules are accumulated, they are promoted as legal provisions after being processed by the country. Statutory law and case law, cored at the legal consciousness of the ruling class, appear alternately.[80] This statement makes sense, but we should notice that ancient Chinese laws have a tenacious tendency towards statutory law, and even precedent rules whose content is mainly legal precedents have been included in codes as much as possible so that

---

[78] See [2], p. 62.

[79] See [57].

[80] See [58], p. 75.

codes and precedent rules are unified, and precedent rules enrich codes. In this sense, ancient Chinese laws are still statutory laws, and legal precedents only play a supplementary and auxiliary role. If codes are broken by precedent rules or precedent rules increase, people will consider it as the inappropriateness of the legal system and criticize it.

The civil law system features statutory law, but as the origin of the civil law system, Roman law was a case law. The French scholar David mentioned that Roman law was a case law when Gaius wrote his noted *Institutes* in the third century.[81] This saying speaks in superlatives, but it is by no means an alarmist talk. Undeniably, case law did exist in Roman law, which was represented as *edictum magistratum*. The Roman's magistrate is the supreme magistrate (*pretor*), also named Justiciar. All pretors should publish specific announcements or orders in writing when they took office to propose their principles and measures for policy guidelines and to hear cases during their term. They should also implement judicial practices after taking office. Pretors did not have the legislative power, but since they were responsible for legislation and the former pretor's edicts had a binding effect on the successors, edicts had no difference from the law in form, so it was called "magistrate law" (*Jus honora Lium*). As one of the sources of Roman law, *edictum magistratum* had a significant influence on the development of Roman law. This was because the state only empowered the magistrate's privilege to punish edicts while not prescribing the content and form of the privilege.

This way, the vision and area were broadened for the magistrates to exert the privilege, and they could thus remedy the shortcomings and defects of the old laws and regulations from reality and made their edicts flexible and effective to reflect the development of Roman law. However, as the imperial power expanded during the Empire, the privilege has been contradictory to the enhancement of the imperial power and thus gradually became a merely nominal right of the pretor. Till 129, Hadrian appointed jurists Sabinus and Julianus to compile all former *edictum magistratum* into a collection as the legal precedents to guide the state's judicial activities. Since then, edicts from the pretors have been rare to see, and pretors could only behave according to the collection, and their original power was canceled. By the third century, statutory law has developed gradually, and codification ushered a peak during the reign of Justinian. Modern civil law countries adopted statutory law following Roman law. Before codification, nonetheless, civil law countries still used case law. The US scholar Alan Watson has conducted an in-depth study on it and compared the legal precedents before codification and those of the common law system, summarizing the following three features: (1) The facts of the cases were not as detailed as those stated in common law. Those facts of the cases impressed people strongly that the recorder believed they only needed to record a few facts related to the law. The reason might be that the fact details between two cases should not be the basis for different judgments, or that the laws, regulations, or principles that made the cases enjoy legal significance only depended on a few basic facts. Under all circumstances, more fixed laws were recorded while very few facts were recorded

[81] See [37], p. 26.

compared to the judgment records of common law. (2) Judgments seemed to be the conclusions of legal doctrines and recorded legal precedents with deliberations, but these doctrines and legal precedents categorized the judgment into a framework of a theoretical system. In other words, courts seemed not to look for a legal answer related to a series of facts but to link the specific practical problems with a series of hypothetical problems for a set of properly linked laws and regulations. The attitude that was divorced from common law was the most important. If a person believed that the life of the law lied or should lie in "experience rather than logic", common law judges would restrict their experience when they fell into the dilemma of urgent case facts. (3) The main purpose of the recorder seemed to state the laws, regulations, and doctrines illustrated by judgments. The focal point of the stress was completely based on generality rather than the concreteness of the law.[82] After codification, statutory law held the absolute authoritative position, and the judges of the civil law system mechanically applied statutory law. Legal precedents must be based on the provisions of statutory law, and people should strictly abide by a judicial syllogism that statutory law was the major premise, the fact of the case was the minor premise, and the judgment of the case was the necessary result by inference. As a result, a legal precedent was merely an individual conclusion derived from the general rules of statutory law, which was of no value, let alone to be the basis for trial. After that, to adapt to the social developments and changes, the civil law system changed its absolute rule doctrine, and the role of legal precedents has enhanced. As the French scholar David mentioned, among countries of the Roman-Germanic law system, the role of legal precedents could not be clearly understood if its relationship with the role of the law was not considered. Since the jurists in these countries tended to refer to provisions, the creative role of legal precedents was always or almost always hidden behind the legal interpretation.[83] David also discussed the difference between case law and statutory law in the civil law system. He said that legal precedents did not allow themselves to create laws and regulations because, according to judges, creating laws and regulations was the work of legislators and the governments or administrative organizations designated to supplement legislators' work. Despite this modest opinions, should we consider that it was the judges that created legal norms? Anyway, two significant differences occurred between the legal norms of case law and those created by legislators. First was the relative importance of the two within a certain system. Legal precedents acted within the frameworks established by legislators, while the purpose of the legislator's humble opinions was displayed in these frameworks. Due to this fact, the influence of the case law was limited. However, among the countries of the Roman-Germanic law system, the situation was the opposite, as recognized by the countries of the common law system.

Second, the "legal norms" established by legal precedents were not as powerful as those established by legislators. They were unstable norms and might be negated or changed at any time when a new case was heard. Legal precedents were free from the restraint of the norms they had proposed. Generally speaking, they even could not

[82] See [50], pp. 61–62.

[83] See [59], p. 125.

quote these norms to defend the judgment they would soon make. If judges applied a norm that they had used in a new judgment, this was not because the norm gained power as it had been used. This norm was not an order. The complete change of legal precedents was always possible, and judges had no obligation to illustrate the reason. The complete change was nothing important because it did not threaten legal frameworks or impact legal doctrines. The norms of legal precedents continued to exist or are applied only because judges—every judge—believed these norms were good.[84] Therefore, the role of legal precedents in the civil law system is minimal. Legal precedents are just the supplements of statutory law and should not exceed the frameworks of statutory law. They are nothing compared with legal precedents in the common law system where the function of legal precedents is to create laws.

The common law system is noted by case law. The common law system is literally named the "British and US law system". Common law has three meanings. First, broadly speaking, it refers to the laws prevailing in Britain after the twelfth century, which is formed under centralization, unified and applied by the state court led by the emperor, and different from the customary law prevailing in Lord's Court in Britain and *The Law Merchant* only applicable for special classes and industries. Second, in the narrow sense, it refers to the case law created, applied, and developed by the British Crown Court after the twelfth century. In terms of the expressive form and ways of production, it was different from the statute law of legislature; in terms of the applicable subject, it was different from the equity of the court of equity. Finally, from the view of comparative law, it generally refers to the legal institution of the countries or regions based on British law and case law as the main legal source, different from the legal institution of the civil law countries or regions featuring statute law and codification in particular. Therefore, common law in the narrow sense is featured by case law, which originates from the twelfth century. The US scholar Ehrmann posited that in Britain, circuit judges of the Crown Court integrated diverse local customs into a common custom when they were on the circuit. After some time, the kingdom's common law was applied as the synonym of customary law. Accordingly, the judge and lawyer class who had greater influences not only created a national legal culture but also integrated the state into an entirety. The creation of common law was a revolution comparable to the all-encompassing codification of law in other countries. In the common law system, customs and court judgments were the most fundamental (although not the only) sources of the law.[85] We can see that common law is characterized by case law and developed from the judicial practice of the British Crown Court. In common law countries, a judgment has special significance. It has a direct effect on specific cases and becomes a precedent that the court should follow when dealing with the same or similar cases in the future. In this way, a chain correlating the judgments of similar cases is formed. However, the factor in connecting the chain is not the judgment but the legal rule contained in the judgment, which is the continuation of the law contained in the previous similar judgments and the legal basis for the judgment of similar cases in the future. Through this way

---

[84] See [59], p. 127.

[85] See [33], p. 44.

is a characterized case law system established. The formation of the British case law has a unique historical background. Britain is an island country with a fewer population, a smaller size, and a single ethnic structure. On the one hand, Britain has not been unified as one country until the ninth century; on the other hand, its unity was easy to consolidate, and it has maintained unity except for the invasion by Denmark when it was emerged into the Danish Empire. As a result, it is easy to implement a low degree of centralization and a high degree of local self-government in a country like Britain. The case law institution was gradually formed during the unification of the legal institution in Britain when the central authority was under the pressure of local governments, and compromised to the local and admitting the existing local customary laws to be the basis for unifying the national legal institution. In the eleventh century, William I, a French Norman Duke, conquered Britain. Before that, Britain had no unified legal institution, and all localities had been using the customary law that was formed and developed since migrating from the mainland to the British Isles. To consolidate the country's unification, after William I ascended the throne, he started to reform the incoherent legal institution, publish the decrees that were uniformly implemented throughout the country, and establish the Crown Court, the national supreme judicial organization. He sent out circuit judges regularly throughout the country and supervised local judicial organizations to apply the unified decrees. Nevertheless, as the customary law system took strong root and the British people were in a strong mood against the conqueror Norman nobility, it was difficult to implement the unified decrees that represented the will of Norman nobility. Thus, the William imperial court had to slow down the legislation process, announce to retain the original customary laws around Britain and allow circuit judges to decide the cases based on local and national decrees and customary laws that did not contradict Norman nobility. To maintain the co-existence of local customary laws and unified national decrees and to keep the unification of the national legal institution, the Crown Court called on circuit judges who were sent out regularly to discuss the judicial situations. It allowed these judges to recognize each other's judgments which would be the basis for similar cases. The Court also regularly published major case judgments as the basis of similar cases for the courts and judges of all levels. After nearly 800 years' development, by the nineteenth century, the "*stare decisis*" was finally formed, and the precedents of superior courts restrained all inferior courts. Under some circumstances, some courts were restrained by their precedents, and in this way, the case law institution was established. The US case law, on the other hand, was the inheritance of the British case law. However, US transformed common law to adapt to its national conditions. In US, the foundation of common law was so deep that even the revolution and hostile feeling towards British things failed to root it out. It is undeniable that US was in danger of adopting the French law (statutory law of the civil law system) after the success of revolutions, but the danger had passed by 1830. USs did not copy all common laws but only adopted the components that their environment did not require them to abandon.[86] Consequently, there remained differences between the US and British case laws.

---

[86] See [35], p. 16.

Through the historical investigation of the development of case law, we can see that the precedent system has played a vital role even for the countries using statutory law. As the opposite of statutory law, case law is unique to the common law system whose charm remains to date.

3.2 *Value Analysis of Case Law*

Case law holds a vital position in the contemporary legal system, the existence of which has a reasonable basis. The value of case law is analyzed as follows.

3.2.1 Adaptability of Case Law

The adaptability of case law refers to the flexibility and variability of case law as a legal form to ensure that the law adapts to social life. The adaptability of case law is opposite to the definiteness of statutory law, which imposes rigidness to the law. In particular, since the formulation and revision of statutory law must proceed with a set of strict legal procedures, statutory law is inevitably lagging. By contrast, judges create case laws, and they can revise laws according to social needs. It must be noted that the adaptability of case law should not be misunderstood as arbitrariness or randomness. Instead, adaptability is based on stability, which is expressed by the complying and change of precedents.

Precedents, also named judicial precedents, refer to the previous judgments of the specific litigation by the court. In every legal system, the opinions expressed by judges in dealing with disputes in the past are of significance to judges dealing with similar cases in the future. If a judge believes that his or the superior court's previous judgments are correct, he has no reason to think that similar results are unsuitable for the unchanging environment. However, judicial precedents mean differently in the civil law system and common law system. In civil law countries, judicial precedents are usually examples to direct things, and these precedents tell people how to interpret statutory law appropriately most. When precedents become the most primary legal sources, as in the common law countries, they are not only to teach judges. As a law that must be observed, it exists independently. For several centuries, British judicial precedents have been what they are as today. They exist not only as a law but also the most fundamental legal source.[87] Therefore, judges follow statutory law in the civil law system, and judicial precedents are merely examples of statutory law. The definiteness of the law is obtained mainly through the long, valid application of codes. In the common law system, however, judicial precedents are legal sources, and the law obtains continuity when people abide by precedents. The Chinese scholar Liang Zhiping has mentioned that British case law was a complete legal system rather than an occasional accumulation of unrelated cases. It was the precedent rule

[87] See [60], p. 155.

that prevented the arbitrariness of case law, which guaranteed the continuity and consistency of the law.[88]

The doctrine of precedents is the basis of legal precedents. In Britain, early at the end of the thirteenth century, judges cited precedents when they handled cases, and by the sixteenth century, the practice of citing precedents has been established as a convention. In the late eighteenth century, the British well-known jurist Blackstone expounded the theory of the binding force of precedents in his work. In the late nineteenth century, as courts were reformed, unified and became systematic, reliable collections of legal precedents occurred, and the doctrine of precedents was established. The doctrine of precedents (*stare decisis*) is the abbreviation of the following Latin: *stare decisis et non quieta movers*, which means to stand by things decided and not disturb settled points. The basic meaning of this doctrine is that superior courts restrain inferior courts, and former precedents of superior courts restrain themselves. In Britain, the doctrine of precedents is expressed in three situations as follows: (1) The judgments of the House of Lords have the binding force on the inferior courts and its previous judgments. (2) The appellate court judgments have the binding force on themselves and the subordinate inferior courts. (3) The judgments of a judge from the high court have the binding force on inferior courts but have no binding force (only persuasive force) on other judges within the high court.[89]

We should first distinguish precedents when complying with precedents, which is called the "distinguishing technique". Case law is not the entire judgment of a case. It means a legal doctrine or rule that the judgment contains and that can serve as a precedent. Meanwhile, precedents are divided into those with the binding force and those without the binding force. In this case, the facts or legal issues in the judgment containing precedents and the facts and legal issues in the current trial cases must be compared and distinguished. This process is called the "distinguishing technique", a term of the common law system. All cases can be divided into facts and reasons, and it is the legal doctrines in the reasons for judgments that have the binding force. The legal statements by a judge during the trial are not always reasons. As a result, it is of great significance to analyze judgments and extract the reasons for judgments. It is generally considered that the following elements are included in each judgment: (1) The decision of the fact of a case is divided into the direct decision and inferential decision.

The inferential decision is made by judges (or the judge, if any) from direct facts or perceptible facts. (2) The statement of legal doctrines applies to the legal arguments resulting from the fact of a case. (3) The judgments combining (1) and (2). For the litigant and the interest persons, (3) is the substantial element of the judgment because it determines the rights and obligations related to the subject matter of the lawsuit, and the decision prohibits the party concerned from filing a lawsuit again. Nonetheless, in terms of the doctrine of precedents, (2) is the necessary element of the judgment. Factually, it is the reason for judgment. Therefore, the reason for judgment is the legal statement applicable to the legal disputes caused by the facts on which the

[88] See [61].

[89] See [62], p. 464.

judgment is based. The other two elements of the judgment are not precedents. The decision in (3) has no binding force (except the direct binding force on the litigant), and the factual decision has no binding force either. Not every legal statement in the judgment has binding force, and only those on the facts on which the judgment is based have. Strictly speaking, all other legal statements are superfluous, which are called "attachments to the judgment". There are two types of attachments to the judgment. The first is the legal statements that are not confirmed or not verified though confirmed as substantial facts. The second is the legal statements that are confirmed by the fact but do not constitute the basis of the judgment. In some litigation, the court makes decisions and further states a broader legal doctrine than the judgment requires. Under this circumstance, only the legal statement applicable to the facts of the case tried by the court is the reason for judgment, and the broader doctrines embodied in the statement are attachments.[90] It should be admitted that distinguishing precedents is complicated. It is through distinguishing precedents that the doctrine of precedents is implemented.

The doctrine of precedents manifests the stability of case law. Every law is stable to some degree, and so does case law. The problem is how stability coordinates with the adaptability of the law to social life, and this is the requirement for flexibility based on stability. A traditional view is that the function of British judges is not creating laws but hearing cases according to existing legal doctrines. The doctrine of binding precedents is thus produced. According to it, judges should take previous precedents as a guide and apply the legal doctrines contained in these judgments. The validity of this doctrine suits the courts of all levels. All courts have relationships, with an inferior court bound by its superior court's decisions and by decisions of the same-level courts. Since the doctrine of precedents has binding force in this system, if cases are always decided according to the eternal principle, an issue on how the law develops arises. In practice, the eternal principle keeps its flexibility through some ways, where two fundamental principles are mentioned: first, the superior court has the right to negate the judgments by the inferior courts and, in some cases, to negate its previous precedents. Second, every legal principle can be changed by legislation; therefore, both judges and countries can change legal principles. Consequently, the possibility of judgments to be voted down and the possibility of limiting the validity of wrong judgments constitute the flexibility of the law.[91] It should be noted that the doctrine of precedents is rigid. Negating a precedent is demanding, especially after the nineteenth century when precedents gradually became clarified and absolutized. After the Second World War, the drastic change in social life immediately made the absolutized doctrine of precedents obsolete. In a time of doubt and uncertainty, people were unwilling to be bound by doctrines and were more concerned about adapting to the rapid-changing social conditions. As social life was uncertain, the theories that ultimately were to satisfy social demands highlighted adaptability. Surprisingly, the adaptability of case law was achieved imperceptibly as judges flexibly applied complicated technique methods, which was opposite to statutory law, which was

[90] See [63], pp.157–160.
[91] See [63], pp.155–156.

revised or supplemented ceremoniously. Judges could recapitulate, compose and state facts in precedents of different levels and expand or narrow the reasons for judgment in precedents to the extent that the text allows. Under some circumstances, judges could identify the differences between the two cases according to the fact and thus disregarded precedents. Judges could degrade the reasons for judgment in precedents to attachments. On the contrary, they could allege attachments as the reasons for judgment and apply them. Even judges did not clarify the reasons for judgment; later courts might also find out evidence. If the later court was superior to the court that created the precedent, the former could also negate the precedent explicitly or implicitly. Lastly, some precedents have not been negated, but they are no longer laws as some condition has changed. All of these are the techniques to maintain the flexibility of the case law system, preventing later courts from applying precedents mechanically. These are conducted in the name of the right of discretion by judges, but society has already imperceptibly revised laws according to social changes by handling individual cases. By respecting traditions, doctrines, and rules, the British people safeguard the stability and consistency of the law. At the same time, by techniques such as citing precedents and declaring judgments, they have changed laws subtly so that laws adapt to social changes.[92] The US doctrine of precedents has never gained the absolute authority it is said to have achieved in Britain. Numerous judgments and conflicting precedents in different jurisdictions undermine the authority of individual judgments. Some subsequent cases existed when society had developed and socio-economic conditions had changed, and the rapid changes often weakened the applicability of precedents.[93] Above all, the US case law shows more adaptability to social life.

3.2.2 Individuality of Case Law

The individuality of case law refers to legal judgments that are made for specific cases, so they possess the nature of individuality. Regarding this, the individuality of case law is unique in sharp contrast to the universality of statutory law. The provisions of statutory law are the statements of general rules. Although existing in case law, general rules are contained in and abstracted from specifics case, so they are differently manifested. Taking an example of the criminal responsibility of mental patients, we can draw differences from the comparison of statutory law and case law. Among civil law countries, the criminal responsibility of mental patients has been specified in special provisions, but there is no definition of mental diseases. The *French Penal Code* defines mental disease as insanity; the *Japanese Penal Code* names it "loss of mind and mental exhaustion", and the *Chinese Penal Code* takes the inability to tell or control as the basis for mental patients to not bear criminal responsibility. Furthermore, from the stipulations of civil law countries' criminal responsibility of mental patients, we can see that French and Chinese penal codes only prescribe the mental

[92] See [61].

[93] See [64], p. 69.

patients who are incapable of criminal responsibility, whereas the Italian and Japanese penal codes involve the mental patients whose responsibilities are relieved. Notwithstanding these differences, the law's expressions on general rules are abstract and generalized. For instance, the highly-condensed legal terms that interpret insanity, loss of mind, mental exhaustion, inability to tell, and inability to control are particularly difficult to implement. By contrast, in case law of the common law system, the criminal responsibility of mental patients is mainly represented by the "M'Naghten rule", which originates from a legal precedent in Britain in 1843. The defendant, M'Naghten, was charged with murder. The case situation is as follows: M'Naghten was confused by a thought that the then Prime Minister Sir Bill was hatching a conspiracy to kill him (there was none indeed) and he should kill the Prime Minister before the "conspiracy" was organized. One day, he shot and killed Drummond, the Prime Minister's secretary whom he mistook for the Prime Minister. After the trial by the court consisting of 15 judges, M'Naghten was considered to have mental diseases and thus was incapable of assuming criminal responsibility, and his killing behavior was "driven by illusion". The court verdict announced that "to establish a defense on the ground of insanity, it must be proved that, at the time of the committing of the act, the party accused was laboring under such a defect of reason, from the disease of the mind, as not to know the nature and quality of the act he was doing; or if he did know it, that he did not know he was doing what was wrong."

The court's judgment arose such extensive dissatisfaction that the issue was submitted to the House of Lords for debates (although the case has never been brought to the House of Lords from the perspective of the judicial function). The result was that all members submitted to the judges some abstract questions about people with mental delusions. Judges' replies were summarized as follows: (1) every man was presumed to be sane and possessed a sufficient degree of reason to be responsible for his crimes until the contrary was proved to their satisfaction; (2) to establish a defense on the ground of insanity, it must be proved that, at the time of the committing of the act, the party accused was laboring under such a defect of reason, from the disease of the mind, as not to know the nature and quality of the act he was doing; or, if he did know it, that he did not know he was doing what was wrong; (3) regarding his knowledge that his act was wrong, judges considered that "if he is informed that the act should not be implemented and the act violates the national law, he should be punished"; and (4) judges noted that if a man committed criminal acts while in a state of psychotic delusion on reality, the treatment to him should depend on the nature of the delusion; however, judges made such a presumption that if a man was in a state of partial delusion and was not insane in other aspects, his responsibility should be considered as if the delusional facts were true. Since the defense of the M'Naghten's case was published, the court had adopted the following rules: (1) When defense reasons for metal diseases were proposed, the burden of proof (as long as it reached the level of reasonable doubt) was on the party denying it; (2) Even though the defense did not propose mental diseases as the grounds of defense, (possibly) the prosecutor's arguing evidence confirmed the mental diseases complying with the M'Naghten rule; (3) When defending the accusation of murder and providing evidence of mitigation of responsibility, the prosecutor might request a proof in order to prove that the defendant is mentally ill; (4) When the prosecutor did induce the proof of mental disease in this way, it must prove the mental disease has reached the level beyond a reasonable doubt; and (5) When the defense induced the proof of mental disease, the prosecution might at any time require rebuttal evidence to prove the diminished responsibility.[94] Since the publication of the M'Naghten rule, even though there have been criticisms from the medical and legal communities, the court still accepted it as a binding, authoritative opinion on the defense of mental diseases. From this rule, we can see that the legal rules of cases law are expounded from legal precedents, which are featured by individuality, and individuality determines the concreteness and comparability of precedents, because applying statutory law is a process from general inference to individual inference, while applying case law is a process vice versa. Case law provides judges with a comparative example that is specific and perceptual for imitation to prevent the spirit of the law from depletion and distortion when the law is applied.

Undeniably, the individuality of case law has defects; that is, legal precedents are numerous and complicated and may become red tapes. In the face of ever-increasing, tremendous amounts of collections of legal precedents, courts must be careful with determining what should be laws because excessive legal precedents blur basic principles.[95] As the collections of case law develop, especially as the computer is introduced, a considerable improvement has been made in this respect. In the preface of the Chinese version of *Legal Research in a Nutshell*, the US scholar Cohen mentioned that US legal research embodied and reflected the struggles for justice and order, which promoted legal development in US. The primary materials of this type of research included some rules that governed US society. The search tool of the book provided the search methods for numerous legal precedents and statutory laws published in chronological order, and the secondary research illustrated US laws by examining the past and present and exploring the future. The source and search method of US law changed as time went by. Most importantly, computerization and microfilm technology have been widely used. While people acquainted the most basic legal form, computerization and microfilm technology have improved people's ability to store and review legal research.

These changes have made it possible to search legal intelligence data when publications being out of control surged.[96] Notwithstanding, the individuality of case law brings about significant troubles to judges who are overburdened by it.

The value of the adaptability and individuality of case law, to some degree, can compensate for the shortcomings of the definiteness and universality of statutory law, so case law has brought about a great interest in China's legal academia. Whether case law holds a place in the sources of China's law triggers deliberations of China's excellent jurists. Of course, there remain disagreements on whether China should adopt the views of case law. Legal precedents are usually called cases in China's legal and judicial communities, and the boundary between the two is blurry. In authoritative

[94] See [65], pp. 89–91.

[95] See [63], p. 156.

[96] See [66], p. 3.

legal reference books, the term "precedent" is adopted, but in this case, it focuses on introducing the legal systems of ancient China or those of the common law system. However, in the current Chinese legal system, precedent is taboo and is replaced by the term "case". For example, according to the precedent article of *Legal Dictionary*, "a precedent is the judgment that can be cited as the basis of hearing similar cases. One of the sources of the law is called case law. The exemplary cases of judgment, precedent rules and precedent cases, and others are legal precedents. As expressed in *The Great Qing Legal Code* in the ninth year of the Tongzhi emperor (1883), 1,892 legal precedents were collected as the basis for hearing cases, bringing cases even greater validity than codes. In the thirteenth century, Britain developed the common law universally applied across the country, most of whose content was compiled by the court's judgments. Traditionally, a precedent was one of the most primary sources of British law. The US law and laws of other countries established based on British law also saw precedents as one of the most vital sources of the law. European countries such as France and Germany strictly distinguished legislation and administration of justice, and judgments were only the results of applying the law, which could not be regarded as the law and did not have a universal binding force. In socialist countries, precedents were not the sources of the law, which were only valued as references."[97] The entry of precedents does not mention the significance of precedents in China's current legal system. The entry of the case is not collected in most legal dictionaries, but case is one of the most popular legal terms in jurisprudence theories and judicial practice. Accordingly, few people have noticed the subtle differences between cases and precedents. It should be noted that Professor Shen Zongling, a famous Chinese jurist, has mentioned the difference between cases and precedents, who said that "literally, the term precedent is more accurate than case. Precedent refers to that a judgment is taken as a precedent for the trial of similar cases, whereas the term case refers to that a case is taken as a precedent for the trial of similar cases. The object of legal research is legal facts. People notice the facts of cases and the representative judgments courts have made, including the ways adjudicators state and analyze the facts of cases, apply laws, conduct reasoning, and arguments having been proposed and judgments having been made based on the facts, among others. Only these legal precedents are valuable to be referred to similar cases, which will even become precedents."[98] In my opinion, Professor Shen Zongling's argument is convincing. However, the argument as mentioned above fails to distinguish cases from legal precedents. In British, both case and legal precedent are expressed by "Case". A case refers to an individual legal dispute, especially the dispute that results in litigation. The term is also a general term of the pleas of one party, arguments, and submission for trials. A legal precedent also refers to litigation or trial, or the general term of the pleas of one party and arguments. In legal works, legal precedent is a report of litigation, including the opinions of the judge or judges who make judgments. In this context, legal precedent is the legal explanation of an issue, which is likely to

---

97 See [67], p. 439.

98 Shen [68], pp. 465–466.

become the precedent of later cases.[99] I believe that a case is the general term of the materials of a case, including the facts of the case (usually called details of the case) and evidence, and it focuses on the statement of the details of the case. On the other hand, a legal precedent refers to the judgment judges summarize based on the details of the case and evidence, and it focuses on the legal evaluation of the details of the case. Consequently, the term "case" covers no concept of "legal precedent" in China.

In recent years, the call for case law has been upsurging in China's legal community. For example, some Chinese scholars have proposed to establish a legal system with Chinese characteristics, giving first place to statutory law with case law supplemented. They believe that the macro pattern of China's legal culture has experienced the developmental stages from arbitrary law (the Shang dynasty), case law (the Western Zhou dynasty and Spring and Autumn Period) to statutory law (the Warring States Period and Qin dynasty) and mixed law (the Western Han dynasty till modern and contemporary times). Mixed law is the unity of statutory law and case law. When statutory law is suitable for social reality, people tend to advocate statutory law and exclude the creation and application of legal precedents; when statutory codes do not exist, or the existing codes do not suit for social life, people create and apply legal precedents to direct judicial activities across the country. As precedent rules are accumulated, they are promoted as legal provisions after being processed by the country. Statutory law and case law, cored at the legal consciousness of the ruling class, appear alternately. With the commercialization of economic life, the democratization of political life, and the increase of international exchanges, China's social life has become more active and diverse, which brings high requirements for legislation and the administration of justice. If we still abide by the old rules of statutory law, we are bound to obstruct the use of law to protect and promote reforms. To do so, we must take the initiative to establish and perfect the system of mixed law.[100] Some scholars have proposed to learn from others, and advocate and gradually implement case law: (1) authorizing the Supreme People's Court the power to promulgate legal precedents. These legal precedents must be approved by the Judicial Committee of the Supreme People's Court and promulgated by the Supreme People's Court Gazettes. Once published, they have the universal legal binding force. When local people's courts encounter the same or similar cases later, they should refer to relevant legal precedents, handle the case qualitatively, and not make opposite or inconsistent judgments. (2) The power to promulgate legal precedents should be strictly controlled, and only the Supreme People's Court is authorized. The aim is to prevent legal precedents from being issued excessively, which impacts the universal implementation of the law. But courts at all levels should be required to accumulate typical cases and conclude the trial experience.

---

[99] See [69], pp. 139–140. According to this book, Case has the first meaning of the law case and should be interpreted into the established case, which is contrary to the second meaning of legal precedent. Otherwise, legal precedent should be interpreted into judgment to correspond to the law case.

[100] See [70, 71].

The Higher People's Courts of provinces (municipalities, autonomous regions) should submit typical cases and controversial and difficult cases to the Supreme People's Court timely for it to grasp the judicial work across the country, find out problems, and deliberate and promulgate legal precedents selectively. The Higher People's Courts can also select the collections of legal precedents of their jurisdictions as the reference for inferior courts; however, these legal precedents do not possess the universal legal binding force. (3) For the purpose of perfecting the socialist legal system and creating conditions for promoting case law, effective measures should be taken to improve the working quality of case handling.[101] Opposite to the above opinions that advocate case law, some opinions oppose the implementation of case law in China's legal circle. For instance, some scholars have mentioned that due to the failure of a deepened research of the substance of the case law system by the scholars who advocate case law, the difference between the legal precedent system in civil law countries—a system where legal precedents play a role in directing judicial activities but have no binding force—and that in common law countries is confused. Not to mention that the legal precedent system in civil law countries has existed for several centuries but fails to break through the status quo. The scholars who advocate the case law system exaggerate the applicability of this system, ignore the difference between the verdicts by China's people's courts and those by judicial organizations in common law countries, and the fact that there has never been and has no form or carrier on which the case legal system depends. Therefore, the suggestion on adopting the case law system in China is not desirable or practical. Based on this opinion, China will repeat the mistakes of numerous precedents and long litigation in common law countries, and judicial localism, decentralism, and individualism will spread in China, hindering the development of China's socialist legal system.[102] It is worth noticing that some Chinese scholars believe the case law system should not be adopted in China, but the role of legal precedents should be strengthened. Professor Shen Zongling said that we must distinguish between case law and legal precedents. In legal works of common law countries, these two terms were interchangeable. For Chinese jurists, nonetheless, they were very different. As their names indicated, case law was a law, whereas legal precedents could be referred to during the trial; however, they were not laws, at least in China. The case law system was not suitable for China's political system. China did not have a long-term and solid historical tradition of case law like Britain or other common law countries, and Chinese judges lacked experience in case law methodology. Moreover, case law had shortcomings. All in all, China should not adopt case law. However, case law also had merits which were exactly the shortcomings of statute law. For example, case law better reflected the principle that all people were treated equally under the same circumstances. Following previous legal precedents also helped improve the efficiency of judicial work. The most distinguished merit of case law was that it was provided with a principle of organic growth to adapt to new situations. By contrast, statute law stipulated general rules and principles applied to special circumstances

[101] See [72].

[102] See [73].

mechanically while losing flexibility. Chinese laws were usually abstract, bringing difficulty to implement. Therefore, it was more necessary to supplement statute law with legal precedents.[103] Regretfully, Professor Shen Zongling did not mention how to supplement statute law with legal precedents, nor did he point out the difference between improving the case system and adopting case law, and if the difference was qualitative or formal, among others.

In my view, the following issues are worth studying on whether China should adopt case law: (1) the issue on the binding force of legal precedents. Adopting case law means admitting the binding force of legal precedents, so following legal precedents become the fundamental doctrine of case law. Then, where does the binding force of legal precedents come from? The binding force of legal precedents differs from claim preclusion (*Res judcata*), which refers to the legal validity of judgments on specific cases, while the binding force refers to the legal validity of similar cases handled later by the court. In the common law system, diverse opinions remain on the source of the binding force of legal precedents, among which the most valuable opinion holds that the binding force of legal precedents is for ensuring the stability of rights, the determination of law, and consistent needs. This is the answer from the perspective of legal value. If take a perspective of the empirical method, the following statement may be more convincing: legal precedents are of the nature of the law, and judges can only interpret and apply preceding laws but not arbitrarily change or revoke them. Judges bear the obligation to abide by precedents.[104] In other words, case law is the outcome of judges making the law. It is a law, so it enjoys the binding force. Then, the question of the boundary between legislation and the administration of justice arises. The Chinese scholars who advocate that legal precedents should not have the binding force say that China's statute law system is strictly divided based on legislative and judicial powers. The legislature makes laws based on meticulous and predictive existing writings to establish the determinative norms of the law. In terms of legislation, pursuing the highly centralized legislation power does not empower the court to create case laws or establish the scope or area of the new sources of the law, nor are judges allowed to create laws.[105] On the contrary, scholars with opposite views argue that since China does not recognize the theory of separation of the three powers, why does it secretly abide by this theory in real life? As a result, the status of the source of the case law should be determined as soon as possible.[106] I believe that the binding force of legal precedents originates from power. However, whether judicial organs empower judgments with binding force is equal to law creation should be studied further. For instance, many issues such as uncertain blank stipulations in legal provisions, the necessary limit of justifiable defense in criminal law, predictability of negligence, other methods for relatively minor, serious, and grave crimes, robbery, and rape have not been provided by the legislature in detail. Why is it not allowed to give judicial organs that define and endow the legal binding

---

[103] See [74].

[104] See [61].

[105] See [75].

[106] See [76].

force the power to fill the legal gap? Even if there are no explicit provisions in the law, it does not violate the legal principle to authorize the judicial organs to create applicable rules with precedents through legislation. Above all, I believe that it does not violate the legal principle that the binding force of legal precedents comes from the authorization of the law. (2) The issue on the legal status of the sources of legal precedents. Moreover, the legally binding force of legal precedents is an issue on the status of the sources of the law. Undoubtedly, legal precedents are the main sources of the law in the common law system. Then, are legal precedents the sources of the law in the civil law system? In the nineteenth century in Europe, state positivism led to the state's monopoly of legislative power, where the separation of powers was strictly implemented and only specifically designated state organs could create laws. According to this principle, the government's legislative power was different from its judicial power. If we aimed to prevent the abuse of power, legislative power must be strictly distinguished from judicial power. Legislative power was limited to the creation of laws, and only the legislature could formulate laws. Since the legislature was the only representative government department directly elected, only it could reflect people's will. The doctrine of precedents was opposite to the principle of separation of powers, so it was abandoned by civil law countries. Thus, in the civil law system, judicial legal precedents were not laws.[107] Clearly, according to the motto that judicial judgments do not produce legal rules, legal precedents are not the sources of the law of the civil law system. However, up to now, the status of legal precedents has changed greatly in the civil law system. For example, the well-known French jurist David regarded legal precedents as one of the sources of the law in the civil law system. He said that in order for us to determine the importance of the court's judgments in the formulation of the law, some existing proposals should be prevented because they tried to stress that law was the only source and negated the qualification of legal precedents as the sources of the law. These proposals would be ridiculous if they were used in countries like France or Germany because legal precedents played a primary role in some fields during the development of the law…and another element should be noticed, namely the existence and development of collections of legal precedents. These collections were not compiled for the use of legal historians or sociologists, nor for the amusement of readers. They were compiled for jurists engaged in practical work, which could only be interpreted from the fact that legal precedents were the real sources of the law. The importance of legal precedents as the sources of the law in the Roman-Germanic legal system was seen by the large quantity and good quality of these collections.[108] Positive[109] and negative[110] opinions remain in China's legal community on whether the status of legal precedents as the sources of the law should be recognized. I posit that it is the historical development trend in the contemporary world that the two law systems learn from, draw close to, and penetrate each other. The monistic or arbitrary theory of the sources of the law

---

[107] See [45], pp. 22–23.

[108] See [59], pp. 24–25.

[109] See [77].

[110] See [78].

does not coincide with the requirements for social development. In this case, China should abandon the traditional view that statutory law is the only source of the law and should leave a place for legal precedents. (3) The issue on the relationship between case law and statutory law. It should be admitted that case law and statutory law are distinct legal patterns, and it is an unchangeable fact that China has basically accepted the pattern of statutory law. When we propose to adopt case law, we do not mean to abandon statutory law. Rather, we suggest giving priority to statutory law with case law supplemented. Even some Chinese jurists have clearly put forward the problem of case law in the sense of overcoming the limitations of statutory law. For example, the Chinese scholar Xu Guodong mentiond that the law had limitations. When the voice for enhancing the legal system became louder, we should understand the law based on objectivity and abandon the thought that legislation was omnipotent. When considering what legislative mode China should adopt, we should also consider the limitations of codes. In the future, China's legislative pattern would be open rather than closed. China, which was deeply influenced by the civil law system, should avoid making the same mistakes already made by civil law countries. Currently, the voice for recognizing case law was much louder, which was beneficial to illustrate the limitations of the law.[111] From this perspective, case law can and should be adopted in China's legal system. (4) The issue on the functions of case law. How to understand the functions of case law if case law is adopted in China? Two opinions remain among Chinese jurists: first, determining the functions of case law as a new legal form of the sources of the law, which aims to compensate for the shortcomings and fill the gap of legislation. Second, the legal precedents of the supreme court are merely the descriptions and explanations of the spirit of the statute law. The supreme court's handling of legal facts is not allowed to contradict statute law, and once legal precedents are formulated, they are of the binding force.[112] Both opinions affirm that case law should be adopted in China, but they have different understandings of the functions of case law. The former holds that case law can formulate legal rules and fill the legal gap. The latter believe that case law only concretizes the significance of specific legal facts and legal provisions, and it is directly operable. Thus, when statute law has already had a tight system, China's legal precedents are generally the descriptions and explanations of the provisions and spirits of statute law, whose validity should be lower than statute law, and the handling of legal facts by legal precedents is not allowed to contradict statute law.[113]

I think the functions of case law should adapt to China's legal system and should not be overvalued or undervalued. But in the criminal law field, the application of case law should not contradict the doctrine of no penalty without a law either. China has stipulated the analogy system, but a consensus to abolish the analogy of no penalty without a law in criminal law revision has been a consensus. In this case, the application of case law should be restricted by the doctrine of no penalty without a law. Some Chinese criminal law scholars argue that criminal precedents should possess the

[111] See [77].

[112] See [75].

[113] See [79], pp. 238–239.

nature of law creation under some special circumstances so that criminal precedents obtain legal validity, and its scope should be limited to the analogy precedents in criminal law that are applicable to Article 79 of *Penal Code* and approved by the Supreme People's Court. China's system of analogy in criminal law is of the nature of law creation. The behavior that judicial organs create law is seen as legal because the power originates from the legislature. As a result, analogy in criminal law, in fact, is seen as an authoritative legislative activity. China is implementing the system of "one case, one report, and one review" system. This helps to strictly control judicial activities. However, it reduces judicial efficiency, prolongs the trial period, and increases repetitive work. Thus, as the law controls judicial activities strictly, all analogical legal precedents approved for the first time should be given legal validity in the future. Afterward, when inferior people's courts or special courts handle similar cases, they can quote judgment basis directly without reporting the cases for approval. They only should report the cases to superior courts for recordation.[114] I hold different opinions to it and the main reason is that as the soul of criminal law, the doctrine of no penalty without a law always possesses an unshakable position to guarantee citizens' rights. For criminal law, no penalty without a law is the principle.

As a flexible method to remedy the shortcomings of statutory law, case law should not contradict the principle, at least in the criminal law field.

We stress that case law should be limited by the doctrine of no penalty without a law in criminal law, but we do not ignore the role of case law. In the revision of the criminal law in 1997, the analogy system was repealed, and the doctrine of no penalty without a law was established. As the doctrine of no penalty without a law was implemented, legal precedents played a role in interpreting the law. In particular, as people have recognized the disadvantages of the normative judicial interpretations universally applied in China, the judicial interpretations of individual cases have been paid increasing attention to. In this case, it is necessary to determine authoritative legal precedents through judicial interpretations of individual cases and give full play to their roles in criminal judicature. Predictably, legal precedents will play an increasing role in directing criminal judicature in China.

3.3 Empirical Foundation of Case Law

When the famous British jurist Maine compared the civil law system with the common law system, he pointed out meaningfully that the world's most noted legal system began from a "code" and ended with a "code". Throughout the history of Roman law, the paraphrasts of the Roman law implied that their system's entity was built on the *Twelve Decemviral Tables*, meaning it was built on statutory law. Apart from this special point in Rome, all systems before the *Twelve Decemviral Tables* were not recognized. The Roman jurisprudence theoretically dated back to a code, whereas British law was theoretically considered to originate from ancient unwritten conventions. This was the main reason that their systems and ours developed

[114] See [80].

differently. These two theories did not entirely coincide with the facts, but they both had produced critical results.[115] Maine's saying that "these two theories do not completely coincide with the fact", means that when laws are developed, they are by no means escaping the stage of being customary laws.

However, once the civil law system surpasses this stage, it will be replaced by codes. A splendid, shining legal palace is then built, and customs are nothing but inconspicuous decorations. By contrast, the common law system always follows customs. Although customs have changed from unwritten ones to written ones, judicial customs that follow old routines and accumulate numerous cases are the soul and essence of the common law system forever. Therefore, the difference between the statutory law of the civil law system and the case law of the common law system is never formal (i.e., written or unwritten). The main feature of the difference between case law and statutory law depends on the philosophical foundation: empiricism. The US scholar Ehrmann pointed out that if customary law and common law were built on human experience, then legislation was a leap to show what behaviors would be adjusted in the future. Customary law never denied itself as the outcome of social power, while legislation was always the first to claim that it could change independently and was powerful enough to promote social and political reforms in all sources of the law.[116] The reasons why case law is built on experience are mainly in the following two aspects:

To begin with, the development mechanism of case law illustrates that case law is the result of the formation of customs and accumulation of experience. Statutory law is not only the outcome of legislation but also that of the revolution. The foundation of case law, however, is the historic continuity of experience. So, following precedents is regarded as a principle, and reform is happening secretly. Regarding this, the British jurist Maine has made excellent arguments, who said that we always saw an organization in Britain which expanded, changed, and improved the law. In theory, however, this organization should not change anything about the existing laws. The process of utilizing completed legislation work was perceptible, however, it was not admitted. In terms of most legal systems in legal precedents and recorded in legal reports, we were used to using doublespeak and holding double, inconsistent concepts. When some facts were brought to the British court for trial, during the whole process of the discussions between judges and defenders, they would never and could never propose to apply any principles other than the old ones or propose any different questions other than those that have been allowed. It was considered a certainty that there must be a law including the facts that were resorted to the law for settlement in some places, and if it could not be found, it was only due to the lack of necessary patience and knowledge or intelligence. Nevertheless, once the judgment was announced and recorded, we were immersed in a new language and thoughts, unconsciously and covertly. At this point, we had to admit that the new judgment had changed the law. If we used a very incorrect statement that was sometimes applied, that meant the provisions that could be applied were flexible enough despite that these

115 See [81], p. 1.

116 See [33], pp. 48–49.

statements have changed. Now, a new legal precedent was added. The legal norms that were concluded based on the comparison of legal precedents were completely different from those concluded from one legal precedent. An old provision has been abolished and replaced by a new one, but this was usually imperceptible because we were not used to expressing the legal formulas derived from legal precedents into correct words; therefore, unless the nature of provisions has been drastically changed, otherwise, it was not easy to notice.[117] Therefore, as a naturally-grown legal organism, case law also abides by the law of evolutionism, which was initially proposed by the British biologist Darwin in his work *The Origin of Species* and introduced into the sociological study by Spencer, who established the theory of social organism and Social Darwinism later. Deeply influenced by Darwinism, the common law system was even called "Legal Darwinism". The US scholar Schwartz has written that on November 9, 1882, an evening banquet was held in Delmonico's in New York City, where Herbert Spencer was treated. Spencer was about to finish his visit to US, and William M. Evarts, the recognized "Prince of US Lawyers", delivered a speech to Spencer to show his respect. Evarts mentioned, "Mr. Spencer, you are better than any of us. In all aspects of social life, we appreciate your work. This faculty of laying on a dissecting board an entire nation or an entire age and finding out all the arteries and veins and pulsations of their life is an extension beyond any that our own medical schools afford." At that time, Social Darwinism was the dominant legal philosophy. All theories were absolutized in the law. Abstract concepts regarding freedom and justice were regarded as the dogma of the constitution, and the *Fourteenth Amendment to the United States Constitution* was seen as the legal recognition of the law of survival of the fittest. It was demanding to read the constitution, if not through the lens of Spence's views. For US jurists, the law displayed so many similarities with the living nature in all aspects and development that it was proper to translate them into the language existing after Darwinism.[118] Indeed, Darwin's evolutionism is the outcome of empiricism, which is apt to interpret case law. Throughout the long history of case law, the wisdom and experience of judges from generation to generation makes it adapt to social environments and changes and develops gradually.

Second, the creation mechanism of case law also shows the importance of experience. Under the conditions of statutory law, judges use deduction to handle legal provisions and individual cases, so the legal precedent is the result of applying provisions of law to individual cases and an example of the legal provisions. The statutory law system requires judges to set out from the law instead of legal precedents to decide cases. Legal provisions are the fruits of the reason of legislators, while legal precedents are the results of the experience of judges. Therefore, setting out from legal provisions means to emphasis and admire reason during adjudication. However, no judge is a blank slate. Judges' previous experience still more or less influences their deductions of each case. In fact, judges are biased by their experience during adjudication, so they are still affected by legal precedents. However, they do not admit the influence under the statutory law system. Case law explicitly admits the role of

[117] See [1], pp. 18–19.

[118] See [35], pp. 116–118.

the experience of judges in judicial activities. The US jurist Pound just called it judicial empiricism and compared it to the legislative rationalism of the civil law system. He said that natural law was a massive power for developing jurisprudence and a superior preparation of the legal principles and systems, which existed in reason, and the current legal system was merely an incomplete reflection of natural law. Thus, the existing laws could be revised and supplemented based on natural law. This theory expresses the jurists' aspirations to improve and supplement the existing legal materials for specific objectives in litigation while not damaging people's beliefs in the law's incomparable authority and persuading the court to accept the result with this method. Without further explanation, you must know what achievements the Roman jurists have made. In the seventeenth and eighteenth centuries, European civil law jurists have applied the same method for the same work. Judicial empiricism has done most things the jurisprudence has done for Roman law. Through prudent, sometimes creative induction, judicial empiricism handled cases one by one. However, many cases of creative judicial behaviors have opened a new page of the legal history or have created a new legal system.[119] In the sense that judicial legal precedents create legal rules, the so-called judicial empiricism by Pound is the same as legislative empiricism.

Experience is the source of understanding, but the experience is inevitably coarse and branded as a practitioner. If experience is not raised to rational understanding, it will be limited by time and space. The empirical nature of case law originates from the handling of individual cases, but it has not been methodized and thus is fragmentary, messy, and lacks formal reason, which is precisely one of the defects of case law. We should not make positive or negative evaluations on case law and statutory law arbitrarily. We must notice that legislation has increased, and more laws have been written into statutory laws in common law countries, which favors the civil law system and has brought changes to British law. As Geldart has said, in the past, statute law was only to correct and supplement the law; however, it would be a means for legislators to express themselves as much as they can.

It is the same as a judge revising the existing legal rules or creating a new rule.[120] It is not asserted whether common law countries will accept the concept of civil law, but as statute law is published and systematized, the influence of civil law penetrates common law. The harmonization of case law with statutory law will no longer be a sack of minutiae, but a major issue concerning the future of case law.

References

1. [UK] Maine, *Ancient Law* (Commercial Press, Beijing, 1954)
2. [US] D. Bodde et al., *Law in Imperial China* (Jiangsu People's Publishing House, Nanjing, 1993)
3. T.C. Tung, *Law and Society in Traditional China* (Zhonghua Book Company, Beijing, 1981)
4. G. Zhang, *New History of Chinese Ideology of Law* (Peking University Press, Beijing, 1991)

[119] See [20], p. 130.

[120] See [37], p. 27.

5. X. Zhao, Legal concept deriving from theocracy. Sci. Law (2) (1991)
6. [Soviet Union] N.M. Diakonov et al., *Commentary on Babylonian Emperor and Babylonian Law* (Renmin University of China Press, Beijing, 1954)
7. [Soviet Union] Nersesyants, *Political Thought of Ancient Greece* (The Commercial Press, Beijing, 1991)
8. [US] Bodenheimer, *Jurisprudence: The Philosophy and Method of the Law* (Huaxia Publishing House, Beijing, 1987)
9. [Italy] Aquinas, *Aquinas Political Writings* (The Commercial Press, Beijing, 1963)
10. [Ancient Rome] Justinian, *The Institutes of Justinian* (The Commercial Press, Beijing, 1989)
11. [France] Rousseau, *On the Social Contract* (The Commercial Press, Beijing, 1962)
12. [France] Rousseau, *Discourse on the Origin and Basis of Inequality Among Men* (The Commercial Press, Beijing, 1962)
13. [Germany] Hegel, *Elements of the Philosophy of Right* (The Commercial Press, Beijing, 1961)
14. P. Gong, *On Marx's Legal Philosophy* (Henan People's Publishing House, Zhengzhou, 1992)
15. *Marx-Engels-Gesamtausgabe*, vol. 2, 2 edn. (People's Publishing House, Beijing, 1995)
16. *Marx-Engels-Gesamtausgabe*, vol. 3, 2 edn. (People's Publishing House, Beijing, 1995)
17. *Marx-Engels-Gesamtausgabe*, vol. 4 (People's Publishing House, Beijing, 1958)
18. *Marx-Engels-Gesamtausgabe*, vol. 1 (People's Publishing House, Beijing, 1965)
19. *Marx-Engels-Gesamtausgabe*, vol. 4, 2 edn. (People's Publishing House, Beijing, 1995)
20. [US] Pound, *Interpretation of Legal History* (Huaxia Publishing House, Beijing, 1989)
21. H. Zhang (Editor-in-Chief), *History of Western Legal Thoughts* (Peking University Press, Beijing, 1983)
22. [US] Pound, *Social Control Through Law* (The Commercial Press, Beijing, 1984)
23. G. Zhang et al., *General Introduction of Legislation* (Law Press China, Beijing, 1991)
24. [US] A. Seidman, R.B. Seidman, *Legal Order and Social Changes* (China University of Political Science and Law Press, Beijing, 1992)
25. C. Hu, Legislation can be fore-running but not advancing. Law Sci. (4) (1991)
26. Q. He, Legislative advance: one of the rules of legal operation. Law Sci. (4) (1991)
27. C. Sun, Basic trend of contemporary legislative behaviors. Law Sci. (11) (1991)
28. Z. Liang, *Searching Harmony in Natural Order: A Study of Legal Tradition in China from a Cultural Perspective* (Shanghai People's Publishing House, Shanghai, 1991)
29. B. Xie (Editor-in-Chief), *Roman Law* (Beijing Peking University Press, 1990)
30. L. Zhou, *Roman Law* (Quzhong Publishing House, Beijing, 1983)
31. [Italy] G. Giuseppe, *The Story of Roman Law* (China University of Political Science and Law Press, Beijing, 1994)
32. G. Xu, Justinian and his legislative career: and on the disadvantages and remedies of code law. Sci. Law (5) (1990)
33. [US] Ehrmann, *Comparative Legal Cultures* (Joint Publishing, Beijing, 1990)
34. [Britain] R.J. Walker, *British Legal System* (Southwest University of Political Science and Law, Chongqing, 1984)
35. [US] S. Bernard, *The Law in US: A History* (China University of Political Science and Law Press, Beijing, 1989)
36. H. Chu, *US Criminal Law* (Peking University Press, Beijing, 1987)
37. [France] D. Rene, *British Law and French Law: A Comparison in Substance* (China University of Political Science and Law Press, Beijing, 1984)
38. Y. Dongfang, Three attributes of statutory law: the balance between right and power and on the adjustment object of modern law. Sci. Law (5) (1993)
39. X. Chen, *Philosophy of Criminal Law* (China University of Political Science and Law Press, Beijing, 1992)
40. [France] Montesquieu, *The Spirit of the Laws*, vol. 2 (The Commercial Press, Beijing, 1963)
41. [US] Nonet, Selznick, *Law and Society in Transition: Toward Responsive Law* (China University of Political Science and Law Press, Beijing, 1994)
42. Q. Liang, *On the Evolution, Gains and Losses of the Compilation of China's Statutory Law* (Zhonghua Book Company, Taipei, 1971)

43. K. Mu, Legal language. Chin. J. Law (4) (1994)
44. [Canada] P.A. Crépeau, Comparative law, legal reform and codification: a domestic and international perspective, in *New Trends in Comparative Law: Proceedings of the International Conference on Comparative Law* (Peking University Press, Beijing, 1993)
45. [US] Merryman, *Civil Law Tradition* (Law Press China, Beijing, 2004)
46. S. Xue, Characteristics and future of Chinese legal system. Res. China Soc. Sci. **1**(4) (1928)
47. [Japan] K. Takeshi, The second task of comparative law to transplant foreign laws, in *New Trends in Comparative Law: Proceedings of the International Conference on Comparative Law* (Peking University Press, Beijing, 1993)
48. C. Wang, Mutual reference and absorption between laws of different countries: an important topic in the research of comparative law, in *New Trends in Comparative Law: Proceedings of the International Conference on Comparative Law* (Peking University Press, Beijing, 1993)
49. G. Su, *Rationality and Its Limitation: Introduction to Weber's Thoughts* (Shanghai People's Press, Shanghai, 1988)
50. [US] W. Alan, *The Making of the Civil Law* (China University of Political Science and Law Press, Beijing, 1992)
51. S. Zhang et al., *Kant's 'Critique of Pure Reason'* (Peking University Press, Beijing, 1987)
52. [UK] Locke, *Two Treatises of Government, The Second Treatise* (The Commercial Press, Beijing, 1981)
53. H. Xie, Comment on legal instrumentalism. China Legal Sci. (1) (1994)
54. *The Shuihudi Qin Bamboo Texts* (Cultural Relics Publishing House, Beijing, 1978)
55. H. Ning, *General history of Chinese Criminal Law*, vol. 2 (Liaoning University Publishing House, Shenyang, 1986)
56. L. Wang, *New Research on the Law of Tang Dynasty* (Shanghai Academy of Social Sciences Press, Shanghai, 1993)
57. S. Wu, Let history predict the future: on the overall spirit and macro pattern of Chinese legal culture. Cass J. Law (2) (1989)
58. S. Wu, *Legal Tradition in China from a Cultural Perspective* (Peking University Press, Beijing, 1994)
59. [France] D. Rene, *Main Contemporary Legal Systems* (Shanghai Translation Publishing House, Shanghai, 1984)
60. Gledon et al., *Comparative Legal Traditions* (China University of Political Science and Law Press, Beijing, 1983)
61. Z. Liang, British case law. Sci. Law (1) (1991)
62. R. You (Editor-in-Chief), *Foreign Legal History* (Peking University Press, Beijing, 1992)
63. [UK] R.J. Walker, *British Legal System* (Southwest University of Political Science and Law, Chongqing, 1980)
64. [US] E. Allan Farnsworth, *An Introduction to the Legal System of the United States* (Quzhong Publishing House, Beijing, 1986)
65. [Britain] J.W. Cecil Turner, *Kenny's Outlines of Criminal Law* (Huaxia Publishing Press, Beijing, 1980)
66. [US] Cohen, *Legal Research in a Nutshell* (The Commercial Press, Beijing, 1994)
67. *Legal Dictionary* (revised), 2nd edn. (Shanghai Lexicographical Publishing House, Shanghai, 1984)
68. Z. Shen, *General Introduction to Comparative Law* (Peking University Press, Beijing, 1987)
69. [Britain] D.M. Walker, *The Oxford Companion to Law* (Guangming Daily Publishing House, Beijing, 1988)
70. S. Wu, On the position of precedents in China's legal construction. Law Sci. (6) (1986)
71. S. Wu, On history predicting the future: on the overall spirit and macro style of Chinese legal culture. Law Sci. (2) (1989)
72. M. Cui, "Case law" is an important way to perfect the legal system. Law Sci. (8) (1988)
73. Y. Gao, China is not suitable for case law system. Chin. Legal Sci. (3) (1991)
74. Z. Shen, Precedents in modern China: a comparative law inquiry. Chin. Legal Sci. (1) (1992)

75. W. Wu, Q. Chen, Legal precedents should not have the binding force in China. Sci. Law (1) (1990)
76. G. Xu, Analysis on process mode of legal limitation. China Legal Sci. (3) (1981)
77. G. Xu, Analysis on process mode of legal limitation. China Legal Sci. (3) (1991)
78. J. Chen, On the sources of the law. Sci. Law (4) (1991)
79. Z. Shen (Editor-in-Chief), *Studies in Jurisprudence* (Shanghai People's Publishing House, Shanghai, 1990)
80. W. You, On the criminal case system in China. Cass J. Law (4) (1994)
81. [Britain] Maine, *Ancient Law* (The Commercial Press, Beijing, 1959)

Chapter 10
Human Nature Foundation of Administration of Justice

The administration of justice is the activity to apply criminal law. Human is the subject of judicial activities, so the judge is the subject of the administration of justice, who is in the core position. The research of judges from the perspective of human nature is of great significance to investigate the human nature foundation of the administration of justice. A judicial activity is a process where judges apply the law, during which two vital links are included, which are statutory interpretation and discretion. Through statutory interpretation and discretion, the law applies to individual cases. Statutory interpretation and discretion are technique-related issues on the application of the law. However, if we limit ourselves to the technique level, we could barely reveal their true values. Only by setting out from human nature can we uncover the general rules of statutory interpretation and discretion on a deeper theoretical level.

1 Judicial Subject

In ancient times, there was the so-called "trial by ordeal". When disputes or arguments happened, people asked for gods to distinguish right from wrong, solving disputes and determining crimes and non-crimes by the power of gods. Ancient Chinese documents recorded that the "trial by ordeal" method existed in the Spring and Autumn Period when the unicorn *zhi* was used to butter the criminals if crimes were difficult to determine. If *zhi* buttered the criminal, the person was guilty and vice versa.[1] Gods acted as judges in "trial by ordeal". Ancient people invited gods to

[1] The ancient Chinese character of the law, according to *Shuowen Jiezi* (discussing writing and explaining characters), "(it) means criminal law. The character has a component of water, meaning that law enforcement should be as just as water. Another component of this character is *zhi*, a mythical creature who rams corrupt officials with its horn and devour them." *zhi* is explained as "a beast. It resembles a goat and has a single horn. In ancient times, it butted people who violated the law."

X. Chen, *Humanistic Foundation of Criminal Law*,
https://doi.org/10.1007/978-981-19-9764-8_10

serve as judges not only because they believed and worshiped the god's justice but also because they did not trust each other. By now, judges are no longer gods; they are humans. Humans have weaknesses, so can we treat humans with the requirements of gods? Certainly not. However, we have reasons to require judges to be impartial and upright. Therefore, we should analyze the human nature of judges correctly and reshape the personality images of judges.

1.1 Personality of Judicial Subject

The understanding of the personality of the judge, who serves as the judicial subject, evolves from divinity to human beings. Classicism idolizes judges by acknowledging (1) the sacredness of the authority of judge's behaviors. Since the law is implemented by judges via specific behaviors, the social authority of the law evolves into the authority of the judge's behaviors at the practice level, and the sacredness and insurmountability of the law sanctify the authority of the judge's behaviors; (2) the impartiality of judge's behaviors. The impartial foundation of the law and the judge's legal position dispels people's doubt about the judge's impartial attitude towards legal affairs; and (3) the legality of the judge's behaviors. The previous points show that the judge's behaviors are naturally legitimate, and judges are always the subject of legal evaluations, who are free from the social evaluation on legality.[2] The idolized understanding of judges is grounded on the presumption of a judge's human nature; namely, a judge is a reasonable person who has free will, who can decide facts and who applies laws impartially and objectively. This is the apotheosis of judges, which ignores the natural characteristic of a judge's personality. As US scholars have shown, about four thousand years ago, after the *Code of Hammurabi*, people believed that judge's decisions and laws came from the Deity. By the end of the nineteenth century, when Holmes established his research, people realized that the law resulted from human experience. At the beginning of the twentieth century, jurists generally considered that judges could be free from the impact of their personalities when making judgments.[3] Meanwhile, positivism actualized judges. For instance, judicial behaviorism did not understand legal phenomena from the abstract concept established for judges by historical practice, traditional theories and doctrines, so the hope of a country ruled by law was no longer based on the illusion deduced by the subjective logic. Judicial behaviorism focused on judges who served as natural persons, or practical behavior as a "political actor" in the judicial procedure, and the basic tendency of judge's behaviors determined by political, social ideology and, values.[4] Legal realism further declared the impacts of individual factors, such as emotion, on judge's behaviors. Legal realists, such as Benjamin Cardoza, Jerome Frank, Tharman Arnold, and others, put an end to the legend of judges who were

---

[2] See [1], pp. 132–133.

[3] See [2].

[4] See [1], p. 136.

automatic judicial instruments and argued that as long as sufficient reasons were applied, the law, as a clear, consistent rule, was easy to find. When a person became a judge, he could not eliminate all his biases or gain resistance to social pressure. How he would behave depended on his personality, experience, attitude, belief, and preference for values.[5] Therefore, positivism has revealed the sacred veil from judges to show their real appearances as natural persons. Also, it stressed the reality and experience of the judge's behaviors while denying the assumption of the free will of the judge's personality.

Classicism judges are of impersonal characteristics while positivism judges are of personal characteristics. Then, are judges impersonal or personal? In my opinion, there remains a contradiction between necessity and reality on this question. Classicism judges are of impersonal characteristics, while positivism judges are of personal characteristics. The image of classicism judges is merely an idealized image of judges. In the sense of reality, as a natural person living in society, a judge was impossible to be otherworldly, so a judge must have a distinctive personality characteristic. Undoubtedly, when we mention the personality factors of judges, we are not to defend them blindly; oppositely, we should prevent these factors from impacting the impartial judgments based on the affirmation of the personality factors of judges. To do so, we should analyze the human nature of judges' activities during the administration of justice.

A judicial activity is a practical human activity during which complicated cognition is contained. Is reason or non-reason playing a decisive role in the judge's cognitive activities? According to Beccaria, the administration of justice is reasoning of syllogism, which is a mere manifestation of human reason. Although Beccaria admitted that the judge's emotional impulsion might impact the judgment, he believed that the impact could be eliminated as long as the judge's right of interpretation was removed. However, according to legal realism, this was nothing but a "judicial myth". Frank, a legal realist, proposed two formulas of judicial judgment. The myth formula was R (rule) × F (fact) = D (decision). The reality formula was S (stimulus, the stimulus about judges and cases) × P (personality) = D (judgment), or R (rule) × SF (subjective fact) = D (judgment). Frank has specifically researched judges' personalities and said that according to psychological principles, the judgment process rarely started from a premise that led to a conclusion. Oppositely, it started from an ambiguous conclusion, setting out from a conclusion and trying to discover the premise that proved this conclusion. Theoretically, a judge set out from the premised legal rules or principles and applied them to reality before making a conclusion, namely the judgment. Nonetheless, as mentioned above, judges were humans, and the normal thinking process of ordinary people (except for a few simple situations) was not determined by the reasoning of syllogism. Judges did not have a different reasoning method only because they worked in the legal area. In most cases, judicial judgments were the same as other judgments, which were made based on temporary conclusions. Frank quoted the former US judge Hutcheson's description of his judgment process that after verifying and deliberating his materials of cases, he started his

[5] See [3], p. 402.

imagination performance. Deliberating reason, waiting for sense and predicting; the intuition to understand the problem became the flash connector between the problem and the decision, and shined the flash along the way on the darkest road for the pace of justice…when sensing or predicting his decision, the judge's behavior was the same as when a lawyer dealt with a case. The only exception was that since a lawyer had a predetermined goal—wining the lawsuit for his client—he only sought for and noticed those presentiments that stopped him on the chosen path, however, a judge, who was only on the path with the uncertain mission of finding a proper solution, would follow wherever his hunch pointed out. Hutcheson also said that a judge made the judgment based on sense rather than judgment and presentiments rather than reasoning, so the reasoning only existed in the grounds for judgment. The most vital impetus of a judgment was the intuition on the rightness or wrongness of a specific case. Once a judgment was made, a smart judge mobilized all his intelligence and mind to justify his intuition and make sure his intuition passed the verification of his criticizers. Thus, he had to rethink all rules, principles, domains, and concepts that were directly or indirectly useful for him to choose those things that, in his opinion, would justify the results he hoped. According to Frank, Hutcheson's descriptions were basically correct illustrations of how judges thought. Frank further stated that if the law was composed of judge's judgments, but these judgments were based on the presentiments of judges, the ways judges obtained their presentiments were the keys for judicial activities. The judgment process of judges was the same as that of ordinary people. When ordinary people made judgments, various hidden factors were acting. Likewise, the judge's judgment process was intertwined with complicated factors determined by every person's features and which were more important than political, economic, or moral biases. The individual features, namely, the features, temperaments, biases, and habits of each judge, were generally termed "individual personalities". Accordingly, Frank concluded that we must thoroughly understand the complex thing we termed "judge's personality" if we aimed to know what judges have made by creating laws and making presentiments. If the personality of the judge was the key factor in the administration of justice, the law was determined by the judge who accidentally trailed the case.[6] We should admit that Frank has correctly stated the crucial role of individual factors when a judge makes a judgment. Nevertheless, Frank exaggerates the role of individual factors to a great extent and even denies legal rules as the foundation of the judge's judgment; instead, he believes the judge's judgment is determined by other unreasonable factors such as emotion, intuitive presentiment, and bias.[7] Clearly, this view is biased. In my view, when a judge makes a judgment, rational and empirical factors, and even non-rational and unconscious factors all play a role in the psychological activities.

Among rational factors, mainly the legal consciousness plays a role. Legal consciousness refers to the professional legal consciousness, namely, the concept of law formed by professional legal personnel and legal experts based on the legal

---

[6] See [4], pp. 108–110.

[7] See [5], p. 150.

ideology of the nature of world outlook and specialized legal knowledge, and accumulated experience in legal practice and activities of applying the law, as well as the understanding of all aspects of the law (including professional legal content) by the competent authorities. The formal legal consciousness is a vital factor in the creation and application of the law.[8] Thus, legal consciousness is crucial in judicial activities, which consists of the foundation of the judge's judgments. An interesting phenomenon is involved: the understandings of the professional knowledge of judges between the classical school of criminology and positivist school of criminology are distinct, leading to the contradiction over the existence and repeal of the jury system in criminal justice. The classical school of criminology negates the necessity of the judge's professional knowledge but advocates the jury system. Beccaria said that an excellent law which establishes assistants to the principal judge, and those chosen by lot; for that ignorance, which judges by its feelings, is less subject to error, than the knowledge of the laws which judges by opinion. Where the laws are clear and precise, the office of the judge is merely to ascertain the fact. If, in examining the proofs of a crime, acuteness and dexterity be required; if clearness and precision be necessary in summing up the result; to judge of the result itself, nothing is wanting but plain and ordinary good sense, a less fallacious guide than the knowledge of a judge accustomed to find guilty, and to reduce all things to an artificial system, borrowed from his studies.[9] Similarly, Hegel is also an enthusiastic advocate of the jury system in the modern administration of justice. According to him, jurors and specialized judges with specialized legal knowledge and experience are different. The juror's primary role in trials is not to solve the legal attribution of the case but to address the fact-finding problem. In this respect, jurors are competent. Consistently, Hegel regarded the traditional "judge superstition" as an absurd concept and negated it determinedly. The main reason was that, first, fact-finding did not involve any legal decision. It was completely a general problem with cognition. Therefore, there was no reason to believe specialized judges could only recognize that fact-finding because everyone who had been educated could do it rather than the people who had received legal education. Second, the judge's behavior in finding facts was, like ordinary people, subjective. In other words, the conclusion displayed in the judge's final judgment was made under inner conviction, subjective belief, and conscience or intuitive knowledge. There was no special magic or secret. Hegel said that it was basic to verify the judge's behavior of finding facts. The two capabilities, as mentioned above, were what jurors were equipped with, and their capabilities were as good as specialized judges.[10] Ferri admitted the merits of the jury system. First, from the political perspective, the jury system by no means represented people's sovereignty because it recognized that the legal right originated from people and should be exercised directly by people. Second, the jury system prevented citizens' right to political liberty from being violated by the abuse of power by the government. The abuse of power by the government was easy exist without jury system

[8] See [6], p. 129.

[9] See [7], p. 20.

[10] See [8], p. 101.

when the government controlled a minority of judges. Furthermore, the jury system was also an approach to affirm the equality awareness of citizens because every citizen might be the judge with whom he shared the same status. Notwithstanding all the advantages mentioned above, Ferri claimed to cancel the jury system in criminal justice which gave the primary reason that jurors were hard to equipped with the professional knowledge that they should have. Ferri pointed out that if legislators asked judges to only answer "yes" or "no", jurors might be as suitable as magistrates. However, he believed that legislators did not ask for the judgments that were without any interpretation like what Kamineni called "the approach of civil judges" but those that could be adjusted on the grounds of reasons, especially in the positivist system of the criminal procedure, which required judges to be proficient in anthropology and criminal sociology and to make judgments that helped correct criminals based on the personalities of criminals and features of crimes. Ferri also disproved the argument that "general reason is better than science for telling the fact, common sense is better than the best intelligence, and general training is better than scientific training" by Beccaria and mentioned that even though we recognized that the fact could be separated from the law, logic and experience had approved it wrong.[11] There is no doubt that the disagreement between the classical school of criminology and the positivist school of criminology towards the jury system reflects the professional requirements for judges. The classical school belittles the role of judges, who considers judges as a machine to apply the law. Hence, every person is competent for this job as long as he is reasonable. On the other hand, the positivist school merits the role of judges, especially criminal judges whose trial object is criminals, and argues that judges should be equipped with professional knowledge of criminal law and other aspects, including sociology and anthropology, so jurors are not competent for taking the post of judges. I make no comments on this argument. In the final analysis, reason holds the dominant position in judicial activities and depends on the social role of judges.

Not only the reason but some unreasonable factors also determine the judge's judgments, which are judges' personality characteristics. US scholars mention that judicial scholars refer to a judge's personality regularly but have never deeply discussed it. If we define personality as all reactions of a person to the people around him, then, without further explanation, many aspects of the judge's background are related to it.[12] A judge is not a purely rational person but an empirical person, so he must be influenced by his personality. As Chinese scholars have mentioned, judges are not rigid machines that apply penalties but men of flesh and blood, so their cognitive activities of applying penalties are impossible to be free from the "physical" and "mental" influences, such as personality, emotion, temperament, experience, moral concepts, legal awareness, political belief, world outlook, and view on life.[13] Through statistics, the founder of US legal realism Frank proved that the judgment was determined by the judge who accidentally heard the case. Based on the investigations of the treatment of thousands of minor criminal cases by the magistrate's court of

[11] See [9], pp. 122, 127, 129.

[12] See [2], p. 161.

[13] See [10], p. 214.

New York City between 1914 and 1916, the differences between magistrates when dealing with similar cases were shocking. Among 546 people who were accused of drinking and dealt with by the same judge, only one person was released, while others (about 99%) were guilty; however, among 673 people who were accused of drinking and dealt with by another judge, 531 people (79%) were not guilty. Among cases of disturbing the order, one judge only released 18% of people, while another released 54% of people. That is to say, people on trial only had a 20% probability of being released if they were heard by the former judge, while more than a 50% probability by the latter judge. The investigation reports concluded that these numbers indicated that trials were determined by humans, which reflected the magistrates' temperament, personality, education, situation, and personal features.[14] These statistics do not demonstrate all problems, but they show that the personality of judges does influence judgments. The experience shows that judges of different psychological features make distinct judgments. Through the study of the psychological features of judges, the Chinese scholar Gu Peidong divides judges into the following five types and concludes the impact of psychological features on judgments[15]: (1) emotional-and-impulsive type. The psychological features of this type are that judges are easily affected by conflicting facts, words and behaviors of the conflicting subject and public opinions and thus have robust mentalities of hatred, detest, sympathy, or concern. Judges with such psychological features are agile in acting and dealing with conflicts. However, these judges tend to be bound by their first impressions. They lack patience and easily bring their emotions to trials and judgments; (2) experience-biased type. This type of judge tends to deal with conflicts intuitively and the more effective their intuitive judgments and behaviors are, the more their experience biases are enhanced; (3) altruistic-for-reward type. This type of judge tends to empathize with people on trial and try their best to provide procedure convenience and protections for the parties concerned and ensure that beneficiaries feel and beware of their altruistic motivations to pay back. This psychology is negative because judges easily give up principles to satisfy the conflicting subject, and, impacted by vanity, they are restricted to choosing and applying judgment approaches by their anticipations of rewards, so the procedure is unjust; (4) mild-and-meticulous type. This type of judge rarely injects their emotions into the conflicts they are engaged in. They are obtuse, which usually influences the antagonistic emotions of the conflicting subject and exerts a buffering effect. During trials, these judges easily find subtle changes in the details of the conflicting facts and the emotions of the conflicting subjects and are patient in guiding and persuading the conflicting subjects. Nonetheless, they are obtuse in judicial actions, leading to the inevitable result of longer trial periods; and (5) defiant-and-self-esteem type. This type of judge tends to be cautious about implementing their judicial actions, paying extra attention to the impacts on their dignity. They have a solid awareness of self-discipline, including their manners and appearance during trials. The weakness of this psychological type is that judges excessively stress the impertinence of the conflicting subjects and other litigators on themselves

[14] See [11], p. 341.

[15] See [1], pp. 168–170.

and the respect of their opinions by other litigators. To sum up, a judge is the unity of a rational person and an empirical person, and the unity of social and personal roles. Although unreasonable factors matter, it is the reason that plays the dominant role during judgments, and the personality of judges has greater influence. The opinion that views judges as trial machines and negates the personality characteristics and reason factors of judges, which views judgments as completely the outcome of sense, is biased. Only when we have a correct understanding of the personality of judges will we establish a scientific mechanism to regulate the judicial subject, eliminate the adverse impacts of the personality factor on judgments, and ensure the impartiality of judge's behaviors.

1.2 Regulation of Judicial Subject

If there is no judge, there is no law. It indicates the importance of judges to the law straightforwardly. Nevertheless, in different law systems, judges enjoy different positions. The differences between the two primary law systems are apparent, which regulate the judge's behaviors in different ways.

Civil law judges are merely megaphones of the law. Regarding this, Merryman has vividly described in his book *Civil Law Tradition* that judges are much like specialized law clerks who, except for exceptional cases, attend trials only to solve litigation and seek apparent legal outcomes from the existing legal provisions. Their role is to find the correct legal provisions and correlate them with the facts, producing solutions automatically from the combination of legal provisions and facts. Judges endow them with legal significance. Therefore, the entire trial process is limited in the framework of pedantic syllogism of formal logic. The image of judges is the machine operator designed and established by legislators, and the role of judges is mechanical as well. Civil law judges are not great men of accomplishment, nor do they have paternal dignity. They are ordinary people. Their images are of civil servants who perform important but non-creative tasks.[16] The negative status of judges in the civil law system is determined by the nature of judicial organizations of the civil law system. Due to the strict separation of powers, the administration of justice is significantly restricted in the civil law system, with judicial organizations being merely governmental bureaucracies that are judicially independent on the surface. On the contrary, case law is the primary source of the law in the common law system, a kind of judgment accumulated by judges when they apply unwritten and customary law to solve disputes. It is neither the interpretation of statute law nor the applied customary law under the recognition of statute law. Thus, it is different from statute law in nature. Regarding case law as the primary source of the law degrades the position of pure legislation. In the administration of justice, the judge's judgments are not based on statute law but on precedent rules, namely the "doctrine of precedents". The judgment of a previous case has the binding force on later similar

[16] See [12], pp. 37–37.

cases. Even though previous judgments are found incorrect, they should still be observed. If cases are different, judges can apply the justice principle of their accord. This means that the external binding mechanism of judges' behaviors are weak, and judges run through all judicial activities, thus having supreme status in the legal structure.[17] Through comparisons, we can see that great differences in the status of judges remain between the civil law system and the common law system. Then, can we say that civil law judges are more restricted because they estimate human nature is evil, while common law judges are less restricted because they estimate human nature is good? It seems incorrect because the doctrine of original sin that sees human nature as evil is a western cultural tradition. Plato has mentioned in *The Laws* that "human nature will be always drawing him into avarice and selfishness, avoiding pain and pursuing pleasure without any reason, and will bring these to the front, obscuring the juster and better. And so working darkness in his soul will at last fill with evils both him and the whole city. For if a man were born so divinely gifted that he could naturally apprehend the truth, he would have no need of laws to rule over him; for there is no law or order which is above knowledge, nor can mind, without impiety, be deemed the subject or slave of any man, but rather the lord of all. I speak of mind, true and free, and in harmony with nature. But then there is no such mind anywhere, or at least not much; and therefore we must choose law and order, which are second best."[18] Plato's thoughts have profoundly influenced the world, particularly with closer integration of the Christian doctrine of original sin in the Roman era, it becomes a deep-rooted traditional thought in western culture. In modern times, almost all Enlightenment scholars and liberal thinkers held that human nature was evil, which led to the doctrine and implementation of the separation of powers. In this sense, the doctrine that human nature is evil is a theoretical premise of the separation of powers.[19] Even in US, when federalists devised the federal polities, they also gave full consideration to this factor and thus set up a system in which state authorities could not transcend their legal authority through the separation and balance of powers between authorities.[20] Therefore, the difference in the status of judges of the two law systems is not equal to that in the understanding of human nature, but to the illustration of different regulations and measures on judge's behaviors.

The regulation of judges in the civil law system is mainly via statutory law. The behaviors of judges, who act as the judicial subject, are restricted by legislation. The administration of justice is subordinated to the thoughts of legislation, which originates from the French Revolution. The thought comes from a hypothesis that legal provisions can be made so clear that judges' creative activities are not needed when these provisions are applied to each case. The restriction on judges is seen as the necessary condition for the unification of the national legal system. Since judges only play a role in applying legal provisions, judicial centralization is seen as the

[17] See [13].

[18] See [14], p. 27.

[19] See [15], p. 179.

[20] See [16], p. 264.

centralization of applying the law.[21] Under this circumstance, judges are subject to the law and can only act within the scope prescribed by the law, so the personality of judges is excluded to ensure the justice of judgments. The regulation of the judge's behaviors has the advantage that judges do not have many rights of discretion, so every case can be treated based on the law. However, the disadvantage is that it excessively restricts judges from acting on their own, which is difficult to give full play to the judge's subjective initiative and thus inevitably falls into the dogmatism of mechanical application of the law. As Chinese scholars evaluate, if too much attention is paid to legislation and rule doctrine is strictly implemented, the right of discretion of judges will be suppressed. The law is definite, united, but rigid, so it is difficult to expect justice for all.[22]

The regulation of judges in the common law system is mainly via procedural law. The common law system pursues the doctrine of "Justice before Truth", where justice can also be interpreted as judgments, which should be understood from the sense of procedural law. The well-known French comparative jurist Rene David said that defendants should enjoy fair trial in procedures, and judgments should only be made following the rules of natural justice. The central idea of British law focused on procedure, with more consideration given to trials than justice. If you followed the procedure that had been carefully prescribed and worked in just ways, British jurists believed you could almost obtain just solutions.[23] In the judicial practice of the common law system, a unique rule of "due process of law" has been developed to an advanced level, from which judges are portrayed as justice to ensure natural justice. It is generally considered that the due process of the law plays a role in ensuring the justice of judgments, but as it is a constraint of the process rather than restricted by statutory law, the right of discretion of judges still lacks. This is also why judges of the common law system are impacted by personality more.

China follows statutory law, so judges must hear cases based on the law and the status of judges is similar to that of the civil law system. But as China's legislation is imperfect, judges have more right of discretion. In this case, statutory law is difficult to regulate judges' behaviors effectively. Furthermore, there is a common problem in China's legal awareness that the civil law system pays more attention to substance than procedure. The procedure, particularly the legal procedure to regulate judge's behaviors, is incomplete, and the effect is greatly reduced in implementation. Therefore, non-observance of the law and difficulty in investigating illegal acts happen sometimes. To solve them, we must improve the mechanism to regulate judges.

---

[21] See [17], pp. 48–49.
[22] See [13].
[23] See [18], p. 337.

2 Judicial Activity (1): Statutory Interpretation

Criminal justice means that it is the law that administrates crimes. In different law systems, the meanings of the law are diverse, with the civil law system primarily referring to statutory law and the common law system mainly referring to case law. Common law countries have statute law, similar to the statutory law in civil law countries. In the criminal law field, the trend of codification arises in common law countries.[24] Hence, for criminal judicial activities, the way to interpret the law becomes a critical issue. Statutory interpretation[25] is never a mere technical issue, and it has close relationships with legal ideas. In other words, scientifically defining the humanistic foundation of the criminal law has great significance to illustrate the theories of legal interpretation and the determine of the rules of legal interpretation.

2.1 *Evolution of Judicial Interpretation*

Statutory interpretation has a time-honored history and tradition. It can be said that on the date when judicial activities occurred, statutory interpretation existed as well. So, statutory interpretation is one of the essential contents of judicial activities. In ancient societies where the law was underdeveloped, statutory interpretation played an essential role in supplementing the weaknesses of legislation.

In ancient China, statutory interpretation existed early in Pre-Qin Period, but relevant historical books have lost. In 1975, *Shuihudi Qin Bamboo Texts* were found in Yunmeng, Hubei, which contained *Legal Questions and Answers*, including 210 bamboo slips and 187 articles. It used the form of questions and answers to clarify some articles, terms, and the aims of articles of Qin law. According to the study by the experts of legal history, since Shang Yang's reform, the Qin dynasty has implemented "the emperor holding arbitrary power", advocating the emperor to establish unified government decrees and officials to interpret statutes. Hence, the *Legal Questions and Answers* could never be arbitrary private interpretations of the law, which should have legal validity.[26] During the Han, Wei, and Jin dynasties, statutory interpretation further developed, which featured "legal erudite", an unprecedented official position to interpret and teach the law, was developed. Many legal works that inspired and interpreted legal provisions were born. Codes were annotated, and annotated articles enjoyed the same legal validity as legal articles.[27] By the Tang dynasty, statutory interpretation reached its heyday. In the first year of the Yonghui era (650), the Emperor Gaozong of Tang ordered Zhangsun Wuji, Li Zeli, Yu Zhining, and other officials

---

[24] See [19], p. 20.

[25] Statutory interpretation is divided into legislation interpretation, judicial interpretation, and academic interpretation, and this section is legal interpretation, which generally refers to judicial interpretation.

[26] See [20], p. 150.

[27] See [21], p. 23.

to formulate 12 chapters, 502 articles of Yonghui law based on the Wude law and Zhenguan law. In the second year (651), the Law was promulgated across the country, which was called Yonghui law, or Tang law as we call it today. To illustrate the legislation principle and spirit of the Yonghui law and interpret the articles uniformly, the Emperor Gaozong of Tang also ordered Zhangsun Wuji, Li Zeli, and other officials to annotate all laws in the Yonghui law, named "Commentaries on the Codes". Approved by the emperor, it was promulgated in the fourth year of the Yonghui era as the attachment to the laws that shared the same validity as laws. Laws and codes were collectively named as *Yonghui Code* and *Tang Code* after the Yuan dynasty.[28] Hence, the *Tang Code* integrated laws and annotations, both a law and a book. Its technique of interpreting laws has reached perfection, which was breathtaking. By the Qing dynasty, directed by pragmatism, the trend of private interpretation of laws sprung up based on the experience of previous dynasties. Incomplete statistics showed that by the end of the Qing dynasty, private annotations of the *Great Qing Legal Code* had been over 130 editions, excluding different editions of the same book. Private interpretations of the law significantly impacted the Qing dynasty's legislation and administration of justice. Whenever the Qing governors revised laws, they paid great attention to the annotations of the *Great Qing Legal Code* by annotators and endowed these annotations with limited legal validity. In judicial activities, when laws and articles were unclear, private annotations were taken as the basis of judgment. Even when laws contradicted annotations, "annotations replaced laws".[29] The system of statutory interpretation with Chinese legal characteristics is an important component of China's legal cultural heritage and should be passed down and learned from.

The statutory interpretation of the civil law system originates from ancient Rome, which is based on legal fiction. "Fiction" (*fictio*) refers to a noun of plea in ancient Roman law, meaning that the defendant should not argue the false testimony of the plaintiff. The British jurist Maine extended "legal fiction" to any assumption that covered or aimed to cover the fact that a legal regulation had changed. The law's wording did not change, but the rules to apply it changed. Maine clearly stated that "the answers of the learned" (*Responsa Prudentium*) in Rome were grounded on fiction. The form of these Responses varied a good deal at different periods of the Roman jurisprudence, but throughout its whole course they consisted of explanatory glosses on authoritative written documents, and at first they were exclusively collections of opinions interpretative of the Twelve Tables. As with us, all legal language adjusted itself to the assumption that the text of the old Code remained unchanged. There was the express rule. *Books of Responses* bearing the names of leading jurisconsults (*jurison-suits*) obtained an authority at least equal to that of our reported cases, and constantly modified, extended, limited, or practically over-ruled the provisions of the Decemviral law. The authors of the new jurisprudence during the whole progress of its formation professed the most sedulous respect for the letter of the Code. They were merely explaining it, deciphering it, bringing out its full meaning; but then, in the result, by placing texts together, by adjusting the law to states of fact which actually

[28] See [22], p. 33.

[29] He [23].

presented themselves and by speculating on its possible application to others which might occur, by introducing principles of interpretation derived from the exegesis of other written documents which fell under their observation, they educed a vast variety of canons which had never been dreamed of by the compilers of the Twelve Tables and which were in truth rarely or never to be found there.[30] This was because the statutory interpretation of jurists was to revise and change the contents of the code, and jurists had the binding force no less than that of the legislation of the legislature, so statutory interpretation had the legislative nature, with the "answers of the learned" considered as law and one of the main sources of Roman law. For instance, during the Roman Emperor period, Augustus designated some jurists to answer legal questions and endowed their opinions with legal validity, and the trials of the supreme pretors and all judges must observe "the answers of the learned". Since then, jurists' "answers of the learned" (*Responsa prudentum*) have become one of the sources of Roman law.[31] The statutory interpretation of ancient Rome was originally monopolized by priests, from whom people understood the procedures of litigation or activities they should follow. People also obtained answers from priests about the legal settlement of certain situations. The magistrates who sought help from priests raised their inquiries to the priest group, and an individual magistrate asked questions to a priest. People designated a person among priests to answer questions to individuals every year. The monopoly power of priests, however, fell apart as history advanced. The *Twelve Decemviral Tables* started to avoid the monopoly of interpretation because it had determined and published relevant rules. As legal knowledge and interpretation were disclosed, people have opened up a path for secular jurisprudence, enabling some people to obtain the authority of legal knowledge and interpretation (not depending on priests). The famous Italian Roman expert on the History of Roman law Giuseppe Grosso has intriguingly explained the continuity between the interpretations by priests and secular interpretations, saying that if people could understand the historical significance of the procedure of communications law and permission of liberal interpretations, they would make changes through historical and legal continuity, which was expressed as that secular jurisprudence still saved the prestige and authority of priest jurisprudence. Originally, the law was the domain of priests who had special knowledge, and only priests could answer questions when there was doubt. Since the third century B.C., [priests have monopolized "sacred law" (*ius sacrum*) until the mid of the first century B.C.], legal knowledge has been transmitted, and people recognized to be directed by those people who joined the dominant position to which the priest group belonged with their profound knowledge and who gained prestige and authority. Therefore, let alone the changes in the degree of binding force (abstractly, all developmental stages may have such problems), legal theories are successive, equivalent to civil law status. Priest jurisprudence in early times was the same as secular jurisprudence, which did not create norms because it had no power to formulate regulations; however, it was the interpreter of traditions, which revealed norms, integrated norms into proper structures, and applied norms

[30] See [24], p. 20.

[31] See [25], p. 30.

to specific situations, or, interpreted norms (*interpretatio*). It did not impose norms on human will; it studied, followed, and adjusted norms with different attitudes. Since interpretation does not impose norms on human will, why is it the source of the law? Giuseppe Grosso said that from the point of form, legal theories had an interpretative function of the knowledge of the "law" (not creative) because it was premised on the existence of the law (*jus*), which was potentially perfect. Nonetheless, in history, this kind of law (*jus*) was a fluid complex, which was connected with its innate structure, and included and solved realistic developmental problems. As we said, it was the legal reflection of social reality, which was restricted by specific and unchanged basic conditions and which maintained organicity and continuity in logic. Later, legal theories took the mission to develop norms. Thus, it performed the function of creating laws and acted as the source of the law from the historical perspective.[32] In ancient Rome, statutory interpretation was not only made by jurists but also directly by pretors (judges) based on "Equity", referring to the behaviors that Roman pretors used laws and regulations, which were established on principles, to replace some old-dated contents in the law. The power of equity enabled pretors to interpret the law.[33] Maine has discussed the difference between equity and fiction, holding that equity could interfere with the law openly and explicitly.[34] In other words, fiction did not change words but contents, while equity could change words and contents openly and explicitly. The Roman pretor is a Roman magistrate, also called Justiciar. This position was set up in 366 B.C., whose authority was to administrate litigation, and lead judicial activities across the country and among provinces. All pretors should publish specific announcements or orders in writing when they took office to propose their principles and measures for policy guidelines and to hear cases during their term. They should also implement judicial practices after taking office. Pretors did not have the legislative power, but since they were responsible for legislation and the former pretor's edicts had a binding effect on the successors, edicts had no difference from the law in form, so it was called "magistrate law" (*Jus honoralium*). *Edictum magistratum* had a significant influence on the development of Roman law. This was because the state only empowered the magistrate's privilege to punish edicts while not prescribing the content and form of the privilege. This way, the vision and area were broadened for the magistrates to exert the privilege, and they could thus remedy the shortcomings and defects of the old laws and regulations from reality and made their edicts a flexible and effective form to reflect the development of Roman law. Based on reason and natural law, pretors interpreted the law by announcements and adapted Roman law to the needs of reality. In the Middle Ages, ecclesiastical law of the civil law countries dominated other laws. In 1140, the friar John Gratian finished *Decretals of Gratian*, which concluded all ecclesiastical decrees that were traditionally patterned and became the main sources of ecclesiastical law. This ecclesiastical law applied a unique way to deal with all legal materials systemically, the way of which was to attach relevant canons to every

[32] See [26], pp. 101–104.

[33] See [27], p. 11.

[34] See [24], p. 17.

ecclesiastical law and regulation, followed by an opposite canon and a "solution", with other ecclesiastical laws attached for comparison or reference. Thus, a unique, successive way for annotations that ran through the book was formed, referred to as "Gratian's ways of annotation". From the end of the eleventh century to the early twelfth century, as the commercialized economy prospered, the Revival of Roman Law emerged and people valued Roman law again. The Revival targeted the interpretation of Roman law when the well-known School of Glossators arose in Italy. It originated in Bologna in Italy, and the founder of the School of Glossators in the early stage was Irnerius (around 1055–1125), and the representative in the later stage was Accursius. The main work of these jurists was to annotate the documents in Roman law. Annotations became more detailed later, including disagreements over annotators, arguments from all aspects, authors' conclusions, relevant cases whose legal rules applied could be referred to, brief standards and definitions that were summarized for memory, and discussions on a legal area, among others. Annotations of Roman law profoundly influence the formation of western legal traditions. The famous US jurist Berman argued precisely that the occurrence of the modern western legal system in the late eleventh century and the twelfth century was closely related to the existence of the earliest batch of universities in Europe, where Western Europe, for the first time, taught the law as a unique, systematic knowledge system (a science), in which scattered judicial judgments, rules, and statute law were studied based on science and interpreted based on general principles and truth, so the entire legal system was based on these principles and truth. Graduates, trained by new legal science from generation to generation, entered the legal affairs departments that formed in the religious and secular countries and acted as consultants, judges, lawyers, magistrates, and legislative drafters in other departments. They endowed legal norms accumulated throughout history with structures and logic using their knowledge so that the new legal system was diverted from all old legal orders that almost mixed with social customs, and general political and religious systems.[35]

The statutory interpretation of the common law system dates back to the Middle Ages. Samuel Thorne has mentioned that in some periods of the Middle Ages in Britain, the opinion of common law on statutory interpretation was the same as that of Roman law and civil law. In the early fourteenth century, common law judges had greater freedom in dealing with laws and regulations. The freedom was so great that it was common for judicial authorities to revise statutory law substantively.[36] In the sixteenth century, statutory interpretation was not bounded by the interpretation of words, and the "mischief rule for statutory interpretation" was evolved from the "Heydon case". The rule was as follows: for the sure and true interpretation of all statutes in general (be they penal or beneficial, restrictive or enlarging of the common law), four things are to be discerned and considered: (1) what was the common law before the making of the Act; (2) What was the mischief and defect for which the common law did not provide; (3) what remedy the Parliament hath resolved and appointed to cure the disease of the commonwealth; and (4) the true reason of the

[35] See [28], p. 143.

[36] See [5], p. 508.

remedy. The office of all the judges was always to make such construction as shall suppress the mischief, and advance the remedy, and suppress subtle inventions and evasions for the continuance of the mischief, and for private benefit, and to add force and life to the cure and remedy, according to the true intention of the makers of the Act, for public benefit. By the eighteenth century, a presumption that advocated the strict interpretation of criminal laws and regulations was established. In the R. v. Harris case, the defendant bit off the victim's nose, but this was not found guilty based on an ordinance of George IV, which stipulated that all "people who illegally and deliberately stab, cut or wound another person" should be punished. The court held that the literal meaning of this ordinance was that the words in the statute pointed towards using a weapon according to the intention of the parliament's legislators; meanwhile, the court also quoted a previous shooting case to strengthen its conclusion.[37] In the nineteenth century, it was generally considered that the responsibility of judges was only to determine the content of regulations made by the parliament and apply these legal wordings to trials. For demanding cases, it was considered the excess of authority if judges supplemented key points to statutes (except that if supplements were not made, the statute would be meaningless) or attached the exceptions for equity. It was considered that the true meanings of statutes were consistent with the meanings conveyed to the judges by the precise meanings of their words, and if it was possible, judges should give full validity to the literal meanings of the words. The objective of judges was to pursue the legislature's intention from the words of statutes, even though the result of the interpretation was detrimental. The court's obligation was to illustrate the law based on the current situation of the law and leave remedies (if needed) to others. It was usually not allowed to even resort to the history of a parliamentary statute as an approach to help determine the meaning.[38] Through the historical investigation of statutory interpretation, we can see that statutory interpretation has played a critical role during the formation and development of all law systems, with unique systems of statutory interpretation having been established.

2.2 *Idea of Judicial Interpretation*

Regarding statutory interpretation, there remain different ideas among legal theories. In the criminal law field, the classical school of criminology and the positivist school have distinct understandings of statutory interpretation.

The classical school is noted for its strict restriction on statutory interpretation. Beccaria even negated the judge's right of interpretation on the law, saying that criminal judges had no right to interpret criminal laws because they were not legislators. He posited that judges should apply the law sentence by sentence without inquiring about the spirit of the law. If "the spirit of the law needs to be inquired about" was regarded as an axiom, Beccaria believed that there was no axiom more dangerous.

[37] See [29], p. 13.

[38] See [5], pp. 510–511.

Adopting this axiom means embracing raging opinions, which have been verified according to him. However, ordinary people regarded it as strange talk. They tended to sense minor troubles and could not sense the fatal and profound result arising from a ridiculous principle that had rooted in a state. Interpreting the law would bring about fatal results because our knowledge and ideas were connected, and the more complicated our knowledge was, the greater divergences of our ideas would have. Every person had his ideas, and regarded things from different perspectives at different times. Thus, the spirit of the law depended on whether a judge was good at logical reasoning and how well the judge understood the law. It also depended on the judge's emotional impulses, the weakness of the defendant, and the relationship between the judge and the victim. It depended on all the subtle factors that could change people's hearts. So, the fates of citizens changed as the court changed. Unfortunate people's life and freedom were sacrificed for ridiculous reasoning or a judge's emotional impulse since judges viewed the ridiculous conclusions from mixed concepts in their minds as legal explanations. We could also see that the same court gave different punishments for the same crime due to the difference in time. This was because instead of having a long-lasting, stable statutory interpretation, people had an indefinite one. Beccaria admitted the law's ambiguity, so strictly abiding by criminal wording might encounter troubles. However, he believed the trouble was nothing compared to the confusion by the impossibility to interpret the law because the temporary trouble urged legislators to revise confusing wording for accuracy and stopped people from interpreting the law arbitrarily, which was fatal and the source of arbitrary judgments and favoritism. Beccaria wrote emotionally that when a code had been published, people should follow every word, and the only mission of judges was to determine whether citizens' behaviors followed statutes. When the rule of right, which ought to direct the actions of the philosopher as well as the ignorant, is a matter of controversy, not of fact, the people are slaves to the magistrates. The despotism of this multitude of tyrants is more insupportable, the less the distance is between the oppressor and the oppressed; more fatal than that of one, for the tyranny of many is not to be shaken off, but by having recourse to that of one alone. It is more cruel, as it meets with more opposition, and the cruelty of a tyrant is not in proportion to his strength, but to the obstacles that oppose him.[39] Deeply influenced by the French Enlightenment scholar Montesquieu, Beccaria claimed to move forward along the glory path of this great man, who showed the same attitude towards statutory interpretation. Montesquieu made it clear that in Republics, the nature of the political system required judges to base on the words of laws; otherwise, explanations that harmed citizens would be made in a case related to a citizen's property, honor, or life.[40] Beccaria, who denied the judge's right to statutory interpretation, only strictly restricted judges from arbitrarily interpreting the law regardless of the literal meanings of the law that resulting in judicial tyranny and to guarantee the safety and freedom of citizens. Nonetheless, the application of the law included interpretation. Even though the interpretation was on the literal meaning, an issue of understanding

[39] See [7], p. 13.
[40] See [30], p. 76.

remained, and the focal point was the limit of interpretation. Beccaria's style of strict statutory interpretation was consistent with his admiration of statutory law. He held that based on the legislator's reason, it was possible to formulate a perfect statutory code, and this was the setting of "rational legislators". The judges' mission was only to apply the law; they had no right to revise the law by interpretation. Even the law was ambiguous, and it should be improved by legislation.

The positivist school of criminology abandoned the classical school's strict interpretivism limited by the wording of the law, which advocated that flexible statutory interpretations could be made if allowed. Ferri admitted the boundary between the administration of justice and legislation, holding that the administration of justice should not transgress legislation, and that the responsibility of judicial organizations was to follow and apply statutory law primarily. Because once we admitted that judges (amateur or professional) could revise the law, freedom would not be guaranteed, and the individual's power would be limitless.[41] Meanwhile, Ferri affirmed that the law was always coarse and inadequate to some extent and was challenging to adapt to social needs. Consequently, the law should allow judges to apply the judicial interpretations of the law case by case. In *General View of a Complete Code of Laws*, Bentham discussed that the difference between strict interpretation and liberal interpretation was that if you entrusted a legislator an intention that was considered necessary when the law was made, this was strict interpretation; if you entrusted a legislator an intention that was ignored due to his carelessness, thus, even though the legislator was asked to interpret the situation, he must have the same intention. You implemented this intention by interpreting the law as if the legislator had stipulated it, and this was a liberal interpretation. According to Bentham, liberal interpretation was divided into expanded interpretation and restrictive interpretation. Expanded interpretation applied laws and regulations to cases beyond the prescription of legal words according to literal meanings, while restrictive interpretation was to make a law and regulation not applicable to cases that were literally interpreted within the scope of the prescription of legal words. Bentham believed that both interpretations were to change laws: interpretation became the circumlocution for changes. As a result, expanding an old law was equal to establishing a new law. On the other hand, restricting an old law meant abolishing the law. The only difference between the changes made this way and general changes was that the former did not exceed the legislator's intention or the legislator's possible intention as long as controversies were not proposed to the legislator, namely, not exceeding the actual or hypothesized intention of the legislator. Therefore, if a new law was formulated, it should be done in this mode and contain some contents of old laws; if a part of old laws was to abolish, even it was just a part, the legislator was supposed to abolish this part if he was confronted a controversy. Bentham did not oppose liberal interpretation. He saw it as a subtle and important division of judicial power that concession to it might be risky but negating it led to damages.[42] The positivist school tended to advocate liberal interpretation in statutory interpretation. A liberal interpretation was not an

[41] See [9], p. 126.

[42] See [29], pp. 29–30.

arbitrary interpretation but had a certain limit. The theoretical basis was that since human reason had limitations, it was impossible to make a perfect statutory code. The facts of cases were distinct, so they were impossible to be utterly consistent with legal provisions. Under this circumstance, the judge's interpretations of the law were necessary, and the right of judicial interpretation was one of the most critical contents of judicial power.

The disagreement between the classical school and the positivist school in statutory interpretation can be concluded as the disagreement between the theory of subjective interpretation and that of objective interpretation. The theory of subjective interpretation holds that laws are behavioral norms designed by legislators for ordinary people, which expresses the subjective willingness of legislators who hope or do not hope, allow or do not allow people to conduct some acts. Therefore, the law should be definitive. And criminal law should specify what acts constitute crimes and what kind and what degree of penalties should be imposed in the form of statutory law. According to the behavioral norms prescribed by the law, people can design their behavioral methods in social life and predict the legal outcomes of their acts. The definiteness of the law urges judges to deal with cases strictly and exert their power within the prescription of the law and prohibits judges from abusing their authority to violate the legal rights of citizens. Even criminals should not be punished improperly, and the safety value of the law is thus guaranteed. Accordingly, every statutory interpretation is the understanding of the original legislative intention of legislators and the discovery of the original legislative intention. Since this opinion on statutory interpretation aims to understand the original legislative intention and tries to understand the subjective conditions of legislators, it is called the subjective interpretivism of statutory interpretation.[43] The subjective theory is based on the following points: (1) legislative behaviors are the behaviors of legislators' intentions, who express their opinions and intentions through legislation. They express their social objectives by the law, which are expressed by statutory interpretation; (2) the legislator's meanings are historical facts that legislative documents can sense. As long as every person is oriented to the historically detectable intention, the ruling or decision of the law enforcement organization will be predictable, so the safety of the law will not be shaken fundamentally; and (3) based on the principle of the separation of powers, the law enforcement organization should rule or decide cases based on the law which the legislature can only formulate. Consequently, legislators' meanings become the decisive factor in applying the law, and statutory interpretation should aim to explore and achieve the legislators' meanings.[44] Objective interpretivism holds that the law is the social outcome and statutory interpretation must coincide with real social life. Thus, the term "objective" refers to the objective needs of reality as the opposition to the subjective conditions of legislators advocated by subjective interpretivism. Objective interpretivism points out that the law is not dead words but behavioral norms that are alive and changing as time and space change. Once legislators promulgate the law,

[43] See [31].

[44] See [32], p. 295.

the law changes temporally and spatially and survives independently. It then gradually loses some properties legislators have given and obtains other properties. The vitality of the law can only be maintained when the law adapts to new social needs. Radical objective interpreters believe that legislative intention is merely a fictional concept. Starting from negating the legislator's intention, he evolved the judge's statutory interpretation into the creation of the law in the name of statutory interpretation, namely, judges creating the law.[45] The basis of objective interpretivism is that (1) since the law is promulgated, it has had no relationship with legislators, and legal thoughts have been determined. Thus, judgments should be based on the law, not something outside the law. Legal models are usually concluded from different legal chapters and promulgated articles concurrently or successively. The fact also illustrates that the law and legislator's (meanings) are not integrated; (2) if we act as the standpoint of objective interpretivism, legal stability will be strengthened. Legal stability is ensured in the interpretation of meanings. Initially, the law was promulgated as customary law was unstable. If statutory interpretation is based on the legislator's meaning, people will turn to cumbersome legislative materials that are not accessible to ordinary people. Consequently, people regulated by legal norms will be unable to understand the law. The law must be oriented at making every person understand it and bear legal obligations, while at the same time, forming its legal relations. In this case, people are easy control administrative power.[46]

Among the ideas mentioned above, radical objective interpretivism deviates from the original meaning of "interpretation", which confuses the boundary between legislation and the administration of justice. It is necessary to define the term "interpretation" scientifically in this context. The term "interpretation" literally means analysis and illustration. In Hermeneutics (or Theory of Interpretation), interpretation (*Hermes*) originates from a Greek myth. Hermes is a mythological Greek deity and messenger of gods. He not only announces god's messages but also plays a role as an interpreter in annotating and illustrating god's edicts. This way, these edicts can be understood and of meanings. Therefore, interpretation mainly was the explanation of god's edicts in the Temple of Apollo Epicuriusat Bassae. Two basic meanings are thus derived: (1) displaying hidden things; and (2) clarifying unclear things.[47] Therefore, interpretation differs from creation but assembles translation, which is based on objects (usually texts) to illustrate the meaning based on understanding. Creation needs a basis, but the object of the basis is not necessarily a text; it is a spiritual creation of social life. Legislation, according to Marx, determines legal provisions based on objective laws. Although Marx coins the term "translation" to explain legislation's reflection of objective laws, it is just a metaphor. Whether legislation reflects objective laws well or badly is an objective standard to evaluate legislation. However, legislators have sufficient freedom when they make laws. Interpretation, on the other hand, is different. It is restricted by texts, different from legislation that establishes the law. It is an illustration of implicitness to explicitness. Statutory interpretation is

[45] See [31].

[46] See [32], p. 298.

[47] See [33], pp. 3–4.

even like this. It displays the meaning that has been or should be included in legal texts (can be called legislative meaning). Accordingly, regardless of the meaning of the legal text, like what radical objective interpreters advocate, negating the existence of legislative meaning is not interpreting but creating the law. Therefore, only by setting out from the special meaning of interpretation can we further explore the problem of how to interpret the law.

Regarding the ways to interpret the law, the debate between subjective and objective interpretivism resembles that between "I explain the classics" and "classics being my footnote" in ancient China. Thus, it is necessary to study it based on Hermeneutics.

At the turn of the eighteenth century and nineteenth century, there was a drastic change from traditional Hermeneutics to modern Hermeneutics. The original form of traditional Hermeneutics was Biblical Hermeneutics, which referred to the process and method that revealed the meanings of God in the *Bible* and other divine classics through interpretation and annotation. The purpose of this religious interpretation determined that the interpretative orientation was the way to discover and understand the intention of God that was assumed to exist in divine classics. The subject of the understanding existed independently prior to understanding, which was beyond the understanding. The purpose of understanding was to discover and reveal the true intention of its subject. Understanding should mobilize all cognition approaches, including the examination of words, analysis of syntax, and understanding of the context, to discover the true purpose of divine classics. Driven by this belief, Biblical Hermeneutics paid extra attention to the "intention" or "the original intention (of God)" hidden in the words of divine classics, developing the examination and interpretation of words and promoting the long development of philology. After Renaissance, as humanism prospered, the interpretative approach of divinity was applied to interpret secular classics, freeing Hermeneutics from the narrow scope of understanding the *Bible* and thus became the general methodology of the humanities and was widely applied to historical science, literature, philosophy, and jurisprudence. In this case, Hermeneutics was no longer limited by the traditional approach of understanding the intention. With philosophical interpretation, interpretation became a philosophical conversion process—the state of mind of the interpreter changed into the artistic conception of the interpreted work through mastering the art of understanding and thus completed the change from traditional Hermeneutics to modern Hermeneutics. Traditional Hermeneutics advocates the theory of "the original intention", which establishes the following three assumptions directly and indirectly: (1) meaning is in work; (2) the meaning of the work exists prior to the understanding of the work; and (3) the significance of the work changes as times changes, but the meaning of the work remains unchanged. By contrast, modern Hermeneutics proposes different three assumptions as follows: (1) the meaning of the work only exists in the dialogues between the work and interpreter; (2) the meaning of the work cannot exist independently of the understanding of the interpreter; (3) the significance of the work changes as times change, so does the meaning of the work.[48] Therefore, a few problems worth studying are proposed:

[48] See [34], p. 58.

First, the relationship between language and meaning is that between speech and meaning. Language is a tool to communicate humans' minds, which is divided into written language and oral language. There is an apparent distinction between the two: written language rules out a context, where people can communicate directly in oral language, for language understanders and language users to understand the language. In direct dialogues, communicators can confirm each other's intention or the original intention directly. As we understand texts, especially the works of different periods, authors are silent apart from the written words. They cannot affirm, verify, deny or revise the communicators' understandings and speculations on their intentions like what they can do in talks. In addition to depending on their understandings of the written language to probe into the intentions of authors, interpreters have no alternatives. Moreover, there is a gap between the authors of texts and the written language of texts. The authors' intentions are always distinct from the words expressed. Then, "meaning beyond words" arises where language fails to precisely express the author's meaning. "Meaning beyond words" displays the limitations of the author's language capabilities, which is also caused by the ambiguity of the language, which is difficult to avoid thoroughly. As a result, there are language barriers to absolutely restore the text's original meaning. In this sense, meaning does not exist in the text but only in the dialogues between the text and the interpreter. The process of interpretation is seen as a dialogue process.

Second, the connection between meaning and interpretation. The second assumption is whether the meaning of the text exists independently of interpretation. In other words, before interpreting the text, shall we determine that the text has already contained the intention or meaning that is independent of understanding, or assume that the meaning of the text is still undetermined, and only understanding can determine it? Suppose we adopt the former opinion, namely, determining that meaning has already been included in the text prior to interpretation and understanding. In that sense, the mission of interpretation is to find the existed original meaning. Whether interpretation succeeds depends on whether the original meaning is revealed or restored in understanding. If we follow the latter opinion, which assumes that the meaning of the text is not determined as time goes by, then the interpretation will be determined to shape and clarify the undefined, ambiguous state of the meaning by understanding. According to the opinions of modern Hermeneutics, interpretation can never find or fully restore the original meaning of the author; also, the purpose of interpretation is not to discover the original meaning. Modern Hermeneutics believes that the existence of text as words and the existence of text as meanings are two different problems. Uninterpreted texts are merely the existence of words, and the meaning of the text exists in interpretation. The meaning of the text, however, can only keep its vitality in interpretation after the author makes it. The meaning of the text is not a postbag filled, sealed by the author, and passed down in interpretation without any change. Through interpretation, history ceaselessly uncovers the postbag and supplements new contents, and changes or removes original loads in this bag.

Finally, the relationship between interpretation and reality. An interpreter is a real person in reality who has "preunderstanding". According to modern Hermeneutics, preunderstanding is also called foreknowledge, which originates from the "horizon".

"Horizon" is a broad concept in modern Hermeneutics that describes the process of understanding. It derives from its literal meaning to refer to the starting point of the understanding, the vision or angle of forming an understanding, understanding the possible prospects of opening to the unknown, as well as the historical and cultural context of the understanding. All constitute the necessary conditions of interpretation, which is called preunderstanding. Therefore, the interpreter is not a blank slate when interpreting a text but has some preunderstanding. So, the meaning of the text changes according to people and time.

From the statutory interpretation perspective, even though it does not pay much attention to the aesthetic value like the interpretation of literary works but the functional value, it still shares similarities with the latter theoretically. Whether statutory interpretation is to explore the original legislative meaning or determine the legislative intention tends to be a hard-solving problem. The common law system does not distinguish the original legislative meaning from legislative intention, which calls them the "intention" collectively, but it has divided them into two meanings: one is the legislature's intention when formulating legal norms, and the other is the objective intention of the laws formulated by the legislature. The former refers to the subjectivism of legislative intention, while the latter refers to the objectivism of legislation intention.[49] The Chinese criminal law community also does not strictly settle the boundary between the original legislative meaning and legislative intention. For instance, some people have defined the original legislative intention as the intention expressed by legislators in legal provisions.[50] Others define the legislative intention as a certain purpose or requirement that the legislator contains in the legal provisions stipulates that the provisions should achieve.[51] The above two definitions show that there is no difference in contents although being called the original legislative intention and legislative intention, respectively. It is worth noting that some Chinese scholars of criminal law advocate distinguishing the two concepts and consider that the original legislative intention refers to the original meaning of legal provisions when legislators make them. On the contrary, the legislative intention refers to the legislative purpose of legislators expressed in the criminal law provisions.[52] In my opinion, this difference is of great significance. Theoretically, legislative intention leaves a robust subjective sense to people, so we advocate replacing it with legislative meaning. Original legislative meaning is subjective and definitive, which is a "dead meaning". Legislative meaning is objective, fluid, and open, which is a "living meaning". In many cases, statutory interpretation takes interpreting the original legislative meaning as its responsibility. In some cases, it is determined by the contradictions between legislative similarities and judicial differences. There is no definite original legislative meaning for a judicial object. As the British jurist Grey said, when the legislature had no intention, it had never considered the relevant legal issues. When judges were not to decide the legislature's intentions but to guess that the legislature

[49] See [27], p. 55.

[50] See [35], p. 21.

[51] See [36], p. 180.

[52] See [31].

had never considered legal issues, there might be difficulties in interpretation when intentions are contained in some circumstances.[53] Therefore, statutory interpretation is not limited to the exploration of the original legislative meaning; it should creatively reveal the legislative meaning and match it to reality. Consequently, statutory interpretation does not mechanically restore the original legislative meaning but takes the initiative to illustrate legislative meaning, including explaining the limitations and expansion of legal provisions within the allowed scope and even the remedies of legal loopholes. As vividly explained by the British Lord Denning, "if legislators accidentally encounter a wrinkle on a legal textile, how do they smooth it out? It is easy, and judges must do as legislators do. A judge can never change the materials of a legal textile but can smooth the wrinkle out."[54]

Among current countries, statutory interpretation is moving from the strict interpretation by the classical school of natural law to liberal interpretation. This is partly due to the characteristics of this period and social changes. The US jurist Ehrmann stated the change that the Byzantine Culture in its heyday, the enlightened despotism in Europe in the eighteenth century, members of the Society of the Jacobins in France, and Napoleon were all unwilling to empower judges with the right to interpret unclear legal provisions. If needed, judges should gain authoritative direction from governmental political organizations. A term in the *Napoleonic Code* went even further, warning judges that when judges heard specific cases, they must not establish general behavioral norms. A century later, in another country—Switzerland, the first article in the Swiss code displayed the opposite model of judicial procedure: the Code governed all legal issues within the scope of the provisions or spiritual provisions, and if there were no applicable provisions in this Code, the judge might determine them according to customary law, and if customary law failed to address the problems, the judge, as a legislator, could determine them based on the rules of his.[55] From legislation expressly prohibiting judges from interpreting the law to explicitly authorizing judges to interpret the law, the change was tremendous. It was the development of the legal culture that dominated the change. During the transformation from strict interpretation to liberal interpretation, legal sociology has played a huge promoting role as scholars found the sociological lens of statutory interpretation. Based on legal evolutionism, the famous Japanese criminologist Makino Eiichi divided statutory interpretation into three developmental stages. The first stage viewed the law as god's orders, and the literal rule was adopted accordingly. The second stage viewed the law as the legislator's will, and logical interpretation was adopted accordingly. The third stage regarded the law as the embodiment of the spirit of the time, so sociological interpretation was taken. The spirit of the time meant real social demands, justice, and kind customs, among others. Therefore, if social thoughts were viewed as a legal context, it was necessary to liberate statutory interpretation from previously fixed formulas.[56] Pound, the founder of legal sociology, claimed that "there

---

[53] See [29], p. 33.

[54] See [37], p. 10.

[55] See [38], pp. 209–210.

[56] See [17], p. 90.

is no eternal law. But there is an eternal goal—the development of the powers of humanity to their highest point. We must strive to make the law of the time and place a means toward that goal in the time and place, and we do this by formulating the presuppositions of civilization as we know it. Given such jural postulates, the legislator may alter old rules and make new ones to conform to them, the judges may interpret, that is, develop by analogy and apply, codes and traditional legal materials in the light of them."[57] The connotation of interpretation changed dramatically in this context, which was the evolution of law from the reproduction of the original legislative intention of the classical school of natural law to the development of the sociological school of the law. Reflected in criminal law theories, the classical school of natural law was the classical school of criminology, which, under the domination of strong rationalism, strove to establish a perfect country ruled by law. Centered on legislation, the ruled-by-law country governed the entire society by formulating perfect statutory codes, while judges were the operators of the law who were not allowed to interpret the law. The interpretation was just the reappearance of the original legislative meaning. The drastic changes in social life and economic life broke the illusory legal Utopia described by the classical school of natural law. The sociological school of the law, on the other hand, changed its attention from legislation to the administration of justice based on the consideration of social interests and advocated giving judges greater right to judicial interpretation, so judges took the initiative to apply the law. Even Pound has said, we should develop and change the law from rigid dead law into living law that suited society. Barlow, the chief president of the French Court of Cassation, said in a speech in 1904 that when provisions were in the form of clear and definite orders without any ambiguity, judges must follow them. When a provision was ambiguous whose meaning and scope were in doubt, if it was compared to another provision, it would lead to contradictory, limited, or expanded contents, and I believe judges had the most extensive right of interpretation at this moment. They did not need to work on the endless discussions of legislators' thoughts when they formulated the provision a hundred years ago; They should ask themselves how these authors would think if they formulated the same provision today. They should also realize that in the face of all the changes that have taken place in France in ideology, customs, legal system, and social and economic conditions over the past century, justice and reason forced people to generously and humanely adapt the legal provisions to the reality and requirements of modern life.[58] As for criminal law, driven by the positivist school of criminology, statutory interpretation was increasingly believed as a method to break rigid rules of the law, which empowered the law with greater flexibility to defend society.

Since China promulgated the criminal law, statutory interpretation, which takes judicial interpretation as its body, has become more frequent. The main reason is that since the promulgation of criminal law, China has entered the reform of its economic system and stepped into a social transition period when criminal legislation seriously lagged behind social life. In this case, judicial activities had no way to implement

---

[57] See [39], p. 145.

[58] See [40], p. 112.

if the law was not interpreted. Accordingly, judicial interpretation has played an essential role in implementing criminal law and thus evolved into quasi-legislation to some extent so that the court was not applying criminal law but judicial interpretation. Facing the frequent promulgation of judicial interpretation, the Chinese criminal law community has conducted deep research on judicial interpretation. Regretfully, the research still lingers on the technical level without advancing to the depth of theory. However, some individual papers have talked about the nature of statutory interpretation and proposed intrusive questions. For instance, some scholars mention that China's interpretation of criminal law should be based on China's criminal law and judicial practice and should absorb the essence of theories of subjective interpretivism and objective interpretivism in a scientific manner to establish China's interpretation theory of criminal law. These scholars hold that the validity principle of China's interpretation of criminal law is the core for establishing China's interpretation theory of criminal law, which is a validity principle of criminal interpretation supplemented by legislative intention and based on the original legislative meaning when the legislative intention is obviously divorced from social reality, and new cases can be solved by criminal law interpretation when necessary.[59] In my view, China's interpretation of criminal law should be based on the practice of criminal legislation and criminal justice in China. On the premise of adhering to the doctrine of no penalty without law and maintaining the authority of criminal legislation, we should give full play to the positive role of judicial interpretation. Above all, the interpretation of criminal law should not be bounded by the original legislative meaning. It should illustrate the spirit of legislation to remedy its weaknesses as permitted by the legislative meaning.

2.3 Rules of Judicial Interpretation

Statutory interpretation is a highly complicated cognitive process. As statutory interpretation is based on certain legal texts, the linguistic features of legal texts have critical relationships to statutory interpretation. First, statutory interpretation is to understand and illustrate linguistic meanings, namely determining the "meaning of the word" (*der Wortsinn*). Undoubtedly, statutory interpretation starts from establishing the meanings of the words. Under normal circumstances, the meanings of the words are consistent with legislative meanings. In some cases, however, they are contradictory, and the former should abide by the latter. Therefore, understanding the ways to determine legislative meanings and the relationship between the meanings of the words and legislative meanings becomes a critical issue in statutory interpretation.

The establishment of the meanings of the words involves the understanding of language. Language is a unique phenomenon of humans and the habitat of both meanings and thoughts. In statutory law, legal meanings are contained in legal texts. Accordingly, statutory interpretation should deal with the legal texts loaded with

[59] See [31].

language initially. Particular language must have references, and the expression of meaning via language must follow language rules. Therefore, usually, we can determine the meaning by analyzing language and words. Individual words do not realize the language expression of meaning, and a complete meaning is expressed by an organic entirety composed of individual words. Therefore, the principle of the hermeneutic circle should be used in statutory interpretation. In Hermeneutics, the principle of the hermeneutic circle was expressed by the German thinker Wilhelm Dilthey most wholly and explicitly, who said, "We understand the meaning of an individual word by seeing it in reference to the whole of the sentence; and reciprocally, the sentence's meaning as a whole is dependent on the meaning of individual words." Therefore, the circle involves the relationship between the part and the whole of the text. Dilthey holds that the relationship between the part and the whole has three meanings: first, the work, including its meaning, style and, structure, is a whole, and the parts of the work, such as chapters, words, and sentences, must be understood in work to obtain significance. Second, through the lens of the historical and cultural background of the work, we can see that the work is part of the cultural background, and must be understood in the historical and cultural background. Third, the relationship between the work and the spirit of the author and that between the language and the language style of the times. In terms of these three relationships, the hermeneutic circle aims to establish meaning relationships between known or experienced parts and the unknown whole.[60] The hermeneutic circle is mainly on systematic interpretation and historical interpretation in statutory interpretation where the hermeneutic circle is the rule that should be followed. According to the Taiwanese scholar Huang Mau-Rung, in legal norms, every expression (*der Ausdruck*), law (*der Rechtssatz*), or regulation (*die Regelang*) should suit the whole legal system; while the whole legal system should ensure that the individual expressions, laws or (and) regulations are understood, which is "the hermeneutic circle". Accordingly, statutory interpretation enjoys "the hermeneutic cyclicity".[61] The cyclicity of statutory interpretation requires statutory interpretation to be not out of context or not to misunderstand the author's original meaning by sticking to the words; instead, systematic and historical approaches should be taken to understand the legislative meanings of legal texts in a comprehensive manner.

Systematic interpretation, also system interpretation, refers to the status of legal provisions in the legal system, namely, the interpretation method of clarifying the intention of norms according to the relevant positions of the articles in the chapters and sections, or the legal meaning of the relevant articles.[62] The fundamental concept of systematic interpretation regards legal texts as an inherently related system, which determines the meanings of texts by integrating the parts into the whole. To do so, a judge must apply the general and (or) (where appropriately) specific meanings in the context of the legal text and determine the scope of the general words in this context. As the British Viscount Simonds said, legal words, especially general words, should

[60] See [34], p. 145.

[61] See [32], p. 289.

[62] See [41], p. 130.

not be isolated from the context because their vividness and content came from it. Therefore, I argue that it is my right and obligation to review every word of the laws and regulations based on the context. The "context" refers to the most extensive meaning. As I have said, the context includes other legal provisions of the same law, preface, current legal situations, other similar laws and regulations, and laws and regulations that aim to remedy unspoken words and that I can understand through legal means.[63] Systematic interpretation is of great significance for determining the meaning of general and fuzzy words. For example, the term "violence" in China's criminal law has rich connotations, ranging from minor injury to murder. There are many violence-related crimes in China's criminal law. For instance, violence methods are defined in the crime of robbery and the crime of disrupting public service; however, their maximum statutory penalties are very distant. Then, can we explain them in the same way? Definitely not. We should base it on the context of the criminal law articles. It is generally considered that the violence of the crime of robbery includes intentional homicide, and that of the crime of disrupting public service only includes minor injury. When words are ambiguous, systematic interpretation helps us understand the meanings of texts correctly. The Japanese scholar Kato Ichiro has said that if legal norms are in the center of the "frame", they are most explicit; the more distinct from the center, the more ambiguous norms are until the boundary of the "frame" is blurry. This is his "frame" theory. "Frame" (*Rahmen*) refers to the scope as the meaning of the law prescribes or the farthest range semantics can reach. When legal provisions are around the frame, meanings are ambiguous and difficult to understand, so systematic interpretation is approached.

Historical interpretation refers to determining the literal meanings of laws and regulations with the help of references in legislation. The legislative intention is determined, and the literal meanings of laws and regulations are further defined by legal proposals, debate records, comments, and historical reports during the legislation. Here involves using external auxiliary materials of interpretation in the common law system. External auxiliary materials mean those auxiliary materials beyond legal texts which are not a part of governmental printed texts, such as the historical background of statute law, dictionaries, written materials, social customs applicable to laws and regulations across the class, interpretations of the same period, and other laws and regulations of similar materials, which are of great significance to investigate legislative intention from the historical perspective. For example, counterfeiting and alternation are two behaviors with different degrees and properties. Article 122 of the Chinese Criminal Law of 1979 only prescribes the crime of counterfeiting the national currency, but is the crime of alternating national currency included? If we answer it, we must refer to external auxiliary materials to make historical explanations. *The Interim Regulations on Punishment for Impairment of State Currency* published by the State Council on April 19, 1951, prescribed counterfeiting and alternation. In drafting criminal law, a careful decision is given to prescribing only one article based on the actual conditions of cases and behavioral detriments. The crimes of counterfeiting of national currency and trafficking in counterfeit national

[63] See [29], p. 66.

currencies are formulated this way, and this is how article 122 of China's Criminal Law of 1979 is made.[64] From Professor Gao Mingxuan's discussion on the legislative background, counterfeiting should not conclude alternation.

Accordingly, historical interpretation is helpful.

Language falls into daily language and professional language, and legal language is a professional language, also termed "legal words and phrases". In most cases, legal texts use daily language, but specific legal language is sometimes adopted. Thus, when deciding meanings, the special connotation of legal language should be considered to avoid confusing it with daily language and triggering unnecessary misunderstandings. Thus, we must follow the rule of prioritizing legal language over daily language, which is that "expressions that are to be interpreted cannot be seen to have legal-specific meanings if there is no sufficient reason; however, if they have been confirmed to have the special meanings, they should be used regardless of the meaning of the same form in daily language."[65] For instance, the term "hoodlum" has two meanings in daily language: in terms of people, it originally referred to a vagrant and later a person who did evil; in terms of things, it means bad behaviors of using obscene means, being unruly, and acting shamelessly. Furthermore, it especially refers to people and things related to illegal behaviors. China's Criminal Law of 1979 prescribed the crime of hooliganism, referring to hooligan activities of affray, stirring up troubles, humiliating women and other activities undermining public order. Therefore, the term "hoodlum" is quite different in legal language and daily language. When interpreting the law, we should only refer to legal meanings rather than daily meanings. In the revision of 1997s Criminal Law, the crime of hooliganism was abolished, and the crime of humiliating women, the crime of affray, and the crime of creating disturbances were formulated, respectively. The revision made these criminal behaviors be defined more easily. However, in 1997s Criminal Law, using literary descriptive language to describe crimes still occurs. For example, when describing crimes of organizing, leading, and participating in crimes of a criminal syndicate nature, the literary language of "playing the tyrant in a locality, doing evil, riding roughshod over and cruelly killing the masses" was used, bringing difficulty to statutory interpretation.

When a legal language has mistakes, the way to correctly interpret is complicated.

There are two opposite opinions among common law countries. There is a legal proverb among these countries asserting that the court has no excuse to negate a general meaning of a word and phrase due to its expectation that the legislature's expected results cannot be satisfied reasonably. Take an example. In R. v. Judges of the City Court of London, Lord Esher said, "as long as legal words are clear and explicit, you shall follow them; no matter if they will cause absurdity, the court is not entitled to inquiry. In my view, rules are always like this. If legal words have two literal interpretations, they are implicit; if one interpretation leads to absurdity, while the other does not, the court infers that the legislature has no intention to case

[64] See [42], p. 168.

[65] Ziembinski [43], p. 311.

absurdity and adopts the other interpretation therefore."[66] The view of adherence to literal meanings of the law does not allow judges to make reasonable interpretations even if those meanings are absurd. For instance, Article 8 of the *Road Traffic Act* of 1972 in Britain prescribed that the police who wore uniforms could require any person driving or attempting to drive motor vehicles on the road or in other public venues to provide respiratory samples. The literal meaning of this regulation was (regardless of attempting to drive) that the police could not require drivers to conduct respiratory testing if drivers were not driving; however, this was impossible. Only when drivers stopped driving could the testing be conducted. In this case, according to the literal interpretation, the law could never be implemented. Therefore, another view claimed that if a judge believed the application of the general meanings of words would lead to absurd results, which failed to be considered the legislature's intention reasonably, then the judge could apply any subsequent meanings of words. The judge put the words implied in legal words into his understanding of legal words and is entitled to add, change, or ignore legal words to a specific degree to avoid obscurity, absurdity, irrationality, impracticality, or incompatibility of the rest part of the law. In Britain, the second view takes an upper position, and the well-known British jurist Denning refers to the faults of legal words as the wrinkles of legal textiles, which states that judges should smooth them out.[67]

Not only does the law have wrong statements, but also the discordance of norms. Suppose the application domains of two norms are compatible, but their regulation domains contradict because the behavior ordered by one norm is prohibited by the other (and vice versa). In that case, we regard these norms as fundamentally contradictory (however quite rare). When these norms share the same application domain, they are contradictory. To eliminate some contradictions, sometimes it is enough to accept such interpretations: the application domain of a norm has been restricted to the specific part of the application domain of another norm.[68] It is also a complex problem to interpret norms when they contradict each other. Under such circumstances, we should not be restricted by literal meanings but explore legislative meanings to reasonably choose to remedy legal mistakes.

Whether statutory interpretation fills the legal gap is also controversial. Legal leaks (*de liicke*) have two characteristics: (1) the quality of the described object has loopholes that affect its function; and (2) the loopholes are not welcomed. Legal leaks refer to the imperfect state of the legal system.[69] They mainly result from the legal blind zone due to the "understatement" of meanings. Then, can statutory interpretation fill legal leaks? There remain two opposite opinions in Britain: the first is the negative theory, as seen in Simonds' statement of filling legal leaks as "the rampant usurpation of legislative right under disguised by interpretation." Lord Merton says, "as long as congressional legislation or order embodies the intention of the Congress or the king and ministers, no matter if it uses explicit words or implicit words that

[66] See [29], p. 40.

[67] See [37], p. 10.

[68] Ziembinski [43], p. 313.

[69] See [32], p. 328.

are necessary, the court should implement these intentions; nonetheless, the responsibility of a judge is by no means to fill subjective loopholes in congressional legislation. If he does so, he is usurping the authority of the legislature."[70] The second is a positive theory. For instance, Austin said, "a judge expands the law to the ignored situations by legislation because these situations are a component of the general legislation even though they have not been prescribed explicitly."[71] Therefore, the focal point of the two opinions is whether filling legal leaks violates the legislative right. The Taiwanese scholar Huang Maotong tries to distinguish statutory interpretation from the statutory supplement, who believes that the administration of justice is a law-finding activity (*Rechtsgewinnvmg*), namely, finding the "major premise" (*der Cbersatz*). The activity is usually divided into two types or stages: statutory interpretation (*Gesetzesauslegung*) and statutory supplement (*Rechtsfortbilduns*). A remarkable difference between the two activities is that the two are relative to the "possible meaning" of the law. In other words, the activities of statutory interpretation are only within the possible meaning; while the activities of statutory supplement lie only beyond the possible meaning except for "intra-judicial leaks".[72] "Intra-judicial leaks" refers to the imperfect status arising from open concepts, which is different from other leaks, and the law has explicitly authorized the court to fill these "leaks". Thus, this "leak" is named the "delegation of filling leaks" (*Delegationslucke*). In China's criminal law community, some scholars hold that criminal law interpretation has the function of filling leaks of criminal law since the law, in terms of its fundamental characteristic, is the outcome of social reality. However, society constantly changes, but the law cannot be revised without particular procedures. In this way, when society has drastically changed while the law remains unchanged, the law and social reality are disjointed. Specifically, when a case finds no applicable rules in the existing law, the law has a leak. Legislators cannot avoid legal leaks altogether. Therefore, judges should refer to legislative intentions and adapt the law to social reality through statutory interpretation to fill legal leaks for each case even though their interpretation conclusions do not coincide with the literal meanings of legal words.[73] In my opinion, the key to addressing the issue of whether statutory interpretation fills legal leaks is to define legal leaks correctly. There are differences between legal leaks and lawless space. Thus, legal leaks are not the erosion of lawless space by judicial administrators but are merely careless omissions of legal provisions. For such legal leaks, I believe they can be filled by statutory interpretation. The Taiwanese scholar Huang Mau-Rung distinguishes statutory interpretation from statutory supplements, considering that statutory supplements can only interpret legal leaks (except for intra-judicial leaks). I disagree with this opinion because statutory supplements are just one of the functions of statutory interpretation, which should and can be included in the statutory interpretation. Moreover, it is inappropriate to take "possible meaning" as

[70] See [29], p. 50.

[71] See [29], p. 31.

[72] See [32], pp. 390–391.

[73] See [31].

the boundary of distinguishing between statutory interpretation and statutory supplements because statutory interpretation definitely goes beyond the literal meanings of legal words, as illustrated by expanded interpretation. Expanded interpretation is the interpretation of legal provisions on an expanded scope or the explanation of articles exceeding the original meanings to some degree.

Whether legal leaks can be filled by judicial interpretation is an issue concerning the definition of judicial authority. Under the setting of "rational legislators," the law is perfect, so legal leaks are impossible to exist. This understanding strictly restricts judicial rights, separating them from legislative ones, which is logically consistent. Nevertheless, the legend of "rational legislators" has gone bankrupt. Soviet Union scholars have said that expecting the existing law to prescribe every criminal behavior without omission is idolatry, a deception of ourselves, and utterly unjustifiable assertiveness and arrogance.[74] In this context, expanding the judicial right to a reasonable extent until it can fill legal leaks through judicial interpretation is feasible and does not violate legislative authority. However, filling legal leaks should not violate the doctrine of no penalty without law, which mainly refers to that "lawless space" is not violated.

3 Judicial Activity (2): Discretion

Discretion is the judge's deduction of facts according to the law when dealing with individual cases. Therefore, the exercise of the right of discretion by judges is the main content of judicial activities. In criminal justice, the judge's right of discretion concerns the life and death of citizens, so it is vital. Therefore, it is necessary to deeply study the theoretical foundation of discretion and its application from the perspective of human nature.

3.1 Evolution of Discretion

Discretion is the process of the judge's operating the law, so discretion is born with judicial activities. As human legal culture advances, discretion has evolved from absolute to extremely strict rules and relative discretion.

The absolute discretion in ancient China is closely related to China's imperfection in legislation. Before the existence of statutory law in ancient China, there was no strict distinction between legislation and administration of justice, when intimidativism of "if the law was not promulgated, it had unlimited power" prevailed.

Laws and regulations were not set in advance and systems were discussed when relevant cases happened, and one system was only for one case. Thus, it was inevitable

[74] Piontkowski et al. [44].

for discretion to be absolutized. After the Spring and Autumn Period, China had statutory law whose legislation was perfected and reached its peak in the Tang dynasty. However, extreme strict rules have never appeared in China's legal history, a critical characteristic of the Chinese legal system. Legalism claims that both emperors and ministers "shall follow the law," including the restriction of "arbitrary judgment of penalties" on judicial officials at all levels. However, perfect systems did not guarantee the restriction, so it was a shell. In the Han dynasty, rituals were introduced into the law, where penalties were determined by the motif of criminals and the "Chun Qiu statute" was established, namely, taking Confucian patriarchal ethics as the criterion for trial cases based on *The Spring and Autumn Annals*, where criminals who had good motif were exempted, and people who followed the law but had evil motif were killed. *Discourses on Salt and Iron* mentioned, "the law is always ignored when cases are heard." Therefore, judicial tyranny in the Han dynasty is severe. By the Tang dynasty, the restriction on judicial officials was improved. For example, the Laws *relating to the administration of justice* in the *Tang Law* prescribed that the administration of justice be quoted from the main bodies of codes, decrees, rules, and procedures. According to *Tang Code*, "criminals are regulated by rules. The law that hears cases shall depend on the main body." So judgments must quote the main bodies of codes, decrees, rules, and procedures. There might be faults if codes, decrees, rules, and procedures were not quoted. The judge who disobeyed to quote them would be flogged thirty times.[75] Additionally, *Tang Law* controlled the right of discretion of judicial officials by punishing illegal settlement of lawsuits. It believed that settling lawsuits based on the law was the main content of the administration of justice. The illegal settlement of lawsuits did harm to the legal system and even the country, so the legal liability of criminals of this kind must be strictly investigated. Based on the features of crimes of the kind, *Tang Law* strictly punished judicial officials based on the principle of sentencing the accuser to the punishment facing the person he falsely accused. Thus, *Tang Law* specifically prescribed the crime of regarding the guilty as innocent and vice versa. Since it established individual, generalized crimes, judicial officials still enjoyed the greater right of discretion. For instance, *Tang Law* stipulated the crime of "doing what ought not to be done". As the note explained, "it is applied if no code, decree, or reason can be applied". *Tang Code* said, "there are so many miscellaneous offenders and minor crimes that it is difficult for laws and regulations to cover them all. In the case of no law or decree, if the crime of 'doing what ought not to be done' is not prescribed, there will be no legal basis. It is established for supplementing omissions and for judicial officials to convict criminals temporarily and discretionarily." Thus, it is seen that the establishment of the crime of "doing what ought not to be done" is to supplement omissions, leading it to be very general. The scope of "doing what ought not to be done" is broad, and the law does not provide identification standards, so we only rely on judicial officials to "convict criminals discretionarily". In ancient times, China was a feudal autocratic country where emperors governed everything and enjoyed both legislative and judicial authority. In order to protect the imperial power, judicial

[75] See [22], p. 416.

officials must be restricted to convict criminals, and it was a necessity to restrict the right of discretion of judicial officials. On the other hand, the right of discretion had to be granted to judicial officials to punish crimes. The paradox has run through ancient China. For instance, US sinologists, when commenting on the legal system of the Qing dynasty, said that generally speaking, Chinese people were not against the practice of determining crimes or penalties through judicial procedures when there was no law or regulation. The role of judicial organs reflected that the focus on the Chinese legal system throughout history was not to enact behavioral norms but to determine proper penalties when wrongful acts recognized by people happened. Most Chinese legal provisions have stipulated charges with a narrow range and determined single, unchanged penalties of these crimes. As statutory punishments only applied to more severe parts of the crimes, the applicable range of legal provisions was usually narrow. *The Great Qing Legal Code* contains several thousand articles, but it still cannot predict severe criminal acts because it applies narrowly. The existence of such a legal blind zone is anticipated. Legislators have adopted two remedies for the legal blind zone: first, the criminal acts that the law has not prescribed are dealt with according to prescribed criminal acts; second, formulating some general legal provisions that are applied extensively.[76] These two remedies have enlarged the right of discretion of judicial officials, in sharp contrast to strict legal rules.

Among ancient countries of the civil law system, it was the customary law implemented before statutory law. If we define the administration of justice from the perspective of statutory law, in this period, the administration of justice was not based on the law but on absolute discretion. As the British scholar Maine said, it was asserted that when humans were born, they could not imagine any legislative organ of any kind or even a definite legislator. The law was not popularized as a custom but as a convention. The judicial judgments made based on facts had the only authority to tell rightness from wrongness, and it was not a violation of a pre-set law.[77] Thus, before a perfect statutory law existed, experience-based judicial discretion enjoyed the central role in legal activities. With the promulgation of the *Twelve Decemviral Tables*, ancient Rome stepped into the period of statutory law, which reached its peak by the time Justinian's code was compiled. At the early time of ancient Roman statutory law, discretion was strictly restricted, and the strict rule doctrine and legal formalism were the legal styles of that time. Giuseppe Grosso, an Italian scholar, has vividly described the formalism in ancient Roman law that the early legal behaviors expressed legal situations by formal language. The formal transfer of property (*manicipatio*), a typical form of transferring things *(res mancipi)*, used a set of patterns that simply expressed abstract behaviors (the validity of behaviors were independent of reasons and might be any reason), that is, a balance-holder (*libripens*) held a scale with five witnesses in presence, and the purchaser stroke the scales with the piece of bronze (*radusculum*) to claim the possession of the thing because he had bought it with the bronze (*aes*) and scale. The initial expression of this form was a behavior, namely, trading things after paying money using

[76] See [45], pp. 421–422.

[77] See [24], p. 5.

formal language. At that time, trade was made by weighing; that is, an essential term was used to reflect the trading activities of weighing coins. Romans' tendency to pay attention to traditions makes Romans keep these early forms even though these forms no longer adapted to specific situations; the Romans still regarded them as a necessary form to produce legal validity that does not depend on specific reasons but only existed as abstract behaviors.[78] Legal formalism determines, to some extent, the strict rule doctrine in judicial activities. Judicial officials have a minimal right of discretion. As society developed, strict rule doctrine no longer satisfied social needs, so ancient Rome stepped into the equity period when judicial officials enjoyed the greater right of discretion. For instance, Ulpian mentioned in the first book of *On Rules* that the responsibility of judicial administers was broad because they could allow the possession of the property, allow one to take possession of others' property, and set guardians for juniors who did not have one, and designate judges for litigants. Javolenus also mentioned in the six books of On Kaci that people who had been authorized judicial administration seemed to be authorized the rights that were necessary to exercise judicial rights meanwhile.[79] Till modern times, as Roman Law revived, civil law countries have formulated a batch of codes successively, and a codification movement was conducted, which moved the world into the strict rule doctrine period. Therefore, the right of discretion of judges was completely excluded, and judges just mechanically applied the law as Merryman depicted. According to Merryman, the trial process in civil law countries was a mechanical operation. Judges were like special law clerks who, except for special cases, attended the court only to solve litigation facts and look for obvious legal results from the existing legal provisions. Their role was only to find the correct legal provisions and correlate them with facts to produce solutions automatically from the combination of legal provisions and facts. Judges endowed solutions with legal significance.[80] No penalty without a law represents the strict rule doctrine in modern civil law countries without law in an absolute sense. According to no penalty without a law, the criminal code should prescribe the composition of crimes and absolute statutory sentences. Judges must not be allowed to decide penalties based on the severity of cases. For example, the well-known Soviet Union criminologist Trainin said that the 1791s *French Criminal Code* limited the judge's discretion prominently, which prescribed absolute definitive statutory sentences. The court's activities were summarized as only determining the existence of crimes and specific criminals, while all other work of the court in assessing crimes before and after trials had been completed by legislators.[81] In the second half of the nineteenth century, civil law countries experienced drastic changes in social and economic conditions and were mechanically criticized by the administration justice, where no penalty without law in the absolute sense developed into that in the relative sense, so the right of discretion was affirmed within some limit and scope.

[78] See [26], pp. 116–117.

[79] See [46], p. 17.

[80] See [12], p. 36.

[81] See [47], p. 19.

The common law system primarily originates from common law, and the right of discretion of judges is naturally reasonable. However, common law has experienced a period of strict rule doctrine. Common law dates back to the twelfth century, before which Anglo-Saxon law prevailed in Britain. In 1066, the Normans conquered Britain and created common law, which was gradually formed by the judgments of royal judges, so it existed in the form of case law over a long period, and there was no statute law. The common law developed in the extremely mechanical, rigid writ system and litigation form. Facts of cases must satisfy the categories of writs, and if writs were inappropriate, lawsuits must be lost. Also, the category of writs was limited. Even if there was a system similar to case litigation, it was impossible to change the writ system's mechanical nature fundamentally. Since the fourteenth century, people have gradually found that some of their rights and claims failed to be fulfilled by the mechanical and rigid writ system of the common law court, so they proposed requests to the British King, Privy Council, the consultation organ of the King and Parliament to uphold justice and take special remedies. The appeals were usually managed by the Chancellor, who was responsible for judicial affairs. When hearing such cases, the Chancellor adopted doctrines and litigation forms different from common law. Chancellor was the King's favorite courtier who enjoyed great authority. When common law flourished, the Chancellor issued orders in the name of correcting the injustice of local courts, who ordered common law courts, and royal courts, to hear cases. Now, the Chancellor personally hears cases in the name of correcting the injustice of common law courts. In 1474, the Chancellor, for the first time, decided cases in his name. Since then, unique trials made by the Chancellor without the participation of the common law court were called equity cases. By the sixteenth century, as equity cases increased, the Chancellor's office finally developed into the court that was named the royal court and that was parallel to common law court, namely, the Court of Equity.[82] Equity empowered judges with greater right of discretion. The right of discretion of judicial ministers at early times, as John Selden commented, constantly changed "depending on the foot length of judicial ministers" and formed into its procedure law in the eighteenth century, with the purpose of eliminating rigidness becoming one feature of this procedure; however, this was contradictory.[83] Therefore, the development of the right of discretion was restricted by social living conditions and was inseparably interconnected with the evolution of the legal system. In any case, however, the existence of equity enabled the British law to possess the dual structure as David said: apart from the common law stipulations by the Westminster's Royal Court (or common law court), there was a remedy called "equity", which revised and supplemented the stipulations of common law.[84] In this way, judges could adjust the law with equity and made the law more adaptive.

Through the historical investigation of discretion, we can see that in different law systems and even different periods of the same law system, the right of discretion is hugely distinct. Comparing the civil law system and common law system, we find

[82] Shen [48], pp. 173–174.

[83] See [49], p. 99.

[84] See [40], p. 309.

that statutory law and case law are determined by the two legal systems, but judges have the smaller right of discretion in the civil law system and the greater right of discretion in the common law system. This is an indisputable fact.

3.2 Basis of Discretion

Should the right of discretion exist? If it should, what is the basis of rationality? This is a critical question worth studying. In criminal law, the classical and positivist schools of criminology have sharp disagreements over discretion.

Generally speaking, the classical school advocates strict rule doctrine and negates the right of discretion of judges. The noted French Enlightenment thinker Montesquieu compared the judgment patterns of different political regimes and considered that the closer a regime was to the republic, the more definitive the judgment patterns were; in the Republic of Bangladesh, elected officers were arbitrary in trialing cases because there was no legal basis, which was a drawback. When deciding cases, the consuls of early Rome were the same as those elected officers in the Republic of Bangladesh. However, they felt it inconvenient and thus formulated explicit laws. In Rome, judges could only declare what crimes defendants committed and punishments of crimes no matter whom the law prescribed them. This could be seen from the laws formulated then. Similarly, in Britain, jurors determined whether defendants were criminals based on the proposed facts. If judges declared the crimes true, they would declare punishments according to the law. A judge was enough to do so with one eye open.[85] Thus, according to Montesquieu, in democratic regimes, judges should take the law as the only criterion to determine crimes and should not possess the greater right of discretion. Beccaria passed down Montesquieu's thoughts and harshly criticized the right of discretion of judges. He pointed out that "the laws only can determine the punishment of crimes; and the authority of making penal laws can only reside with the legislator, who represents the whole society united by the social compact. No magistrate then, (as he is one of the society,) can, with justice, inflict on any other member of the same society, punishment that is not ordained by the laws. But as a punishment, increased beyond the degree fixed by the law, is the just punishment, with the addition of another; it follows, that no magistrate, even under a pretence of zeal, or the public good, should increase the punishment already determined by the laws." This is the first conclusion of Beccaria by studying the origin of punishment and the power of punishment.[86] To prevent judicial tyranny of judges, Beccaria has proposed the doctrine of no penalty without law. As Chinese scholars have mentioned, Beccaria and French Enlightenment thinkers set out from the ethics of the bourgeoisie, attacking the asceticism and Godism that killed freedom and dignity while proposing their political and legal claims, which were reflected in criminal law as follows: implementing the doctrine of no penalty without law,

[85] See [30], pp. 76–77.

[86] See [7], p. 11.

opposing judicial tyranny, formulating unified, codified criminal law, and excluding the old sources of law (religious laws, traditional customs, and personal opinions).[87] Concerning the classical school of criminology, Hegel holds different views from Beccaria, who excluded the right of discretion of judges completely. Hegel proposed "contingency of law," saying that the law and the administration of justice contained contingency, which was an aspect of them in nature. The reason why he said so was that the law was an ordinary stipulation applicable to individual events. If someone opposed the contingency, he might be talking about an abstract thing. For instance, the severity of penalties made it impossible for penalties to adapt to any stipulation, and thus all decisions were arbitrary. The arbitrariness, however, was inevitable.[88] The arbitrariness, as Hegel said, referred to judicial discretion. The judge's discretion was within the scope of the law. As Hegel has mentioned, the law did not affirm the final stipulation required by reality but let judges make decisions. It only limited judges between the maximum and minimum limits, which, however, did not help solve problems because the maximum and minimum limits were integers, not preventing judges from making a limited, purely positive stipulation; by contrast, it was the responsibility of judges to decide penalties between the maximum and minimum limits.[89] In contrast to the classical school, the positivist school tended to expand the right of discretion of judges to individualize penalties. Ferri made the following comments on the classical school's opinions of ignoring the individual difference of the right of discretion and therefore negated that judges had the right of discretion based on individual difference: the classical school believed that all burglars were "larceners", and all killers were "murderers". Legislators saw no specific individuals, and individuals only appeared in judges' minds. For scholars and legislators, criminals were just living specimens that judges could stick a criminal law provision on their backs. Apart from exceptions mentioned in criminal codes and rare human mental conditions, all other cases were only used as grounds for judges to choose a provision applicable to criminal specimens from the criminal code. If it were not article 407 but 404 stuck on the criminal's back, the appellate court would be against any change in number. If the specimen was still alive and said, "it may be important for you to choose which article to apply to me, but if you carefully study the conditions that force me to seize other's properties, you may realize that the importance is schematic." The judge would answer, "the future administration of justice may be like this but not now. You broke article 404, so this number will stick to your back based on the law. When you leave the court and go to jail, another number will change for you because your personality completely disappears in front of the law representing social justice." Accordingly, the person's personality was unreasonably killed and retained in jail for deteriorating treatments. If the person followed the same old disastrous road and committed another crime, the judge might stick another provision on the original crime, such as adding article 80 or 81 providing for

---

[87] See [50], p. 73.

[88] See [51], pp. 223–224.

[89] See [51], p. 223.

recidivism to the offense provided for in article 404.[90] Ferri also discussed the reason to expand the right of discretion of judges from the special nature of criminal justice. He said that in criminal law, it was not or should not be a merely legal, abstract logic-related issue to apply laws and regulations to specific cases like how it was in civil law. It must apply an abstract legal provision to people alive from a psychological perspective. This is because criminal judges could not separate themselves from the environments or social lives to become a legal instrument that was mechanical to some extent. Every criminal judgment depended on acts, actors, and the social situations that acted on them rather than statutory law. Now, we have an opportunity to address the old problem of the judge's authority (right of discretion; as noted by the citer). Regarding this problem, we have moved from one extreme to another and from the Medieval arbitrariness to Bacon's motto of respecting the law and judges. According to Bacon, the best law left minimum space for judges to think, and the best judge left minimum space to judge cases independently. If the function of criminal judges, as it was nowadays, was always to conduct illusory quantitative research on the moral responsibility of the defendant based on the Byzantine's equivalent rules for attempted, accomplice, and confrontational crimes; in other words, if the law applied to crimes instead of criminals, the judge's authority should be restricted by the length of sentences as what legal provisions had stipulated, like Chinese law's precisely stipulation of the length and thickness of bamboo sticks (this had the same reputation as the single cell in the Chinese penal system). On the other hand, if a criminal trial was a physiological and psychological investigation of the criminal and the crime that was informed of degrading to the subordinate position—criminals should be advanced through the lens of penalty—criminal code apparently should be limited within some basic rules of defense, means of social sanctions, and components of felonies and minor crimes. At the same time, judges should enjoy greater freedom allowed by scientific, empirical trial materials so that they could try the defendant based on anthropological knowledge.[91]

The disagreement between the classical school and positivist school over the right of discretion lies in the way to view the human factor in judicial activities primarily, directly related to the understanding of human nature.

Should the human factor be included in judicial activities? Here involve the relations between human and law, and in a broader sense, the relations between the rule of man and the rule of law. In the Spring and Autumn and the Warring States Period, there were debates over the rule of law and the rule of man. Although their concepts were completely different from those as we say today, the debate was about whether law or man mattered more. The rule of law in the Spring and Autumn and the Warring States Period referred to a country being ruled by law, which was advocated by Legalism. The oppositions were the rule of rites, rule of virtue, and rule of man. The opposition between the rule of law and the rule of man is about the relationship between man and law, which has the nature of jurisprudence, namely, whether human or law has the decisive role in governing the country? Is the role

---

[90] See [52], pp. 37–38.

[91] See [9], pp. 120–121.

of man more important than the role of law or vice versa?[92] Generally speaking, Legalism stresses the role of law and opposes the rule of man, who believes that the law is the objective standard to measure merits and demerits and decide penalties and awards, which is the pattern and example of everything (by Shen Zi). In contrast, the rule of man is ruled by the heart that is arbitrary, inconsistent and has no objective standard. It is a misunderstanding for Legalism to criticize that the rule of man is arbitrary. Although the Confucian school advocates the rule of man, it does not negate the role of law. It stresses the role of man more. Particularly remarkable, Xun Kuang has made a comprehensive, objective analysis of whether man or law had a decisive role in governing the country, and his opinions are as below: (1) Xun Kuang made clear at the outset that "there always exists a man governing the country but not an unchanged law." He means that the man rather than the law plays a key role in governing a country, and only good rulers govern the country well. The law is critical to a good-governed country, and Xun Kuang also said that "the law is the starting point of realizing great governance". Therefore, the quality of law completely depends on the governor; (2) It is the man who masters and implements good laws, which are just dead letters otherwise. He further pointed out that "Hou Yi's archery method does not disappear, but he cannot make future generations into archery masters. Dayu's legal system still exists, but the Xia dynasty cannot govern the world forever. So the rule of law alone cannot govern the country, nor can it be implemented naturally. A country exists when it has talents in governing the country. Without talents, the country will perish"; and (3) State affairs are complicated, and always change, so the law cannot contain everything, nor can it change at any time. It is man's flexible application and prompt decision that solve these affairs. Therefore, Xun Kuang said, "So the emperor formulates the law and minsters to settle state affairs. The responsibility of officials at all levels is stipulated, and officials communicate with each other, so there will be no schemes, undiscovered good deeds, or mistakes. No one but a man of good character can make it." If there is a man of good character, even if the law and responsibility are not in place, "the law is prioritized if it exists. If not, good men are recommended, so even though there lacks the law, everything is in order." If there is no man of good character, "even though the law is complete, it is inflexible and fails to address emergencies, triggering chaos." Thus, a conclusion is made that "there are chaos when the law is in place, but there has never been chaos when men of good characters govern the state."[93] Xun Kuang saw the contradiction between the limits of the law and the complexity and variability of society. The role of man must be stressed to overcome the contradiction. Thus, Xun Kuang proposed some important jurisprudential concepts and statements, namely "laws must be promoted by man", paying attention to the human factor in the administration of justice. "The law is prioritized when it exists, and if not, good men are recommended", which analogized similar legal provisions when the law had no explicit stipulations to compensate for the weaknesses of the law. Therefore, the rule of law stresses "classics", while the rule of man focuses on "authority", in which

[92] See [53], p. 231.

[93] See [54], pp. 87–88.

"classics" are defined by the law and "authority" is operated by men. "Classics" without "authority" is a reduction to rigidness, and "authority" without "classics" is inflexibility. Both opinions, as we see, are one-sided. In ancient Greece, the argument between the rule of man and the rule of law also existed. It is generally considered that Plato advocates the rule of man, while Aristotle, the rule of law. Plato's thought of the rule of man is mainly reflected in his work *The Republic*, which advocates that the saint governs politics and philosophers govern the state. He believes that excellent people can easily find the rules of commerce, market, contract, public security and, harbor, so there is no need to formulate laws for each. Furthermore, the state governing authority, especially philosophers (when the law does not provide for the king and judges), enjoys the greater right of discretion, who can publish decrees and laws at their will.[94] Plato advocates the rule of man primarily because he thinks the law is rigid and fixed, failing to adapt to changes. The law, meanwhile, is strongly based on principles and cannot be applied to every special example. Generally, the law has rigidity, which restricts politicians from reigning over, so he is against the rule of law. By contrast, politicians govern states relying on their knowledge, so they make every necessary measure to adapt to changes and special needs. Thus, Plato strongly advocates the rule of man. Plato has deeper understanding of the law and admits that the rule of law is "the second best" politics in *The Laws* he writes in his late time. However, Aristotle opposes the rule of man and states that "the rule of law shall be better than the rule of man." The reason is that the rule of man mainly lies in: (1) that the law is made after careful considerations of the majority of people or their experience. Compared to the opinion of a man or the minority, that of the majority is correct; (2) that the law is unsentimental and impartial; (3) that the law does not talk and lie like men who change their statements every day, and it is stable; and (4) that the law is expressed via norms, in particular via words, and it is definitive. Aristotle, on the other hand, sees the limitations of the law, so he pays attention to the human factor in judicial activities. He mentions that the law is a public measurement, but like a man, it can not predict all possibilities in life. However, even though the law is universally uncertain, it is still an irreplaceable regulator of political relations. When the universal principles of the law are not suitable for individual occasions, we must correct defects and fill the gap the former legislators have left. He names the way to overcome the general adverse consequences as "according with the reason or law." The nature of "according with the reason or law" is as follows: when the law is not satisfactory due to its universality, we revise the law according with the reason or law. It is impartial to accord to the reason or law; however, we should not understand it from the literal meanings of the law but from the spirits of legislators. Even though he has legitimate rights, an impartial person will not harm others based on the literal meanings of the law. Instead, the person will apply the law freely as legislators have done when formulating the law.[95] From the argument between the rule of law and the rule of man, we can see that apart from some extreme supporters of the rule of a man who negate the role of law fundamentally and those of the rule of law who

[94] See [55], pp. 5–6.

[95] See [56], p. 194.

negate the role of law, most people show both positive and negative attitudes to the role of law, who only have different focal points. Supporters of the rule of man stress man while despising the role, and supporters of the rule of law are opposite.

No matter the stress on the law or man, understanding human nature is involved. The understanding of human nature by the supporters of the rule of law falls into two aspects: (1) the preference and advocate of human reason. They believe that the law can regulate all human behaviors, which is reflected by an ancient Chinese saying that "justice has long arms"; (2) the inference that human nature is evil. For instance, Han Fei, a Legalist philosopher, claimed that human selfishness could not be changed by human power, and it was impossible to "transform intrinsic evil nature to develop acquired nature of goodness". Only the law bound the intrinsic evil nature. The understanding of human nature by the supporters of the rule of man is opposite: first, they case doubt on human's rational capability. According to them, the limitations of the law are inevitable. As the saying "the law is limited, but the sensibility is infinite" reflects, it is impossible to regulate infinite sensibility by limited laws. As Plato has mentioned, the differences between humans and their behaviors and endless and irregular activities in human affairs do not allow a universal and pure rule, and no technique has formulated a principle that deals with constant changes.[96] Second, they infer that human nature is good. For instance, Mencius's doctrine of kingcraft of "commiserating government" is based on the goodness of human nature. Because human nature is kind, social order is built on the charismatic power of the ruler's moral personality, and self-discipline is more potent than discipline. Human nature is not absolute for certainty, and the theories of goodness and badness of human nature can transform and even integrate. For example, Plato's "philosopher politics" in early times was grounded on the goodness of human nature, so he believed that to restrict philosophers by legal provisions was like forcing an experienced doctor to plagiarize the provisions from medical textbooks.[97] However, in his late times, he turned to that human nature was evil, who considered that human was born to pursue individual interests but not public interests, so there must be a law to sanction or punish human evil behaviors.

It should be said that the law has limitations objectively, which is determined by the limitations of human's rational capability, so we must admit that human has a positive role in judicial activities, and the right of discretion of judges is a necessary premise for the administration of justice. In this sense, it is not desirable to completely negate the human factor in judicial activities like what the classical school of criminology has done. However, it is hard to prove whether human nature is good or evil, but it is better to presume that human nature is good than evil. If the power is not restricted, it must be corroded. Therefore, the right of discretion of judges should not be unlimited. More importantly, the transformation from the negation of the right of discretion by the classical school to the affirmation and expansion by the positivist school is based on the significant changes in criminal concepts. With regards to this, the well-known Soviet Union criminologist Trainin has incisively discussed that

[96] See [57], p. 36.

[97] See [58], p. 92.

if like what the classical school has said that the basis of criminal responsibility should be exact behaviors that have been described in the previous law, the role of the court could reduce to the minimum, which would be accurately applying the law. After (the positivist school) criminals were prioritized, a completely different situation was caused in which legislators could not meet criminals, so criminals only dealt with the court whose authority was expanded.[98] The classical school studied crimes and attributed crimes to a purely legal category, which only stressed the jurisprudential analysis of crimes. As Ferri has said, the classical school treats crimes as legal problems and focuses on the legal analysis of the name and definition of crimes while ignoring the personality factor against a certain background. This way, the entire criminal code is merely a logarithmic table to calculate penalties in the final analysis.[99] Judges are only to calculate the term of imprisonment based on the recognized criminal facts. Accordingly, judges have a minimal role in this criminal judicial system. The positivist school fulfills the significant transformation from crimes to criminals, has transformed judicial objects from crimes to criminals, paid special attention to the physical detriment of criminals, and determined the responsibility of criminals based on their physical detriments. These are individual penalties, which require giving judges the greater right of discretion and stress the role of judges in judicial activities. As Ferri has mentioned, if there are no good judges to implement the code, there will be no great effect even for the most academic and noble code. However, if good judges implement it, even though the code is not perfect, it does not matter.[100] Afterward, liberal jurisprudence further stresses the role of the administration of justice while belittling the legislative function, even claiming to discover the law liberally. For instance, one of the founders of liberal jurisprudence Eugen Ehrlich holds that it is insufficient for judges to depend on state-formulated statutory legal rules. Every rule that has been made is incomplete, and when it was made, it was outdated. We can hardly manage the present, let alone the future. Those responsible for applying the law are people of their nations and eras, who apply the law based on the spirit of their nations and eras rather than the intention of legislators or the spirit of the past. Eugen then proposes two ways of judgment: the traditional technicism, which strictly observes the ways of judgment in statutory law, where judges are bound to obey a rule that pre-determines all things. And the liberal judgment he advocates, is based on the law discovered by judges instead of statutory law. The distinction between the two ways of judgment is not mainly that liberal judgment may transcend the regulations of statutory law, but the way of doing so. The technicism way of judgment provides that the never-changing legal method is the only way to fulfill the task while liberal judgment notices the huge creative power of judges, so the latter does not see judges as arbitrary and advocates giving play to judge's personality.[101] The above idea stressing the creative power of humans in judicial activities is desirable because the law, in the end, is the realization of judicial

[98] See [47], p. 24.

[99] See [52], pp. 24, 34.

[100] See [9], p. 120.

[101] See [11], pp. 276–277.

activities. Nevertheless, the nature of the administration of justice determines that judicial discretion is subordinated to the law, so if we put too much stress on it, there will be a potential danger of judicial tyranny. As some scholars point out, It seems that the purpose of statutory determination, consideration, or judgment is to make the statutory penalty adapt to individual crimes as far as possible, that is, the consistency between crime and punishment, to ensure the principle of legality of penalties. However, serious opposition occurs and the right of discretion is expanded, which opens the gate for the inconsistent measurement of penalties that breaks the rule of law. Therefore, the right of discretion of judges is both the lock to ensure the legal system of criminal law and the key to tyranny and the destruction of the legal system of penalties. The lock and key are in the hands of judges.[102] Thus, the right of discretion of judges should be limited to a necessary extent.

The Chinese criminal law and judicial practice indicate that Chinese judges have the greater right of discretion, mainly reflected in the following aspects: (1) principle stipulations leave room for discretion. There are many principle stipulations in China's criminal law depending on judges to be implemented, so judges are endowed with the greater right of discretion, as shown in criminal law that, the necessary limit is the boundary to distinguish between justifiable and excessive defense. The necessary limit in this context is a principle stipulation. As to how to determine the necessary limit of justifiable defense, it all depends on the judge's judgments; (2) blank stipulations leave room for discretion. Blank stipulations account for a considerable number in China's criminal law. When there are blank facts about crimes, judges should fill the blank based on relevant economic and administrative laws and regulations to provide the legal basis for blank facts. As relevant economic and administrative laws and regulations are not complete, however, the determination of these crimes relies on the judge's understanding of policies and regulations, which is subjective; (3) general stipulations leave room for the right of discretion. Laws and regulations should be specific, but China's criminal law has many general stipulations, such as "serious circumstance". The term "serious circumstance" is available everywhere in criminal law, whose connotation and extended meaning are so general that there is no definition. It can be a boundary to distinguish crimes from non-crimes and a standard to distinguish felonies from minor crimes. Ordinary citizens by no means know the exact meaning, and even judicial personnel, except for the existing judicial interpretations, have to refer to their experience when handling cases; and (4) optional stipulations leave room for discretion. Most of China's stipulations of statutory penalties and sentencing in criminal law are optional. For example, punishments for a crime are applicable to multiple types and degrees of penalties. Sometimes the range is so huge that five principal punishments are applied together, or principal and accessory punishments are applied in combination, leaving huge space for judicial personnel to choose from. Take another example. The stipulation of statutory circumstances by China's criminal law only prescribes consideration in sentencing without further limits. Sometimes, lighter, mitigated, or exempted punishments are

[102] See [59], p. 537.

in parallel, and since there is no explicit stipulation of the applicable conditions, judicial personnel have to decide by themselves according to circumstances. The fact shows that China's judicial personnel must enjoy some right of discretion, but the excessive right of discretion is not good to guarantee the legal interests of citizens. The current level of social development and situations in China demonstrate that the reasons why judicial personnel should enjoy some right of discretion, as Chinese scholars mention, are mainly based on the following[103]: (1) the purpose of penalty in China. The purpose of applying penalties to criminals is to prevent crimes. The prevention includes general prevention and special prevention. General prevention is to punish criminal behaviors for maintaining the maximum deterrence of penalties. Special prevention, by contrast, while punishing crimes, should consider the individual situations of criminals and determine the social detriments and the difficulty to transform criminals based on the analysis of these situations before prescribing the proper remedies so that sentencing is suitable for individual situations. Individual situations are different for each criminal, which legislators could not predict and prescribe in the law, so actual situations are only considered by judges, so it is necessary to empower some right of discretion to judges; (2) China's national conditions. China enjoys a huge territory and a large population, where the development of localities is imbalanced and criminal behaviors are diverse. The detriment of the same criminal behavior is greatly different, so it is impossible to give completely established penalties for the same crime. Therefore, statutory penalties are relatively determined, and ambiguous concepts are applied to some legal terms to expand the connotation of the law. Then, judges need to enjoy the greater right of discretion; (3) the ability of humans to understand things. The ability of humans to understand the objective world is both infinite and limited. Humans cannot understand all existing things clearly, nor is it possible for them to precisely and meticulously predict future things. Laws made by legislators are realistic, and are based on social reality, so future situations are impossible to be considered. The law that is to make should apply to future circumstances; however, the criminal form in the future may be inconsistent with the situation at the time of legislation, and some may even be very different. As we aim to maintain the law to be effective during a period, the law has to be general, and we can only use relatively definite statutory penalties to adapt to the crimes in the future; and (4) the normative characteristic of the law. The law is the regulation to direct people to act. As a behavioral norm, it must be simple, clear, and easy to read and understand. If absolute statutory penalties are adopted in criminal law, all sentencing situations must be listed one by one, which is impossible and not allowed by the normative nature of the law. Like traditional Chinese medicine shops, those criminal codes are impossible for people to understand and thus fail to fulfill their goal to regulate human behaviors. Determined by the above factors, the existence of the right of discretion of judges is objectively necessary. Undeniably, the right of discretion without limits also leads to judicial tyranny. Therefore, the right of discretion should be limited to a necessary extent.

[103] See [60], p. 258.

Judicial discretion can be limited by both legislative and judicial aspects. From the perspective of legislation, judges should be left with appropriate discretion. If legislative stipulations are too strict and trivial, there will be no space for the discretion of judges, and the rigid law is hard to adapt to the complex and ever-changing social needs. By contrast, if legislative stipulations are too coarse and flexible, judges will have the excessive right of discretion, leading to judicial tyranny. The crux is to hold a limit, which is of great significance to limiting discretion. In my opinion, for some critical issues on the boundary between crimes and non-crimes, legislation should provide stipulations as straightforwardly as possible. For other issues, legislation can be flexible to ensure the impartiality and authority of criminal law and give criminal law some flexibility. Regarding the administration of justice, the exercise of the right of discretion should be provided for operative stipulations and normalized in the procedure. It is better to uniformly prescribe them through judicial interpretation for some critical issues to ensure judges exercise the right of discretion impartially.

3.3 Operation of Discretion

Beccaria has summarized the judicial activities of judges into the syllogism logical reasoning as follows: the major should be the general law; the minor the conformity of the action, or its opposition to the laws; the conclusion, liberty or punishment.[104] Beccaria's judicial syllogism is against the right of discretion of judges, which is premised on the perfect stipulations of the law. In this case, the judicial activities of judges are simple and mechanical, but this is a "judicial Utopia". Judicial activities are never as simple as what Beccaria thinks. Due to the shortage and weaknesses of legal provisions and the complexity of cases, the judicial discretion of judges is an operative process involving cognitive, psychological, and logical factors.

Discretion is the application of the law, so it possesses the general characteristics of the application of the law. The application of the law is one of the most vital contents of legal adjustment, which supplements the attribute of the execution of the power of legal norms with its execution of power, ensures the fulfillment and implementation of legal norms, and ensures the adjustment of relations in such a manner of applying individual laws and subordinating norms so that the adjustment continues and ends. The application of the law falls into three primary stages: (1) determining the fact (determine the factual basis of the case). Here involves the analysis of the fact, evidence, and verification, namely, the behavior to obtain the information of the fact; (2) selecting and analyzing legal norms (determine the legal basis of the case). This stage refers to the behaviors relevant to legal norms, including finding the definite texts of normative documents, checking the legal validity of documents, and explaining documents, among others. It also includes filling the legal gap; (3) reflecting the case's decision in the document of the application of the law. In this stage, judges should decide the legal case based on the analysis of the fact

[104] See [7], p. 12.

and legal norms, which is reflected in the document of the application of the law. The decision has a particular form and should be implemented. The first two stages are preparations, which are the reflections of the understanding of the law and constitute the basis of the application of the law, namely, factual basis (the first stage) and legal basis (the second stage). The valid application of the law is to decide the case and apply the law.[105] Therefore, as the application of the law, judicial discretion has the following features:

First, judicial discretion is a process of absorbing the law. The law can only play a role in social life when applied. Otherwise, the law is merely a pure linguistic form and lifeless "dead letter". The application of the law transforms the law from "dead letter" to "living letter". Accordingly, first of all, there is an absorption process of the law in judicial discretion, which includes the understanding and interpretation of the law, manifested as a "law-finding" process. The absorption of the law in judicial discretion puts forward some requirements for legislation; that is, the law must be absorptive and operative. In fact, not all laws are operative. Inoperative laws are difficult to be absorbed and thus are hard to apply, leading to the legal emptiness or automatic invalidity of the law. The operability of law refers to whether operating the law is possible or feasible, or extensively refers to the possibility of the application of the law. Generally speaking, if a feasible method exists, which applies a legal provision to specific cases, then the legal provision is operative; otherwise, it is inoperative. The feasible method means the operative rule or method that can be implemented. Broadly speaking, it is the method that the law has stipulated in advance for each step, and that ends within limited steps when the law is applied. By "having been stipulated by the law in advance for each step", it means the explicit stipulation that has been prescribed by previous rules to direct every step. Feasible methods also require themselves to be completed within finite steps, so endless ones are not operative. The non-operability of legal provisions includes the non-operability of legal concepts and legal norms established by legal provisions. If there is no feasible method to determine whether any phenomenon or behavior is the object of a legal concept or whether it has the characteristics of the phenomenon or behavior reflected in the legal concept, the legal concept is said to be inoperable. The non-operability of legal concepts is undecidability. Feasible methods are the demarcation criteria and judgment methods the law prescribes. If there is no feasible method that applies a legal norm to specific cases, the legal norm is inoperative. Without loss of universality, the non-operability of legal concepts and norms is collectively called the non-operability of the law.[106] Due to the non-operability of some laws, some laws fail to be applied in the administration of justice, which is common in China's criminal justice.

In judicial discretion, not only is inoperative law not absorptive, but the operative law is not a simple pigeon-holing process, where the choice for legal articles, namely the issue of "law-finding", exists. In most cases, as long as the law has clear and operative provisions, it is not hard to understand and determine it. Under some complex

[105] See [61], pp. 714–715.

[106] See [62].

situations, however, "law-finding" is a significant issue for judicial discretion. Moreover, as long as the law suitable for the case has been found, judicial discretion is more than half successful. The choice of legal provisions is not arbitrary but in strict accordance with the internal logic of the legal provision system, so legal doctrines must be followed. According to criminal law theories, the application doctrine of the overlap of articles provides a doctrine for law finding. The overlap of articles refers to that due to the complex stipulations of criminal law articles, there is a subordinated or cross relationship in the content of the constituent elements stipulated in several laws. The overlap of articles is a theory of the relations among articles that answer which article is to apply when multiple articles apply to criminal behaviors.[107] The choice of articles occurs when articles overlap. The choice, however, is not arbitrary but determined by the internal logic of the overlap of articles. Among the discussions on the overlap of articles, there are arguments on whether articles can be chosen with aggravating punishments.[108] Till now, the issue has not been agreed upon. Thus, the choice of articles is a complex issue and should be based on the law and reason. Otherwise, judicial *ultra vires* are certainly caused.

Second, judicial discretion is also a process of recognizing facts. Judicial discretion is to apply legal norms to specific cases, so recognizing the facts of cases is critical. When we apply legal norms, all the facts related to the objective reality of legal cases are the object of true judgment. The concept of objective reality is not only the fact per se but the social, and legal significance of facts (especially social detriments of illegal acts). The fact of the objective reality also includes the law and the rights and obligations of the subject. In conclusion, all the objective facts that constitute the rational aspects of applying the law are the object of truth judgment when we apply the law.[109] When recognizing the facts of cases, we must follow the general principle of epistemology, according to which cognition is the reflection relationship between the subject and the object. As a subject is a social person who has consciousness and a brain (with sensory organs as his tools) to think, the subject's cognition to object (concept reflection relationship) must happen during the interaction between the subject and the object (practice process). The nature of the relationship is that the subject understands or reflects the object and forms a concept image of the object in its brain; the object is understood or reflected by the subject and becomes a part of the subject's concept. The subject's cognition of the object or the reflection relationship is a concept relationship different from the practice relationship. It does not change the object's existence form in reality but reproduces the object in the form of a concept in the subject's brain to form a concept, which is a conceptual form for the subject to understand.[110] Therefore, cognition is only a reflection process for the subject to understand the objective fact, and we must adhere to the principle of objective authenticity. Objective authenticity requires that judges must accurately reflect the objective facts in judicial activities. The principle

[107] See [63], p. 13.

[108] See [64, 65].

[109] See [61], pp. 706–707.

[110] See [66], p. 163.

of taking facts as the basis in China's criminal law indicates that the impartiality and legitimacy of the law can be guaranteed only when facts are reflected objectively. The recognition of facts in judicial activities has a feature different from the general understanding of the law. The feature is that those objective facts in legal cases have limitations in the object and content. Unlike theories, our task is not to reveal the nature, connection, and intermediary of facts or to determine the objective regularity, social, political, and economic essence of the phenomenon. The factual situations in the judicial investigation are within a strictly prescribed and legally determined scope, which is not limitless and inclusive of the content of the phenomena it can discover.[111] The feature of judicial cognition determines that only affirmation can be given to the facts of cases that are significant to the application of the law in judicial activities. Western scholars have a penetrating conclusion that "the law only cares about basic facts; everything else is ignored because it has nothing to do with the application of legal rules."[112] The basic fact, manifested in criminal justice, is the recognition of the facts of crimes and criminals that reflect the social and physical detriments of the behaviors and actors. Judicial cognition must follow certain legal rules, which are primarily the proof rules and procedure rules as procedural law prescribes. These legal rules are of great significance to correctly understanding the facts of cases. In China's criminal justice, adhering to the truth is an emphasis. There is no doubt that adhering to the truth is correct, which is also the value goal of criminal justice. However, people have limited cognitive ability, and not every "truth" of the "fact" can be correctly "sought for" by people. Consequently, it is necessary to draw the support of legal rules. For example, the presumption of innocence is one of the rules that helps us understand the truth.

Finally, judicial discretion is a process where legal provisions and facts of cases couple with each other. According to the Soviet Union jurisprudence theories, the coupling process of legal provisions and facts of cases is called the decision of legal cases, which can be illustrated from three aspects: (1) it is a process of formal logic. From the perspective of formal logic, the decision of legal cases is reasoning that brings the specific facts (the situation of the case) into legal norms. Thus, the decision of cases integrates the two preparatory stages and combines the factual and legal basis; (2) it is a process of creation. The decision of legal cases is, first of all, to apply universal rules to special daily life, to connect norms with the situations in daily life. According to legal norms and within the scope of legal norms, the competent authority adjusts individual social relations based on the direction legal rules have prescribed; and (3) it is an activity for the competent authority to exercise state power. Deciding legal cases is exercising state power, which includes thoughts and orders. Through deciding legal cases, a new factor, which ensures the law to be adjusted, legal obligations to be performed comprehensively and accurately, the subject rights to be fulfilled, and the law to be adjusted to the end, is added to the legal adjustment mechanism.[113] Therefore, the coupling of legal provisions and facts of cases is a

[111] See [61], p. 708.

[112] Peter and John [67], p. 11.

[113] See [61], pp. 728–730.

process of adapting a general legal provision to an individual case. The process is the specific operation of judicial power that contains complex legal reasoning.

Criminal judicial discretion is a process of applying criminal law, which involves the execution of the right of discretion of judges. China's criminal law community tends to restrict the right of discretion of judges to the discretion of penalties. For example, according to Chinese scholars, the right of discretion is that when judges hear criminal cases, on the premise of adhering to the doctrines of no penalty without law and of strictly observing the law, they have the right to choose punishment methods suitable for the criminal acts and the individual characteristics of the criminals according to criminals' circumstances within the legal scope prescribed by law.[114] Some scholars define the right of discretion of judges as the power or responsibility that the law gives judges (including judicial organs) to decide the penalty to the criminal defendant fairly and reasonably within the legal scope according to the principle of suiting punishment to crime and the purpose of the penalty. The scope of the right of discretion of judges, however, is not limited to the discretion of penalties, which also includes the discretion of crimes whose scope contains four aspects as follows: (1) In the critical state of crimes and non-crimes, it is the right of discretion that determines the nature of the case, including 1. whether some critical behaviors constituting crimes are decided at the discretion of judges when judicial personnel and lawyers have disagreements. 2. The provisions of criminal law on certain circumstances constituting crimes and their consequences are very general, and the nature of such critical behaviors is at the discretion of judges; (2) In the critical state of punishments and non-punishments, the right of discretion decides whether to punish. Once a behavior constitutes a crime, it is equipped with the nature of being punished. But deserving a penalty does not mean punishments must be applied to every criminal in judicial practice. China's criminal law expresses that judges can exert exemption of criminal penalties to criminals if the circumstances of the crimes are minor and that sentences are not needed. Apart from this, criminal law also expresses that judges have the discretion to decide whether to apply the non-penalty method and what kind of non-penalty method to the person exempted from criminal punishment; (3) the right of discretion to choose the type and degree of statutory penalties. China's criminal law pursues a relatively definite legal punishment system, in which the general provision of criminal law only makes principle provisions of heavier, lighter, mitigated, or exempted from punishments. However, in specific provisions of criminal law, there are many types of penalties for specific crimes and an extensive range of penalties, so judges have extensive discretion within the range; and (4) the right of discretion in other aspects. In order to adapt to the varied and complicated needs of criminal cases, China's criminal law has some "other" provisions for expanding the adaptability of legal provisions. These "other" provisions include specific circumstances of incompletely listed articles. If such circumstances happen, judges can exert the right of discretion following the spirit of legislation: citing the provision, expanding the interpretation of the provision based on the original meaning but exceeding its literal meanings, and flexibly applying the

[114] See [60], pp. 251–252.

provision.[115] To sum up, the concept of the right of discretion by arguers contradicts the scope they list. I hold that the right of criminal discretion should cover conviction and sentencing. The discretion of conviction means that judges can decide the nature of critical behaviors between crimes and non-crimes according to the law. In China's criminal law theories, conviction refers to the activity in which the judicial organ identifies the behavior to be tried and the constitution of the crime stipulated in the criminal law.[116] During conviction, legal provisions mainly refer to constitutive elements of crimes. Any behavior that meets the statutory constitutive element is a crime and vice versa. In this sense, there is no space for judges to exert discretion. Nonetheless, legal provisions of the constitutive elements are not always explicit; sometimes, there are general, named evaluation elements in the Soviet Union criminal law theories. Evaluation elements are variable, distinguished from the invariable elements with definitive contents. To a large extent, their contents depend on the legal consciousness of legal personnel who apply the law. These people should consider the requirements of criminal law and the situations of specific cases. These variable elements are more like the changing situations evaluated by the investigative organization, procuratorial organization and the court, so they are conditionally called evaluation elements. When the constitutive element of a crime is the evaluation element, the court should determine the consistency between the fact of the case and the element and what the element refers to at the beginning. For instance, to determine whether the abuse of authority causes significant loss, we must first make clear how we understand "great loss" under current conditions. Legislators endow judicial personnel who apply the law with the power to solve this problem.[117] When the constitutive element of a crime is the evaluation element, judges have the right of discretion of conviction. The execution of the right of discretion of conviction is concerned with the boundary between crime and non-crimes, so it must be carefully treated.

The discretion of sentencing refers to that judges can decide whether the criminal should be punished and to what extent the punishment is given according to the facts of cases and the individual situations of criminals. As countries globally have abolished absolute statutory penalties, criminal law usually prescribes relatively definite statutory penalties. Thus, judges have the right of discretion in sentencing, which includes: (1) whether to sentence; (2) the type of penalties; and (3) the choice of the degree of penalties. Based on China's criminal law stipulations, judges have the considerable right of discretion in sentencing. Currently, positive discussions have been made on scientific methods of sentencing in China's criminal law circle that have proposed mathematics sentencing and computer sentencing.[118] After the computer sentencing is adopted, the arbitrariness in sentencing has reduced dramatically, exerting a positive role in the comprehensive balance of sentencing. In this case, however, does the right of discretion of judges exist? Our answer is positive. This is

[115] See [68].

[116] See [36], p. 11.

[117] See [69], p. 141.

[118] See [70], pp. 615–618.

because although computer sentencing is introduced, the subject of sentencing is still judges. A computer is an auxiliary tool for sentencing, which is impossible to replace the role of judges in sentencing. Undeniably, inconsistency happens sometimes in sentencing with not enough attention given. Therefore, a reform of the sentencing system should be conducted, and learning from foreign countries is particularly critical. For instance, US has guides on criminal sentencing. Guides are not a part of the criminal code but separate legal documents to illustrate the exact meanings of each word, phrase, and paragraph to provide detailed, specific standards for sentencing. Guides aim to restrict judges from excessively exerting the right of discretion in sentencing. Chinese scholars have mentioned that the idea of using guides should be affirmed. While maintaining the content, system, and structure of the criminal code, guides provide specific, practical, detailed, and specific standards for criminal sentencing, displaying the complex behavioral phenomena with quantitative relation. Additionally, the whole system of these guides is strict and complete, and the contents of guides are meticulous and explicit, which controls the judgment difference due to the subjective arbitrariness of judges and leaves room for the discretion of judges. Also, guides propose sufficient reasons and allow judges to divorce from themselves.[119] So, we should learn from it. However, as China has a vast territory and a large population where political, economic, cultural, and national differences exist among regions, criminal situations are also very different. Thus, it is difficult to establish a unified, meticulous, strict sentencing standard across the country. Even so, we should try our best to balance the sentencing to unify the legal system.

References

1. P. Gu, *Social Conflicts and Litigation Mechanism* (Sichuan People's Publishing House, Chengdu, 1991)
2. [US] T. Hans (Editor-in-Chief), *Legal and Criminal Psychology* (Quzhong Publishing House, Beijing, 1986)
3. [US] H.J. Vetter et al., *Introduction to Criminology* (Knowledge Publishing House, Beijing, 1992)
4. Z. Shen, *Modern Western Jurisprudence* (Law Press China, Beijing, 1983)
5. [US] Bodenheimer, *Jurisprudence: The Philosophy and Method of the Law* (Huaxia Publishing House, Beijing, 1987)
6. [Soviet Union] C.C. Alekseyev, *General Theory of Law*, vol. 1 (Law Press China, Beijing, 1988)
7. [Italy] Beccaria, *On Crimes and Punishments* (Encyclopedia of China Publishing House, Beijing, 1993)
8. S. Lü, *The Study of Hegel's Legal Thought* (People's Public Security University of China Press, Beijing, 1989)
9. [Italy] Ferri, *Criminal Sociology* (People's Public Security University of China Press, Beijing, 1990)
10. Z. Zhou, *Principles of Criminal Law* (Law Press China, Beijing, 1990)
11. Z. Shen, *Modern Western Jurisprudence* (Peking University Press, Beijing, 1992)

[119] See [71], p. 235.

12. [US] Merryman, *Civil Law Tradition*, 2nd edn. (Law Press China, Beijing, 2004)
13. K. Yang, A comparative study on the status of judges. Legal Sci. (4) (1993)
14. *Selected Materials of the History of Western Legal Thoughts* (Peking University Press, Beijing, 1983)
15. G. Zhu, *Restricting Power with Power: A Commentary of Western Decentralization Theory and Decentralization System* (Sichuan People's Publishing House, Chengdu, 1987)
16. [US] Hamilton et al., *Federalist Papers* (The Commercial Press, Beijing, 1982)
17. Y. Xu, *Comparative Criminal Procedure Structure* (Modern Press, Beijing, 1992)
18. [France] D. Rene, *British Law and French Law: A Comparison in Substance* (China University of Political Science and Law Press, Beijing, 1984)
19. H. Chu, *US Criminal Law* (Peking University Press, Beijing, 1987)
20. *The Shuihudi Qin Bamboo Texts* (Cultural Relics Publishing House, Beijing, 1978)
21. L. Wang, *New Research on the Law of Tang Dynasty* (Shanghai Academy of Social Sciences Press, Shanghai, 1993)
22. W. Qiao, *Study on Tang Law* (Shandong People's Publishing House, Jinan, 1985)
23. M. He, Private statutory interpretation and its methods in Qing Dynasty. Cass J. Law (2) (1992)
24. [UK] Maine, *Ancient Law* (Commercial Press, Beijing, 1984)
25. B. Xie (Editor-in-Chief), *Roman Law* (Peking University Press, Beijing, 1990)
26. [Italy] G. Giuseppe, *The Story of Roman Law* (China University of Political Science and Law Press, Beijing, 1994)
27. H. Guo, *Comparative Study of Statutory Interpretation* (Renmin University of China Press, Beijing, 1993)
28. [US] Berman, *Law and Revolution: The Formation of the Western Legal Tradition* (Encyclopedia of China Publishing House, Beijing, 1993)
29. [Britain] C. Rupert, *Statutory Interpretation* (Southwest University of Political Science and Law, Chongqing, 1986)
30. [France] Montesquieu, *The Spirit of the Laws*, vol. 1 (The Commercial Press, Beijing, 1961)
31. P. Wang, On the validity of criminal law interpretation in China. Sci. Law (2) (1994)
32. M.-R. Huang, *Legal Methods and Modern Civil Law*, 3rd edn. revision (National Taiwan University, Taipei, 1993)
33. R. Zhang, *Exploration of Meaning: Contemporary Western Hermeneutics* (Liaoning People's Publishing House, Shenyang, 1986)
34. D. Yin, *The Fate of Understanding: On Hermeneutics* (Joint Publishing, Beijing, 1988)
35. B. Zhao et al., *Application and Perfection of Criminal Law* (Law Press China, Beijing, 1989)
36. Y. Wang, *Introduction to Conviction* (Renmin University of China Press, Beijing, 1990)
37. [Britain] Denning, *The Discipline of Law* (Quzhong Publishing House, 1985)
38. [US] Ehrmann, *Comparative Legal Cultures* (Joint Publishing, Beijing, 1990)
39. [US] Pound, *Interpretation of Legal History* (Huaxia Publishing House, Beijing, 1989)
40. [France] D. Rene, *Main Contemporary Legal Systems* (Shanghai Translation Publishing House, Shanghai, 1984)
41. R. Yang, *Legal Methodology,* Revised edn. (San Min Book, Taipei, 1987)
42. M. Gao, *The Birth and Development of the Criminal Law of the People's Republic of China* (Law Press China, Beijing, 1981)
43. [Poland] Ziembinski, *Practical Logic* (Quzhong Publishing House, Beijing, 1988)
44. [Soviet Union] A.A. Piontkowski et al., *History of the Criminal Law Sciences of the Soviet Union* (Law Press China, Beijing, 1984)
45. [US] D. Bodde et al., *Law in Imperial China* (Jiangsu People's Publishing House, Nanjing, 1993)
46. *Fragmented Selection on Civil Law: On Judicial Jurisdiction, Judgments and Actions* (China University of Political Science and Law Press, Beijing, 1992)
47. [Soviet Union] A.H. Trainin, *General Theory of Constitution of a Crime* (Renmin University of China Press, Beijing, 1958)
48. Z. Shen, *General Introduction to Comparative Law* (Peking University Press, Beijing, 1987)

49. Gledon et al., *Comparative Legal Traditions* (China University of Political Science and Law Press, Beijing, 1983)
50. F. Huang, *Beccaria and His Thoughts of Criminal Law* (China University of Political Science and Law Press, Beijing, 1987)
51. [Germany] Hegel, *Elements of the Philosophy of Right* (The Commercial Press, Beijing, 1961)
52. [Italy] Ferri, *Positive School of Criminology: Three Lectures* (China University of Political Science and Law Press, Beijing, 1987)
53. G. Zhang, "The rule of law" and "rule of human" in the spring and autumn and the warring states period, in *Collected Essays on the Rule of Law and the Rule of Man* (Quzhong Publishing House, Beijing, 1981)
54. G. Zhang, *New History of Chinese Ideology of Law* (Peking University Press, Beijing, 1991)
55. R. Wang, L. Cheng, *Theory of Rule of Law* (Shandong People's Publishing House, Jinan, 1989)
56. [Soviet Union] Nersesyants, *Political Thought of Ancient Greece* (The Commercial Press, Beijing, 1991)
57. H. Zhang (Editor-in-Chief), *History of Western Legal Thoughts* (Peking University Press, Beijing, 1983)
58. [US] Sabine, *A History of Political Theory*, vol. 1 (The Commercial Press, Beijing, 1986)
59. Y. Gan, P. He, *Foreign Criminal Jurisprudence*, vol. 1 (Peking University Press, Beijing, 1984)
60. Z. Zhang, *On the "Right of Discretion" of Judges in Sentencing, in Criminal Law Development and Judicial Perfection* (People's Public Security University of China Press, Beijing, 1984)
61. [Soviet Union] C.C. Alekseyev, *General Theory of Law*, vol. 2 (Law Press China, Beijing, 1991)
62. H. Wang, On the non-operability in the law. J. Comp. Law (6) (1994)
63. X. Chen et al., *On the Overlap of Articles of Law* (Fudan University Press, Shanghai, 1993)
64. Y. Feng, On the aggravating choice of the overlap of articles of law. Law Sci. (4) (1984)
65. K. Xiao, Aggravating choice is not for the overlap of articles of law. Law Sci. (8) (1984)
66. Z. Xia, *Introduction to Epistemology* (People's Publishing House, Beijing, 1986)
67. [Britain] S. Peter, S. John, *Legal Values in Western Society* (People's Public Security University of China Press, Beijing, 1989)
68. Z. Li, On the right of discretion of criminal judges and its reasonable control. China Legal Sci. (4) (1994)
69. [Soviet Union] B.H. Kudryavtsev, *General Theory of Conviction* (China Prospect Publishing House, Beijing, 1989)
70. X. Chen, *Philosophy of Criminal Law* (China University of Political Science and Law Press, Beijing, 1992)
71. G. Li, *Comparative Study on Punishment against Freedom* (Jilin People's Publishing House, Changchun, 1992)

Postscript

In 1991, when I finished the *Philosophy of Criminal Law*, I felt like waking up from a dream because I had expressed all my ideas, and my mind was blank. Although in the concluding words of *Philosophy of Criminal Law*, I left a foreshadowing that "for myself, the philosophy of criminal law in the sense of natural law is an eternal temptation, or maybe a major topic to discuss in the future," I had no idea what the topic would be. From then on, I have looked through books to replenish and accumulate my thoughts and searched for the next academic objective. One day, accidentally, I found a book titled *Sociological Theory: Explanation, Paradigm, and Ideology* by the US sociologist W. D. Perdue. It analyzed people, schools, and thoughts from a unique perspective of assumption and paradigm, and the assumption of human nature arose my great interest. According to it, human nature, as we referred to, was a concept of fundamental human qualities sociology could ascertain. Human nature was reality-originated abstractness, and the qualities it explored would vanish as all external influences wore off. According to sociology and other disciplines, all assumptions, as mentioned above, focused on disputable issues such as determinism and voluntarism, self-interest and social man, reason and emotion, and hedonism and humanitarianism, among others. The analysis of all sociologists starts from their assumptions of human nature before their sociological ideas were stated. The analysis method inspired me immediately: can this method also be introduced to the theories of criminal law? Then, I saw the sayings by the British philosopher Hume in *A Treatise of Human Nature* that "science has relationships with human nature more or less. No matter how distant disciples are from human nature, they come back to human nature in some way." Undoubtedly, as a discipline, criminal law should have relationships with human nature, so the value of criminal law can only be revealed when it is examined from human nature. Then, where should the human nature analysis of criminal law start? Hitoshi Otsuka, a Japanese criminal jurist, inspired me with a saying that "the contradiction between the classical school of (criminology) and the positivist school of (criminology) originates from their different understandings of the human nature of criminals, who act as the subject of crime. Crimes are conducted by human beings, and punishments are imposed upon human beings. Therefore, we must take human nature into account since the

X. Chen, *Humanistic Foundation of Criminal Law*,
https://doi.org/10.1007/978-981-19-9764-8

subject of crime is human. The understanding of human nature determines the nature of criminal law." Accordingly, I came up with a topic: Humanistic Foundation of Criminal Law. In the beginning, it was just the title of a paper. I was about to write a paper themed on it. I started it in June 1993; however, I dropped it when finishing the half because I felt it difficult to carry on. Several months later, I braced myself to continue it, and a ten-thousand-character paper was completed in December. Then, I sent it to the Chinese Journal of Law, where the paper was published in the fourth issue of 1994. The research on the human nature of criminal law could have ended after the paper was completed. By May 1994, however, a publishing house planned to publish a series of books on criminal law, and the person in charge asked me to name a title. I, who has not given full expression to my views on the human nature of criminal law, named "Humanistic Foundation of Criminal Law". The name was approved, and I planned to write a book. To write the book, I started to read and think again and began to write in June 1994. The writing was a spiritual exploration. Although I racked my brains all day, the process was unexpectedly smooth, and I spent only four months finishing it. It was scheduled to write 300 thousand characters, but when I sorted out my scripts, I found it had already been over 480 thousand characters. From a ten-thousand character's paper to an over 480 thousand character's book, it was not only the increase of characters but, more importantly, the accumulation of thoughts, the sublimation of theories, and the expansion of ideas.

My writing style is unique, with the book title set first before the system of the book planned. The system is a focal point because it is both the narrative system of writing and the logical system of theories. The book was scheduled to have ten chapters, each chapter has only one title, and the contents were not devised. As I determined to write a chapter, I would think how many sections there would be, what questions would be discussed, and how many characters I would write for each question. This way, tasks were assigned tier upon tier, and I would think and read while writing. Once I started writing, I was so excited that I would not stop until finishing a whole section. As can be seen, I wrote books without deep consideration but with great randomness and inspiration. It was only when a chapter was finished that I knew how to express my ideas set in advance and to what extent these ideas would be expressed. Since inspiration was transient, I had to force myself to write a flood of ideas down as quickly as possible before they were gone. Otherwise, when inspiration passed by, I might not write anything. Consequently, I devoted my entire energy and thought even though I spent not much time writing. Overall, I did not write the book smoothly or with great facility.

In the postscript of *Philosophy of Criminal Law*, I raised the idea of constructing the professional food trough of criminal law, considering that the superficial and broad evaluations of the professional food trough are suitable for criminal jurisprudence and even the entire jurisprudence. As a rigid discipline, criminal jurisprudence should be equipped with its professional trough, and without strict professional training, a person is not allowed to have a bite. This is to safeguard criminal law's academic and scientific nature. However, my idea was criticized by two voices: one argued that professional trough might be adverse to the popularization of the theories of criminal jurisprudence, leading to the negation of the practicability of criminal jurisprudence.

The other argued that professional trough might hinder the improvement of criminal law views, especially resulting in the negation of the humanistic nature of criminal jurisprudence. My idea is that I proposed professional trough since China's research on criminal law theories was superficial. I was not against the practicability of criminal jurisprudence. Till now, I still insist that the recession of criminal law theories was not due to the distance of criminal law from reality but exactly the excessive secularization of criminal law or it being secularized excessively. The crux of the problem lies in the way to stop the loss of the professional properties of criminal law theories. Therefore, constructing a professional trough of criminal jurisprudence is the foundation for criminal jurisprudence to develop independently, which is a rational examination of the normative content, the carrier of criminal law, by criminal law. My *Philosophy of Criminal Law* is thus an effort to construct a profession trough of criminal law. Nevertheless, I never believe that criminal law theories will stay at this level. In my opinion, as a discipline, criminal jurisprudence should also have its humanistic connotation and express the concerns on human nature and value, which are the origin issue of individuals and society. As a result, attaching more importance to the humanistic connotation of criminal law theories is the foundation for criminal jurisprudence to develop, which is what my theory is interested in. The *Philosophy of Criminal Law* is in the name of philosophy but has nothing much to do with philosophy, which is a shame. And it is because that I realized this that I categorized the book to the domain of philosophy of criminal law in the sense of positive law in the postscript of *Philosophy of Criminal Law*. After it was published, I swore to write a book about the philosophy of criminal law in the sense of natural law, although I could no longer name it the "philosophy of criminal law". I had no idea of what the philosophy of criminal law was in the sense of natural law, but I have set a criterion to verify it, that is, the philosophy of criminal law in the sense of natural law should be a work of criminal law without a provision of criminal law. Notwithstanding that whether the *Humanistic Foundation of Criminal Law* belongs to the philosophy of criminal law in the sense of natural law remains to be verified by history, at least the criterion that "without a provision of criminal law" is achieved, which is comforting. I say so not because I hate criminal law provisions, but precisely because I have believed that provisions are critical and particularly for a normative discipline like criminal jurisprudence, whose provisions are the starting point and final destination of criminal law research. In the preface of the *General Theories of Criminal Law*, I expressed to establish a discipline of criminal law provisions and made unremitting efforts, as shown by the book *Research on the Overlap of Articles of Law*. Maybe I will write a book only about provisions one day, which is also my long-planned target.

The book's writing is not only a satisfaction of my interest in philosophy but, more importantly, an opportunity of my experience. My interest in philosophy originated from a random chance when I was 20. In September 1974, when I turned 17, I became a member of educated youth after graduating from high school. I was fond of literature, so I killed the dullness and loneliness of rural life with literature. In December 1976, after finishing the educated-youth life for two years, I was arranged to work in the Public Security Bureau, and I was under 20. During a trip in August

1977, I met a companion, who was a railway stevedore, a member of educated youth and shared a similar age with me. He read a book with great interest at night, and I noticed it was a tutoring book on *Anti-Dühring*. After communication, I knew that he was interested in philosophy. Although working as a stevedore, he had read a lot of Marx's and Lenin's works and had profound political aspirations and lofty pursuit of life. He had great interests in martial arts, literature, and so on. He could do authentic *Tongbeiquan* and was adept with both the pen and the sword. After a talk for the night, I developed interests in philosophy and admiration of him. Back from the trip, when I started to read Marx's and Lenin's works, the college entrance examination system was restored in December 1977, and I participated in the examination immediately. When applying for the majors and universities, I put the philosophy of Peking University as my first major and school, journalism of Fudan University as the second, and law of Peking University as the third. I was enrolled by the Department of Law of Peking University partly because I worked in the Public Security Bureau. Anyway, I did not fulfill my dream to study philosophy. Studying at Peking University, I have read a lot on western philosophy, like Hegel's works, enraptured but not fully understood. Hegel's works at that time were different from those today, and I had difficulty understanding them. Since the accidental encounter with the stevedore, I have never met him, and we had occasional communication by letters. In early 1982, I was admitted to Renmin University of China to study for my master's degree and received a letter from him, from which I knew he had returned to his hometown and worked as a martial arts coach in the Commission for Physical Culture and Sports. Meanwhile, he was self-studying law and taking the correspondence course in the law major of East China University of Political Science and Law and asked me a few questions on law. I replied to him quickly and agreed to meet in his hometown during the summer vacation. However, he never came to me, and I never received his message. In 1984, I received my master's degree and continued my doctorate in the Department of Law of Renmin University of China. One day, when I read *China Legal Daily* in my office, I was attracted by a full-page news report on cracking down on a crime. When I saw the name of the principal criminal, I was shocked. It was the railway stevedore I met by accident! Exactly. He was arrested when participating in a provincial-level match as the coach. After reading the news, I understood that he premeditated to steal a precious cultural relic in the Palace of the Taiping Heavenly Kingdom in his hometown. To do so, he had read such a lot of works on the history of the Taiping Heavenly Kingdom and local activities of the Taiping Heavenly Kingdom local chronicles recorded particularly that he even became an expert in the history of Taiping Heavenly Kingdom. At the same time, he dug into the science of cultural relics to be familiar with the values of cultural relics. When everything was ready, he stole all cultural relics in the Palace one day in 1980, which became a major case shocking the province. The case was pending until his partners confessed it in 1984, and he was arrested. Calculating the time, I realized that when he wrote to me in 1982, it was over a year since he conducted the crime. There was no doubt that he studied law for evading legal sanctions. After that, he was sentenced and went to jail. When he was released from prison, he joined the business world and became rich. The story is true and by no means my fabrication. I know many talents who are brilliant but become criminals. This makes me further think of human nature: are citizens and criminals only one step away? Humans have reason, which makes them both noble and degenerate, and the degeneration is even more horrible. Thus, human reason has boundaries, and we cannot equate reason with goodness. Humans have experience, who are attracted by food, sex, wealth, and fame. Without self-control, humans can barely resist these temptations. With the realistic thinking of human nature, I developed theories to form the basic ideas of this book. I always feel that the previous interpretations of crimes are superficial, which are difficult to illustrate criminal phenomena in reality. Therefore, it is necessary to explore the humanistic foundation of criminal law from the human nature perspective. This is not only a theoretical but also a realistic issue.

It is out of the theoretical deliberation of thinking the humanistic issue of criminal law through the lens of philosophy that many philosophical contents are included. Roughly calculated, the book has around 480 thousand characters, covering criminal law, legal principle, and philosophy, which accounts for one-third respectively. Accordingly, when writing the book, I could not control myself from exploring philosophy. This is a severe professional transgression, and I could not help asking myself: is this a work on criminal law? In particular, the transgressed philosophical part is just at the amateur level, and I was afraid of being laughed at. The only encouragement was my exploration spirit on theory: since it was an adventure, it was inevitable to make mistakes. If I was afraid of mistakes, I would not enjoy the splendor at the peak of mountains. This soothed me a lot. I have read extensively, but I have been sticking to a principle that I read those books not related to criminal law as a scholar of criminal law, so everything should be based on criminal law so that I could not go so far as to encounter a great calamity in the ocean of knowledge. However, there was an exception as to the issue of free will. I should think as a scholar of criminal law and think professionally from the perspective of philosophy. It was so important that I could not abandon the philosophical part, and I took a risk. The only soothing thing is that although the book is mixed with many contents about philosophy, jurisprudence, sociology, psychology, ethics, biology, and other disciplines, all are overflowed from the thoughts of criminal law and are organically related to criminal law. So at least people will not feel disorderly if they are appropriately arranged in the book.

British jurists Peter Stein and John Shand have quoted a saying in the preface of the book *Legal Values in Western Society* that the only difference between people "without the philosophy" and people "with the philosophy" is that the latter understand what philosophy is. The saying is profound, which can be applied to jurisprudence and criminal law specifically. Philosophy is the most tempting content in jurisprudence. Departmental laws, including criminal law, civil law, and administrative law, except for their professional troughs, share the same philosophy, which can be promoted to jurisprudence and even higher-level philosophy. We can never say philosophy does not exist in our research domain. It is there, and the key is whether you can discover it.

I have no idea if I have fully expressed what I should say, but it is time to stop. Maybe, I may write my next book better if there is one. The postscript ends here.

Chen Xingliang
October 31, 1994
In the Yingchun Garden Residence in Beijing Tower Courtyard

Bibliography

1. [Japan] O. Seiichiro, *Theory of the Element of a Crime* (People's Public Security University of China Press, Beijing, 1991)
2. [Soviet Union] A. Guseynov, Г. Irellitz, *Brief History of Ethics* (Renmin University of China Press, Beijing, 1992)
3. [Britain] Bentham, *Theoretical Basis of Penalty,* British edn. (1843)
4. [Germany] Filanjili, *Criminal Legislation Study,* German edn. (1788)
5. [Japan] K. Eameji (Editor-in-Chief), *Dictionary of Criminal Law* (Shanghai Translation Publishing Corporation, Shanghai, 1992)
6. [US] Hoy, *A Philosophy of Individual Freedom: The Political Thought of F.A. Hayek* (Joint Publishing, Beijing, 1992)
7. [Britain] Huxley, *Man's Place in Nature and Other Essays* (Science Press, Beijing, 1971)
8. Compiled and Translated by the Teaching and Research Section of the Section of Foreign Philosophy of the Department of Philosophy of Peking University, *Philosophy of Western European Countries in the 16th–18th Century* (Joint Publishing, Beijing, 1958)
9. [Germany] Engels, *Anti-Dühring* (People's Publishing House, Beijing, 1970)
10. [Soviet Union] Weyman, *The Great British Materialist: Thomas Hobbes* (The Commercial Press, Beijing, 1962)
11. *Marx/Engels Collected Works* (People's Publishing House, Beijing, 1956–1985)
12. J. Zhang (Editor-in-Chief), *On Liberty* (Shanghai People's Publishing House, Shanghai, 1990)
13. J. Guo, *A Few Basic Issues About the US Criminology* (People's Public Security University of China Press, Beijing, 1992)
14. [US] Turner, *The Structure of Sociological Theory* (Zhejiang People's Publishing House, Hangzhou, 1987)
15. T. Qu, *Law and Society in China* (The Commercial Press, Beijing, 1981)
16. Z. Shen, *Jurisprudential Research* (Shanghai People's Publishing House, Shanghai, 1990)
17. [Italy] Selected and Compiled by Schipani, Selected Translation of Civil Law, *Jurisdiction, Trial and Judicial Action,* vol. 2 (China University of Political Science and Law Press, Beijing, 1992)
18. *Collected Theses on the Rule of Law and the Rule of Man* (Quzhong Publishing House, Beijing, 1981)

X. Chen, *Humanistic Foundation of Criminal Law*,
https://doi.org/10.1007/978-981-19-9764-8

Index

X. Chen, *Humanistic Foundation of Criminal Law*,
https://doi.org/10.1007/978-981-19-9764-8

R

S

T

U